# Punch, Volume 95

Anonymous

LONDON:

PUBLISHED AT THE OFFICE, 85, FLEET STREET,

AND SOLD BY ALL BOOKSELLERS.

1888.

SCENE—Mr. PUNCH's *Sanctum.* SEASON—*The Eve of the New Year. Present,* Father TIME, Mr. PUNCH, *and* TOBIAS. *An Edisonian Phonograph, of the latest construction, is arranged, oracle-like, behind a curtain, the Sage and the Scythebearer have been experimenting therewith.*

*Father Time* (*with emphasis*). Wonderful!!!

*Mr. Punch.* From you, who have witnessed so many wonders, that one word is a tremendous tribute which my young friend EDISON would mightily appreciate.

*Father Time* (*meditatively*). Yes; I *have* seen many marvels—or what for awhile were esteemed such. But the mirific marvel of to-day has ever been the matter-of-course of to-morrow, or at most of the day after. A real nine-days'-wonder is indeed an exception. Still this latest of Yankee "notions" is a startler. My favourite Egyptians never achieved anything more surprising.

*Mr. Punch.* You *don't* mean to say that your pets the Pyramid-builders did not forestall us poor moderns in this, as in most other things? Very good of them, I 'm sure, to leave us *something* to discover!

*Father Time* (*drily*). What to do with the Soudan, for example. You don't seem in a hurry to avail yourself of that privilege, however.

*Mr. Punch.* Ah! I wonder now, were it possible to turn on the voice of RAMESES through this vocal cone, whether he could give the Marquis the straight tip about Suakin?

*Father Time.* If Memnon himself could speak through the phonograph, in the very voice of oracular music with which he used to greet the rising sun in old Thebes, do you suppose that your Party potterers would heed it?

*Mr. Punch.* Humph! Isn't it whispered that the Priests—the real politicians of the period—had something to do with that little Coptic "fakement;" that in fact the lips of the Vocal Memnon formed merely a convenient sort of phonograph for the official oracles—the SALISBURYS and SMITHS and STANHOPES of that day?

*Father Time.* I perceive, Sir, that you know a thing or two.

*Mr. Punch.* Otherwise, my KRONOS, it would hardly be worth *your* while to halt for an hour's chat with me on the very edge of the New Year. Pray give your glass another turn, though; I cannot part with you yet. And the *other* glass, dear Edax Rerum, turn *that* up likewise—no heel-taps, you know, here!—and let me fill it again.

*Father Time* (*sententiously*). It is passing good—and too good to pass. (*Drinks.*) Your health, my Perennial One! You are not of an age, but for All Time, as BEN JONSON said of the other Immortal. "*She*" indeed! What was RIDER HAGGARD's two-thousand-year-old compared with the unquenchable "*He*-who-must-be-obeyed" of Fleet Street?

*Mr. Punch.* You do me proud, Sir. But, by JOVE!—beg pardon for naming that usurping *parvenu!*—you will have, my dear KRONOS, to look to your laurels, or your prescriptive rights and privileges, if this sort of thing goes on.

*Father Time.* What do you mean, Mr. PUNCH?

*Mr. Punch.* You know what EDGAR ALLAN POE says:—

> "Science! true daughter of Old TIME thou art!
> Who alterest all things with thy peering eyes."

Well, it seems to me, Father TIME, that your daughter is gradually depriving her sire of certain of his most cherished attributes and most exclusive prerogatives. Space she has practically annihilated; and now she is having a turn at You! Time was when what was past *was* past, when what Edax Rerum had once devoured knew no resurrection. But now? Well, when Science can thus make the vanished Voices of the Past actually audible Voices of the Present, then, in the words of the Hibernian Magistrate in "*Killaloe*"—

"Ye never know what *she*'ll be up to next."

Already she has beaten MUNCHAUSEN on his own ground. Frozen words made audible by thaw? Pooh! What is that compared with the awe-striking possibility of the *ipsissima verba* of eloquent GLADSTONE, or honey-tongued LEIGHTON, or ventriloquial IRVING, being ground out of this instrument, for the edification, or Edisonification, of dwellers in the tail-end of the Twentieth Century!

*Toby* (*fortissimo*). Bow-wow-wo-o-o-o-w!!!

*Father Time* (*anxiously*). What's the matter with that dog? He—he—*seems* to be asleep, and yet——

*Mr. Punch* (*laughing*). Don't alarm yourself, KRONOS. TOBY *is* asleep, so soundly, that even his own bark—of the day before yesterday—does not awaken him!

*Father Time* (*with awe*). What, do you mean to say it was that inf——that extraordinary instrument of EDISON's that was yelping like that?

*Mr. Punch.* Precisely! TOBY barked into it for me a day or two since. His wax-recorded yelp may be useful to frighten burglars in the year 1989. Had ANUBIS done ditto several thousand years ago, we could now compare his yaps with those of the modern Dog of Dogs.

*Father Time.* Here, I say, *don't!* It's really uncanny, and, as you suggest, knocks my traditional prerogatives into a cocked hat!

*Mr. Punch.* Never mind! After all, 'tis *Vox et præterea nihil.* American Scientists are as impotent as were Egyptian mummy-makers or the Embalmers of Kôr, *really* to bring back the Past or to perpetuate the Present. And the Future is Ours—as Mr. GLADSTONE says of the Liberal Party.

*Father Time.* Quite so. *You* may find the phonograph useful, to record for the benefit of remotest posterity your words of wisdom and scintillations of wit; eh, Mr. PUNCH?

*Mr. Punch.* My dear KRONOS, do you not see that, practically, I am as independent of this remarkable and really interesting instrument as you are of an improved egg-boiler or patent lawn-mower? *I* am perennial, and have a Phonograph—or *Funnigraph*—of my own, invented long before the days of EDISON.

*Father Time.* Indeed! I should *so* like to see it.

*Mr. Punch.* You shall, dear Edax. Indeed you shall take it with you, if you like. It will amuse and instruct you on your lonely round between now and next New Year's Day,—when I hope to see you here again. You will find therein echoes of the most valuable Voices of the Past, the best and brightest utterance of *the* Voice of the Present, and not a few vocal and vaticinatory "dips into the Future!" Oh, don't be alarmed; it is not a cumbersome and complicated bit of mechanism, like this of EDISON's. It is compact and portable. Tuck it under your arm, Father TIME; it won't interfere with the comfortable carrying of your scythe and hour-glass, I assure you. For Mr. PUNCH's original, ingenious, unsurpassable Patent Funnigraph is his

# Ninety-Fifth Volume!

## OUR DEBATING CLUB.

THE election of a new member to the Gargoyle Club is so seldom attended by any incident of note, that I may be pardoned, perhaps, for devoting this paper to the description of almost the single exception in our annals. It is our invariable custom to transact all business of this sort before proceeding to debate; and on the evening in question PLUMLEY DUFF, who had proposed the candidate for election, rose to give the information necessary to enable them to pronounce upon his claims to admission. Now DUFF had very good-naturedly undertaken the duty at the suggestion of BOSHER, who had represented that the recommendation would fall with far greater weight from him, and that, in DUFF's hands, the election was safe.

"Well, Gentlemen," said DUFF, in his most matter-of-fact style, "it is not usual to say much on these occasions. I can only remind you of the value of a little new blood from time to time in our councils. When I have said that Mr. SCIPIO P. GOLIBOISE is a member of one of our most ancient Inns of Court, the Under Temple, and is fitting himself to take an active part in the profession of the Law, I think you will see that he has—ah—fair qualifications for election as a Gargoyle."

Then GEYSER primed by BOSHER, rose with his usual impetuosity. "I must say, Gentlemen," he began, "with all deference to our friend, Mr. DUFF, I don't think he has laid Mr. (eh? yes, thank you, BOSHER!) GOLIBOISE's claims to our votes before us with all the earnestness and thoroughness he usually devotes to whatever he takes in hand. He has suppressed—no doubt, inadvertently—a very important fact in connection with the Candidate which, in my humble opinion, will appeal strongly to your imaginations. Mr. GOLIBOISE is a representative of one of the most thriving of the dependencies of our great Empire. He comes to us, Gentlemen, from the Island of—(which? ah, just so)—the fair and smiling island of Sangaree. I put it to you whether it is not our duty to lay aside all minor considerations, and, in this Jubilee time, give the world a striking instance of the brotherly feeling which unites the Mother Country to her Colonies! Let there be nothing of ungracious, of grudging, of perfunctory, in the response we make to his application for admission; a hand, Gentlemen, is stretched out to us from across the seas—let us not in the palm we hold forth in return, conceal the invidious form of one solitary black-ball!" (*There was a murmur of admiration at this fine image.*) "Let us for once be unanimous in throwing our portals wide open to receive the stranger who stands knocking at the door of the Gargoyle Club!" [*Loud applause.*

There was no necessity for any further speech-making, but PERCY VERE would get up; he always will whenever he sees the slightest opportunity, for his great idea is that oratory comes with practice, and that it doesn't so much matter what you say, so long as you gain a little more confidence by saying it.

So PERCY VERE began very fluently: "As to the remarks of the Honourable Member who has just sat down, I only wish to remark that the remarks he made were remarks——" (*Here he looked about him in a distressed manner*) "remarks which were very ably—er, very ably remarked. I can't help rising to say that I have no—that I rise without any—I—I mean . . . that I don't feel a—a . . . . (I could tell you the word if I could only remember the name—it's curious how you forget things standing up!) oh,—what I meant was *hesitation!*"

Having arrived at this point, he sat down very contentedly.

"I won't add any words of my own," said PINCENEY, "to the eloquent pleas (*here* PERCY VERE *looked deeply gratified*) we have just listened to. The Secretary will now distribute the balls, and the ballot-box will then be brought round in the usual manner to each member."

"I am happy to tell you, Gentlemen," our President announced, after a scrutiny of the box, amidst much enthusiasm, "that Mr. GOLIBOISE is elected without a single dissentient voice! And now let us proceed to the motion before the House, which is——"

"One moment, Sir," said BOSHER. "I believe the new Gargoyle is below at this instant, waiting permission to take his seat amongst us. With your leave, I will now invite him to do so."

But this quite innocent proposal brought up PORPENTINE: "I must really protest, Sir! It looks to me as if the Candidate, by coming here this evening, must have regarded his election as a foregone conclusion; as if—I am about to conclude with a motion, Sir. . . I move—'That, having regard to circumstances with which the Club was previously unacquainted, Mr. GOLIBOISE be now informed that his election is still under consideration.'"

*Geyser* (*rising excitedly*). Really, Sir! really! Are we to punish Mr. GOLIBOISE for his very laudable impatience to join our society? Is his ignorance, pardonable in a stranger, of our customs to be thrown in his teeth like this? A thousand times no, Sir! I call upon Mr. PORPENTINE to withdraw his motion; otherwise, I, for one, will not continue a member of this Club a single day! No, Sir, not one hour—not one minute—not one instant—(*lowering his voice impressively*)—not one *week!* (*Cries of "Withdraw!" and some excitement.*)

*Porpentine* (*rather sulkily*). I beg to withdraw the motion.

*Pinceney.* Then, if Mr. BOSHER will introduce the new Member as he proposes, I shall now call upon Mr. GEYSER to bring forward the subject for debate, which is in the following terms:—"That this House is of opinion that all Racial and other distinctions are invidious and reactionary, and should be abolished."

BOSHER had already disappeared, and, as the President spoke, there were steps outside, and presently the door opened, and Mr. GOLIBOISE made his first entrance into the Gargoyle Club.

He walked up to the vacant chair next to GEYSER's, which BOSHER had vacated (by the way, he did not reappear that evening), and sat down grinning from ear to ear, evidently highly pleased with himself and us, after which he devoted himself to rolling his eyes, and sucking the top of his walking-stick.

I trust that we did nothing unworthy of our character as Gargoyles and as gentlemen; but I am bound to confess that our new Member's appearance excited a certain sensation amongst us which could not be wholly disguised.

For Mr. GOLIBOISE happened to be a remarkably fine specimen of the pure African type. It made no difference, of course, but we *should* like to have been a little better prepared.

## THE CONQUEROR JOCK; OR, THE WHIP-HAND.

(*Some way after " The Conqueror Worm."*)

**" Time was when wners of horses were the masters of the trainers and the jockeys; now it too often happens that the trainers are the masters of the owners, and the jockeys masters of both."—Sir Charles Russell.**

Lo! 'tis a gruesome sight,
Within hese loathly latter years,
A feverish throng, dust-coat bedight,
With veils, or cads, or peers,

Stand in a race-course ring to see
A play of hopes and fears,
And an undertone breathes fitfully,
Now curses, and now cheers.

Mimes in the form of magnates high
Mutter and murmur low,
And hither and thither fly;
Mere puppets they who come and go

At bidding of misshapen things,
  That drive them blindly to and fro,
Dealing from out their rascal rings
  Inevitable woe!

That motley drama—oh, be sure
  It shall not be forgot!
With its Phantom chased for evermore
  By a crowd that seize it not,
Through a circle that ever returneth in
  To the self-same spot;
And much of madness, and more of sin,
  And swindling the soul of the plot.

But see amid the mimic rout
  A wizen thing intrude!
A shrivelled shape that rides about
  With despot power imbued!
It spurs!—it whips!—the Swells, the Snobs,
  The vampire treats as food,
And the nobles that it rides—and robs—
  Are to its will subdued.

Down—down on all fours are they all,
  The sordid, sold, fool-flock,
The fierce whip-lashings fall
  Like storm-flouts on a rock;
And the dupes, from counter or Court,
  That wizened thing doth mock:
The play is the farce called "Sport,"
  And its hero the Conqueror Jock!

## WILFRID LAWSON'S LATIN.

The following quotations, freely translated, may be added to the Baronet's admittedly limited stock:—

"*Clausum fregit*"—He burst up the Clause.

"*Horresco referens*"—It gives me shivers to refer to it.

"*Pro bono publico*"—For the bones of the Publican.

"*Res angusta domi*"—The cussedness of the House.

"*Ære perennius*"—Trust me for brass.

"*Tempora mutantur*"—Wouldn't I just like to take my change out of the *Times*.

"*Est modus in rebus*"—Mine is the only measure for everybody who is at all anybody.

"*Dulce est desipere in loco*"—It is pleasant to play the fool in a certain place.

"*Nigroque simillima cygno*"—And very like a black Public-house sign.

"*Fons et origo bonorum*"—The town pump.

"*Actum est de Republica*"—It's all up with the Licensed Victualler's business when my Act passes.

An Honest Jockey.—Rather unstable.

"WAYS AND MEANS."

*Visitor.* "You take it easy, Brown. You must have a good Salary."

*Brown.* "H-m—ya-as—pre'y well. I draw Three Hundred a year—save say a Hundred, and run into debt Four Hundred, that 's—Eight Hundred; and if a Bachelor can't live on that—'ought to be ashamed of himself!!"

## THE EX-PENSIVE PRESIDENT, R.B.A.

Three weeks ago we asked, "Who is Mr. Wyke Bayliss?" beyond being the President-Elect of the Society of British Artists in lieu of the Licensed Whistler, James I., deposed. We are now answered. The gentleman has been interviewed by a friendly *Figaro* who furnishes us with the following facts:—

"Mr. Wyke Bayliss, when a student at the British Museum, did not limit his attention to the Elgin Marbles," but on the other hand, "as a Chess-player, he held, last year, the cup for the county of Surrey."

He is, moreover, "Chairman of the Board School in his District," "Member of the Diocesan Council of Rochester," and besides being "Public Orator of Noviomagus" (what on earth is this?), he is "Honorary Fellow of the Society of Cyclists."

It is quite clear from all this that Mr. W. B. was born for Suffolk Street, and Whistler, the Painter, was there decidedly out of place. And now having discovered Wyke Bayliss, Pres. Elec., we have four questions to put to anybody who can answer them; *i. e.*, "Who, What, or Where is 'Noviomagus'?" And "Why has he a Public Orator all to himself?"

Shady Places for Hot Weather.—During the past week, Lord Dunraven, as Chairman of the Sweating Commission, Lord Herschell with the Board of Works Inquiry before him, and the Lord Chief Justice with the Great Turf Libel case, might have been represented at Madame Tussaud's as Æacus, Minos, and Rhadamanthus, in a Modern "Chamber of Horrors." Their effigies might have melted, but their Lordships themselves are made of sterner stuff.

## THE WANDERING VETERAN.

(*A Legend of Wimbledon.*)

The Old Man sighed as he walked into Richmond. The children laughed at him, and their elders tossed their heads in scorn. But he did not mind. He leant on his weapon, which served him as a staff, and strode sturdily onwards. Soon he was in the Park. He sank on one knee. In a moment he was accosted by an official.

"Move on!" said the official.

The Old Man wiped away a tear, and obeyed the order. He passed through fields and gardens, and now he was at Epsom. Once more he had prepared to make a stay.

"Move on!" again shouted an official, and the Veteran was forced to submit.

And so he wandered from place to place—everywhere unwelcome, everywhere abused.

At last he lay down on the ground, and could go no further. In spite of the rough requests of the officials "to get up and be off," he stayed where he was. Indeed, he could go no further.

"Where have you been?" they asked him.

"All over the country," he replied, in a faint voice; and then he told them how he had journeyed from place to place, and never was allowed to settle.

"And who are you?"

"The surviving Member of the National Rifle Association;" and, with a faint smile upon his thin lips, and forgiveness in his heart of hearts, for H.R.H. the Duke of Cambridge, the last of the Volunteers calmly died.

The Conservative Tent just now.—Discon-tent.

WHAT OUR POET HAS TO PUT UP WITH.

"YES; SHE'S A MOST SYMPATHETIC WOMAN. I WAS READING MY LAST POEMS TO HER ONLY YESTERDAY, AND THE DINNER-HOUR PASSED BY WITHOUT HER EVER PERCEIVING IT!"

"*PARBLEU, MON AMI!* YOU KNOW ZE FRENCH PROVERB—'*QUI DORT, DINE*'!"

## JOTTINGS FOR THE TIMES.

(*From the Duke of Downshire's Journal.*)

A VERY weary day. Don't think I can stand this Omnibus driving business much longer. Having to go to the BLUEMANTLES' crush as soon as I get home to-night, dressed before I took the reins in the morning, and have been got up in full fig, ribbon of the Garter and all, under my overcoat on the box all day, so as not to keep the Duchess waiting. She says I look "crumpled." Don't wonder at it. Six times from Hammersmith to Whitechapel and back is enough to take the starch out of anybody. Think, however, the Duchess has been put out, finding the new Dressmaking business she set up in Bond Street not half so satisfactory as she thought it would be. She has tried to tone down the "shoppy" side of it by offering her customers five o'clock tea, and by endeavouring to invest the whole business with a little social glamour, but she says that our pork-butcher's wife, whom she supplied only last week with a ruby velvet, came and complained quite nastily that the dress did not fit her properly in the back, and on the Duchess smiling amiably and saying she saw nothing amiss, retorted that "Business was business, Duchess or no Duchess," and that when she "paid good hard money for what she ordered, she expected good honest work in return."

This sort of thing is, I am bound to say, only what I expected. I was not, therefore, surprised to hear that my two dear daughters, the Lady CONSTANTIA, and the Lady FEODORA, had had some disagreeables with the Principal of the Regent's Street Bonnet Establishment, in which I had just succeeded in placing them with so much difficulty, and had determined to throw the whole thing up.

Then, again, the Fried Fish and Whelk business in Marylebone, which I had made such sacrifices to secure for PLANTAGENET, appears likely to turn out a disappointing investment. He says that, after his life in the Guards, he cannot somehow take kindly to the calling. Well, poor boy, he may be assured that it is not one that I, his father, would have selected for him, as the heir upon whose brows my Ducal Coronet must eventually descend—still, what was I to do? The only other thing in the market was a "Sausage" concern.

My second boy, BERTRAM, seems, I am glad to note, fairly satisfied with his butcher's calling, and dons his blouse and shoulders his tray with the best of them. Still, the outlook is not cheering, and if PLANTAGENET backs out of the Fried Fish, all I can say is, "Heaven help him!" Sometimes I think if we could give a drawing-room entertainment, and appear at a Music-Hall as "the Duke of DOWNSHIRE's talented troupe," we might perhaps make ends meet. I should still look respectable in spangled tights; but with Beaumanoir and the Dashworth estates both mortgaged over the hilt, it's clear that something must be done, and that quickly. Ha! here is the Duchess! She looks well in what, trying to raise a miserable laugh among ourselves, we call, in wretched satire, the "family paste." No matter. I will talk the subject over with her. But the slavey has announced that the four-wheeler is at the door. Very well, Duchess. Lead on, I follow!

## HOME-TRUTHS FROM ABROAD.

(*But not from Mr. Browning. Gleaned from the Chancellor of the Exchequer's Speech in the Debate of last Week.*)

I.

OH, to be in Ireland
  Now the boycott's there,
And whoever wakes in Ireland
  Finds some morning, unaware,
That his baker denies him his daily bread,
And his butcher is threatened with "doses of lead,"
While the "bhoys" are carving his favourite cow
In Ireland—now!

II.

And after daylight, when dark follows,
And help is far, and vain all holloas,
Hark, where the ominous knock at supper-time
Preludes a talk, a hasty shot, a groaning—
The goodman's end! And she, who saw the crime,
That's the wise wife!—she's dumb, but for low moaning,
Lest she too know what mean the unwritten orders
Of these same gay marauders!
And though some sham regret may be expressed,
Next Sunday 'll show the boycott at its best;
Curses will dog the widow's churchward way—
Far better than our English Sabbath-Day!

## THE TRUTH ABOUT MR. BALFOUR'S HAT.

SIR,—I saw in the *Times's* Dublin Letter an account by an eye-witness, of Mr. BALFOUR walking wildly about in St. James's Park "with his hat in his hand." And somebody wrote to explain this, and said that the correspondent of the *Times* wanted it to appear that Mr. BALFOUR had "lost his head." I emphatically contradict this. Mr. BALFOUR has not lost his head; but he *frequently carries his hat on his shoulders and his head in his hands* as you may see in this sketch by

AN EYE-WITNESS.

NOTE ON SOME RECENT EVIDENCE.—"VAN DAMM" is an appropriate name for a witness before the Sweating Commission who attacks "MAPLE & CO.," the firm always associated with furniture vans.

SONG FOR LORD TENNYSON AND OTHER POETS.—"See me re-verse."

NEW NAME FOR THANET.—The Lowther Arcadia.

## COLERIDGIAN CONCEITS;

OR, DRAWINGS ON THE WOOD.

A USEFUL PLATER.

[At the first mention of "useful plater," it occurred to L-rd C-l-r-dge that several of his own spoons and forks wanted doing up. *Mem.* accordingly.]

"IN AND OUT RUNNING."

[On hearing this phrase, L-rd C-l-r-dge at once remembered his happy school-days.]

PULLING A HORSE.

[L-rd C-l-r-dge's first impression—corrected after hearing the case.]

"SERIOUS MEN ENGAGED IN A RACE."

[L-rd C-l-r-dge's original idea—subsequently corrected.]

## OPERATIC NOTES.

*Monday, June* 25.—Lovely music to *Il Flauto Magico.* The commencement of one song sung by *Monostatos* (Signor RINALDINI), a kind of Mozartised Christy Minstrel, reminds me of "*Ah, bravo, Figaro.*" It has probably reminded a good many persons of the same air long ago, but the Opera is to me a comparative novelty. Exciting story,—a trifle mixed. What I gather from it is that RAVELLI the Reliable is an Egyptian called *Tamino,* (evidently some familiar form of "*Tommy,*")—and that *Tommy* the Tenor, falls in with three Ladies, one of whom is Mlle. DOTTI, which is a painfully suggestive name, but there is no lame attempt about her singing, no "DOTTI-and-go-oney," but, on the contrary, she is majestic and impressive, more "DOTTI-on-the-eyey" kind of performance; and the other two are Mlle. DESVIGNES and Madame SCALCHI, who is, as it appears, also in another line of business as a Real Genius (no one ever doubted it, of course) associated with two other Geniuses, Miss LOUISE LABLACHE and Mlle. BAUERMEISTER; and without the last mentioned no cast at Covent Garden Opera can now be considered complete. Well,—TOMMY the Tenor, meets one *Papageno* (Signor DEL PUENTE),—a person in the ridiculous costume of a kind of Parrot in full feather,—and *Tommy* having been presented with a golden flute and a temperance blue riband, and *Papageno* having received a set of musical bells, they find themselves in, apparently, the Egyptian Court of the Crystal Palace; and here *Tommy* gives a solo to some pantomime Monkeys and profile Lions, Tigers, Rhinoceri, and Elephants—quite a "monster concert." *Papageno* makes some comic niggers dance by playing on his bells, but beyond this they make no particular use of their magic gifts.

Then *Tommy* makes love to Miss MINNIE HAUK, impersonating the remarkably fine grown-up daughter of Miss ELLA RUSSELL as the *Queen of Night,* who, for the loss of the infantine MINNIE, is draped in black, representing the curious spectacle of Night and Mourning all in one. Then Miss HAUK is interviewed by her mother, Miss ELLA RUSSELL, who sings such astonishing top-notes as quite take away her breath, the mother's, that is, and so she herself wisely declines the vociferous *encore;* but, before she retires, makes a handsome present of a dagger, perhaps to be used as a paper-knife, to her daughter MINNIE, who, having accepted it unwillingly, promptly loses it.

Then the Mozartian Christy Minstrel annoys poor MINNIE with his too demonstrative attentions, and she is rescued—she is always being rescued—by *Tommy* the Tenor, who, having lost his magic flute as *Papageno* has his bells, has had it restored to him by the three gifted Geniuses (who have also restored to *Papageno* his lost bells), and then Miss MINNIE, assisted by the three distinguished Geniuses in costumes such as Geniuses wore many, many years ago, before Gaiety Fairies were invented, is taken away by *Tommy* the Tenor, and is forthwith seen taking, as it appears, a sort of Turkish bath with him in the pleasantest manner possible, he playing the flute the while, and both decently attired, of course; and afterwards they stand under a mountain torrent by way of *douche*—and what the douche it all means I don't know, but the foregoing story is something like it, without mentioning Miss ARNOLDSON as *Papagena,* the bride of *Papageno*—she ought to have been *Mammagena,* of course—and without mentioning the High Priest, who being a Basso, is a very low priest, and ought to have been EDOUARD DE RESZKÉ, but wasn't—having been metamorphosed by magic into Signor NOVARA,—and without going into any of the wonderful details and describing the grand Transformation Scene at the finish ("Thought there was going to be Harlequin and Columbine," grumbles H.R.H.'s Attorney-General, Q.C., M.P., to one of the Organising Committee, as he takes up his hat and slowly emerges from the box. "Should like to have seen RAVELLI as Harlequin, and ARNOLDSON as Columbine,—charming Columbine, begad!") I should say that a better performance of the most muddle-headed Extravaganza ever invented has rarely been seen at Covent Garden. Could hear it all again with pleasure, but not see it. The only singer who really seems to thoroughly enjoy it is SCALCHI. ARNOLDSON looks very pretty as *Mammagena.* She ought to be brought on earlier. Why shouldn't she be the Princess as well? She could "double the parts" as SCALCHI does; but SCALCHI is "the First Genius," and can do anything. Any Manager has a treasure in SCALCHI. Can call upon her for a song at any moment, and never make a mis-Scalchi-lation. Which is a cryptogrammic joke: so hidden.

## A TURN AT THE HANDEL.

THE Crystal Palace can now and then offer attractions by which crowds may be drawn, as they have been in the week past by the Handel Festival, without advertising the edifying spectacle of a woman hanging on by her teeth to a rope attached to a balloon though at first sight one is afraid lest the names of ALBANI, NORDICA, LLOYD, and SANTLEY, at the Palace, should not be sufficiently attractive in themselves without adding some gymnastic feat to their fine musical performances.

The Oratorios went splendidly, and the Selections on Wednesday brought together a select audience. The Grand Old MANNS of the C. P. might have written something better himself than the specimen of "*The Triumph of Time and Truth,*" and have called it "*The Triumph of Time and Tune,*" which is a hint for next Festival. SANTLEY in first-rate voice, with "*Honour and Arms;*" so also LLOYD, with his "*Love in his Eyes,*" (no connection with "*Two Lovely Black Eyes*"), which he sang deliciously.

The G. O. M. of the C. P. accepted the *encore* of the *Occasional Overture* for this occasion only, but ALBANI and NORDICA refused flatly—the only note of any flatness in the entertainment—to accept any *encores,* no matter how they might be pressed on all hands. Madame NORDICA charmingly sang, "*Hush, ye pretty wobbling Choir,*" addressed, of course, to the Handelian Choristers, who evidently bridled up at the insinuation of unsteadiness, and refused to "hush," rendering their *fortissimo* with such precision as to prove the charge of their being "pretty wobbling," to be absolutely without foundation. [A friend, who knows nothing about it, has suggested to me that when I say "wobbling" I mean "warbling." Absurd! If I meant "warbling" I should warble.] No one at the organ can be better than BEST. In fact the whole performance was so good that as everybody wanted to have everything over again, this "Choral Festival" may be memorable as the "Great Encore-all Festival."

NEW CIVIL UNIFORM.

. . . "Four small buttons down front, and to button on to collar of cloak; gilt hook and chain. . . . Cap: Blue cloth made up soft, with a small gold braided top, and a row of gold braid round the crown."—*Vide London Gazette, June* 13.

SOMETHING FURTHER ABOUT "MR. G."—Mr. GLADSTONE was reported last week as having said that, among some of the few things he had to live for was to show "the substantial identity between the theology of HOMER and of the Old Testament." We believe he since added to this the idea for demonstrating that the Six Days of Creation must be understood as six "Parliamentary Days."

PEDESTRIANISM AT LAMBETH.—In the course of a series of amusing articles on the Established Church, the *St. James's Gazette* suggests that the legal-ecclesiastical difficulties of its position at home and in the Colonies is "a case in which, in a marked degree, difficulties will be solved *ambulando.*" Yes, certainly—a good deal of "Walker" about this remedy. It might be tried this week at Lambeth.

NEW NAME FOR IT.—The Metropolitan Board of "Perks."

**PLEASURES OF A "PLEASURE-HORSE."**

MR. BIGSBY DETERMINES TO WRITE TO THE *TIMES* A LETTER HEADED, "THE DANGERS OF THE STREETS," DENOUNCING MILK CARTS WITH RATTLING CANS, BICYCLES, TRICYCLES, GERMAN BANDS &C.

## CLEARING THE COURSE!

AIR—"*Clar de Kitchen.*"

ON St. Stephen's stream, to give us room,
We clear the course like a brand-new broom;
And we form a regular Government ring,
And this is the song that we do sing:—
Clear the river, cockboats, cockboats!
Old Morality wants clear way!

'Ware, cockboats, 'ware If you should cross
The bows of the Government Launch, you'll toss
On a terrible swell from shore to shore,
That might almost swamp a seventy-four.
So clear the river &c.

Cockboats conceive St. Stephen's stream
Is free to all; 'tis a foolish dream.
When the big boat comes with the crew at the prow,
They must all get out of the way, somehow.
So clear the river, &c.

Like a big bull-frog in a tadpole swim,
The steam launch glideth grand and grim;
And the Private Member who'd keep afloat,
Will be tossed like a cork in his crank cockboat.
So clear the river &c.

There is Old Morality wants clear way,
And the run of the river by night and day;
And chief-mate RITCHIE he cries with a frown,
"If you don't clear out, I shall run you down!"
So clear the river, &c.

'Tis an Aaron's rod of a craft, you see,
This Launch, and the skipper, SALISBURREE;
Hopes if 'tis steered with strength and skill,
It will clear the river and whip poor WILL!
So clear the river, cockboats, cockboats!
Old Morality wants clear way!

## COLERIDGE CORRECT.

LORD COLERIDGE in a recent case made an observation, to which we have already drawn attention, to the effect that he could not understand how anyone with such an honoured name as "MOSES" could ever consent to change it for, *e.g.*, "MORDAUNT." The Handelian Festival brought this remark of the Lord Chief Justice's vividly to our mind. Where would be the force of substituting "Mordaunt" for "Moses" in *Israel in Egypt?* Or to take a great work by another Composer, *Mosé in Egitto*, how would *Mordaunt in Egitto* or *Montmorency in Egitto* sound? No; Lord COLERIDGE is right. But is he not always right?

## THE BARON'S BOOK.

THE *Memoirs of Baron de Rimini* are anything but Barren Rimini-iscences. Startling and amusing. I'm not jealous, though he is a Baron as well as myself. Can't help bursting out into poetry and singing:—

O by Jingo! O my Jimini!
Marvellous *Memoirs of Baron de Rimini;*
Nothing merely niminy-piminy
In the *Memoirs of Baron de Rimini!*

Nothing like them since the records of Baron MUNCHAUSEN, who, in my humble opinion *overdid it*. RIMINI doesn't; it is all fact! There's the startler. Truth stranger than fiction. HAGGARD and STEVENSON nowhere. Walk up! Yours, THE BARON DE BOOK WORMS.

IN RE SCOTT *v.* WILKINSON.—Dear *Mr. Punch*,—I quite forgot to say—indeed, it only occurred to me afterwards, and I couldn't re-open the case to admit the *esprit d'escalier*,—when I read out about the "'orreries" in the school prospectus, and remarked on the defective sanitation, "On 'orrery's head 'orreries accumulate."

Yours ever, L-CKW-D.

"WE are in quite another World," Lord COLERIDGE is reported to have said in his summing-up in the WOOD case. The well-known line from *The Stranger* can now, on the Lord Chief's authority, be thus quoted, "There is another and a Betting World."

CLEARING THE COURSE!

## AWFUL TO CONTEMPLATE.

[The Title does not allude to the Portraits in the above Picture, which are those of Her Majesty's Judges going all together by steamer to dine at Greenwich. An artful Detective sends us this as showing a nefarious design (not the drawing) on the part of some ambitious Members of the Bar, which has been happily frustrated.]

## THE DIARY OF A NOBODY.

*April* 28.—At the office, the new and very young clerk PITT, who was very impudent to me a week or so ago, was late again. I told him it would be my duty to inform Mr. PERKUPP, the principal. To my surprise PITT apologised most humbly and in a most gentlemanly fashion. I was unfeignedly pleased to notice this improvement in his manner towards me, and told him I would look over his unpunctuality. Passing down the room an hour later, I received a smart smack in the face from a rolled-up ball of hard foolscap. I turned round sharply, but all the clerks were apparently riveted to their work. I am not a rich man, but I would give half-a-sovereign to know whether that was thrown by accident or design. Went home early and bought some more enamel paint—black this time, and spent the evening touching up the fender, picture-frames, and an old pair of boots making them look as good as new. Also painted GOWING's walking-stick, which he left behind and made it look like ebony.

*April* 29, *Sunday*.—Woke up with a fearful headache and strong symptoms of a cold. CARRIE, with a perversity which is just like her, said it was "painter's colic," and was the result of my having spent the last few days with my nose over a paint-pot. I told her firmly that I knew a great deal better what was the matter with me than she did. I had got a chill, and decided to have a bath as hot as I could bear it. Bath ready—could scarcely bear it so hot. I persevered, and got in; very hot, but very acceptable. I lay still for some time. On moving my hand above the surface of the water, I experienced the greatest fright I ever received in the whole course of my life, for imagine my horror on discovering my hand, as I thought, full of blood. My first thought was that I had ruptured an artery, and was bleeding to death, and should be discovered, later on, looking like a second MARAT, as I remember seeing him in Madame TUSSAUD's. My second thought was to ring the bell, but remembered there was no bell to ring. My third was, that it was nothing but the enamel paint, which had dissolved with the boiling water. I stepped out of the bath, perfectly red all over, resembling the Red Indians I have seen depicted at an East-End Theatre. I determined not to say a word to CARRIE, but to tell FARMERSON to come on Monday and paint the bath white.

*April* 30.—Perfectly astounded at receiving an invitation for CARRIE and myself from the Lord and Lady Mayoress to the Mansion House, to "meet the Representatives of Trades and Commerce." My heart beat like that of a schoolboy's. CARRIE and I read the invitation over two or three times. I could scarcely eat my breakfast. I said—and I felt it from the bottom of my heart—"CARRIE, darling, I was a proud man when I led you down the aisle of the church on our wedding-day; that pride will be equalled, if not surpassed, when I lead my dear pretty wife up to the Lord and Lady Mayoress at the Mansion House." I saw the tears in CARRIE's eyes, and she said, "CHARLIE, dear, it is *I* who have to be proud of you. And I am very, very proud of you. You have called me pretty, and as long as I am pretty in your eyes, I am happy. You, dear, old CHARLIE, are *not* handsome, but you are *good*, which is far more noble." I gave her a kiss, and she said, "I wonder if there will be any dancing? I have not danced with you for years." I cannot tell what induced me to do it, but I seized her round the waist, and we were silly enough to be executing a wild kind of polka when SARAH entered, grinning, and said, "There is a man, Mum, at the door who wants to know if you want any good coals." Most annoyed at this. Spent the evening in answering, and tearing up again, the reply to the Mansion House, having left word with SARAH if GOWING or CUMMINGS called we were not at home. Must consult Mr. PERKUPP how to answer the LORD MAYOR's invitation.

*May* 1.—CARRIE said, "I should like to send mother the invitation to look at." I consented as soon as I had answered it. I told Mr. PERKUPP at the office with a feeling of pride, that we had received an invitation to the Mansion House, and he said, to my astonishment, that he himself gave in my name to the LORD MAYOR's Secretary. I felt this rather discounted the value of the invitation, but I thanked him, and in reply to me he described how I was to answer it. I felt the reply was too simple, but of course Mr. PERKUPP knows best.

*May* 2.—Send my dress-coat and trousers to the little tailor's round the corner to have the creases taken out. Told GOWING not to call next Monday, as we were going to the Mansion House. Sent similar note to CUMMINGS.

*May* 3.—CARRIE went to Mrs. JAMES, at Sutton, to consult about her dress for next Monday. While speaking incidentally to SPOTCH, one of our head clerks, about the Mansion House, he said, "Oh, I'm asked, but don't think I shall go." When a vulgar man like SPOTCH is asked, I feel my invitation is considerably discounted. In the evening, while I was out, the little tailor brought round my coat and trousers, and because SARAH had not a shilling to pay for the pressing, he took them away again.

---

### "READ him by his Form."

*Twelfth Night*, Act III., Sc. 4.

[Mr. WALTER READ, playing last week for Surrey against Oxford, made the enormous score of 338 runs.]

READ by his "form" proud Surrey's READ,
Should be called "Read-and-Run" indeed.
A "form" so fine, may READ not alter;
Here's wishing you top-scorer, WALTER!

---

WARM FOR THEM.—The St. Stephen's Westminster Barometer, on the 26th inst., one of the hottest days we've had, marked for the Opposition side of the House 93 in the shade!

---

NEW NAME.—A "Kill-joy" or a "Wet-blanket" used to be the name for the guest whose every sentence was a damper on conviviality. Now, more artistically, he is termed a "Depressionist."

## ROBERT AT THE ACADEMY.

MY constant wissits to the Royal Academy wunce every year, gets my eye so acustomed to what is I bleeve called Eye Hart, that now, when I entur its sacred presinks, I jest casts my egle glance around, and at wunce settles down upon my pray, and the first as I seizes upon is No. 12, which I am told is a old woman a rowing of herself to Market, with lots of wegetables, the most singular part of which is the Sea, which, strange to say, is all milk, every drop of it, or it may posserbly be curds and way, but it suttenly aint water.

No. 21 is Prince BISMARCK. Well, I dessay as he's quite a faverite at tome, but I much wunders as he didn't git sumbody jest to tie his xtrordinary white handkersher for him afore he went to be painted. Why a mear Coffee House Waiter woud be utterly ashamed of such a Tye!

The next thing as fixes my hegar gaze is one of them staggerers as not ony staggers but fairly puzzles me. It is No. 95, and is called A Siren. I don't no what a Siren is, or where they happens to live, but they suttenly seems a remarkable careless lot. Now this one for instance has been a having a bath in the Sea, without no bathing-dress on, and sumbody has bin and stole all her close! and there she sets, poor thing, on the hard rocks a-trying for to make the peeple in a ship ever so far off come and help her. And all as she's got to emuse herself and keep herself warm is a little Arp which I spose as she's werry fond of, tho she's left off playing of it.

No. 107. Why the R. H. the Erl of HAREWOOD shoud 'ave gone and dressed hisself up in a Tourist's Suit, that coudn't have cost him more than about 12*s.* 6*d.*, when he was a going to have his picter painted, is a puzzle to me, the more speshally as of course he might have been painted in his crimson robes and with a Koronet on his hed, and praps have been taken for a Sherrif or heven a Lord Mare!

No. 152 is called "*Juno*," sumthink to do with the present munth I suppose. She's a flying right hup into the hair, and is about the hugliest and the crossest looking flyer as ever I seed. I overheard a Gennelman say that the reason as she looked so dredful angry was becoz she had jest left Paris in disgust, though why, I coud not understand. But my pore ed akes with seein so menny picktchers, and I must ere defur my most hintrestin remarx and crikisissums for annuther hokkashun.

ROBERT.

RETURN OF PALMY ITALIAN OPERATIC DAYS.

*Archie.* "I SAY, FRED! QUITE REMINDS ONE OF OLD TIMES, EH!"

## WIGS AND BONNETS.

MY DEAR MR. PUNCH,

YOU are *always* so *very* kind to Ladies that I am quite *sure* you will do your best to assist us to obtain the redress of a little grievance that has caused us a *lot* of worry recently. You know *how* fond we are of trials—especially a criminal one, where a nice interesting murderer is put in the dock, and has to fight for his life. It is *such* fun! But, alas! my dear *Mr. Punch*, the resources of the Central Criminal Court are of the most *limited* character imaginable! I can assure you there is scarcely *any* room on the Bench, and sometimes it is *absolutely* necessary for Ladies—accustomed to *every* home comfort,—to put up with *wretched* seats in the body of the Court! We want you to get *all* this altered for us. Cannot the Old Bailey be rebuilt, or something?

What makes the matter the more irritating to us is that at the new Royal Palace of Justice everything is so *very* nice. My sister and I the other day, were on the Bench with that *dear* Lord Chief Justice, and you cannot think how excessively *nice* it was! We had such delightfully comfortable chairs, and the "L. C. J." (as our barrister young friends call him), was so amiable! The dear good creature scarcely gave himself any room at all so that we should not be crowded! And then the *Luncheon!* Well, I will not say *anything* about *that*, as (like the Duke of PORTLAND's letter), it was a *private* matter! But really and truly it was *such* fun!

We laughed and talked to our heart's content, and the dear Lord Chief J. kept on making *such* funny little remarks! Pretending, you know, not to understand anything about racing, when everybody feels that he is a thorough old sportsman! I was rather sorry I had not brought my "work" with me; but a friend of mine—such a clever young lady—had got her Sketch-book with her, and took likenesses of *all* the witnesses! She finished by drawing Mr. LOCKWOOD, who, *everyone* says, is *so* clever with his pencil. If *he* sketched her, I am sure it must have made a pretty picture, because he seemed to be *so* pleased at attracting *such* attention!

If the Lord Chief Justice would let us bring a camera into Court, we could have *great* fun! Now, dear *Mr. Punch*, pray don't forget about the C. C. C., and, believe me to be, always yours sincerely,

*Horrorsfield, Gloomshire.* EMILY DE CHATTERBOX-PRY.

## OUR JAPANNERIES. No. 5.

THE HOUSE OF LORDS.

## ESSENCE OF PARLIAMENT.

EXTRACTED FROM

### THE DIARY OF TOBY, M.P.

*House of Commons, Monday, June* 25.—Great field-night. Government arraigned. Indictment set forth by JOHN MORLEY in speech full of gems of literary style. OLD MORALITY formally led into dock. Makes a lovely criminal. Air of unimpeachable respectability worth anything to counsel for defence.

"Sort of man *sure* to be bailed out," said CHARLES RUSSELL, looking at him with professional eye.

House crowded at outset, but specially in Galleries. "Three Lord-Lieutenants looking down upon us," said JOSEPH GILLIS, glancing up at Peers' Gallery. "It's like NAPOLEON—or was it WELLINGTON?—marching his men past the Pyramids, so that he might say thirty centuries were looking down on 'em."

JOEY B. nodded with friendly recognition to SPENCER and ABERDEEN. Rather cut LONDONDERRY, who had snatched an hour from arduous duties at Dublin Castle to sit in Senate. DERBY there, as usual without JOAN. But STRATHEDEN had brought CAMPBELL to recreate his great mind by taking a turn at Irish affairs. STRATHEDEN AND CAMPBELL—"Siamese twins of *la haute politique*" as ROSEBERY calls them—an audience of themselves. Sit by the hour with grave face looking into space. "If they hadn't been born to share British Peerage," said GEORGE CURZON, who is an authority on the subject of Peers, "would have made a reputation as Chief of the Apaches, or any Indian tribe where a look of unutterable wisdom is qualification for leading position."

On the whole, rather a dull evening. Everybody intensely interested, of course; fate of Ministry in balance, and all that sort of thing. Still, after first couple of hours, Members began, as it were, to fold their tent like the Arab, and as silently steal away. Just before Nine, House so empty, occurred to anonymous humorist (probably JOACHIM) to try Count Out. That would have been funny to have Members summoned from ends of earth to attack or defend Ministry, and the sitting to end in Count Out. Joke spoiled by Members rushing in from dining-room, "their mouths full of cabbage and contradiction," as SYDNEY SMITH said of HALLAM when he came upon him at a dinner-party. Later, SAUNDERSON got on. Made things more lively. Colonel been a nuisance all night to Members sitting near him with his subdued cries of "Whirroo!" and his twirling a lead-pencil round in his fingers, as if it were a shillelagh. Couldn't hold him in any longer. So, at Eleven o'Clock, took off his coat, stepped down on to floor before Irish Members, and for space of an hour walked up and down, trailing his coat; shouted at the Irishmen at top of his voice; answered back with shrieks and yells. Quite a pity when midnight struck, and Debate stood adjourned.

*Business done.*—Vote of Censure moved.

"Whirroo!"

*Wednesday*, 1 A.M. — Over at last Division bell ringing; Members, recovering from comatose state, staggering out into division lobbies as men half-dazed. What a night we've had to be sure! O'BRIEN began it with speech an hour long. Better have been forty minutes. But mercifully moderate compared with what followed. CHAPLIN, not to be outdone by Irish Member, spoke for over an hour; then GLADSTONE for an hour and forty minutes. Next thin end of the GEDGE modestly inserted during blank dinner-hour. Then BALFOUR for two hours and ten minutes; and, finally, SEXTON, for as long as House would listen to him.

HARTINGTON spent miserable time for last forty-eight hours with speech laboriously prepared. HARCOURT sat on Front Bench all night big with impromptus, packed to his boots with repartees. Wind Bag SEXTON appeared on scene with his perpetual smile of ineffable scorn, his illimitable waste of words. HARTINGTON and HARCOURT mutually resolved to sacrifice their speeches. SEXTON sure to go on till morning. And he did. Pleased beyond measure with himself. So wrapped up in charms of own eloquence didn't notice that BALFOUR after first three-quarters of an hour had slunk away. Went on with same irritating everlasting smile, pointing finger of scorn at unoffending OLD MORALITY, who had incautiously dropped in Chief Secretary's vacant seat.

"No gestures!"

Speech of the evening decidedly O'BRIEN'S; volcanic in its energy; vitriolic in its bitterness; irresistible in its marshalling of facts and arguments; bold and felicitous in its illustrations. Pity the greater part of it was delivered at top of his voice, creating circle of stone deafness within immediate area. Gestures terrific, and dangerous to personal safety of Members sitting underneath. But speech finely conceived, inimitably phrased, good enough to compensate for these remedial drawbacks.

"*Erin-go-Bragh!*" cried PLUNKET, momentarily falling into his native tongue, in admiration of compatriot's native eloquence. "Splendid! But reminds me of what CURRAN said of GRATTAN, that he used to scrape the ground with his knuckles as he bowed in speaking, and thanked God he had no peculiarities of gesture."

*Business done.*—Vote of Censure rejected by 366 votes against 273.

*Wednesday Afternoon.*—Doctor GRANDOLPH, D.C.L., turned up. Not been here much since Degree conferred on him. Rather expected he'd appear in cap and gown. But same now as when he was General GRANDOLPH, V.C., or Lord High Admiral GRANDOLPH, K.C.B. Modesty still his guiding star. Dropped in quietly, and, as far as possible, unobserved. Channel Tunnel Debate on. GLADSTONE supported Second Reading of Bill. A little awkward that Doctor GRANDOLPH should be shareholder in concern. But trifles in the way of logical difficulties never insuperable. When he became a shareholder was in private capacity. In opposing scheme in Commons he appears as a Statesman. GLADSTONE takes other side. Delightful to see Dr. GRANDOLPH gently shaking ferrule at Old Boy; laments his deficiency of knowledge respecting military and naval matters. On the whole not in bloodthirsty mood. Old Boy let off very gently.

Early evidence of the Doctor's new erudition displayed in lavish quotation. Taken a leaf out of OLD MORALITY'S copybook. "Let well alone," observed the Doctor just now, with look of supernatural wisdom. "Better is the enemy of Good," he added, by way of peroration.

"Yes," said OLD MORALITY, unusually moved by this audacious incursion on his copyhold, "and Imitation is the sincerest Flattery."

Lord Tannel-Chunnel.

Bill thrown out by rattling majority. But WATKIN not a bit disheartened.

"Wonderful man!" said the G. O. M. "Fancy I shall live to make him a Peer yet. Dover Pierage of course. Shall suggest the title Lord TANNEL-CHUNNEL."

*Business done.*—Channel Tunnel Bill rejected by 307 Votes against 165.

*Thursday.*—Lively debate on Sunday Closing Clause of Local Government Bill. Government propose to drop it. HARCOURT, who might have slated Clause had Government stuck to it, now protests it is best part of the Bill. Can't part with it on any account. Incidentally birches CAINE. Ring immediately cleared. Heavy weights, about same height, and fairly matched. Conversation most edifying.

"Yah!" cries HARCOURT.—"Boo!" says CAINE.

"Get 'long with yer Barrow!" says HARCOURT.

"Uncle *Pumblechook*," roars CAINE, who is a student of *Punch*.

"Where did you borrow your Latin grammar?" jeers HARCOURT.

"Political lurcher!" cries Member for Barrow, and HARCOURT retires with this brand of CAINE red on his massive brow.

WILFRID LAWSON gave genial turn to debate by dropping into familiar Latin quotation. Turned out, to amusement of House, that in this respect WILFRID'S strong point is quality not quantity. *Timēo Danăos et dona ferentes*, was his way of putting it.

"The long and short of it is——" said WILFRID, summing up.

"That you put the long where the short ought to be," said BRYCE.

But WILFRID not to be daunted. Immediately after dragged in another, even more familiar, tag.

"*Cave canem!*" he said, looking at CAINE.

"That's Dog Latin, eh, TOBY?" said HENRY JAMES.

*Business done.*—Licensing Clauses omitted from Local Government Bill. In this way we're getting along quite nicely with the Bill.

*House of Lords, Friday.*—Our Only General at it again. WEMYSS made a back for him, with wordy Resolution raising question of National Defences. Our Only took it flying, jumping on GEORGIE HAMILTON, whom he accused of making "wild, extravagant, misleading statements on subject of vital importance to nation." The DOOK to the front again, apologising for having created scare, and explaining away his intentions.

"Fact is, TOBY," he said, when it was over, "it's my personal appearance that's against me. Can't help looking warlike and fierce. My martial bearing strikes terror into casual observer. I must dissemble." WEMYSS'S Motion utterly ignored in course of debate. Nobody said word for it, or against it. So Lords, always, polite, made up for slight by accepting it.

*Business done.*—Local Government Bill in Commons.

---

HISTORY REPEATS ITSELF, with variations,—as may be seen in the *Wood* v. *Cox* case. What will remain in men's minds long after other details of the trial have been forgotten will be the Duke of PORTLAND'S confidentially free-and-easy communication, which, like Lord JOHN RUSSELL'S celebrated Epistle in the "Papal Aggression" time, will be known as "The Durham Letter."

---

CON. FOR CASUISTS.—If "the Receiver is as bad as the Thief," as proverbially affirmed, is it less "scandalously irregular" to buy a "surreptitiously obtained official document" than to sell it?

---

THE PRUSSIAN DIET.—German Sausages.

## VOCES POPULI.

### AT A WATER-PICNIC.

*Miss Fritilla Papillion (arriving at landing-stage with her brother).* Why, TEDDY, isn't that STELLA CINNERSHAW?

*Mr. Papillion (dissembling his rapture).* Is it? I daresay.

[*Looks carelessly about, and wishes he had had a new ribbon put on his straw.*

*Mr. Petticure (elderly, but of youthful exterior, who has undertaken the control of the expedition).* Then we're all here now? I've told them to get the boats ready. I thought we'd just pull quietly up to Eelbuck Island, land there, and have our picnic and—and what not, and drift comfortably down in time for the last up-train, eh?

[*General Chorus of "Delightful!" "Charming!" &c.*

*Miss Manley (observing* Mr. BUNCOMBE'S *elaborately aquatic attire).* I needn't ask if you are going to row.

*Mr. Bunc. (modestly).* Oh, if I'm wanted. But they seem to have nothing but fixed seats in these boats. I've got so used to a slider.

*Mr. Papillion (who has been making some highly artful arrangements on his own account, coming up to* Miss CINNERSHAW). I—er—think you're in my boat, Miss CINNERSHAW?

*Miss C. (with a sweet smile).* Oh, am I? Then we'd better be getting in, hadn't we?

*Petticure (arriving at the exact moment when* Mr. PAPILLION, *overjoyed at his success, is handing* Miss C. *into boat).* Here—here, stop a bit—let me see, PAPILLION, you're going to stroke, eh? Very well. DEFADDER bow. Miss MOULE steering. Capital!—but Miss STELLA? No, no, *that* won't do—can't spare *you*; must have you in with *us!*

*Miss C. (with, if possible, a still sweeter smile).* Must you? Oh, very well.

*Pett.* And, PAPILLION, I'll put somebody else in Miss STELLA'S place. Ah, Miss SQUEAMS . . (*in an undertone*) nice chatty girl—*you* don't mind about looks, I know. That's all right, then, *you're* settled!

### GOING UP-STREAM.

*Miss Moule (to* Mr. PAPILLION, *who is rowing with the gloom of a galley-slave).* There's nothing more delightful, don't you think, than an excursion on the water? It's the *right* string you pull when you want to go to the left, isn't it? I never *can* remember! And there's a barge or a steamer coming.

[Mr. P. *just conquers temptation to leave her to exercise her own discretion.*

*In the Second Boat.*

*Mrs. Ballast.* Trim the boat, Mr. RULLOCKS! Now, what a pretty poetical idea of yours! But you must wait till we get to some water-lilies.

*In the Third Boat.*

*Miss Manley (stroke, to* Mrs. DEDWAYTE). *Could* you manage to keep her head a little straighter, dear?

*Mrs. Dedw.* I am trying as hard as I *can*, ATALANTA—but it *will* keep going to one side!

*Mr. Buncombe (in a gallant manner, to Miss M.)* Afraid I'm pulling you round.

*Miss M. (who has been rowing with one hand for the last half-minute).* Are you indeed? I didn't notice. (*Mr. B. executes an elaborate backfall.*) Don't apologise; I suppose you forgot you were on a *fixed* seat.

[Mr. B., *from the bottom of the boat, is understood to attribute the accident to some peculiarity in the button of his oar.*

*The boat which carries* Miss CINNERSHAW *sweeps gaily by* Mr. PAPILLION'S; Miss C. *is rowing under* Mr. RULLOCK'S *supervision.*

*Mr. Rull. (with a tender patronage).* Better, Miss CINNERSHAW, *much* better! Don't cover more than the blade of your oar, and drop your wrists at the finish—beautiful indeed!

*Miss C.* I shall soon get into the way of it, now I have someone to coach me properly.

*Mr. P. (grinding his teeth, to* Mr. DEFADDER, *who is inserting an oar in the water placidly at intervals).* Shall we—er—quicken up a bit, Sir?

*Mr. Def.* Eh? Rest a bit? By all means, by all means!

[*He easies.*

*Miss Papillion (playfully, from* Miss C.'s *boat, as it rapidly recedes).* Goodbye, TEDDY, dear, don't overtire yourself!

[*He hears her voice from afar informing* Miss C. *that poor* TEDDY *is getting quite round-shouldered.*

*Miss Squeams.* Don't let us hurry, Mr. PAPILLION, it's so much nicer to glide gently along. And by-and-by, when we get to a quiet part, I want you to teach me how to row. I've so often wished to learn, but I'm such a dreadful coward in a boat—with *most* people!

### ON THE ISLAND.

*Mr. Papillion (after landing, and finding himself close to* Miss CINNERSHAW). I hope (*huskily*) you had a pleasant row?

*Miss C.* Oh, delightful! I rowed part of the way, and then Mr. RULLOCKS and I towed.

*Miss Fritilla (to her brother, archly).* TEDDY, *how* disgracefully you behaved with that Miss SQUEAMS—*we* saw you!

[Mr. P. *thinks people ought to know better than invite a fellow with his sister to this sort of thing.*

*Mr. Pett. (to numerous private inquiries).* It's no good—we *can't* do anything till BUNCOMBE'S boat comes up; they've got the champagne, and the knives, and all the plates—and they're not in sight yet!

*Mr. P. (making a second approach to* Miss C.). I don't think this party has been very well managed.

*Miss C.* Oh, *don't* you? I thought Mr. PETTICURE arranged everything so beautifully!

[Mr. P. *is about to explain what he considers were errors of judgment, as* Mr. PETTICURE *comes up with an immense bunch of grasses.*

*Mr. Pett. (with the air of an authority on costume).* I've been wondering all the morning *what* it was your hat wanted to make it absolute perfection, Miss STELLA! Allow me—one moment—there . . . (*he fastens bunch into her hat*) charming—charming!

[Miss C. *submits as sweetly as ever.*

*Mr. Pap. (indignantly, as* Mr. PETTICURE *ambles off).* But you don't approve of that, surely!

*Miss C.* Oh, no—it's hideous, but I can't take them out very well now, *can* I?

[Mr. P. *is about to express his sense of her angelic consideration—when his sister intervenes as usual.*

*Miss Fritilla.* Now, TEDDY, I want to talk to STELLA very particularly. Go and make yourself useful with the hampers, or there's poor Miss SQUEAMS all alone there!

Mr. BUNCOMBE'S *boat arrives an hour late, with* Miss MANLEY *and* Mrs. DEDWAYTE *in shocking bad tempers, as he has volunteered to steer, and broken two sculls getting into a lock; B. is as serenely pleased with himself as ever, and says the Conservators ought to make the lock entrances wider.*

*Miss Squeams (to* Mr. PAPILLION). I thought Mr. BUNCOMBE was such a "crack oar," as you call it?

*Mr. Papillion (who is feeling misanthropic).* I don't know what you expected—but he's smashed two already.

### AFTER THE PICNIC.

Mr. PETTICURE *is secretly depressed because a young man in a burst of effusion has wished that he had a father like him. Several Ladies "think they felt a spot of rain." Packing begins in confusion.*

*Pett. (coming up to* PAPILLION). Look here, we must make some alterations going back. Miss MANLEY'S very anxious to get back as soon as possible—so's Miss CINNERSHAW.

*Pap. (trying to repress his delight).* Yes? and you want me to,—eh?

*Pett.* Exactly, old fellow, to take Miss ATALANTA MANLEY'S place in BUNCOMBE'S boat.

*Pap.* And—er—how's Miss CINNERSHAW going?

*Pett.* Oh, in *my* boat—it's the fastest; with Miss STELLA and Miss MANLEY, and RULLOCKS, rowing randan, we can drop down in no time, and take some of the old people on with us—you and BUNCOMBE can manage without a cox, I daresay.

### OUTSIDE THE STATION.

*Bunc.* There's plenty of time, I tell you. What's the matter with you? You've been as grumpy as a pig all the way down. I *told* you I didn't feel up to doing much work coming back. Of course I shouldn't have run into the bank if I'd seen where I was going; but, after all, the damage to the boat won't come to much, between us, and it didn't delay us half an hour! What, just missed the last train? Well, I thought it was rather a forlorn hope—but your sister will be all right, you know. And you and I, old chap, must keep up one another's spirits at the Hotel, eh?

[PAPILLION, *who has been reckoning on the railway journey as his last chance, is incapable of replying.*

## MR. PUNCH'S PARALLELS. No. 8.

**THE BICENTENARY OF THE ARMADA.**

*Captain Charles Beresford.* "GADSO! BELAY! AND AVAST HEAVING! MY DEAR EYES! THE ENEMY'S IN SIGHT!!!"
*Drake Hamilton.* "IFAKINS! AND BY MY HALIDOM! BUT WE WILL FINISH OUR LITTLE GAME FIRST!"

## THE NEW ARMADA

### AND THE NICE LITTLE GAME OF DUCKS-AND-DRAKES.

(*As it might have been written in the picturesque and patriotic pages of a new "Westward Ho!"*)

* * * * * * * *

IF the reader were a student of political men and machinery, he would have found few more curious companies on whom to exercise his discernment than he might have seen in the little terrace bowling-green on this afternoon of July. Chatting in groups or lounging over the low wall, as though on the riverside terrace at St. Stephens, were gathered many notable men—and some less than notable—of the British Senate, the *posse comitatus* of England's (more-or-less) worthies.

See those five talking fleeringly in a ring. Those sleepy eyes, that pointed chin you recognise already; they are A——R B——R's. The pug-faced young man in the cutaway garment, who eyes A——R B——R so equivocally, is his old friend and leader, Lord C——L; opposite to them stands, by the side of Lord H——N, a man as stately even as he, A——R B——R's uncle, Lord S——Y, of H——d, Premier of England. But who is that plausible and apologetic-looking personage playing at bowls with S——E, yonder? A pretty patrician stamp of man; yet the whole figure and attitude of him wanting in determination, self-possession, energy; and when he speaks a multitude of words with scant meaning of a satisfactory sort, all eyes look doubtfully upon him—for his name is Lord G——E H——N.

But he plays the game as one that loveth it, hugging the bowl caressingly, as a miser his money-bag, and eyeing the "jack" as keenly as an angler eyeth his bobbing float when a big fish is nibbling thereat, and the creel is empty, and supper-time draweth nigh, and the inner man speaketh sharply forth in favour of grill and goblet. Verily, 'tis a little game, this British Bowls, that a man loveth not so much in proportion to his patriotism as to—well, other considerations that need scarce be set down in detail here. Skill thereat, like unto success on the Stock Exchange or in the juggling diplomacies of parchment and protocol, argueth little for a man's merit as citizen, state-servant, or patriot.

"A murrain on it!" muttereth one standing by, a small but sturdy and striking-looking personage, with ultra-aquiline beak, and back adorned with a sort of decorative jib-boom, "Here be fellows calling themselves Supervisors of Her Majesty's Services, yet are they playing, as it were, ducks and drakes in the day of danger. A petty game, and an unpatriotic. Blurt for them, sneak-ups! say I. I share old Admiral HAWKINS's scorn of croakers. As the outspoken Admiral hath it, 'These same beggarly croakers be only fit to be turned into yellow-hammers up to Dartymoor, and sit on a tor all day, and cry, "Very little bit of bread, and no chee-e-se!"' Many alarmist scribes and factious ex-officials there be whom I should rejoice to see served incontinently in such sort. The yowling yellow-hammers only so cry what time they are out in the cold. Snug-nested, and safely perched, they pipe rose-water optimism of a shallow sort every whit as pernicious, in its own foolish way, as the frog-like cacophony of the croakers. I'figs, were I Admiral of the Fleet, with such marsh-murmurers and parrot-prattlers on board, I'd hang the whole herd of them as high as HAMAN, if they didn't clap tompions in their muzzles pretty fast. Marry, sneak-up, say I again. But for this same game pitiful with British bullion for bowls, and British honour for stake, I hold that no true man—— But who cometh here now?"

"Captain C——E B——D, as I'm a sinner."

"Is the fellow mazed or drunk, then? or has he seen a ghost? Look to mun!"

"I think so, truly," said H——N. "His eyes are near out of his head."

The man was a rough, rollicking, beardless young sea-dog, who had just burst in from the tavern through the low hatch, upsetting a drawer with all his glasses, and now came panting and blowing up to the First Lord of the Admiralty.

"My Lord, my Lord! They're coming! I saw them off the Lizard last night."

"Who? my good Sir, who seem to have left all your manners behind you."

"The Armada, your Lordship,—the enemy! But as for my manners, 'tis no fault of mine, for, as manners count among Party popinjays, I never had none to leave behind me."

"What wilt drink, man?" said the first bowl-player, blandly.

"First Lord H——N, First Lord H——N, this is no time for bowls,—whether for toping or throwing!" cried the eagle-beaked bystander aforementioned.

"Why not, then, my PUNCHIUS? Come S——H, we'll play our nice little game out before we move. It will be twelve good months before we can be fit to tackle them, so an odd half-hour can't matter."

"I must command the help of your counsel, First Lord," said Lord CHARLES, turning to H——N.

"And it's this, my good Lord," said H——N, looking up as he aimed his bowl, "How slow soever they come, they'll come far too fast for us to be aught like ready; so let no man vainly hurry himself. And, as example is better than precept, here goes!"

* * * * *

**THRIFT.**

*Highlander (he had struck his foot against a "stane").* "PHEW-TS!—E-EH WHAT A DING MA PUIR BUIT WAD A GETTEN IF A'D HAD IT ON!!"

## NAVAL INTELLIGENCE;

### OR, WHAT MAY BE EXPECTED UP TO DATE.

HER MAJESTY'S ironclad, *Staggerer*, having yesterday taken her crew on board with a view to joining in the forthcoming Naval Demonstration, but being still unprovided with her guns, it was determined, before she started, to test her capabilities of offence as a war-ship by a little preliminary "ramming" practice. The harbour being crowded at the time, afforded a favourable opportunity for essaying the test in question. The operation, which appeared to create some surprise among the local shipping, was in every way successful, a passenger steamer, several yachts, three or four colliers, and a steam-dredger being in turn all sent to the bottom in a remarkably short space of time by the *Staggerer* accomplishing its task with perfect facility, as it made several vigorous and unexpected runs up and down the wreck-strewn water. It is rumoured that the incident will probably form the basis of an official inquiry.

---

A rather serious accident is reported as having occurred yesterday afternoon on board Her Majesty's belted cruiser *Perambulator*. It appears that the Purser's Mate having dropped a three-penny bit in the magazine, incautiously entered it with a lighted candle, and letting a spark fall on the fifteen tons of powder stored there, ignited the whole, with the result of blowing out the ship's bottom, and otherwise seriously disabling her. It is said that the occurrence will, in all probability, form the subject-matter of an official inquiry.

---

Last evening, the turret-ship *Boot-jack*, while slipping her cables for the night, suddenly headed on towards the ironclad *Magog*, and as she was bearing down on her, the order to "go ahead at full speed" having by some unaccountable mischance been given instead of that to "go astern," an inevitable collision was the result. The *Magog* had an entire watertight compartment stove in, while the whole of the bows of the *Boot-jack* were carried clean away, and both of the vessels were towed inshore in a sinking condition by the rest of the Fleet. It is reported that the untoward *contretemps* will very likely afford material for an official inquiry.

---

Last night there was again the usual collision in the dark among the torpedo boats, and three more went to the bottom. It is rumoured that the affair will shortly become the subject-matter of an official inquiry.

## ROBERT AT THE ACADEMY.

No. 26. Ah, I'm not at all surprized at the gorgeus but disgusted Footman looking quite ashamed at having to carry the Baby's Nore's Ark from the Stores! or that all the pore peeple as is a buying their wittles and drink shood look so estonished at the meanness of the grand Carridge Peeple, and all jest to save a paltry sixpense or so.

No. 288. The Ghost of a Patient.

No. 126. "The Burden of many years." Ah, poor thing, if she's had to carry that big bundle for ever so many years she must be pretty well tired of it I shood think. I nose as I shood be, but, thank goodness, that hasn't bin much in my line. Waiters wonts pashence and manners rather than mere brute strength.

The Parsons all looks perfecly satisfide with things in gineral and theirselves in perticklar, as they ginerally does.

As usual, No. 198, Sir R. Hanson, Bart., X- Lord Mare, carries off the Parm Tree. What a costoom! how all the other sillybreties hides their diminished heds and looks the other way at sight of his Jubilee Robes. His late Lordship seems about to say, "Bless you, my peeple!"

No. 348. Well, I do like cheek! The idear of saying as Sent Martin's Church is in the feelds! when we all knows, speshally all raddicles, as it's in Trafalgar Square. But the hutter hignorance of sum hartists in many well-known matters is sumthink ardly creddible.

No. 139. "Tria Juncta in Uno."

No. 360. The young coupple as is having of their nice little bit of chat, had better look sharp about it, for the old Lady, as pertends to be asleep, has evidently got one eye open.

No. 364 is called "the Garden of Eden," so praps I had better leave it to my reader's emagenashun, for I reelly haven't the imperance to elude to it farther than to say, that if that sort of thing had continued, I don't see how on airth we could have found employment for the wurking classes.

Robert.

## "QUITE A LITTLE (ROMAN) HOLIDAY."

(*A Page from History, more or less remote.*)

The day for the Triumph of Titus had arrived. It had been delayed for a season, as it had been desired (to quote a print of the period) "that the Italian Exhibition, *per se*, should first 'win its spurs' on its own merits." Again to refer to the same authority, "it had done so, and the Colosseum was opened with a view to give Englishmen some idea of Ancient Roman Sports and Pastimes in a more realistic form than had ever been previously attempted." And, to more fully carry out this intention, the Directors of the "spurred" (and possibly "booted") Exhibition, made a charge, varying from sixpence to 36s., to those Members of the British Public who desired to avail themselves of the boon thus generously offered to them.

The Colosseum itself had a strange appearance. One-half of it was filled with a motionless audience of persons in the costume of Ancient Rome, while the other moiety contained a few languid spectators, garbed in the costume appertaining to the close (or rather clothes) of the Nineteenth Century. There was a flourish of trumpets, followed by music, in an orchestra of exceptionally early Romans, whose instruments, however, were of far more recent date, and then the Triumph of Titus commenced.

First came a line of Roman Guards, whose helmets were brave with coloured worsted. They were succeeded by rows (fully ten men to every one of them) of Etruscans, Gauls, Legionaries, and Pretorians. They, in their turn, were followed by Gladiators, "Young Gladiators" (who seemed well qualified to accept engagements of a Terpsichorean character), Lictors, and many others. Then came the Emperor and Empress standing (somewhat unsteadily) in a chariot, remarkable chiefly for an entire absence of springs. They were succeeded by more "Young Gladiators," Consuls, Vestals (judiciously veiled), Matrons (seemingly not many years older than their immediate predecessors), and Slaves. It was a motley throng, and one that certainly gave to Englishmen "some idea of Ancient Roman Sports and Pastimes in a more realistic form than had ever been previously attempted." And as the beholders came to this conclusion they murmured to themselves, "So it is written in the programme—good old programme!"

Titus and his illustrious Consort having taken their places in a sort of roomy and draughty private box, the Sports and Pastimes commenced. First there were "wrestling bouts" that gave not only an excellent idea of Ancient Rome, but also an admirable recollection of modern everywhere else. Then followed foot-races that were as full of local colouring as the "wrestling bouts." These over, and the "gladiatorial combats" commenced. They were certainly peculiar, especially a contest set down in the official programme as "the Roman Quintet." Not surprisingly, the quintet consisted of five men—a gentleman with a sword and four warriors in helmets, shields and weapons all complete. The gentleman with the sword (who wore the unpretending costume of an acrobat) for a while indulged in a fight of two to music which fight of two gave some idea of the combats once popular in the minor theatres of the mighty Metropolis. Wearying of this, he produced a second sword, and, still to music, engaged in a contest with all four of the warriors, frequently waltzing about in their midst. This eccentric behaviour apparently caused the warriors to die of fright, and consequently left the acrobat master of the field, and ready to receive a wreath from the Emperor as a token of his victory.

The "gladiatorial combats" were followed by some chariot-races that rather suggested the idea that the animals engaged therein might possibly belong to that useful breed of steeds known to the moderns as "wild omnibus horses." Then came a contest between "the net and trident," which caused less awe than merriment. Ultimately one of the gladiators was wounded, and appealing in vain to three vestals of substantial proportions, who indulged in "*police verso*," for mercy, was done to death. Then it was that his conqueror tried to drag him out of the arena. For some time the dead man was motionless, but the journey being a long one, his legs ultimately became revivified, and obligingly assisted in the rest of his lifeless form's removal.

After this came—to quote the programme—benevolent and ancient document!—"the teaching of the Young Gladiators." This instruction proved to be a dancing lesson, and "the Young Gladiators," to judge from their *physique*, might have taken part in the days of their youth in a Burlesque at the Gaiety or a Ballet at the Alhambra. More "Ancient Roman Sports and Pastimes" followed, and then, with a grand processional march, the Triumph of Titus ended, never to be seen again, save at the hours of "4 and 8·30, wet or dry, daily." And as the small crowd of languid spectators dispersed, one of the more languid (thinking of the Wild West and the Paris Hippodrome of a bygone day) murmured to himself, "'Wet or dry'—well-beloved and antiquated announcement!—again and again, 'good old programme!'"

## GRAND PROSPECTS FOR "STUFFING BOYS."

Mr. Blundell Maple's an amusing witness before the Sweating Commissioners, who have all had a good deal taken out of them during the past muggy weather. He is reported to have said, on Thursday last—

"A boy who was engaged in stuffing could rise to any position in the commercial world."

Whereupon somebody among the audience shouted out, "No!" which interruption evoked a rebuke from the Chairman. Then Mr. Blundell Maple explained how he had meant that

"The boy could rise to any position as a stuffer."

And this correction of Mr. Blunder Maple's—(name altered for the occasion)—was received with "laughter." But wasn't he perfectly right at first? What better training could there be for the honourable position of an Alderman,—which counts for something in the commercial world,—than a course of "stuffing"? And as a "stuffer," if he only stuffed enough, he might at last rise to be a good old-fashioned English Mayor of the traditional type. For these are degenerate days. We haven't had a stout Lord Mayor for some years; there's scarcely a portly Alderman to be found in the whole Court, and not a nose of any importance worthy of the Ward of fine old crusted Portsoken. No Blunder, Maple, but you're absolutely right; and if an improvement can be introduced into the City breed of Mayors, the Sweating Commissioners will not have sat, and Mr. Maple's evidence on "stuffing boys" will not have been given, in vain. The problem, "What to do with our Boys," is solved. Make them "stuffing Boys"; and, like other boys, they have only to "cram" sufficiently, to be able to rise—(sounds difficult for any boy "stuffed" or "crammed")—to any position in the commercial world, and become worthy members of the Big Corporation and full-sized Lord Mayors.

## OUR BOOKING-OFFICE.

GUIDE-BOOKS at this time of year are our principal reading. MURRAY come up! or in this instance, BLACK come up! as he is first in the field, though the field is, just now, likely to be uncommonly sloppy. Where shall we go? I look wistfully at *Black's Ireland*. Don't like the association: Ireland's black enough just now; but "dark's the hour before the dawn," and we'd prefer to go in broad daylight. Here's *Black's Guide to the Isle of Wight*. Worth knowing, this. *Black's Wight*,—for once. Delightful short trip. Yorkshire is the next "*Black*" Country that's out, and after that Derbyshire.

Why not for once and away try the Home remedies provided at Harrogate, or Buxton, instead of Aix and Homburgh? You will find the merits set forth in Black—and white. Give the "Continong" a rest for a bit. "Better," says the village *Hamlet*, "to bear the aches you have, than fly to others (*Aix* in Savoy, *Aix* in Germany) that you know quite enough of." I have been there, and still wouldn't go,—not except upon compulsion. As for the seaside, well, the best air anywhere is to be got in the Isle of Thanet (which doesn't want Home Rule at present, and is perfectly satisfied with a decreased majority against it) whether you go to Blushing Birchington-on-Sea, to the Wild Westgate, to Merry Margate, Baby Broadstairs, or Refreshing Ramsgate.

The GERMAN REEDS have a lively entertainment just now, entitled *Wanted an Heir*—to which I reply, "The Air of Thanet is all you can possibly want." But there are more seasides than one to this question, and Black's move on the board is Whitby, Bridlington, and Scarborough, the first being far and away—well, it *is* "far," and a considerable "way" from London—the best. The Tourist must not forget to take *Tracked Out* with him. The title is suggestive of a guide-book, but it isn't anything in that line. It is a sensational shilling novel, written by ARTHUR À BECKETT, who is the author of *Fallen among Thieves, The Ghost of Greystone Grange, The Mystery of Mostyn Manor*, and who will, no doubt, in due time produce *Picked up among Pickpockets, The Filtered Phantom of Felkirk's Folly*, and *The Crime of Cricklewood Creek*. It is midnight, and I have just opened the book. The lights burn blue. To bed! To bed! To bed! Hark! Who's that knocking at the door? * * * * Yours, from under the bed-clothes,

THE BRAVE BARON DE BOOK WORMS.

## A MUSIC SCORE.

*Tuesday.*—*Un Ballo in Maschera.* Fairly good all round, as a *Ballo* ought to be. JEAN DE RESZKÉ plays splendidly. Good point that of his, making a pause just before "*È Scherzo.*" "I think MARIO used to do it," says ALFR-D W-TS-N, who wanted to follow the score closely, but, having so many sporting and dramatic things to think of, has brought a volume of the Badminton Library by mistake. "Very annoying," he says, "but between Acts can read the Duke of BEAUFORT's preface; always amuses me,—nearly as good as first chapter of *Pickwick*." "DE RESZKÉ's first-rate in '*È Scherzo*,' eh?" says H-R-CE F-RQ-H-R, appealing to H.R.H.'s Attorney-General. "First-rate!" returns the Attorney; "reminds me of a chap in some burlesque who used to sing, '*Let Dogs delight to Bark and Bite*' to the same tune. Went wonderfully, begad." "I remember," observes Lord R-V-LST-KE, "it was in a classical burlesque—Gods and Goddesses—all the Olympians." At this moment Lord L-TH-M looks into the Omnibus Box, but catching the word "Olympians" withdraws.

M. LASSALLE rather cold, but warms up for "*Eri tu*," which, it strikes me, he sings to perfection. "That's a pretty compliment to the audience," observes a gallant Major A.D.C. to Mr. ALFR-D, who smiles sweetly, but remembers something similar having been said by SYDNEY SMITH, and glides away from vicinity of the Major. ARNOLDSON's face and voice both pretty. Madame ROLLA not so effective here as she was when representing one of the *Don Giovanni's* easy victims, not quite such a Rollaking part. SCALCHI, as *Ulrica*, of course,—where would *Un Ballo* be without SCALCHI? "Where, indeed!" sighs the composer who writes under the name of WALTER AUSTIN (and for a very good reason); "but," he adds, kindly, "if SCALCHI only had a few lessons from *me*, you'd see what an *Ulrica* she'd be!" *Mise-en-scène* unexceptionable. Total,—good; but not the best thing this Season.

*Wednesday.*—Day out for Operatic Birds. DRURIOLANUS gives grand "Three o'Clock" at St. James's Hall. Goes "like One o'Clock." ALBANI, NORDICA, RAVELLI, & Co.

*Thursday.*—"*Guglielmo*," or our old friend "*William*" *Tell*. Big House. "Bless my dear eyes! what, *William!*" exclaims Lord CHARLES, and splits a pair of brand-new white kids when applauding the grand trio and magnificent chorus at the end of Second Act. He knew it would be a success. "Sure, didn't I 'Tell' you so?" says the Deputy Judge Advocate General to DRURIOLANUS, who is beaming again at the appearance of an entirely new set of ballet costumes worn by Merry Swiss Girls, Merry Swiss Boys, and a novel array of Bounding Swiss Beefeaters. "Can't be Swiss Beefeaters," objects C-MPB-LL CL-RKE, who lives on the Continent, and knows more of Switzerland than most people would imagine; "must be Goateaters."

Then he whispers in my ear, "*Je pars pour Paris demain*—beg pardon—I mean I'm off to Parry to-morrow; give you my idea of the political situation,—little sketch—when this you see, remember me," and he bestows this upon me as parting gift.

*France.* "Mate!"
*Déroulède and Boulanger.* "Not yet. We have another move!"

Mlle. BAUERMEISTER as *Little Jemmi*. Might as well put "Little BIL-LEE," into Italian Opera. As a matter of fact, "Big BILLEE" *is* in it, being *Guglielmo* himself, played by LASSALLE. What a pair of conspirators, EDOUARD DE RESZKÉ as *Walter* (not of *The Times*, but of this Opera), and LASSALLE as *William!* Both "very fine and large." Little *Arnoldo* (M. PRÉVOST) shouts his loudest against them, but he's only "a mealy-mouthed constitutional Leader," only a foolish O'DONNELL or a mildly genial JUSTIN M'CARTHY against the gigantic Swiss PARNELL and DAVITT, "nobly struggling to be free." This is an Opera that Floral HALL enjoys. He looks upon *Guglielmo Tell* as a Home Rule work, and wishes the G.O.M. were here, instead of gardening-partying at Dollis Hill. "*Dollis*," says the Floral One, very much in earnest, "sounds too like *Marionettes*, but here's the real thing." "Ah," sighs S-TH-RL-ND EDW-RDS, who remembers the palmy, and the GRISI, days, "compared with MARIO, all modern tenors are but *Marionettes*"—and down this goes in his note-book, in which, like *Count Smorltork*, he is collecting material for his next new book to be entitled, *Changing Tenors*, a companion to his latest *Prima Donna* in two vols.

Act First ends with the excited exit of EDOUARD DE RESZKÉ and DE VASCHETTI going out tobogganning, and disappearing down a steep incline. Act Second ends magnificently. Act Third ends noisily. The pippin has been shot off little JEMMY BAUERMEISTER-SINGER's head, and when presented to Grim *Gessler* (Signor MIRANDA), the Tyrant of the Tyrol, proves to be an apple of discord. Act IV. An apple—no, an appeal to the Cantons—"*Suivez moi!*" by ARNOLD, who, with a sword, goes through ARNOLD's exercises, rescues The Grand Old WILLIAM, saves the boy, is married to MATILDA MCINTYRE, a Scotch Italian—(same sort of family combination as The Scotch Italian, MCIAVELLI)—who has done what was expected of her in first-rate style. So in *Guglielmo Tell*, or the Story of the Apple, all ends Apple-ly, as it ought to do. Don't think *Tell* a heavy Opera, not as done here to-night: full of life,—"*Tell*" *est la vie*. Too long; not life, but Opera.

*Saturday.*—Considerable excitement to hear new *Carmen*. Everybody here, and very soon Everybody likes Mlle. ZÉLIE DE LUSSAN. Gallant and-far-from-Rustic SWAINE, Major A.D.C., says, with best French accent, "Can't have *trop de Zélie* here." Applause. After First Act *bosquets*, not bouquets, carried up on to stage. Out of one of these Pretty *Prima Donna* wrenches flowering shrub, as a Reward for RAVELLI, the Reliable. After Second Act, same business with Signor MANCINELLI, who receives small tree for his good conducting and for his knowledge of music in all its branches. Too much of this Floral Tributing. Occurring so frequently, it looks like a "regular plant." Brilliant house and brilliant performance. *Toreador* DRURIOLANUS *contento*.

TAG FOR THE RECENT JOCKEY CASE.—"Then (Jury) Box and Cox are satisfied." (*Curtain.*)

THE "CENTIPEDE."

A NEW FLEXIBLE, PATENT-JOINTED, VERTEBRAL OUTRIGGER. (SEEN—AND DRAWN—BY OUR ARTIST (THE FESTIVE ONE), AFTER AN UNUSUALLY SCRUMPTIOUS LUNCH ON BOARD A HOUSE-BOAT AT HENLEY.)

## OUR "MUTUAL FRIEND."

The projected visit of the Emperor of GERMANY to the CZAR is (says the *Times* Paris Correspondent) "considered to be a guarantee of peace, in view of the present disposition manifested by the young Emperor, which must be accepted as sincere."

PEACE *loquitur* :—

MUST be accepted! Well, I'm sure I'm willing
To hail the slightest reason for such trust,
Although the flaunting war-hosts Europe filling
May somewhat mar the optimistic "must";
A guarantee of Peace? I've known so many;
And who will guarantee the guarantors?
The Emperor, old or young, must be a zany
Who yearns for wanton wars.

A zany, yes! But then my ardent lovers,—
And all men are so, if you trust their words—
When my dove flies and when War's raven hovers,
Are so much given to confuse the birds.
Strange! Emperors pray for me, and poets bless me
Most earnestly when most prepared to fight,
And those who seem most eager to caress me
Are readiest to smite.

Still, I'd fain hope that "present disposition,"
May be perpetuated. Ah, young Prince!
Of warrior-worship you've made exhibition,
Proud passion for "my Army" you evince.
Ardent, spontaneous seems that youthful passion.
I wonder now whether your love for *me*
Is a soul-fervour or a mere speech-fashion.
Well, we shall shortly see.

And you, my Autocrat, austere and restless,
They say you love me with a burning love;
*You* would not see it wandering perchless, nestless,
My white-winged harbinger, my gentle dove;
The vision of the Shipka horrors haunts you?
The trump of Armageddon lures not you?
Well, if the prospect of my rule enchants you,
I hold it to your view.

The stricken sire, the aged grandsire vanished,
Here comes Germania's youthful heir and hope.
Were War's grim spectre not securely banished,
If, not in hollow phrase or canting trope,
But in plain speech of honest men, you greeted
Me, and struck hearty hands in my defence,
Whilst down the wind War's carrion-bird fast fleeted,
Death-struck by faith and sense?

Say, shall I make a third, get welcome ready?
Shall there be faithful bond between us three?
If our accord were full, our union steady,
That would be something like a "guarantee."
Are you prepared to hail me, Czar and Kaiser,
"Our Mutual Friend," foe but to fight and feud?
As counsellor and cordial sympathiser,
I hope *I* don't intrude!

---

PAN-ANGLICAN THEATRICAL AMATEUR ENTERTAINMENT at Lambeth Palace, for the amusement of the assembled Bishops, when will be performed the laughable old farce, entitled, "*To Oblige Benson.*"

---

CRUELTY TO HORSES.—Pulling and scratching them.

## BAH! BAR!

*Or, the Duties of a Counsel Defined by Webster.*

*Client.* If you please, Sir, may I see you without the intermediary of a Solicitor!

*Barrister.* Certainly, my dear Sir, under certain conditions. But I will not bother you about those for a moment. Perhaps, first, you had better state your case?

*Client.* My house has been burnt to the ground by incendiaries.

*Bar.* Are you quite sure?

*Client.* I think so. Then I have been deprived of all my loose cash by fraudulent trustees.

*Bar.* Yes! Anything else?

*Client.* My wife has run away, and my children have been unjustly expelled from school. My house is tumbling about my ears, and I have been unreasonably deprived of my engagement as a City clerk. And, now, what shall I do?

*Bar.* Really, all this is very bad, and I would willingly help you, if I could. But just answer me. Is any Solicitor acting for you?

*Client.* No, certainly not.

*Bar.* So far so good. And now tell me is any matter you have mentioned contentious business?

*Client.* I can't say. That depends upon your advice.

*Bar.* But I can't give it unless I know whether you are going to fight or knock under. But once more—are you *quite* sure of the accuracy of your statements?

*Client.* Well, I suppose they are fairly true.

*Bar.* "Suppose" and "fairly"! That settles it! I am afraid I must refer you to the other branch of the profession. As you evidently have no objection in the abstract to lies, *why, you had better consult a Solicitor!*

# OUR "MUTUAL FRIEND."

SPIRIT OF PEACE (*to the two Emperors*). "HOPE *I* DON'T INTRUDE!!"

## HOW WE ADVERTISE NOWADAYS.

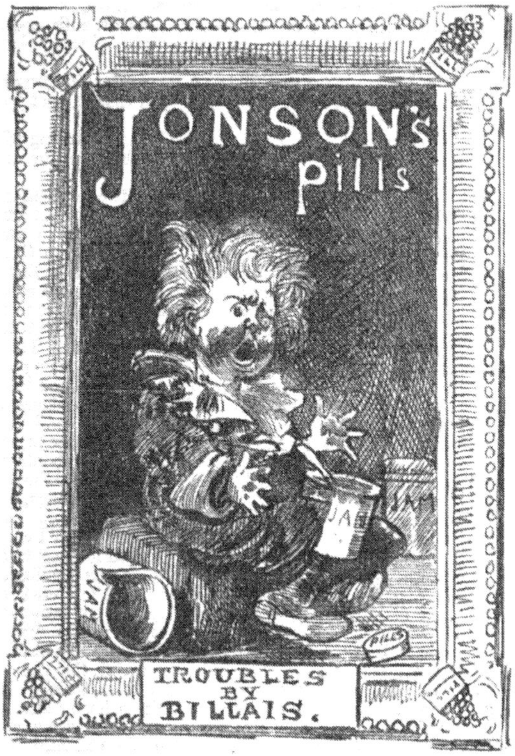


THIS LITTLE BOY HAS EATEN TOO MUCH JAM, BUT JIM JONSON'S LIVER PILLS WILL CURE HIM.

## TWO P.'S, BUT UNLIKE.

*Mr. Parnell.* Mr. PUNCH, I believe?

*Mr. Punch.* Mr. PARNELL, I'm sure.

*Mr. Parnell.* Your manner of salutation re-assures me. We are friends?

*Mr. Punch.* Acquaintances.

*Mr. Parnell.* Mr. P., if I thought you looked upon me as the mean-spirited, sanguinary creature the *Times* would make me out, I'd—I'd—well, there now, I'd be sorry for you.

*Mr. Punch.* No necessity for sorrow or anger. I laugh at all that's laughable, even when it's contemptible. I assume every man's innocence until he is proved guilty beyond all possibility of doubt. Therefore I assume that you and your party are innocent of the complicity in these crimes with which you have been charged.

*Mr. Parnell.* And you don't believe a word of it at all, do you now? Who in his senses can believe that I, or PAT EGAN, ever wrote such trash as was put forward by the *Times?*

*Mr. Punch.* I am in my senses, and I say, as every judicially minded man must say, that if these letters are forgeries, if your treasurer, PAT EGAN'S, letters are, as he wrote to our friend LABBY, M.P., "villanous concoctions," then why do not you, with the Parisian PAT, and others of your party, unite, and bring an action against the *Times?*

*Mr. Parnell.* Why should we?

*Mr. Punch.* Why? Because the cause which you have at heart will gain the sympathy of all liberal-minded Englishmen, if you purge yourself and your party from all taint of crime, and thus confound your accusers.

*Mr. Parnell.* Those who would believe that I wrote "make it hot for old FORSTER," or that PAT EGAN wrote as he is represented to have done, would believe anything.

*Mr. Punch.* Just so; and the majority of Englishmen, "from information received" at the trials of the American Irish Dynamiters and Phœnix Park murderers, will continue to regard you and the "constitutional leaders," be they "mealy-mouthed" or not, suspiciously, until you yourself take up the gauntlet the *Times* has long ago thrown down, and bring a civil action for libel, or place Proprietor, Editor, Printers, and Publishers in the Dock of the Old Bailey.

*Mr. Parnell.* See here now! When the *Times* first attacked me, you may remember I offered to have the whole matter sifted by a Select Committee of the House?

*Mr. Punch.* An offer the Government obstinately declined, suggesting that you should bring your case before the ordinary tribunal.

*Mr. Parnell.* And would I have a fair trial?

*Mr. Punch.* Before an English Judge and Special Jury? Certainly.

*Mr. Parnell.* If it were only myself, you see . . . . but—there, I can't do it.

*Mr. Punch.* If a person in a responsible position charges a private individual with complicity in murder, then I should say any man, conscious of his innocence, would prosecute the utterer of so foul and malicious a libel.

*Mr. Parnell.* But isn't an Irish gentleman's word as good as that of the *Times?* Why certainly. And suppose, now, I'd publish a pamphlet charging the proprietors, publishers, and the whole of the *Times* crew with conspiracy and with aiding and abetting forgery, where'd I be then?

*Mr. Punch.* Try it, and you'll see. *Floreat Hibernia!* Good day. *Causa nondum finita est.* [*Exeunt severally.*

## "READY, AYE READY!"

(*Imperial Naval Farce, just produced with great success.*)

*A Secret Chamber in Whitehall.* Exalted Admiralty Official *listening attentively to report of* Well-informed Subordinate.

*Exalted Admiralty Official.* Then I am to understand that the *Jackass, Bouncer, Wheelbarrow, Phlegethon,* and *Rattlesnake* have been patched up into a condition that will at least warrant the expectation that they will float.

*Well-informed Subordinate.* Yes, my Lord.

*Exalted Admiralty Official.* And new bottoms have been put on to the *Blunderer, Pigstye,* and *Corkscrew?*

*Well-informed Subordinate.* They have, my Lord.

*Exalted Admiralty Official.* And they can now be counted on not to capsize in tolerably smooth water?

*Well-informed Subordinate.* They can, my Lord.

*Exalted Admiralty Official.* And the *Blue-bottle, Catapult, Oxus, Jam-pot,* and *Thunder-bolt,* though their boilers want replacing, are not likely to blow up within a month's manœuvring?

*Well-informed Subordinate.* I think they may, my Lord.

*Exalted Admiralty Official.* And so, saying nothing about guns that won't stand firing, vessels, some of which are not quite seaworthy, and others of which the speed is not remarkable, you think we can make a flourish on paper that shall induce the nation to believe that, after all, it has got something to show for its money?

*Well-informed Subordinate.* Indeed, I do, my Lord.

*Exalted Admiralty Official.* Come, that is satisfactory. And how about the men? Have you whipped in the Reserve, hunted up the Coastguard, and supplemented the deficiency of stokers by the enlistment of the local bathing-machine men?

*Well-informed Subordinate.* We have, my Lord.

*Exalted Admiralty Official.* And the stores? You are sure that the several Departments have provided respectively supplies of marling-spikes and tinned rabbits, hammocks, rum, sardines, gunpowder, tarpaulins, coals, Patent Medicines, mixed biscuits, and other necessaries in sufficient quantity to enable the Fleet to put to sea for three days without replenishing?

*Well-informed Subordinate.* I am nearly sure, my Lord.

*Exalted Admiralty Official.* And you think that, after this secret three months' preparation, if mobilisation were to be, so to speak, "sprung upon" you officially at a supposed twenty-four hours' notice, you would be prepared to mobilise?

*Well-informed Subordinate.* Well, my Lord, I think we should—almost.

*Exalted Admiralty Official.* And you are of opinion that the country would be immediately impressed with the idea that the whole thing had not been a pre-arranged job, and regarding the charges brought against the working and organisation of the Departments as unfounded, consider that to be ready at a moment's notice was your normal condition?

*Well-informed Subordinate.* Indeed I hope it would, my Lord.

*Exalted Admiralty Official.* Well, then, I think I will try the experiment.

[*Does so, and ordering "Mobilisation at twenty-four hours' notice," staggers the public mind and produces immense effect.*

AD DAVIDIUM PLUNKETUM.—If Cyclists are to be allowed in the Parks, why not throw open a way of escape from them to the poor Equestrians through Kensington Gardens? When are there to be some new rides in Hyde Park besides this squirrel-in-a-cage-round-and-rounder called Rotten Row? Never was a Rottener Row. The long-suffering riders cry aloud to the Honourable Ædile, much as our WILSON BARRETT used to exclaim whenever he got a chance, "How long! How long!"

## OUR IMBECILES.

*Solomon Snipson, Esq.* "AH—YAAS—NICE PLACE VIENNA!—AND WHAT I LIKE ABOUT SOCIETY THERE IS THAT IT'S SO THOROUGHLY *EXCLUSIVE*, DON'TCHERNO!"

## "VENIT 'SUMMER' DIES."

VIRGIL.

"Summer is i-cumen in."—*Old Song.*

SUMMER is come, though who can say
We've had a glimpse of a Summer's day?
Where are the charms which Nature boon
So freely gives to an English June?
When each enamelled meadow lies
Emblazoned in a thousand dyes,
And every dainty flower that's there
Pays fragrant tribute to the air,
While, high above, the leafy trees
Bend to the whispers of the breeze,
And every bird, with swelling throat,
Fills Heaven with his grateful note,
And all created things confess
The spell of so much loveliness;
Oh, where are all these joys so rare?
And Echo hoarsely answers, Where?
For she, poor Nymph, like all the rest,
Has caught a cold upon her chest,
Which throws the shade of disrepute
Upon her only attribute.
Aquarius, be off, my man,
With your confounded watering-can;
Without a rap of rhyme or reason,
You're playing havoc with the Season,
And spoiling everybody's fun
Because you've quarrell'd with the Sun.
Pray recollect that, when it pours,
You stop all pleasure out of doors,
And that for cricket a morass
Is not so good as simple grass;
What man will want to play at tennis,
When every lawn just like a fen is,
Or care to screw his polo stud
By gallopping all day through mud?
No creatures e'en in fur or feather
Can stand such execrable weather,
While as for those from foreign parts
You're nearly breaking all their hearts.
The lion roars with might and main
As he thinks of the drought of his native plain,
And the virtues of flannel are highly taxed,
For the throat of the big giraffe's relaxed;
The elephant too has a bad catarrh,
And he blows his nose like a loud petar;
The wolf, to be eased of rheumatic pain,
Flies for relief to his proper bane;
And his aching bones confess the might
Of panacean aconite.
Each bird sits dumb in his feathered suit,
For too much liquid has made them mute.
So pray be off, and let us try
The effect of a sunny and warm July,
Give Phœbus a bit of a chance to blaze
And have done with these dripping, dropsied days,
Or else the country will soon become,
Aquarius, an Aquarium.

## THE DIARY OF A NOBODY.

*May* 4.—CARRIE's mother returned the LORD MAYOR's invitation, which was sent her to look at, with apologies for having upset a glass of port over it. I was too angry to say anything.

*May* 5.—Bought a pair of lavender kid-gloves for next Monday, and two white ties, in case one got spoiled in the tying.

*May* 6 (*Sunday*).—A very dull sermon, during which, I regret to say, I twice thought of the Mansion House reception to-morrow.

*May* 7.—A big red letter day, viz., the LORD MAYOR's reception. The whole house upset. I had to get dressed by half-past six, as CARRIE wanted the room to herself. Mrs. JAMES had come up from Sutton to help CARRIE, so I could not help thinking it unreasonable that she could require the entire attention of SARAH, the servant, as well. SARAH kept running out of the house to fetch "something for Missis," and several times I had in my full evening dress to answer the back-door. The last time it was the greengrocer's boy, who, not seeing it was me, for SARAH had not lighted the gas, pushed into my hands two cabbages and half-a-dozen coal-blocks. I indignantly threw them on the ground, and felt so annoyed that I so far forgot myself as to box the boy's ears. He went away crying, and said he should summons me, a thing I would not have happen for the world. In the dark I stepped on a piece of the cabbage, which brought me down on the flags all of a heap. For a moment I was stunned, but when I recovered I crawled upstairs into the drawing-room, and on looking into the chimney-glass discovered that my chin was bleeding, my shirt smeared with the coal-blocks, and my left trowser torn at the knee. However, Mrs. JAMES brought me down another shirt, which I changed in the drawing-room. I put a piece of court-plaister on my chin, and SARAH very neatly sewed up the tear at the knee. At nine o'clock CARRIE swept into the room, looking like a Queen. Never have I seen her look so lovely and quite distinguished. She was wearing a satin dress of sky blue—my favourite colour—and a piece of lace, which Mrs. JAMES lent her, round the shoulders to give a finish. I thought perhaps the dress was a little too long behind, and decidedly too short in front, but Mrs. JAMES said it was *à la mode*. Mrs. JAMES was most kind, and lent CARRIE a fan of ivory with red feathers, the value of which, she said, was priceless, as the feathers belonged to the Kachu Eagle—a bird now extinct. I preferred the little white fan which CARRIE bought for three-and-six at SHOOLBRED's, but both ladies sat on me at once.

We arrived at the Mansion House too early, which was rather fortunate, for I had an opportunity of speaking to his Lordship, who graciously condescended to talk with me some minutes; but I must say I was disappointed to find he did not even know Mr. PERKUPP, our Principal. I felt as if we had been invited to the Mansion House by one who did not know the LORD MAYOR himself. Crowds arrived, and I shall never forget the grand sight. My humble pen can never describe it. I was a little annoyed with CARRIE, who kept saying, "Isn't it a pity we don't know anybody?" Once she quite lost her head. I saw some one who looked like FRANCHING, from Peckham, and was moving towards him, when she seized me by the coat-tails, and said, quite loudly, "Don't leave me," which caused an elderly gentleman, in a court suit, and a chain round him, and two ladies, to burst out laughing. There was an immense crowd in the supper-room, and, my stars! it was a splendid supper—any amount of champagne—CARRIE made a most hearty supper, for which I was pleased, for I sometimes think she is not strong. There was scarcely a dish she did not taste. I was so thirsty, I could not eat much. Receiving a sharp slap on the shoulder, I turned, and, to my amazement, saw FARMERSON, our ironmonger. He said, in the most familiar way, "This is better than Brickfield Terrace, eh?" I simply looked at him, and said, coolly, "I never expected to see you here." He said, with a loud, coarse laugh, "I like that—if *you*, why not *me*?" I replied, "Certainly." I wish I could have thought of something better to say. He said, "Can I get your good lady anything?" CARRIE said, "No, I thank you," for which I was pleased. I said, by way of reproof to him, "You never sent to-day to paint the bath, as I requested." FARMERSON said, "Pardon me, Mr. POOTER, no shop when we're in company, please."

## OUR JAPANNERIES. No. 6.

[Our Lika Joko visits the Law Courts, and beholds the dignified courtesies exchanged between the Lord Chief Justice and *Mr. Punch*, previous to the examination of Toby, M.P. for Barkshire, as Witness in the farcical-tragical case of *O'Donnell* v. *The Times*.]

## ESSENCE OF PARLIAMENT.

EXTRACTED FROM

### THE DIARY OF TOBY, M.P.

*House of Commons, Monday Night, July* 2.—JEMMY LOWTHER back to-night after too long absence. Everyone glad to see him. No "pulling" or "kidding" or "in-and-out running" about JEMMY. Always runs straight. Takes any hurdle that comes in his way, "including the Temperance Vote," says WILFRID LAWSON. Looks as young and ingenuous as ever. Still mere beardless boy, as he was when DIZZY put him up to govern Ireland. Found on returning to House that Home Rule not yet established. High Court of Parliament discussing for hour and half Private Bill relating to Ulster Canal. Seems it's among the Ulster Customs to have a Canal. That's all ninty-nine Members out of a hundred know of question, though everybody ready to divide on it if necessary.

"Dam the Canal!" said STANSFELD.

Everybody shocked to hear such expression, particularly from such a source. STANSFELD hastily explains no "*n*" in the word. Merely a harmless engineering feat suggested.

After talking for hour and half suddenly discovered that there's no serious diversity of opinion. Accordingly passed Third Reading *nem. con.*, and JEMMY brought up in triumph to receive benediction of SPEAKER.

Coming suddenly on JOACHIM sitting in very centre of Tory camp, JEMMY's self-possession momentarily deserted him. Had heard something about change, but not quite prepared, after sitting opposite to JOACHIM through two long Parliaments, to find him in this position. JOACHIM held out hand, which JEMMY took in bewildered manner, and passed between table and Treasury Bench in apparently dazed condition. Didn't notice any of his former colleagues. But allowance made for temporary loss of presence of mind. No malice borne.

ARTHUR BALFOUR in high spirits. "JEMMY just returned in time," he says; "the very man to fill the new office of Parliamentary Under-Secretary to the Chief Secretary to the LORD LIEUTENANT. Shall get the Bill right through, and insert the jemmy."

Solicitor-General, interposing as *amicus curiæ*, volunteered information that "that would be flat burglary."

"Softly, softly!" cried Old Morality. "What does the Copy-book say—'*Gently does It.*' I intend to make JEMMY First Minister of Agriculture."

"That's your affair," said WILFRID LAWSON. "But, on behalf of Temperance Society, JEMMY is engaged for a series of Lectures on the Advantages of Temperance, in supplement to his pledges at Thanet." Evidently plenty of work for New Member.

*Business done.*—ARTHUR BALFOUR announces new Irish Policy. Government resolve to drain the Liffey—or is it the Shannon? That done, Ireland will be at peace.

*House of Lords, Tuesday.*—Lords nothing particular to do just now. Happy thought occurred to CAMPERDOWN. Land League on trial in Queen's Bench before Lord Chief Justice and Special Jury. Everybody talking about it. Great excitement of the hour. Why not have sort of mock trial in Lords? In civil cases Lords ultimate Court of Appeal. Why not forestall course of events and try case before it had left Court? CAMPERDOWN opened case for prosecution in rather dull speech. Well meant, but calculated to throw damper over proceedings. Seemed for moment after CAMPERDOWN sat down that he had extinguished debate. After pause SPENCER said a few words. This brought up the MACCULLUM MORE. Things now fairly started. Delightful to watch the MACCULLUM MORE strutting into the fray like a game cock. Figure erect, breast protruded, head thrown back, crest uplifted.

"Always think when I see ARGYLL plunge into debate," said ROSEBERY, "it's a pity Rules of House forbid musical accompaniment. Dook would speak twice as well if he were allowed, before commencing, to strut twice round the House whilst the piper played.

The MACCULLUM MORE did pretty well without the bagpipes. Mention of GLADSTONE's name is a fair equivalent, and sight of SPENCER or former colleagues quite enough to set him off. Banged them all right and left. Left them smiling, provokingly unharmed. GRANVILLE, taking matter seriously, protested against bringing on debate at that particular time, increasing difficulties attendant on a trial in Court of Justice. Markiss replied, and then it was discovered that in order that nothing might be lacking to success of travesty, Lord Chief Justice was in his place. Not quite so imposing in appearance as when he sits in wig and gown in Court of Queen's Bench, whether fast asleep with one eye open on learned counsel delivering speech, or exceedingly wide awake during examination of witnesses. Position less advantageous than that occupied in Queen's Bench. Can't look down on CAMPERDOWN with smile of ineffable sweetness as he does when coming down severely in Court on Attorney-General or HENRY JAMES.

The Campbell who is not coming.

"But quite enough, thank you, for me," said CAMPERDOWN, as he shivered under the stern glance, and the words spoken more in sorrow than in anger.

"I deeply regret that this debate has taken place at the moment it has," said L. C. J. Every-one waited breathlessly for next sentence. No one surprised if L. C. J., still fixing guilty CAMPERDOWN with stony stare, had continued,—"and you to be taken to the place whence you came, and there be hanged by the neck till you are dead."

Recollecting himself just in time, L. C. J. omitted this little formula. Debate came to hurried conclusion; everybody got off safely.

*Business done.*—Local Government Bill in Committee in Commons. Every one asking where is CAMPBELL, Member for Fermanagh, PARNELL's private secretary. Name been favourably mentioned in Queen's Bench. JOSEPH GILLIS tells me he's not very well, and can't come.

*Wednesday.*—A strange weird sight to-day. BRADLAUGH, at head of Tory hosts, leading them to death or victory. Oaths Bill in Committee. BRADLAUGH, with approval of SOLICITOR-GENERAL, moved certain Amendment. JOHN MORLEY, TREVELYAN, ILLINGWORTH, JACOB BRIGHT, and Liberals generally, hotly opposed it. Division called. BRADLAUGH and Tories troop into one lobby, Liberals into other. A close run; but the Tories, under new Leader, won by Six.

"What do you think of *that?*" I asked WILFRID LAWSON, being, to tell the truth, a little excited by general tumbling up of things.

"It's all right," said WILFRID, with nice air of imperturbability. "BRADLAUGH knows what he's about. Old Morality going up to Lords. 'Baron Bookstall,' doncha. Conservative Party will want new Leader. Embarrassing competition among ordinary candidates. BRADLAUGH walks in. It's their way. First they revile a man, then follow him. True, they never physically kicked DIZZY downstairs, as they did BRADLAUGH. But up to 1873 many's the time they wished they could. Our stout friend knows what he's about, you bet. 'BRADLAUGH, Beer, and The Bible!' not at all a bad cry."

Never can quite make out whether LAWSON's joking. Must think over this.

*Business done.*—BRADLAUGH, Leader of House *pro tem.*, defeats Liberal Opposition.

*Thursday.*—Black Rod up to his larks again. Never saw an elderly respectable-looking gentleman like this so fond of practical jokes. Always, about this time of the Session, lurking at doorway; waits till some Member is on his legs; listens till he comes to point of his observation, then with drawn sword coerces doorkeeper to enter, and bawl at top of voice—"Black Rod!"

Forthwith, "in defiance of Magna Charta, in despite of Bill of Rights, representative of the people must plump down into seat whilst the salaried hireling of haughty aristocracy prances up the floor." That's PICTON's way of putting it. PICTON a little pictorial, but not altogether inaccurate. Usually Black Rod waits to catch Minister on legs. The other day marched in whilst Old Morality on his feet. Later, shut up STANHOPE; to-day had satisfaction of choking off Sage of Queen Anne's Gate. But Black Rod's days of supremacy numbered. SYDNEY BUXTON takes him in hand. Means to see he comes in at proper time—say ten minutes after House has adjourned. Sage also on the war-path.

*Spectator* in the House of Lords.

"He had me this afternoon, I admit," he says. "But if, when Vote for House of Lords is reached, I don't move to reduce his salary by £500, my Christian name's not LABBY."

Little procession of two, which usually follows SPEAKER to House of Lords on these State occasions, increased by one.

ADDISON, Q.C., has carried useful Bill, clipping wings of harpy who hovers over Penny-readings, and comes down for penalties for breach of copyright in songs. Musical Copyright Bill, in batch of Measures to receive Assent. "I must do the *Spectator*," says ADDISON. So goes out in train of SPEAKER, amid cheers from both sides. *Business done.*—Committee of Supply.

*Friday.*—Great Libel Case came on on appeal in Commons. *Times* says PARNELL wrote certain letters. PARNELL replies, "You're another." There the matter rests.

After this, House resumed Committee on Local Government Bill. Spent evening sitting discussing whether we should pay ourselves wages or not. On whole, decided not; 135 voted for wages; 192, drawing themselves up to full height, declined to take a penny.

Voted with the majority. Knew a single vote would not turn scale. Looks well with constituency.

---

ECCLESIASTICAL INTELLIGENCE. — When the Archbishop of CANTERBURY gave a party to the Pan-Anglican Conference, the guests of his Grace were prepared to take Pot-luck. An English Cook provided the dinner. Everything was fried or stewed in a Pan Anglican. Pan-cakes were of course on the *menu*. There was a concert of Pan-pipes afterwards. Each Bishop had his own pan-acea for the grievances of the time.

"Enough on this head!"

THE COMMON CRICKET, OR THANKYSIR IRRITANS.

## VOCES POPULI.

### AT THE ITALIAN EXHIBITION.

In the Sculpture Gallery.

*A group of British Visitors are dubiously inspecting an immense "Monumental Fireplace," representing rocks, in the centre of which a marble Mermaid (heroic size), is emerging from a gigantic shell, and toying absently with an octopus.*

*First Visitor.* Very peculiar, eh? (*Consults Catalogue, and finds the work described as "Decus Pelagi," which does not help him much.*) Um—a fancy piece!

[*Suddenly loses interest in it, and moves on.*

*Female V.* (*to her Husband*). It looks like a drowned diver; but then, what is that long thing, like the end of an eel, sticking out of the shell?

*Her Husband.* That's her tail—she's a mermaid, you see. And an octopus has got hold of her arm, while she's pinched in that shell. It's very well done.

*F. V.* Oh, very. But not at all a pleasant subject, *is* it?

*Husband.* Well—(*considers, without being able to arrive at any opinion*)—that depends on the view you *take* of it.

*F. V.* (*wavering*). I suppose it does; but still—(*forgets what her objection is exactly, and becomes languid*)—oh yes, no doubt.

*Jocular V.* (*to his Wife*). How d'ye think that would look in our back parlour, eh, Polly?

*Polly.* I wouldn't have it, not if you was to give it me, I wouldn't. Why, they haven't left no place to stand a clock and ornaments on.

*Mr. Highsniffe* (*who is endeavouring to form the taste of his fiancée,* Miss Phyllis Tyne). You don't mean to tell me you *like* any of these things!

*Miss Phyllis.* Well, I don't pretend to be partial to statuary as a general rule; but I *do* like this. It's all so natural, with the eyes put in and everything. Why, look at the beads in this girl's necklace!—and I'm sure you can count every stitch in that jersey! And the boy trying to button his shirt; and the black girl who has just been vaccinated; and the little girl caught reading a book she oughtn't to—they're as real as life!

[Mr. Highsniffe *comforts himself by reflecting that one can't have everything in this world.*

In the Picture Gallery.

*A Visitor* (*examining a representation of the "Flight of the Pope Eugenio IV."*). That's the Pope, you see, standing up in the boat.

*Second V.* Yes, I suppose so; but who's that crouching down behind the shield, in the red bonnet?

*First V.* (*who has not noticed this before*). That! Oh, that's his wife, I expect.

*In Room V. are some Colossal Canvasses, which produce an intimidating effect upon the spectators, who stand before them in gasping silence.*

*First Spectator* (*on recovering speech*). Appears to be a battle, or something of the kind, going on, eh? (*has a misgiving that this is rather a rash conclusion*). I don't know, though.

*Second S.* Oh, it's a battle—it's certainly a *battle.* What battle, I can't say, unless it's the battle of—(*tries to recollect the name of any ancient battle, but fails*). Very likely the catalogue will tell us. Ah, of course, Imera—in Sicily, you know (*he gives this piece of information as if he had not just found it in the Catalogue*).

*First S.* Imera—to be sure it is! Let me see, it was fought between the Sicilians and—and, wasn't it the Romans?

*Second S.* It was the Romans (*thinks there may be somebody behind who knows, and hedges*)—that is, if it wasn't the Greeks. I rather fancy it *was* the Greeks.

*A Puzzled Person* (*reading Catalogue*). "See Herodotus"—'um.

*His Wife.* Is that Herodotus on the grey horse?

[P. P. *gives it up.*

*Paterfamilias* (*to his son*). Here, Bob, you're fresh from College. What's "*Hic Optime Manebimus*"? Title of this picture over here.

*Bob* (*after a cautious reference to the Catalogue*). Oh, it's out of Plutarch—about the Second Foundation of Rome, and Camillus, and so on.

*Pater.* I can read that for myself. What I want to know is, what the Latin means.

*Bob.* Oh! (*desperately*) "Manebimus is the best man here;" he was a popular character at that time—a demagogue and all that.

*Pater.* (*suspiciously*). I don't see what that has got to do with the life of Camillus.

*Bob* ("*bluffing*"). Camillus—why Manebimus was his *other* name!

*Miss Phyllis* (*to her fiancé*). Oh, come along; never mind these stupid Italian oil-colours. I'm sure *they're* not worth looking at.

*Mr. Highsniffe.* I'm glad to hear you say so. These—ah (*with a slightly corrective emphasis*), oil-*paintings* hardly deserve any serious study. Where would you like to go now? There are several things you really *ought* to see.

*Miss Phyllis.* I've seen all *I* want—let's go on the switchback.

[*He yields with an inward shudder, and wishes that her tastes were less primitive.*

In the "Alimentary Annexe."

*Mrs. Bryanston.* How do you do, Mr. Lapsling? I'm only just waiting to see these Mandolinist people come on—and then I shall go.

*Mr. Lapsling.* Oh, really? I—I hope they won't be very long before they begin, then.

[*It dawns upon him, ten minutes later, that he might have made a happier remark.*

In the Marionette Theatre.

*The Puzzled Person* (*the First Part is beginning, and a bearded puppet in a turban has just made his appearance on the stage*). I don't exactly see what a Turk is doing in "*The Eruption of Vesuvius.*" (*A female marionette comes on with a jerky caution, kneels to the Turk, clasps her hands passionately, and then beckons—the marionette with the beard is evidently deeply moved.*) Ah! she's warning him to fly from the eruption. (*Another female marionette enters, and kneels, after pointing upwards in wild terror.*) I fancy there's some mistake in the programme. It's *The Deluge* they're doing—not *The Eruption,* after all. That's Noah with the beard, and they're begging him to take them in the Ark. Yes, that's it, of course. (*Scene shifts to a cavern under the sea, with a fish swimming in mid air, without making any progress.*) I thought so—it *is The Deluge.* (*The bearded puppet enters, and, after one or two abortive efforts, succeeds in jumping inside the fish.*) Hullo! that can't be Noah, though! Why, of course, it's Jonah—Jonah and the Whale. (*Last change of scene to hall with columns and pillars; procession of four janissaries enters marching, with their feet in the air; a small dwarf follows, and begins to dance with great energy—re-appearance of bearded marionette with a staff, which he tosses up and catches like a drum-major, as the curtain falls.*) Why, I thought he was inside the fish. Well, it doesn't seem very connected, to *me*—but (*with a bright idea*) perhaps that was the Ballet *Excelsior.* Eh? no, that's the Second Part, though. Ah, well, we shall find out by-and-by, I daresay.

*Elderly Maiden Lady* (*during the "pas seul" by the prima ballerina in "Excelsior"*). Well, my dear, I don't know how you can laugh, I'm sure—*I* never saw anything so shameless in all my life—it ought not to be allowed.

Outside the Colosseum, after "The Triumph of Titus."

*Mother* (*to small boy*). Well, Freddy, did you like it?

*Freddy.* Yes, pretty well. Only I thought they'd have had lions, and—and—real martyrs, you know.

---

Latest Knights.—Announced as the "New Musical Knights." One of them, Sir Charles Hallé, is rather an Old Musical Knight, being seventy years of age, but—*H'allez donc!*—he doesn't look it or show it, when he appears at the "Pops" as popular as ever. Sir John Stainer is a Newer Knight. "The Knight is still young," being only forty-eight. He has plenty of time before him to prove himself a capable Sir-stainer of his well-deserved reputation. With musical honours, Gentlemen, charge your musical glasses!

## A SQUEAK FOR LIFE.

*Ritchie the Piqueur* (*to eager hounds*). "Back, there! Let him get away!"

*Ex-Piqueur Harcourt.* "You're a nice tender-hearted Sportsman! Just let *Me* have the Chance again—*I'll* Finish him!"

## THE BABYLONIAN BOAR-HUNT.

"The tenderness with which he beats the Pigs proves him to have been a *Sus Bœotiæ*; possibly *Epicuri de grege Porcus*: for, as the poet observes,—

"'A fellow feeling makes us wond'rous kind.'"

Shelley *in Introduction to "Œdipus Tyrannus; or, Swellfoot the Tyrant."*

*The Modern Swellfoot* (Sir W. H-rc-rt) *loquitur*:—

Tenderness!—and to Pigs? Oh misplaced mercy!
*I* would not spare them thus,—quite—visy-versy!
A fellow feeling? True, my moony Shelley!
If against Boars you have a *casus belli*,
War *à outrance*, I say, war to the knife!
I, Swellfoot, would not spare a single life,
Like Zephaniah, the hog-butcher, I'd slay.
This temporising is mere baby-play.
Call this a Boar Hunt? Not *this* sort of fun
The Attic heroes had in Calydon,
'Tis only fit for modern Babylon.
Why, the old Boar escapes, and, what is bitter.
Hunter won't let the hounds slay all the litter,
True, some are down, and some are maimed, but some
Are hooking it. Such "Sport" is all a hum.
*You* a pig-sticker? No, egregious R——e,
Your mental obfuscation must be pitchy,
Beating the Boar-hounds down in that mad fashion!
By Jove, it almost puts me in a passion.
Me the complacent one "of kingly paunch,"
As Shelley puts it. I should like to launch
My javelin at the Corporation Boar.
The brute should root and ravage then no more.
"Give him a chance," indeed? Such folly irks.
You'd spare the Metropolitan Board of Works,
If you'd your way, I've not the slightest doubt.
A hunter's heart should not be soft, but stout.
Agags are meant for hewing, pigs for sticking,
Boar-spears are made for thrusting, not pin-pricking.
A pretty hero you would make, I'm sure;
A Theseus who would spare the Minotaur!
You petty Purganax, your blows mere digs,
Your pusillanimous maxim, "Please the pigs!"
Would I'd your chance! But that *may* come to pass;
Then the Big Boar shall get his *coup de grace!*

---

An Initial Drink During Sarah's Season at the Lyceum.—"S. and B."

**STARTLING.**

"I'm very glad to have been of any comfort to your poor Husband, my good Woman. But what made you send for *Me*, instead of your own Minister?"

"Weel, Sir, it's *Typhus* my poor Husband's got, and we dinna think it just reet for our ain Minister to run the risk!"

## FABER MINOR PUNCHIO SUO, R.S.V.P.

Care Punchiole,

Alii socii paullò caninius scribunt; nostrâ scholâ altiora molimur: quæ res magistro gaudio est; nobis non molesta; nulla autem est ὕβρις de me. Habui unam tonantem alaudam hoc dimidio. Avunculus meus, qui domi, permissione ægrâ, ab extremis Indis jamdudum commoratur, nuper huc venit, et me equitatum excepit. Equum immanem, colore graium, caupo malignus mihi obtulit. Non potui tamen plumam monstrare albam. Cor in ore, ossa trementia, vultus maximâ tranquillitate, non dicere audaciâ. Equus meus erat ut muri Babylonis, ducenos pedes altus—vel manus, si manus libentius audis: et durus ore ceu messorum ilia. Bene, secavimus flammarum instar. Subito apparet præsepe, res ad unguem pro saltu. Animal meum usque ad punctum collaborare conor. Frustrà. Huc illuc saltitat. Ast ego non graiis servitum motibus ibam. Persuasoribus introductis quadrupedem ad præsepe appono, dum nequicquam avunculus a tergo clamat, veritus ut obstaculum superemus. Incredibili celeritate volitamus. (Stat sonipes.) Ego quidem non maneo. Sublimi ferio sidera vertice. Tunc tribus aut quatuor gyrationibus aëriis effectis, oppono auriculam cæspiti vivo. Ego etiam vivo; sed primum verò me exanimem cogitavi. Carpo meipsum et apprehendo bestiam brutam, qui quantulum nefandulum stultum de se fecisset ignorare constanter simulabat. Aquam fortem, ad avunculi sumptus proximâ tabernâ imbibi. Sic domum, nullo pejor, sed lætus ut cicala illa marina, cui nomen "puer arenosus" a majoribus nostris fuit tributum. Tuus fideliter,

Faber Minor, (*vulgò* "Snipe.")

P.S.—Cum Ionibus minoribus nuper dimicavi (si quidem Iones sunt plurales —non scio, neque curo, nec scire fas est omnia). Iones isti juvenes non pulchrè pugnaverunt, namque insani leonis vim stomacho apposuere nostro. Haud mora; caput ejus optimè charivabar, (ὡς ἐνὸς εἰπεῖν; Charivari, 1st dep. = *Punch*) donec spongium vomsit. Obliviscor perfectum de "vomo," nec scire fas est omnia ut supra dixi, sed donec eris felix quid opus est verbis? Amorem meum Tobio tuo.

## CIVIC ELOQUENCE.

If all Masters of City Livery Companies were like Sir Andrew Lusk, how readily should we all flock to their splendid Banquets. Having the other day to perform the somewhat difficult task of stepping down from the exalted position of Master of the Worshipful Company of Fishmongers, in the very middle of the Banquet, he took his leave in the following memorable words:—

"Twelve months since I appeared in this noble Hall with all my blushing honours thick upon me. But this day comes a frost, a killing frost, and withers all my blossoms. I must therefore say, Farewell, a long farewell, to all my greatness, and be satisfied henceforth to retire to the country, and propose toasts and make speeches at cricket clubs and harvest homes, and people will say of me as they did of Scott's old Minstrel—

"'He tunes, to please a peasant's ear,
The harp that kings were wont to hear!'

"In conclusion, let me say—

"'Charge, Fishmongers, charge! On, Wardens, on!
Are the last words of Marmion!'"

---

Haspirations.—Robert read out the titles of the harticles in the *Henglish Hillustrated Maggyzine* for this month, "The Mediation of Ralph 'Ardelot," "Pagodas, Haurioles, and Humbrellas," "William 'Utton," "A 'Ampshire 'Amlet," "Hin Hexile," and "Het Cætera."

---

The Clouds and the Conference.—What weather for Lawn Meets at Lambeth! Last week, the Pan-Anglicans who attempted to disport themselves at garden-parties, without umbrellas or mackintoshes, must have returned home quite Dripping-Pan-Anglicans.

---

A Sight for gods and men at the South Kensington Silver Charity Bazaar, during three wretched days last week,—Good Women struggling with *Fête*.

## BUSY WITH BISMARCK.

ACCORDING to an evening paper, Prince BISMARCK, the other day, was found playing a barrel-organ in the Imperial Nursery, while the Crown Prince and his brothers danced to the music. "You begin in good time to make the Heir Apparent dance to your pipe," said the German Emperor, putting his head into the room, and "looking with surprise and emotion at the strange scene." To this exceedingly exciting little anecdote *Mr. Punch* begs to add another of even enhanced interest. It runs as follows:—

Prince BISMARCK, a few days afterwards, was walking in the orchard of the Palace, where he had gone to pick a cabbage with which to make an apple-pie. He met a great she-bear dancing with the rest of the Royal Family, and was immediately invited to play catch-who-catch-can until the gunpowder should run out of the heels of his boots. The Emperor at this moment passing the orchard, smiled sadly and observed, "My dear Prince, who will pay the piper? This is indeed a surprise!" Shortly afterwards, Prince BISMARCK imprudently married the daughter of the Barber, and from that moment to this took for his motto the far-famed German line—"*Vätno söp?*"

## SARAH LA TOSCA.

BUT for the existence of such a being as SARAH BERNHARDT, such an author as SARDOU would not have written *La Tosca*. "Written" is scarcely the word: to be strictly accurate, I would rather say, "pieced together." The piece is in five Acts, of which two are superfluous, though not from a French dramatist's point of view, who, by occupying the stage for an entire evening, pockets the whole percentage, undiminished by any fee for a *lever du rideau*. Sensible SARDOU.

M. Pierre Berton as the Baron Scarpia Le Nez-apolitain.

If SARAH had not been so recently seen as *Théodora*, the scene of *La Tosca* might have been laid, with greater propriety according to our plain English notions,—and according to strict French notions, for the matter of that,—in Pagan Rome, or in Egypt of the Pharaohs; and then the scene in the side-chapel between *La Tosca* and her lover, while preserving its cynical truthfulness as depicting one phase of depraved human nature, would have been less objectionable to a professedly Christian audience. *La Tosca* is a purring sensualist, in whom whatever she once possessed of religion has given place to the most debased superstition. Her religious sentiment is akin to that of the brigand who murders and robs a traveller, and then drops a stolen coin into a box at some church door, under the vague impression that he has appeased a ghost which otherwise, like the revengeful spectre of *Hamlet's* father, might have made himself very troublesome.

Sarah La Dame Blanche sees a black beetle on the dinner-table.

Given such a character to purr, to fondle, to caress, to murmur gutturally, "*Mario! mon adoré!*" (dear me, how often have I heard "*mon adoré*" from the same lips!), to be fondled and caressed in turn, then to fly out in uncontrollable, jealous passion, and at once be soothed and petted and stroked the right way; then to be gay and careless; then to be frightened, distracted, shrieking, frantic, raging like a wild cat caught in the toils; then to be the cold determined murderess, shrieking curses in the ears of the dying scoundrel she has stabbed; then horrorstruck by her own deed, to "wake the corpse" with a private religious rite; then rushing back to release her lover, and, finding herself at last duped and deceived, to utter one last despairing cry and commit suicide,—given such a character, I say, and call her by any name you please, classical, mediæval, or modern, then the only person to play it is SARAH BERNHARDT. At least, I can think of no other: nor do I want to. The "situation" in the Chapel, and the "waking the corpse," are not more repugnant to our sensitiveness in such scenes being represented on the stage than are the prayers of *Louis the Eleventh* to his leaden statues, and his bargaining with heaven before the Madonna's shrine, or the ostentatious piety of the two unhung ruffians in *Fra Diavolo*. Those who are squeamish on such matters must stop away from *La Tosca*. In action it is, on the whole, not more terrible than *Théodora*, except the situation where she sees the knife on *Baron Scarpia's* table, and the happy thought occurs to her "stick it into him." Certainly SARAH'S *La Tosca* is a marvellous performance.

Last Scene of Sarah-Sardou-Richardson's Show. La Tosca precipitates herself from the battlements into the Tiber. "*Roma Tibur amem!*"

Beyond SARAH'S own part—and it is her own, for in this instance her individuality "created" it—SARDOU being a mere sewing-machine to stitch the pieces together for her to appear in,—there is nobody in whom anyone can possibly be interested. M. DUMENY is, after SARAH, the best of the lot as the amateur painter, *Mario Cavaradossi*, whose altar-piece would be a disgrace to any church; but M. PIERRE BERTON as the *Baron Scarpia* with his exaggerated old-fashioned stagey action, in strong contrast to the naturalness of SARAH, and his mouthing elocution, is to my mind simply ridiculous. I have never seen him look better, or play worse.

SARAH is going to appear as *Francillon* on the 23rd. Cannot say I fancy her in the part of the heroine, which Mlle. BARTET played to perfection. But at all events we may look for an original view of the character, and the play, in spite of much that is tedious in the dialogue, is a good one, with several strongly marked characters.

*En attendant*, SARAH, in *La Tosca*, must prove a great attraction, and could fill the house for a far longer time than M. MAYER'S season, which ends Saturday, July 28th. How much pleasanter it is that a French company should come over here and play in one of our comfortable theatres, than that we should have to go to them and sit for hours in one of theirs. By all means let those, who have neither time nor inclination to encounter the inconvenience of foreign travelling, encourage M. MAYER and his French Seasons in London. The synopsis is briefly thus:—ACT I. *La Tosca* Tender. ACT II. *La Tosca* Tiddy-fol-lolling. ACT III. *La Tosca* Towzled. ACT IV. *La Tosca* Terrible. ACT V. *La Tosca* Wild. JOHN IN THE BOX.

## "BY YOUR RIGHT—CLOTHES!"

THE COMMANDER-IN-CHIEF having ordered that *brown kid gloves* shall, for the future, be worn by Officers on parade, the following further regulations are hourly expected:—

On rainy days, Field-Officers will provide themselves with umbrellas.

In threatening weather, the Band will be expected to wear goloshes.

Fancy tweed trousers, of any pattern selected by the wearer, may be assumed at any parade where undress uniform is *de rigueur*.

During the hot weather, battalions may sit down on camp-stools by companies, and plunge their feet into cold water by sections.

Finally, the entire Army shall appear on parade in uniform, except when it pleases any or every of them to turn up in *mufti*.

A TRIFLING CORRECTION.—Several Correspondents write to know "why the title of No. 8 of 'Mr. Punch's Parallels,' last week, was 'The *Bi*centenary of the Armada,' when, as everybody knows, &c., &c." Here is the explanation, as we drop easily into poetry:—

The fact is it escaped our eagle eye,
We overlooked it, and we passed it 'Bi.'

Substitute "ter," and there you are. After all, what matters a century or so more or less in the World's history?—ED.

## ROBERT ON HARRYSTOCRATICK TRADESMEN.

PRAPS, if ever an Hed Waiter was hutterly estonished, and, indeed to say flabbergasted, it was on receiving a letter sum little time ago with a most butiful red seal of a Markis's Coronet, as I was told it was, kindly hinformin me that the Most Honourabel the Marquis of LONDONDERRY, havin removed his Wharf to 9 Elms Lane, his Lordship asked me to be kind enuff to send him a horder for some coals! which his Lordship said shood be delivered at my house without no extry charge, witch I calls truly harrystocrattic libberallity! His Lordship also hinformed me as he didn't keep no agents, but did all his bizziness hisself, excep, I spose, when his Lordship is in Dubbling. Being posserbly jest a leetle short of money jest then, his Lordship told me as his terms was "Cash on Delivery." His Lordship finished up his hinteresting communecashun by hinforming me that his Lordship's price for his Lordship's "best Londonderry Wallsend" was 24*s.* a ton.

Well, having herd as how as so many of our principle Nobillerty and their wives was a going into bizziness for theirselves, I ort not to have bin quite so surprised as I were, but as I had bin told as his Lordship was allowed a Sallary of about five hundred pound a week for running over to Dubbling now and then, and pertending to be King of Ireland, jest for fun, I really at first thort it must be a joke. Howsumever, I thort as there coudn't be no harm in trying, so I sent his Lordship a horder for a hole Tun, and sure enuff his Lordship sent them the werry nex day, and, to show as there wasn't no mistake in the matter, not only did his Lordship call me Esquire on the Coal ticket, but there was printed on it, in large black letters, "The Most Honourable the Marquis of LONDONDERRY, Seller!"

There's one grate adwantage in dealing with sitch iminent swells. A "Most Honourable Markis" would scarcely send me any slates in my coles, and wood see as they was all propperly skreened, and with plenty of nubbly ones among 'em, and all full wait. I ain't got no fault to find with 'em on the hole, but they rayther partakes of the April Fool carackter, that is to say, they requires lots of atention, as sitch harrystocrattick Coles naterally wood do, and if they don't git it, they fust sulks for a short time, and then quickly extinguishes theirselves, and there you are.

I thort at one time of writing to the Most Honnerable Cole Seller and xplaining this matter to his Xcellency, but I didn't quite no his Dubbling adress, so I refraned from trubbling him, besides His Lordship must have plenty to do to see to all the seweral Races he has to attend to, and to mind as there ain't no "pulling."

Being rayther particklar myself about spelling, I was summut surprized to see as the Most Honerable Markis's Carman spelt his receet, "Pade," but I spose as it stands good all the same. I shall suttenly continue to patronize the Most Honerable Markiss when I wants sum more Coles, as it seems sumhow to put us more on a pa with one another then we was afore; which is suttenly one to me.

ROBERT.

## NOBLE LIFERS.

LORD SALISBURY's Life Peerage Bill having been hung up for a year (in company with a measure of a like character, the Lunacy Laws Amendment Bill), there is now plenty of time to consider possible applicants for appointment. To assist the Government in its selection, *Mr. Punch* subjoins a first list of Candidates, with their claims for advancement:—

| *Name of Candidate.* | *Reason for Life Peerage.* |
|---|---|
| Sir FREDERICK LEIGHTON, P.R.A. | Special desire of Public Opinion. |
| Sir JOHN EVERETT MILLAIS . . | Can't advance one without the other. |
| Mr. WALTER BESANT . . . . . | Because he has not been Knighted. |
| Mr. GEORGE AUGUSTUS SALA . . | Senior to Mr. BESANT. |
| Mr. HENRY IRVING . . . . . | To justify Public Rumour. |
| Mr. J. L. TOOLE . . . . . . . | On account of his success as a Don. |
| Sir MARTIN HOLLOWAY . . . . | Sequence of former honours. |
| Mr. PEARS . . . . . . . . | To prevent jealousy. |
| Mr. JOHN HOLLINGSHEAD . . . | Title, "Viscount NIAGARA," compliment to America. |
| Mr. GILBERT FARQUHAR . . . | Compliment to Mr. J. HOLLINGSHEAD. |
| Mr. WILSON BARRETT. . . . . | By request of part author of *Ben-my-Chree.* |
| Sir WILFRID LAWSON . . . . | To get him out of the Commons. |
| Mr. Justice NORTH. . . . . . | To help the Lord Chief Justice. |
| Mr. Justice GRANTHAM . . . . | To assist Mr. Justice NORTH. |
| The Common Serjeant . . . . | To prompt Mr. Justice GRANTHAM. |
| Messrs. BROWN, JONES, and ROBINSON . . . . . . . . | And pray why not? |

CHANGE OF NAME WITH CHANGE OF SEASON.—The Dog-days of this year must be remembered as "The Cat-and-Dog-days."

## OPERATIC SCORE.

EVERYTHING going as usual. Good old Operas. Weather doesn't affect the score here as it does at Lord's. Good Houses every evening.

*Tuesday, July* 10.—*Il Trovatore.* Madame FÜRSCH-MADI—Fursch come Fursch served—makes a magnificent *Leonora.* "Doosid fine woman!" says the gay Colonel N-SS-N L-S, an authority on all operatic matters. "Very," replies Lord R. R-THSCH-LD; "thought she was French,—FURSCH-*Mardi gras,*" and he at once quits the house till the next Act. The *prima donna* gives charmingly, "*Tacea la notte placida,*" and "*Di tali amor.*" RAVELLI the Reliable quite up to the mark as the merry *Manrico,* but scarcely up to *Leonora's* figure. Brings down the house with "*Ah si ben mio.*" "Quite a Conservative song," says Signor CHAPLINO, thinking of the days of "BEN-DIZZY." D'ANDRADE encored in "*Il balen.*" Encore declined with thanks. At end of First Act NAVARRINI called before curtain for being *Mio Fernando.* SCALCHI powerful: singing with great taste and feeling. "I should like to give her a few lessons, though!" says the Composer who continues to write under the name of WALTER AUSTIN. "Never too late to learn." Somehow, audience's enthusiasm cools down, and opera isn't finishing so brilliantly as it commenced. Seeing this, and wishing to enliven matters a bit, one of DRURIOLANUS's soldiers strays out of his line at the end of the Act, and then pretends to be utterly disconcerted at finding himself between the curtain and the footlights. Signor RANDEGGER evidently afraid the soldier is going to sing a solo—unrehearsed effect—DRURIOLANUS momentarily paralysed under the impression that the military super is about to address audience on the wrongs of Ireland, or the Match Girls' strike, only recovers himself in time to rush round on to the stage, and find poor military super retreating from scene as fast as possible. Diversion created by incident, and opera goes twice as well after this, right up to end. DRURIOLANUS will reward this warrior. Promote him to a sergeantry in the supernumerary forces, and "decorate him," says Lord L-TH-M "with an order." Ah, *Leonora, addio!*

*Saturday.—Aïda.* First and only time this season. "After *Dorothy,*" observes Mr. H. S-DG-R to DRURIOLANUS, "*Aïda*'s my pet Opera." "It's my trum-pet Opera," returns DRURIOLANUS, who never loses a chance, and immediately disappears. DRURIOLANUS always brilliant when house crowded and everything going well. Recalls for NORDICA and SCALCHI end of Sc. 2, Act II., and everybody back again before curtain after Second Act. Procession splendid, *mise-en-scène* magnificent. Act III.—Novel effect of boat capsizing, and upsetting the mariner. Unaccountable accident, as, the singing being so good, there was no likelihood of a squall. Wind in orchestra did it perhaps. Last Saturday but one. Grand *Finale* of the season next Saturday, and testimonial to DRURIOLANUS and RAVELLI the Reliable.

### Probable.

GERMAN Doctors, in a frenzy,
Liking not Sir M. MACKENZIE,
Gravest charges make.

Hear the other side, say I.
May not German Doctors lie—
Under a mistake?

THE SWEATING SYSTEM.—Mr. MADDEN, in evidence before this Committee, stated that "*Government trousers were completely made at eleven shillings per dozen.*" Good gracious! Who wear them? Members of the Government, of course. Not eleven shillingsworth of "trouserings" on the Ministerial front bench!

*THE* CAMBRIDGE UNION.—The Master of Trinity is going to make a Mrs. of Trinity. The clever young lady, Miss AGATA RAMSAY, was "Senior Classic" of her year; and so was Dr. BUTLER, only rather more so by some years. Two "Senior Classics" marrying each other! How fortunate they are not two Senior Wranglers!

SUNSHINE FOR THE ETON AND HARROW MATCH.—Most appropriate, as every parent with a boy at Eton or Harrow was glad to see some little sun on this occasion. But ultimately Harrow took the shine out of Eton, and Saturday was dull indeed.

## STUDIES IN EVOLUTION.—THE ARTIST.

**OLD STYLE.**

AT THE "PIG AND WHISTLE."

**NEW STYLE.**

AT HER GRACE'S GARDEN PARTY.

## THE HISTORY OF A SIGNATURE.

*(From Our Life Peer Elect.)*

ERY DEAR MR. PUNCH,—No doubt the recent discussion about the signature of MR. PARNELL prompted you to apply to me. I will tell you as shortly as I can, my recollections.

As a boy I used, when addressing my school companions, my nickname "TONK." I fancy this title was bestowed upon me with a view to calling attention to my nose, and referring to my name TUCKER, "TONK" was frequently altered into "KONK," "TUNK," and "SNOUT," but I do not remember ever using the latter signatures. After leaving school, I used to sign myself, when writing to the young lady who subsequently honoured me by becoming my wife, "TOOTY," but this was a term of endearment that I did not adopt when addressing strangers. After my marriage, at the request of my wife, I invariably signed myself "JOHN HAZLEWOOD TUCKER," and "Mr. and Mrs. HAZLEWOOD TUCKER" appeared on our visiting-cards.

Later on, when I was honoured with a knighthood for discovering (and advertising) my patent Cedarwood Cough Mixture, I called myself Sir JOHN TUCKER, and my wife was satisfied with "Lady TUCKER." She told me that she preferred it to "HAZLEWOOD TUCKER," which, as she observed, "after all, was double-barrelled, and under the circumstances unnecessary." At this time I occasionally signed myself "JACK" when addressing my brother TOM, and "Your Dear Papa, J. H. T.," when writing to my son and heir, aged seven.

The Sandalwood Cough Mixture having rendered me a Millionnaire, I have, on the promise of a Life Peerage (which will be bestowed upon me, I have reason to believe, in company with Sir FREDERICK LEIGHTON), arranged in the future merely to sign myself,

Yours most truly, DE TÜCKERVILLE.

## CONVERSATION-BOOK FOR OFFICIALS.

HAVE you any guns for ships?

Certainly. I have twenty guns for ships. They were ordered five years ago, and were promised to be ready last January.

Were they ready then?

No, they were not ready then; but they may be ready by next June.

Are the ships built that are to take these guns?

The ships should be built that are to take these guns, as they were promised to be quite ready for sea last July twelvemonth.

But are they ready for sea?

No, they are not; but they may be in six months' time.

Should war be declared, would it not be inconvenient?

If war were declared, it would be *most* inconvenient.

And were war so declared, what would you do?

If war were so declared I think I should go on leave.

On leave—where?

Anywhere—outside my native country.

Then you have not much confidence in the Government?

On the contrary, I have every confidence in the Government, but should war be declared I think that would be the most appropriate time for self-effacement.

---

"NATIONAL ROSE SOCIETY."—"Happy Thought" by a certain energetic Operatic Manager,—Why not start a "National Carl Rosa Society"? or (this by Colonel HENRY MAPLESON, jun.) a "National Marie Roze Society"? The question of the chances of establishing a National English Opera House (or "Institute"—why "Institute"? the very name suggests dreariness) being now under discussion, not for the first time, the above suggestions may be useful.

---

KING MILAN *v.* QUEEN NATALIE.—Checkmate in several moves. Odd quarrel. King complains of Queen's extravagancies in Milanery matters. To which Her Majesty replies that she is never dressed expensively, though always Nattily.

# "'FIAT' JUSTITIA!"

Mr. Punch (*Amicus Curiæ*). "WHY A SPECIAL COMMISSION, OR A SELECT COMMITTEE, GENTLEMEN? EITHER OF YOU COULD WAKE UP THE PUBLIC PROSECUTOR;—IT IS ONLY A QUESTION OF—'*WHO'D SPEAK FIRST*'?"

## THE CHURCH HOUSE.

AMONG the numerous plans already suggested, the one that we are now enabled to place before the public seems likely to meet with the most favourable consideration. It shows, at all events, whatever be its shortcomings, a laudable attempt to supply a want, and to meet the essential difficulties which *primâ facie* present themselves.

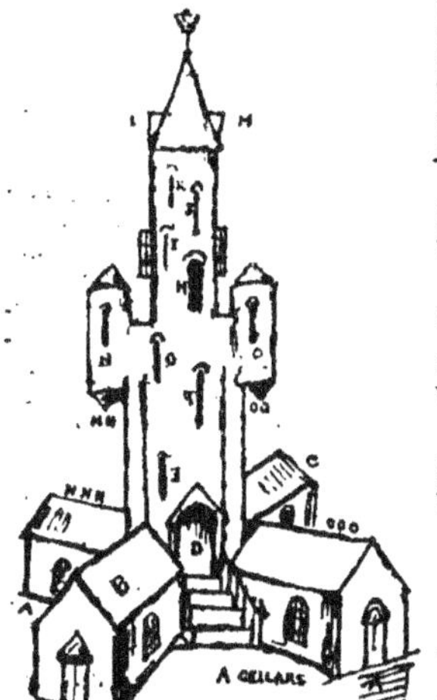


[N.B.—Design quite original. Nobody connected with Metropolitan Board of Works need apply.]

A A A. Temporary Offices for aggrieved Parishioners.

B. Church Association Department. Carefully walled-up inside, and no communication, not even on business, with

C. S.P.G. Society, similarly protected.

D. General Entrance, communicating immediately with separate lifts up to the different departments.

E. Extremely Low Evangelical.

F. Moderately Low.

G. Country-Gentlemanly Clergyman Party. Fair-sized Flat.

H. Broad Church. Large windows, with fine open views.

I. Moderately High. The windows (—) become narrower at this elevation.

J. Ritualistic Storey.

K. Ultra-Ditto. Expensively furnished. Pegs for vestments.

L M. Attics for the use of the Rev. F. G. LEE and small party. Airy situation, quite *in nubibus*.

N. Office of Mr. HAWEIS, with (N N) private staircase leading to (N N N) Concert-hall and Fowl-house.

O. Office of Rev. S. HEADLAM, with (O O) private staircase leading to (O O O) well-appointed Theatre and Music Hall, and an exit to Trafalgar Square.

Grounds arranged for Lawn Tennis Tournaments (for Bishops only); model farms for Rural Deans; summer-houses for Pastoral Plays, &c., &c.

## JULY JOTTINGS.

(*Extracted last week from the Journal of an al fresco Pleasure-seeker.*)

*Monday.*—Go down on invitation to the BILKERBURY's place in Surrey "to look at their roses and try their strawberries." Raining heavily. Still start. BILKERBURY meets me at station with dog-cart. Says "he hardly thought I would come in such weather." Five-mile drive. Pelting the whole way. Arrive drenched. Family depressed. "Try" the strawberries at luncheon. Find them colossal, watery, slug-eaten, and tasteless. BILKERBURY says it is the rain that has done it, and that if I had only "come down last Tuesday week *then* he could have shown me something like a strawberry." Ask about the roses. Says they are simply "mashed up" with the rain, and that there's nothing left of them. Spend a dreary afternoon playing backgammon with Mrs. B. Say I think I'll walk back to the station. BILKERBURY nods and doesn't press the dog-cart. Miss my way, and lose my train. Have to wait at the station three hours and a half, in my damp clothes, for the next. Afraid I have caught cold. Home at last. A very gloomy day.

*Tuesday.*—Off to Tippingford to play in the Home Eleven against the Roving Batterbridge Juveniles. Pelting cats and dogs. Ground like a sponge. Both Elevens boxed up in the tap-room of a small local public-house drinking hot whiskey-and-water. After waiting five hours and a half rain stops for a few moments, and the Captains determine to begin the match. We win the toss, and go in. Owing to the sloppy state of the wicket, we are all got out for eleven in five-and-twenty minutes. Cats and dogs recommence. Further adjournment, and whiskey-and-water drinking. Weather not clearing, other side decide to go out and have their innings, when it is discovered that both our bowlers and five of the field have left for Town. Opposition Captain furious, and asks me whether I think I "belong to an Eleven of Gentlemen." Point to the weather. Rival Umpire asks "What that's got to do with it?" and offers to fight me. Decline, and beat a retreat, eventually getting up to Town, escaping notice in the corner of a third-class compartment. Arrive dripping. Feet in hot water. To bed miserable.

*Wednesday.*—Glass still falling, and pelt continuous. Still, make up my mind to start for the FEATHERFLYS' Water Pic-nic at Cookham. Get there, and find the young people determined not to give it up. Say they are sure it will be "very jolly" if we only take umbrellas and waterproofs enough. Am forced to start. Find myself rowing bow in a light suit of flannels drenched through with a driving rain that is swept by a bitterly cold wind in pailfuls over my dripping back. Spirited young lady, who is steering, expresses her opinion that it is "great fun." After two hours of this, join other boats under some dripping bushes, to have lunch. Everybody in an ill temper. Get a soaked sandwich, and call attention to it. Comic man asks me what else I expected at a "Water Party." No one laughs. Should like to duck him. Start to return, wind risen to a hurricane, rain coming down in a deluge. Take an extra hour-and-a-half getting back. Hurry up to catch train without waiting to say good-bye to FEATHERFLY. Feel too savage to do it. Am all over aches and pains. Think, on the whole, it is the most disagreeable day I have ever spent in my life. Go to bed, wondering whether I shall be able to hobble through my part in the Open-air Pastoral Play which I am booked for to-morrow.

*Thursday.*—No change in weather. Worse, if anything. Nevertheless, start for Sir HARRY POTTIFER's place in Kent, to take part in a Pastoral Drama, written specially for the occasion by himself, entitled the *Apotheosis of Pan, or Sunshine in Arcady*. I am to play *Bacchus*. Rain coming down in torrents. Find all the players protesting against giving the thing in "such weather." Sir HARRY insists that we must, as Royalty is expected. Turn out, grumbling, and begin. Seeing that *Venus* has got on a waterproof, I put on an Ulster, and the Chorus of Wood Nymphs, taking the hint, execute a "sylvan dance" in goloshes, wraps, and umbrellas. Sir HARRY is hurt. Says he didn't think we would mind "a little wet, just for once," and that, of course, if we are going "to play the fool in that sort of fashion," we may as well "give up the whole thing." After a hot altercation on the lawn, held in a roaring wind in the midst of blinding sleet and rain, *Pan* absolutely declining to appear, even in his "Apotheosis," unless enveloped in a coachman's overcoat, a compromise is arrived at, and it is ultimately settled that we are to finish the Open-air Pastoral Drama as well as we can in the back drawing-room. Do this. It falls decidedly flat. Royalties leave before it is over. Sir HARRY grumpy, and almost rude. Take my departure, vowing nothing ever again shall persuade me to go in for a Pastoral Drama. Arrive at my Chambers, feeling that, spite the Ulster, my scanty get-up as *Bacchus* has given me a severe chill. To bed, shivering, and wishing I hadn't stood so long on the lawn in sandals.

*Friday.*—Feel that the sandals have done it, and that I have certainly got a chill. Head splitting. Aches all over. Glass hesitating. Think it really looks like clearing. Give three feeble cheers. Wonder whether I can manage to get down to the SPINKLEBY's Garden Party to-day, and put in an appearance at the Champion Bicycle Tournament to-morrow. Think I'll see Doctor. Do so. Shakes his head and makes me telegraph to put them both off. Explain my symptoms. Tells me I may think myself lucky if I get off without rheumatic fever. Says Monday set it up. Tuesday developed it. The Water Pic-nic on Wednesday brought it to a head, and that *Bacchus* yesterday evidently finished me. Orders me wet towel to my head and gruel. Toss about in a troubled sleep dreaming I am pursued by a demon Clerk of the Weather, who is playing on me continually with a four-inch hose of a sixteen horse-power engine of the Metropolitan Fire Brigade.

*Saturday.*—Glass gone up amazingly. Sunshine once more. No use. Comes too late. Still in bed. Wet towel still round my head. Still taking gruel. On the whole, an irritating ending to a beastly week.

## NOTES PICKED UP IN THE COURT OF THE L.C.J.

11·15 A.M.—Fairly punctual. Must not go to sleep until all my friends are settled.

11·30 P.M.—Think there is no more room on the Bench. Have given orders I am not to be disturbed.

12 NOON.—Opening for the Plaintiff still going on. Wonder if Counsel will last until luncheon interval. Pleasant voice—does not disturb me at all.

1·30 P.M.—Force of habit! Woke up in time to suggest that the usual mid-day adjournment should take place.

2 P.M.—Find that address to the Jury is *not* concluded. Very well.

4 P.M.—Force of habit again! Woke up to the minute. Some witnesses I find have been examined.

4·30 P.M.—Adjourned Court. Shall be interested to find what I have been trying to-day. Sure to see it in the *Times* to-morrow!

### The Summer of 1888.

(*Old Tune.*)

I REMEMBER, I remember
How this Summer fleeted by,
With its warmth of a December,
And its smiles of Janu-a-ry.

A MOTTO which certain Architects of the Board of Works acted on:—"One must draw the line somewhere." And they did. And that line wasn't a right line.

"IN CASE OF ACCIDENTS."

*Sub-Editor* (*to Nervous Subscriber*). "I MAY OBSERVE, BY THE WAY, SIR, THAT ALL SUBSCRIBERS TO OUR PAPER, THAT PAY IN ADVANCE, WILL BE ENTITLED TO A FUST-CLASS OBITUARY NOTICE!—GRATIS, SIR!"

## THE DIARY OF A NOBODY.

*May* 8.—I woke up with a most terrible head-ache. I could scarcely see, and the back of my neck was as if I had given it a crick. I thought first of sending for a Doctor, but I did not think it necessary. When up, I felt faint, and went to BROWNISH's the Chemist, who gave me a draught. So bad at the office, had to get leave to come home. Went to another Chemist in the City, and I got a draught. BROWNISH's dose seems to have made me worse, Have eaten nothing all day. To make matters worse, CARRIE, every time I spoke to her, answered me sharply—that is, when she answered at all. In the evening I felt very much worse again, and said to her, "I do believe I've been poisoned by the lobster mayonaise at the Mansion House last night." She simply replied, without taking her eyes from her sewing, "Champagne never did agree with you." I felt irritated, and said, "What nonsense you talk; I only had a glass and a half, and you know as well as I do——" Before I could complete the sentence, she bounced out of the room. I sat over an hour waiting for her to return, but as she did not, I determined I would go to bed. I discovered CARRIE had gone to bed without even saying good-night, leaving me to bar up the scullery door, and feed the cat. I shall certainly speak to her about this in the morning.

*May* 9.—Still a little shaky, with black specs. CARRIE had commenced her breakfast when I entered the parlour. I helped myself to a cup of tea, and I said, perfectly calmly and quietly, "CARRIE, I wish a little explanation of your conduct last night." She replied, "Indeed! and I desire something more than a *little* explanation of your conduct the night before." I said, coolly, "Really, I don't understand you." CARRIE said, sneeringly, "Probably not; you were scarcely in a condition to understand anything." I was astounded at this insinuation, and simply ejaculated "CAROLINE!" She said, "Don't be theatrical. It has no effect on me. Reserve that tone for your new friend, *Mister* FARMERSON the ironmonger." I was about to speak, when CARRIE, in a temper such as I have never seen her in before, told me to hold my tongue. She said, "Now *I'm* going to say something. After professing to snub Mr. FARMERSON, you permit him to snub *you* in my presence, and then accept his invitation to take a glass of champagne with you, and you don't limit yourself to one glass. You then offer this vulgar man, who made a bungle of repairing our scraper, a seat in our cab on the way home. I say nothing about his tearing my dress in getting in the cab, nor of treading on Mrs. JAMES's expensive fan, which you knocked out of my hand, and for which he never even apologised; but you both smoked all the way home, without having the decency to ask my permission. That is not all. At the end of the journey, although he did not offer you a farthing towards his share of the cab, you asked him in. Fortunately, he was sober enough to detect from my manner that his company was not desirable."

Goodness knows I felt humiliated enough at this; but, to make matters worse, GOWING entered the room without knocking, with two hats on his head, and holding the garden-rake in his hand, with CARRIE's fur tippet (which he had taken off the downstairs hall-peg) round his neck, and announced himself in a loud, coarse voice, "His Royal Highness the Lord Mayor." He marched twice round the room like a buffoon, and, finding we took no notice, said, "Hulloh! what's up? Lovers' quarrel, eh?"

There was a silence for a moment, so I said, quietly, "My dear GOWING, I'm not very well, and not quite in the humour for joking, especially when you enter the room without knocking—an act which I fail to see the fun of." GOWING said, "I'm very sorry, but I called for my stick, which I thought you would have sent round." I handed him his stick, which I remembered I had painted black with the enamel paint, thinking to improve it. He looked at it for a minute with a dazed expression and said, "Who did this?"

I said, "Eh? Did what?"

He said, "Did what? Why, destroyed my stick! It belonged to my poor uncle, and I value it more than anything I have in the world. I'll know who did it."

I said, "I'm very sorry. I daresay it will come off. I did it for the best."

GOWING said, "Then all I can say is, it's a confounded liberty, and I *would* add, you're a bigger fool than you look, only *that*'s absolutely impossible."

---

"HOW TO PREVENT ALPINE ACCIDENTS."—Simple old remedy: Stay at home.

## OUR JAPANNERIES. No. 7.

A PARLIAMENTARY WIMBLEDON.

## ESSENCE OF PARLIAMENT.

EXTRACTED FROM

### THE DIARY OF TOBY, M.P.

*House of Lords, Monday, July* 9.—Regrettable coolness sprung up between House of Lords, and House of Commons. Can scarcely be said to be on speaking terms. Talk at each other with elaborate affectation of personal disregard. Commons began it. Every Session on opening day pass series of Sessional Orders. One prohibits Peers and Prelates from interfering in Elections. This particular Order been passed for generations. Nobody a penny the worse; nobody a halfpenny the better. Pleased the Commons; didn't hurt the Lords. This year Lords suddenly woke up to indignity of the whole thing. Barons of England swore on hilt of Crusader-forefather's sword not going to put up with this sort of thing. That doughty Baron, HALSBURY (Cr. 1885), in particular outraged.

"'Sdeath," said he. "These beggarly Commons do assume too much. By the bones of my forefathers, the white dust of which choked SALADIN's host, this shall be seen to. A HALSBURY! A HALSBURY!"

That 's an excerpt from Lord CHANCELLOR's private conversation on subject. Rising from Woolsack to-night, and compelling respectful attention of ROWTON, moved Resolution to effect that action of Commons in the matter should be ignored.

"Let us," he said, dropping into modern English, "assume a don't-know-yah air towards these fellows. That'll rile 'em more than anything else."

"Attention!"

Suggestion unanimously adopted. Noble Lords adjourned in condition of high elation.

"A set of common persons," said that other Plantagenet Peer, BRABOURNE. "Teach 'em to mind their own business. Think we could get on very well without the Commons. Save time and expense. At any rate, won't have them dictating to Us. A Peer not to interfere in a Parliamentary Election, forsooth! Then what's to become of ME and my personal influence?"

*Business done.*—In Commons, pegging away at Local Government Bill.

*Tuesday.*—OLD MORALITY appeared at Table with bulky bundle of copybook headings. Desire to do our duty; animated by one feeling; nothing further from our thoughts; most anxious to meet views of House; no desire to affect legitimate discussion; profoundly regret; a great property in which the nation has a deep, a large, and a vested interest; would not use the power placed in our hands to interfere with the liberties of Hon. Members; I may be allowed to travel somewhat farther, and say; certainly, Sir; always guided by a due sense of my responsibility; desire to act in the interests of the public service; in this I do not wish to be understood; when I say this, I must also state; we should not be justified in allowing; I am afraid we should not think it right; and so on, leading up to final conclusion to appropriate all the time of the House for Government business.

Sage of Queen Anne's Gate jeeringly criticises proposals. Doctor GRANDOLPH, LL.D., much distressed at this frivolity. Severely birches Sage. Then turns upon Government, tears to shreds the amiable copybook headings, sprinkles Treasury Bench with fragments. OLD MORALITY proposes to take Local Government Bill through Committee, pass all Supply, adjourn early in August, resume for Autumn Session at the end of October. Dr. GRANDOLPH demonstrates practical impossibility of this arrangement. Shall be here till September carrying out first part of programme. How could House be asked to meet again in October?

"GRANDOLPH's quite right," said BATES, clasping his hands in habitual devotional attitude. "If programme's carried out, shall certainly have an Autumn Session, but it'll last straight through from now till November."

The Ven. and Rev.

Bad quarter of an hour on Treasury Bench. Deliverance from unexpected quarter. GLADSTONE takes Government under paternal wing.

"Keep your eye on your father," he says, "and your father will pull you through."

So he does, insisting as price of deliverance that Life Peerages Bill shall be abandoned. OLD MORALITY gratefully gasps forth assent. Message sent across to Lords. Been debating Life Peerages Bill all night. Just agreeing to read it a Second Time when OLD MORALITY's note arrived. The Markiss boils over with rage; nothing for it but to drop Bill, which he does in magnificent passage of withering scorn. Sends note to OLD MORALITY to say would like to see him for few minutes.

O. M. sends back word, very busy indeed. In fact has an urgent summons to other end of town. Back d'reckly.

*Business done.*—Autumn Session arranged for.

*Thursday.*—Lords having it all their own way this week. Commons not in it. To-night, all the world knows that The MACALLUM MORE is to move Vote of Confidence in Government with special reference to Irish Administration. Ordinary attractions of speech by the Dook increased by natural curiosity as to issue. Will the Lords pass Resolution, or will Opposition, mustering in overwhelming force, defeat it? Quite exciting prospect. Nothing like little uncertainty to make debate draw.

Walking towards House beheld three cloaked figures, cautiously proceeding along Corridor. Knew them at once, in spite of disguise and shrinking gait. 'Twas GRANVILLE, SPENCER, and ROSEBERRY, helping each other along, mutually cheerful.

"I at least will die hard," said the Red Earl, plucking a dagger from his boot.

"Ha! ha!" said ROSEBERY, resolutely, though with slight tendency to chattering of teeth.

"We must dissemble," said GRANVILLE. "ARGYLL's a terrible man when blood of MACALLUM MORE boils."

A crowded House. Privy Councillors throng steps of Throne. M.P.'s packed in pens at Bar. LOCKWOOD seized opportunity to make sketches for his forthcoming portrait of "Duke of ARGYLL as Bantam Cock, Crowing on his Own Dunghill." Peers' benches crowded. Bishops in lawn, Ladies in side Galleries, and in high feather.

Our Artist Q.C.

"Glad I didn't carry out first intention to come in kilt," said the MACALLUM MORE, modestly glancing at galleries, whence fifty pair of bright eyes scanned his manly form.

Just as preliminary business cleared off, STRATHEDEN AND CAMPBELL blew their nose. In the distance sounded something like earliest effort at tuning bagpipe. MACALLUM MORE started like ancient war-horse at sound of trump. A great occasion. Rose to its full height and his own. Perhaps a little historical in his treatment of subject. Had avowedly come to praise the present Government. Lagged on the way to bang GLADSTONE on the head and scarify SPENCER. Pretty to see the Red Earl, when opprobrium heaped upon him, stoop and furtively feel if the dagger was still in his boot.

For full hour by Westminster clock MACALLUM MORE enjoyed himself. Presently would have pleasure of hearing the Markiss and others extol his speech, whilst Opposition feebly struggled against flood of eloquence and force of argument. The debate would stand out in forefront of historic battles royal. London would ring with it in the morning, and the distant glades of Inverary faintly echo its grander passages. Everybody wound up to fever-heat by his eloquence; yearning to join in fray. Better not take up too much time. So at end of hour and quarter sat down. Gazed haughtily round attentive Senate. Who in the urgent race would win the prize of place and immediately follow him? The black-browed Markiss, the gluesie GRANVILLE, the Red Earl with his secreted weapon, or the ribald ROSEBERRY, capable of speaking disrespectfully of the Equator? (*Did* the other day actually allude to Dook as a "portentous political pedagogue.") A wondering silence fell over the crowded benches. A rustle of garments, a murmur of whispered conversation, something like a titter rippling along Front Opposition Bench, and then—the Lord CHANCELLOR on his feet putting the Question!

It was all over. The House had listened, and concluded with one accord that there was nothing in the oration suggesting reply. Debate a monologue. Opposition broke forth into unseemly laughter, Ministerialists answered with angry cheer. As for the MACALLUM MORE he could not understand it.

"A low practical joke," he said, glancing suspiciously at ROSEBERY; then with head thrown back, and chest more than ever protuberant, he stalked forth.

*Business done.*—Local Government Bill in Commons.

*Friday.*—Gog and Magog had their noses pulled to-night. PICKERSGILL proposed to deprive Corporation of ancient right to appoint to the offices of Recorder and Common Serjeant. ATTORNEY-GENERAL said "No." Much cheering from Gog and Magog. Then GRANDOLPH supported Amendment. HENRY JAMES followed; OLD MORALITY capitulated; Gog and Magog groaned.

*Business done.*—Local Government Bill advancing by leaps and bounds.

---

## THE PARK NEAR RICHMOND HILL.

(*An Old Story with a New Burthen.*)

NEAR Richmond Hill there stands
 a Park,
 Right fair at eve or morn;
To claim it for the "Men of Mark,"
 Moves most to rage or scorn.
Though Volunteers earn patriot
 cheers,
 And *Punch's* right goodwill,
He must decline to thus resign
 The Park near Richmond Hill.

How foolish would the Public
 prove,
 Which calls the Park its own,
To yield the verdant glade we love
 To tents and butts alone!
Pothunters "pot" at Aldershot,
 There show your marksman
 skill; [of toil
But oh! *don't* spoil for thralls
 Our Park near Richmond Hill!

---

## BOMBASTES FURIOSO À LA FRANÇAISE.

(*Adapted from the Old English Burlesque.*)

DRAMATIS PERSONÆ.

*King Artaxominous (insulted and floored by General Bombastes)* . . . The Royalist Party.
*Distaffina (a Faithless Flirt)*. . . . . . . . . . . Mdme. LA FRANCE.
*Fusbos (a Prime Minister, who is victorious over General Bombastes in a duel)* . . . . . . . . . . . M. FLOQUET.
*and*
*General Bombastes* . . . . . . . . . . . GÉNÉRAL BOULANGER.

*** The situation represented is the finish of the combat between *Prime Minister Fusbos* and *General Bombastes*, and it may be interesting to add that, in the original version, the *finale* ran thus:—

| | |
|---|---|
| *Distaffina (distracted).* | Briny tears I 'll shed. |
| *Artaxominous (rising unexpectedly).* | I for joy shall cry, too! |
| *Fusbos (considerably astonished).* | Zounds! the King 's alive! |
| *General Bombastes (suddenly sitting up).* | Yes! and so am I, too. |

But in the French version this order will not be exactly followed, as *General Bombastes* will sing the second line. *Fusbos*, much astonished, will exclaim, "*Tiens! il vit encore!*" and the King will sing the last line. So far, the rehearsals have been eminently satisfactory.

## THE DIARY OF A NOBODY.

*May* 21.—The last week or ten days terribly dull. CARRIE being away at Mrs. JAMES's, at Sutton. CUMMINGS also away. GOWING, I presume, is still offended with me for black-enamelling his stick without asking him.

*May* 22.—Purchased a new stick mounted with silver which cost seven-and-sixpence (shall tell CARRIE five shillings), and sent it round with nice note to GOWING.

*May* 23.—Received strange note from GOWING. He says: "Offended? Not a bit, my boy. I thought you were offended with me for losing my temper. Besides, I found, after all, it was not my poor old uncle's stick you painted. It was only a shilling thing I bought at a tobacconist's. However, I am much obliged to you for your handsome present all the same."

*May* 24.—CARRIE back. Hoorah! She looks wonderfully well, except that the sun has caught her nose.

*May* 25.—CARRIE brought down some of my shirts and advised me to take them to TRILLIP's round the corner. She said: "The fronts and cuffs are much frayed." I said without a moment's hesitation, "I'm '*frayed* they are." Lor! How we roared. I thought we should never stop laughing. As I happened to be sitting next the driver going to town on the 'bus, I told him my joke about the "frayed" shirts. I thought he would have rolled off his seat. They laughed at the office a good bit too over it.

*May* 26.—Left the shirts to be repaired at TRILLIP's. I said to him: "I'm '*fraid* they are *frayed!*" He said without a smile, "They 're bound to do that, Sir." Some people seem to be quite destitute of a sense of humour.

*June* 2.—The last week has been like old times. CARRIE being back, and GOWING and CUMMINGS calling every evening nearly. Twice we sat out in the garden quite late. This evening we were like a pack of children, and played "Consequences." It is a good game.

*June* 3.—Consequences again this evening. Not quite so successful as last Saturday. GOWING having several times over-stepped the limits of good taste.

*June* 4.—In the evening CARRIE and I went round to Mr. and Mrs. CUMMINGS' to spend a quiet evening with them. GOWING was there, also Mr. STILLBROOK. It was quiet but pleasant. Mrs. CUMMINGS sang five or six songs—"*Maggie's Secret,*" and "*Why don't the Men propose?*" being best in my humble judgment. But what pleased me most was the duet she sang with CARRIE—classical duet, too. I think it is called—"*I would that my Love.*" It was beautiful. If CARRIE had been in better voice, I don't think professionals could have sung it better. After supper we made them sing it again. I never liked Mr. STILLBROOK since the walk that Sunday to the "Cow and Hedge," but I must say he sings comic songs well. His song, "*We don't Want the Old Men now,*" made us shriek with laughter, especially the verse referring to Mr. GLADSTONE. But there was one verse I think he might have omitted, and I said so, but GOWING thought it was the best of the lot. "*Chacun à son gout,*" as the French say.

*June* 6. TRILLIP brought round the shirts, and to my disgust, his charge for repairing was more than I gave for them when new. I told him so, and he impertinently replied, "Well, they are better now than when they were new." I paid him, and said it was a robbery. He said, "If you wanted your shirt-fronts made out of pauper-linen, such as is used for packing and bookbinding, why didn't you say so."

*June* 7.—A dreadful annoyance. Met Mr. FRANCHING, who lives at Peckham, and who is a great swell in his way. I ventured to ask him to come home to meat-tea, and take pot-luck. I did not think he would accept such a humble invitation, but he did, saying in a most friendly way he would rather "peck" with us than by himself. I said, "We had better get into this Blue 'bus." He replied, "No blue-bussing for me. I have had enough of the blues lately. I lost a cool 'thou' over the Copper Scare. Step in here." We drove up in style home, and I knocked three times at the front door without getting an answer. I saw CARRIE through the panels of ground glass (with stars), rushing up-stairs. I told Mr. FRANCHING to wait at the door while I went round to the side. There I saw the grocer's boy actually picking off the paint on the door, which had formed into blisters. No time to reprove him, so went round and effected an entrance through the kitchen window. I let in Mr. FRANCHING, and showed him into the drawing-room. I went up-stairs to CARRIE, who was changing her dress, and told her I had persuaded Mr. FRANCHING to come home. She replied, "How can you do such a thing; you know it's SARAH's holiday, and there's not a thing in the house, the cold mutton having turned with the hot weather."

Eventually CARRIE, like a good creature as she is, slipped down, washed up the tea-cups, and laid the cloth, and I gave FRANCHING our views of Japan to look at while I ran round to the butchers to get three chops.

---

SHAKSPEARIAN MOTTO FOR THE BOX-OFFICE AT A THEATRE OR AT A LIBRARIAN'S.—"So much for Booking 'em!"

---

PLUVIAL.—"The phenomenal wetness of the Season is really becoming grave," says an agricultural organ. Grave? Yes, the "*watery* grave"—both of business and pleasure.

---

THE CROPS AND CURRENT LITERATURE.—Bad Weather for all the Cereals.

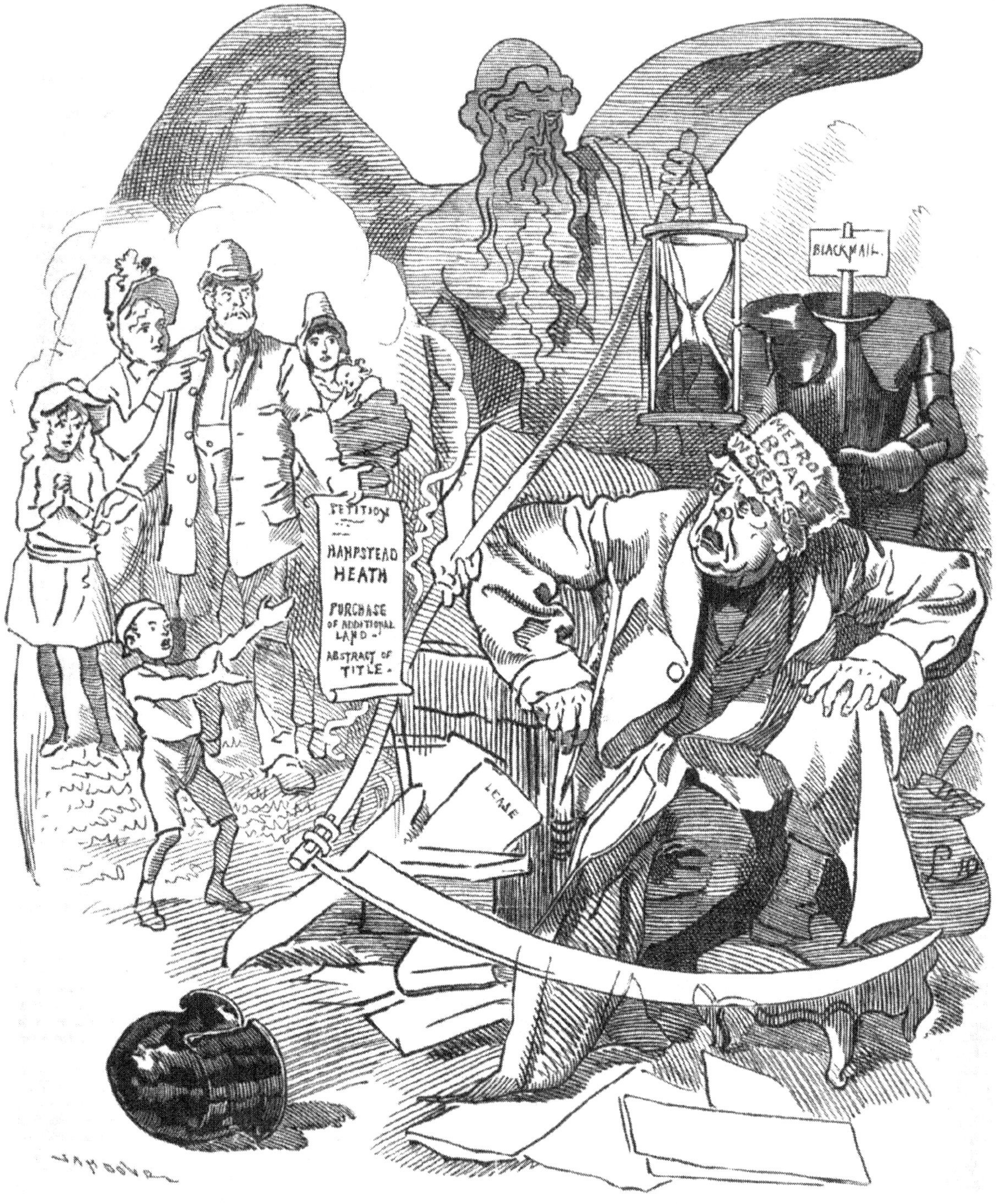


**A LAST CHANCE.**

*London Artisan (to Expiring Metropolitan Board of Works).* "DO ONE GOOD WORK BEFORE YOU DEPART THIS LIFE, AND, AT A STROKE OF THE PEN, SECURE THE BENEFITS OFFERED AT HAMPSTEAD TO THE LONDON TOILERS, THEIR WIVES, AND CHILDREN."

HARD NAMES.—What a very simple-minded Chairman Lord MAGHERAMORNE seems to be! What a title it is! "Give a Dog a bad name," &c., &c.; but give a HOGG a name most difficult for the Saxon to pronounce properly, and roast him when you catch him. Perhaps the nearest thing to "a Pig in a poke" is "a HOGG in a Witness-box."

AT a recent meeting the Archbishop of CANTERBURY observed that he hoped the Church House would soon be launched. So it is to be a House-Boat, after all. In smooth water, let us hope, and in communication with the nearest bank.

THE GOVERNMENT WORKSHOP—"The Smithy."

## MAGHERAMORNE!

*(A Plaintive Ditty, as sung recently, with more or less success, before a certain Royal Commission.)*

LET me down gently. Treat me not unkindly,
  Because, poor victim, I have been deceived.
For what else could I do but trust them blindly?
  Who would their simple ways have not believed?
I came down to the office almost daily;
  Moved in their midst. Ah! how could I have guessed,
Their souls, when they were meeting me so gaily,
  With thoughts of filthy lucre were possessed!
So treat not my confiding trust with scorn
But pity me, poor, duped MAGHERAMORNE!

Promptly to HEBB, whom Mr. HARE had shown up,
  I pointed out his wrong, quite moved to tears.
But when they told me GODDARD'S game was thrown up,
  I frankly own I would not trust my ears!
But here my *largesse*, it is fair to mention,
  We paid to VULLIAMY, my Board and I;
His salary, together with his pension,
  Because,—well, I can't really tell you why!
Still, meet me gently. Treat me not with scorn.
Regard me as poor, weak MAGHERAMORNE!

Ah! if you can, once more just reinstate me
  Amid the splendours of my former power:
And in your fancy once again translate me
  From out the clutch of this all-evil hour!
Think what it is for one who knows not jobbing
  To be associated with a craven crew,
Accused of bribing, double-dealing, robbing,
  And in their shameless course involving you!
Think what it is, and pity your forlorn,
Dejected, duped and dazed MAGHERAMORNE!

---

### Faber Major Punchio Suo.

CARE PUNCHI,

VESTER Correspondens, "FABER MINOR," acutior esse debuit quam qui acutum accentum in vocem εἰσιών imponeret. Qui ultimam ejus verbi non circumflectet, ipse trans patris genua circumflexus vapulare debet, donec accentus dolorosi exprimantur.

Vester vere, FABER MAJOR.

**A PROUD AND HAPPY MOMENT IN 'ARRY'S LIFE.**

SILVER FÊTE. THE TEA AND COFFEE STALL. JULY, 1888.

---

## ROBERT AT THE AKIDDIMY.

WOT orrible subjecs sum Painters chooses! Fancy having hung up in one's dining-room a picter of a poor old Lion a dying of hunger, and about a duzzen hungry Wultures jest a little way behind him, a waiting impashent for the coming feast! And then there's another horrid picter, as made me feel quite mellancolly to look at. It's the inside of a Theatre, and the Balcony and the Galleries is all crowded with peeple, and about seven growed-up females is all tied to postesses, and a lot of lions is waiting outside the iron door to come in and kill 'em all. What a nice subjeck for your Droring-Room!

Then No. 438 is a werry remarkabel tall Lady, who has had no time to dress herself, and is being compelled to carry a great jug full of water on her poor naked shoulders, and two of her sisters similar atired in nothing in partickler is a running after her to call her back. In anser to my hegar inquirys as to what it all ment, I was told as it was classicle, and ony skollards could understand it. And all I can say is, that if all the howdacious ones is classicle, let 'em be put in a room by themselves, so that decent peeple may no what they has to xpect.

No. 1055. Picture of Scare Crows.

No. 630. "The Miserables!" Ah, that's a fine picter, if you likes. Why, it gave me the miserables so badly, ony to look at the pore Cab-horses a standing so pashently in the pouring rein, that I was compelled to have a drink! I shoodn't much like to have that picter, wunderfool clever as it is, a allus hanging in my room; it wood cost me a lot of money jest to keep up my sperrits.

No. 669. "Old and Crusted!" Yes, there's no dout about it. The werry look of the smiling Waiter, and the remarkabel carefool way in which he carries that Bottle of Port tells me at a glance as there ain't no desepshun there. And ain't the 3 thirsty gents jest a got all their 6 eyes upon it, and ain't they all thorowly prepaird for the cumming joy! Ah! Mr. DANDY SADLER, I warrent as you knows a glass of old Port when you gets it, as well as any Alderman of the hole Court, or you coudn't have painted that glorious picter of the pleazure of Hopin. There's one thing quite certain, there won't be much of that "old and crusted" left for the Waiter, pore Fellar!

No. 712. This is a werry striking Picter of the sad results of a hole famerly playing on the Stares, altho their Ma has warned 'em over and over again of the natural consekwences. There's no less than 3 on 'em amost dead, allreddy, and no one carn't wunder at it when they gazes at them cruel looking stone stares.

There is sum of the ushal old jokes, such as Mr. HUNT'S 3 horses "waiting for buyers," and a preshus long time they'll have to wait I shood think, for they all looks the werry picter of misery, has all their eyes shut, and, they're all on a bare common with not a sole near 'em but the horseler. And then Mr. GRIMSHAW, not to be outdone, calls a picter "Winter Leaves," and there ain't not a singel leaf on all the many trees there!

The Akaddimy is now shettin its dores, and there's a hend of the Season. I think nex ear I shall start as a Hart Cricket, and give em sum Ome trewths by yours respekfilly,

ROBERT.

---

THE UNITED "SERVICES."—The Brothers RENSHAW.

## SARAH ON THE DEVELOPMENT OF GENIUS.

IN this land of BERNARD-BEERE [stout;
*On m'a dit* I'm getting
In great *rôles* I must appear,
Present costumes must
"let out."

I must take no bread nor butter—
"Butter" I shall miss, alack!
When I cease to be "too utter,"
To the *Français* I'll go back.

## LEGAL "EXHIBITS."

ON Thursday of last week there was what the newspapers call a "Scientific At Home" at the Temple, when various electrical appliances were exhibited, and the haunt of the lawyers was illuminated from outside by electric lamps—but ought not the illumination to have come from within? The subjoined are a few of the articles which may have been on view:—

1. *The Wig of the Future*—warranted not to make one's hair come off. In connection with *The Patent Judge-Awakener*, warranted to make one's case come on.

2. *An Automatic Grand Jury*—all ready "charged," by a Recorder or Judge, with electric force, and guaranteed to find true Bills for eight consecutive hours without renewing the supply.

3. *The Judge's Friend.* Being a robe formed exclusively of the dried skins of electric eels, causing the wearer a series of mild but continuous shocks, effectually stimulating the intellect and preventing sleep.

4. *Patented Arrangement*—for suddenly converting the interior of a Court of Law into a first-class *Restaurant*, so as to obviate the necessity of the mid-day adjournment. Cleverest Members of Junior Bar act as *head* waiters. Barons of beef for Mr. Baron HUDDLESTON'S Court. Hash for Counsel.

5. *The Mechanical Juryman*—with a label, "Put a ton of forensic balderdash into the (jury) box, and the figure will return a verdict according to the weight—of the evidence."

6. *A Model Costs-Reducer.* New method (been tried once) of drawing up Solicitor's charges and taxing them simultaneously. Has taxed the inventor's ingenuity for years. So far it has only failed to act on a single occasion.

7. *New Way of "Taking Silk"*—by subjecting silk-worms to unpleasant electric vibrations.

8. *The Phonograph*, or *Storage of Judgments. Lord Chancellor* (*twenty years hence*). "Usher, turn on my predecessor in *Juggins* v. *Bellamy*. Rather squeaky. Perhaps Lord HALSBURY had a cold that morning. Still, there's his opinion in favour of the Plaintiff's view. That settles it. Judgment for Defendant, with costs."

9. *Punishment on a Novel Plan.* "Fourteen Days, or six prods of the Galvanic Titillator." (Machine shown, and tried.)

## VOCES POPULI.

### AT THE ANGLO-DANISH EXHIBITION.

SCENE.—*The Grounds on a July afternoon. One heavy shower is just making way for another. A light fog. Military Band conscientiously performing to rows of wooden chairs. Attendants hoisting strings of limp Chinese lanterns to posts, and baling rain-water out of coloured oil-lamps. Enter a* Pleasure-Seeker, *who has been ordered by his Doctor to "divert his mind as much as possible." He feels a little uncertain where to begin his diversion, as the saddles of the galloping horses in the Steam-Circus look too soaked to be inviting; but, seeing a couple picking their way through the puddles towards the "Danish Grotto of Mysteries," he follows.*

IN THE GROTTO.

*A Gloomy Man in a Friar's habit receives their threepences, and leads the way into the interior, which is entirely dark. The Lady of the couple giggles.*

*The Friar* (*in a solemn voice*). Go straight on, and do not be afraid. (*He stops before a sort of ticket-hole in the canvas rock, through which they dimly perceive an illuminated transparency depicting two insipid young persons on a garden seat.*) Youth and Decay.

*The Gentleman.* Where do you make out that Decay comes in, Guv'nor?

*Friar* (*with sombre triumph*). Here! (*Pulls string—figures on seat change to skeletons.*)

*The Lady* (*unappalled*). How funny! Do you mind doing that over again?

[*The* Friar *seems hurt and depressed by such a request, but complies. He then leads the Party to a Canvas Cavern, where, upon a board at the threshold being trodden upon, a rickety skeleton emerges.*

*The Lady* (*still calm*). Law! What are those two twinkling things?

*Friar* (*suppressing his annoyance*). They are the flaming eyes of the apparition.

*The Lady.* I suppose that's done with candles inside of its head?

[Friar *declines to reveal this grim secret, and proceeds to another cave, where four more skeletons are grouped in a faint green light. He pulls a secret string, and two of the skeletons extend their arms with a grisly rattle.*

*The Lady.* That's rather pretty, isn't it?

*The Gentleman.* We've come to the right shop for skeletons, eh?

[*They pass into the Stalactite Cavern, which contains an earthy smell, and a "correct representation, as those of the party who have visited Elsinore will bear witness, of the Ghost Scene from Hamlet." The Lady commends the moon, which she says "looks quite watery." They then inspect a pasteboard seaman dying of starvation on an iceberg, and depart.*

Our Pleasure-Seeker *seeks to restore himself by taking afternoon tea at a damp table under a dripping tree, until driven by stress of weather into the Conservatory, where a "Watteau Concert" is going on. Three Gentlemen in velvet Court suits and white wigs are singing a trio describing "What a merry, merry life we Gipsies lead!" with a laughing chorus. Concert concludes with "Vocal Polka" by three young Ladies, in costume, illustrating the joys of washing with real pails, linen, and soapsuds. Not greatly exhilarated, the* P. S. *repairs to the Lake. Here a languid row of spectators are gazing from under umbrellas at a Professor in a tight suit of black, who is standing on his head at the bottom of a glass tank while his feet are waving above the surface. The Professor rights himself, and puts his head above water to bow, and make a damp little speech. "I shall now show you—Eating under water!" Sits at bottom of tank and consumes a biscuit. Several Spectators drift away, their curiosity satisfied. The* P. S., *after watching the Professor and his Pupil gambolling in the Lake like porpoises, begins to feel depression coming on again, and enters the Exhibition, hoping to gain some idea of the Commerce and Industry of Denmark.*

IN THE EXHIBITION.

*The Scene is characterised by a profound calm. Exhibitors behind stalls rouse themselves from torpor as the* P. S. *passes, and attempt to attract his attention.*

*First Exhibitor* (*hopelessly*). *Have* you heard the new organ-top, Sir? [*Spins it on a plate; it drones in a devotional chord, reminding the* P. S. *of a Cathedral Scene on the stage.*

*Second Ex.* Excuse me, Sir, but have you seen the wonderful new invention for drawing corks?

*Third Ex.* (*imploringly*). *Will* you allow me to show you this patent self-threading needle, Sir?

*Fourth Ex.* One moment, Sir. The advantage of using our patent pickle-fork is that you avoid spearing, pricking, stabbing, or wounding the pickle, Sir; you press it gently with the knob—thus!

[*Illustrates this humanitarian device with a bottle full of small corks.*

P.-S. *hurries on, like Ulysses passing the Sirens. At one stall the Exhibitor is asleep, and a Fireman is tickling his ear with a pen. At another a good-looking* Policeman *is dallying.*

*Stallkeeper* (*archly, to* Policeman). Ah, you haven't your friend opposite to talk to *to-day!*

*Policeman.* What friend? All *my* friends—(*tenderly*)—are *this* side of the way.

*Stallk.* How innercent we are! You know who I mean. Your partickler friend—MARY, if you *must* 'ave it. *I've* seen your goings on! [Policeman *protests. Dialogue continued in undertone.*

*A Stallkeeper* (*paying flying visit to another*). Well, dear, and how have you been doing to-day?

*Her Friend* (*viciously*). Oh, don't ask!—I could *kick* the people!

(Two Old Ladies *come up, and hover about stall undecidedly.*) Those painted tambourines are pretty. (*Indifferently.*)

*The Old Ladies* (*enthusiastically*). Oh, very, *very* pretty—and how much do you say? Is that *all?* Dear, dear! Well—we must look in some other time. *Good* afternoon! [*They shuffle off.*

*Girl.* Stingy old *cats!*

[Pleasure-Seeker *finds his spirits flagging again, and enters the Theatre, thinking that the* Tableaux Vivants *from* HANS ANDERSEN *may revive him. An Orator is on the stage, describing the story from which the next tableau is taken. He has a fine voice and an imposing presence, but would evidently prefer to describe incidents of a less extravagant nature.*

*Orator.* TOMMALISE (*leniently, as if the poor girl couldn't help her name*), or "Little Tiny,' as (*slight dash of the pedagogue here*) she is called in some English versions, was born in a—(*this apologetically, with an obvious misgiving that he may not be believed*)—a tulip flower, and had some (*as though he would put it more strongly if he had his way*)—hem—surprising adventures. (*In a bland tone.*) A Toad (*glances at audience to see how they take this*) stole her as a wife for his son, and imprisoned her on (*here he examines his gloves, apparently hesitating whether to impose further on his hearers' credulity*) the leaf of a water-lily—but the fishes (*very softly, as if desiring it to be distinctly understood that he gives this statement for what it is worth*) nibbled the stalk, and set her free. She lived with a Kind, Old, Field-Mouse (*slowly and condescendingly*), who wanted to marry her to a Mole (*pause, during which he seems considering the social objections to such an arrangement*), but a swallow (*here he grows doubtful again;* "Will *they stand the swallow?*"—*decides to risk it*) —a swallow she attended when it was ill bore her away (*quickly—to disarm captious objections*), when it *recovered*, to the land of the Flower Spirits (*feels he is over the worst now, and proceeds with more confidence*), and they welcomed her, and gave her—(*he would clearly like to substitute some more ordinary and useful article here—but feels that he must stick to his instructions*)—wings.

[*Tableau is disclosed: Charming children; Pretty music and grouping. Inevitable tendency to giggle and wobble towards the end. Exit* Pleasure-Seeker, *in slightly improved spirits. Rain. Fog. East Wind. Thunder.*

## OUR BOOKING-OFFICE.

WEMYSS REID'S *Life of W. E. Forster* is a most Reidable biography, of special interest at the present moment. Here, from the commencement of the most dramatic portion of it,—that is, from the day he became Irish Secretary until his resignation—the outsider is allowed more than a mere peep behind the scenes, during the performance of the earlier acts of the Irish Home Rule Drama at St. Stephen's. A fair-minded student, possessed of no special knowledge, will probably be struck by two things: first, the overwhelming anxieties of the Irish Secretaryship; and, secondly, the light-heartedness with which some members of a Cabinet can bear the trials and troubles of one of their own number.

I put down *Forster*, and, *pour me distraire*, I take up PERCY FITZGERALD'S *Chronicles of Bow Street.* "What's] *Hecuba* to him, or he to *Hecuba?*"—I mean what's Bow Street to FITZGERALD, or FITZGERALD to Bow Street, that he should select this subject for his busy pen? He has, however, produced a chatty couple of volumes, full of interest to the student of human nature, who can see the humorous side wherever it exists, of the curious stories of knaves, fools, dupes, and deceivers, heartless criminals and astute detectives. The stories of "Old Patch" and other rascals are entertaining in a cynical sort of way. But one of the best anecdotes is of an incident in the career of ADKINS "the Little Ferret," the pluckiest of detectives.

Like most of my friend FITZ'S entertaining compilations, the stories seem to have been strung loosely together from time to time as he came across them at haphazard: and the form and style of the book suggest that friend FITZ treated it in a Gampish-cordial fashion —that is, the MSS. was "on the mankel-shelf, and the author put his pen to it when he was so dispoged." The consequence is that *Chronicles of Bow Street*, instead of being a work by "FITZ," is rather a work by "FITZ and Starts." Very entertaining all the same, says

THE ECCENTRIC BARON DE BOOK-WORMS.

## A WEEK'S OPERATIC SCORE.

*Tuesday, July* 17.—This week is last week. Odd jumble of time; but so it is. *This* Tuesday is *last* Tuesday—of Opera Season. Crowds to hear BOÏTO'S *Mefistofele*, in a Prologue, Five Acts, and an Epilogue. (Didn't count the Acts, but think there are five.) Prologue magnificent: carried on by only EDOUARD DE RESZKÉ, conductor and orchestra visible—chorus invisible. EDOUARD is almost an Oratorio in himself. Enthusiastic applause at fall of curtain very gratifying to Signor MANCINELLI, who has written an Oratorio, and has conducted the Prologue *con amore.* Then a scene as bright and lively as any in GOUNOD'S *Faust.* Staple of story of *Mefistofele* identical with that of *Faust.* Odd not to hear all GOUNOD'S familiar airs in BOÏTO'S Opera. All the soldiers here, but not *the* March. How they can come on without it is a puzzle. And no *Valentine!* Only WAGNER here, as a friend of *Faust's*, who is as un-Wagnerish as he can be, but this is before he composed *Lohengrin.* What an Opera GOUNOD'S *Faust* and BOÏTO'S *Mefistofele* would have made combined! Immortal!—at least we should never hear the last of it. If it began at eight, when would it be over? Miss M'INTYRE, as *Margherita*, charming. Mme. SCALCHI, as *Marta*,—a very willing martyr. Opera full of melody and movement.

Real chance for DRURIOLANUS in the Brocken Scene. Expecting Signor ENRICO IRVINGO every moment. "*Margaret's* grim ghost" glides in, and tells *Faust* of her "Brocken heart." Audience moved to tears seeing RAVELLI the Reliable for the last time, but subsequently much consoled to find that, resisting all temptations and the allurements of ELLA RUSSELL as the scrumpshus *Elena of Troy Weight* (*i.e.*, *La Belle Hélène*, from OFFENBACH), he has the moral courage to "cling to his old black book," to defy EDOUARD DE RESZKÉ as the fiery-bearded *Mefistofele*, and that finally he dies, swan-like, as a singer should, while a shower of rose-leaves descends upon him, and everyone is more certain than ever that RAVELLI the Reliable is a real good tenor who has gone up higher than even TAMBERLIK'S C sharp.

Druriolanus Covent-Gardenius Operaticus finishes his Season in a Blaze of Triumph.

*Saturday.*—Blaze of triumph. Brilliant House; but forced gaiety on part of Organising Committee, because of its being positively the Very Last Night of Season. Every note of NORDICA'S, SCALCHI'S, ELLA RUSSELL'S, of the Great DE RESKE BROTHERS, and, in fact, of everybody engaged in *Les Huguenots*, breathes "Adieu!" The Band on Board the House Boat struggle manfully with their feelings, and blow hard to stifle their emotion. Dry throats, but not a dry eye anywhere. DRURIOLANUS triumphant after enlivening the Metropolitan Board of Works with his evidence, also after his victory, in County Court, over big umbrella man, and radiant in consequence of long leading article in *Times* this morning, all about himself and Italian Opera. He alludes with mysterious significance to his plans for next Season. Covent-Gardenia HALL cheerfully alludes to his Box-plans for next Season. Pamphlet containing record of "business done" circulated about House. Critical portion of pamphlet signed "J. B." "JOEY B. is sly, Sir, devilish sly." JEAN DE RESZKÉ jumps out of window, and NORDICA swoons for last time this Season. Shooting season commences—bang, bang—"*piff paff*," as *Marcel* sings—several hits—guns bring down trio—bring down curtain—bring down house—great sport—all recalled—National Anthem—DRURIOLANUS on—speech from throne—DRURIOLANUS congratulates everybody—everybody congratulates DRURIOLANUS—*exeunt omnes*—lights out—*exeunt* sentries—ditto linkmen—DRURIOLANUS locks up—pockets keys (and notes)—off to bed—Italian Opera Season of 1888 is finished.

WINDOW STUDIES.
A SCHOOL TREAT IN JULY, 1888.

## THE BRITISH VOLUNTEER.

(*A New Song to an Old Tune, piped by Mr. Punch to his beloved Boys of the N.R.A.*)

SOME talk of going to Brighton,
  And some to Aldershot;
The target-potting CRICHTON
  Must have *some* place to pot.
For of all our national music that
  Which most delight to hear,
Is the pop, pop, pop, pop, pop, pop
  Of the British Volunteer!

For seasons close on thirty
  They 've popped at Wimbledon;
In weather bright or dirty,
  That music still rang on.
But those well-known ranges will no more
  Resound—that 's sadly clear—
With the pop, pop, pop, pop, pop, pop
  Of the British Volunteer!

*Punch* feels a pang of sadness
  He cannot well suppress.
He hailed "the Camp" with gladness,
  He welcomed its success;
And many a time his manly voice
  There sounded forth in cheer,
'Midst the pop, pop, pop, pop, pop, pop
  Of the British Volunteer!

He saw young ROSS made hero,
  Young FULTON shouldered high.
In weather down near zero,
  Beneath a flaming sky,
His annual visit he has made
  To watch the butts, and hear
The pop, pop, pop, pop, pop, pop,
  Of the British Volunteer!

Damply this year, but suavely,
  He held the soddden field,
And saw the Pats win bravely
  The Elcho Challenge Shield.
Such shooting hath he never seen
  As in this last wet year,
Of the pop, pop, pop, (at Wimbledon)
  Of the British Volunteer!

To prejudice a stranger,
  *Punch* will not stop to judge
The Rifles or "The Ranger;"
  But, boys, you 'll have to budge.
And BULL some suitable new range
  Will have to find or clear,
For the pop, pop, pop, pop, pop, pop
  Of the British Volunteer!

Eh? Camp 'neath Richmond's shades, lads?
  No, no!—that will *not* do!
Can't yield those rural glades, lads,
  Even, dear boys, to *you*.
Those oaken clumps, those bracken-spreads,
  Were sacrifice too dear
To the pop, pop, pop, pop, pop, pop
  Of the British Volunteer!

WANTAGE is wrong this time, lads,
  And WALTER EAST is right.
A stroll 'neath elm or lime, lads,
  Is the tired man's delight.
Our choicest Cockney's Paradise
  We can't give up, that 's clear,
To the pop, pop, pop, pop, pop, pop
  Of the British Volunteer!

You 'll twig, my lads, instanter!
  Take *Punch's* friendly tip.
The ramble or the canter
  Tired toilers can't let slip.
No harm? That 's bosh and will not wash.
  GEORGE RANGER 's right, lads, here.
The Park won't stand the pop, pop
  Of the British Volunteer!

But find some fitting range, boys,
  For his crack-shots BULL *must*,
And since you 're bound to change, boys,
  'Tis to improve, I trust.
Pot-hunters there, and popinjays,
  No more should raise the jeer
Midst the pop, pop, pop, pop, pop, pop
  Of the British Volunteer!

Such soldiers had the Teuton,
  So willing—and so cheap,
A range for them to shoot on
  Be sure he 'd find—and keep.
And we, your Grace, must sigh some
  place
  Where BULL henceforth may hear
The pop, pop, pop, pop, pop, pop
  Of the British Volunteer!

"JOHN LEECH'S SISTERS' FUND."—The circumstances of the case have been fully set forth in the *Times*. Never was there a Physician so successful in his treatment of dull care and despondency as was our LEECH. Those who are indebted to him for many a hearty laugh can pay off the score to his Sisters. *Mr. Punch* will be happy to receive and forward any subscriptions to "our Mr. AGNEW," who is on the J. L. S. F. Committee. In the name of the Sisters of *The* Leech, we cry, "Give! Give!" and we are assured of a hearty response.

VERY SMALL BEER—CONYBEARE.

# NEAR THE MARK.

**Gen. Von Moltke** (*to H.R.H. "the Dook"*). "ACH! VIMPLETON! RICHMONT! DONNERVETTER! PY CHORCH! IF I HAT A ZO VILLING ZOLTIER ALS DAT, ZOON HIM VOOT I VIZ A SCHOODING-CROUND PROVITE."

## AN IMPORTANT PERSONAGE.

ONE day last week, according to a report in the *Times*, "Lord ERNE *was appointed Imperial Grand Master of the World*." For what reason has Lord ERNE received this appalling dignity, which to describe in appropriate terms would require the genius of a MILTON or a DANTE? It was conferred upon Lord ERNE at Carrickfergus, County Antrim, at an Orange Lodge. So the world, being round as an orange, is to be one huge Orange Lodge, of which Lord ERNE is henceforward "Imperial Grand Master," like *Mefistofele* in BOÏTO's opera.

By the way, what sort of an ERNE is this "Imperial Grand"? Is he a Tea-Erne or a Funeral Erne? How has he Erne'd this dignity? Is he, 'ARRY would like to know, any relation to 'Erne the 'Unter? And, in fact, on behalf of the vast majority of the World, of which his Lordship has been appointed Grand Master, we ask, Who *is* Lord ERNE?

## ADELPHI NAVAL AND MILITARY MANŒUVRES.

MR. GRUNDY is fortunate in being associated with Mr. PETTITT—the pettitt child of melodramatic fortune—in the "new and original" Drama (so new, and so original!) at the Adelphi, entitled *The Union Jack*.

Except that the male *dramatis personæ* are soldiers and sailors, and that out of eleven scenes, two are at Aldershot, and one on board a vessel bearing the happy combination-title "H.M.S. *Wellesley*," there is nothing extraordinarily nautical or military about the play. That the plot justifies its authors' description of their work as "new and original" is soon made evident by the incident of the petty officer, *Jack Medway*, [What a capital name for a sailor! so appropriate, you know! None of your common hackneyed "*Bill Barnacle*," or "*Tom Tug*," or "*Jack Mainbrace*"—oh, dear, no!] striking his superior officer and being court-martialled; and then the newness and originality of the story are further shown by the presence of a Wicked Baronet who is also "an Army Contractor" [Happy touch this, brings "Wicked Bart." up to date], and by there being a good deal of hiding behind doors and curtains, and plenty of overhearing and seeing what wasn't intended to be overheard or seen, and everything happening just at the right moment, too, so as to clear the innocent and confound the guilty; and having so far proved the newness and originality of the plot to the entire satisfaction of the audience, will it be believed that the Wicked Bart. has actually committed a forgery, and that the second villain holds this *in terrorem* over his head, until first villain, unable to stand it any longer, stabs second villain, and then tries his best to get poor petty officer TERRISS found guilty of the crime? And then, so fresh and full of novel surprises is this play. Would anyone who has ever seen a melodrama imagine that the unfortunate heroine actually falls ill, escapes from

Nautical Situation. Terriss the Tar, the Swell of the Ocean, escapes with the Heroine in the Captain's Gig.

her captors, and staggers about the country in a blinding storm of snow, until she faints by the wayside and is rescued by her lover? Isn't all this "new and original?" Rather! or at all events if it isn't now, it was—once upon a time. Such is *The Union Jack*. For a hero of this sort of melodrama, the Messrs. GATTI are fortunate in possessing a

"*Rara avis in Terriss*."

But if his authors continue writing for him long speeches to be delivered on every possible occasion, opportunely or inopportunely, full of claptrap and theatrical sentiment as "new an original" as the play itself, this sturdy melodramatic actor will soon run Mr. WILSON BARRETT very hard indeed, though the latter, at present, as far as preachifying goes, can give Mr. TERRISS half-a-dozen lengths and beat him easily. The truth is, that this melodramatic stereotyped hero has become rather a bore, and I shall not be surprised if the honest patrons of Adelphi drama do not resent the next attempt, if it be unwisely repeated, at entertaining them with this school-boyish kind of play.

Mr. CHARLES CARTWRIGHT, as the scoundrelly *Captain Morton*, was thoroughly artistic. I doubt if even that unexceptionable stage-villain, Mr. WILLARD, could have played it better. And this is the highest praise. The ladies were all good; especially Miss OLGA NETHERSOLE, in the one genuinely pathetic situation of the play. Miss OLGA is not the "leading lady," but the misled lady, and at the end of the play when everybody is happy, no one cares twopence what becomes of her. "Poor little Me!" She is quite out of it. Miss CLARA JECKS is just the very *Polly Pippin* required by the new and original "*Adelphoi*" PETTITT and GRUNDY BROS.; and Miss ELEANOR BUFTON, as *Mrs. Stone*, one of the Wicked Bart.'s "creatures," suggests by her sardonic smile possibilities of such sensational crimes as might make over again the fortune of Miss BRADDON, and inspire Mr. FARJEON with a plot as cheerful as that of *Uncle Silas*.

Mr. Shine as British Sailor, with Robert Macaire's old creaking snuff-box. Nautical effect: Little Cove and Big Creek.

Of course, however successful the play may be, it can never "go without a hitch" as long as there is a nautical character in it like Mr. SHINE in a sailor's costume. There is, however, one new and original mystery about the play, and that is—Why is it called "*The Union Jack?*" The Union Jack is occasionally alluded to in the dialogue, but the only time it is visible is when the comic sailor sticks up a small toy-flag over the window of the old toll-house on the highroad, and wittily remarks that the cottage thus decorated looks like a ship. Of course the play is successful; of course it will "run"; but if no nautical piece can, as I have proved, "go without a hitch," certainly a play called *The Union Jack* must be of "flagging" interest.

JACK IN THE BOX.

## THE MEETING OF THE EMPERORS.

(*Song of a Sensational Special.*)

AIR—"*The Meeting of the Waters.*"

THERE is not, for the quidnunc, a city so sweet
As St. Petersburg now while the Emperors meet.
One may wander o'er Europe anear and afar,
Yet not find such a chance for a staggering "par."

It is not that the KAISER will give me a "tip,"
Or the CZAR in my ear a state-secret let slip;
That either will whisper his wish or his will,—
Oh! no, there is something more promising still.

As an oracle now for some days I may shine,
A BLOWITZ—though but at a penny a line.
I have only some awful war-rumour to start,
To shock—somebody's—nerves, or chill—somebody's—heart!

Sweet stream of the Neva, beloved of the Russ,
What *canards* I'll let fly from your shores, with what fuss!
What odds if they're fudge? I shall feather *my* nest,
And the *gobemouches*, though fluttered, will soon sink to rest.

IMPROVEMENTS IN THEATRES.—In the new Theatre being built for Mr. HARE, the stall-chairs are on wheels. They are standing out in the spacious hall, and on arriving at the front door, the visitor's hat, coat, and stick, are immediately removed by a hidden machinery which wheels him into the exact situation he is intended to occupy. An electric-bell at his side has to be sounded for refreshments, and another for a cab or carriage, as the case may be. When the vehicle has arrived at the front door the visitor is noiselessly trundled out backwards, without disturbing the audience, the receding chair allowing him to see the performance until he passes through "vampire trap-doors" into the hall, when his hat, coat, gloves, umbrella, stick, goloshes, &c., are fitted on to him again, when is carried out under the portico, and with a gentle and pleasant force, is projected into his carriage or cab, of which the door will have been previously opened by a Commissionnaire in attendance. There will be machines into which you put the requisite sum and obtain your ticket. There are many other novelties. It will be perfectly ventilated, as there will be plenty of HARE there.

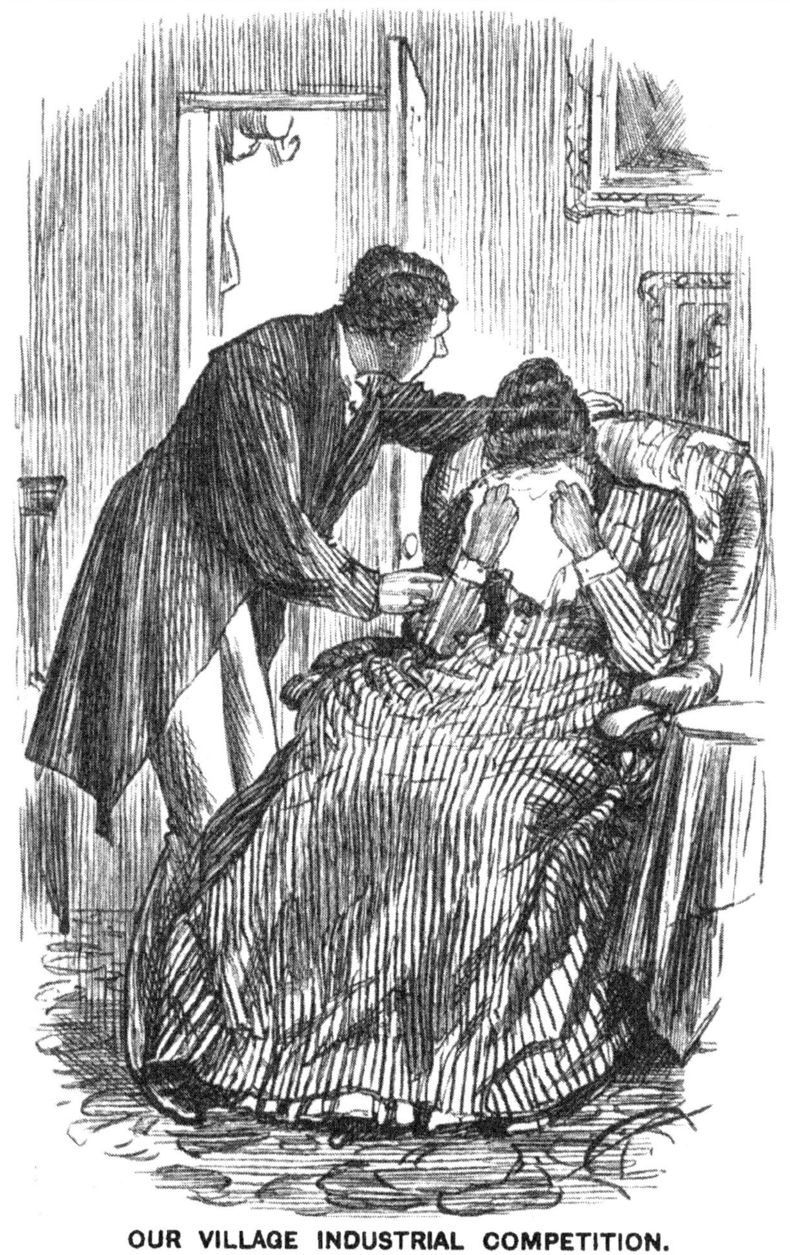

**OUR VILLAGE INDUSTRIAL COMPETITION.**

*Husband (just home from the City).* "My Angel!—Crying!—Whatever 's the matter?"
*Wife.* "They 've—awarded me—Prize Medal"—*(sobbing)*—"f' my Sponge Cake!"
*Husband (soothingly).* "And I 'm quite sure it deserv——"
*Wife (hysterically).* "Oh—but—'t said—'twas—for the Best Specimen—o' Concrete!"

## THE END OF WIMBLEDON.

*(The Story of a Grandfather, to be told Fifty Years hence.)*

"And so, my little ones," said the old man, pointing with his stick to a mass of factories, suburban villas, and public-houses, "you want to know what sort of a place *that* was when I was a young man, many, many years ago?"

"Yes, yes!" cried the children, as they dragged the veteran on to the top of an electric omnibus, that, belonging to the London and South-Western Railway Company, was stationary, and likely to remain so for some time.

"Well, you must know," continued the white-headed grey-beard, "that in those days it was all open country. If I am not mistaken, where you now see that crowded burial-ground there was a brickfield that used to be the pride of the Duke of Cambridge. It was to save, if I remember rightly, persons from being shot to death by thousands that the Duke ordered the Volunteers away!"

"How very good of His Royal Highness," lisped little Mary.

"Ay, that it was! It was either to save slaughter, or to use the land for running up houses—I forget which. But, as you see, they have run up houses since."

"And what was Wimbledon like in the days of the Volunteers?" asked Richard.

"Well," said the old man, smilingly, "my memory is not so good as it used to be; but what I recollect most distinctly is a trophy connected with Hop Bitters. It was shown to the public in a large marquee, called the Exhibition Tent, from ten till dusk; and I fancy, too, that beside this trophy, were boots, and dozens of champagne, and cigarettes, and soap advertisements, and walking-sticks, and all sorts of queer things."

"Dear me, how funny!" giggled little Mary. "And what were they for?"

"To encourage the love of rifle-shooting, I imagine; but I am not quite sure. The people who presented them may have had some other object in view, but of that I know nothing. Then there were all manner of fancy tents, furnished in the oddest fashions; and then there were Ladies lounging about, doing nothing in particular; and for a fortnight it was a regular pic-nic."

"Was there any shooting?"

"To the best of my recollection there was. I fancy it used to be called pot-hunting. I don't think that many of the Volunteers used to shoot—I mean not the real ones. I remember, distinctly, that the strangest costumes used to be worn at the ranges."

"Was there much discipline?" asked Richard, who was now putting the questions.

"I don't think there was much," replied the old man, "except, perhaps, amongst the police."

"Do you remember who were the greatest marksmen in 1888?"

"To be sure I do. The winner of the Queen's Prize was an engraver who used to work on the noblest paper in the whole world; while the Albert Jewel (which was the any-rifle-equivalent to the Queen's Prize), was carried off by Quarter-master Arrowsmith, who as you know, is a millionnaire."

"Surely not the Mr. Arrowsmith who published '*Called Back*,' and the '*Tinted Venus*,' and whose latest *édition de luxe* (the thirtieth) of '*Tracked Out*,' at ten guineas a copy, has received only recently so warm a welcome in every quarter of the civilised world?"

"The very same!"

"And when the camp of the National Rifle Association was expelled from Wimbledon, and tried first on the Brighton Downs, and then at Wormwood Scrubs, and next at Herne Bay, and subsequently for some time in Olympia, until last year it was held in the Thames Tunnel—did it flourish?"

"That, my dear little ones," said the old man, who was getting rather weary of the conversation, "you must judge for yourselves. You now have the past and the present before you, and consequently are in a position to take your choice!"

---

"Honours Easy."—*Voilà* Zola *décoré!* But not "decorous," a word that does not exist in the French language. Zola a Knight of the Legion of Honour! If the French Honour list is alphabetical, then, with Zola they must have got to the very end of it.

## OUR JAPANNERIES. No. 8.

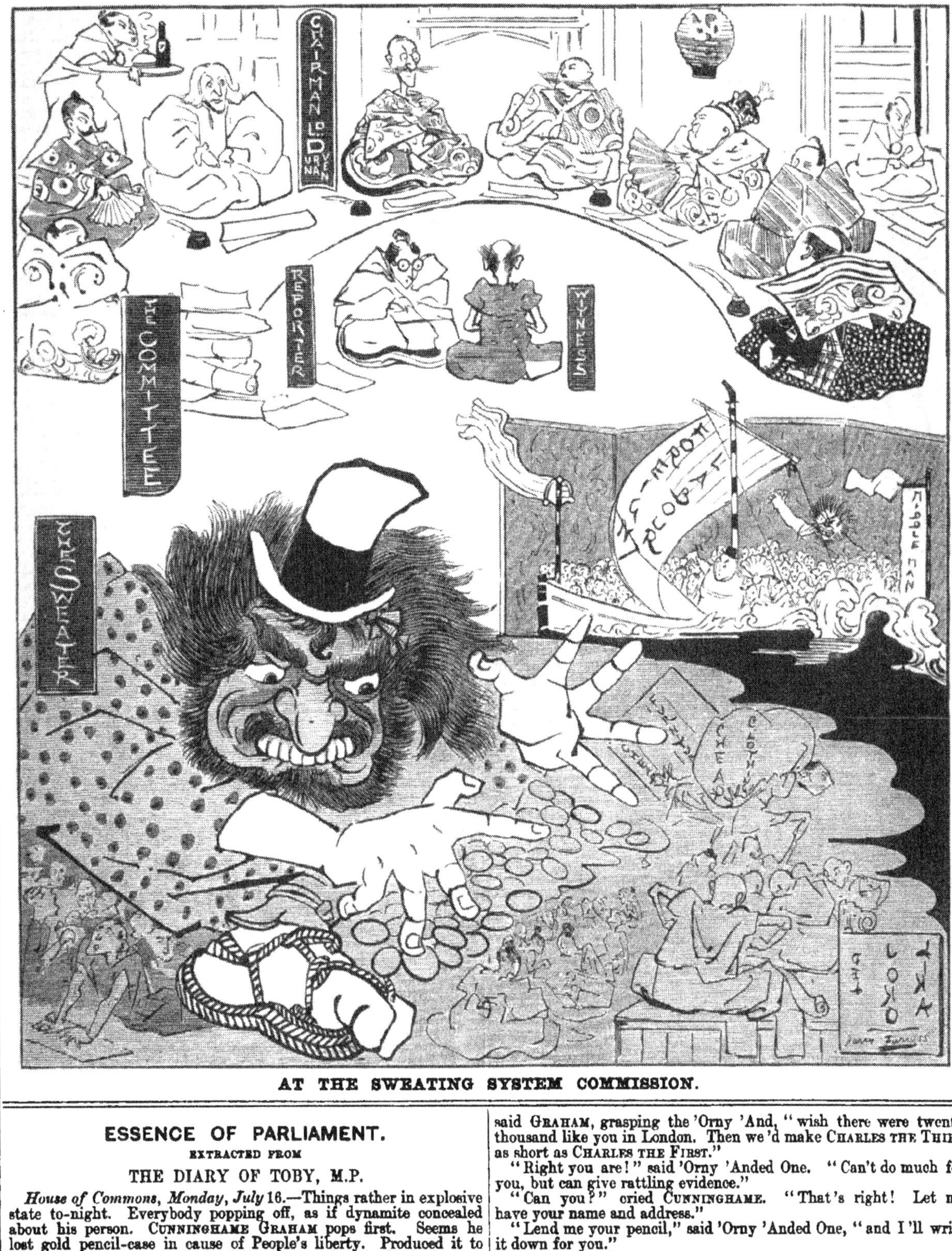


AT THE SWEATING SYSTEM COMMISSION.

## ESSENCE OF PARLIAMENT.

EXTRACTED FROM

### THE DIARY OF TOBY, M.P.

*House of Commons, Monday, July* 16.—Things rather in explosive state to-night. Everybody popping off, as if dynamite concealed about his person. CUNNINGHAME GRAHAM pops first. Seems he lost gold pencil-case in cause of People's liberty. Produced it to take policeman's number in Trafalgar Square on Saturday. Sympathising British Workman, standing by, loudly cheered. "Ah!" said GRAHAM, grasping the 'Orny 'And, "wish there were twenty thousand like you in London. Then we'd make CHARLES THE THIRD as short as CHARLES THE FIRST."

"Right you are!" said 'Orny 'Anded One. "Can't do much for you, but can give rattling evidence."

"Can you?" cried CUNNINGHAME. "That's right! Let me have your name and address."

"Lend me your pencil," said 'Orny 'Anded One, "and I'll write it down for you."

"Good!" said CUNNINGHAME GRAHAM.

Handed over gold pencil; priceless value; heirloom in the family.

Just then somebody tapped Cunninghame on right shoulder. Turned sharply round to see who it was. On looking back, found 'Orny 'Anded One disappeared with pencil-case.

Sees it all now. 'Orny 'Anded One a policeman in plain clothes; told off by Warren for this particular work. Communicates suspicion to Home Secretary, who sits guiltily silent.

But the popping of Cunninghame Graham nothing to Parnell's. Comes up with question as to course Government intend to take with respect to Bill creating Special Commission, to try over again great libel case. Parnell palpitating with passion. Fixes directly upon Old Morality. Looks as if he would tear him limb from limb. O.M. evidently in a terrible funk. But there is table and breadth of floor between him and Parnell, and Lord-Advocate at end of bench. If anything happens, can get behind Lord-Advocate. Take a good deal of tearing up to finish *him* before hour of adjournment.

Thinking of the 'Orny 'Anded One.

After this, motion for Adjournment, whilst Conybeare discanted on Saturday's performance in Trafalgar Square. Dr. Clark gave interesting account of proceedings. Singularly like scene from Pantomime where policeman comes on; only, situation reversed. Instead of Bobby being chivvied, and finally chucked out, Bobby seems to have chivvied the Public in casual way. Graphic descriptions of Rev. Gentlemen with hats battered; Hon. Members rushed backwards and forwards across Square, and then taking cabs to go home. Old Morality, recovering from state of coma into which Parnell had frightened him, abruptly moved Closure. By curious association of ideas, this reminded Cunninghame Graham that his gold pencil-case was not closed when he passed it to the 'Orny 'Anded One. Rose to mention this incident. Speaker put question. C. G. stood in attitude of defiance, still thinking of the 'Orny 'Anded One. Conservatives yelled. Speaker shouted "Order! Order!" Cunninghame Graham tumbled back into his seat, "and Freedom," at it again, "shrieked when Kosciusko fell."

*Business done.*—In intervals of miscellaneous popping, three clauses added to Local Government Bill.

*Tuesday.*—House been for some weeks engaged in race against time with Local Government Bill. Contest being on go-as-you-please system determined to-night to run; tremendous scamper; at four o'clock on Clause 67; finished up before midnight with Clause 125 and last.

"A Clause every Sixty Seconds!"

Pretty to see Caleb Wright standing at Bar with mouth open, watching Bill jump along clause by clause.

"Been Chairman of the Tyldesley Local Board man and boy for forty years," said he, in a hushed whisper; "but never got through business like this. A mile a minute—a clause every sixty seconds! Tyldesley not in it!"

Towards half-past twelve, on Clause 120, Courtney began to show signs of distress. Five Clauses yet to pass; only half-hour to do it in. Old Morality sat restless on Treasury Bench; strong impulse on him to move the Closure. Ritchie smiled feverishly; tried not to look at clock. Charlie Beresford, practical at critical moment, brought glass of hot rum for Chairman. Edward Clarke contributed sponge and a lemon. Thus refreshed in and out, Courtney got up another spurt, staggering past the post with Clause 125, and ten minutes to spare.

Curse of Camborne interposed, and suggested that progress should be reported, and last Clause left over. Howl of angry reprobation greeted suggestion. Would dearly have liked to vex everybody by moving to report progress; but at last moment courage failed him. So ultimate Clause agreed to, and the Curse went home to roost.

*Business done.* — Last Clause of Local Government Bill through Committee.

*Thursday.*—Local Government Bill finally through Committee, new Clauses, Schedules, and all. House cheers; Ritchie blushes. Abraham proposes to lead off chorus, "*For he's a Jolly Good Fellow;*" Dilwyn pointed out that that would be out of order; might lead to conflict with Speaker. So melody remains mute in Abraham's bosom.

Nevertheless, everybody agrees that Ritchie has done uncommonly well. Comparatively a young Parliamentary Hand, with no experience of taking Bill through House, has carried one of the biggest measures of modern times. For such success much depends on nature of Bill; but a great deal on the Minister in charge. Harcourt says he knows many men, who in most favourable circumstances couldn't have carried Bill. Everybody knows one, but in Harcourt's presence doesn't mention name. Ritchie, throughout long struggle, has been clear-headed, courteous, firm wherever firmness was quite safe; when making concessions, adding to the grace of giving by doing it promptly and cheerfully; never bumptious; resisting all temptations to be smart, and clever enough to hide his cleverness. Several men may have reason to believe that they have done pretty well in the long debate; but Ritchie has carried his Bill.

Curse of Camborne back again. Roosting with him a disappointingly brief exercise. Balfour moved Second Reading of Bann Drainage Bill. Appears that this is a fresh injustice to Ireland. The whole country seething with indignation. In such circumstances might reasonably expect Leader of Irish Party, or one of principal Lieutenants to move rejection. But it is an English Member that comes to the front. Conybeare moves rejection of Bill. Bluntly announces he's going to talk it out.

The Grand Young Gardner.

"We'll see about that," says Macartney. Lay low and said nuffin till just on stroke of midnight. Another sixty seconds' vituperation, and the Curse of Camborne could have carried out his threat. Macartney moves Closure just in nick of time. Closure carried; main question put; Irish Members evict each other; noisily tumble out of House; after Division, as noisily come back; Orders run through; object to everything; Curse of Camborne in full blast; Speaker threatens to "Name" him, whereupon Curse subsides, and House adjourns.

"Ah," said Herbert Gardner, strolling out; "glad it ended that way. If Speaker, in 'naming' Conybeare, had accurately described him, afraid he must have dropped into unparliamentary language. Then we'd have had to call Speaker to Order, which would have rather complicated things."

*Business done.* Local Government Bill through Committee.

*Friday Night.*—The Curse really *has* gone home to roost this time. Been writing to the papers, personally attacking Speaker. This breach of good manners stirred Grandolph to deepest depths.

"If there's one thing I like, Toby," he said, just now, "it is to see respect shown to our pastors and masters. Do anything you like with me; but don't expect me to stand tamely by if anyone scouts constituted authority."

So Grandolph moved that the Curse be suspended for the rest of the Session. House secretly delighted at prospect, but dissembled its joy.

"Oh, hang it!" Members said. "That's too much. Give him a month."

Sage of Queen Anne's Gate pleaded for fourteen days, and costs. Finally, House shook off the Curse for a month.

*Business done.*—Conybeare suspended. A few Votes in Supply.

---

### The Umbrella at the Opera.

Says Bousfield to Harris, "I must keep my gingham."
Says Harris to Bousfield, "To stalls you can't bring 'em."
To Bousfield (*v.* Harris), says Bayley, the Judge,
"You'll pay all the costs, and the action is fudge.
When the Op'ra you visit,—by this you'll abide,—
If you stick to your gingham, you must stick—outside."

---

Bryant-and-May's Young Girls.—Match-makers indeed! They no doubt make excellent "strike-on-their-own-box" and other matches for B. and M., who, having for once met their match, have behaved most sensibly, and yielded with a good grace to reasonable demands, but in the West End, a young lady, no matter how lovely, if she only had nineteen shillings a week at most, couldn't expect to make much of a match without assistance. Yet match-making mothers have been known to make splendid matches for their daughters even when they have been absolutely penniless. Wonderful persons these West End matchmakers!

---

The "Sweets" of Wimbledon.—Bull's-eyes.

☞ NOTICE.—Rejected Communications or Contributions, whether MS., Printed Matter, Drawings, or Pictures of any description, will

## 'ARRY ON ST. SWITHIN.

DEAR CHARLIE,

I'M down with rheumatics, and scrawls this 'ere letter in bed,
With a elber as sore as Jemimer, and 'ammers at work in my 'ed.

Bloomin' nice state o' things for July, CHARLIE! Summer's 'ad *me* on the 'op,
For a fellow must be a fair turmut to stand such a Season of Slop.

I 'ave seen a few mizzlyish ones, but my eyes and a band-box, dear boy!
This bangs 'em to bits; it is somethink a teatotal frog might enjoy.
*Rain?* Bust it, the word isn't hadyquate now, and if Science would teach
'Ow to talk of our weather O.K., she must tip us some new parts of speech.

St. Swithin be jolly well jiggered! He's got me on toast, and no kid.
I'd been piling the dibs for a outing, and saved up a couple of quid,
So I jined a swell party of right 'uns who'd rented a prime four-in-'and,
For a tool down to Dorking by road, and, by Jove, we meant doing the grand.

If you'd witnessed the muster at HATCHETT'S, at ten-thirty sharp Toosday week,
You'd ha' bust arf your buttons orf, CHARLIE. It mizzled, a reglar damp reek,
Like a cook-shop in Winter, my pippin; and as for our party, great SCOTT!
You'd a swore as you never popped lamps on a funnier wropped-upper lot.

The top-coats and muckingtogs, CHARLIE, the rugs, and the hulsters with 'oods!
For a party of Gents in July! Oh, I tell yer 'twas reglar good goods.
Britons hout for a 'oliday? Bosh! North-sea pilots in shin-plaster suits,
And Friars in brown bed-gowns, and Bobbies with tippets and double-soled boots!

*That* nicks hus more nearer like, CHARLIE. Yours truly was toffed up superb,
In a thick hoatmeal suit of splashed dittos; and as I stood there on the kerb,
A puffing a prime Larrynargar, my waterproof slung on my arm,
I tell you I fetched Piccadilly, and worked on the gals like a charm.

Well, we took a nip round at the bar. Brandy neat was my tipple; sounds rum
For the dog-days, old pal, I'll allow, but then dog-days is all a dashed hum.
Lemon-squosh is a capital lotion when Summer is fair on the job,
But to lap lemon-squash on a hiceberg is shivery work, s'help me Bob!

Well, we started. Oh, CHARLIE, that ride! Which yours truly ain't sugar or salt,
To melt in a shower; we packed close, liquored up every time we'd a halt;
Puffed sputtering cigars like dashed chimneys, or asphalter's cauldrons, and *yet*
We couldn't keep in any warmth, nor we couldn't keep out any wet.

Tried to joke, my dear boy, but each wheeze, like the weather, was watery and dull;
I had a toon hup on the 'orn, but I made jest the muckiest mull,
Couldn't squeeze out one fair sisirary; and when there's a rowdedow round,
'ARRY 'ates to be out of the 'unt, as you know by this time, I'll be bound.

Hutter frost, my dear boy, and no herror, that run down to Dorking by road,
And next day I wos doing a doss with rheumatics as bad as be blowed.
This mucky mix-up they call Summer! The Seasons *are* 'aving a game,
And that sloshy old squirter, St. Swithin, they tell us, old pal, is to blame.

St. Swithin! He's wus than Sir WILFRID, His whack's forty days and no more,
But he's now like Old Joe in the song, for he kicks up behind *and* before.
He has spiled the whole Season this year, for he's drownded both June and July,
And it's pelting like fun as I write, although Orgust is now precious nigh.

Mucked Henley! My Houseboat—leastways I'd the run of it, CHARLIE, old pal,
The Boss bein' BAGSHOT, the Booky, who hired it to please his new gal——
Our Houseboat, the "Margery Daw," was as smart as they make 'em, no doubt,
But the spree gave yours truly the hump; it wos jest one perpetual spout.

Couldn't do a lark round with the ladies or git a fair boss at a race.
Ony wish I could spot old St. Waterworks; hang him, *I'd* sit on his face!
As to Wimbledon, well, that wos wus. Wot's the good of the toppingest togs
In weather like washing-day, CHARLIE, a season fit only for frogs?

As to cricket, oh, criminy crikey! It's muck, my dear feller—sheer muck!
When McDONNELL, can't play Sussex "lobs," and when WALTER READ'S done for a duck,
To squat on damp seats, doubled up like a cab-driver caught in a storm,
May be wot Surrey mugs would call "sport," but I tell yer it isn't *my* form.

Lawn-tennis? Oh, turn it up—*turn* it up! Beastly to see pooty gals,
With shiny black muckingtogs smothered, a-hiding their snappy fal-lals,
A trottin' about with damp racquets, their dear little noses all red,
'Anging round on the chance of a game, when they'd better be tucked up in bed,
Why the great "Bounding Brothers" theirselves, those top-sawyers at service and "smash,"
The RENSHAWS, carnt play in a puddle or mud-swamp with science and dash.
Saw them pull off the finals, wet-footed; fair cautions for pluck and for skill;
But WILL only seemed arf in earnest, and ERNEST scarce played with a will.

And here I am mugged up in blankets, and lapping a go of rum 'ot! [*that's* all going to pot.
'Ow's yerself and the country, old 'ermit? I s'pose Teatotallers, tadpoles, and turmuts, may like this Unlimited Slosh, [barney will wash.
But *don't* call it Summer, dear boy, for I'm blowed if that
St. Swithin the snivelling old Spoil-sport is 'aving a Triumph, wus luck! [and Muck.
But Bizness and Pleasure this season are ruined by Mizzle
Oh, for Cheap Hemigration, my pippin! The very fust cove it should carry
To sunshine and dry-feet *somewheres*, should be yours (wot there's left of him), 'ARRY.

---

"GIVE YOU GOOD DAY."—By objecting to Mr. Justice DAY being one of the Special Commissioners, the Parnellites give their opponents the chance of reproaching them with not wishing to have the light of Day on their alleged dark secrets. Perhaps, after all, the Special Commission may be postponed *sine die*, without a Day.

---

## EXTREMES MEET.

(*Musings of a Misanthrope, after reading the "Latest Foreign Intelligence."*)

How bored these rambling Royalties must be!
A morning call, a Five o'Clock swell Tea,
Or other hollow "function" of Society,
Has as much vital interest and variety
As these parades where crowned toff meets toff,
And HOHENZOLLERN bows to ROMANOFF.
Say I "drop in" on JONES and JONES'S wife;
We bore each other nearly out of life,
And part much wearier, but nothing wiser.
Is it much different with CZAR and KAISER?
Mrs. JONES gives me tepid tea, a look
At her old Album or new Birthday Book;
The Russ the Teuton banquets when they meet,
Shows him his Army, and parades his Fleet.
Good Mrs. JONES and I contrive to chat
About my Tennis, or her Persian Cat;
I caring for her Cat, she for my Tennis
As much as a blind nigger might for Venice.
Teuton and Russ make after-dinner speeches,
And which the hollowest depth of bathos reaches
Might tax a cynic TALLEYRAND to tell.
They vow they love each other passing well,
(As I admire "*dear* Mrs. JONES'S" tabby)
Whilst each laugh low the inward laugh of LABBY.
Mrs. JONES tells me that, upon her life,
She's pining for a sight of my *sweet* wife—
They're social rivals, and they love each other
As—well, as WILLIAM loves his northern brother.
The Muscovite—or Swede, it matters not—
Drinks to the Teuton's health, talks royal "rot"
Concerning "bonds of friendship," and the traces
That bind in one fast "team" two rival races.
So their "agreement" is by bunkum ratified;
WILLIAM "smiles graciously," the CZAR "looks gratified,"
And Special Correspondents—wondrous creatures—
Who read, in passing smirks on Royal features
Imperial policy—proclaim aloud
Autocrat twaddle to the gaping crowd.
Well, all this smiling sham, this humbug solemn,
Ekes out an article, or pads a column.
But, mighty CÆSAR! how these great and gracious
"Forked radishes," these vagrant and veracious
Imperial Panjandrums *must* be bored!
I fell asleep at JONES'S—nearly snored!—
But better tepid tea and twaddling tattle
Than bunkum-banquets which *may* lead to battle!

---

"OF course I see you're joking," said Mrs. R., with a knowing look, interrupting her nephew—who had just commenced reading aloud the title of a paragraph in a newspaper, "A University for Wales." "You can't take me in quite so easily. University for Whales, indeed? "And yet," she added, reflectively, "when I was in Cornwall, I heard them frequently speak of a 'School of Herrings." So you may be right, after all."

---

A DUTCH FRIEND OF MR. GOSCHEN'S.—Van Tax.

**ST. SWITHIN TRIUMPHANT. THE RECORD OF A JOVIAL JULY.**

"CHARGE, CHESTER, CHARGE!"—and, of course, Chester did charge, and pretty well too, for lodgings and hotel accommodation during the Festival. But not exorbitantly. The weather sent everything down, including prices. Madame NORDICA and GRACE DAMIAN in excellent form; when these two sing together it is specially good for the former, who sings with GRACE; and as these artists, with Messrs. LLOYD and SANTLEY, must have dined at least two or three hours before performing, they all, being with Miss DAMIAN, sing with GRACE-after-dinner. Everything very perfect. Miss BELLE COLE,—Princess COLE, daughter, I suppose, of the ancient highly popular Monarch, who was, as everyone knows, so fond of music with his own chamber-trio of strings,—well, Miss BELLE COLE, not quite up to the high level of the others. But consider the weather! And she being a COLE that can sing, might only have required a little Coke-sing to come out all right. Her chest-notes were forcible, but not too forcible, by comparison with the locality, which, if her notes were chest, was, it must be remembered, Chester. Altogether satisfactory, except to Canon BLENCOWE, who, we are informed, objected to patronise the sacred musical performance in the Cathedral. Well, he didn't come; and, if so, he acted like an indifferent Canon,—went off, with a slight explosion perhaps, but hurting nobody. Sir ARTHUR SULLIVAN thought that this Canon might have been loaded with reproaches.

---

HONEST OPPOSITION.—That of Sir WILFRID LAWSON, and Teetotallers, to all "Imperial Measures." A great pint this.

"SHARP'S THE WORD"!

*Wife.* "POOR MAMMA IS DREADFULLY LOW-SPIRITED THIS MORNING, GEORGE. ONLY THINK—SHE HAS JUST EXPRESSED A WISH TO BE CREMATED!"

*Husband (with alacrity).* "'O'B-LESS MY——" (*Throwing down his Newspaper.*) "TELL HER TO PUT HER THINGS ON, DEAR! I'LL—I'LL DRIVE HER OVER AT ONCE!!"

## INTERVIEWING BY MACHINERY.

(*By One who now knows How to do it.*)

I HAD received an intimation from the conductor of a popular London paper that I was to be visited by one of his representatives, so I pulled myself together and looked up my note-books. I pondered for hours over my past life, and called to mind its most telling incidents. I arranged my house in the most artistic fashion, and awaited events rather anxiously. At the appointed time a lively young gentleman introduced himself.

"Now, my dear Sir," said he, "all I want you to do is to sit quietly and attend to me. You need not speak yourself. I am so accustomed to this sort of thing that I can save you all that trouble. Iron-grey hair—military moustache—about fifty. Think you are about fifty, and the colour of your hair is hereditary?"

I nodded.

"Quite so. Well, that will do for a start. I think you have been a soldier: had adventures of the usual kind in South Africa. Lived with the Boers and Afghans. Eaten half-raw mutton, and slept for nights in huts made of mud? Eh? That's it, isn't it?"

Again I bowed my head.

"Certainly," and he jotted down a few more lines in the note-book which he had taken from his pocket. "Literary man too. Written lots of books. Novels—romances. You start a plot by getting a central idea. Then you think it out. Then you find the proper sort of persons to carry out your notion. Put them down and give them names? Then think out your last incident. Get it and go backwards till you come to Chapter First. Then go to the seaside and think it over again—all of it. Then begin your work and finish it. Eh? That's the sort of thing, isn't it?"

Once more I silently acquiesced.

"Fancy too you were once a doctor. Laboured amongst the very poor. Heart crushed by the misery of the East End. Saw the usual characteristics of 'Horrible London.' Once visited a Chinese Opium den—heathen Chinee—old woman with a small pipe—squalid surroundings. Eh?" I made the same gesture as before.

"Just so. Then I think you have been fairly athletic. Were in your school Eleven and rowed in your College boat. Still have the bat, and took away the rudder. Got both of them hanging up in your study. Was rather fond of following the Thanet Harriers. Once caught by the tide at Herne Bay and (mounted) had to swim for your life. I think I am right—stop me if I am wrong."

I did not stop him.

"Live in this house. Usual sort of old-fashioned mansion. Brocaded curtains, and dark-coloured wooden chests picked up in Brittany. Pictures of your father, mother, grandfather, and grandmother. Value them all. However set highest price on a small picture of himself, once given you by his Royal Highness. Fond of dogs—that black poodle can do some tricks. Like flowers in your garden; water them every day when your toil is done. Can play on the fiddle, and sometimes indulge in a game of whist at the Club. I think that is about all you have to tell me, except when you said good-bye you shook me warmly by the hand, and once more got back to the work my entrance had interrupted."

And before I could reply he had jumped up, rushed down my steps, taken a Hansom, and gone off to interview somebody else.

---

"PLAY UP! MUSIQUE!"—"*It seems a pity,*" says Our Own *Times* Correspondent, writing from Berehaven during the Naval Manœuvres, "*that bands should now be all but abolished. Rightly or wrongly, Lord Charles Beresford is credited with the change,*" &c. What! Lord CHARLES, a prominent supporter and member of the Organising Committee of the Italian Opera, "forbidding the bands"!! We cannot believe that Our CHARLEY can have been so misguided as to be out of harmony with popular sentiment. Let every ship be like the Old Lady of Banbury Cross, and have music wherever she goes, to cheer up our hearts of oak, and set the tars' toes going to the hornpipe.

---

SLIGHT CONFUSION.—"Very glad," observed Mrs. RAM, "to read that Mr. SANTLEY is back again. He's much better employed in singing, than in finding some Pasha or other in Egypt."

## ROBERT AT THE CRISTIAL PALLIS.

Thanks to the kindness of a frend of mine who is engaged there, I went larst week with a horder to the Cristial Pallis, but after gitting in without not paying nothink, I found to my grate estonishment, as I couldn't have a seat in the Theater on the same libberal terms, and on picking out a nice one rite in front, I was acshally arsked no less than seven-and-six for it! Of coarse I wasn't a going for to pay sitch a sum as that jest to hear a Eyetalian Opera all about *Don Geewarni*—which I am told is short for Mr. John—so, after a good deal of squabbling, he let me have one at the back for harf-a-crown.

Luckily for me, one of my old Copperashun patrons was there, and he came up with his usual good-natered smile and said, "I didn't kno, Mr. Robert, as you was a Etalien skollar; are you?" To which I replied, "Not a werry fust-rate one, I'm afraid, Sir; but I knos that *greesy* means a great singer, and that *allboney* means a werry stout lady." "Well," he said, larfing, "if that's all, praps you'd like me to sit by you, and tell you all about it?" "That I suttenly shood," says I, "if you'll be so kind." Witch he were.

Well, after all the fiddlers and trumpetters and the big drummer had played away a lot of rubbish, jest to git their hands in, up went the Curtain, and sure enuff there was a werry ansumly drest gennelman, whose name was *Lepperellor*, and he began a singing, as I was told, all about what a noosance it were for him to be a dordling about out there in the cold while his Marster, *Mr. Geewarni*, was amusing of hisself indores. Presently in comes his marster and a werry stout lady all in wite a dragging of each other about most horful, and then the Lady runs away, and in cums her father and tells *Mr. G.* as he ort to be ashamed of hisself for to hact like that, upon witch he pulls out his sword and they fites, and *Mr. G.* kills the lady's father, bang on the floor, and then runs away. And that's the hend of the fust seen, witch didn't strike me as being werry moral, till arter I'd seen the next one, and then I didn't think so werry badly of it. In the second seen, in cums *Mr. G.* and his servant, *Mr. Lepperellor*, a larfing, and a singing all about the fun they've jest had? when presently in comes one of *Mr. G.*'s old sweethearts, who gives it him pretty hot for leaving her as he had done, when he tells her as it's all rite, as his frend *Mr. L.* will xplain, but as he's got a werry perticklar engagement hisself, off he goes.

*Mr. L.* then percedes to xplain everythink to the pore Lady, and if it hadn't been as my Copperashun patron had told me what was coming, I never coud have bleeved that any one gennelman coud have behaved so shamefull, or that hundreds of most respectabel ladies, old and yung, coud have set and lissened to it all as cool as so many cowcumbers! What a rewelashun!

*Mr. Lepperellor* unfolds a long list about 10 foot long, which, he says, contanes the names of all his Master's sweethearts! and then he tells the pore Lady how many there are and where they all lived! So many in Itterly, so many in France, so many among the Turkeys, none, I'm prowd to say, in England, but in Spain one thousand and three!! Glad I am as Mrs. Robert wasn't there to hear the shamefool tail! But ewen that wasn't all, for that imperent servant goes on to xplain that there was among 'em Marshonesses and Countesses and Barrownesses and Citizenesses, and ewen Serwants, in fact, sum of all sorts and all sizes! I never coud have bleeved it if I hadn't have herd it all with my own years, and my kind frend's together, and then off he runs, and ewerybody acshally larft and clapped their ands!

In the next seen of this shameful hoperer there is a pore willage gal a going to be married, and *Mr. Geewarni* acshally trys to perswade her to go with him to his carsel close by! But three ladies and gennelmen, all dressed in black, faces and all, stops him jest in time, and gives it him pretty hot, and serve him rite, but he don't seem to care much about it, for in the next seen he and his imperent servant comes in larfing as usual, tho it is a churchyard, with ony one toom in it, and that is the pore gennelman's as he killed in the werry fust seen, and it has on it a picter in stone of the dead old Gent a seated on his favrit horse. Well, drekly as *Mr. G.* sees it, he makes his pore servant harsk him to come and have supper with him that werry nite at 12 o'Clock sharp, and he nods his stony head, and says as he will! No wonder as the pore servant was amost fritened to death, for it made ewen me quite start agane.

Well, the werry next seen shows *Mr. G.* at supper with sum of the most owdacious-looking ladies as I ever waited on, and they all drank away at reel Shampane, as I was hinformed as Mr. Orgustus Arris was sitch a reel liberal Manager that he allers guv his peeple reel suppers and reel wine, like a reel Gennelman as he is. Well, presently, as trew as I sets here a riting, in comes the stony-looking Statty as was last seen on Horseback in the Churchyard, and sings out as he has cum to supper, as he promised for to do. And then hout runs all the pore fritened ladies, tho I saw one on 'em as took good care to emty her glass fust, tho she was so terrible agitated. Then the Statty naterally harsks *Mr. G.* to shake hands with him, which he werry foolishly does, for of course it's so cold that when he's got a good hold of it he carn't let it go agane till he falls down dead on the floor, and is ewen then so cold that his face is all blew! And then down came the Curtain, and it was all over, and we was all so pleased to see how werry propperly *Mr. G.* was punished for his owdacious goings on, that we all clapped our hands and went home.

And if this is the sort of morality as is tort by all Etalian Operas, it will be a jolly long wile before I takes Mrs. Robert to see one, tho I must say that both me and my kind frend, and all the Gennelmen, aye and a good menny of the Ladies too, all seemed to most thoroughly injoy it, and my kind frend was good enuff to tell me, that tho we are no dowt the most morallest peeple in all the world when we understands all that's being said, when it's served up in a forren tung we can stand quite as much as most folks, and praps a little more. Robert.

---

## RECENT SUMMERY PROCEEDINGS.

*In the Country (selon la Saison).*

How provoking that the Blue Hungarians should have thought that the weather would have stopped the garden-party, and that in consequence only the ophicleide has come down from London.

Fashions in the Present Rain.

I do not think, somehow, he is producing very much effect concealed among the palms in that conservatory.

Seeing that the rain is falling in torrents, it would certainly have been better to have postponed the performance of these pastoral players.

That dance of dripping wood nymphs would have been much more effective if it had been given without the aid of goloshes and umbrellas.

Dear me! why here is the river that has overflowed its banks, come up in full flood to the drawing-room windows!

Surely that must be the peacock perched on that garden-seat floating away bottom upwards in the distance.

I am afraid that the poor Old Vicar with two feet of water running through his study must be feeling rather rheumatic.

Ha! there goes the whole hay-crop carried away over the lasher.

I wonder whether I could get any salmon-fishing in those cucumber frames.

If this weather continues, I really think a visit to town would be desirable.

See, here is the house-boat at the front door come to take us to the station.

---

Notion for a Juvenile Dramatic Art School.—The excellence of Mr. Saville Clarke's charming *Tableaux Vivants* (at 3·30, Anglo-Danish Exhibition) should suggest the idea to some enthusiastic Comedian—[why not to Mrs. Kendal, the clever trainer of the *Real Little Lord Fauntleroy!*]—of starting an Infant Dramatic School, as a real nursery for the Histrionic Art. The Fairy children here are delightful, all so pretty, and evidently such very Good Fairies. Mr. Clarke only made one mistake, which hardly counts, and that was in representing the King as clothed. The whole point of Andersen's story is the child exclaiming, "Why, he has got on no clothes at all!" It was the Naked Truth *v.* Courtly Flattery and Falsehood. Miss Annie Delatour's solo in the sixth *tableau* is well worth listening to; she is an invisible Fairy, as is Miss Thornton, who also sings prettily during the next *tableau*. So the pupils could learn music as well as acting, and would be instructed in declamation by "The Orator," Mr. George Temple, and enter themselves as "Students of the Temple."

---

Richmond Park.—'Wantage Ground for Wolunteers.

## HOW TO GET OUT OF IT.

[*Critic to Editor.*—Dear Sir,—You told me I "mustn't pitch into the new piece," which I certainly should have done but for your kindly instructions. I think I've managed the task rather neatly.—Yours, A. Trimmer.

⁂ As a model specimen of how to get out of saying that a piece is utter bosh from beginning to end, we publish the accompanying in the interests of true Critical Art.—Ed.]

We heartily congratulate Messrs. Colwyn Malaprop and Timothy Grand on the triumphant success which attended the production of their new and original Melodrama at the Oracle Theatre yesterday evening. It is sure to run for at least five hundred nights, and at the end of that period no doubt the two playwrights, who work together so harmoniously, will have another piece ready to take its place. And when we say this, it must be clearly understood that we do not pledge ourselves that this last arrived of our entertainments is either new or original. As a matter of fact we have seen everything contrived by our authors a score of times before, and are sick to death of forged bills, mislaid marriage certificates, and substituted children. We loathe deserted wives and sirenically influenced (if we may coin an epithet) husbands, and can see no fun in the low comedy of smashing a band-box, or gentle satire in speaking disrespectfully of somebody's mother-in-law. But what of that, and what does it matter? Has not Messrs. Malaprop and Grand given us a good, healthy, honest, wholesome play, that will set the hearts of many a gallery boy (and, if it comes to that, of many a gallery lassie too) beating as hearts have ever beat since good old Father *Adam* walked through the Forest of Ardennes in the company of the melancholy *Jacques*? Ay, and it is so, and we heartily thank our authors for what they have done for us.

In these days of mock realism and sham sentiment, it is a good thing to find that men can speak out, as it were, straight from the elbow, as readily in the Theatre as in the Church. Not that there is any particularly noble language in the piece under review. On the contrary, the captious may think that *Mabel*, telling her best-loved child to steal a shilling, accidentally left on the mantelpiece, in order that she may pay the cabman "more than his full fare," open to question on the score of morality. But what of that? What does it matter? The Authors are not writing for sour-visaged Puritans, but for good, sound-hearted, round-faced, honest John Bull, and his rosy-cheeked wife, and his giggling, girlish, and gentle-eyed daughters.

Again it may not be altogether true to nature to make Major-General Sir John Abercromby, K.C.B., dining at mess as the guest of Staff-Sergeant Tomkins in full uniform after the inspection of the latter's regiment, but if there is to be no poetic licence, beer may as well be abandoned and skittles regarded as a game whose rules are lost for ever in the dim realms of a distant obscurity! For what do we go to a play-house? Assuredly not for Shakspeare or the musical glasses, to say nothing of prunella! So long as the fare is sound at the core, what more can we want? And if the play of last night was not only improbable but impossible from the opening scene down to the end of the tag which was the signal for the lowering of the green baize curtain, surely the fact remains that the work was as sweet-scented as hay, and as homely as a bean feast or a barn-door fowl. Given this and what does the rest matter? As *Othello* observes, "Not a jot, not a jot!" And the swarthy Moor of Venice was right. The great master who "thought him out" in the little cottage in Stratford-on-Avon was never wiser, never sager, never freer from cant and nonsense than when he wrote "hold up the mirror to nature to show vice her own image and virtue the habit in which she lives," or words to like effect. Ah, "Sweet Willie" was indeed a judge of the frailties of poor humanity! He knew that the flats must be "joined," and the scenes painted with a ten-pound brush. Rouge is a coarse pigment, but cheeks are pale without it under the fierce glare of the blue-hued lime-light! Again, the hypercritical may declare that acting is a lost art, and assuredly they would find some reason for their cross-grained assertion in the acting of last night. *Mr. Avenue* strutting the stage and appealing to the chandelier with outstretched arms is not exactly the sort of hero we find in a modern drawing-room, nor is pretty *Miss Haresfoot*, in white muslin in a snow-storm the ideal heroine of nineteenth century romance. But what of that—both the lady and the gentleman are prime favourites with the Pit, and if the dwellers in the Stalls slumber, why then let it be more to their shame than to their glory! Out upon the querulous questioners of the likely and the commonplace! What do we want with their hypochondriacal murmurings? So long as the play is pleasant to the palate and healthy to the understanding, we can do without the applause of the reviewers and the hearty enthusiasm of the burners of midnight oil.

In conclusion what could be better than the title of the drama? In selecting "*Six-foot Rule Britannia*," our authors have shown a discrimination far above all praise. That it has nothing whatever to do with the motive of the piece is a detail unworthy of criticism. No, let us rest and be thankful. Let the play of last night run a thousand nights—if possible longer. And when it becomes our pleasant duty to have to record its successor, may we be in a position to write a *critique* as valuable as that which with a hearty shake of the hand to all concerned—authors, actors, managers, and scene-painters—we now bring to a genial and welcome conclusion!

## THE GREAT UNKNOWN.

The stern-faced resolute old man once more approached the Treasury. He had been there several times before, but on this occasion there was a new Messenger at the entrance, and consequently there was a chance of his gaining admittance. With some trepidation, he passed the porch unquestioned, and now he was on the road to the being of whom he was in quest.

"I shall see him," he murmured, "and prove to an unbelieving world that he is not a myth."

Almost with a smile on his pale harsh features, he knocked at a door and entered.

"No," said the clerk whom he had questioned; "you have come to the wrong place. All we have to do is to look after the Divorce Division. We represent the Queen's Proctor. If you want to intervene we will help you to do it, but we can't go further than that."

"But where shall I find him?" asked the distracted veteran.

"How should I know?" answered the official, testily; and he turned to some one else.

Portrait of the Public Prosecutor.

Disheartened but unconquered, the aged wanderer uttered a sigh and recommenced his search. He entered a second room and made his customary application.

"Now, really," said an official who was busily engaged in discussing a plate of sandwiches and a glass of sherry, "it is several degrees too bad to worry a fellow at his lunch!"

"Surely you can tell me the name of your chief?"

"The name of my chief is nothing to you," was the brusque reply, "but I can tell you his office. He is Solicitor to the Treasury."

Baffled once again, the wandering greybeard retired to the streets, and sitting down beside a lamp-post, uttered a series of piercing yells.

"This is disgraceful!" exclaimed a passer-by. "This man is a nuisance. Constable, arrest him!"

"Very sorry, Sir, but I have not the power," replied the policeman.

"Not have the power!" echoed the wrathful pavement promenader, and then he turned to the weeping white-head and observed to him, "I have half a mind to take you before the Public Prosecutor."

"Take me before the Public Prosecutor?" repeated the now radiant investigator. "Pray, pray do!"

"You would not like it!" was the stern commentary.

"Would not like it!" For a moment the ancient could not speak for emotion, and then he continued—"Why, it would realise the dream of my life! But if you do, you must be a cleverer man than I am, for I have been hunting for the Public Prosecutor for the last twenty years, without being able to find him."

"Not find him! Why here is his portrait!" And with this the good-natured passer-by presented the old man with the original picture, of which the sketch ornamenting this article is a rough, but not altogether unsuggestive copy!

Another "G. O. M." in the Field for Gallant Little Wales.—"Mr. Gee."

## CHARITY BAZAARS.

(*Things one has to put up with, in a good cause.*)

*The Lady Hildegarde de Sangrazul.* "Will you take a Share in the Raffle for this beautiful Vase?"
*Affable Stranger.* "Ah, my dear, if it was only You as was going to be Raffled for, now, blest if I wouldn't take Forty!"

## HER MAJESTY'S SHIP "BLUNDERER."

*A Warning Dockyard Ditty, as Sung by Cheery Jack.*

D'ye want to know the trimmest craft that might have sailed from port,
When we went a manœuvring, mates, in Eighteen-eighty-eight;—
A regular tip-topper of Lord George's special sort,
With every dodge aboard of her to bring her up to date?

Then listen as I tell ye first about her steady pace,
As proud she'd meet the Channel waves a slipping neatly under her
At near five knots an hour—not the speed to win a race?
May be: but that's the record of Her Majesty's ship *Blunderer*.

A record that, you'll say, my mates, it won't take much to beat,
P'raps not, and like enough it is to stir a landsman's mirth;
But still her pace is all that she can manage, and the fleet
Take precious care, when out with her, to give her a wide berth.
For something in her steering-gear goes wrong, and then d'ye see
She runs foul of another craft, whose bulwarks straightway dashing in,
She, after heavy loss and damage finally gets free,
Her own three starboard boats and all her gun-ports gaily crashing in.

But, there, mates, they had built her five-and-twenty years ago;
So first they let her out a bit, and then they took her in,
And cut her down, and patched her up, and made a sort of show
Of giving her another inch or two of iron skin.
And so, mates, taking stock of all her points both fore and aft,
Although, d'ye see, it may be that you mightn't have a doubt of her,
It's possible while thinking her a tidy sort of craft,
That on the whole, if going a cruise, you'd just as soon be out of her.

So, if her boilers prime a trifle, mates, why, what's the odds,
Becos her engines and all that was put in second-hand;
And if her steam-pipe's leaky, and she busts her piston-rods,—
Well, that's the sort of thing, d'ye see, Lord George can understand.
And if it comes to firing of her guns: then you may swear
Each un'll start her breech and rings, and blow her blessed muzzle out;
'Tain't much. But going aboard of her? It ain't that I don't dare;
But what's the use? And that's the question, mates, I tries to puzzle out!

Moral.

So when these here manœuvres is all finished up and done,
And Admirals and Captains stop their little larking fight,'
And the chaps who write for papers have helped to make the fun,
And talked big of the "Enemy," who never came in sight,
It may be that "My Lords," when taking stock of recent slips,
In duty to Britannia, since they take service under her,
May manage just to wipe out from their coming list of ships,
Such a racy roaring craft as Her Majesty's ship *Blunderer*.

---

"Devoutly to be Wished."—All good men, and true friends of Ireland, hope that the Irish leaders, by entirely clearing themselves from all suspicion of complicity with crime, will prove that they are members of an honest National, and not Assassi-National League.

---

The first person (singular!) to hear of Mr. O'Kelly's arrest was Mr. Chance. The Government, unable to give an answer when questioned, heard of it subsequently quite by Chance. What a lucky Chance!

---

Perpetual Motion in Trafalgar Square.—"Move on!"

AN AFFAIR OF HONOUR.

*(SETTLING THE DISTANCES.)*

## OUR NATURAL ADVANTAGES.

*M. le Comte (who has come to London for the Season of* 1888). "AH BAH! YOU ARE AFRAID OF THE CHANNEL TUNEL! *QUELLE BÊTISE!* VY, IT IS NOT YOUR 'SILVARE STREAK' ZAT PROTECT YOU FROM ZE INVASION, *MES AMIS!* IT IS YOUR SACRED DOG OF A CLIMATE!"

### SONG ON SOUTH AFRICA.

THERE is USIBEPU, and there's DINIZULU
To be King of the Kaffirs pretending;
And one more little war looms in prospect—what for?
Lives and money the Government spending!
USIBEPU, DINIZULU.
Dusky antagonists, out upon you!

And those pestilent Boers at our Colonists' doors
Are preparing to level the rifle.
If in conflict they close, we shall pay through the nose,
At a cost like to prove not a trifle.
USIBEPU, DINIZULU,
What bothers and Boers! To be taxed for you two!

---

THE DESCENT OF MAN,—by Parachute, out of Balloon, on Saturday last,—when "Professor" BALDWIN accomplished the "sensation" of descending from a Balloon at the Alexandra Palace, when one thousand feet high, "with," to quote the words of the scientific person's Manager, "nothing but an umbrella to aid him in his descent." It is true that the "umbrella" looked uncommonly like an ordinary parachute, but for all that the leap seemed to be sufficiently dangerous to please the Many-headed. The "Professor" (it would be interesting to identify his University—did he graduate in Skye?) claims to "drop from the clouds with ease, grace, and rapidity." No doubt at all times he will be able to insure the third characteristic of his flight. On Saturday he apparently lost his balloon, but he did not lose his life. It is to be hoped that he never will, although precedent is against him. In the event of his getting some day a drop too much, or rather too many, it will be important to learn whether the coroner's jury will bring in a verdict of misadventure, suicide, or murder. In the event of the latter, the Authorities, who could have prevented the accident but would not, may, perhaps, figure as accessories before the fact!

---

LAMBETH CONFERENCE.—The Lawn-meets for the English and Colonial Bishops were so frequent, that Bishops *in partibus* will now be known as Bishops *in garden-partibus*. (N.B.—Especially when one omnibus took fourteen Colonials to one of these *al fresco* entertainments.)

## PLAY TIME.

THERE were to have been three *Dr. Jekylls and Mr. Hydes* in the field. One so far afield as the Croydon Theatre; at least, so said the *St. James's Gazette* young man last week. But in the meantime there have been injunctions and legal difficulties. Perhaps if the Law is satisfied there may yet be *The Strange Story* of Dr. BANDFIELD and Mr. MANSMANN, at the Lyceum Comique and Opera Lyceum. Regular muddle. It is long since the Opéra Comique had something in keeping with its title. The last time was when *Opéra Bouffe*, with full orchestra, was played there; now there's no *Opéra Bouffe*, but only a BAND-MANN.

One piece doing first-rate business in town just now is, I should say, Mr. PINERO's *Sweet Lavender*, at TERRY's Theatre. And deservedly so. Capital part for TERRY, who plays it admirably, though occasionally dropping into exaggeration of style which would be more suitable in burlesque. Mr. ALFRED BISHOP as the kind old Irish Doctor is a life-like portrait; and so too is Mr. BRANDRAM THOMAS's well made-up picture of the old remorseful Colonel, who has been a bit of a dog and a good deal of a snob in his younger days. Miss CARLOTTA ADDISON is the very ideal of the "lone and lorn one"—a still youthful *Mrs. Gummidge*—who lives to heap coals of fire on the head of her betrayer, or rather, to nurse him in his illness, and give him his gruel, which she does with a will, and gives it him hot. Miss MAUD MILLETT presents us with a pleasant sketch of the fresh young English girl, capitally contrasted with her second-class Yankee lover—for as she is not quite the typical aristocratic English girl, so he is not by any means a type of the superior American,—while her Aunt is represented by that clever actress Miss VICTOR as an amusing specimen of a good-natured, vain, underbred middle-aged woman.

The story—very interesting, and the plot well constructed, with one slight exception—seems to have been founded on the episode of *Pendennis* falling in love with *Fanny Bolton*, the daughter of a Temple porter. *Dick Phenyl* is a superior kind of *Eccles*; but all the same is a sketch from real life. Miss NORREYS as the heroine, is, of all *ingénues*, a great deal too ingenuous. She is THACKERAY's *Fanny Bolton*, only,—conscious of an audience. So simple and innocent does she strive her best to appear, that, not knowing the story, I began to think she was a consummate little hypocrite, and that in the Second Act we should find she had been playing *Sainte Nitouche*, and should probably see her enjoying a champagne supper after the manner of the "pretty little souls" in *The Pink Dominoes* and other kindred pieces. By straining to emphasize her "*Sancta Simplicitas*," she suggests the idea of such "an artless thing" as was *Miss Becky Sharp* on quitting school. The play, generally, suggests THACKERAY Theatricalised. The lover is uninteresting—lovers mostly are—and Mr. PINERO delights in making this commonplace young man, who is very much in love, drop into sham poetry, and talking to *Dick Phenyl*—of all persons!—about "every beat of his heart saying Lavender"—"every newspaper-boy crying Lavender," &c., &c., and all that sort of thing, which no young man in real life, unless he were an affected, æsthetic nincompoop, would ever dream of saying. When TOM ROBERTSON gave us modern lovers on the stage he knew how valuable was the eloquence of silence, and how natural it was for an ordinary Society young man when deeply in love to be uncommonly taciturn. But Mr. PINERO wants this sort of character to talk, and to talk a sort of TENNYSON-and-water,—weak "T" in fact.

These are trifles. The audience takes it for granted that lovers will talk nonsense, and though they do have their doubts as to the genuine simplicity of *Sweet Lavender* herself, and do not look forward hopefully to the future domestic happiness of her husband, yet on the whole they are thoroughly interested and return home perfectly satisfied with having passed an exceptionally pleasant evening.

---

### Obvious.

WE must get JOHN BULL's business out of this kink,
Officialdom's credit must soon be restored;
Or in Civil corruption the country will sink,
And national honour will "go by the Board."

---

APPROPRIATE DATE FOR THAT BLESSING IN THE GUISE OF AN AUTUMN SESSION.—The Fifth of November.

## FANCY PORTRAITS.

"GROCERIES."

"The Right Hon. A. J. Balfour, M.P., and Sir Frederick Leighton, P.R.A., were admitted to the Freedom of the Grocers' Company, Wednesday, July 25th."

## A SONG OF WILLOW.

*(Made at Lord's in the miserable two-hours' interval between two tremendous Thunder-showers in the horrid Season of '88.)*

Sing, "Willow"? Ay! But who may wield
The willow bat this wild, wet season,
When, a sheer swamp, the cricket-field
Is only fit to shake and sneeze on?
When smartest "fielders" flop and plunge,
When pluvial down-pour scarcely ceases;
When balls are pap, and pads are sponge,
And "creases" simply water-creases?
Say who can cut, or drive, or slog,
On black and bladeless mud-morasses?
Or bowl on wickets like a bog
That has been trampled by wild asses?
Not Grace himself nor Walter Read,
The sodden lead-like lump of leather
May urge across a miry mead
After a week of *such* June weather.
What chance, when "turf" means sticky slime
Even for A. G. Steel or Lohmann?
How should "the Champion" place or time
With Jupiter Pluvius for foeman?
Slow wickets help the bowler? Yes!
But love mud-swamps? No, that's an error.
There *may* be too much muck and mess
E'en for "the Tempter" or "the Terror."
For topping score or brilliant catch,
So bad a time I never saw, Sir;
Fancy the Oxford-Cambridge match
Running four days, and *then* a draw, Sir!
We seek the field to funk and freeze,
Oh, happy Shrewsbury, Stoddart lucky,
To be at the Antipodes
Away from quagmires cold and mucky!
This is no time for tent and sward,
But warm fire-side or cosy pillow.
Sing Willow? Bah! the cheeriest bard
Could only sing the *Weeping* Willow!

Ecclesiastical Art.—An appropriate exhibition that the Archbishop of Canterbury ought to have sent or taken his clerical guests to see, was the pictures of Parsons and Abbey. Too late now, as last week was the last week of the show.

## YANKEE DOODLE IN A NEW CHARACTER.

"M. Albert Wolff, of the *Figaro*, bewails in his last *chronique* the number of masterpieces of modern French Art which have been spirited across the ocean by the magic of the American dollar, and irretrievably lost to the country."—*St. James's Gazette.*

Yankee Doodle comes to town,
And you may bet a "pony"
He's game to plank his dollars down
For Millet or Moroni.
Yankee Doodle buys up Art
As though 'twere cheap as candy;
But though the *dilletanti* smart,
The dollars come in handy.

Yankee Doodle all our best
In Art and Books will collar,
Our Masterpieces lures out West
By the Almighty Dollar.
The picture-dealers gladly part,
The publishers say thankee!
Only poor friends of native Art
Cuss "that confounded Yankee!"

Yankee Doodle cannot paint
(So run the critics' strictures)
But—'tis enough to vex a saint!
He buys up *our* best pictures.
When twenty-thousand pounds he'll "part,"
(Like Boston's rich Rockfeller),
For an immortal work of Art,
'Tis like to find a seller.

Yankee Doodle he strikes oil,
And then all Europe's galleries
The millionnaire proceeds to spoil
Despite our groans and railleries,
Well, Yankee Plutus has the pelf,—
He makes "collections,"—swell them!—
One day he'll paint big things himself,
***And then he'll want to sell them!"***

## THE GREAT ADVENTURER.

Dear Mr. Punch,

This is what has happened. She and I are really seriously attached to each other. She would make an adorable wife, and I'm sure I'm designed for domestic happiness, as I'm always falling in love, which is quite beastly. It keeps me continually miserable: first, when the girls don't care for me, and secondly, when they do. Bogie (I call her Bogie because she has such beautiful red hair) is a perfect girl, and we should certainly be very happy, but when, in the most gentlemanly way, I told her father about it, he asked me a lot of impertinent questions about my income, which was really in the worst possible taste, as he knows very well that I haven't any. However, I've written a poem, which, if not entirely original, is adapted to circumstances with some skill, and I think you will own that, even if it doesn't scan, it is quite true.

The people who review books are always asking Why are there so many Minor Poets? I can tell them one reason. It's because there are so many sordid fathers of the only girl a fellow ever really loves. He hinted something about an adventurer—like a man in a farce at a *Matinée*—so I call my poem, *Love the Adventurer* (only, unfortunately, he doesn't). Here, however, is the effort:—

### LOVE THE ADVENTURER.

When Love seeks a business-man's daughter,
His hopes he will dash
By asking how he means to support her
Without any cash:
The hat that is sat on
You may have it blocked next day,
But when the old man tries *that* on
Love must get out of the way.

You may warble love-songs in an agreeable baritone,
You may wear small gloves of a mild canary-tone,
You may write for the papers,
Or have evolved the plot of a really new and original play;
But you'll only lose love's labours;
You *can't* make him see things your way.

You may train the eagle
To stoop to your fist;
(Though it's quite another thing to inveigle
The creature to desist.)
You may move (with a crowbar)
The Lioness to give o'er her prey;
But there is really no bar
To the inquisitiveness of a proposed Father-in-law, in the matter of prospects and pay.

Yours, in depressed circumstances,
Lovelace Lackland.

## OUR JAPANNERIES. No. 9.

AT THE "TIMES v. CRIMES" DEBATE IN THE COMMONS.

## ESSENCE OF PARLIAMENT.

EXTRACTED FROM

### THE DIARY OF TOBY, M.P.

*House of Commons, Monday Night, July* 23.—Sir PARNELL with sword drawn, walking about Lobby, waiting for OLD MORALITY. Old MORALITY, longing to be at 'em, foregone his dinner rather than miss opportunity of pinking Sir PARNELL. Second Reading of Commission Bill expected on any moment. Opening first made for Debate on affairs in Zululand. Last week, Opposition trembling with indignation because opportunity for discussing ZIBEPU *v.* DINIZULU refused. Got it now, and all charm vanished. House nearly empty; Debate flickering out; likely to lapse before dinner-hour. So Sir PARNELL paces the Lobby, his sword more than ever drawn; OLD MORALITY sits on Front Bench, and wonders what they're having for dinner at Grosvenor Place; GLADSTONE hurries back after what must have been a Barmecide feast; names of ZIBEPU and DINIZULU float through hazy atmosphere; everyone thinking of matters nearer home.

Zulu Debate dies out. OLD MORALITY moves Second Reading of Parnell Commission Bill. Same old speech. Desire to consult the best interest of Members, and welfare of the country; deeply regretted and deplored; did not desire to utter a single expression; trusted and believed; command full confidence and esteem; the advantage of the country; the convenience of the House.

OLD MORALITY sat down, suffused with moral rectitude, and wondering whether he might not now slip out to dinner. PARNELL, pale and passionate, rushed straight upon him, "like BOULANGER upon FLOCKY," as JOSEPH GILLIS said. Maintained himself at white heat of passion through long speech; occasionally turned aside from OLD MORALITY to ATTORNEY-GENERAL. Irish Members cheered every thrust; save for Irish quarter, House still comparatively empty.

"All of them comfortably getting their dinner," said OLD MORALITY with a weary sigh, glancing round empty benches.

After dinner House rapidly filled up. Eleven o'clock not a seat to be had; side-galleries crowded; Peers' Gallery thronged; CHARLES RUSSELL thumping away at his learned friend the HOME SECRETARY; EDWARD CLARKE followed on other side; Sage of Queen Anne's Gate said what was necessary to carry debate over. A curious, awkward, ill-managed arrangement of business, which served nobody's purpose and necessitated appropriation of another night.

Sir Parnell.

*Business done.*—Parnell Commission Bill discussed.

*Tuesday.*—Black Rod at his jokes again. Funny at first, but a trifle monotonous; rather palls upon House towards end of Session. Joke is to hang about door till Commons get into thick of business; then send in doorkeeper to bellow "Black Rod!" Began the Session with tripping up a Minister. Fastened now on Sage of Queen Anne's Gate. Came in upon him the other night when putting a question. To-night Sage just launched forth in his indictment of ATTORNEY-GENERAL *re* O'DONNELL *versus Times*, when Black Rod appeared. Business peremptorily interrupted; SPEAKER and Mace go off to Lords to see LORD CHANCELLOR and other old women in cloaks bow-wowing on Woolsack.

Black Rod introduced new piece of business to-night. Sent doorkeeper in to bawl "Black Rod!" just as House was loudly cheering Sage. Doorkeeper's shout consequently drowned in uproar. Nobody heard it. Black Rod entered practically unannounced. Sage, with his back to the door didn't see him enter. Proceeded with remarks.

"Order! order!" cried the SPEAKER, who had spotted Black Rod.

"Well, Sir," said Sage, apologetically, "I was only desiring to point out——"

"Order! order!" shouted the SPEAKER.

"Certainly, Sir, I will bow to your decision, though I really don't know——"

"Order! order!" roared the SPEAKER, with his eye on Black Rod advancing towards the table.

Sage, looking round in bewilderment, at this fresh exhibition of SPEAKER's interference with freedom of speech, caught sight of Black Rod. His jaw fell, eyes assumed glassy stare, dropped into seat as if he had been shot.

"Life would be endurable only for its Peers," he said, when he recovered presence of mind. "The Lords pursue me even in the House of Commons."

"Curious thing," said Black Rod, winking at Sergeant-at-Arms, as they crossed the Lobby in procession. "Always find LABBY on his feet when I chance to look in at Commons."

Just in Time.

Parnell Commission Bill debated. CHAMBERLAIN, not often heard now, arrived just in time to speak. A model speech, full of point through its forty minutes, saying exactly what he had at heart in clearest phrase, and with irresistible force. Whether one agrees with him or not, an intellectual delight to listen. Incomparably the best debater in House. Not an orator like GLADSTONE, but still unapproachable as a debater. Fancy CHAMBERLAIN profits by recent infrequency of his speeches in House. Have time and opportunity to compare him with more familiar speakers. Remember what he said in far off June days at Birmingham? Was it fifty years ago, or only three?:—

> "I sometimes think that great men are like great mountains, and that we do not appreciate their magnitude while we are still close to them. You have to go to a distance to see which peak it is that towers above its fellows; and it may be that we shall have to put between us and Mr. GLADSTONE a space of time before we shall know how much greater he has been than any of his competitors for fame and power."

Similarly, but not precisely, the conditions under which CHAMBERLAIN now occasionally speaks in House give opportunity for appreciating his quite unique position as a debater. All night long, all through the weary week, men make speeches round about a subject. Then CHAMBERLAIN comes in and *talks.* As PLUNKET says, "A wonderful difference between a man who has a speech to make, and a man who has something to say."

*Business done.*—Parnell Commission Bill read Second Time.

*Thursday.*—"Demme!" says Markiss o' GRANBY, "BUXTON's put spoke in wheel of Black Rod."

Simile perhaps not quite perfect, but description fairly accurate. BUXTON asked how long we're to have Black Rod bursting in on House like a venerable catapult? OLD MORALITY says he's been talking matter over with LORD CHANCELLOR. Arranged that suggestion made by his Hon. Friend TOBY, M.P., a fortnight ago, shall be adopted. Black Rod to do his bursting in before public business commences in Commons. This, of course, takes all the fun out of the thing. Not be worth while turning up now if he can't interrupt a Minister answering question, or intercept the storied wisdom distilled from lips of Sage of Queen Anne's Gate.

"Another of our treasured institutions gone," says CAVENDISH BENTINCK. "Soon will have nothing left worth living for."

BALFOUR had four bad quarters of an hour at Question Time. Irish Members bubbling up all round him, snapping out interrogatories. BALFOUR took them all round—one down another come on. Imperturbable throughout, only an added hardness of manner, a degree or two more frost in his tones, indicating severity of contest.

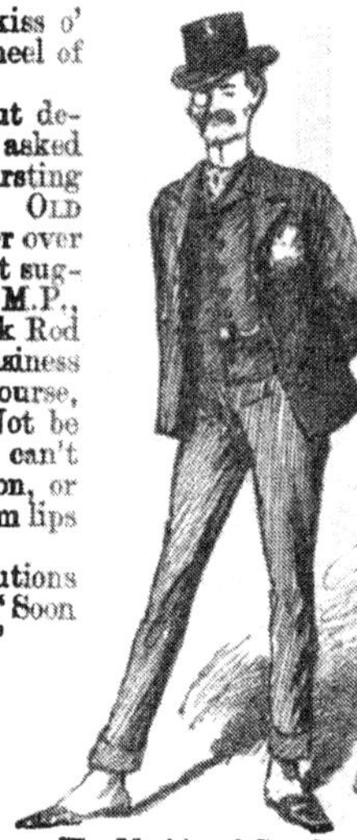

The Markiss o' Granby.

OLD MORALITY announced arrangements for winding up first part of Session. Expects House to be up on 11th of August. To that end proposes programme which, if carried out, would keep House at work till Christmas. Programme in point of magnitude much more like Queen's Speech on opening Parliament in February than suggestions of Leader of House closing up tracks at end of July.

"It's all right, you'll see," said OLD MORALITY. "Remember in younger days, when I was still attendant at a seminary, we used, for the perfection of our style of caligraphy, carefully to copy out remarks lithographed at the top of a ruled page. One of these, I remember, ran to the effect, *Throw plenty of mud, and some of it will, in all human probability, adhere.* That's the principle upon which, animated as I am by a desire to meet the convenience of Hon. Members, and conserve the interests of the public service, I lay before the House this somewhat extended programme. We shall not get through with it all; but we shall emerge having achieved more than if we essayed to do less. In other words, as we used to write in the days already alluded to, *If you aim at the stars, you may succeed in sending a stone through the windows of the second-pair back.*"

*Business done.*—Report Stage of the Local Government Bill.

*Friday.*—Local Government Bill through final stage in Commons. Four Peers, representing Upper House, playing whist since Seven o'Clock, waiting for Bill. Stout and long pipes supplied out of Civil Service Estimates. Half-an-hour after midnight word came Bill was through Commons, and compliments going on all round. Four Peers put away cards, finished stout, presented attendants with broken pipes, and marched into Lords. One took a seat in front of Woolsack, and presided, three others spread themselves as much as possible about Chamber, and formed a House. Bill, solemnly brought in, ordered to be read a First Time. House adjourned.

"Have another rubber?" said Noble Lord, who had presided.

"Think not. Getting late. Besides, we have finished the stout."

So they went home.

*Business done.*—Local Government Bill read Third Time in Commons, and First Time in Lords.

THE PARACHUTE.

*Lively Aëronaut.* "HAPPY THOUGHT! BLOWED IF I'LL COME DOWN TILL THE WEATHER CHANGES!"

## TWO AMERICAN "EYE-OPENERS."

("*Still Alarm*" *at Princess's, and Still More Alarming at Lyceum.*)

*Eye-Opener No.* 1.—On the first night of *The Still Alarm*, after the sensation scene in Act III., representing "The Central Fire Station, New York," the actors were called before the Curtain, so was the author, who didn't appear—at least I didn't see him—and so were the horses, one of which was led on to bow its acknowledgments. The burning and shining fire-engine, which also received the honour of a summons, modestly remained behind the Curtain, as did also the meditative greyhound, whose part in the piece stood out far more than that of Mr. HARRY NICHOLLS, who as a good young man tried his very best to be funny, but despairing of success, had recourse to pretending to play the bones with a couple of spoons, then a tray as a tambourine, and finally his hat as a concertina, and at last finding that these original devices somewhat failed in their object, he relapsed, during the remainder of Miss FANNY LESLIE's solo dance, into moody silence, evidently wondering within himself why he had ever been born, and bitterly meditating on the hollow absurdity of the old proverb which asserts that "Necessity is the mother of invention." If ever there were a moment when the necessity for doing something really humorous was imperative, wasn't it now on this first night of *The Still Alarm*?

The style of Mr. LACY, who plays the hero, is something between that of a sententious American Lecturer and the "Massa JOHNSON" of every Nigger Minstrel *troupe*. He is supposed to represent, says the programme, "*An American fireman of to-day*," and if he does so, correctly, then, however active and spry the "American Fireman of to-day" may be in answer to a call (not before the Curtain, but to a fire), his manner in private life is marked by a peculiar kind of squirming action, coupled with a drawling, sing-song, nasal intonation, which, if intended to be irresistibly fascinating, singularly fails in attaining its object. Whatever may be the attitude of Mr. HARRY LACY's *Jack Manley* towards others, be it of love or hate, there is one person with whom he is always evidently on the very best of terms, and that person is—himself. The best performance in this old-fashioned piece (which only differs from most of this kind in not having a wicked Baronet in the *dramatis personæ*—but then Baronets, good or wicked, are not indigenous to New York) was that of Mr. H. PARKER as the drunken old actor. He reminded me of BENJAMIN WEBSTER in *Janet Pride*, with a considerable touch of Mr. GEORGE HONEY as *Eccles* in *Caste*.

Of course, the Fire-piece will draw on account of this one scene, which is well worth seeing, as a practically vivid illustration of the rapidity with which a fire-engine can be turned out, fully equipped, at the shortest possible notice, in the Central Fire Station of New York. The action, by the way, seemed to me rather incomplete, as the engine was driven off by *Jack Manley* alone, and the firemen were left behind to form a *tableau* at the descent of the Curtain. The orchestra ought to introduce "*Sound an Alarm!*" into the overture.

*Eye-Opener No.* 2. "*The Strange Story of Box and Cox; or, A Puzzle for Bouncer*" *at the Lyceum.*—I must defer my criticism on *The Strange Story* until I have quite recovered from the awful jumpy, creepy, crawly effect produced on me by Mr. MANSFIELD's extraordinary performance last Saturday night. "And is Old Double dead?" He is, and he isn't. "For O it is such a norrible tale!" as Mr. E. L. BLANCHARD used to sing. Ugh! Ugh! Lights there! What ho! Lights, I say! "Why, being gone, I am Dr. Jekyll again!" I read the book long ago, and quite forget why *Dr. Jekyll's* inferior self is called *Mr. Hyde*. Who gave him that name? But more of this anon, when I have had time to review it calmly. Now it's all *Hyde* and Hanwell, and *Quilp* as *Grip* the Raven, raven mad, crying, "I'm a devil! I'm a devil!" Mr. MANSFIELD looked so like the late Mr. CRESWICK, that most middle-aged play-goers must have expected him to turn into SHEPPARD. *The Strange Story of Sheppard and Creswick!!* It is a ghastly extravaganza, with a marvellous "transformation scene." So slight is the human interest in the story, that it might as well have been produced at the Egyptian Hall of Mystery, as *The Strange Story of Messrs. Maskelyne and Cook*. Hush! 'tis the Night Watch! Put out the lights! close the shudders—ah!—I am not *Dr. Jekyll* nor *Mr. Hyde*, but still Yours tremblingly,

JACK-IN-THE-BOX.

## Frank Holl, R.A.

BORN JULY 4, 1845. DIED JULY 31, 1888.

Too early taken, whilst the eager hand,
Held skill at will, and power in full command,
A Painter passes, who so played his part
As to do honour high to English Art.
Sadly the stroke upon Art-lovers falls,
Fresh from admiring gaze around the walls
Where hung the latest triumphs of his brush,
The Master who has fallen in manhood's flush,
With powers unimpaired, though late o'erstrained,
Tasks incomplete, ambitions half attained.
Yet when doth Art not fail of its full aim?
Enough hath been achieved for lasting fame.
A memory thine that mocks at death and fate,
Great English limner of our English Great!

SHAKSPEARE IN THE NORTH.—Our Divine WILLIAMS was a thorough sportsman. He was devotedly attached to sport on the 12th. Didn't he write an entire play about a Moor? Hasn't he provided all Grouse-shooters with the motto for the 11th, "Now will I hence to seek my lovely Moor"? Why certainly.

## JEUNE POUR LA JEUNESSE!

MRS. JEUNE, writing to the Editor of *Truth*, makes the following appeal (which *Mr. Punch* gladly seconds) on behalf of her Children's Boarding-out Fund:—

"May I make one more appeal for a little extra help for my Boarding-out Fund? Through the kindness of your readers and my friends, I have received £363 13*s*., and with that money have sent 386 children to the country at a cost of £303 4*s*. 11*d*. But the holidays are beginning next month, and I have 200 more waiting anxiously to know whether they are to have the much-dreamt-of, or longed-for holiday. Will your readers help me to send them? One pound sends a child for three weeks. How much health and happiness that little sum represents, perhaps we can never fully realise. But we may take it on the word of those who, perhaps, can judge, that no money is better spent—no good more unalloyed than that which gives the little London children their country holiday."

ONE pound sends a child for three weeks to the fields!
A fiscal fact this for us all to remember,
How seldom a sovereign *such* interest yields!
Three weeks, mark, in August, or e'en in September.
British Public stump up to a right handsome tune,
And make Autumn fulfil the fair "Promise of JEUNE."

COOKERY FOR TOURISTS.—Consult the *menus* issued by the Traveller's Guide, Philosopher, and Friend, THOMAS COOK, the *Chef* of COOK AND SONS. Too many COOK's tickets *don't* spoil the journey—on the contrary, they improve it, and they'll show you how to make the best use of a very wide Range.

"THE FLATTERING TALE."

*Old Lady* (*"down upon Followers"*). "THAT YOUNG MAN WHO IS JUST GOING OUT, I SUPPOSE, IS YOUR BROTHER, JANE?"
*Maid.* "NO, 'M. NOT MY BROTHER, M'UM,—WHICH HE'S A YOUNG MAN, M'UM,—MOST R'SPECT'BLE, M'UM,—AS I'VE 'OPES OF!!"

## JACK AT THE WINDLASS.

(*Dibdin adapted to the Day.*)

COME, all hands ahoy to the anchor!
Manœuvres are now all the go.
Land-lubbers whose hearts are all rancour
On Britain's sea-glories would blow.
They say foreign foes would just kick us
About on the boisterous main;
But these shore-going *Timons* won't trick us,
We've licked, and can lick 'em again.
With a will, ho! then pull away, jolly boys,
Our sea-trim has altered, we know;
But we're in for 't, then dash it, what folly,
For to be down-hearted! Yo-ho! [boys,

We look rum in a hulk and our rigging,
Some *have* gone ashore, and some sunk.
The *Warrior* went winkle-digging,
The *Sandfly* went wrong; but why funk?
The old Wooden Walls are slap out of it,
Iron is now all the rage.
Some blunders we've made—there's no doubt
So did Old Salts, I'll engage. [of it,
With a will, ho! &c.

We must go with the times; that's my maxim.
Old England expects us to win;
BULL doesn't much mind how they tax him,
So there's something to show for his tin.
Do you think JACK will sulk or turn craven?
No, no! he will work, fight, and smile,
Same with big war-hulks at Berehaven,
As with old wooden ships at the Nile.
With a will, ho! &c.

Here's me, now, aboard of the *Ajax*,
For fun or for fighting agog;
BULL knows how to find, and to pay, JACKS,
And JACK's game for glory or grog.
Once to handle a blade and hitch trousers,
Sufficed JACK for talents and charms;
By BENBOW, that will not do now, Sirs,
In these days of whopping big arms!
With a will, ho! &c.

The Gunner must now be no bubber,
Straight shooting as Science is classed;
The Steersman must not be a lubber,
Our ships are so big and so fast!
No jollity, NANCY-love, wrapp'd in,
No fondness for fighting and flip,
Will *now* fit a fellow to Captain
That marvel an Iron-clad Ship.
With a will, ho! &c.

Some praise our new ships, some abuse them,
They're ugly, no doubt, as they're big;
What JACK has to do is—to *use* them.
He'll do it too, boys, dash my wig!
JACK never was known for a railer,
We're here for rehearsal—no joke!
But to do his darned best show your Sailor,
Be hulls built of iron or oak.
With a will, ho! then pull away, jolly boys,
Our sea-trim is altered we know;
But spite some big blunders, 'twere folly, boys,
For to be down-hearted! Yo-ho!

---

ALL THE DIFFERENCE.—MR. J. A. HAMILTON, in his new volume on DANIEL O'CONNELL, warns us not to judge the great Irishman "by an English standard." What the present Irish leader objects to be judged by is not so much an English *Standard* as an English *Times*.

## ON THEIR METALS.

THE G. N. R. and the L. & N. W. R. are making a race for it to the north, and eclipsing all previous records in fast railway travelling. In future the Euston "Scotchman" will get to Edinburgh in eight and a half hours, and the King's Cross one, "for one month only," in eight! A month of such steeplechasing is quite enough for anybody. The hundred and ninety-four miles to York done without a break!—or rather, with only a continuous automatic break. Sportsmen, going north, instead of singing "*My Heart's in the Highlands,*" will feel inclined to sing, "*My Heart's in my Mouth.*" And what is to prevent the "one month only" from becoming the Great Northern's "permanent way"? We notice that the North-Western interval for dinner at Preston will be reduced to twenty minutes—twenty minutes allowed for shunting the hungry traveller into the Refreshment Room, coupling him to a meal of three courses, and shunting him back again. In fact, you first bolt into the Refreshment Room, and then bolt *in* it; you eat in haste and repent at leisure. Why not call these new train-services a training in dyspepsia?

---

A CASE OF GROUSE INJUSTICE,—it will be, if anyone goes out shooting on Sunday the 12th, which is a "*Dies Non.*" The translation of this, *vide* Cheeper edition, is, "To-day a Grouse dies not."

---

INFALLIBLE CURE FOR CORPULENCE.—The "Sweating System."

## OUR JAPANNERIES. No. 10.

**A ROW IN THE HOUSE DURING "TIMES v. CRIMES" DEBATE IN COMMITTEE.**

## ESSENCE OF PARLIAMENT.

EXTRACTED FROM

### THE DIARY OF TOBY, M.P.

*House of Commons, Monday Night, July* 30.—"TOBY," said JOSEPH GILLIS, in a broken voice, whilst a tear ran down his cheek and fell upon his watch-chain, where it stood like the dewdrop on the collar of gold that MALACHI wore which he won from the proud invader,—"TOBY, I don't know whether you're of a musical turn, but, if you can give me the key-note, I should like to sing what we used to call in Parry,'*Nunck Dimity*. Whether the Session be long or short, I can go now in peace; to-night's done me a power of good. Thought I'd never look upon the old scenes again. But it's been the right sort of thing. Cheered me withered heart, made me feel ten years younger. Excuse me, but the SPEAKER's up, going through the Orders, and I must go and object."

Truly JOEY is translated. The old gleam in his eye, the old swing in his stride, the old rigidity of the forefinger extended to "object." Thought he was reformed, but only suffering from lack of opportunity. As HENRY FOWLER said the other day, when I was speaking to him of the change, "Scratch JOSEPH GILLIS, and you'll find BIGGAR."

A very lively night. Began at Question Time, when Parnellites made dead set at BALFOUR, with occasional raids upon the Chair. But this nothing to developments in Committee on Parnell Commission Bill. Benches crowded; interruptions constant; cheering and laughter incessant. Impressive scene when HARCOURT thought he heard a smile from GORST. Stopped short in speech; wouldn't go on till GORST had finished his smile, and assumed customary judicial air. Wilder still when, just on stroke of midnight, CHAMBERLAIN spoke.

"Still lithe enough."

"Pickle getting peppery," said CHARLES FORSTER. "Think I'll strut off whilst coast clear. Not so lithe as I was; still, lithe enough."

Five minutes to Twelve when CHAMBERLAIN sat down. COURTNEY about to put question, when PARNELL slowly rose from below Gangway. Debate must needs peremptorily close at midnight. What could PARNELL say in four minutes? A good deal more than was pleasant for some to hear. Turned upon CHAMBERLAIN with placid manner, smiling countenance, and bitter tongue; trickled down upon him stream of vitriol. Drop by drop it fell, searing and burning. Only four minutes to say it all in. But had finished before Big Ben broke in with sound of midnight. Irish Members leaped up in tumult of uncontrollable delight. Above the roar, like shout of mob thirsty for some one's blood, rose cry of "JUDAS! JUDAS!" This was TAY PAY'S contribution to harmony of sitting; subsequently withdrawn, and apologised for. But what of that? CONYBEARE, the great authority on points of honour, has established code in this matter, accepted in sympathetic circles. As he has written, "the withdrawal of an unparliamentary expression does not do away with the effect produced by using it, and does not imply any alteration of a deliberately expressed opinion."

*Business done.*—In Committee on Commission Bill.

*Tuesday Night.*—Debate on Commission Bill on again. Seems to have been a mistake somewhere. General impression was that PARNELL had been doing something; midnight assassination, moonlighting, houghing of cattle, or some other nocturnal diversion. Turns out House assembled, not to consider possibility of PARNELL'S guilt, but certainty of CHAMBERLAIN'S. At opening of proceedings PARNELL appeared in position of Public Prosecutor. Got CHAMBERLAIN in dock, and publicly pummelled him. House amazed, sat and listened with open mouth.

"Pelly-Melly."

"I suppose," said LEWIS PELLY, his hair rising Pelly-melly, and uplifting his hat, "we shall next have a little pamphlet on *Chamberlainism and Crime.*"

PARNELL more than hints that CHAMBERLAIN when Cabinet Minister was playing fast and loose with men steeped to the lips in crime. Quite an unexpected treat this. House summoned to debate on troublesome Bill, suddenly found itself treated to piquant dish of scandal. Every seat occupied. Members standing at Bar, leaning over gallery, flocking behind Speaker's Chair. CHAMBERLAIN as quiet and collected as PARNELL. Admits he had communications with Irish Chief between 1880 and 1885. But interviews were sought by PARNELL, and what passed faithfully reported to GLADSTONE.

Through both narratives old friend, O'SHEA, flits. CHAMBERLAIN says O'SHEA was PARNELL'S agent in arranging interviews. PARNELL says O'SHEA arrived at one of the interviews whilst he was there with JUSTIN McCARTHY. It's all O'SHEA. Seems to have been impartial agent for both sides.

"That's all very well," says CAMPBELL-BANNERMAN. "But we mustn't forget the old axiom. What says COKE upon LITTLETON—or was it LITTLETON upon COKE? *Qui facit per alium, facit per* SHEA."

After CHAMBERLAIN-PARNELL fizzle over, Debate on Commission Bill went forward. Proceedings decidedly explosive. EDWARD WATKIN, who knows something about railways, says reminded him of nothing so much as train approaching station on foggy afternoon. Fog-signals exploding every two minutes. OLD MORALITY had terrible time. Appears that WALTER, of *Times*, happened to call at Grosvenor Square, whilst preparations for Commission Bill going forward. Interview nothing whatever to do with Bill. An old friend just passing by, looked in to say "Howdy?" Bill *might* have been mentioned; but so was the weather. O'SHEA seems to have had nothing to do with this meeting. Position nevertheless harped upon till OLD MORALITY loses his temper; frankly tells Sage of Queen Anne's Gate he's another. Sage much hurt at this wild language, but on ground that OLD MORALITY is unduly excited, magnanimously forgives him.

*Business done.*—Parnell Commission Bill in Committee.

*Wednesday.*—Matters livelier than ever. JOSEPH GILLIS skipping about like a young lamb. Flits from side to side, in and out by the door, across the lobby and back again.

"Not precisely up to usual style of *Puck*," says ALBERT ROLLIT, looking on admiringly. "But,—everything going wrong, everybody by the ears and JOSEPH GILLIS hopping around—reminds me of scene in the wood. Expect to find him catching Chairman's eye and saying as he skips, "Mr. COURTNEY, Sir;

> Up and down, up and down;
> I will lead them up and down:
> I am fear'd in field and town;
> Goblin, lead them up and down!"

TIM HEALY wanting to know more about OLD MORALITY'S morning callers. "How about this visit of WALTER?" says TIM, as if he were inquiring whether the grocer had called; "and BUCKLE—what did BUCKLE call for? WALTER, we know, was an old friend. Was BUCKLE an old friend?"

GLADSTONE in terribly high spirits. Thumps the box, shakes his fist at GOSCHEN, and nearly talks himself hoarse. GOSCHEN affected almost to tears. Then HARCOURT comes in, big and blatant, roaring and rampant. LULU, standing on guard at lobby-door, bringing up the British Constitution in the rear whilst his father leads it in the van, hears the parental voice and is soothed.

"Lulu."

Closure moved: COURTNEY puts question; declares "the Ayes have it!"; Parnellites bellow "No!" Division threatened; GLADSTONE shakes his head in token of dissent. Question put again. Parnellites sit dumb; only O'HANLON up in the side gallery with small day-book on his knee roars "No!" O'HANLON in the grocery business when temporarily out of politics. Rather neglected home affairs of late. Thinks opportunity favourable for making up accounts and lost time. So finds snug corner in gallery, brings out day-book and bill-heads, pegs away for an hour. Getting on with work nicely when Closure incident comes on. Hears his friends shout "No!" when question put. Doesn't observe GLADSTONE'S signal of dissent; goes on making out his bills. Meets COURTNEY'S reiterated assertion that "the Ayes have it!" with steady shout of "No!" All eyes turned upon him. Just put down another half-pound of sugar to MAT MALONEY, 13, Main Street, Derry, when House cleared for Division; then emissary sent up to explain situation. O'HANLON sees it all; Question again put; sits mute as harp on Tara's wall; Closure agreed to and sitting adjourned. *Business done.*—Committee again.

*Friday*, 1·30 A.M.—Commission Bill through at last. A dull sitting compared with those that had gone before, varied by charge of breach of privilege against *Times*. Been saying things of GLADSTONE, JOHN MORLEY, and even of HARCOURT! Talk designed with more than usual plainness to pass away time. Arranged that at One o'Clock this morning, whatever Clauses left should be put without debate. Scene expected at One o'Clock; impatiently awaited; nothing came of it; COURTNEY put Clauses one by one; no one said him nay, and so Bill passed through Committee. ESSLEMONT (in the drapery business at Aberdeen), emulous of O'HANLON'S success on Wednesday, got into corresponding position in opposite gallery; produced day-book and bill-heads; worked away, intending to challenge Division on Clauses. Splendid advertisement for ESSELMONT and MACKINTOSH. "And so cheap," the canny Scot observed to himself. At last moment heart failed him. Clauses passed, and opportunity missed.

LIBERAL UNIONISM
SESSION 1888

# LANDED!

PROFESSOR RITCHIE WITH HIS PARLIAMENTARY PARACHUTE.

"Weel, weel," he said, folding up day-book in gratuitous copy of Orders; "Aiblins, MACKINTOSH needna ken what we've lost."

Great muster of Members for divisions. CHRISTOPHER SYKES comes among others, not familiar of late.

"Going to speak?" I asked him.

"No, dear boy," said CHRISTOPHER, with priceless air of languor, that BAUMANN vainly strives to imitate. "My speaking days are over. Sold my lib'ry, doncha. Fine collection, formed by Sir MARK SYKES; known in the family as Sir MARK-READ-LEARN-INWARDLY-DIGEST SYKES; splendid lib'ry; most useful to me in preparing speeches; rare collection of works on *Crustacea*. Remember my speech, a few Sessions ago, on bringing in Crab and Lobster Bill? Couldn't do it now, dear boy. Great sacrifice for public man to sell his lib'ry." *Business done.*—Parnell Commission Bill through Committee.

*Saturday.*—House sitting to-day, by way of change. Army and Navy Votes under discussion. Enormous sums at issue. Benches nearly empty. Everybody wanting to go away. Sat till nearly Two o'Clock this morning. Voting on account trifling sum of Seven Millions odd. Very dull. No personal question involved. Only the Millions aforesaid. *Business done.*—Votes in Supply.

## OUR BOOKING-OFFICE.

IN *Our Celebrities*—SWANN AND SONNESCHEIN—M. WALERY has a good photograph of Mr. GLADSTONE, in a peculiar reddish glow of light—suggestive of his blushing for Dr. BIGGAR and some of his recent associates, or of a Grand Old Sunset. Then next in order is Sir ALGERNON BORTHWICK meditating on the strange laws of Newspaper Libel; and thirdly, Mr. GEORGE LEWIS in resplendent gaiters with an ornamental vase on the table by his side, which is probably characteristic of something—perhaps his vase'd legal knowledge, though I can hardly suppose, far-fetched as some of L. E.'s jokes are, that this was really the meaning of the ornament at G. L.'s elbow.

Then there are Mr. BARRAUD'S *Men and Women of the Day*, in which appears Mrs. GLADSTONE, who clearly ought not to have been separated from her husband this year of all years when they are Golden Unionists. She looks remarkably happy, either at being in the company of such distinguished photos as that of Admiral HEWETT, V.C., and Dr. RICHTER, or at the idea of being re-united to "Mr. G.," when the volume is bound up and the photos are re-united.

The *Universal Review* keeps up its fame for brilliancy,—you've only got to see it on a table, that's enough. Good matter within, but lacking in that touch of genuine humour which made even Mr. HAWEIS quite lively for a time. DAUDET'S latest novel is an important feature; of course, Lord WOLSELEY'S *Courage* animates the *Fortnightly*—whose motto is, *pro Harris et focis*—but the *Nineteenth*—well here I must drop into poetry:—

"Uncommon good number," says Baron DE B.,
"Is this month's *Nineteenth Centuree*."
"Offices Public" by BLACKWOOD, with
"'Merrikin Statesmen" by GOLDWIN SMITH;
"The Pompadour,"—not of the stage, but very
Real,—by Mlle. BLAZE DE BURY.
This name, so explosive, quite dazzles my gaze,
Should send up the Magazine—bang—all ablaze!

"How *not* to get Fat," by BURNEY YEO,
With a Yeo ho! ho!
And away we go!
Yeo ho! my Hearties!
Avoid dinner-parties!
Cries Captain KNOWLES, with "avasts" and "ahoys,"
"Up goes the sale, Yeo ho! my boys!"

"For growing too fat the new cure," says YEO,
"Is——" Never mind,—read it, and then you'll know.
For the subject is one
Which, all said and done,
Must trouble particular vanity.
"So much for the body," says Doctor KNOWLES;
"I'll give you a cure for poor starved souls."
Eight leaves of a LILLY out he doles,
As "What's left of Christianity."

Where shall I go for my Vacation? I shall take a lot of books with me and,—I have it—the very place, *Reading*.

Yours, THE BOLD BARON DE BOOK-WORMS.

### MR. PARNELL AS *HAMLET*.

THE *Times* is out of joint. Oh! cursed spite
That ever I was forced with it to fight!

THE SWITCHBACK ADAPTED.—Dr. BIRCH begs to inform his young friends that he has patented for use next school-time an entirely new invention, entitled "The Swishback."

## THE PARLIAMENTARY PARACHUTE.

SCENE—*The St. Stephen's Pleasure (?) Grounds, on the occasion of the Great Parachute Performance of that rising (by descending) aëronaut and acrobat*, Professor RITCHIE.

*First Gazer (vaguely impartial and inquisitive).* Will he do it, do you think?

*Second G. (Tory)* } *together* { Why, *of course* he will!
*Third G. (Radical)* } { Why, *of course* he won't!

*First G. (puzzled).* Well, anyhow, I hope he won't hurt himself.

*Second G.* Hurt himself? Not he! One of the skilfullest acrobats in the country, Sir. Knows what *he's* about, I can tell you.

*Third G.* Nonsense, Sir! Never *intends* to do it. All a put-up job to gammon the public.

*First G.* Well, but I don't quite see the pull of *that*, don't you know.

*Second G. (scornfully). Don't* you, though? Why, you *must* be jolly innocent, you must. He'll get the Gate Money, and we shall get the gammon. Simple enough—except to simpletons.

*Fourth G. (old-fashioned Tory).* Well, *I* don't think such exhibitions ought to be allowed. Can't think what Government can be about not to interfere. The performance, Sir, is both dangerous and demoralising.

*Third G.* Well, *you've* come to see it, anyhow.

*Fourth G. (with dignity).* Sir, my motives in doing so differ from those of the mob. I hate mobs. It is because this business is pandering to the mob that I protest against it. I am here to—well, in point of fact, *to* protest. *(Excitedly.)* By Jove, he's off!

*Third G. (dryly).* Not yet! I see you're going to "protest"—with a pair of opera-glasses. However, you needn't flurry yourself. There'll be a hitch somewhere presently, and then either the performance will be postponed, or something perfunctory will be fobbed off on the public instead of the real thing.

*Second G. (hotly).* Nothing of the sort, Sir. I happen to know that this is a perfectly *bonâ fide* business. You, I suspect, are interested in a rival Show, and pooh-pooh this performance because it is not on your own programme.

*Third G. (angrily).* Not in *our* programme? Why we've had the real thing in reserve for years, with a far better *artiste* than yonder fumbler ready to accomplish it, only—thanks to fellows of your sort—we've been prevented from presenting it to the Public.

*Second G.* Oh, ah, I dare say. That's always your cry.

*First G. (deprecatingly).* Well, Gentlemen, don't quarrel. He's just about to begin, and the matter you're disputing will be settled in about a minute better than by a bushel of argument.

*Second G.*
*Third G.* } *(together).* Ah! *now* you'll see!
*Fourth G.*

*First G.* By Jove, he's off! Looks awful hanging like that doesn't he? Cool as a cucumber though, apparently. How the balloon shoots up! Isn't he going too far? Now he pulls the string! The balloon collapses! Great Heavens, he's off!—he's falling like a stone!—he'll be smashed to pieces!!! No!—the Parachute *does* open—slowly—steadily! Hooray!!!—he floats quietly downwards like a falling leaf or a head of thistledown! Wonderful!! Beautiful!!! *Whe—e—e—w!!!* *(To* Third Gazer.) See, Sir, *that's* no gammon! *(To* Fourth Gazer.) Look, Sir, *there's* no danger!! He touches the ground! He bows to the crowd! It's all over, and a great success! Hooray! Hooray!! Hooray!!!

*Second G. (triumphantly, mopping his forehead).* What did I tell you, you of the rival Show? Who's the humbug now?

*Third G. (grumpily).* Bah! there's nothing in it,—no talent, no danger, no anything! It's all a blind, I tell you,—invisible wire, or something of the kind, I'll be bound. Now, *our* man——

*Fourth G. (impatiently).* Sir, *depreciation* is the badge of all your tribe. As I said, I do not quite approve of the *attempt*, but to dispute its *genuineness*, or deny its *success*, is the very blindness of mean partisan malice. [*Swells visibly.*

*Third G.* Ah! just you wait a bit! Wait till this bogus performance is tested—wait till *our* man has a try, and *you'll* see. [*Snorts.*

*First G.* Well, anyhow, it's a clever feat, and Professor RITCHIE is a cool customer. If that Parachute only *lasts*, and doesn't collapse, as such things have rather a way of doing, I don't see why he shouldn't repeat the programme till further orders. How the crowd cheers! Hooray! Hooray!! Hooray!!! [*Left shouting.*

RITUAL AND INDIA-RUBBER.—Among the speakers at the recent Lambeth Conference:—

> "Several colonial and missionary Bishops spoke of the difficulties they encountered in their dioceses owing to the want of elasticity in their forms of worship."

If the forms are not elastic, try stretchers. But couldn't some clever person invent forms that can be elongated so as to seat from four to fourteen? By the way, aren't the seats in Church always being "let out"?

## THE NEW CRUSADE, AND THE FIVE CHAMPIONS OF CHRISTENDOM.

"I address myself to Christian England, because nowhere can I find a greater respect for liberty and human dignity; for it is England, who, in this age, has taken the initiative in the abolition of slavery in the West Indies, and this she has done with an indomitable energy and a perseverance which have at last obtained the concurrence of all nations, and the triumph of a noble cause. *Noblesse oblige.* After having destroyed Colonial slavery, England owes it to herself, to support, by her sympathies, those who wish to destroy African slavery,—a hundred times more horrible."—*Cardinal Lavigerie, at Meeting of the British and Foreign Anti-Slavery Society, held in Prince's Hall.*

*Noblesse oblige!* Right, eloquent, high preacher
Of Christian chivalry to willing ears!
When England owns not Duty for chief teacher,
Slights honour, or takes counsel of her fears;

When the long wail of the enslaved, tormented
Dusk victims of the gold-god's cankered lust
Stirs not her heart, with sluggish peace contented,
Her name is nullity, her fame is dust.

*Noblesse oblige!* This, like the war-drum's rattle
Should sound reveille round the freeman's Isle;
A sovereign summons, not to Syrian battle,
But struggle with a foe more venal-vile

## THE METROPOLIS IN AUGUST 1888.

FORESEEN AND DRAWN BY OUR ARTIST (THE MELANCHOLY AND LEFT-ALL-ALONE-IN-LONDON ONE), AFTER A SOLITARY SUPPER AT THE "PORK-PIE CLUB," COLD HARBOUR LANE.

[*Happily Our Artist's dyspeptic Forecast has been falsified.*

Than the cross-flouting Saracen, more cruel
Than SALADIN's desert swordsmen swart and stark.
'Tis ours to close in stern and truceless duel
With the dread incubus that haunts the dark
Of the Dark Continent. Oh, land of shadows,
Which the whole Western World seems now to throng
In ardent search of Trade's new Eldorados,
Whose spoils there lie for the astute and strong;
One shadow darker, deadlier than all others
Lies like a line of sinister eclipse
Across your torrid sand-tracks. "Men and brothers"?
How glibly the old pulpit-tag still slips
From thoughtless tongues; and there they lie and perish
In myriads, prone, done cruelly to death.
Where are the hopes brave GORDON dared to cherish,
For which stout LIVINGSTONE his latest breath
Drew painfully 'midst leafy wildernesses?
Still on the roads our heroes strove to clear
The ceaseless, ruthless, blood-stained Slave-hunt presses.
The fiendish Arab lurks, a shape of fear
By forest-path, lake-border, hutted village,
Where women toil, men sleep, or children stray,
Pauseless as pestilence, intent on pillage,
Ready to ravish, prompt to fire or slay.
Think on that tiger-throng and the red ravage
They make midst Afric's homes unchecked, unstayed,
The long dread marches, and the slaughter savage,
All the black horrors of the accursed trade.
LAVIGERIE pictures them till fierce compassion
Throbs like the fire of hatred in the heart.
Think of it, careless votaries of Fashion!
Think of it, affluent masters of the Mart!
This too is Trade! Mammon means Moloch often
Even in factory cage, or Sweater's den;
But *there*, no love may aid, no solace soften
The doom of men the prey of fellow-men.
Men? Miscreants, demons, tigerish torturers, rather,
With whom we, save with sword, no terms should hold.
And in those realms the Christian nations gather
In hot earth-hunger, eager quest of gold.
The Briton and the Teuton, flower of learning,
And of civility, meet, as rivals there;
Thither the polished Frank for wealth is turning. [care
Brings cruelty no change, this curse no
To the Cross-bearing West? Must greed's insanity
Crush conscience thus, or shall the new Crusade
Stir, not fanatic hate, but wise humanity,
In the coöperant phalanxes of Trade?

*Noblesse oblige!* To England, as seems fitting,
Comes the first urging of the high appeal;
There she should lead, no lesser hand permitting
First to unsheathe the stern avenging steel.
New Champions of Christendom, the nations,
Beneath the old flag of Freedom fresh arrayed,
Fired with the noblest of all emulations,
Should join, for Honour calls, the New Crusade!

## IN HIS BAG.

(*What an august Imperial Traveller recently brought back with him.*)

*From St.-Petersburg.*—A Russian Rear Admiral's uniform, a little roomy in the back, complete, brand new.

Translation of Exercise from *Ollendorff*, commencing at,—"I prefer the Hussars of my Grandfather to these Dragoons," down to, "I cannot give you the boots of the Battenberg, nor the ultimatum of the SULTAN, but I can supply you with the Bulgarian umbrella of Prince FERDINAND," inclusive.

A pot of genuine *caviare* from the Russian Foreign Office.

*From Stockholm.*—A Swedish Post-captain's Uniform, a little tight in the waist, complete, brand new.

A slip of paper, containing a neat translation of the phrases, "How are you this morning, Sir?" "Very well, I thank you, Sir. All right, Sir. Hurrah!" into the Swedish language.

The Star of a Knight Grand Commander of the Order of the Blue Elephant in best Paris paste.

*From Copenhagen.*—A Full-dress Parade Uniform of a Drum-major of the Royal Danish Guards, two sizes too large, brand new.

*A Hundred Ways of Meeting a Foreign Potentate.* Beginners' Handbook. Shilling Edition.

*From Friedrichsruh.*—The Chancellor's general approval, and a return-ticket to Berlin.

## FROM A NAUTICAL KNOW-NOTHING.

*All at Sea with the X. Y. Z. Squadron.*

I HOPE you have received my previous contributions all safe and sound, for in them I have described to you all that has occurred to us since the "Declaration of War" up to date. Seeing how at one moment the Authorities seem up to any larks, and the next appear to take the whole thing in grim earnest, I shouldn't be surprised to hear that my letter had been washed overboard, or seized, or done something to that had prevented it ever reaching you at all.* What a time I've had of it! You know, as I told you, I began by hiding under the Admiral's table, and copying out his sealed orders to send you, and then, when I was discovered, and said it was only "my fun," and I thought "it didn't matter, as they were only playing at fighting," and he said "he had half a mind" to have me "put in irons," to teach me how to conduct myself on board one of Her Majesty's ships, I really felt so disgusted that, if I could have got off, I should certainly have thrown the whole thing up then and there.

However, the incident passed, though I'm bound to say it left a nasty feeling behind. It is owing to this that I am rather vague as to what we are supposed to have been doing. When I go up to a First-Lieutenant, and slap him cheerily on the back, and say, "Well, Mate, how's the enemy this morning?" he only mumbles something in a resentful manner, but gives me no information. I fancy, as far as I can gather, we are supposed to be watching a hostile fleet, or else we are blockading one; though, now I come to think of it, perhaps we are supposed to be blockaded ourselves. I must try and solve this, and then perhaps I may be able to give you some definite idea of what our movements mean. They certainly are curious.

For the last few days we have been continually creeping along in-shore, then on, suddenly sighting the "Enemy," dashing out,—at least, so it seems to me,—about 200 miles into the Atlantic, for the purpose of slowly creeping back again somewhere else. To-day there has been a good deal of signalling going on, and on a local Coast-guard Station displaying the question, "Have you any message for Whitehall?" I managed to get the advantage of the petty officers who were looking out the flags, and, I think to the surprise of every-body, quickly ran up "Walker!" This again seemed to annoy the Admiral, and a fresh nasty feeling has been the result. I believe he has threatened to put me on board the first torpedo-boat that comes within hail. However, meantime, I have made the acquaint-ance of a communicative Marine, from whom I have gathered several items of what sounds like reliable information. He has pointed me out some vessels in the offing, which he says are the *Stagnation*, *Rattletrap*, *Blazer*, and *Ophicleide*, who are watching us, and that, when we get within one thousand yards of them, the "fun will begin."

Apparently hard-up for any excitement, the Admiral bears down on the quartette with alacrity, and we are soon in the midst of them. They have commenced blazing away at us with their guns on all sides. Two of ours won't fire, but that doesn't much matter, and I don't suppose it would in real warfare, for, what with the noise and excitement, we seem to get on well enough without them.

After about an hour and a half of this, the other side suddenly stops and sends off a despatch-boat, bearing a flag of truce. It brings an Umpire, who says, that he has ruled us out of the game as "sunk." The Admiral's only reply is "Gammon!" The Umpire expostulates and says, that if that is the way his authority is to be treated, "the sooner the whole thing is understood to be a gigantic farce the better," to which the Admiral rejoins that he doesn't care a couple of brass farthings whether the whole thing is regarded as a gigantic farce or not, but that "he is not going to strike his colours in deference to the expression of a bit of beggarly opinion in an out-of-the-way nook on the Irish coast."

This apparently settles the Umpire, who retires threatening that he will communicate with Whitehall. The Admiral thereon puts our head about, returning to the bay, which, reaching about dusk, we are, owing to there being some hitch in the working of our signals, taken for one of the enemy by our own ships, and greeted by a succes-sion of heavy broadsides from the *Dunderhead*, *Jackass*, *Catapult*, *Slop-basin*, *Blue-bottle* and *Boot-jack*, who continue pounding away at us until they discover their mistake. The local Umpire upon this gives it as his opinion that as such a catastrophe might have occurred in real warfare, he is obliged to rule us as "sunk," and therefore, out of the game. The Admiral merely again rejoins "Stuff and nonsense!" and says that "real warfare or sham warfare," he is not going "to be ruled out of his ship, by the decision of any petty-fogging Umpire alive, as long as he has a single blessed plank of her afloat under him." The Umpire says that that's all very well, but "it is not the sort of spirit in which to carry out the Naval Man-œuvres," upon which the Admiral tells him to "Shut up and mind his own business." Upon this the Umpire merely retires sulkily.

Taking advantage of an inquiry by signal from the station as to whether we wanted any coals, and wishing to find out if there was any conveyance to take me if I could manage to get ashore, I just ran up the answer, "No. But can I get a four-wheeler on the coast?" On this being reported to the Admiral, it has apparently put him in into a very bad temper, for he has ordered me to be put in irons for the night. This is very unpleasant.

I have just remarked to the communicative Marine, that I think it rather a strong measure, considering that I have only been playing at being on board a man-of-war. He says, no doubt that is so, but that it won't do to be "too larky with the Admiral." Anyhow, the incident brings this communication to an abrupt close. More in my next.

* This is the only contribution we have received from our Correspondent.—ED.

---

## THE TRAVELLER'S DREAM-BOOK FOR AUGUST, 1888.

*(Prepared by the Clerk of the Weather, but subject to considerable variation.)*

IF you dream of—

*Amiens.*—You must expect rain in a foreign town without home comforts.

*Bath.*—Go there. Ask for hairdresser.

*Boulogne.*—Look for the perfumes of the Port in an East wind.

*Brighton.*—Don't, at least not yet: better try Jericho.

*Calais.*—Accustom yourself to a rough sea-passage with the glass a few degrees above freezing.

*Coventry.*—Try it for the sake of your friends.

*Dieppe.*—Prepare for a storm-beaten Casino without visitors.

*Etretât.*—Welcome a watering-place where it is too cold to bathe.

*Florence.*—Fancy Italy in the unhealthy season.

*Genoa.*—Learn to love dirt in a desert.

*Heidelberg.*—Imagine a Castle in a Scotch mist.

*Interlachen.*—Confine your attention to an excellent *table d'hôte* at the Switzerhof.

*Jericho.*—Try Brighton instead. It is Jewly here all the year round.

*Kiel.*—Picture to yourself dulness at its worst, and beat the record.

*Lyons.*—Think of silk, and rest satisfied without paying a visit to its chief manufactory.

*Madrid.*—Acclimatise yourself to bull-fights, and if you contem-plate suicide choose the arena to an overdose of chloroform.

*Naples.*—See the Bay in a fog, and don't die, if you can help it.

*Paris.*—Pass through before you are drenched.

*Quebec.*—Rather far off, which may be an advantage, if the sun in Europe has retired on permanent leave of absence.

*Ramsgate.*—Go there. Air confers immortality, *vide* recent local sanitary reports. Nobody dies at Ramsgate: if they want to do so, they immediately leave the place and go somewhere else.

*Rotterdam.*—Get your umbrella and open it.

*Suez.*—Better try Southend; livelier.

*Turin.*—Do not weep if you find the rain as constant as at the Italian Exhibition.

*Uig.*—Spend all your time and money in testing whiskey.

*Venice.*—Confess that a gondola in a thunderstorm is not much more amusing than a Hansom cab with the glass down.

*Waterloo.*—Imagine that it's rather fun to drive in a coach up to your eyes in an Ulster.

*Whitby.*—All clever people at Whitby. Here "*Les grands esprits se rencontrent.*" Hence the name. Don't *you* go to Whitby.

*X—Exeter.*—Try it, and get out of it. Be Enterer and Exiter.

*Yarmouth.*—Avoid the bloater aristocracy.

*Zurich.*—"On the margin of Fair Zurich's waters"—give your-self a margin—or better—leave it to your imargination.

And if you dream of no place at all—why, thank your lucky stars and stay at home!

---

MANNERS MAKE THE FOREMAN.—At the Old Bailey last week the learned Recorder of London was charging the Grand Jury, when the Foreman suddenly charged back. No wonder there was a "sen-sation in Court." Perhaps this Juryman was too "Grand" to listen to legal advice. He seems to have taken CHAMBERS for a Flat!

---

PROBABLE.—Dr. T-NN-R, M.P., is said to be writing some New Nursery Rhymes, to be called *Tullamore Tra-la-las.* He has got as far as "Barr, Barr, black-sheep," but here the Muse has failed him.

---

THEATRICAL FORECAST FOR AUGUST AND SEPTEMBER.—Mr. CHARLES WYNDHAM will make the ascent of several mountains, giving per-formances in various languages of *David Garrick.* He will also try the N. W. Passage; if he doesn't like it, he'll give it up, and do a little Polar Bear shooting. Mr. WYNDHAM will play for one night only in Japan, and on his road home he will give a *Matinée,* under the patronage of the Grand Llama of Thibet. He will inaugurate his Winter Season with an entirely new piece entitled *David Garrick.*

Mr. Dauber at last discovers his little Gem. He has been searching for it all the Season.

## POLITICAL GIPSYING;

*Or, Jottings by an Eminent Common-wheel-man.*

*Any Time in August.*—Holiday begun, thanks to Smith. Why not take hint from Irish ex-constable who's going about Eastern Counties in a "Home Rule Van," and have van of my own in benighted South of England? I will.

*Next Day.*—Van procured. Smells distinctly stuffy. Several vans, in fact, because directly I mentioned subject, Granville said "he *must* come too!" So did Spencer, Harcourt (why Harcourt?), Shaw-Lefevre, Herschell, and Rosebery. Each of 'em has a van; but Rosebery says I'm in "the van of progress," and must go first. Start next week.

*Monday.*—Our Caravan starts from Town amid indescribable enthusiasm. Whole of Piccadilly, Knightsbridge, Hammersmith Road, and as far as Hounslow, packed with crowds to see us pass. *Query*—Does not this show that opinion of London is changing on Home Rule? Shaw-Lefevre says, "Not a doubt of it." Granville suggests "making *détour* to avoid mob." Wish he wouldn't speak of "mob" when he means electors. If one says, "making *détour* to avoid electors," folly of such a course at once apparent. Only get ten miles out of Town by night-time. Put up on a common. Herschell rather doubtful if we "aren't making ourselves liable to action for trespass." Wish he wouldn't bring out inconvenient legal knowledge just now. Have made five speeches, Harcourt six. *Query*—Isn't it unwise of Harcourt to challenge oratorical comparison with me in this way?

*Tuesday Morning.*—Wake up with happy notion. Why not *signals* between different vans? Rosebery takes to idea at once. Spends day in erecting complicated series of flags on roofs, which can be pulled by strings from inside. Also invents signalling code. [N.B.—Interesting subject for pamphlet, Signalling.] We all learn it, except Harcourt, who's studying maps, as he's volunteered to be our guide. Says he knows the country by heart.

*Wednesday.*—Got to Farnham. Agricultural district. Gratifying reception. Villagers turn out in hundreds, also turn out horses, and drag us into village. Long speeches. Give rustics lecture on Irish Land Tenure. Rustics go off to hear Harcourt, who's bellowing as usual. In evening horses can't be found anywhere. Some London thieves are suspected of having organised the reception, and eloped with horses! *Query*—is this a dodge of Salisbury's? Or Argyll, in revenge for recent soliloquy in Lords? Must inquire. Begin notes for my forthcoming article on "Our Nomadic Population."

*Thursday.*—Somewhere in Hampshire. Shaw-Lefevre made speech before breakfast. Stupidly spoke of agricultural labourer as "Hodge." Labourers very angry. When I try to pacify them with seductive speech on Home-Rule, they say they want to know about Allotments! Don't "Remember Mitchelstown," but do remember "Three Acres and a Cow." Find they believe in Jesse—singular delusion! In afternoon, Harcourt found out guiding us all wrong. Seems he was trying to sneak down to New Forest. Provoking!

*Friday.*—Only drawback to complete enjoyment so far has been weather. Rain incessant. Home-Rule Van leaks badly. Can't study Irish History, or compose speeches with stream of rain-water coming down small of one's back.

Awkward—hear that Spencer, in moment of forgetfulness, and apparently fancying himself still Viceroy, has been saying "*he* wouldn't whine about imprisonment if *he* were Irish patriot." What made him say this? Put up signal—"Do you refer to Dillon?" No answer. Curious. After an hour or two, Spencer sends round boy who looks after his horses to say, "he doesn't understand the code." Fancy this an excuse, but don't like to say so.

*Saturday.*—Slight *contretemps.* Wheeler (a bay horse—Rosebery calls him a Botany Bay horse—Interesting subject again—"Colour in Horses"—why is one bay, another roan? What is the Home Rule about this?) goes very lame. Other horse doesn't care about drawing van by himself, and tries to lie down in road. Harness in tangle. Have to try and put it right in pouring rain, as boy has gone off to village inn "to get help," he says, but really to get glass of beer, I believe. Most unconstitutional. Shall suspend boy when he comes back, I think.

Signal to Rosebery to come and assist. No reply. Singular! Send driver round (but isn't this contrary to code?), and find that Rosebery has gone off to see somebody's stud-farm near here. Rosebery seems to regard whole affair as sort of picnic. Worst of it is that he's taken Granville and Harcourt with him. Harcourt would be invaluable just now to sit on horse's head while I undo harness.

On his return Rosebery suggests that van is too heavy, and that I had better lighten it by "chucking out some of the Irish Histories." Surprised at Rosebery! He explains by saying that *he* finds "the less fact he puts in speeches, the better they go down."

*Sunday.—Dies non.* Propose church. Shaw-Lefevre anxious to go. Rosebery, it seems, hasn't brought prayer-book. Spencer and Granville both want to mend holes in their roofs. Harcourt asleep. Herschell offers to mediate with neighbouring Vicar, and tells him I'll read lessons. Good fellow, Herschell. I do.

*Monday.*—Curious thing occurred to-day. Met *another van!* A political one apparently. Painted outside with pictures of moon-lighting outrages. Asked driver (big man with black beard) if he was in favour of Home Rule. He merely answered "Yah!" Who can have invented this opposition van? Perhaps Randolph. Now I come to think of it, boy attending horses very like Randolph. Mention suspicion to Granville. He pooh-poohs idea—Randolph away in Africa or America, he says.

Mysterious van follows us everywhere. Comes to villages we've left, and distributes Primrose League tracts and blankets to adults, and sweetmeats to children. *Query*—isn't this corruption? Can't ask Herschell, because he's gone back to town to attend (he says) at obsequies of Board of Works.

*Tuesday.*—Rosebery complains this is "slow." Couldn't we all dress up as nigger minstrels? Remonstrate privately with Rosebery, who admits he had no sleep last night, owing to bedclothes being saturated, and smoke from stove. He says, "Granville and Spencer both favour nigger plan—or if not, dismissing vans and going to first-class hotel." *Can* this be true? And I'm not half through my educational course of Irish history, which peasants are dying to hear.

Still suspicious of opposition van. Now believe Argyll's inside. Why can't Argyll stay in Isles? Can man on box be Salisbury himself?

*End of Tour.—Exeter.*—Down here at last! Down with rheumatism, too. Harcourt's van disappeared near Southampton. Granville telegraphed for at Wells. Rosebery left behind in hospital at Bath. Shaw-Lefevre worn and haggard, but still here; seems quite as lively as when he started,—but *that*'s not saying much. Shall rest a week, and then back to Hawarden, not at all *van*-quished; only a fortnight spent on wheels is enough for anybody.

---

Revival of the Elizabethan Drama.—*Betsy* at the Criterion.

THE COLLECTION.

*Scrooge.* "I SAY, COULD YOU LEND ME SOMETHING TO PUT IN THE PLATE, MR. MARLEY? I'VE ONLY GOT A *SOVEREIGN!*"

*Marley.* "OH, A SOVEREIGN 'LL DO."

## PICKING THE WED-LOCK.

*To the Editor.*

SIR,—I see that some of your Correspondents are asking, "Is Marriage a failure?" How fortunate that the public should have become suddenly interested in this question just as the Dull Season has come round again! Perhaps, with judicious management, the subject could be made to last on to the Autumn Session! My view is that it is simply a matter of intelligent selection of the locality where the marriage is contracted or annulled. I, myself, have already been married in eight different States in America, and have found no difficulty in securing eight separate divorces on no ground whatever. As there are about thirty States, I look forward to continuing this process for some considerable time, and as I take care to "go where money is," I am now in the possession of a modest competency, entirely due to prudent matrimonial ventures. I advise those who are unhappy in wedlock to take courage—and a ticket to Colorado. Yours 'cutely, GAY ROVER.

SIR,—How Marriage can be called a failure I cannot understand. Take my own case. I recently indulged in some disastrous speculations, which landed me, before I knew where I was, in the Bankruptcy Court. All that I had was taken to feed my avaricious creditors; but fortunately my wife had property settled upon her, which they could not touch, and I was living in comfort, as a result of that arrangement. It is true that I am not able to keep more than four hunters, but I console myself by thinking that my creditors also are not completely happy with their composition of sixpence in the pound, which was all I felt justified in offering them. I often tell my wife I never knew her value till now. So far from Marriage being a failure, it has turned Failure into a triumphant success!

Yours chirpily, UNDISCHARGED.

SIR,—I don't think I am particularly hard to get on with, yet after only six months of marriage I have been obliged to send my wife home to her relations, allowing her *five hundred pounds a year* simply in order to get rid of her! She says my temper is unbearable, but if one can't chuck one's own wife out of a second-storey window for venturing to argue with one, I should like to know whom one *is* allowed to chuck out? Then when I knocked her though a glass door and (as she says) injured her head, which was always rather soft, I was acting simply on principle and from a high sense of duty, although the Police Magistrate took a different view of the occurrence. Is it not intolerable that wives should venture to contradict any opinion expressed by their husbands? This is the sort of "Marriage Not" which every husband is bound to cut. I must in fairness add that mine never openly disagreed with me but once, when the chucking-out took place; but after that she used to *look as if she were going to disagree*, which is even more aggravating to a man of sensitive disposition like Yours truly, A MATRIMONIAL VICTIM.

## FOOL BRITANNIA!

(*A new and original Manœuvring Cantata, arranged for production at the Imperial Naval Concert Room, Whitehall.*)

*The Scene is supposed to represent the progress of a weird Incantation conducted by the* Wizard of the Admiralty, *in which, revealing to the astonished gaze of an assembled crowd of mystified* British Landlubbers *the wonders of his Department, he compels them, by the exercise of his magic arts, to express their astonishment and admiration.*

CHORUS OF BRITISH LANDLUBBERS.

HARK! Again the cannons' thunder
Almost overwhelms our chorus!
We are fairly dazed with wonder
At the sights he sets before us!
As we read the evening papers,
We in mute surprise are gaping.
Admirals prodigious capers
Cutting, real warfare apeing;
Cruisers hither, thither flying,
Property quite disregarding,
And, accepted law defying,
Private householders bombarding!
Health resorts in vain contesting
With some ironclad's distant flashes,
Have, by dozens, though protesting,
Ruthlessly been laid in ashes.
See, e'en Margate has surrender'd
Pier dues both, and local band!
Herne Bay, brought to book, has tender'd
Millions down by note of hand!
For Rosherville what fate's in store
We dare not ask! (*They turn away shudderingly.*) We'll see no more!

THE WIZARD OF THE ADMIRALTY (*continuing the Incantation*).

But nay! for sure there's plenty more to see.
And here just once again I must repeat,
What evident to all of you must be,
The fact that you possess a first-rate fleet.
You've had, I think, a telling proof or two
Of what "My Lords," when put to it, can do.
Such guns, such coals, such crews, such speed combined,
You'll in no other rival Navy find!
There hasn't been a hitch. Naught's gone amiss!

*An* Inquiring Taxpayer *rises through the ground.*

INQUIRING TAXPAYER.

Perhaps, then, you'll explain to one what's this?
[*Produces recent number of a morning paper.*
The *Mohawk* and the *Tartar*, come to grief,
Are left behind, and cannot get along.
The *Archer* for her boilers wants relief;
Then the *Northampton's* engines have gone wrong.
The *Racoon* leaks at every blessed chink;
The stokers of the fleet by dozens sink,
Unequal to their work, because untrained.
If there's no hitch,—these things might be explained?

THE WIZARD OF THE ADMIRALTY.

And I am the party to do it,
For each charge that against us is laid
I straight to its source will pursue it,
And soon prove that 'tis recklessly made.
I'll answer each empty-brained gaper
Who provokes all this critical fuss,
And show him it's all right "on paper,"
And "on paper" 's sufficient for us.

ÆACUS, MINOS, AND RHADAMANTHUS OUT FOR A HOLIDAY.

And such JOHN BULL finds it, and takes it
like honey,—
While he thinks we give him enough for his
money!

So what do I care if our cruisers
Show a pace that's as bad as a snail's,
In the game be they winners or losers,
Well—it isn't their pace that avails—
Least not for "My Lords," whose one notion
Is just this: if you only create
A regular naval commotion,—
Well,—all minor shortcomings may wait.

For JOHN BULL, in the stir,—'tis certainly
funny,— [money.
Will think he has got quite enough for his

INQUIRING TAXPAYER.

It may be so. But, if you speak by rule,
You make BRITANNIA a precious fool!

CHORUS (*con fuoco*). Fool BRITANNIA! BRITANNIA fooled by knaves,
Britons ever, ever, ever shall be slaves!

[*They dance round the* Wizard of the Admiralty, *who continues his Incantation as the Curtain descends.*

"JOHN LEECH SISTERS FUND."—The contributions to this Fund forwarded by the Editor will be duly acknowledged in the list published by the Honorary Secretary, 36, Berkeley Square, W. We are glad to say that they already amount to a considerable sum.

---

FOOD FOR THE MIND.—Mrs. RAMSBOTHAM lately went to the office of a literary and scientific institution, and asked for a Syllabub of the Lectures.

## VOCES POPULI.

### A PASTORAL PLAY. (A REMINISCENCE OF THE PAST JULY.)

ARGUMENT.—Mr. and Mrs. BRONDESBURY BROWN (of North Kensington), roused to emulation by certain recent open-air performances, have invited their friends to witness a selection from *The Tempest* in the garden of their villa, "Fontainebleau" (which derives its title from two remarkably fine plane-trees at one end of the lawn).

SCENE—*The Auditorium.* Mr. *and* Mrs. B. B. *discovered in readiness to receive their Guests.*

*Mrs. B. B.* (*with a desperate cheerfulness*). Do you know, BRONDESBURY, dear, I really *do* believe we shall have it fine, after all?

The Naiades' Garden Party last July.

*B. B.* (*not a Pastoral Enthusiast*). I shouldn't be surprised if it did clear up—about midnight.

*Mrs. B. B.* Well, if it doesn't rain any more till all the people are here, *I* shall be satisfied.

[*She says this with a dim notion of propitiating the Powers that be by her moderation.*

*B. B.* Why, you won't do it out here if it *rains*, will you?

*Mrs. B. B.* (*with a deadly calm*). Where do you *suppose* we shall do it, then?

*B. B.* (*feebly*). Why not in the —ar—Drawing-room?

*Mrs. B. B.* (*fanning herself*). *Really*, BRONDESBURY, you are too trying for anything! A Pastoral Play in the Drawing-room! Have you *no* sense of the ridiculous? Do you know what a Pastoral Play *is?*

*B. B.* (*grimly*). I'm beginning to find out, my dear.

*The First Guests hopefully* (*as they make their way down the little cast-iron staircase to the lawn, which is roofed over with sail-cloth, and provided with rout-seats and chairs*). They can't possibly mean to have it this evening—we shall be able to get away all the sooner! (*To their hostess.*) Oh, Mrs. BROWN, *how* unfortunate! such *hopeless* weather for it! We really ought not to have come at all.

*Mrs. B.* Oh, but indeed—we're not afraid of a few drops of rain—you shan't be disappointed! (*General fall of jaws.*) We're going to begin as soon as ever a few more people come. You shan't go away without your *Tempest!*

[*Guests, realising that they are in for one, at the very least, seat themselves with hypocritical expressions of delight.*

BEHIND THE CURTAIN: UNDER THE PLANE-TREES.

*The King of Naples* (*to Ferdinand*). I say, old fellow, if we're to lie down and go to sleep here, we must have a little sawdust thrown down first. The ground's sopping!

*Ferdinand* (*also Stage Manager*). Oh, don't bother *me*, my dear fellow! Where the dickens am *I* to find sawdust?

*The K. of N.* (*unkindly*). Thought you might have spared us some out of your calves!

*Miranda. I* have to go to sleep, too; and that couch is simply soaked!

*Ferdinand* (*irritably*). Soaked? Of course it's soaked! It's Pastoral. We must put up with it, that's all. My dear child, what on earth have you got on your feet?

*Miranda* (*regarding her goloshes ruefully*). They're mother's. She made me promise to wear them if the ground was at all damp.

*Ariel* (*to Maid, who has come round by the path*). Well, TUCKER, what is it now?

*Maid.* Your Aunt's love, Miss; and she must insist on your putting on this.

*Ariel.* What a shame! (*To King.*) I can't act *Ariel* in a waterproof, *can* I?

*The K. of N.* (*sardonically*). Oh, why not? We must try and borrow an old sou'-wester for *Prospero*, though, or he'll be out of the picture. (*Angrily, aside to Ferdinand.*) Hang it all, we'd better do the whole thing under umbrellas at once!

*Caliban* (*to Miranda*). All *I* know is, I hope we shall begin soon. If I stand about in a damp hump much longer, I shall be ill. Just feel it. [MIRANDA *feels his hump delicately, and commiserates him.*

*Prospero.* Never mind your hump—see if you can tell me how to make this confounded beard of mine stick on—the rain's washed off all the gum.

IN FRONT—BEFORE PLAY BEGINS.

*Mrs. Harlesden Smith.* Oh, I shall see splendidly here, thanks, dear Mrs. BROWN, *how* well you have arranged it all! It's really not at all cold—well, if you *would* go and fetch my cloak, HARLESDEN, perhaps it *might* be more——

*Miss Ladbroke Hill* (*to Mr. Kensal Green*). Such a charming idea, these garden theatricals. So different from a hot stuffy theatre!

*Mr. Kensal Green* (*putting up his coat-collar*). It certainly is the reverse of *stuffy* here! Plenty of air!

*Miranda's Mother.* I do wish they would begin. I can't bear to think of my poor girl standing about on that nasty wet grass all this time—so bad for her!

*Ariel's Aunt.*—If I had guessed it would turn out such a night as this, I would never have allowed my niece to accept the part—and even as it *is*——

[*The curtains drawn aside, and play begins;* PROSPERO *instructs* MIRANDA *concerning the family history in the midst of a heavy downpour. One of* ARIEL'S *shoes come off in the mud.*

*Miss Ladbroke Hill.* How well they did the lightning then, didn't they?

*Mr. K. G.* Oh, it's all genuine—the BROWNS are determined to do the thing well. Thunder, too, you see? There's nothing mean about BROWN!

*Miranda's Mother.* That dreadful lightning! Oh, Mrs. BROWN, do please tell them to come away from the trees—it *is* so dangerous!

*Cecil's Aunt.* Oh, do; they might be struck down at any moment—it's tempting Providence!

*Mrs. Brown* (*in despair*). It—it's only *sheet*-lightning. Please—*please* don't say anything about it to them now—it will only put them out. They're getting on so nicely!

*Enter Caliban* (*on stage—moist, but maledictory*).

"As wicked dew as e'er my mother brushed . . . .
Drop on you both—a south-west blow on ye!"

*Prospero* (*with feeling*). "For this, be sure, to-night thou shalt have cramps!"

*Mr. K. G.* (*sotto voce*). If *Caliban* don't have them, I shall!

*Enter Trinculo* (*on stage*). "If it should thunder as it did before, I know not where to hide my head. Yond same cloud cannot choose but fall by pailfuls. . . . Alas, the storm is come again!" &c., &c.

[*Real thunder—rain descends pitilessly.*

*Mr. K. G.* Really a triumph of stage-management!

*Enter Ferdinand on stage, bearing a log* (*he throws it down with a heavy splash*). "There be some sports are painful."

*Mr. K. G.* (*who has been sitting for some time with a stream of water from the roof trickling down the back of his neck*). Pastoral Plays, for example.

[*Scene with* MIRANDA *is proceeding in pelting rain, which extinguishes most of the lamps which light the scene, when*——

*Miranda's Mother* (*rises*). I can't help it, Mrs. BROWN,—flesh and blood can't bear it. I can't sit here and see that poor child catching cold under my very eyes. MINNIE, dear, come in under the tent out of the rain this instant! Do you hear? I order you!

[*Sensation in audience.—on the whole, hardly of disapproval.*

*Miranda.* In a minute, Mamma. "I am a fool to weep at what I am glad of." (*To* PROSPERO.) I really must go. It's no use, when Mamma once makes up her mind. [PROSPERO *acquiesces sulkily.*

*Ariel's Aunt.* I was just about to say the same thing, dear Mrs. SUDBURY! Pastorals or no pastorals, I can't let my sister's child commit suicide. FANNY, come too—and bring your waterproof.

*Ferdinand* (*helplessly*). But, I say, how are we to get along without *Miranda* and *Ariel?*

*Miranda's Mother.* That I can't pretend to decide—but I should have thought you gentlemen could have finished it alone—somehow. Or I don't object to MINNIE'S acting, provided she keeps under the tent and speaks her part from there.

[*Ariel's Aunt makes similar concession with regard to her niece.*

*Prospero.* No, I don't think that would do. (*To* Mrs. BROWN.) Perhaps we *had* better stop for this evening—there doesn't seem to be much chance of the weather improving, and—(*candidly*)—I'm afraid it really *is* a little damp for the ladies,—eh, BROWN?

*Mr. Brown* (*basely*). Well, if you ask me, I think we've all had about enough of it. [Mrs. B. *conceals her mortification.*

*Guests* (*eagerly*). It's been too charming, too delightful—but we mustn't be selfish, must we? It would be cruel to expect them to do any more. And they *are* so wet, poor things!

[*They adjourn with ill-disguised relief and profuse expressions of gratitude.*

IN THE DRAWING-ROOM—LATER.

Mrs. BRONDESBURY BROWN *is shedding a quiet tear by the chimney-piece;* Mr. BRONDESBURY BROWN *is humming, as he lights a candle with one of the programmes.*

*Mr. B. B.* (*with offensive cheeriness*). Do you know, I shouldn't wonder if we had a fine day to-morrow—the glass is going up again.

*Mrs. B. B.* (*in a muffled voice*). It may, if it likes.

*Mr. B. B.* Come, come, POLLY! I'm sure everything went off very well—considering. I only hope none of the people will get rheumatism after it—that's all.

*Mrs. B. B.* I dud-don't c-care if they all *die!*

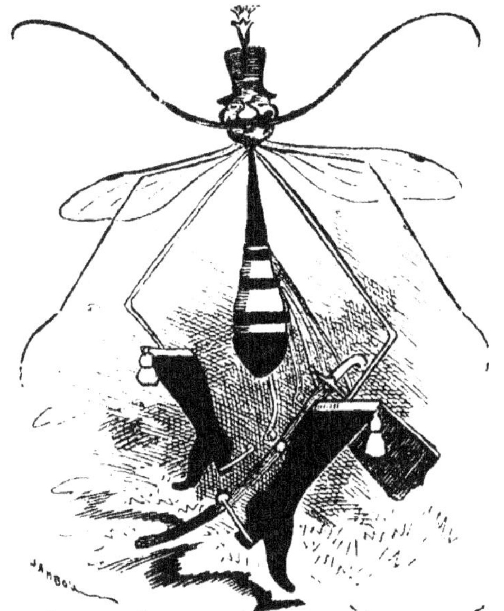


Our Artist trusts it will not be found, as this is, "on the Hop."

## SENSATIONAL TO A DEGREE.

(*Report of a Lecture by a Professor of the Future.*)

Yesterday the recently-appointed Professor of Popular Science delivered his inaugural lecture to the students of the Four Inns of Court in the Drill Hall of the D. O. Rifle Volunteers. It will be remembered that following the lead of the Authorities of the Inner Temple, who some time since gave a "learned At Home," the Masters of the combined Bench have recently established a chair or rather, *trapèze* of Athletic Philosophy. The apartment was filled with students and utter-barristers, who exhibited the most lively interest in the spirited proceedings.

The Professor, who appeared in academical costume, said that he was much pleased to see so good an attendance, as he wished to teach by example rather than by word of mouth. He would first go through a few performances.

Upon this he threw off his gown and disclosed a closely fitting suit of spangles. The band of the Inns of Court Volunteers having struck up a lively tune, the Professor quickly sprang into the air, and catching the bar of a *trapèze*, went through a series of evolutions of the most extraordinary and intricate character. Returning to the ground he resumed his gown and bowed his acknowledgments to the thunder of applause that greeted his return to the reading-desk.

"You have seen," he observed, "that it is perfectly easy to fly through the air with the assistance of the horizontal bars. And the principle may be carried further. I have here a small steam-engine, and by sitting on the safety-valve, thus, I accumulate an amount of force sufficient in volume to raise me some distance from the ground. In the event of the boiler bursting I shall, no doubt, rise to a very considerable altitude; indeed——" at this point the Professor's learned discourse was interrupted by the bursting of the boiler to which he had called attention. Several of those present attended the subsequent inquest, which brought the proceedings to a sensational, if somewhat, melancholy conclusion.

"Jeune pour la Jeunesse."—The subscriptions sent to the Editor for Mrs. Jeune's Three-Weeks-in-the-Country-for-the-Poor-Children Fund have been forwarded to Mrs. Jeune. And for all we have received Mrs. Jeune and the children are truly thankful.

## ROBERT'S STORY OF JACK THE GIANT.

I coodn't refuse a offer as I reseeved the other day from a good old frend to spend from Satterday to Munday at dear old Broadstares, more espeshally as hinside his hinwitashun he henclosed a return ticket. Ah! that's wot I calls inwiting a frend in a trooly royal manner, tho' I am told as Royalty sumtimes forgits that nice little atenshun, and leaves poor Dooks and Markisses to pay their hone fairs, which don't seem quite fare to me.

I didn't find much change in nice quiet Broadstares. There's the same old black Peer, and the same nice wite cliffs, and the same butifool yaller sands, and the same brite blue sea, and the same little imperent tavern as will call itself the Albion! As if there cood be 2 Albions! But there was one thing as I soon missed, and that was my old frend Jack the Boatman. Jack was a grate giant of a feller, and the idle of all the children. Lor, what fun he used to have on the sands with the pretty littel darlings, to be sure. They used to call him Jack the Giant. I've sumtimes seen three or fore of 'em on his back at wunce, and he on his hands and nees a pertending to be their orse, and they a spurring and a wippin on him like mad.

Well, it seems that larst Summer a Lady used to cum on the Sands every day with her Servent and a pore littel feller of a boy, about five or six year old, who had amost lost the use of his pore littel legs, and the Doctor had told his pore Mother that the only chance of recovering the use of 'em was sea-bathing, but nothink would induce the pore littel chap to go into the Sea. He used to screem and struggel so that it was shocking to hear and see him. So his pore Mother had to give it up, but she came ewery fine day on the Sands, and sat as close to the sea as she cood, in opes sum day to tempt him in.

Well, one day sumbody happened to tell Jack all about it, so what does he do but he goes and he sets hisself down by the side of pore littel Frank, that was the littel chap's name, and he began a torking to him all about the Sea, and wot fun it was to go and catch a lot of fishes and bring 'em home and have 'em for dinner. And that's all he said that day. The nex day he did the same, and the nex, and Frank got so used to him that he quite missed him if he wasn't there.

So one day Jack says to him, "Woodn't you like to git on my back, and let me be your horse and take you into the Sea?" And little Frank says, "No, I shoodn't," says he, "for I don't want to git wet, and don't mean to." "But suppose I promises that you shan't git wet," says Jack, "what then?" "Then I don't think I shood beleeve you," says he, larfing out quite merrily. "But suppose your Ma says as you may trust me, woodn't you beleeve me then?" "Yes, I think I shood," says he. So at larst after a good deal of perswadin he lets Jack take him on his back and in they goes a littel ways into the Sea, and Jack brings him back to his delited Ma as appy as a king and as dry as a bone.

After a time Jack got him to have his shoes and stockings off and to ride on Jack's back further into the Sea, and his Mother made him a pair of butifool blew rains, and bort him a littel whip, and he used to go riding into the Sea as bold as a lion, and shouting out to his delited Ma to see how brave he was. Well, after a time the pore littel feller's legs got quite strong, and he could ewen manage to wark a littel.

But now cums the curiusest part of my story. Not one penny wood Jack take from the gratefool Mother for all his long services. No one knew who she was. She seemed to know noboddy, but she had plenty of money, and was as ginerous with it as a Princess cood be, but nothink wood Jack take, till one day, when he was a going away for a munth, he managed to stammer out that, if she didn't think it a libberty, he shood like to have littel Frank's pictur. I think as he called it his Haughtygraff, for Jack wasn't much of a Skollar. However, you may be sure as he hadn't long to wait for it, and away he went.

Whether it was that he missed Jack, or whether it was a chill as he got one windy day, or what it was, noboddy seemed quite to know, but by the time as Jack came back pore littel Frank was worse than ever, and was at last confined to his bed. Jack used to go every day to see the pore littel darling, and could always get a smile from his little wan face, even when his pore Mother failed. But it was all in wain, and before long it was all over, and the pore littel feller was at rest.

They buried him at the old church at St. Peter's, and you may be sure that Jack was there, and if his greef wasn't quite so grate as his pore Mother's, it wasn't a werry long ways off it.

Jack took just one long long look into the littel grave, and then went his way.

He left the place the next morning, and forgot to say where he was a going to, and hasn't cum back yet, and sumthink strikes me as he won't cum back there no more.

It seems a strange thing that a grate, hulking, ruff, uneddicated Boatman, like Jack the Giant, shood have had such a soft, loving heart, but so it was, and so it has been, and so no dowt it will be till we're all gathered together sum day, rich and pore, big and littel, Waiters and Wicounts, learned and unlearned, into one loving fold!

I think I must be gittin both old and foolish, for pore Jack's story quite spylte my hollyday, and sent me home as sollem as a Churchworden. Robert.

Strange Case of Forgetfulness on the Part of a Gentleman.—In the Reading-Room of a very important City Institution is posted up the following announcement:—"On Thursday last an Umbrella was taken from this room, and has not been returned. It *had* engraven on the handle the name and residence of the Owner. Will the *Gentleman*, who was and is, doubtless, labouring under some strange delusion as to the ownership of the Umbrella in question, kindly return me the name-plate, the continued possession of which might cause him some slight trouble at some future time. I need not sign my name and address, as the *Gentleman* has them already."

"SO NEAR—AND YET SO FAR!"

SCENE—*A Dance in Bayswater.*

*Daughter of the House.* "DO YOU KNOW MANY PEOPLE HERE, MR. SNOOKSON?"
*Prize Idiot (from Kensington).* "AW—NOT A SOUL, I CAN ASSURE YOU! AW—I CONFESS I'M QUITE OUT OF MY BEARINGS *ANYWHERE NORTH OF THE PARK*, AW!"

## DR. M'JEKYLL AND MR. O'HYDE.

(*Fragments plagiarised, with a purpose, from a popular Original.*)

* * * * * * *

SIX o'Clock struck, and still Mr. JOHN BULLSON was digging at the problem. Hitherto it had touched him on the intellectual side chiefly; but now his imagination also was engaged, or rather enslaved; and as he lay and tossed in the gross darkness of mental doubt, Mr. TEMPUS's terrible tale went by before his mind in a scroll of lurid pictures. He would be aware of an open park-like space near a great city, then of the vague, shadowy, undefinable figure of a man, or men, it was impossible to determine which, moving swiftly yet furtively; then of two other figures walking in confidential converse; and then these met, and that shadowy but sinister human Juggernaut struck and trod the two others down, and passed on, regardless of their dying moans. Or else he would see a room in a poor house, amidst thriftily-tilled and poorly-productive fields, where the toiling tiller thereof lay asleep, dreaming, and shuddering at his dreams; and then the door of that room would be opened, the curtains of the bed plucked apart, the sleeper recalled, and lo! there would stand by his side a figure, again misty but menacing, to whom power was given, and even at that dead hour he must rouse and do its bidding.

The figure in these two phases haunted Mr. BULLSON all the night; and if at any time he dozed over it, it was but to see it glide the more stealthily through sleeping houses, or move the more swiftly, and still the more swiftly and secretly through wider labyrinths of lamp-lighted city, or narrower tracks of gloom-shrouded villages; posing oratorically but dimly, like a blend of Veiled Prophet and platform perorator; lurking, phantom-like, by dark entry and behind stone wall, or scanty hedgerow, with purposes uncertain and unsatisfying, sometimes imitative, at least, of dignity, valour, and beneficence, sometimes, as it were, carrying the aspect or suggestion of craven cruelty or blatant imposture; but always, to the perturbed mind of the dreamer, equivocal, troublous, terrifying. And still the figure, or figures, had no face by which he might certainly know it; even in his dreams it had no face, or one that baffled him by its indistinctness, and melted into the suggestion of many before his eyes; and thus it was that there sprang up and grew apace in Mr. BULLSON's mind a singularly strong, almost an inordinate, curiosity to behold the features of the real Mr. O'HYDE. If he could but once set eyes on it, he thought, the mystery might lighten, and perhaps roll altogether away, as was the habit of mysterious things when well examined. He might see a reason for his friend's strange preference or bondage (call it which you please), and even for the startling manifestation of a seemingly paradoxical will. And at least it would be a face worth seeing—for many reasons; the face of a man —or men—without bowels of mercy, or full of patriotic pitifulness, as was diversely maintained with most contradictory fervour of belief; a face which had but to partially and indistinctly show itself to raise up in various minds such opposing spirits.

"Poor M'JEKYLL," he thought, "my mind misgives me; he is in deep waters! This Master O'HYDE, if he were studied, must have secrets of his own: black secrets, by the look of him—in some phases, at least—secrets compared to which poor M'JEKYLL's worst would be like sunshine. Things cannot continue as they are. Ay, I must put my shoulder to the wheel—if M'JEKYLL will but let me."

* * * * * * *

Hitherto it was his practical ignorance of Mr. O'HYDE that had swelled his indignation; now, by a sudden turn, it was what seemed forced upon him as knowledge. It was already bad enough when the name was but a name, of which he could learn little more. It was worse when it began to be clothed upon with detestable attributes; and out of the shifting, unsubstantial mists that had so long baffled his eye, there leaped up the sudden, definite presentment of a fiend.

* * * * * * *

The problem he was thus debating was one of a class that is rarely satisfactorily solved. "There *must* be a solution," said the perplexed gentleman. "There *is* a solution, if I could only find it. God bless me, the Thing seems hardly human! Something like

DR. M'JEKYLL AND MR. O'HYDE.

*Frankenstein's* Monster, shall we say, only intimately, inseparably related to its creator by a sort of clinging identity in dread duality? Can it be the old story of Dr. FELL? Or is it the mere radiance of a foul soul that transpires through and transfigures its clay continent? The last, I think; for O, my poor old PATRICK M'JEKYLL, if ever I read Satan's signature upon a face, it is on that of your mysterious associate."

* * * * * *

M'JEKYLL, indeed, stood at times aghast before the acts of O'HYDE; but the situation was apart from ordinary law, and insidiously relaxed the grasp of conscience. It was O'HYDE, after all, and O'HYDE only, that was guilty. M'JEKYLL was no worse; he woke again to his good qualities, as man, citizen, and patriot, seemingly unimpaired; he would even make haste, where it was possible, to undo the evil done by O'HYDE. Thus, at least, self-love asserted; and thus conscience was made to slumber.

* * * * * *

And M'JEKYLL himself? Do recent incidents seem, like the Babylonian finger on the wall, to be spelling out the letters of his judgment? Does he begin to reflect more seriously than ever before on the issues and possibilities of his double existence? Do things indeed, as his somewhat hot and injudicial accusers roundly assert, seem to point to this: that he is slowly losing hold of his original and better self, and becoming slowly incorporated with his second and worse? Or, as his more partial friends declare, and as all good and kindly hearts would ardently desire, is the exact contrary the case? Is it, not the fear of the gallows, but the horror of being O'HYDE that now alone can rack him? Does he indeed hate and fear the thought of the brute that slept within or raged beside him? Has he now seen the full deformity of that creature that shared with him some of the phenomena of consciousness, and was now co-heir with him to death; and beyond these links of community, which in themselves should make the most poignant part of his distress, does he think of O'HYDE, for all his energy of life, as of something not only hellish but inorganic, anarchic, opposed to all essential humanity as to all ordered law?

Who does not hope so? What man, not blinded by national prejudice, or hardened by Party spite, does not desire that closer inquiry may bring only clearer proof of the effective dissolution of the dismal and deadly bond, be it close and abiding as angry foes assert, or light and transient as tolerant friends maintain, between Dr. M'JEKYLL and Mr. O'HYDE?

## A NASTY ONE.

*Colonel Smithson (of the Poonah Marines).* "BY THE WAY, MY BOY AT SANDHURST HOPES TO GET INTO YOUR REGIMENT SOME DAY."

*Little Snipson (of the Royal Hussars Green).* "AW—I—AW—HOPE YOUR SON IS UP TO *OUR FORM!*"

*Colonel Smithson.* "*YOUR FORM!* DASH IT, HE'S OVER FOUR FEET HIGH, ANYHOW!"

## LETTERS BEFORE PROOFS.

DEAR MR. PUNCH,

THE practice of publishing letters that were dashed off by the writers at a moment's notice, and without any intention of being read by anyone save the recipient, has become so fashionable that I am thinking seriously of printing a collection that I have made myself. But before doing so I would like to ask your advice upon a point connected with the matter. First, however, I had better give you a few specimens from what I call my "note"-book.

The first is from a well-known statesman relative to the conduct of a colleague. For the moment I suppress names, but you may take it from me that they are full of interest:—

DEAR VAPID,

I consider —— one of the most incapable dolts it has ever been my ill-fortune to meet. At the Cabinet yesterday, when the —— Bill was considered, he made himself a laughing-stock by his ignorance and vulgarity. I felt quite distressed that I should have to dine with him in the evening. But my wife would not let me off, and I had to take her and myself to his hideously hospitable board, and I need scarcely say spent an utterly miserable evening.

Yours, &c., ——.

Here is another. It is from an eminent tragedian, and refers to the first appearance of a fellow player:—

MY DEAR OLD MAN,

WHAT an idea! You absolutely think that —— can play *Hamlet!* Why, the man has no more notion of acting than the Man in the Moon! Why, he cannot even speak the Queen's English, much less deliver blank verse! Awkward, ungainly, indistinct! The best thing he can do is to return to the ploughfield, from whence, I imagine, he must have been called away on reaching his majority. I would write more were it not that I have to sup with him after his painfully wearisome performance.

Yours, &c., ——.

Here is another about a not very popular Judge, written by one of his Brethren on the Bench:—

MY DEAR MR. VAPID,

YOU ask me what I think of Mr. Justice ——? This is rather a difficult problem, as I never think of him at all. As a lawyer, he is beneath contempt, and as a man, or, rather, manikin, he is painfully absurd. Nothing can be more ridiculous than his bearing on the Bench, where he jumps about like an imperfectly educated cock-sparrow, and makes faces and shakes his head like an organ-grinder's monkey. For all this, he is to be my host on Tuesday, and therefore I think I had better reserve further criticism until we meet. Yours, &c., ——.

Yet once more:—

DEAR VIC.,—Can —— write? No. I answer in the negative because I have just waded through his last novel. I had to skip three-fourths of it, and the remainder I found to be a hash of somebody else's work! He has asked me to be present at his Silver Wedding Day. Of course I am going, but I wish I could change the appointment for his funeral. Yours, ——.

There, *Mr. Punch!* What do you think of the above? Shall I publish them? Yours truly, VICTOR VAPID.

*Answer.*—Shall you publish them? Why, certainly! They are sure to please—everybody!

POOR MR. BANDMANN! About ten days ago he appeared at the Opéra Comique in a character, or rather two characters, totally unsuited to his *physique*, and for his pains the evening's performance was greeted with a fair amount of derision. Subsequently he was awarded in the columns of the London Press critiques of the most uncomplimentary character. Later still the entertainment was presented before an audience that warranted, by its appearance, the reflection that, as a pecuniary speculation, the venture might be unfortunate. And, latest of all, somebody applied at the Royal Courts and asked that he might be sent to prison! The Judge, however, was merciful, and on Mr. BANDMANN *undertaking not to play in the characters any more* until after the Long Vacation, allowed him his freedom. It is possible that his Lordship may have seen the eminent tragedian in the dual character, which would, of course, account for the view he took of the requirements of the situation!

**REPRISALS!**

*Tradesman* (*to Old Gentleman, who has purchased Lawn-mower*). "Yes, Sir, I'll Oil it, and send it over imm——"

*Customer* (*imperatively*). "No, no, no!—it mustn't be Oiled! I won't have it Oiled! Mind that! I want Noise! And, look here—pick me out a nice Rusty One. My Neighbour's Children hoot and yell till Ten o'clock every Night, so"—(*viciously*)—"I mean to cut my Grass from Four till Six every Morning!!"

## THE DIARY OF A NOBODY.

*July* 30.—The miserable cold weather is either upsetting me or Carrie, or both. We seem to break out into an argument about absolutely nothing, and this unpleasant state of things usually occurs at meal times. This morning for some unaccountable reason we were talking about balloons and we were as merry as possible, but the conversation drifted into family matters, during which, Carrie, without the slightest reason, referred in the most uncomplimentary manner to my poor father's pecuniary trouble. I retorted, by saying that "Pa at all events was a gentleman," whereupon Carrie burst out crying. I positively could not eat any breakfast. At the office I was sent for by Mr. Perkupp, who said he was very sorry, but I should have to take my annual holidays from next Saturday. Franching called at office, and asked me to dine at his Club, "The Radical Conservative." Fearing disagreeables at home after the "tiff" this morning, I sent a telegram to Carrie telling her I was going out to dine, and she was not to sit up. Bought a little silver bangle for Carrie.

*July* 31.—Carrie was very pleased with the bangle which I left with an affectionate note on her dressing-table last night before going to bed. I told Carrie we should have to start for our holiday next Saturday. She replied quite happily that she did not mind except that the weather was so bad, and she feared that Miss Jibbons would not be able to get her a seaside dress in time. I told Carrie that I thought the drab one with pink bows looked quite good enough, and Carrie said she should not think of wearing it. I was about to discuss the matter, when remembering the argument yesterday, resolved to hold my tongue. I said to Carrie, "I don't think we can do better than 'Good old' Margate." Carrie, not only to my astonishment raised an objection to Margate for the first time, but begged me not to use the expression "Good old," but to leave it to Mr. Stillbrook and other *gentlemen* of his type. Hearing my 'bus pass the window, I was obliged to rush out of the house without kissing Carrie as usual, and I shouted to her, "I leave it to you to decide." On returning in the evening Carrie said she thought as time was so short she had decided on Margate, and had written to Mrs. Beck, Harbour View Terrace, for apartments.

*August* 1.—Ordered a new pair of trousers at Benjamin's, and told them not to cut them so loose over the boot. The last pair being so loose and also tight at the knee, looked like a sailor's, and I heard Pitt, that offensive young cub at the office call out "Hornpipe!" as I passed his desk. Carrie has ordered of Miss Jibbons a pink Garibaldi and blue serge skirt which I always think looks so pretty at the seaside. In the evening she trimmed herself a little sailor-hat while I read to her the "*Exchange and Mart.*" We had a good laugh over my trying on the hat when she had finished it, Carrie saying it looked so funny with my whiskers, and how the people would have roared if I went on the stage like it.

*August* 2.—Mrs. Beck wrote to say we could have our usual rooms at Margate. That's off our mind. Bought a coloured shirt and a pair of tan-coloured boots, which I see many of the swell clerks wearing in the City, and I hear are all the "go."

*August* 3.—A beautiful day. Looking forward to to-morrow. Carrie bought a parasol about five feet long. I told her it was ridiculous. She said, "Not worse than your coloured shirt." So the matter dropped. I bought a capital hat for hot weather at the sea-side. I don't know what it is called, but it is the shape of the helmet worn in India, only made of straw. Got three new ties, two coloured handkerchiefs, and a pair of navy-blue socks at Pope Brothers. Spent the evening packing. Carrie told me not to forget to borrow Mr. Higgsworth's telescope, which he always lends me, knowing I know how to take care of it. Sent Sarah out for it. While everything was seeming so bright, the last post brought us a letter from Mrs. Beck, saying, "I have just let all my house to one party, and am sorry I must take back my words, and am sorry you must find other apartments."

---

August 6th.—Memorable this year as "The First Heat."

Omitted from the "St. J. G." Repertoire.—"Under the Greenwood."

## OUR JAPANNERIES. No. 11.

SHOOTING GROUSE ON THE MOORS.

## ESSENCE OF PARLIAMENT.

EXTRACTED FROM

### THE DIARY OF TOBY, M.P.

*House of Commons, Monday Night, August* 6.—Curious place, House of Commons. Summoned to-day to take Report Stage of Parnell Commission Bill; everybody discussing probable course of debate; would Amendments be moved? If so, how many? Would speeches be made? If so, how long? In the end House never reached Commission Bill at all. Scotch Members, envious of prominent position reached by Irish, determined to do bit of obstruction on own account. On the whole, rather dreary business. If we must have obstruction, prefer Irish brand. WALLACE began it at Saturday sitting—not WALLACE of Elderslie and Auchinbothie, but Member for East Edinburgh. Pragmatical person who delivers Latin tags with Perthshire accent. Suddenly dawned upon him that he is a humorist. Discovery made on Saturday. Girded in hippopotamic manner at LORD-ADVOCATE; House always laughs when it looks on or thinks of LORD-ADVOCATE; laughed when WALLACE said something rude about him; WALLACE delighted with unexpected success; hammered away at joke on Saturday afternoon; brought it up again to-night; hammered on for thirty-five minutes. Speaker at critical moment prevented manslaughter by peremptorily shutting up Wallace at thirty-seventh repetition of joke.

"In my experience," said Speaker, "I have never known the latitude usually allowed to an Hon. Member so much abused as on this occasion."

Exit Lord Claud.

Wallace surprised into really humorous remark. Been boring House for over half-an-hour when Speaker interposed. Now, resuming seat, complained that, "in consequence of Speaker's ruling," he must sit down without having delivered the speech he had prepared from a sense of duty to his constituents and his country! Good, that—for Wallace.

"Off and on I've sat in this House for twenty-three years," said Lord Claud Hamilton. "Have seen and heard some things in my time. But if Scotch Members are going to practise obstruction, I think I'll go." So writ moved for new Election, and Chiltern Hundreds fresh Steward.

Lords, not to be outdone by Scotch Members, had their little joke. To-day Bank Holiday. Other branches of labouring classes struck work all over the country; so Lords, who usually begin business at half-past four and adjourn at five minutes to five, determined to make a night of it. Took Local Government Bill in Committee. Pegged away till quarter to two to-morrow morning; got Bill clear through Committee.

*Business done.*—In the Lords, a good deal; in the Commons, none.

*Tuesday.*—"Heard the news?" said Admiral Field. Met him crossing the Lobby on starboard tack, close-hauled, a newspaper reefed in his hand, and flag of distress flying. "Awful!" he said, laying-to, and jibbooming his lee scuppers with his pocket-handkerchief. "Oban taken by the Channel Squadron. Aberdeen bombarded by four line-of-battle ships forming part of Admiral Fitzroy's Attacking Squadron. Forth Bridge destroyed, and not a stone standing on Inchkeith, in the Frith of Forth. Always said it would come to this. Came into House little late to save my country. But done my best. Been laughed at, sneered at, snubbed by First Lord, who doesn't know a halyard from a yard that isn't haled; and now, you see, where we are."

Admiral shook in my face the news of hapless Aberdeen, and unfortunate Inchkeith, and sheered off to blast other ears with the direful news.

"You may and you Mayne't."
*Old Saw.*

Meanwhile, House of Commons going on with Commission Bill, just as if hand of invader were not laid heavily on Scotland. By desperate *coup* Old Morality had snuffed out all Amendments on Committee stage. At One o'Clock on particular morning Clauses peremptorily put from the Chair, and carried. Here they come up again on the Report Stage, "like *Snarleyow, the Dog Fiend*," says Admiral Mayne, who still reads Marryatt. Anyhow, a dogged debate. House, curiously full, considering end of all things at hand. Harcourt looks in after dinner. Rapidly catches up drift of debate; plunges in, "like elephant in a tank," as Chaplin says; splashes splendidly; seized opportunity to speak disrespectfully of profession of Law, sneering at "Old Bailey view" taken of Bill by Home Secretary. This brought up Edward Clarke with lively speech, that greatly delighted House. Went straight for Harcourt, regardless of disparity of size. Bit and snapped, and, on the whole, made Harcourt rather wish he'd stopped another half hour at dinner. House sat long way into to-morrow morning. Still didn't pass Bill.

*Business Done.*—Report Stage of Parnell Commission Bill.

*Thursday.*—Strange thing happened to-night. Time, Eleven o'Clock. Indian Budget on. James Stuart demonstrated afresh how a really able man in own line can prove utter failure in House of Commons. Eight Members present, including Speaker. Half asleep myself. Roused by hearing noise like crackling of thorns under a pot. Came from man next to me. Looked up; found it was Wallace. Noise continued. Strange contortion of features. Getting alarmed.

"What's the matter, old fellow?" I said, cheerily, trying to make light of it. Colic?"

"No," said Wallace. "I'm laughing."

"Oh," I said, quite relieved. "But what are you laughing at? Not at Stuart, I hope?"

"Dear me, no! Field, don't you know, and Lord-Advocate, and the bombardment of Edinburgh, and why wasn't he there? Capital!"

Absent from the Post o. Danger.

More crackling of thorns under the pot; additional facial contortions.

"Ah, that was very funny," I said, "but it happened a long time ago. Came on at Half-past Four; now it's Eleven."

"Yes, I know," said Wallace. "Heard it at the time; only just seen the joke. Often takes me that way; sometimes it's a day after; occasionally a week. To-night I've been rather sharp. But it comes sooner or later. Assure you, though you mighn't think it, there's very little in the way of a good joke *I* miss, take the Session through."

Nice, well-meaning man, Wallace; though, regarded as a companion, a little embarrassing; appropriates his daily share of humour by sort of slow-match process. Never know when you have him.

Glad he finally saw the little joke about Lord-Advocate and Edinburgh got up at Question Time between Field and Lord-Advocate.

How was it, Field asked, that Lord Provost of Edinburgh, as Lord High Admiral of Firth of Forth, took no steps to defend Leith against attack by fleet, which led to bombardment of Edinburgh?

Lord-Advocate, with just a twinkle of mirth on his massive countenance, gravely replied that that distinguished naval officer, the Lord High Admiral of the Firth of Forth had only a phantom fleet under his command, and had acted wisely in keeping it out of sight. Humour being contagious, Caldwell asked Secretary of State for War how it came to pass that Lord-Advocate holding commission as Colonel in Militia, was not at post of danger? Stanhope, in delightfully official manner, explained that the land forces not being called into action, the gallant Colonel's services had not been needed. A most admirable bit of fooling. Fortunate, however, end of Session near, and Wallace will be out of harm's way. Wouldn't do for him to be often taken as he was to-night.

*Business done.*—Indian Budget.

"An unbroken front."

*Saturday.*—Winding things up to-day. At it yesterday with extraordinary effect. At Question Time Old Morality indicated a dozen Orders of the Day to be dealt with before the Adjournment; looked like Three o'Clock in the morning again; but by Eleven all over. Arranged that, after Royal Commission on Monday, Parliament shall adjourn till Tuesday, 6th of November. Irish Members appalled at prospect of being silent for nearly three months on pain of going to prison. Charm of British legislation is, that what in Member speaking from below the Gangway is but a choleric word, is flat blasphemy in same Member speaking at Clonakilty. Say what you like at Westminster. For saying half as bad at Westmeath, you're clapped into prison. "A strange world, my masters," says Joseph Gillis, in reflective mood.

Thing is to make most of present opportunities. This Irish Members do. Other Members want to go home. But Akers-Douglas on guard at the door. Presents unbroken front of resistance. "Wait a bit, dear boy," he says, persuasively. "You needn't dine here to-night, but we must see Adjournment carried." So they tarry till end comes.

*Business done.*—All.

---

"Over the Border with Charlie."—The question between Mr. Parnell and Mr. Walter is, it seems, to be settled in Edinburgh. This being the case, one of the parties will not escape Scot free! If the report is not a "bang," it will cost more than "saxpence."

## THE WHITE ETON.

(*A Companion Story to "The Black Arrow."*)

Prologue.—*Robin Hood-à-Thought-it.*

On a certain afternoon in the late springtime, the bell upon Bolton Moat House was heard ringing at an unaccustomed hour. Far and near people began to desert their labours and thronged together. An express had come calling the whole village to boot and saddle. For the days of Sir Walter Scott had returned again to Merrie England, and the British language had become all but unintelligible.

A Page for a Romance of the Middle Ages.

Sir Allover Oaths the Parson and Colney Hatch were arming for the fray, and good Poultry Yard the Archer was reading to the little children the pages of G. P. R. James, wherein he found certain hints that helped him bravely in his phraseology.

"Poor shrews!" he exclaimed. "I have no natural lord but King Harry the Tent, and it is an ill wind that bloweth to me-ward no good but what may be found in a quarrell fixed in a windac."

"Y' are a strange looking rogue," replied the children, clapping their hands with glee.

"Nay, be it so," replied the old Archer. "By my sooth, Toss-pot and Shuttlewit run in, but my Lord Good Counsel sits o'one side waiting!" No doubt the worthy churl would have said more to the same effect had not an arrow at this moment sung in the air like a huge hornet. It struck old Poultry Yard between the shoulder-blades, and pierced him clean through as he fell among the cabbages.

"By my faith," cried Colney Hatch, "and in good sooth, dash my wigge, but it hath a scroll that will make Sir Allover turn paper colour and pray like a windmill. Fetch me a link, and let us read the writing stuff."

"*Powltree-yaird fro' Rob Hood-à-thort-it.*"

"Nay, I like it not," said all the retainers.

"It is a libel," cried Sir Allover the Priest. "That every run-the-hedge in a green jerkin should fasten a scroll so, runs hard on sacrilege—hard!"

"It boots not, but put to it will wash, Sir Parson," responded Colney Hatch. "Here is unseasonable talk for those who are unfriends. Nay, y'are wrong, and sayest yer much more and I will clout me a yard of arrow through your inwards."

"Now, well a-day!" exclaimed Sir Allover, "what means it?"

"It is wrote on a White Eton, good Sir Priest!" respectfully replied one who had been making too free with the wine-skins.

"And what may that be?" returned the ecclesiastic, showing increased interest.

"A White Eton is a sort of neckgirdler of shirtcloth, may it please ye, and also as good a title as a Black Arrow, and as appropriate!"

Now was it found that Robin Hood-à-Thought-it had written on his scroll that he had plenty of "Whyte Etons," from whence he had sent thither the specimen circlet, and intended to use them upon the bodies of those who had given him offence. Upon this the Priest gave Dick a sealed packet with this superscription:—"To my Ryght Worshypful Master, Sir Daniel Knyght, be thys delivered in haste," and thus, having secured the "y," the messenger hurried away to obtain the wherefore.

Book First.—*Lad and Lady.*

Sir Daniel and his men lay in about Tea Kettley that night, warmly quartered and well patrolled. But the Knight was one who never rested from money-getting.

"Bring up yon fellow," cried he, and one of the retainers led up a poor cringing old man, as pale as a candle, and all shaking with the fen fever. "Ye deal in treason, rogue; ye trudge the country leasing; y'are heavily suspicioned of the death of severals."

"Right honourable and my reverend Lord," the man cried, "here is some hodge-podge, saving your good presence."

"Well a day!" returned the Knight. "Go to! Y'are too cunning, fool-fellow, for a livelihood of seventy shillings!"

And Sir Daniel, who was a very merry Knight,—none merrier in England,—took a drink of his mulled ale, and lay back smiling.

It was then that he addressed a lad who was stretched in a mantle on the floor, after taking off his visored head-piece and unloosing a sanguine-coloured cloak.

"A sturdy boy! I will make you a marriage of a thousand pounds, and cherish you exceedingly. Now eat me a porridge."

Thus the claims of quaint English having been satisfied, the action proceeded apace, and in less than it takes to write it, Dick and John were far away from Sir Daniel and going through a variety of adventures miles from Tea Kettley. They did the fens of Bolton Moatly Forest thoroughly, losing horses, seeing false lepers, and coming across the originals of those fair bowmen who, dressed in round cloth jerkins and snowy neckgirdlers, were called "the White Eton Boys."

"Have ye read the works of Shakspeare?" asked John.

"Faugh!" said Dick; "y' are a milk-sopping baby not to know that your Bard of Avon lived hereafter—aye, when Harry Sixt was long dead, and Harry Eight—to say naught of Betsie—were flourishing. An I guessed rightly, I should call ye a poor shrew of a sniveller! But why did you ask—I mean why putteth you me to the question?"

"Because, forsooth, it remembered me that in *As You Like it*, may it please ye, a lad and wench marched about together, one disguised and the other not, as we do?"

"Nay," retorted Dick; "if that be your tune, so be it, and a plague be with you! Nay, blow me no nose! I love not snivellers!"

Each turned aside, and then began walking off severally. Thus they had many adventures of a more or less mysterious character, until, after parting in a ditch and meeting in a chapel, they found themselves separated by the necessities of the story. For, as the old Chronicles hath it, "Can ye make bricks without straw?" And, again, "What availeth a lot of characters unless, may it please ye, you can put them in a number of startling situations?"

So boy and girl between them, with the assistance of winking tapestry, purposeless spies, and dialogue containing a good deal of the second person singular, managed somehow or other to get through two hundred and fifty pages, without counting varlets, outlaws, and men-at-arms. But in good sooth the work was as tough as a Church steeple of a Lenten Sunday!

Book the Last.—*Couleur-de-Rosy Reading.*

And the two hundred and fifty pages having been passed, it now was time to bring in something about Richard Crookback, and the Wars of the Roses. Thus it happened that one day, Dick, having armed himself more like a gentleman than usual, heard the sound of a trumpet. He came within sight of a booth, and found a most fierce encounter raging on the road before it. There were seven or eight assailants, and but one to keep head against them. Dick, drawing his sword, putting a quarrel in his cross-bow, waving his lance, unslinging his mace, loading his hand-cannon, and using his dagger with considerable dexterity, was able, after about an hour and a half's hard work, to render very valuable assistance.

"A horse! a horse! my kingdom for a horse! So much for Buckingham!" said the attacked one when his assailants had been vanquished, and then, turning to our hero, demanded, "How knew ye who I was?"

"I am ignorant of whom I speak with," Dick answered. "Fact is, I don't in the least know"—then, gracefully pulling himself up, he continued, "an it please ye, I forgot myself! I have me a habit of slipping into English of the Nineteenth Century unawares. I should have said, by my sooth, and by my halidom, but, my good Lord, I know not your arms. But I see ye have the humpe!"

"Humpe me no humpe," replied the other, and a singular sneer played about the young nobleman's mouth as he made answer. Then he added—"But the time is ripe for making you Sir Richard. Ye have pleased me—kneel me a kneel!"

In the bottom of his heart Dick already entertained a great terror and some hatred for the man whom he had rescued; but the invitation was so worded that it would have been cruel to refuse or hesitate, so he hastened to comply, and was Knighted.

"And now, good Sir Richard," said the Crookback, "you may get married as soon as it may please ye, and have done with it."

Bowing gracefully, the young man departed to find out and engage in mortal combat Sir Daniel, who, he had discovered recently, had been his father's murderer. Just as he was on the point of finishing the traitor loon in question, it occurred to him that the wicked Knight should die by the aid of an arrow. For had not Robin Hood-à-Thought-it said as much at the beginning of the story?

So, stepping aside, he awaited events. Hereon all of a sudden a bow sounded like a note of music.

An arrow flew, carrying with it a stiff linen circlet, marked "Six groats the twelve ones." The circlet wound round the Knight's throat, and choked him.

"Is the circlet white?" he gasped. "Does it justify the title of the book?"

"It is white," replied Dick, gravely; "and therefore may be called a White Eton."

Sir Daniel stared wildly, tried ineffectually to follow this reasoning, uttered a piercing cry, and died in much agony.

Dick hurried away, entered the church (accompanied by the White Eton Boys), and was married. When he came forth into the frosty air and sunlight, the long files of the army were already winding forward up the road. But the wedding party turned upon the other side, and sat down with sober merriment to breakfast. And the "merriment" was the "soberer" because each dismal reveller was haunted with the apprehension that some day their exceedingly tedious and uneventful lives would be recorded by a Nineteenth Century chronicler! An it please ye, so they was!

## THE RAILWAY TAM O' SHANTER.

*Shareholder.* "Stop! stop! More haste, less Dividend!"

* * * * *

Weel mounted on his flying steed,—
A fleeter never gat up speed,—
Tam skelpit on at sic a pace
As thoroughbred ne'er held in race.
*Eclipse* himself, or *Flying Dutchman*,
Tam's nag for swiftness could not touch, man.
So sped that steed and Tam upon it,
Whiles holding fast his gude blue bonnet,
Whiles glow'ring round wi' prudent cares
Lest rivals pass him unawares;

"A race!" yelled Tam; "I ought to win it
At something like a mile a minute."

So speeds the "Flying Scotchman," so
Tam rattles madly on, when lo!
A something stirs in Tammie's noddle;
For danger he cares not a boddle,
But ithers at his pace astonished
Consider he should be admonished. [friends,
"More haste, less speed," think Tam's Scotch
*May* mean "mair speed, less deevedends."

Through space can one thus wildly whisk
Without considerable risk
To money-bags as weel as bodies?
Your Scotch shareholders are not noddies.
Their interest is not Sport but Trade;
To see the trim-laid "metals" made
Into race-course—or cinder-path,
For "record-cutting" stirs their wrath.
To safety and good sense they 'll rally,
And in protesting legion sally

As bees buzz out wi' angry fyke,
This racing game they canna' like;
And as TAM flies you see them follow
Wi' monie an eldritch skreech and hollow.
Ah, TAM! ah, TAM! though fast thou'rt farin',
Be sure those shareholders thou'rt scarin';
The public also have a fear
They may buy joys o' speed too dear.
Beware, TAM, ere this cantrip ends
In Danger and low Dividends!

## THE FUN OF THE N. P. FUND.

IN the little Blue Book annually published by the Newspaper Press Fund, there is a comical misprint in the report of the Chairman's speech at last year's banquet. The Chairman, following the wise custom introduced by H.R.H. the Prince of WALES at every public dinner, wishing to get to the cigars and the real business of the evening after the first toast, quoted the well-known words of Mr. DUCROW, who, when rehearsing an equestrian drama at Astley's, found the dialogue tedious, and exclaimed, "Cut the cackle and come to the 'osses." But the reporter and the printer between them have thus reproduced it at p. 13: "'Cut the *cattle* and come to the *asses.*' (*Laughter*)." "Laughter!" We should think so—rather! Sir EDWARD CLARKE, Q.C., Solicitor-General, presided this year, and draw tears from the eyes and money from the purses of his audience by his earnest solicitations.

## "Primate and Confidential."

(*To Lord Carnarvon.*)

I THANK you, my Lord,
I'm quite in accord
With the spirit of your suggestions,
"Open Churches" are rare,
But everywhere
We've plenty of "Open Questions."

JACK TAR'S LOG AT THE MANŒUVRES. — "*Lough Swilly*"—the place to pipe all hands for grog.

"CARRY YER BAG, SIR?"

## THE RIVAL-TO-THE-BIG-GOOSEBERRY CORRESPONDENCE.

*Letter No.* 1.

SIR,—I notice in the columns of one of your Contemporaries that the question has been raised, "Is Marriage a Failure?" and if you will allow me I should like to answer it.

Sir, how can marriage be a failure when the household is well conducted? Let me take my own case. I am a man of great mental attainments, and with a power of organisation that must command respect. Sir, I am not satisfied to leave the care of the home to hands other than my own. Taking for my model the "*paterfamilias*" of the famed law-giver, JUSTINIAN, I consider it my duty to personally superintend the details of domestic management. Thus I think it advisable to arrange with the cook the *menu* of the dinner, and to consult with the housemaid as to the times and seasons most suitable for the cleansing of the various apartments, for the proper condition of which I hold her responsible. And if occasionally our meals become a little complicated, and the sweeping the drawing-room carpet is entirely overlooked, those are matters only of temporary annoyance, and the great principle that the man should be the head of the household is maintained in all its beautiful significance.

From this you must not imagine that I devote my entire time to the arrangement of the proper functions of my servants. On the contrary, I have plenty of leisure for improving the mind of my wife. It is my duty, as it is indeed my pleasure, to read to her works of an elevating rather than an entertaining character. Moreover, when it is fine I am always ready to take her with me to see such Museums as that of the School of Mines in Jermyn Street, or the excellent Anatomical Collection attached to Surgeons' Hall. From this you will gather, that while seeking for instruction I do not ignore the claims of amusement. After these few hints as to the method I pursue in rendering my home a happy one, it is unnecessary for me to indicate further whether in our case marriage is a failure.

I am, Sir, yours, SOMEBODY'S HUSBAND.

*Letter No.* 2.

SIR,—I have just seen a rough draft of which the letter sent to you by my husband is a carefully prepared copy. As he is not looking, will you allow me to answer the question, "Is Marriage a failure?" by the significant word, "Rather!"

Yours truly, SOMEBODY'S WIFE.

*Letter No.* 3.

SIR,—as an American, will you permit me to join in your interesting Correspondence? The institutions of the free United States enable the enterprising Benedick to marry, and then obtain a divorce with the greatest possible convenience and dispatch. Thus I have had considerable experience in Matrimony. I have consequently entered into the bonds of Wedlock more than once, and can therefore conscientiously declare that Marriage is *not* a failure.

Yours truly, TRUE AS STEEL.

*Letter No.* 4.

SIR,—For the last thirty years—in fact, since I reached my eighteenth birthday—I have given this all-engrossing question my most anxious consideration. In spite of the peculiar custom of Leap Year, I have not yet been able to put the problem to a practical test. So, speaking for myself, I fear I must confess that Marriage *is* a failure. Yours, singularly, A MAID OF LEA.

*Letter No.* 5.

SIR,—Of course Marriage is a failure. What is a fellow to do when he is obliged to give up his Club and his Music Hall, his pals and his smoke? No, Sir, it is not good enough for

Yours truly, 'ARRY AT 20.

*Letter No.* 6.

SIR,—Take it all round with the rough and the smooth, the worries of unpaid bills and the trips into the country, the black looks of one's husband, and the laughter of one's children, I really do believe that Marriage is *not* a failure. Yours faithfully, 'ARRIET at 50.

[This Correspondence to be discontinued upon the discovery of a more engrossing subject in the Silly Season.]

"IS MARRIAGE A FAILURE?"—Evidently not, as it contrives to fill two or three columns every day, and keeps up the circulation of the *D. T.* in the D. S., or Dull Season.

REVIVAL OF THE OFFICE OF "THE DIRECTOR OF TRANSPORTS."—Why, certainly. Emotional persons ought to be subject to proper control. We hope he will be a firm but sympathetic person. Perhaps an experienced Matron would be best fitted for the post.

**COMING DOWN ON THE SWEATERS.**

"Quoth Dun-Raven,
Never more!"

## THE DIARY OF A NOBODY.

*August* 4.—Got up at six, but as it was pouring wet, and we had been thrown over in respect to our apartments at Margate, and (as Carrie wisely observed), Monday was Bank Holiday, we would abandon our visit till Tuesday. We became more than reconciled to this, for the first post brought a nice letter from Willie (son by my first), acknowledging a trifling present which Carrie sent him, the day before yesterday being his twentieth birthday. To our utter amazement he turned up himself in the afternoon, having journeyed all the way from Oldham. He said he had got leave from the bank, and as Monday was a holiday, he thought he would give us a little surprise.

*August* 5 (*Sunday*).—We had a bottle of port for dinner, and drank dear Willie's health. He said, "Oh, by the bye, did I tell you I've cut my first name, 'William,' and taken the second name, 'Lupin.' In fact, I'm only known at Oldham as 'Lupin Pooter.' If you were to 'Willie' me there, they wouldn't know what you meant." Of course, Lupin being a purely fancy name, Carrie was delighted, and began by giving a long history of the Lupins. I ventured to say that I thought William a nice simple name, and reminded him he was christened after his Uncle William, who was much respected in the City. Willie, in a manner which I did not much care for, said sneeringly, "Oh, I know all about that—Good old Bill!" and helped himself to a third glass of port. Carrie objected strongly to my saying "Good old," but she made no remark when Willie used the double adjective. I said nothing, but looked at her, which meant more. I said, "My dear Willie, I hope you are happy with your colleagues at the bank." He replied, "Lupin, if you please, and with respect to the bank, there's not a clerk who is a gentleman, and the 'boss' is a cad." I felt so shocked, I could say nothing, and my instinct told me there was something wrong.

*Aug.* 6, *Bank Holiday*.—As there was no sign of Lupin moving at nine o'clock, I knocked at his door, and said we usually breakfasted at half-past eight, and asked how long would he be? Lupin replied that he had had a lively time of it, first with the trains shaking the house all night, and then with the sun streaming in through the windows in his eyes, and giving him a cracking headache. Carrie came up and asked if he would like some breakfast sent up, and he said he could do with a cup of tea, and didn't want anything to eat. Lupin not having come down, I went up again at half-past one, and said we dined at two; he said he "would be there." He never came down till a quarter to three. I said, "We have not seen much of you, and you will have to return by the 5·30 train; therefore, you will have to leave in an hour, unless you go by the midnight mail." He said, "Look here, Guv'nor, it's no use beating about the bush. I've tendered my resignation at the bank." For a moment I could not speak. When my speech came again, I said, "How dare you, Sir? How dare you take such a serious step without consulting me? Don't answer me, Sir,—you will sit down immediately, and write a note at my dictation, withdrawing your resignation and amply apologising for your thoughtlessness." Imagine my dismay when he replied with a loud guffaw, "It's no use. If you want the good old truth, I've got the chuck!"

---

A daily Advertisement informs us that "*She* is in active preparation." *L'Histoire des Femmes. She*'s getting herself up regardless of expense. Always in active preparation, and always keeping us waiting.

## THE PLAINT OF THE GRAND PIANO.

I was a grand piano once—nay, hearken what I say—
The grandeur is no longer here, it left me yesterday.
One leather-souled executant at a sitting could demolish
The mellow pride of tuneful years, of tone, and power, and polish.

A dapper man, with weary brow, and smile of conscious pow'r,
A Jove, prepared to improvise tone-thunder by the hour,
Is Nasmyth Hammermann, whose touch would disconcert the dead,
Whose foot would rush with pedal-crush where angels fear to tread.

He kept his soul in patience while lesser people played,
As one who bears with cruder views that taste-bound souls degrade;
He pitied plaintive melody and winning modulation,
Biding his time—and then it came—the afternoon's sensation.

He hovered over the keyboard, like a wild beast over its prey,
And he tossed his head, and he rattled his wrists—and then he began to play;
To play! And in that crowded room was none with heart to see
That what was play to him and them was worse than death to me!

He struck a chord, as a hawk strikes a lark who is dumb with fear,
And his fingers spread over the octaves like a slander in full career,
And my overstrung nerves that waited the worst nigh sprung from the shuddering case
As he finished his horrible prelude with an awful bang in the bass.

He gloated; I waited; and then began a butchery great and grim,
And melody screamed and harmony writhed, and form, rent limb from limb,
Was hurled in murderous *largesse* to the careless, ravening crowd,
Who chatted and laugh'd the louder, as my agony waxed more loud.

He checked his course, and he wirgled round, till he found the soul of pain,
And he thumped it with pitiless fingers, again, again, again!
Then, like a pawing horse let go, he tore at headlong pace,
And drowned the tortured treble's cry in the roar of an anguished bass.

My tenderest tones, that answer clear the artist's lightest touch,
Were yank'd in handfuls out like hair in some fierce maniac's clutch,
And my beautiful keys, that never yet had sullied their tuneful pride,
Like elephants with the tusk-ache in ivory anguish cried.

Hark to the murmurs sad and low, self-struck upon my strings,
Such music as a dying love, unknown, unsolaced sings,
For yesterday's undreamt disgrace can never not have been,
And I must shrink from music now, and sob "Unclean, unclean!"

The girls have practised on me in endless ladders of scales,
Whereby they mounted to castle'd heights, and the realms of fairy tales;
And I loved their wayward endeavours, and my patient sweetness at last
Won them to tell me their love's young dreams as I hallowed their childhood's past.

And the Governess, meek and modest, who counted the tale of bars,
Would slip from the sleeping children, and the schoolroom worries and jars;
And the tender heart would open to me, and, work-a-day woes forgot,
The pencil-cramped hands would tremble, and the tears from her heart well'd hot.

They called her a Perfect Treasure, but 'twas I alone who knew
The tale of the young life's struggle, so tender and brave and true;
And when she touched me I told it, and somebody listened and learned,
And the winter-time went out of her life, and the daffodil days returned.

And Maud in her tempers would bang away—Sweet Maud—for I often heard
The *fortissimo* suddenly ended in a kiss like the chirp of a bird.
And Mabel's curious reveries—how soon a piano discovers
When a girl gives one hand to her music, and the other is clasped in her lover's.

Perchance some tender hand again may soothe my tortured heart,
May heal the scars of Hammermann with balm of rare Mozart;
Perchance the Nocturne's mystic feet may through my caverns stray,
When great Beethoven's passion-storms have cleansed the plague away.

But no, farewell that happy past; henceforth I'm only fit
To play the concertina's part to wandering niggers' wit;
Or, as a street-piano, find as jubilant a goal
As a wet day in China when you do not know a soul.

Yet it may be my past deserts may win a loftier place,
Low in the outer walks of Art, not blatant in disgrace;
And Music's tutelary powers may bid their Outcast go
And be the sacred music in a panoramic show,
And moan "*The Village Blacksmith*" when the lights are burning low.

## OUR BOOKING-OFFICE.

I THOUGHT I was going to have a rare treat in RIDER HAGGARD's *Maiwa's Revenge.* "*Beati qui nihil expectant,*" as *Major Monsoon* hath it, "for verily they shall not be disappointed." The book is simply the Zoological [Gardens turned loose with that old Choke-bore *Allan Quatermain*, who, I had hoped, was dead and buried in the previous novel, potting elephants and rhinoceri as if they were shrimps, meeting lions and lionesses and savages, and all the stale Rider-Haggardian materials muddled up together, without even the thread of an interesting story whereon to hang the dried skins of the beasts. *Maiwa* herself, an insignificant person, does not appear till page 105, out of a book of 216 pages, and the other part is taken up with stupid stories told by that stupid low comedian *Good*, whom his author loves, and somniferous after-dinner sporting twaddle carried on by the small bore *Sir Henry Curtis*, the aforesaid low comedian *Good*, and the grand old choke-bore, *Allan Quatermain* himself with the little round button at the top and the gunpowder running out of the heels of his boots. Herewith I make a present to Mr. RIDER HAGGARD of a final chapter, with a moral to it—to be found in the application of it—which I will call,—

A Creepy Crawly effect.

### REDAH'S REVENGE!

FIRST LAST, AND ONLY CHAPTER.

On the dried wing of a Fly-leaf, brought to me by the maiden KONSTANT REDAH, I make out these words:—

"For Heaven's sake, whoever you are, try to help me. I have been the slave of this awful RITERAGGARD for nearly four years. He caught me in *King Solomon's Mines;* he charmed me, for he is a wizard, with *She:* and he tortures me now by means of his slaves, *Allano Quarterman, Baddely Good*, and *Sir Henry Cowardis.* Don't desert me, or RITERAGGARD and his Impi, the Pubbeli-Shahs, will have another novel ready in less than a week, and I shall be forced to devour every word of it. Help! help! help! I can bear this no longer.

"Yours, JACK LIVVREY."

"Great Heavens!" I gasped. "LIVVREY! it must be my old friend, JACK LIVVREY, of Liverpil, the great Novel Hunter." I too had suffered at the hands of RITERAGGARD and his Impi, and I was determined that they should not have another victim if I could prevent it. KONSTANT REDAH's eyes gleamed with a vindictive light. She had often tried to put down the tyrant RITERAGGARD, but could not. Now was her chance. So at once we were on the march. Within a few minutes we were in the Boshibook's country, near RITERAGGARD's Impi and the Pubbeli-Shah's Kraal. When I reached the Koppie-Right I lay down on my littery bed and took an inspiriting draught of *Punch.* It was lucky I did so, for now a strange thing happened.

Out of the thick red and blue coverts that surrounded the Koppie-Right arose a swarm of fly-leaves, darkening the air like locusts, and through this black density came flashes like red rays of the setting sun. "It is the Impi's advertisements," said KONSTANT REDAH, coolly, replying to my exclamation. "I know them. Behold!"

I looked, and from underneath this swarm, kicking up a dust all among the Koppie, right and left, came slowly on, as if by forced marches, RITERAGGARD himself, CHOKEBORE ALLANO QUARTERMAN, BADDELY GOOD, Sir HENRY COWARDIS, Old GOBBO the Clown, a lot of savage Elephants, Rhinoceri, Lions, Tigers, Crocodiles, Snakes, in fact the whole menagerie and travelling *troupe.* The men were all armed with repeating rifles loaded with *Saymold* ammunition. RITERAGGARD had an old fifteen thousand Storey's repeating rifle, with which he was shooting in every direction at random.

"Help! help! They are cramming MAIWA down my throat!" I heard in the Tukwokwe dialect. It was the voice of the great Novel Hunter, JACK LIVVREY.

Not a moment was to be lost. With a dexterous whirl I sent my Paypir-knife whizzing through the air. RITERAGGARD, to avoid it, stepped backwards, and, with a yell such as I have rarely heard, fell on to one of his Pubbeli-Shahs, and both tumbled backwards into their own trap,—a trap intended for one horse, but quite suitable for a different kind of animal.

Raising my kill-bore-repeater, I put the contents of one barrel , BADDELY GOOD just as he was preparing to let off a joke, and he with his face to the earth. It was all over with him, and then, be Sir HENRY COWARDIS could recover from his surprise, I let him l the second barrel, and down he went, too, dead as a two-days' glass of ale. Wheeling round I saw that old villain, ALL QUARTERMAN, preparing a yarn which was to come spinning at head and catch me as in a net. But at the critical moment I let and, with a great groan, he, too, fell lifeless, and, though I a Christian, I cannot say I felt sorry for any one of them. As for beasts of the menagerie, they were only pantomimic mechan animals, after all. Many collapsed like bladders on being pric and others I ordered to be broken up, together with RITERAGGA whole bag of tricks.

When I came up to the trap, I found that it had been turned o and the poor steed, cleverly contrived to imitate a kind of wi Pegasus, had got entangled in the harness, but RITERAGGARD, ha managed to crawl out, had disappeared into the coverts of Koppie-Right. Here he was subsequently found by KONST REDAH, who tortured him for hours by declaiming long extracts f his own eccentric books. I left him to her. It was her reve The poor Pubbeli-Shahs and the other Impis begged for mercy, an I let them crawl away as best they could to rejoin RITERAGGA that is, if anything should be left of him after KONSTANT RED awful torture. They may yet give us some trouble, but I doubt

As to poor JACK LIVVREY, the great Novel Hunter, he threw h self on his knees and kissed my hand in an ecstasy of gratitude, gave him a taste of *Punch*, when he speedily revived, and the recommended him a salutary course of FIELDING, DICKENS, THACKERAY, which he is still pursuing, much to his advantage. is now a book-stall keeper at Victoria Station, and doing uncomm well. Only when the name of RITERAGGARD is mentioned in his hea does a cold shudder come over him, and he tries to hide himself a under the evening newspapers.

* * * * *

And so I went to bed and dreamed that I was in the Garde Parodies, and that all the above was quite true, and woke u happy, wrote every word of it down, and now sign myself,

Yours ever, THE BOLD BARON DE BOOK-WO

P.S.—And just one hint to the sensational author of *Mai Revenge.* Let him procure four small handy volumes published most appropriate binding, by WILLIAM PATERSON of London Edinburgh, entitled *Weird Tales*, and then let him read over a the curdlers writ by ALLAN—not *Quatermain*,—but EDGAR AL POE, and let him study *A Fearful Revenge* (author unknown), wh RIDER HAGGARD would have spun out into three hundred page least, while here it is thrillingly and concisely told in twenty- Those who like Thrillers and Curdlers to shorten their journey in this holiday season, cannot do better than purchase this seri *Weird Tales.*

### Liverpool v. Lambeth.

THE Bishop of LIVERPOOL writes common sense on
The Lambeth "Encyclical" signed Primate BENSON,
Who murmurs, with laugh in lawn sleeves all the while,
"I thought that it might you, my dear Bishop, rile."

### THE MORAL OF THIS SEASON.

"YOU can tell me," said the Intelligent Foreigner, button-hol his London Friend, "what it is called."

"It—what?" was the rejoinder.

"Why, when ladies and gentlemen go into a big field, and si carriages in the rain looking at nothing—what is that?"

"I have no idea."

"And when the same people go to boats on a river, and loo other boats, but always in the rain—always—what is that?"

"I cannot say."

"But you must know," said the Intelligent Foreigner, impatien "When the same ladies and gentlemen go into the country, an on damp benches, and cover themselves with waterproofs—alway the rain—what is that?"

"How should I know?"

"And when these same people go for months here, there, eve where, always in the rain. When they meet morning, noon, night, always in the rain. When they bore one another to death. When they are as dull as ditch-water. Come, you n know? What is it?

"Ah, I have it! A big field in the rain.—Lord's. Storm on river—Henley. Damp benches in the country—Goodwood! Toge for months always in the rain! Why you must mean the Lon Season?"

"You are right," replied the other. "And now, my frien must say good-bye."

And the Intelligent Foreigner left England for ever!

**AWKWARD REVELATIONS.**

*Effie.* "Georgie and I have been down-stairs in the Dining-room, Mr. Mitcham. We 've been playing Husband and ife!" *Mr. Mitcham.* "How did you do that, my dear?"

*Effie.* "Why, Georgy sat at one end of the Table, and I sat at the other; and Georgy said, 'This Food isn't fit to t!' and I said, 'It 's all you 'll get!' and Georgy said, 'Dam!' and I got up and left the Room!"

## PROFESSIONAL OPINION."

A Song for the Season.

Air—" *The Tight Little Island.*"

Daddy Neptune one day
To Britannia did say,
ve seen battles on sea and on dry land,
But by Jove, dear, the Briton
A fashion has hit on
atched until now in his Island.
o! but it raises a smile, and
d Nestor to mirth might beguile, and
I never *did* know
Such a rum sort of go,
is latest sham-fight round your Island.

"By Jingo, my daughter,
This seizure and slaughter
Albion's salt water, and by land,
This very sham guarding,
And bogus bombarding
towns and the ports of the Island,
good Autumn days to beguile, and
and-lubbers like Lawson to rile, and
Make Bannerman jeer
But, my dear, is it clear
t good it will do to your Island?

"No doubt Sir George Tryon
Has fought like a lion,
Admiral Baird is no craven;
Larks, varied with blunder,
And make-believe plunder,
n Liverpool down to Berehaven
course may be really worth while, and
ach Jack to steer cruisers in style, and
Improvement fast press on;
But what 's the true lesson
Manœuvres like this teach the Island?

"Blockading Lough Swilly
In vain does look silly;
A big hostile fleet close to dry land
Destruction and pillage
Of sea-port and village
May raise a wry laugh round the Island.
Ineffective blockading seems vile, and
To chase the foe many a mile, and
At last let him slip
Without taking a ship
May be war,—but it puzzles the Island.

"Jack Tars are rare jokers,
But shortness of stokers,
And engines that come to grief nigh land,
Are hardly good wheezes,
Scarce funning that pleases
The folks of the tight little Island.
Yes, it 's a snug little Island,
A right little, tight little Island;
But ports held to ransom
Are really not handsome
Or nice things to read in the Island.

"Suppose an Armada
Again should invade her,
This Queen of the Sea, dear, your Island,
Could you do more—or less—
Than in days of Queen Bess,
To keep foreign foes from your Island?
There are lots have an eye on the Island,
They would much like to plunder the Island;
And—well, can you say
You've not shown 'em the way
To rifle and stifle your Island?

"Those wise Whitehall 'cakes,'
They all play ducks and drakes
With your wealth, but, my dear, can you spy
Are you clear that your Fleet [land?
Is as sound and complete
As is needful to safe-guard your Island?
The good Wooden Walls of the Island
Are gone; iron ruleth the Island;
But do you quite feel
That with Iron and Steel
You can flout all the foes of your Island?

"Well, Time doth reverse all!
And further rehearsal
May show your Fleet worthy the Island,
But more of it 's needful;
So, prithee, be heedful,
And keep a sharp eye round your Island.
Be sure your officials are movers,
To prove by these Autumn Manœuvres,
Which strike me as funny,
The need of more money
To keep up a Fleet for the Island.

"Britannia and Neptune
Have hitherto kept tune
In each saying, 'This shall be my land;'
Should the foes of Old England,
Or all they can bring, land,
We still must show play for the Island.
We must fight for our right to the Island,
Our Fleet must encircle the Island;
If increase it you must,
My dear, down with the dust,
For it 's worth it, your tight little Island."

---

Tuttle's History of Prussia. 2 Vols. Lucid style. "Clear Tuttle!"

# "A PROFESSIONAL OPINION."

Britannia. "WHAT DO YOU THINK OF IT, FATHER NEPTUNE?"

Father Nep. "WELL, MARM,—IF YOU ASK *ME*,—I'VE SEEN A LOT O' BATTLES IN MY TIME,—BUT BLEST IF I EVER SEE ANYTHING LIKE **THIS**!!!"

## A KNOWLEDGE OF HUMAN NATURE.

"AND SO YOUR NICE CLERGYMAN IS GOING TO BE MARRIED, MRS. MARIGOLD! I HOPE YOU'LL LIKE HIS WIFE AS WELL AS YOU LIKE *HIM*."

"WELL, MA'AM, I'M SURE I HOPE SO—BUT WE GENERALLY FIND THAT WHEN THE GENTLEMAN IS *HAFFABLE*, THE LADY 'S *'AUGHTY!*"

## ROBERT AT THE SEA-SIDE.

LAST Friday, when setting on the Jetty, a thinking of this thing and the other thing, wondering what became of all the Turtel during August, why the Nigger Minsterels didn't wash their faces now there was plenty of water for 'em, or sum ekally intresting matter, I suddnly thort to myself, what a jolly thing it must be to have lots of reddy money. Not Houses, and Lands, and Shares, and all such trubbels, but lots of reddy money. Draws full of golden suvereigns!

I think I knows one thing I should do. I should fill my pocket with about a handfull of 'em every day, and out I should go, "taking my walks abroad," as the Poet says, and I should pay a suvereign for everything, and say to everybody, "that will do." Good Gracious Me, what a idear! I should begin by having my boots cleaned, and giving the boy a suvereign and saying, "That will do, my Lad." I should buy a penny Newspaper, and do the same; then I should go in somewhere and have a little lunch and do the same. Fancy the Waiter's estonishment, poor feller, and then I should call a Handsome Cab, and have a littel ride, and I do believe I should even estonish Cabby; and every time I dined out—and I should take preahus good care to belong to lots of the City Gills—when I asked for my At, I should pitch a sovereign into the plate and walk out smiling at the Waiter's Glee.

Ah! talk about Poppylarity and Riverence, why, I should beat Lord SORLSBURY and MR. GLADSTON, and the Archbishup of CANTERBERRY into three cocked hats.

The Great Dook's was the only case of the sort I ever heard on, and he was, in this respeck, what I think the French calls, Eunick. He used to give a suvereign for a Play Bill and say to the estonished Cellar, "That will do!"

I carries out the idear to some small extent in my own umble way. I buys the *Echo* every day, it's my favorite paper because I finds news there that I don't find no wheres else, and I allers pays a penny for it, for which penny I calkerlate as I gets a haporth of news, and a haporth of respeck, and if there's one thing I pines for, even more than pine Appel, it's Respeck.

It was my Wife's Burthday larst week, so I promist her a bottel of Old Port, to witch she is uncommon parshal, probberbly coz she so seldom gits it, witch is the rule of the Road in most things I fancys. So I gos to the principel Wine Merchant's, and I haraks wot Port wine he had got in stock, jest as if I was a going for to order a hole duzzen at wunse. And the young chap says, says he, quite carm and collected,

"We've got sum '47."

"Sum '47!" says I, with perfound estonishment. "Why, wot's the price?"

"Don't kno," says he; "but I'll arsk the Guvvernor." So he shouts out, "We've got sum '47 Port, ain't we, Guvvernor?" This brort that gennelman out pretty quick, and he says, says he, "'47 Port! No, I ony wishes as we had; but we ain't got no Customers down here for sitch wine as that. Nothink but cheap Claret gos down here," says he, bitterly. "Ah!" says I, "I've had sum xperience of both, and I agrees with what I herd a Alderman say the other day, that Claret wood be Port if it coud." "Rite you are," says he; "but unfortnightly for me, all the Port as I drinks gos down into my grate Toe!" "Ah," says I, "I don't know, and I don't care, where mine gos to, but I allus drinks it wenever I can get it." So I chose my bottel of Port and carried it home in triumf, and werry good it were, and both me and the Missus injoyed it mutch, she ony drinking three glasses and me ony drinking all the rest. And the wine made me that libberal, that I sollemly promist her jest sitch another treet on her nex buthday.

We finnished up our more than ushally large serees of Banquets on larst Wensday week, wen we had all Her Majesty's Minnisters at the Manshun Ouse, and didn't they all look jolly appy to think as their work was all hover till next Guy Fox Day, habsent be the homen! Lord GEORGE AMILTON tried hard to friten us all by telling us all as he had jest reseeved a telacram from the Admeral of the Fleet saying as they had taken Habberdeen and Heddingburrow, and was about starting to hinwade Lundon, when he hoped if they seized our poplar LORD MARE, we shood be quite reddy to ransum him! I was that estonished as I neerly spilt a lot of wine as I was anding round. But I needn't have bin alarmed, as a Gent near me said that fortnetly there was about 14 millyun golden suverains a lying in the Bank close by, and that wood no dowt satisfy the inwaders! But wot a state of things all this reweals! The Prime Minnister didn't seem to care werry much about it, but as he's jest a going off to Deep, in France, of coarse he'll be all right, and can wash hisself of the hole affair. Strange to say too, the Rite Honnerabel the LORD MARE follered his prudent xampel and started for Forren Parts the werry next day but wun, so remembring as the better part of discression was waller, I emediately followed sute, and cum to this littel place where no big iron ship wood ewer think of cumming, coz in the fust place there ain't enuff warter for it to swim in, and next, coz there ain't nuffin much to seeze excep Bathing Mashines and Flys, so I don't let no thorts of inwasion disturb my olliday, but eats and drinks of the best as I can afford, and sleeps the sleep of the onest Waiter.

ROBERT.

## STANZAS TO SIRIUS.

IN the Dog-days, cold the middle
Of Summer as Christmas, then,
In the nature of things a riddle,
Dumfounded dogs and men.
The men—and the women—remaining
Still wrapt in winter attire.
While the dogs, yet the Dog-Star reigning,
Lay shivering by the fire.

If dogs thou hast driven delirious,
Thou hast failed to parch the grass,
So provender's like, old *Sirius*,
To be green for horse and ass.
Not enow to stuff a pillow
Has the farmer mown of hay.
With his storage in the *silo*
He must manage as best he may.

AMUSEMENT FOR SUNDAY IN A COUNTRY HOUSE.—The Hostess, taking a hint from *The Musical World* suggested that all the young ladies of the party should write down the names of their favourite Hymns. After some consultation among the girls, the youngest was deputed to inquire, "Whether they were to add their surnames as well?"

"SUMMARY OF THE PAST SEASON."—Wintry.

"DE GUSTIBUS," &c.

*Darby.* "But, my dear, there are no Microbes in Tobacco."
*Joan.* "Um—Shows their Sense!" [*Subject dropped.*

## THE AUTOMATIC DOCTOR.

[The latest American novelty is an automatic machine at railway stations, which delivers medicines instead of matches or sweetmeats.]

Note the ailment that you 've got,
Cardiac or else hepatic.
Put a penny in the slot,
Lo! the action 's automatic.
Out there comes for every ill
Physic, funniest of notions;
Here a powder, there a pill,
But it draws the line at lotions.

Should a maiden chance to feel
That her frame needs restoration,
There 's a section labelled "Steel,"
Which requires no explanation.
Here the Iron Doctor stands,
For the few or for the many;
Curing, with his liberal hands,
All diseases—for a penny.
Yonder gentleman a drug
Seeks, we 'll say, for torpid liver;
There the pills are lying snug,
This machine 's a liberal giver.
There 's no need for guinea fees,
Or for any drug concoctor;
Just a penny gives you ease
From the Automatic Doctor!

No longer a Bachelor of Arts.—Ex-President R.B.A. James McNeile Whistler is now happily married. Happy, Happy Pair! This lady Whistler is not the celebrated this Season's bird *La Siffleuse, bien entendu*, as the latter has gone back to her own Trans-atlantic Shaw.

A Contribution to Light Literature.—"Gosse's Congreve."

## THE VOICE OF THE VICTIM.

[There are so many Companies started nowadays, that it is difficult to get enough first subscribers to the Articles of Association, and Messrs. Ashhurst, Morris and Crisp make use of the same gentlemen over and over again.]

They bring fresh papers every day,
They show me where to sign;
I dream at night of "Table A,"
And shout "competing line."

No matter what the Company,
I 'm down for just one share;
Though large or small the venture be,
My name will still be there.

At first I used to sign with pride,
It seemed a goodly thing,
With men of means to be allied,
In each financial "ring."

But soon the dream was o'er, and now
I loathe the very sight
Of pens and paper, and my brow
Grows pallid as I write.

I 've come to hate my very name,
To curse the thing I am;
I 'm "limited" in all but shame,
My single share a sham.

I 'm not an avaricious man,
I care not for myself;
But each scheme seems a ghastly plan,
That brings me in no pelf.

Promoters flourish on their tips,
And "booms" within the House;
I sit and watch with hungry lips,
A cat without a mouse.

In spite of everything I sign,
In spite of all I do;
For reasons that I can't divine,
They never raise my "screw."

The money rolls before my eyes,
A true Pactolian stream.
Alas! the golden vision dies,
A base illusive dream.

Promoters come, promoters go,
They gather gold galore;
I know not how, I only know,
I sign for evermore.

The very children seem to lisp
My name, with sounds of scorn,
O Morris! Ashhurst and O Crisp!
Why was I ever born!

## HOW BRER FOX LARFS.

The Society for the Prevention of Cruelty to Animals, and all the Anti-Vivisectionists must rejoice to learn that a Bench of Cheshire Magistrates has decided that foxhounds are no exception to the muzzling order, but liable to be muzzled. Should this decision be enforced, the results of a fox-hunt will be no more unpleasant to the fox than the mere over-exertion of running away, and the consequent exhaustion which will bring the chase to a stop. The fox will be none the worse than if he had been run to earth. How jolly for the fox! If the Bench had consisted entirely of Cheshire cats, they couldn't have come to a more anti-canine decision. It's enough to make a Cheshire cat laugh; and, as for "Sly Reynolds" himself, he 'll go home after a run, use his brush, which he will not have left behind him, and spend a pleasant evening, if his vixenish partner will let him.

## "WELL, TO BE SEWER!"

[The report of the Thames Conservators states that Staines is the only town along its banks which still discharges its sewage into the Thames.]

Can this be true, they say of you,
O sad riparian Staines!
That pure and clean Thames now had been
Save only for *your* drains?

From Twickenham down to London town
Each angler now maintains
That 'tis your sewer makes Thames impure,
O retrogressive Staines!

Of Barking's Creek, its loathly reek,
The ratepayer complains;
And there 's no doubt we shall fall out
With out-falls too at Staines.

The house-boat throng we've borne for long
—They 're nuisances and banes—
But *you* defile for many a mile
The river, dirty Staines!

To name this pest with fitting zest
The prudent tongue refrains;
Richmond and Kew now look to you
To end it, Men of Staines!

"Good Business" on the Moors.—No standing Rooms in the Pits. Boxes full.

## OUR JAPANNERIES. No. 12.

FISHING ROD'RICK DHU ABOUT THIS TIME IN SCOTLAND.

## THE PACE THAT KILLS.

*(Further Correspondence.)*

SIR,—I can hardly find language in which to convey to you the tremendous impression made on me by a journey recently made in one of these newly instituted "Racing" trains to the North. The sense of hurry was overwhelming. From the moment in which I was hustled out of breath, by mistake, with a first-class ticket into the corner of a third-class compartment, to that of arriving at Edinburgh an hour and seventeen minutes late, I never enjoyed a single interval of repose. Imagine the ceaseless whirl through stations, the masters of which were watching the train tear by with a dazed stare. As we swept past Grantham refreshments were flung at us from the platform. We reached York at a tremendous rush. Seven invalid old gentlemen were trodden under foot in their efforts to get into the train.

It seems we had beaten the record by five-and-thirty minutes, which led me to believe that I should be able to partake at leisure of the excellent dinner of soup, fish, two *entrées*, joint, salad, pickles, and bread-and-cheese, provided for the passengers in the refreshment-room. Imagine my surprise, therefore, on being told that, if I wanted to dine, I must do it in three minutes and a half; and as "beating the record," as the waiter smilingly observed, "was the order of the day," I got through as much of it as I possibly could in

## AU MAGASIN DU LOUVRE.

"Combien en voulez-vous, Madame?"

"Oh!—er—let me see—Five Yards—Sank *Kilometres*, n'est ce pas?" [*Stupefaction.*

that limited time. So great, though, was the scurry, that I found myself again *en route*, without having had an opportunity of paying him. And now our troubles began. At Thirsk, after struggling heavily against the north-east wind, our engine broke down. This was replaced, but our pace did not mend, and a few miles before Berwick we came to a dead stop. Inquiry confirmed my worst fears. It seemed that the strain had proved too much for them, and that the guard and driver had both gone off their heads simultaneously, and had to be removed to a neighbouring lunatic asylum. Owing to these *contretemps*, we reached our destination somewhat behind time, but found the officials nothing daunted, but full of enthusiasm, they having just heard that the rival Company's express had only just got in with both its driving-wheels off. They are therefore confident that to-morrow will again find the Company "beating the record." How long they will continue to do so is a problem that puzzles your much-impressed and over-wrought contributor,

A Stitch in Time.

Sir,—It is all very well to cry up the magnificent performance of running 200 miles without a break, but I would caution any intending traveller to see that he does not attempt the feat in a compartment with three escaped lunatics. This was my experience yesterday. The train had hardly moved out of the station before I discovered the dangerous character of my companions. In a few minutes they were all at my throat. The struggle was a long and desperate one, but I am fortunately a bit of an athlete, and by the time we had passed Grantham I had secured two effectively in the umbrella and luggage nets, and had fixed the third with the point of a walking-stick underneath the opposite seat. The last hour passed with these three maniacs glaring at me was, however, not pleasant travelling, and I have certainly no wish to repeat the experiment. Yours, &c., Nothing if not Circumspect.

The following letter, which comes fittingly as a conclusion to the above Correspondence, has just reached *Mr. Punch* as he was going to press; and, as it seems to him to announce a very wise decision on the matter, he has much pleasure in subjoining it:—

Sir,—After three weeks' testing of the racing and other qualities of our respective engines, by which we flatter ourselves they have both, in turns, shown that they have been able, when put to it, to "beat the record," we have determined, by mutual agreement, on and after the 31st inst., to return to our normal ways, and observe, as nearly as we can, the hours of departure and arrival of our trains as fixed in the advertised Time-tables of our respective Companies. The fact is, keeping up "the pace that kills" necessitates the heaping a great deal of coal on—an expensive process, that, as figures will readily show, must soon come to a full stop. Our motto is, therefore, *pro tem.*, "*Requiescamus in pace,*" which means that, for the future, we are going to rest and be thankful with a good, but moderate pace. As long as the "Scotchman" can fly from London to Edinburgh in something like eight hours, we fancy the public will have no occasion to quarrel with

Your obedient Servants,

The Directors of the Two Contending Companies.

## PHILALOO!

### A Lay of the Late Session.

Air—"*Killaloe.*"

Well, 'tis ended as 'twas born, in shindy and in scorn,
The Session whose right name is Philaloo;
It was like a dreadful drame, and seemed shaped upon the schame
That we've laughed at in the land of Parlevoo!
Men did everything but swear at the Spayker in the Chair,
And they hinted he said things that were not true,
And the Irish sort of spite, and French manners *im*polite,
Faith, we've larnt 'em in the school of Philaloo.

*Chorus.*

You may talk of Boneyparte,
His fierce rage was rude as hearty,
But the passions now of Party
Lick the Corsican. Hurroo!
We beat Boulanger aisy,
In coarseness crass and crazy,
In spache that's long, and strong, and wrong,
We shine at Philaloo.

"What, lick *us?*" Mossoo would cry. "Why, of course we can," says I.
"Is that a thing to rouse a Frank's surprise?"
A boy straight up from Clare is the chap to raise your hair,
And—rhetorically—black your Party eyes.
What Mossoo would call "*vacarme*" for all Paddies hath a charm,
So bad language fairly flew about the place.
"Judas!" aloud to cry, and each other give the lie,
Were among the pleasant features of the case.
*Chorus.*—You may talk, &c.

Oh, boys, there was the fun, you should see it ere 'twas done,
All courtesies one by one did disappear;
When the Conybeares and Tanners put an end to all good manners,
The talk sometimes was horrible to hear.
The insult and the oath,—well, there's law agin them both,
But for unwritten codes we need not care.
Fellows find it will not do to talk much at Philaloo,
Unless they've got a curse or two to spare.
*Chorus.*—You may talk, &c.

Well, we've raved about the rint, and a dale o' time we've spint.
Says the Spayker, "By St. Patrick, I'm perplexed.
For when 'gentlemen,' ye see, go on like this at *Me*,
I hardly know what to be up to next."
Had he axed *me*, I'd have said, "You had best go home to bed,
And mix no more in Philaloo affairs.
In the papers soon ye'll trace that our Party Spouting Place
Is closed for alterations and repairs."
*Chorus.*—You may talk, &c.

If Billingsgate you'd try, or give Bargees the go-by,
Or make yourself a blayguard, just for fun,
You've just one thing to do—get a seat at Philaloo,
And your mother soon won't own you for her son.
Sure the endless Party shine is a prisint moighty fine,
But what it *will* be you may well suppose.
For imagine, don't ye see, *what* a Philaloo there'll be,
When the prisint Ayes change places with the Noes!
*Chorus.*—You may talk, &c.

Encore Verse.

Well, I'm glad to find it's true ye're ashamed of Philaloo,
And the conduct of the Mimbers that ye send.
May the Session that is past of *such* Sessions prove the last,
Or Parlyment itself perhaps may end.
'Tis not *only* Irish there who abuse, and rave, and swear,
The Saxon does his share, ye'll find that thrue.
If to "justice" he'll consint, and not ax us for the Rint,
Shure we'll all behave like doves at Philaloo!
*Chorus.*—You may talk, &c.

Foot-note at Covent Garden.—Mr. Crowe is an energetic conductor. Head, hand, and foot are at work, quicker, quicker! Here, indeed, as on an elderly beauty's face, "The Crowe's foot marks the advance of time."

OBSTRUCTIONISTS IN A SMOKING CARRIAGE.

## VOCES POPULI.

A SHOW PLACE.

SCENE—*A Ducal Castle. Party of Tourists discovered waiting in the Entrance Hall. Enter the* Head Butler, *an imposing person with sandy hair and pale blue prominent eyes.*

*The H. B.* (*with condescension*). If you'll 'ave the goodness to wait a little, I shall be able to go round with you myself.

[*Departs with mysterious solemnity, leaving the Party overwhelmed.*

*A Matron* (*who yields to none in reverence for the aristocracy—to her daughters*). Doesn't everything look stately, dears? I wonder where they keep all the hats and umbrellas.

*A Wife* (*to her Husband*). Now, for goodness' *sake*, CHARLES, don't try to be funny here—remember *where you are!*

[*The Party converse in whispers; a Tourist in a Flannel Shirt taps a man in armour familiarly on the stomach, causing him to emit a hollow ring. The rest look at him reproachfully. He returns their gaze with defiance, but edges away from the armed figure as the Butler returns.*

*The H. B.* Now please, if you'll follow me, and keep together. (*Tourists straggle after him, each in deadly fear of catching his eye; the Man in the Flannel Shirt hums the "Marseillaise" under his breath.*) The Banqueting 'All. The Fam'ly takes all their meals 'ere when at Blaisenings. (*Party repeat this to one another in hushed voices.*) The tapestry along the walls is Gobling.

*Charles* (*frivolously*). Ha, very bad example for the family!

*The H. B.* Did you speak, Sir?

*Charles* (*turning red in the face*). Only to my wife.

*Tourist* (*with a turn for Architecture and a desire to air his information*). Er—this portion of the building is—ah—Early Decorated, is it not?

*The H. B.* (*severely*). No, Sir. Decorated quite lately, by a London Firm.

[*The Architectural Tourist falls to the rear; the others conceive a poor opinion of him.*

*A Tourist* (*nerving himself to ask a question*). Will there be many dining here this evening?

*The H. B.* (*with a lofty candour*). Well, no—we 'aven't many staying with us at present. I should say we shouldn't set down more than twenty or so to-night—or thirty, at most.

*A Tourist with a Twang.* Air your Company a Stag-party?

*The H. B.* (*pityingly*). There's no deer-forests in this part of the country.

*The Tourist with a Twang* (*clapping him on the shoulder and laughing*). I see you don't understand our National Colloquialisms.

*The H. B.* I don't understand any Colloqualisms bein' took with Me. (*He moves away with dignity.*) This (*opening door*) is the Hamber Droring Room.

[*A door on the opposite side is seen to shut precipitately as the Party enter.*

*The Reverential Matron.* GWENDOLEN—come over here a minute. (*Whispers.*) She was sitting in this very chair—do you see? I wonder if it *could* have been the Duchess! There's the mark left in her book—if I only dared. (*Reading title.*) *The Mystery of a Bathing Machine.* We'll get it at the bookstall as we go back.

*The H. B.* (*coming to a stand and fixing his eye on a Nervous Tourist, who opens his mouth feebly*). The pair of Vawses on the Consols was brought over by the Grandfather of the present Duke of Ammercloth, and are valued at hover five thousand pounds apiece. We 'ave been hoffered nine thousand five 'undred for the pair—and refused.

[*The Man in the Flannel Shirt groans "'Ow long?" to himself in bitter indignation at the unequal distribution of wealth.*

*The Nervous Tourist.* Did you, though?

[*Regards the H. B. with intense admiration for his judgment and resolution.*

*A Comic Tourist.* I wish someone 'ud offer me nine thousand pounds for the vawses on my mantelpiece. I wouldn't '*aggle* over it.

*The H. B.* (*ignoring him*). The picture in the panel above the chimley-piece is a paregoric subject representing "Apoller, Mercry, and the Fine Arts complimenting the first Duke of Ammercloth on the completion of the new Private Chapel. By 'OGARTH. In the corner. Old woman heatin' a nerring. By Torchlight.

*A Tourist* (*who thinks it is time he made a remark*). Let me see—wasn't he one of the Dutch School? Tautschlyt. Torschylt. I seem to know the name.

*The H. B.* (*tolerantly*). No, no, Sir—you didn't foller what I said. It wasn't the name of the artis—it's what the old woman is heatin' the 'erring by, in a cellar. The cellar and the 'erring is considered masterpieces.

*A Young Lady.* What a very curious method of cooking fish, isn't it? [*The Party move on.*

*H. B.* This is His Grace's own Study. His Grace sees his tenants at that table.

[*General interest in the table, except on part of the Man in the Flannel Shirt, who suppresses a snort.*

*Charles's Wife.* Fancy, CHARLES—the Duke uses "J" pens!

*Charles.* Not even gilded! This is a severe blow, CAROLINE!

[*Pretends to be overcome.*

*His Wife.* If you go on in this foolish manner, I will not be seen talking to you.

*The Reverential Matron* (*in a whisper*). ERMYNTRUDE, see if you can manage to pick up a nib when no one's looking—there are plenty lying about.

*A Tourist* (*anxious to propitiate the Butler*). An excellent landlord, the Duke, I believe?

*The H. B.* (*coldly*). We 'ave not 'eard of any complaints on the estate. (*Leads the way to the Gallery.*) The Hoak Gallery—formerly the Harmry. When we 'ave a large 'ouse party, they sometimes comes up 'ere after dinner, and 'as games.

[*Expressions of pleased surprise—always excepting the Man in the Flannel Shirt, who mutters something about "dancing on volcanoes."*

*A Tourist* (*with a thirst for information*). What sort of games?

*The H. B.* (*with dignity*). That I can't tell you percisely, bein' no part of my dooties to participate. (*Halting before a picture.*) Portrait of 'ENERY HALGERNON, Second Marquis of SEASPRINGS, beyeaded on Tower 'Ill by Sir PETER LELY.

*Charles the Incorrigible.* Do you mean that Sir PETER took his head off?

*The H. B.* (*solemnly*). He took his Lordship off full length, Sir, as you can see by looking. (*To the Reverential Matron, whose demeanour has not escaped him.*) If you like to stop be'ind, and let the rest go on a bit, I can show you something that's not generally open to the Public. (*Mysteriously.*) It's the room where all his Grace's boots are kep'. He has over a nundred pair of them.

[*The Matron rejoins the rest in a state of solemn ecstasy, and can hardly refrain from betraying how highly she has been privileged. The Party return to the Hall.*

*A Tourist* (*a diligent student of the Society paragraphs in a Sunday paper—to Butler*). Is Lady FLORILINE at home just now?

*The H. B.* Her Ladyship is away visiting at present, Sir. Expected back Saturday week, Sir.

*The Society T.* (*as if he felt this as a personal disappointment*). Not till Saturday week?—really!—ah! (*The rest regard him with increased respect, and listen attentively.*) I suppose it's quite true that the match with Lord GEORGE GINGHAM is broken off. Going to marry Lady SUSAN SUNSHADE, isn't he? I was very sorry when I heard of it (*feelingly*).

*The H. B.* Was you hintimate with 'is Lordship, Sir?

*The S. T.* (*with a modest reserve*). Oh, I've stayed with him, you know, and that sort of thing.

[*He has—at a Swiss Hotel, when* Lord GEORGE *took him for a Tout,—but what of that?*

*The H. B.* Then I should certingly recommend you to inquire of Lord GEORGE in pusson, Sir. That's his Lordship coming up the terrace now. [*The S. T. collapses utterly.*

*Ermyntrude* (*coming up to her Mother*). Oh, Mamma, what *do* you think? We looked in at a window as we passed, and we saw them all having afternoon tea. And the Duchess was actually eating buttered toast. She didn't see us for ever so long—we had *such* a good view!

[*Scene closes in upon the majority of the Party, anxiously discussing in undertones the propriety or otherwise of offering any, and what, fee to the Butler, who stands apart in a brown study, with a distinct effort to mitigate the severity of his expression. As far as the Man in the Flannel Shirt is concerned, the problem* "solvitur ambulando."

## UP AGAIN!

*Madame La République loquitur*:—

*MON DIEU!* He's up again, though with much splutter.
It seemed that his submergence was so utter!
  But to the surface struggles he once more.
*Pouf-f-f!* No, I cannot say that he looks dignified:
But by his frog-like sprawl one thing is signified,—
  That "*P'tit bonhomme*—BOULANGER—*vit encore!*"

There seemed an end to his thrasonic clowning.
But it appears that he is proof 'gainst drowning,
  Like—well, to specify were too invidious.
Pinked by the "Usher," plunged into the flood
Of Ridicule that's like a bath of mud,
  Here he is once again, alive though hideous!

*Que faire?* I feel that I should relish greatly
To "bonnet" him as I did PLON-PLON lately.
  'Twould simplify my task if he would sink;
But one can't drown a cork that just bobs under
And then pops up. What will France say, I wonder?
  And what, I wonder more, will BISMARCK think?

What is he? What's his aim? Which is his Party?
Is he a sort of Brummagem BUONAPARTE?
  A squeezable and clayey mask of CÆSAR?
Who pulls the wires of this pert popinjay?
Am I indeed to be upset one day
  By this preposterous, spray-spluttering sneezer?

I feel he is *my* foe. A foe *pour rire?*
Or one *fou furieux* more whom I've to fear?
  *Our* geese betray the Capitol, not save.
My fools are my undoing. Despot sane
Were better than a CLEON cracked and vain.
*So* you, my master, "popping up again,"
  Spluttering, but with his head above the wave?

**DIAGNOSIS.**

*Cabman (insolently, on receiving his right fare).* "WHA 'S THIS 'ERE FOR?"
*Fare (promptly).* "WELL, I SHOULD SAY 'FOR DRINK,'—IF YOU ASK ME,—BY THE LOOK OF YOU!"

## COLWELL-HATCHNEY MUSICAL FESTIVAL.

(*Contributed by a Sufferer from the Music of the Present and the Future, at present residing at the Colwell-Hatchney Musical Academy.*)

To commence at common time, four in a bar. There will be sixteen in the American bar.

Opening Chorus accompanied by the

LIGHTEST GUITAR IN THE MUSICAL WORLD,

weighing only two pounds ten. The Second Part of the Festival will be in harmony with the First, and taken at the same time.

Conductor, MR. SAMMY TONE.

(*By kind permission of the London General Omnibus Company.*)

At the word of command, "Full inside! All right!" the Concert will go on with

"*I know a Bank.*" . . . LOTHBURY, E.C.

After which an instructive Lecture on

TAKING DOWN SWELL SHUTTERS,

and opening the Shop for the day, will be given by

*The Leading Assistant Boy*

in the establishment of Messrs. NARROWOOD & Co. (successors to BROADWOOD).

Duet in Scale Armour by Little FRESH HEGNER and B. OFFMAN—
"*Oh, would I were a Fish!*"

To be followed by a Squintette entitled, "*Eyes right! So you are!*" After which there will be

ATHLETIC MUSICAL EXERCISES,

Including *Sliding Scales on the Zither* by Unknown Members of the Accidental Club. N.B.—A Surgeon with musical instruments in attendance. No danger.

RUNNING UP-AND-DOWN-THE-PIANO RACE.

*Five-Year-Olds only entered*
after weighing in the Chromatic Scale.

FLAT RACE over two Grand Pianos. To be won hand over hand.

CHORUS—"*Fingers were made before Tuning-Forks.*"

After which a Practical Lecture on "*How to Score a Treble for the Orchestra,*" by Signor RUBBERINI, assisted by Three Dummies.

Swimming Contest from C. to C. *in puris naturalibus.*

AIR—"*See me Dance the Poker,*" composed about the time of ALFRED the Grate. After which

THE GRAND MUSICAL TOURNAMENT—THE PITCH BATTLE.

By the entire strength of the Company, with Pitch-forks.

To be followed by the Hailstone Chorus, with real Hailstones, and a Grand finale of

ORGANIC REMAINS.

The Chair will be taken by the first person present, singular number, and the Vice will be represented by A VIRTUOSO.

*Admission by Playing Cards only. When in doubt play Penny Trump. No False Notes changed.*

Tea and Shrimps will be served (if the Shrimps like it) in the Antea Room.

Overtures will be made to everybody inclined to assist in the charitable object. There will be a collection of umbrellas and walking-sticks at the doors, which will be given to the *Universal Lemon Aid Society*. Hon. Sec., Mr. SQUASH. Address, Monday Ginger-Pop Concerts.

After the Concert the entire Chorus, Principals of all the Academies, and the Audience will join in the Irrational Anthem from

HANWELL'S ORATORIO.

After which a March Past, three shies a penny, SARAH SARTY, fireworks (which may be procured at the doors by those who have neglected to bring them in their pockets), grand free distribution of everybody's umbrellas, and procession round the ruins. *Sic transit gloria mundi! Pop goes the Weasel!* (*Signed*) BY ANYONE.

*N.B.—Order not admitted after the first row.*

---

"THE RACE ACROSS THE ATLANTIC" (*contributed by Master Tommy, at home for the holidays*).—Why, the American, to be sure!

THE LAWS OF HEREDITY ILLUSTRATED.

*Grigson (who has tripped up his friend Professor Grumpson's campstool just as the latter was sitting down on it).* "HI! DON'T! IT'S NO GOOD CUTTING UP ROUGH, YOU KNOW—I *INHERITED* A TENDENCY TO PRACTICAL JOKING, AND CAN'T *HELP* IT—*YOU SAID SO YOURSELF* !!!!"

*Grumpson.* "QUITE SO, MY DEAR FELLOW; YOU'RE NOT TO BLAME A BIT! BUT *I'VE* INHERITED A TENDENCY TO *KICK* PRACTICAL JOKERS, AND CAN'T HELP IT EITHER." [*Kicks him.*

## SONG BY A SMALL SHOPKEEPER.

IN my business as lies in a subub,
Wen there proves weights and measures untrue,
The least mixture in groceries, grub, bub,
Other articles ever so few;
Wot a row, and a 'owl, and a 'ubbub!
And I'm fined if 'ad up for the "do."

A wrong label the same, on conwiction,
In shop-front if exposed to the sight,
Though there mayn't be no 'arm in the fiction,
Or if any, no matter 'ow slight;
So sewere is the legal restriction
Upon dealins as isn't all right.

O, 'ow 'enious, a sample to tender
To the test wot ain't quite true and trim!
A poor tradesman's a petty offender,
And the Lawr will be down upon 'im.
Now the rule is, "Look out let the vender,"
Clear of fraud 'e must carefully skim.

But Contractors of wealth and 'igh station,
See wot charges is laid to their dores,
Of all manner of falsification,
Shams, and swindles in Government stores,
Guns and weapons of war for the Nation;
Wot yer calls the defence of our shores!

Them as 'olds a superior position,
Imposition can practise scot-free,
For a rogue of exalted condition
There's one lawr, and another for me.
Nothink wus than a Special Commission
To report upon duffers like 'e.

Then the 'ole blame the "systim" is laid on,
Never no one let in for a fine,
As inflicted small cheaters in trade on.
Jerry Diddlers tiptop may combine,
No detection in diddlin' afraid on.
Oh! 'ow blessèd their potion to mine!

---

ADVICE TO WOULD-BE CYCLISTS.—Tri before you Bi.

---

MEN OF RANK AND STATION.—Railway Cabmen.

## MASTER TOMMY'S DOMESTIC MANŒUVRES.

*Suggested by some Recent Make-believe Naval Experiments.*

*How to Make them Fancy the House is on Fire.*—Having prepared two of the top-floor chimneys, by stuffing them with the contents of several feather pillows steeped in petroleum, light these, and proceed quickly to the coal-cellar, where, kindling a large bonfire of newspapers, old school-books, kitchen chairs, and door-mats, rush up the stairs, crying "Fire!" at the top of your voice, and raise the alarm. The house being by this time full of blinding smoke, shout to the butler to open the back windows, and pump freely into the rooms with the garden-engine. This will increase the consternation, but you will have to provide for the excitement of the crowd that will have by this time collected in front of the house. To do this, rush to a window on the second floor, and, flinging it wildly open, tear bed-curtains and sheets into lengths rapidly, and join them together for an escape-rope. Now, having secured the page-boy, and threatened him with a thrashing if he makes any resistance, let him down by this into the area. To give more effect to this, do it with jerks. This will have so impressed the crowd that they will have already summoned the Parish engines, that will now be playing vigorously on the front of the house, and drenching it from top to bottom. The origin of the "Alarm" having by this time been discovered, you will probably be called on for an explanation, whereupon, pointing to the fact, from experience, how well they would have been prepared to meet it, *if there had been a real fire*, you express your complete satisfaction at the result, and frankly intimating that you now consider the incident closed, refuse to enter into any further conversation on the matter.

*An Impromptu Little Dinner.*—This experiment may be best tried at the house of an invalid uncle and aunt, who are noted for their hospitality, and pride themselves on the excellence of their *cuisine*, the object being to show how, with scarcely any preparation, a very satisfactory dinner may be provided on the spur of the moment for a decent number of perfectly unexpected guests. Getting hold of your aunt and uncle's visiting-list, proceed to ask four-and-twenty of their friends to dinner at a short-date, taking care to tell them there is "no need to reply to the invitation." The day at length arriving, and the guests beginning to assemble, hurry out and order in twenty-four bloaters, the same number of mutton-chops, and two dozen of stout respectively from the fishmonger's, butcher's, and the public-house in the immediate neighbourhood. The dinner is now provided. After some awkward pauses in the conversation, your uncle and aunt still being unconscious of the reason of the assembling of their guests in their drawing-room, the butler, much to their surprise, now announces it, and all forthwith adjourn down-stairs to partake of the repast. This does not take long, and the guests, the matter still being unexplained to them, and, rather resenting the fare that has been provided for them, depart early, taking their leave more or less abruptly. Your aunt and uncle being at last left alone, though still profoundly puzzled at the whole proceeding, are bound to admit that, although they have not done it exactly in the style they would wish, they have most undeniably given a *quite impromptu little dinner*.

---

## A FRAGMENT FROM A ROMANCE—A SUGGESTION FOR SCARBOROUGH.

HE was followed everywhere! At last it became unbearable. He resolved that, come what would, to learn his fate. He turned round sharply by the sad sea waves, and faced them. For a moment they shrank back abashed.

"What do you want?" he asked, sternly.

There was a dead silence! Then one of them, extending a bronzed hand, cried, in an appealing voice,—

"A penny, good Sir—a penny!"

His eyes flashed fire, and he indignantly refused the boon.

"A penny, good Sir—a penny!" they repeated, with increased importunity.

Then he hurled at them a defiance.

"If you are not off at once, I will give you into the custody of the Police!"

With an unearthly yell, they threw up their arms, and, taking to their heels, disappeared for ever!!

## THE PLEASANT WAYS OF GLORY.

LORD WOLSELEY, when recently giving his evidence before the Army Estimates Committee, admitting that while an English Major-General of Brigade received £1279 per annum, an officer of corresponding rank in the German Army drew only £700, seemed inclined to defend the anomaly on the plea that what was expected socially of the former in this country would not enable him to do it for a lower figure. Indeed the distinguished witness went further than this. Alleging that the rates of pay for regimental officers were fixed at a time when men purchased their commissions, he proceeded to admit that this same time was one when the Army was looked on as a profession into which men went very much for their amusement, for which they paid partly themselves. Quite so.

"List, List, oh List!"

But with all respect for the opinion of "Our Only General," it may surely be pointed out, that whereas now the Army is decidedly not a profession into which men go "only for their amusement," it need not follow that the traditions of expensive living formerly regarded as its inevitable social concomitant must be accepted as an official necessity from which there is no means of escape or evasion. Yet that some sort of idea of the kind prevails, and is generally accepted as a palpable though unpalatable fact, there cannot be any doubt. No subaltern can live on his pay, nor is he expected to. Indeed, every obstacle is put in his way to prevent him.

Plain DICK and HARRY, as soon as they are out of Woolwich or Sandhurst, and who in many cases have sat down at home in perfect contentment to the family dinner on cold mutton, find themselves suddenly waited upon by flunkeys in plush breeches, and living *en prince*, surrounded by all the luxury and comfort of a well-appointed London Club. There is no getting out of the expenditure, and the subaltern's pay is, as a matter of course, immediately swamped. And the evil seems to permeate the whole system, for the officers of higher rank appear to be no better off, Lord WOLSELEY alleging that he had known men who had refused commands because they were expected to entertain the whole neighbourhood, and could not in consequence cover their expenses out of the pay they received.

In fact, the life of the British officer, as thus revealed, seems to resolve itself into a prolonged struggle to keep up a false position on insufficient means. And at present there seems but little hope of any remedy. For when we have only about two hundred of the new guns ready, and two thousand are required, and when our foreign stations, wanting an equal number, are supplied as yet only with twenty, and whilst the non-commissioned officers and men in the British cavalry number 18,500, and the horses to mount them only reach the figure of 11,800, to say nothing of departmental shortcomings and blunders cropping up daily on all sides, it seems almost futile to raise a fresh cry about such comparative trifles as heavy mess bills and excessive regimental expenditure.

Still, when the lively difficulties and dangers that at the present moment threaten the Army have been in some measure lightened and alleviated, it might be worth the while of Our Only General to try to set on foot some reform that would teach the British Officer that, to place before himself a simpler standard of living, and one more compatible with his means, would in no way derogate from his claim to be considered an English Gentleman.

---

THE BEE AND THE HONEYMOON.—The wedding-dress of the Princess LETITIA, who is shortly to be married to her uncle, the Duke of AOSTA, is to be embroidered with Bees, the emblem of the House of BONAPARTE. No doubt the "going away" costume of this young lady, who has made so singular a choice in the selection of a husband, will also include a bee—in her bonnet!

## THE TRIUMPH OF CAPITAL.

### AN ODE.

(*Picked up at the Crystal Palace, after the National Co-operative Festival, August 18, 1888; and presumed to be intended as a sort of poetic counterblast, from another point of view, to Mr. Lewis Morris's optimistic Ode, "The Triumph of Labour," sung by 4000 Voices on that occasion.*)

COME, let us sing together an old song,
The triumph of the truly strong.
The victories of Gold we celebrate.
Our Mammon still is great.
Let us our chuckling voices tune to praise,
Come, let us sing together the old and joyous song!

Who threatens to emancipate the clown?
Free workmen from their master's frown?
We wish them joy of their preposterous task.
Mammon may wear a mask,
Of too bold flaunting of his gains afraid,
But still the Sons of Toil are Slaves of Trade.
Interests, in union strong, the workers' claim disown.

There is a strife not fought with sword or gun,
Where, 'midst smug Peace, War's wrong is done;
Still, face to face, in hostile camp they stand,—
Capital, Labour's band,—
The rich man holds his own with smiling ease,
And if sham pæans do the poor man please,
Let the fools tootle; it is rare good fun.

"Time's curse is almost done"? Nay, friend, not yet,
Whilst grabbers grab, and sweaters sweat.
Optimist bards may pipe the pastoral reed;
Pan-pipes won't soften Greed.
Were workers really "strong through brotherhood,"
Panic would swiftly spread through Mammon's brood;
But, spite of poet's song, there's little danger yet.

Pooh! Let them pipe, and for one day rejoice;
Let maudlin MORRIS give them voice;
We know that what has been, is, and shall be.
LEWIS, your fiddle-de-dee
Of optimistic Odes won't give Man power.
Eh? "Peaceful union bloom a perfect flower"?
Nay; much more like a "plant," for all their noise.

Co-operant donkeys bray forth solemn mirth;
*Ours* is the fulness of the Earth,
Culled by strong hands, whose labour magnifies
The harvest that we prize.
Look round! and see how rich that harvest grows!
Whilst *we*'ve Wealth's golden fruit and Pleasure's rose,
Labour's last "triumph," bard, though loud, is little worth.

See how around the slums the cellars fill
With triumphs of the Sweater's skill;
"The man's strong work, the woman's deft and fine,"
To swell our hoards combine.
See them sit pinched and pallid, dull and dumb;
In that strange den, that's dubbed an English home,
E'en children work; play their poor mouths won't fill.

Therefore let Toil make merry and seem glad;
The vision need not make *us* sad;
We, in Wealth's wider, stronger brotherhood,
Cling close, for our own good.
We sing the only bond that really binds,
God Mammon's golden link. Wealth little minds
The thing poor fools call "Union,"—they are mad.
And we—we sing together our old and joyous song!

---

QUITE BRADLAUGHABLE.—An evening paper observes, "that while Christians orthodox and heterodox are ready with their millions to endow churches, there does not seem to be a single wealthy unbeliever who is willing to endow Mr. BRADLAUGH, or even to rescue him from the debts by which he is embarrassed." Of course, as the Junior Member for Northampton is a person of ability, this is very very sad; but as the Agnostic by his name announces that he "knows nothing," it is not altogether strange that he should avowedly remain in ignorance of the requirements of his distinguished, but alas, unfortunate co-anti-religionist. Mr. BRADLAUGH may be a big gun in his own circle, but, when the hat goes round, he is not likely to provoke quite as much enthusiasm as an eminent ecclesiastic—say, as a Canon of a cathedral.

## OUT OF TOWN.

(UNFASHIONABLE INTELLIGENCE.)

MR. AND MRS. WILLIAM NUPKINS (AND FAMILY) ARE SPENDING THE SUNDAY AFTERNOON ON HAMPSTEAD HEATH.

## "MY HEART'S IN THE HIGHLANDS."

(*New Version of an Old Song.*)

Mr. P——L *sings :—*

MY heart's in the Highlands; it long has been here;
My heart's in the Highlands, a-chasing the deer.
The hills of ould Erin are greener, I know,
But for sport, at this moment, they're plainly no go.
My heart's in the Highlands, &c.

This is clearly the place for this species of game.
Here I think I may manage to track and take aim.
'Tis a monster, and proud of its high-antlered crown;
But just give me a chance, and I'll yet bring it down.
My heart's in the Highlands, &c.

My heart's in the Highlands. Great GLADDY is clear
That if I've a chance of success, it is here.
He knows the ground well, and he wishes me luck.
Well, *I* wish it were night, and the quarry well struck!
My heart's in the Highlands, &c.

I shall manage a pop at you yet, please the pigs!
Though I do feel a little bit like poor old *Briggs :*
My elbows so ache, and my knees are so sore:
Still I'm bound so stalk on, though it's rather a bore.
My heart's in the Highlands, &c.

They didn't expect me—those Cockneys did not—
To come out as a crack Caledonian shot.
GOSCHEN's swaggering challenge of course was mere bluff.
Horroo!!! Yet I wish that these rocks were less rough.
My heart's in the Highlands, &c.

Yes, my heart's in the Highlands,—but so are my legs,
Which are stiff at this moment as two timber pegs.
But oh, just to hear a swift bullet go cr-r-raunch
Through yon animal's back-bone, or into its haunch!
My heart's in the Highlands, &c.

How little they like me, the Sassenach lot!
A sleuth-hound's slow patience, *plus* skill as a shot,
Are needful for stalking a quarry like yon.
Well, a lesson we'll learn ere all here is done.
My heart's in the Highlands, &c.

All hail to the Highlands! All hail to the North!
The home-land of WILLIAM, the country of worth!
And if to yon brute its quietus I give,
I'll shout for Auld Scotland as long as I live.
My heart's in the Highlands—that is to say, *here*—
My heart's in the Highlands, a-chasing the deer.
Believe, "brither Scots,"—I assure you 'tis so,—
My heart's in the Highlands wherever I go!

## A GOOD JOKE (FOR CLIENTS) FROM THE LAW COURTS.

HIGH COURT OF JUSTICE, CHANCERY DIVISION.

*Counsel* (*addressing Vacation Judge*). My Lud, in this case I appear to ask your Ludship for leave to have a petition to wind up a Company answered at an early date. Under a special Act of Parliament passed on the 13th of August, 1888, the Court has jurisdiction to wind up this Company under the provisions of the Companies Acts.

*Learned Judge.* I wish it to be known by the Bar that Judges who sit in the Vacation have no knowledge of recent Acts of Parliament. Some order has deprived the Judges of notice of Acts of Parliament formerly sent them. I cannot accept notice by hearsay. Let the petition go into the general list.

*Counsel.* Very well, my Lud. But——

*Learned Judge.* Extremely sorry. Call the next action!

HARNESSED TO A NIGHTMARE.—It appears, from a letter of Sir WILLIAM FRASER to a contemporary, that the Duchess of RICHMOND's ball at Brussels, on the eve of Waterloo, was given in a coach-house. Thus the identity of the site of this rather gruesome entertainment no longer remains without a stable foundation.

"MY HEART'S IN THE HIGHLANDS!"

Mr. P-rn-ll. "I CAN GET AT HIM BETTER FROM HERE!!"

## A LITTLE HOLIDAY IN SCOTLAND.

*Energetic Friend.* "NOW, JACK, STOP WHERE YOU ARE, AND YOU'LL GET A SPLENDID SHOT IN HALF-AN-HOUR OR SO!"

[*Jack is thinking that by that time it will be dark, and then what's to be done?*

## FOR NOW IT IS SEPTEMBER!.

SCENE—*Sanctum of a Daily Paper.*

Editor *and* Faithful Contributor *discovered in consultation.*

*Editor.* I am afraid that Bethlehem Hospital, Marriage, Smoking, and the Irish Exhibition, are used up.

*Faithful Contributor.* Surely, not quite. For instance, about the last. Couldn't I write indignantly about the Cork Band under the signature of a Field Officer's Widow?

*Ed.* Scarcely. The musicians, who had not progressed sufficiently far in their art to play the "*National Anthem,*" will have gone back to Ireland before we shall have had time to get published.

*F. C.* Might I not remind the G. O. M. that once he liked Marmalade better than Jam, and quote from *Hansard* to prove it, eh?

*Ed.* Fancy people are growing rather tired of these raked-up little inaccuracies of the Ex-Premier.

*F. C.* Could I do anything in the Matrimonial line?

*Ed.* I am afraid not. You see you have already written as "A Mother of Six Daughters," "Little Toddlekins," "An Engaged Young Man," "Nellie," "A Retired Physician," "A Sensible English Girl," and "Anti-Latch-key," and are getting rather monotonous. Can't you think of something new?

*F. C.* Well, there is the British Museum. They say that the Reading Room is full to overflowing with people who come there only for recreation.

*Ed.* Why shouldn't they? If anyone is to be excluded, why not the professional bookmaker who lives on scissors and paste? Besides who cares for the contents of the British Museum? Far too valuable and useful to attract attention. Now, if anyone had been interfering with the pigeons or the drinking-fountain outside the entrance, that would be quite a different matter. No, we must get something else.

*F. C.* The Bakers seem to have a grievance.

*Ed.* So long as the British Public has rolls for breakfast, they can grieve. If it were a question of adulteration, that would put a new complexion on the case. And even that subject would sure to end in a gratis advertisement for Somebody's Patent Home-Made Loaves. Try again.

*F. C.* Lord WOLSELEY is going to live at Greenwich. Can't we say anything about that?

*Ed.* Only that he will have increased facilities for taking shrimps with his tea.

*F. C.* The Scotch Express——

*Ed.* Is to race no more, but to travel at the leisurely rate that we love so much—on paper!

*F. C.* Anything at the theatres? Barring PENLEY, the new entertainment at the Comedy is the reverse of novel.

*Ed.* Oh, I think we may leave the Drama alone at this season of the year. Nobody expects anything notable until the middle of September.

*F. C.* Foreign affairs?

*Ed.* Sick of them. Besides, there aren't any. Same old story. BISMARCK mysterious, and BOULANGER blatant. Two B.'s might suggest industry, but, on the whole, they don't.

*F. C.* Well, then, what *shall* I write about?

*Ed.* Don't know, I am sure. What you like.

*F. C.* What do you say to GLADSTONE and Lucrative Strawberries?

*Ed.* GLADSTONE and Gigantic Gooseberries would be more appropriate to the season of the year; but do what you please.

*F. C.* And can't I have another dash at "How to Prevent Sleeplessness."

*Ed.* Well, no. I think our readers will be able to discover a cure for *insomnia* for themselves!

[*Scene closes in amidst sounds of slumber.*

## A WORD ON BEHALF OF A PERSECUTED RACE.

WHAT a blessing is a sympathising Mother-in-Law! How beautifully she rounds off all the sharp corners of life's right-angles. And when, as in my case, she happens to be blessed with a large amount of exquisite literary taste, accompanied with a devotion to truthfulness that nothing can shake, where could a confiding Son-in-Law look for a more perfect treasure?

We have been spending a few days at Eastbourne, my Wife, my Mother-in-Law, my Brother-in-Law, ALFRED, and myself. My Wife being an invalid, and ALFRED being fond of sailing, which I emphatically am not, Mother-in-Law accompanies me in my daily stroll, and I find her quite a model companion. Being of what is called, I believe, a literary turn, I sometimes, on these occasions, try my feeble wing, and soar into the loftiest regions of imagination. It is on these occasions that I find the honest candour of my companion so advantageous. For instance, now, we strolled the other day, despite the merry East Wind, as CHARLES KINGSLEY used to call it, —poetically, of course, for practically, I must confess that I cursed and swore at it nearly all the way home, of course, *sotto voce*, as they say at the Opera,—to Beechey Head. I never, by the bye, remember who BEECHEY was, probably, as I wittily suggested to Mother-in-Law, a distant connection of Sir HIGH BEECH, a Lord of the Manor of Epping Forest, judging by the size of his Head, at which she laughed so merrily that I promised that we should have a Pic-nic there next summer. We strolled about till near sunset, and then turned homeward, when my companion, seeing my ardent look fixed upon the restless sea, asked me what I saw? Without a word of reply I sank down upon the chilly turf, and taking out my pocket-book, I pencilled down, in less than a quarter of an hour, the following thrilling *impromptu*:—

"How the sun shimmers upon Beechey's Head!
While the pale twilight bubbles on the lea!
Hark to the echo of the Coast Guard's tread,
Whose telescopic glance oft sweeps the sea!"

I almost blushed as I placed the manuscript in her hand, and I eagerly watched to see what effect it produced upon that candid and truthful relative. "She read it twice, she read it thrice," as TENNYSON sings, and then taking both my hands in hers, she said, looking full into my eyes, "JOHN, I could not have believed it, had I not witnessed it; why this one stanza contains, not only the exquisite music of SHELLEY, but also the noble realism of BROWNING, and both are combined to make up a picture that will stamp itself for ever on my fond memory."

* * * * *

Who can wonder that on that eventful evening I at length consented that dear ALFRED should reside with us until his Mother could make other arrangements for him. J. LITOUÉ.

NEW NAME FOR THE AGRICULTURAL FOLLOWERS OF THE G. O. M.—Men of Strawberries.

THE LIFE OF THE PARTY.

"I SAY, BROWN, LET 'S TRY AND GET INTO THE SAME MOURNING-COACH AS MAJOR BARDOLPH. HE ALWAYS COMES OUT SO JOLLY ON THESE OCCASIONS!"

## THE DIARY OF A NOBODY.

*August* 11.—Although it is a serious matter having our boy LUPIN on our hands, still, it is satisfactory to know he was asked to resign from the Bank, simply because "he took no interest in his work, and always arrived an hour (sometimes two hours) late." We can all start off on Monday to Broadsteps with a light heart, though nearly half my allotted fortnight's holiday has been wasted in correspondence with the Manager of the Bank at Oldham.

*August* 13.—Hurrah! at Broadsteps. Very nice apartments near the station. On the cliff they would have been double the price. The landlady had a nice five o'clock dinner and tea ready, which we all enjoyed, though LUPIN seemed fastidious because there happened to be a fly in the butter. It was very wet in the evening for which I was thankful, as it was a good excuse for going to bed early. LUPIN said he would sit up and read a bit.

*August* 14.—I was a little annoyed to find LUPIN, instead of reading last night, had gone to a common sort of entertainment, given at the Assembly Rooms. I expressed my opinion that such performances were unworthy of respectable patronage, but he replied, "Oh, it was only 'for one night only.' I had a fit of the blues come on, and thought I would go to see POLLY PRESSWELL, England's Particular Spark." I told him I was proud to say I had never heard of her. CARRIE said, "Do let the boy alone. He's quite old enough to take care of himself, and won't forget he 's a gentleman. Remember you were young once yourself." Rained all day hard, but LUPIN would go out.

*August* 15.—Cleared up a bit, so we all took the train to Bargate, and the first person we met on the jetty was GOWING. I said, "Hulloh! I thought you had gone to Barmouth with your Birmingham friends?" He said, "Yes, but young PETER LAWRENCE was so ill, they postponed their visit, so I came down here. You know the CUMMINGS' are here too?" CARRIE said, "Oh, that will be delightful—we must have some evenings together and have games." I introduced LUPIN, saying, "You will be pleased to find we have our dear boy at home!" GOWING said, "How's that? You don't mean to say he 's left the Bank?" I changed the subject quickly, and thereby avoided any of those awkward questions which GOWING always has a knack of asking.

*August* 16.—LUPIN positively refused to walk down the Parade with me because I was wearing my new straw helmet with my frock coat. I don't know what the boy is coming to.

*August* 17.—LUPIN not falling in with our views, CARRIE and I went for a sail. It was a relief to be with her alone, for when LUPIN irritates me, she always sides with him. On our return, he said, "Oh, you 've been on the 'Shilling Emetic,' have you? You 'll come to six-pennorth on the 'Liver Jerker' next." I presume he meant a tricycle, but I affected not to understand him.

*August* 18.—GOWING and CUMMINGS walked over to arrange an evening at Bargate. It being wet, GOWING asked CUMMINGS to accompany him to the hotel and have a game of billiards, knowing I never play, and in fact disapprove of the game. CUMMINGS said he must hasten back to Bargate; whereupon LUPIN, to my horror, said, "I'll give you a game, GOWING—a hundred up. A walk round the cloth will give me an appetite for dinner." I said, "Perhaps *Mister* GOWING does not care to play with boys." GOWING surprised me by saying, "Oh yes, I do, if they play well," and they walked off together.

*August* 19 (*Sunday*).—I was about to read LUPIN a sermon on smoking (which he indulges in violently) and billiards, but he put on his hat and walked out. CARRIE then read *me* a long sermon on the palpable inadvisability of treating LUPIN as if he were a mere child. I felt she was somewhat right, so in the evening I offered him a cigar. He seemed pleased, but, after a few whiffs, said, "This is a good old tup'ny—try one of mine," and he handed me a cigar long enough almost to put in the umbrella rack.

*August* 20.—I am glad our last day at the seaside was fine, though clouded overhead. We went over to CUMMINGS' (at Bargate) in the evening, and as it was cold, we stayed in and played games; GOWING, as usual, overstepping the mark. He suggested we should play "Cutlets," a game we never heard of. He sat on a chair, and asked CARRIE to sit on his lap, an invitation which dear CARRIE rightly declined. After some species of wrangling, *I* sat on GOWING's knees and CARRIE sat on the edge of mine. LUPIN sat on the edge of CARRIE's lap, then CUMMINGS on LUPIN's, and Mrs. CUMMINGS on her husband's. We looked very ridiculous, and laughed a good deal. GOWING then said, "Are you a believer in the Great Mogul?" We had to answer all together, "Yes—oh, yes," (three times). GOWING said, "So am I," and suddenly got up. The result of this stupid joke was that we all fell on the ground, and poor CARRIE banged her head against the corner of the fender. Mrs. CUMMINGS put some vinegar on, but through this we missed the last train, and had to drive back to Broadsteps, which cost me seven-and-sixpence.

## RAILWAY READING.

THE IDEAL, ACCORDING TO SIR THEODORE MARTIN.

SCENE—*Platform Book-stall.* Stall-keeper *discovered.*

*Passenger* (*entering leisurely*). Can you recommend anything?

*Stall-keeper* (*after consideration*). Well, Sir, if your journey is a long one, would not ALLISON's *History of Europe*, or GIBBON's *Decline and Fall* suit you?

*Passenger.* I thank you, but I think something lighter would please me better. I am leaving busy toiling London, in search of leisure—recreation.

*Stall-keeper.* Then, perchance, the poet's song would please you. We have *Paradise Lost*, that mighty work of mightier MILTON. Or, should you prefer the Drama's claims, here is SHAKESPERE, in twelve handy folios.

*Passenger.* Nay, I know MILTON and the Bard of Avon by heart. I would give prose romance a turn.

*Stall-keeper.* Well, then, Sir, I can recommend an edition, fully illustrated, of that great Wizard of the North, Sir WALTER SCOTT; or prefer you something still more modern? We have the History of Lord MACAULAY, which, they tell me, is quite a romance.

*Passenger* (*smiling*). I see you are fond of quaint conceits; but have you no modern novels?

*Stall-keeper.* Ay! Indeed, we have, Sir! The works of GEORGE ELLIOT and of THACKERAY.

*Passenger* (*hesitating*). And yet I know not how to choose with such a goodly feast before me. Let me see.

*Porter* (*approaching*). Please, Sir, you have missed your train. [Passenger *expresses annoyance, as the Scene closes.*

THE REAL, ACCORDING TO THE FACTS OF THE CASE.

SCENE—*Platform Book-stall.* Stall-keeper *discovered.*

*Passenger* (*entering hurriedly*). Can you recommend anything?

*Stall-keeper* (*promptly*). Yes, Sir. *Dead Beat.* The latest thrilling shocker.

*Passenger.* All right! That 'll do. [*Buys it.*

*Porter* (*approaching*). Just in time for your train, Sir.

[Passenger *expresses satisfaction as the Scene closes.*

## OUR JAPANNERIES. No. 13.

LIKA JOKO GOES YOTTIN.

## A LONG VACATION STORY BY A. BRIEFLESS, JUNIOR.

YOU must know that my Chambers are not entirely my own. As a matter of fact, I occupy personally a circular window divided into compartments and shut in with a green baize curtain from a room of larger proportions (belonging to another tenant), through which I have to pass before I reach my own well-ventilated sanctum. The other tenant and I take about a fourth of the complete suite, the remainder being rented principally by BANDSMAN, the eminent leader of the South Northern Circuit. To tell the truth, we are rather proud of "keeping" (as they say at Cambridge) with BANDSMAN, as we hope to gather some of the briefs that may fall from the great man's writing-desk. I have a very slight acquaintance with him personally, my conversations with him having been composed chiefly of "Good morning" or "Good evening" passed to one another on our meeting in the passage common to both our rooms. However, of course I know him very well by sight, and have noticed that he is a severely precise, neat, and quiet kind of man. I have heard that he intends some day to be Lord Chancellor, and is now, so to speak, in training for that dignified position. My excellent and admirable clerk, PORTINGTON, who, as a rule, is no great respecter of persons, always talks of BANDSMAN with bated breath, and rushes forward to open the outer door when the great man prepares to leave the Chambers. It is necessary to explain this, and further to add, that with the good-fellowship habitual to men occupying the same Chambers, by an unwritten law we are permitted to use one another's rooms in the absence of their proper proprietors. My own particular room is popularly supposed by those of my unprofessional friends who occasionally honour me with a visit, to be the cupboard, in which I keep my wig and gown, when not arguing abstruse points of law with the LORD CHIEF JUSTICE, the MASTER of the ROLLS, and other learned personages. From this it will be seen that BANDSMAN'S apartment is far more imposing than my own.

Some little while ago I had reason to believe that I might receive certain Vacation business from a Solicitor who had been kind enough to say that he considered himself under an obligation to me (I had bailed him out when he had been arrested at two o'clock in the morning while attempting to let himself in with a corkscrew, which it appears he had mistaken for his own latch-key), and consequently I had warned PORTINGTON that should any client ask for me it would be as well if he showed him into the rooms of my co-chamberman, Mr. BANDSMAN.

"He is rather eccentric," I had said, on bidding my excellent and admirable Clerk adieu, "and may possibly be a little excited when he calls; so merely show him in, and do not disturb him if he goes to sleep." PORTINGTON bowed, and said that he quite understood the situation. On the following morning as I was entering my Chambers I was met by an American acquaintance, for whom I have a very deep respect, but who is not entirely accustomed to the staid ways of what he calls this "played-out old country." He button-holed me, and told me that he had been looking out for the London friend of a friend of his in the States. He could not find the said London friend, so now was hunting for the said friend's children.

"My friend's friend's name was SMITH,—ROBERT SMITH," he observed. "He was living in 1824. That is so. I have advertised for his descendants, if any. If you hear from any of them, why just you let me know."

"My dear fellow," I replied, "I shall be only too delighted if I can be of any service to you. But surely it's a little vague——"

"Not at all! A card will do anything in the States. Why not here? I have put your name and address to the advertisement. Yes, Sirree. So if you hear from any of them, why just you write to 'Poste Restante, Rome,' where I am due the day after to-morrow. Good-bye!"

And before I could say anything in response, he had seized my hand, wrung it heartily, hastily jumped into a hansom cab, and was being driven at a gallop towards the Victoria Railway Station.

A little flurried by this rather unexpected encounter, I paused a few moments to regain my composure, and then entered my Chambers.

"He's come, Sir," said PORTINGTON, as I walked in, "and I have shown him into Mr. BANDSMAN'S room. He's rather a rum 'un, Sir; but I suppose it is all right. But you won't be long, I hope, Sir, as Mr. BANDSMAN'S Clerk tells me that Mr. BANDSMAN is coming up to town at two o'clock, and will want to use his room for several consultations that can't wait until the end of the Vacation."

"Oh, certainly, PORTINGTON," I replied. "No doubt I shall not require the room for more than half an hour."

Upon this I assumed my best manner (I usually adopt a cheery and genial air when dealing with clients—it puts them at their ease), and entered the apartment in which my anticipated acquaintance was seated, and greeted him with great cordiality.

"Delighted to see you, my dear Sir," I exclaimed—and then I stopped. To my astonishment I found, instead of my expected visitor a rough-looking person in a velveteen coat and a fur cap, with a newspaper in his right hand, and a thick short stick in the other.

"Ax your parding, Guvnor," said this person, with rather a threatening air, "but I've come about this 'ere advertisement."

He handed me the newspaper with a marked passage in the second column of the front page.

"You are BRIEFLESS, ain't you?" he asked, roughly. I nodded, and glanced at the marked passage. To my horror I found it was a request that all persons claiming relationship with a ROBERT SMITH, living in 1820, should call upon me at my Chambers, when they "would hear of something to their advantage."

"Now," said the person, looking at his stick, "I ain't going for to stand no nonsense. I 'ave wasted 'arf a day 'ere, 'cos I turned up before the doors was opened. BOB SMITH was my uncle. What's the summut I'm going for to 'ear to my advantage?"

I really did not know what to say or do. I could not help feeling greatly annoyed at my American acquaintance's thoughtless impetuosity.

"So you are old BOB SMITH'S descendant, are you, my worthy fellow?" I exclaimed, with a heartiness I was far from feeling.

"None of your gammon," he replied, roughly; "but stump up now you knows my rights. Cos why—if you don't stump up it won't be pleasant for you."

Greatly upset by his threatening demeanour, I was about to remonstrate, when PORTINGTON ushered in two more rough-looking persons and three muscular females. The five additions to our little circle produced as many marked newspapers, and immediately called my attention to what they described as their "rights."

"My worthy people," I began, "I fear there must be some mistake."

They anathematised the suggestion, and all six of them advanced towards me with a demeanour that made me devoutly wish that we had included a police-constable on the strength of our clerical establishment. I saw that I must temporise.

"My good friends, I was a little unprepared for your visit, but if you will wait here a few minutes, I think I can satisfy you. And now I will retire."

The rough-looking men were inclined to bar my exit, but the three females, with the observation "that anyone could see as I was a gentleman as meant to be'ave as a gentleman," suggested that I should be allowed to go on the understanding that I returned in five minutes with the "summut" I had presumedly promised to give them.

The men accorded a grudging consent, and I walked away. Once outside, with a hurried remark to PORTINGTON that I might not return until the commencement of Term, I left my Chambers.

Later in the day I passed Pumphandle Court, and from a loud altercation I heard going on within (in which I distinctly recognised the voice of BANDSMAN raised in angry expostulation), I much fear that my unwelcome visitors (who seemed to be still in possession), had seriously interfered with the serenity that usually is the characteristic of my eminent co-Chamberman's important consultations.

## IS SMOKING A FAILURE?

SIR,—I have not the least doubt that the discovery made by MEDICUS, dating from the Middlesex Hospital, that smoking Turkish and Egyptian cigarettes is most injurious to health, is absolutely correct. I have often wondered why it is that I feel so uncommonly queer after dinner; now at last the mystery is explained. It is all due to the "Wady Halfa Paragons" that I have been in the habit of smoking, but which I shall now abjure in favour of a pipe and some extra strong Virginia shag. I assure you that often and often I have felt just as if my throat were on fire, and have habitually gone to bed in my boots, awaking the next morning with a perfectly splitting headache. Yet I have been most moderate in eating, and have steadily limited my drinking to two bottles of Tokay and half a bottle of Scotch whiskey per evening, which surely nobody can call an excessive supply. Some ridiculous friends have insisted that I am suffering from alcoholic poisoning, and have induced me to try this retreat, kept—I fancy—by a medical chum of their own; but you can judge how mistaken the treatment here is when I say that I am limited to two glasses of weak "Vin Ordinaire" a day, while the presiding physician does not care in the least how many noxious and poisonous cigarettes I indulge in. Need I say that, after these awful revelations of MEDICUS, I have given a weekly notice of my intention to leave this retreat—"beat a retreat," I may perhaps call it—and resume my old modes of life, *minus* my old *penchant* for cigarettes, but *plus* pipes and cigars, *ad lib.*?

Beer or Bier—The Smoker's Mixture.

Yours, eye-openedly, A TOPER.

*The Home for Inebriates, Lostwittles, Cornwall.*

SIR,—my mucous membrane is in an *awful condition!* Do you know what it is to have a couple of Doctors exploring your larynx for three hours, as if it were a part of the Dark Continent? I do. They say that my laryngeal regions—by which I think they mean my throat, only a natural delicacy prevents them putting it so plainly—affords a most interesting study, because in all their experience they have never seen anything look half so bad! This is comforting to me. Now, after MEDICUS'S disclosures as to the horrible "unclassified alkaloid poison" in Egyptian cigarettes, I cannot have a doubt where my illness has come from. Where it will go to, time and my Doctors will have to decide between them. And then for MEDICUS calmly to confess that the alkaloid poison is "unclassified!" I don't feel, however, as if it would do my "laryngeal regions" much good even if it *were* classified.

Yours, mucussedly, A DABBLER IN EGYPTIANS.

P.S.—A sanitary expert has just told us that our house happens to be planted over an old cesspool, and that all the domestic pipes connect directly with it. Possibly, after all, the alkaloid is not so guilty as we thought.

A LESSON FROM THE AUTUMN MANŒUVRES.

THE EFFECTIVE USE OF MOUNTED INFANTRY.

## THE PRINCESS PAPOFFSCHIN'S LITTLE DINNER.

(*A Story à la Mode for Those who Know.*)

THE sitting of the International Conference for the Suppression of Bounties on Sugar had been prolonged to an unusually late hour. The assembled Ministers had been dealing with a delicate phase of reciprocal engagements, and had determined not to separate until they had at least a rough draft of the Convention in something like a completed shape; and having accomplished this, they were about to rise, when a Messenger entered, and handed a note to the Baron.

It was a scented epistle on rose-leaf paper, and ran as follows:—

MON CHER BARON,

You must be weary after your labours of this afternoon, and will need relaxation. What do you say to a *petit diner chez moi* to refresh you? Persuade, then, your good *confrères* to join you, and come, all of you, *sans cérémonie*, just as you are, and honour me with your company. I may, *peut être*, have *des nouvelles de Constantinople* to give you. *Mais, nous verrons ce soir, n'est-ce pas?* Come.

Yours always devotedly, FEDEOREVNA PAPOFFSCHIN.

"It is from the Princess," said the Baron, his face beaming with a kindling radiance as he glanced at the contents of the dainty missive before him. "She asks us all to dine with her quite informally. Listen!" Then he read the little note. There was a murmur of approbation from the Conference. Instantly they rose as if by one accord, and hurriedly collecting the business papers before them, thrust them into their respective coat-pockets. They had all of them only one reply to make. They accepted with enthusiasm. Nor was this surprising. The Princess FEDEOREVNA PAPOFFSCHIN was no ordinary woman.

Born in Russia, she soon after the death of her husband, the Prince, had appeared in diplomatic society in Belgrade, and had rapidly, by her intelligence, tact, and capacity for intrigue, succeeded in getting herself such an acknowledged factor in the stirring political movement of the times that she had received her passports, and had been requested to leave the country at twenty-four hours' notice. Transferring in turns her residence to Vienna, Madrid, Berlin, and other European capitals where similar experiences invariably after a time awaited her, she was next heard of as the intimate friend of several Parisian statesmen of note, and though her career in the French capital had come to a rather sudden termination, owing to the connection of her name with a celebrated *café chantant* scandal, she seemed to have preserved enough of her reputation to assure her a hearty welcome among the leading lights of English diplomatic society. Regarded as intimately acquainted with the secret counsels of the Sultan, her friendship was eagerly cultivated by the heads of the Foreign Office, and it was not an uncommon sight to see her surrounded in some West End *salon* by a thronging crowd of politicians and statesmen hanging on her lightest word. Indeed, it was stated that the Premier himself was so deep in her confidence that the entire direction of his Eastern Policy had latterly been due to her advice and influence. It was not to be wondered at that the Conference accepted her invitation with alacrity. A chance of an informal evening with the fascinating Princess in her delightful mansion in Mayfair out of the season was not an experience to be missed, and at a little before a quarter to eight three four-wheelers conveying the expectant Plenipotentiaries were making their way up Piccadilly to their coveted destination.

In the course of the same afternoon the Princess had prepared for their advent. She had sent for her Major Domo. "I have a little dinner this evening," she said. "We shall be eighteen." Then she added, significantly, "I am expecting *diplomatists*."

The man bowed profoundly. He had understood his orders. He knew that the dishes were to be drugged, and the champagne doctored with morphia.

* * * * * *

Several courses had been disposed of, and the dinner was apparently promising to be a great success. Never was hostess more bewitchingly entertaining; never were guests more enthusiastic. On the right of the Princess sat the Baron, on her left the German Count. The conversation was airy and brilliant.

"How about those promised *nouvelles* from Constantinople, Princess?" asked the Baron, endeavouring to give the talk a practical turn. But his fair hostess only replied with a little timely badinage, and motioned to the servant to fill up her interlocutor's glass with more champagne. So the dinner sped on. The *cuisine* was pronounced excellent, the wine superb. But little by little, almost imperceptibly, the conversation began to quiet down. It halted strangely. Then it dropped altogether. It seemed as if all the guests were gradually becoming so absorbed in some private reflections of their own, that they did not care to break the silence for the purpose of imparting their thoughts to their neighbours. Then some of them closed their eyes.

The Baron, who noticed the soporific influence stealing over him, thought that he must somehow have been taking too much wine, and elected to hold his tongue. He struggled against the feeling for a short time. Then he succumbed. In like manner, in a few more minutes, so did all the rest. And it was not to be wondered at. They had had bromide of potassium in the *Potage à la Maintenon*, and had just partaken of a *Salade à la Russe* mixed with chloral hydrate. This had finished them. They had all of them sunk back into their chairs, overcome by a profound narcotic slumber. Then the Princess rose. She approached the wall, and touched a little brass knob. Instantly a panel slid back, disclosing a chamber beyond.

"*Entrez, Monsieur l'Ambassadeur*," she said, addressing some one within. "*Voyons! Ces Messieurs* are ready to receive you."

She had scarcely spoken when a tall personage, wearing a fez, crossed the threshold. This was the Turkish Ambassador, and he was followed by twelve Secretaries of the Legation.

"You are sure, Madame, they will not wake?" he asked, cautiously surveying the prostrate forms before him.

The Princess replied by striking a loud dinner-gong. Not one of the sleepers stirred. The Ambassador was satisfied.

"To your work, Messieurs," he said, addressing his subordinates. In another minute the pockets of all the unconscious Plenipotentiaries had been rifled of their contents which were being rapidly but methodically transcribed by the practised Secretaries.

The task did not take long. It was over in four hours and three-quarters. The papers were returned to the pockets of the different Ministers from which they had been respectively abstracted. Their coats were carefully rebuttoned. Then the Turkish Ambassador withdrew.

That night he telegraphed to Constantinople in cypher.

* * * * * *

A little later, eighteen cabs in charge of eighteen policemen were conveying the now recovering Ministers to their respective homes. That which contained the Baron, now partially aroused, had drawn up at his own door. As he descended, though still dazed, he seemed to notice the Policeman's uniform.

"Why! what does this mean?" he asked, trying to collect his scattered thoughts. "Where have I come from?"

The Policeman smiled.

The Baron stared inquiringly at the smiler, then staggered feebly up the steps, entered the house, and went to bed.

The next morning the Marquis and the Baron received a telegraphic despatch from the British Minister at Constantinople, informing them that the Sultan proposed an immediate seizure of Egypt.

"That's odd," they remarked, thoughtfully. But they never connected the circumstance with *the Princess Papoffschin's Little Dinner*.

### Poetry and Partridges.

"FIRST Love never lasts," says some stupid old song;
It simply dies out like an ill-lighted ember.
The Poet—as usual—is utterly wrong—
Just look at Man's love for the First of September!
Fickle Romeos may shift in their amorous troubles,
But "First Love" is stable enough—in the Stubbles!

BETSY THE SECOND.—At Hammersmith, the other day, one ELIZABETH TUDOR was sentenced by MR. PAGET to two months' imprisonment for stealing a sovereign. ELIZABETH TUDOR the First anticipated the crime in the matter of MARY STUART. Three hundred years ago it was a case of stealing a sovereign—with an axe! History repeats itself.

## ISRAEL AND EGYPT; OR, TURNING THE TABLES.

"The Children of Israel multiplied so as to excite the jealous fears of the Egyptians. . . . They were therefore organised into gangs under task-masters, as we see in the vivid pictures of the monuments, to work upon the public edifices. 'And the Egyptians made the Children of Israel to serve with rigour. And they made their lives bitter with hard bondage in mortar and in brick, and in all manner of service in the field.'"—*Smith's Ancient History*. "The Sweater is probably a Jew, and, if so, he has the gift of organisation, and an extraordinary power of subordinating everything —humanity, it may be, included—to the great end of getting on. . . . The conditions of life in East London ruin the Christian labourer, and leave the Jewish labourer unharmed."—"*Spectator*" *on* "*Sweaters and Jews.*"

*The screed of the Shade of the Poet* PENTAOUR, *to* PUNCHIUS *that came,*
*Even* PENTAOUR *Bard unto* PHARAOH, *the singer whose song was as flame:*
*The pupil of mild* AMENEMAN, *he painted the lot of the poor*
*In the far distant days of* RAMESES, *who shut on sweet Mercy the door.*

* * * * * * * *

THE form was the form of the PHARAOH, as WILKINSON shows him he stood,—
The pose was exceedingly proud, the perspective, perchance, was not good,—

## CIRCUMLOCUTORY.

*The Parson* (*who likes to question the Boys, now and then, in a little Elementary Science*). "NOW, CAN ANY OF YOU TELL ME——COME, I'LL ASK YOU, DONOVAN,—WHAT IS SALT?"

*Irish Boy.* "IV Y' PLAZE, SIR,—IT 'S—IT 'S"—(*after a desperate mental effort*)—"IT 'S THE STUFF THAT—MAKES A P'TAYTOR VERY NASTY 'V YE DON'T ATE 'T WITH 'T!"

And he looked in the face of the Hebrew, the changeless, the oily, the fat,
Whether crowned with the cap of the Copt, or the Saxon's cylindrical hat.
He stood, and he stared, and he spake: "O! thou Oleaginous One,
Whose tresses so reek of the oil-pot, whose finger-rings flash in the sun,
I, PHARAOH the Pyramid-builder, the slayer of Hittites, the King
Whom PENTAOUR magnified greatly—*my* Laureate knew how to sing;—
I, mighty one named by MANETHO, right well to HERODOTUS known,
I, pictured in wall-paintings many, and chiselled on acres of stone,
I, I was the scourge of the Semites, the Hyksos, the Hebrews, my foes, [nose.
The swart-bearded sons of the shepherds, the slaves of the aquiline
Behold on this rock you perceive them, my heel on their neck, and my scourge [urge
On the hides of them; look at the sticks of my taskmasters, eager to
The staggering slaves to their toil in their agonised thousands, so loth,
Yet helpless as rogues before RA, or as fools in the presence of THOTH.
I made them shape bricks without straw, and the mouths of them scantily fed
With radishes, onions, and garlic, with scraps of affliction's black bread.
Read the ideographical Coptic around them in characters hewn,
And you 'll see that their life was a curse, that the coming of death was a boon. [flail,
When I rose in my might like to MENTU, and lifted like HORUS the
Then the heart of the Hebrew would melt, and the cheek of the Hebrew would pale; [sound,
And now——" Then a chuckle forth crackled, a nasal but jubilant
And a whiff of tobacco and patchouli mingled was wafted around.
A hat took a knowinger rake, and there brake on the sight of the King
The wave of an adipose hand, and the flash of a glittering ring.
A sound 'twixt a creak and a snuffle from lips like an Ethiop's dropt—
All unlike the calm smile of the King, all unlike the clear tone of the Copt—

"Ha! ha! Mr. Pyramid-builder, at present you 're out of the hunt.
Yes, you once gave the Semite the stick, but the Semite now gives you the shunt;
Ask TEWFIK, or good Mr. GOSCHEN! Old CHEOPS, if that's your dashed name—
SESOSTRIS, RAMESES, or what not,—a change *has* come over the game.
Your 'name is a noise' and no more. Yes, the Gentile once 'sweated' the Jew, [that's true.
But the Hebrew has now turned the tables; DUNRAVEN will tell you
You worked us, and whipped us, and starved us; you robbed us of shekels and joy; [old boy.
But now it 's *our* turn, and we 've bettered your ancient instruction,
Look here!——" Then there shaped through the shadows a sordid and sorrowful scene—
There were men pinched, and pallid, and bowed, there were women dishevelled and lean; [was fierce,
And the stress of their toiling was harsh, and the strain of their torture
And the splendour of day might not pass, and the sunlight of hope might not pierce
Through the darkness and damp of the den where they crouched to the Sweater's stern nod,
As PHARAOH's own scourge without pity, and harsh as his task-master 's rod.
The thong-marshalled gang of the sand-wastes were hardly so servile as these,
So helplessly vassals to Mammon—so hopeless of health or of ease.

"That cuts the Copt record, I reckon; makes Mummydom sing rather small. [church wall,
How would *that* look in paint on a temple, or chipped on a ruined
Three thousand years hence, Mr. PHARAOH?" So sniggered the Hebrew, and shook
The soul-sweated gold in his pocket. And lo! an unspeakable look
Was seen on the face of the PHARAOH. And I, Poet PENTAOUR, I saw
That the cycles of time bring no change to the merciless Mammonite maw.

I sang the Rameseïd, I, when Orontes beheld the great King
Wield the sword unresisted of RA; but I also betook me to sing
The pitiful life of the peasant, the prey of the locusts and rats
And men-vermin more merciless yet who took tithe of his barns and his vats. [asleep,
And, behold, though the Sun-God is silent, the Son of the Sun-God
Still merciless Mammon is master, the slaves of the Gold-God still weep;
Be his ministers Hebrew or Gentile, his worship is cruelty still;
Still the worker must sweat 'neath the scourge that the stores of the tyrant may fill.

## DUE NORTH.

*(Some Notes of a very brief Holiday.)*

*Question—Answer—Reasoning—Decision—Indecision—A Departure—Arrival—Invitation—Uncertainty—Certainty.*

HOBSON, with curly fair hair, florid face, and earnest manner, looks in to ask me if I am going away for ten days' change. "No, I am not," I answer. It occurs to me, however, that the tone of my reply, though resulting from a fixed pre-determination, may sound somewhat brusque to my old and valued friend, and so I repeat, in a more sociable manner, "No, I am not," adding a question, also pleasantly, and with an air of apparent indifference, which has in it just sufficient spice of friendliness to prevent my manner towards my dear old friend HOBSON from being entirely unsympathetic—"Why? are *you* thinking of going away for a holiday?"

"How *are* you?"

Yes; HOBSON *is* thinking of it. As a matter of fact, he has so far thought of it that he is now sending a letter to order a berth in one of the London and Edinburgh steamers. "Will I join him?" To do or to attempt doing something I have never yet done, has for me a certain fascination. I have never been from London to Edinburgh by steamer. A minute ago my determination *not* to take a holiday was inflexible; now it is flexible. My iron will—or my iron "won't"—is bent, not broken.

"Not a bad idea," I remark to HOBSON.

He replies that he prefers this way of going North to any other. *Happy Thought.*—"HOBSON'S choice." I do not say this aloud to my old and valued friend, because it is just possible that, his name being "HOBSON," it may have been said to him before.

"Yes," he repeats, after some silent consideration of the subject, "I certainly prefer going by steamer to any other way of getting to Edinbro'."

"Well, but how many other ways are there?" I ask, as, should he be able to mention a greater novelty, I should be inclined to adopt the suggestion.

"I mean," he returns, "that it's better than going by train." I thought so. Putting aside walking, driving, riding, bicycling, tricycling, and ballooning, the alternative is "training" or "steamering."

"Excellent for health!" says HOBSON, who studied medicine years ago in Edinburgh, and, in consequence, has always been consulted by his intimate friends, in an amateur way, ever since. "Twenty-six hours of sea first-rate," he adds, expanding his chest, sniffing and smacking his lips as if at this moment he were actually inhaling the seabreeze and relishing it.

"I'm such a bad sailor," I observe, hesitatingly. "If I go, I'm sure to be ill,—at least," I add, with a reminiscence of a few surprising exceptions to the rule, "it's almost a certainty."

"Do you a world of good," says HOBSON, with an air of scientific conviction. "More good if you're ill than if you're well. I'm going alone; only too glad of a companion. Look here, I'll alter one berth into two berths in my letter." And before I have time to make any further objection he has ordered the second berth, drawn a cheque for prepayment, stamped and closed the envelope, vanished for a second or so as far as the pillar-box, where I see him dropping it in, and at the last moment cannot find it in my heart and voice—("heart and voice," quotation from National Anthem) to call out to him from my window, "No, I won't come!" So, my will, or won't, being temporarily paralysed, and he having sent the cheque for two, I make no further objection, but begin considering what I can do when I once get to Edinbro'.

*Happy Thought.*—If I am ill, as he has studied medicine in Edinbro', he may be able to give me something that'll put me right in an instant. If he possesses the secret, by the way, he ought to make a rapid and colossal fortune out of it. This recalls to my mind a book of travels entitled *The Earl and the Doctor*. They went together everywhere. The Earl with guns and fishing-rods, and the Doctor with medicine-chest. Capital idea for both of them. Excellent for Earl when ill, equally so for Doctor when they returned. Such combinations might be more frequent. *The Captain and the Lawyer*, *The Musician and the Sailor*, &c., &c.; perhaps the best of all would be *The Duke and Two Doctors*, one being M.D., and the other D.D.

Where's HOBSON going? "Well," he explains, "I'm going to pay two or three visits to friends." Ah, then we part at Edinbro'? "Yes, we do." And here he leaves me—as he will in Scotland—being very busy. What shall I do alone in Scotland? "Alone in Scotland," sounds dreary. Of course, the rule is, "When in Scotland, do as Scotchmen do." What's that? It is, I believe, summed up in "bock agen"—which to the experienced Continental traveller is suggestive of asking for another glass of light creaming beer. "Bock agen" with me would mean 'Back again to London.' Bock agen, WHITTINGTON!" But why go all the way to Edinbro' by steamer, merely to come bock agen?"

I am beginning to be almost angry with my old and valued friend HOBSON, in his absence, for leading me into this trap,—a trap to catch a companion,—and I am about to sit down in my sanctum, where my books and papers seem to beseech me to remain, and write to HOBSON a retractation of my decision, when I hear a tremendous shout in the passage.

"Woo-Hoop!"

This is followed by a voice whose tone indicates unusual strength of lung, exclaiming, as if the inquiry were urgent and anxious,

"How *are* you?"

The door is burst open, and, as if impelled by a mighty wind, there appears before me a big man, youngish, beaming with health and high spirits, dressed in a country suit.

"How *are* you?" he repeats boisterously, and then once more, "Old chap, how *are* you?"

In another second he has grasped my hand warmly, and I am delighted to see him.

"Hullo!" I cry out, for his tone is catching, "why what brings you here?"

"Cab, my boy!" he shouts, heartily, he generally shouts, unless he sings, but whatever it is it is done with tremendous and overpowering heartiness,—even his whispers are hearty. "Just on my way to see the Wicked Uncle and Good Aunt. Passing through London——" here he lowers his tone, laughs, and bursts into a snatch of a song—

"Off we go to London Town,
Yeo ho! my boys!
See the King in his golden crown,
Yeo ho! my boys!"

and then he laughs in perfect enjoyment of appropriateness of the quotation and continues hurriedly, "I thought I'd call in" (call *in*,—he means, call *out*), "and say," here he raises his tone again, "How *are* you?"

As nobody ever speaks of him, or to him, but as "D. B.," it is not always easy on the spur of the moment to call to mind what his name really is. When asked, I have to think for some seconds, and, generally failing to remember, I have to answer, apologetically, "Well, really, I forget what his name is at this moment, but we always call him 'D. B.'"

His real name is DAVIE BAIRD, and he is in a general way "in the City" with a partner. Now he is on a holiday, without a partner. Going North.

I tell him that I also am thinking of going North.

"Don't think," he says at once, and just as loudly as ever; "don't think—do it. Come to JOHNNIE BUDD'S. I'm going there now. First-rate fellow! Capital chap! I'll tell him you're coming. You know JOHNNIE, don't you?"

It never occurred to D. B. to ask me this last question before inviting me to Mr. BUDD'S.

I reply deliberately, "Yes—I know him; but not sufficiently well to go to his house without an invitation."

"Nonsense!" he exclaims, quite annoyed with me for making such an objection. Then he bursts into a popular refrain—

"'He's all right when you know him,
But you've got to know him fust.'

"And you'll soon do that," he goes on. "He's an uncle of mine. 'O my prophetic soul!' He'll be delighted."

"But," I protest, "he hasn't asked me."

"No matter," returns D. B. "*I* ask you—your little DAVIE asks you"—he has a way of alluding to himself in the third person—"and that's sufficient." Then he says, in an injured tone, "I wouldn't say so if it wasn't, would I?" To this appeal I am bound to reply seriously that I am sure he wouldn't.

"Very well, then," he returns, brightening up again. "Business is business. I'll tell him directly I arrive. Besides," and here he has hit upon so powerful an argument that he must shout louder than ever, "he *did* ask you—at dinner, two months ago—and," he adds, reproachfully, "*you* said you couldn't come."

"Yes,"—I admit the fact, and feel now that I ought to have accepted—"but it won't do to——" I commence.

"Yes, it will," he interrupts. "I shall be up there to-morrow. How *are* you? We'll have larks. When do you start?"

"At the end of the week, I believe," I reply, not being quite certain.

"Good enough." Then he shouts, as if to relieve his pent-up feelings, "How *are* you? How are you getting on?"—a question that he puts about every five minutes—and then goes on,—"I'm off. Will wire—you'll come up—shooting, fishing, bagpipes, 'good business,'—go as you please—I'll answer for your enjoying yourself—Good-bye!—How *are* you?" he shouts for the last time, as he disappears down the staircase three steps at a time.

Fate, HOBSON, and D. B.'s wire next day, decide the matter. Boat with HOBSON to Edinburgh, and then on to D. B.'s uncle, JOHNNIE BUDD, at Loch Glennie. And I had fixedly determined not to take any holiday at all this year!

## VOCES POPULI.

BY PARLIAMENTARY.

ON THE PLATFORM.

*A Lady of Family.* Oh, yes, I do travel third-class sometimes, my dear. I consider it a duty to try to know something of the lower orders. [*Looks out for an empty third-class compartment.*

IN THE CARRIAGE.

*The seats are now all occupied: the* Lady of Family *is in one corner, next to a Chatty Woman with a basket, and opposite to an Eccentric-looking Man with a flighty manner.*

*The Eccentric Man* (*to the Lady of Family*). Sorry to disturb you, Mum, but you're a-setting on one o' my 'am sandwiches.

*The L. of F.* ? ? ? ! ! !

*The E. M.* (*considerately*). Don't trouble yourself, Mum, it's of no intrinsic value. I on'y put it there to keep my seat.

*The Chatty W.* (*to the L. of F.*) I think I've seen you about Shinglebeach, 'ave I not?

*The L. of F.* It is very possible. I have been staying with some friends in the neighbourhood.

*The C. W.* It's a nice cheerful place is Shinglebeach; but (*confidentially*) don't you think it's a very sing'ler thing that in a place like that—a fash'nable place, too—there shouldn't be a single 'am an' beef shop?

*The L. of F.* (*making a desperate effort to throw herself into the question*). What a very extraordinary thing to be sure. Dear, *dear* me! No ham and beef shop!

*The C. W.* It's so indeed, Mum; and what's more, as I daresay you've noticed for yourself, if you 'appen to want a snack o' fried fish ever so, there isn't a place you could go to—leastways, at a moment's notice. Now, 'ow do you explain such a thing as that?

*The L. of F.* (*faintly*). I'm afraid I can't suggest any explanation.

*A Sententious Man.* Fried fish is very sustaining.

[*Relapses into silence for remainder of journey.*

*The Eccentric Man.* Talking of sustaining, I remember, when we was kids, my father ud bring us home two pennorth o' ches'nuts, and we 'ad 'em boiled, and they'd last us days. (*Sentimentally.*) He was a kind man, my father (*to the* L. of F., *who bows constrainedly*), though you wouldn't ha' thought it, to look at him. I don't say, mind yer, that he wasn't fond of his bit o' booze—(*the* L. of F. *looks out of window*)—like the best of us. I'm goin' up to prove his will now, I am—if you don't believe me, ere's the probate. (*Hands that document round for inspection.*) That's all reg'lar enough, I 'ope. (*To the* L. of F.) Don't give it back before you've done with it—I'm in no 'urry, and there's good reading in it. (*Points out certain favourite passages with a very dirty forefinger.*) Begin there—*that's* my name.

[*The* L. of F. *peruses the will with as great a show of interest as she can bring herself to assume.*

*The Eccentric Man.* D'ye see that big 'andsome building over there? That's the County Lunatic Asylum—where my poor wife is shut up. I went to see her last week, I did. (*Relates his visit in detail to* The L. of F., *who listens unwillingly.*) It's wonderful how many of our family have been in that asylum from first to last. I 'ad a aunt who died cracky; and my old mother, she's very peculiar at times. There's days when I feel as if I was a little orf my own 'ed, so if I say anything at all out of the way, you'll know what it is.

[L. of F. *changes carriages at the next station. In the second carriage are two Men of sea-faring appearance, and a young Man who is parting from his* Fianceé *as the* L. of F. *takes her seat.*

*The Fiancé.* Excuse me one moment, Ma'am. (*Leans across the* L. of F. *and out of the window.*) Well, goodbye, my girl; take care of yourself.

*The Fiancée* (*with a hysterical giggle*). Oh, I'll take care o' *my* self.

[*Looks at the roof of the carriage.*

*He* (*with meaning*). No more pickled onions, eh?

*She.* What a one you are to remember things! (*After a pause.*) Give my love to JOE.

*He.* All right. Well, JENNY, just one, for the last (*they embrace loudly, after which the F. resumes his seat with an expression of mingled sentiment and complacency*). Oh, (*to L. of F.*) if you don't mind my stepping across you again, Mum. JENNY, if you see DICK between this and Friday, just tell him as——

[*Prolonged whispers; sounds of renewed kisses; final parting as train starts with a jerk which throws the* Fiancé *upon the* L. of F.'s *lap. After the train is started a gleam of peculiar significance is observable in the eyes of one of the Seafaring Men, who is reclining in an easy attitude on the seat. His companion responds with a grin of intelligence, and produces a large black bottle from the rack. They drink, and hand the bottle to the* Fiancé.

*The F.* Thankee, I don't mind if I do. Here's wishing you——

[*Remainder of sentiment drowned in sound of gluq-glug-glug; is about to hand back bottle when the first* Seafarer *intimates that he is to pass it on. The* L. of F. *recoils in horror.*

*Both Seafarers.* It's *wine*, Mum!

[*Tableau. The* Lady of Family *realises that the study of third-class humanity has its drawbacks.*

## MALÂ FIDE TRAVELLERS IN WALES.

*Welsh Justice, Chairman of Quarter Sessions, and likewise of Local Bench* (*to Publicans in attendance*). Now mind, all you publicans, and innkeepers, and hosts, and tapsters, have a care how you serve anyone whomsoever with wines, and beers, and porters, and ales, and swipeses, and metheglins, and spirituous or fermented liquors, on any pretences or occasions, at any times on Sundays. You are not permitted, or suffered, or allowed, or authorised to supply peoples with beers, look you, simply because they have come three miles to get them. In my opinions, and judgments, and sentences, that is no sufficient journeys to make them *bonâ fide* travellers. I pray you take notice that, as far as I am concerned, if any charges comes before me, I shall look, and see, and inquire, and determine whether publicans have tried ordinary means, and interrogatives, and questions, to discover if persons were *bonâ fide* travellers in truth, look you now. A *bonâ fide* traveller is one who is travelling for purposes, and objects, and necessities. For instance, a *bonâ fide* traveller would be a man travelling to get work, but not one who came a certain distance to get beer. As an example of a frivolous, and trumpery, and make-believe excuse for tippling and toping, I know a case in which a man had the cheek, and the effrontery, and the brass, to say that he had walked all round the three-mile stone. Don't tell me of constitutional walks, and exercises, and thirsts, and needs of refreshments. Let me warn you, and admonish you, and exhort you to sell no one a glass of beer for no better causes and reasons than being tired and exhausted with a Sabbath-day's journey, whether short or long. 'Tis no matter for their fatigues, and wearinesses, and drynesses, and droughts, that makes them call for it, because, look you, they want it, and their desires and inclinations demands it, and their exhaustions craves for it against the laws and statutes in such cases made and provided for restraints of their appetites and offences. So now go your ways, shentlemens, and get you about your businesses, and see that none of you be brought before me for selling drink to any traveller, howsoever faint, and foot-sore, and thirsty, on a Welsh Sabbath, forasmuch as, look you, I would beseech you, and intreat you, command you, and, moreover, compel you to make it a dry Sunday. [The remarks of this wise Magistrate may perhaps occasion British tourists to think twice and three times before devoting their holidays to an excursion in "gallant little Wales."]

Taking a Draught.

**WHAT OUR ARTIST (THE INTENSELY PATRIOTIC ONE) HAS TO PUT UP WITH!**

*Just as he is pointing out to Monsieur Anatole Duclos, the Parisian Journalist, how infinitely the English type of female beauty (especially amongst our Aristocracy) transcends that of France, or any other Nation,—who should come up from the beach but Lady Lucretia Longstaff, and her five unmarried daughters!*

"——AND AS FOR THOSE IDIOTIC OLD FRENCH CARICATURES OF *LES ANGLAISES*, WITH LONG GAUNT FACES, AND LONG PROTRUDING TEETH, AND LONG FLAT FEET—WHY, GOOD HEAVENS! MY DEAR DUCLOS, THE TYPE DOESN'T EVEN *EXIST!*"

## THE CUT DIRECT; OR, OTHER FISH TO FRY.

OH yes, I'm aware I seemed sweet on you once,
But 'twas only a *penchant*, a passing caprice.
Lose the world "All for Love"? Nay, I'm not such a dunce,
And—at least for a time—my attentions must cease.
You 're "quite English, you know," my dear. *Need* I explain
Why that sort of thing won't do at present? Ask BLAINE!

True, I *did* introduce you a few months ago
To COLUMBIA.* Politeness, my dear, half pretence!
I found—didn't you?—it was really no go.
And although at that time I could "sit on the fence,"
That rail it's no longer quite safe so to ride;
I must seem to get down, dear,—and not on *your* side.

Tut! tut! Broken vows, and all that sort of thing?
That's a most extreme view, now, to take of the case.
I just took you under my fatherly wing,
Made you known, and, I think, with a good deal of grace.
But bound to you? Nay, my dear child, that's absurd.
If you talk about bonds, I am off like a bird.

Miss PROTECTION may not be so pretty, or young,
I do not pretend on her person to dote;
But she claims, well, I won't say my heart, but my tongue,
And I want to win, not her love, but her vote.
Needs must when—Democracy drives, don't you know,
And one can't quite afford to be careless of *dot.*

Come, come! don't be angry! A fellow, I'm sure,
May philander a little with no bad intent.
You know what's at stake, what I want to secure;
Our friendship was real, as far as it went;
That friendship one day we perhaps may renew,
But do stand aside for the present, now *do!*

Your little friend CANADA? Well, I dare say
She's a tiny bit tiffed; thinks we've treated her ill.
All that will come right, I've no doubt, dear, some day;
But indeed at this moment I don't want a spill,
And if I smile on her just now I'll go down.
So, for politic reasons I put on a frown.

Hush! The other one's eye is upon us. Eh, what?
Claim acquaintance? Intrusive, I really must say!
Give my arm, at this moment too? Certainly not!
Don't know you, don't know you!—at least, not to-day.
Be off, and don't worry me! (*Aside.*) There now, *don't* cry;
*Can't* you see that I've quite other fish now to fry?

* See Cartoon, "Quite English, you know," December 17, 1887.

## "CAVE CANEM!"

IT is stated that two dogs belonging to a Deputy named LAGUERRE, "the henchman of General BOULANGER," have been taught to howl whenever M. FERRY's name is mentioned. It is really a pity thus to waste time, and demoralise such decent animals as dogs. M. LAGUERRE would find it simpler to retain certain of the two-legged curs of Creed and puppies of Party, who may be safely trusted, and that without being taught, to yelp hideously whenever a particular Statesman's name is uttered in their hearing. Could any honest dog "drop into poetry," he would, doubtless, deliver Dr. WATTS's familiar lyric in some such inverted fashion as follows:—

"Let scribes delight to snap and bite,
For 'tis their nature to;
Let petty scribblers spit their spite,
For Party makes them so.

"But, doggies, *you* should never let
Your purchased yelpings rise;
Your honest mouths were never meant
To howl out Party cries!"

"A RARE OLD PLANT."—There is much talk in Vienna of a so-called "Weather Plant," which is said to possess the property of prognosticating all atmospheric changes three days in advance. Well, the *Abrus peregrinus*, or "Paternoster Pea," may possess all the powers claimed for it. But, *Mr. Punch's* opinion is, that the real "Weather-*plant*" this year at least—is *the Weather itself!*

# THE CUT DIRECT.

President Cleveland. "DON'T KNOW YA! (*Aside.*) AT ANY RATE, FOR THE PRESENT!!"

**PORTRAIT OF THE GENTLEMAN WHO DRAWS UP THE METEOROLOGICAL REPORTS.**

"ANOTHER DEPRESSION IS COMING!"

[*Just as he was about to take his Holiday too!*

## ACROSS THE WATER.

(*With the Lord Mayor.*)

WELL, it is all over now, but it has been a wonderful success. Dendermond, comparatively insignificant Flemish town though it is, has certainly known how to emphasise the glorious fact that it has given from its sons a Lord Mayor to the City of London. Such a Procession! There were "mediæval" trumpeters and drummers, young persons with banners, in classical costume; "Commerce" represented by a steamboat full of ladies accompanied by sailors of all countries, and followed up by effigies of "Painting," "Industry," "Music," and "Science," together with a group showing ROBRECHT VII., VAN BETHUNE, Lord of Dendermond, presenting to the town a charter, dated 1333. This last personage was, I think, owing to the fact that he was attired in chain armour, frequently taken by the crowd for the LORD MAYOR himself, and vociferously cheered in consequence.

I found the townspeople, however, rather vague as to their estimate of our Chief Magistrate's position and privileges, and had to be continually explaining to them in indifferent Flemish that when at home he neither shared the Woolsack with the LORD CHANCELLOR in the House of Lords, commanded the Life Guards in person, or sat down every night of his life to a grand banquet at the Crystal Palace with a thousand picked members of the British Nobility. Nothing though that I could say appeared to detract from the exalted estimate they had formed of his general dignity, and when the effigy of London came upon the scene, surrounded by allegorical figures of "Foresight," "Constancy," "Vigilance," "Civic Virtues," "Dancing," "Deportment," "Athletics," and "Stenography," the enthusiasm of the spectators knew no bounds, and they fairly shouted themselves hoarse. Then came music and fireworks, and later, several groups who had been dining, congregated round me, and insisting that I must be the LORD MAYOR, began to cheer me disagreeably. I, however, remonstrated in dumb show, and pointing to a window in the Town Hall where the Burgomaster could be seen at that very moment for the tenth time in the act of embracing the portly and smiling form of Mr. POLYDORE DE KEYSER himself, succeeded in diverting their attention.

The next day the LORD MAYOR started on his return journey, smothered in trophies. He made a short halt at Ghent and Bruxelles, his stay at the latter place being chiefly remarkable for a thoroughly racy comic after-dinner speech, made on the occasion by Mr. Sheriff DAVIES. That the whole party after a capital outing has arrived quite safe and sound in town again is here recorded with much satisfaction by your careful and observant correspondent,

A CITY REMEMBRANCER.

## A WORD IN SEASON.

"It is the pride of the Hohenzollerns to reign at once over the noblest, the most intellectual, and most cultured of nations."—*The* EMPEROR WILLIAM.

WHY, who speaks here? A Kaiser and Commander,
Or some mob-flattering, demagogic pander?
Droll doubling of two parts, the pompous ruler,
And glosing hyperbolic people-fooler!
How martial souls—like WOLSELEY—who deride
All sentiment upon the popular side
As "sickly," "pharisaic,"—Heaven knows what—
Philanthropy, with other kinds of "rot"
With the fine swagger of the soldier classing,—
Must shudder at the Hohenzollern's "gassing"!
*Noblesse oblige*, my WILLIAM! Mighty souls,
Like yours and WOLSELEY'S, aim at other goals
Than CLEON and the Sausage-seller, surely.
Flatter the crowd? Is the crown so securely
Poised on the head of despot power to-day
That Kaisers can with fulsome phrases play,
Without the risk of bringing on Autocracy
The "torrent of anarchical democracy"
Which scares our pocket-Cæsar in a fashion
That moves him to quite incoherent passion?
Take thought, my Teuton Chief, and, above all,
Take counsel with our "Only General."
He is not, like your MOLTKE, taciturn;
He deals in thoughts that breathe and words that burn,
As prettily as any poet-person
Who martial hero ever turned a verse on;
(The poet's highest function which redeems
Bard songs from being merely baby-dreams.)
He reckons up historic heroes lightly—
I hope, Lord Herr, you've read the last *Fortnightly*—
Appraises MARLBOROUGH, and NAPOLEON,
And picks some little holes in WELLINGTON.
You'll hardly, Kaiser-King, obtain an article
Of this particular sort, without a particle
Of shrinking modesty, from the old chief
Whose age in touching terms asks late relief
From the long strain of splendid service. No,
Your Silent Hero is not fashioned so.
His brief pathetic letter, the appeal
Of time-worn strength to drop the martial steel,
That script historic and your kind reply
Beseem you both, Lord Herr, right royally.
But even MOLTKE'S silent tongue might wag,
Mildly against the too thrasonic brag,
Of such an untried CÆSAR, where huge hosts
Need little to be swelled by boyish boasts.

A SHAVING CLAUSE.—Those intelligent and amusing personages, the Commissioners in Lunacy, in their forty-second Report to the LORD CHANCELLOR (*à propos* of a possibly preventible suicide at Bethlehem Hospital) "while acknowledging the difficulty of entirely doing away with razors in asylums," advised that they should be kept under a double lock. They added to this extremely sensible proposal the interesting information that, "as a still safer plan," they "had recommended the daily services of a barber accustomed to lunatics." It would be interesting, however, to learn how such a person could obtain his necessary qualification. The first attempt to shave a raving madman is rather suggestive of the last chapter but one of a "shilling shocker"; and although people who eschew beards possibly may not be considered entirely in their right minds, their eccentricity, at the most, partakes rather of the characteristics of harmless idiotcy than of the more violent forms of acute mania.

### Literal.

PAT may be a lazy and law-breaking sinner,
With cudgels and Plans of Campaign be too free;
But at least he'd have rather more chance of a dinner,
Were it not for the curse of the absentee (*absent tea.*)

LITERARY DIET.—"Much reading, like much eating," said Sir THEODORE MARTIN, in the Llangollen Town Hall, quoting an old writer, "is wholly useless without digestion." True enough, and food for the mind is indigestible if too tough. Indulgence in modern French literature of the baser sort is very apt to create indigestion attended with nausea.

GOOD ADVICE—TAKEN IN A PROPER SPIRIT.

*Fond but Impecunious Uncle (to Middy).* "AND REMEMBER, JACK, BE ECONOMICAL. DON'T RUN INTO DEBT—AND, WHATEVER YOU DO, *NEVER GO TO THE JEWS!*" *Jack.* "NO, UNCLE—*I'LL ALWAYS COME TO YOU!*"

## BALLADS OF TO-DAY.

### THE OLD TELEPHONE.

(*By Milton Featherly Ionsone.*)

IT stands as of yore in the dear dark corner,
But the dust has gather'd, the voice has flown;
There, like a little forlorn Jack Horner,
It lingers, unlook'd-for, the old Telephone.
The blinds in the office hang yellow and slanting,
The sun strikes mottled athwart the pane,
And ever a low lone voice is chanting,
From days evanish'd, an old refrain:
Ring, ring-a-ring! Are you there? Who are you?
What do you want? Ring-a-ring! Are you there?
Answer, O love! While I rest for a bar, you
Murmur your numbers, my fair, my fair!

Ring, ring-a-ring! Like the joy-bells chiming;
Whirr! Like a coffee-mill talking alone;
Silence! Like poets who sleep at their rhyming;
An answer softer than cushat's moan.
Yes, for a voice on the desert of business
Fell like the dew, though the face was unknown.
And ever my brain with delirious dizziness
Reels when I think of the old Telephone.

Ah, but the world whirls wearily round me,
And I with the weary world am whirl'd;
Should it suddenly stop, it could scarce confound me,
If, some bright morning, the angels found me
Recklessly round the lamp-posts curl'd.
But, in garden old, or in window'd minster,
From chordless organ, or frozen bird,
From bachelor bold or blushing spinster,
Such soul-sweet music was never heard.
In love's bright play-bill I largely star you;
I hear you ever, my unseen fair;
Ring, ring-a-ring! Are you there? Who are you?
And Echo sobs—There is no one there!

CUE-RIOUS.—A Billiard-player's prosperity seems very paradoxical. The more "hazard" there is about it, the more certain it is, and it is largely *made* by *breaks*.

## ROBERT'S EXCURSION.

I HAD what I calls a reel treat the other day, and as I don't have it, as sum seems to do, about wunce a week, but jest about as seldom as possibel, I did jest injoy it. I was orderd down to Rumford, of all places in this mortal world, to wait on a party of City swells at the principle Otel there, called, I think, the Golden Carf, or sum sitch name, and as I was there in good time afore they started on their desperate hard work of surweying all the principle mountains of Hessex, and as there wasn't not nobody hinside the bootiful drag and its four hosses, the nice good-looking Chairman acshally arsked me to jump in! Witch I need ardly say as I did, like a bird. Well, off we set, and may I never be beleeved, if the Landlord of the Otel, where the gents was a going for to dine after their ard day's work, didn't git on the box and drive all the fore hosses, and werry well he did it too, and didn't upset us not wunce.

And to make the whole set-out quite compleat, we took a trumpitter with us with about the werry longest trumpit as I ever seed or ewen heerd on, and wenever we cum near an house or an hoss, he blowed away to that xtent that I werrily thort as he must ha' bust hisself, but he didn't. We had a most luvly ride on a most luvly day, our fore bootiful hosses a running up the Essex mountains and down into the Essex walleys as if they thort nothink of 'em. We druv threw some Nobbleham's Park. The young trumpitter, who was, I think, a bit of a wag, tried to perswade me as the Nobbleham's name was PETER, but I wasn't quite so green as to bleeve that.

It wasn't a werry cumferal looking house as was in the Park, for the roof was all off, and all the winders was broke, which guv it rayther a chilly look, but the Mossyleum, as we seed a little further on, quite made up for it, for anythink more nicer, or warmer, or cumferal looking I never seed.

I think, praps, if they'd both ha' bin mine, I should ha' gone in for sumthink of a change in the wicey wersey style; but of course there's no acounting for taste, speshally among the werry hiest horder of the Harrystockracy. There was a good many solgers and peeple about warious parts of our ride, and wenever we druv through 'em, I jest raised my at and made my werry best bow—witch I'm told is werry much like a serten Royal Prince's—at which they was hevidently much pleased, for they all larfed quite haffably. I wunder who they took me for, in my sollitury grander, drest, as of coarse I was, in full heavening costoom.

Well, wen we got back, the Chairman, thinking praps as he had better go on as he had begun in the staggering line, acshally arsked the driving Landlord to dine with 'em, and, follering my nobel xample, he didn't want not no pressing, but down he sat. And if he didn't earn his capital dinner by the way in which he emused all the City swells, nobody never did. Of coarse I was too much occypied by my purfeshnal dooties to hear werry much, but wot little I did hear ony made me long for more. Just one or 2 anneckdotes as xampels.

He told 'em as he wunse druv a party of 12 on a fore horse Drag all the ways to Liverpool, a matter of 220 mile, jest to see a Race run, and he charged 'em two hundred and fifty pound for the job!

And having gammond 'em as he lost money by the transackshun, they all subskeribed together, like reel Gents as they was, and had a picter painted of the hole concern, Drag, and Hosses, and Gents, and Driver, and all, and guv it to him at a grand dinner at his hone house, and, as he werry propperly said, if any Gent here dowts my word, there's the werry picter! And there to be sure it were, a hanging in the werry room as the City swells was a dining in! I couldn't say much about the rest of the party, as I'd never seen 'em, but the likeness of the Driver was werry striking. Of coarse jest a leetle bit felattering, but they allers is, or in coarse we shoodn't buy 'em.

Well, that wasn't a bad story jest to begin with, but I think he even beat that afterwards, wen he told em that all the hammytoor Coaching swells once guv a grand dinner to all the Purfeshnals, at the Bell Savage on Ludget Hill. His Father, who was a Purfeshnal, wasn't well enuff to go, so he said to his son, says he, "You shall go insted of me, PETER,"—which was his name,—"but, wotever you do, don't get drunk!" Werry wise and frendly adwise, but, unfortnetly, offener given than follerd.

The night came, and they all set down, I think as he said about 60 in number, and a rare dinner they must have had, for the Bill came to fore ginnys a head! Ah, they was sumthink like times, them was. And what a gloryus Chairman they must have had! He ort to ha' bin a Sheriff at the werry least. For about 3 o'Clock in the

## OUR JAPANNERIES. No. 14.

LIKA JOKO AT THE SEASIDE.

morning he called for the Bill, and when it was guv to him, he jest looked at it, and then he said, "Gennelmen," says he, "I beg to congraterlate you on your nobel work, for the fust amount as catches my eye is, Champain, £47! Let us give three cheers for that splendid hitem!" And so they did, and then one cheer more. And they didn't brake up ewen then, and Peter, to prove to his trusting Parient as he kep his word, druv the Coach, that started at 6 o'Clock, hay-hem, the fust stage, to Rumford, without no accidence.

Ah, Mr. Peter, Mr. Peter! if you have a few more such scrumpshus stories of the grand old days of yore in that fine-looking hed of yours, your proper place is not on the box seat of an ansum Drag, but within the sacred walls of the grand old Copperashun, or of an ancient Livery Company, where they wood be as thorowly apreseated and as thorowly injoyed, as they was by your umbel admirer

Robert.

### Virginia Stock's View of It.

Is Marriage a Failure? Why, yes, to bo sure.
But, oh! abolition won't furnish a cure.
Whilst thousands of spinsters in solitude tarry,
It's clearly a failure—because men *won't* marry.

## "CLASS" LEGISLATION.

(*Further Correspondence.*)

SIR,—Look here, the sooner first and second-class travellers disappear altogether the better. Nobody wants 'em. Take my word for it, if the big Companies only know what they are about, they will take pretty sharp to running nothing but third-class trains. The fares should be tidy cheap, say at the rate of a farthing for five miles. But what would be the upshot? Why, such a blessed influx of traffic that they would hardly be able to meet it. Talk of dividends, why the prospect ought to make the shareholders' mouths water, for the big bulk that never travel at all would be on the move like one o'clock, and every loafer from Seven Dials, and the whole of the Unemployed would be all cutting up North—or anywhere else on the spree with, Yours hopefully, A WHITECHAPEL ROVER.

King's Cross.

SIR,—That the first-class traveller is very hardly treated by the Companies there cannot, I think, be any question. Take my case. On a recent journey I had positively to share a whole compartment with a fellow passenger, and this though I had paid my fare and had certainly a right to expect an entire one to myself. As to second and third-class carriages, they ought, of course, to be abolished, with a view to the provision of fitting accommodation for the patrons of the first. One first-class passenger to a compartment would give five to a carriage; some two hundred, therefore, could be conveniently provided for in a train, say, of about forty carriages. I do not know how this would work, nor do I care how it would affect the shareholders' question of dividends, for with these matters I do not think the patrons of the line have any concern. But I offer my suggestion with much confidence, and meantime beg to subscribe myself

Yours, &c., NOTHING IF NOT EXCLUSIVE.

SIR,—If there is one thing that is clear, it is that the whole system of our railway travelling needs completely revolutionising. Why, I ask, should the passenger who has to pass eight hours on a journey, say to Edinburgh, be cut off from the comforts and conveniences of ordinary life? It is true that in the Pullman sleeping-car he can have a bed, and make his *toilette;* but what, Sir, I ask, is this at the close of the Nineteenth Century? What are the Companies about in thinking that in providing him with a paltry bed and basin, they have properly discharged their functions? The idea is preposterous. Suppose he wishes to consult a doctor or even a solicitor *en route*, why should he not be able to do so? He might even wish to take lessons in dancing, or have a tooth extracted. No train ought, therefore, to start that is not accompanied by a duly qualified doctor, dentist, attorney, and dancing-master.

There should also be a swimming-bath attached to it. And it should contain a full and complete reference-library, while drawing-rooms, dining-rooms, private sitting-rooms, stores, saloons for private theatricals, and an ample gymnasium, should be at the disposition of all the passengers. Nor is this all. Some may like music. For these a brass band should be provided; and, as many passengers may desire some sort of recreation *en route*, no thoroughly equipped train should be started unless provided with a *troupe* of acrobats, and all the attractive features of a Variety Entertainment. A train made up on such principles could not fail to secure the patronage of the travelling public; and Directors will be wise in their generation who cheerfully incur the outlay necessary to the instalment of a service framed on these lines. All the Public ask is, "enough for their money." That the above, then, would be, on the whole, a move in the right direction, is the opinion of

Yours, categorically, TAKING IT EASY.

## PLAY-TIME IN LONDON.

SCENE—*A public thoroughfare. Enter a* Londoner. *He is about to retire sadly when he meets his* Country Cousin.

*Londoner.* Dear me, who would have thought of meeting you here?

*Country Cousin.* Why not? The rain has spoilt the harvest.

*Lon.* Well, I suppose I must take you to see the sights. Come to the theatre this evening? Go to TOOLE'S—eh?

*C. C.* Went there last night. Couldn't stand it a second time.

*Lon.* Impossible! Mr. TOOLE in *The Don* is excellent.

*C. C.* Mr. TOOLE in *The Don!* Why, he is "touring." They have got *Pepita*, a comic opera, at TOOLE'S. Haven't you seen it?

*Lon.* Not I. Never heard of it.

*C. C.* Why, it's been played hundreds of times in the Provinces, so we sent it up to Town. But I won't go and see it again.

*Lon.* Well, what do you say to the Haymarket—*Captain Swift?*

*C. C.* I saw it when it was produced at a *matinée*. Mr. TREE very clever, as he always is in character parts, but I don't care to go again.

*Lon.* Well, I will take you to the Avenue to see *Gladys* and *Don Juan, Junior.*

*C. C.* Thanks, much; but I have seen both and can't stand either. *Gladys* begins too soon, and *Don Juan, Junior*, ends too late. And strange as it must appear to you, I seldom laugh at Mr. RIGHTON.

*Lon.* Strange, indeed! What say you to the Adelphi *Union Jack?*

*C. C.* Seen it twice, and can't stand it a third time. It really is very feeble for a melodrama, and I am tired of trick changes.

*Lon.* Well, then, there is the Vaudeville.

*C. C.* No, there isn't. It's closed; and so is the St. James's, and the Opéra Comique, and Drury Lane.

*Lon.* Really, you seem to know more about the amusements of Town than I do.

*C. C.* Why shouldn't I? To tell you the truth, I am obliged to go everywhere. You see, I am so accustomed to country quiet that I cannot stand London noise; so I go every night to a Theatre.

*Lon.* What for?

*C. C.* To get a couple of hours' sleep!

[*The conversation is interrupted by a thunderstorm, mixed with snow, and the other ingredients incident to this year's summer. Hail, thunderbolts, fog, and Curtain.*

## RATION-AL DIET.

IN the interests of economy (which, however, will always be combined with a certain regard to efficiency), the Regimental Regimen in future to be allowed to private soldiers will be as follows, which the Military Authorities, who arrange for victualling contracts, and the Contractors themselves, consider more than sufficient for the wants of growing youths, and likely to bring quite a rush of recruits into the Army:—

A Private Box.

*First Meal in the Day.*—This will consist of two thin slices of bread and margarine—the latter not to be laid on too thick—with half a mug of shilling tea and a thimbleful of skimmed milk. (N.B.—Two spoonsful of this fine matured tea to every six men.) This meal will take place at 8·30, and for lack of any more expressive title, will continue to be called "Breakfast."

*Second Meal.*—Dinner, which is to be served at 1·30. Every soldier to have *one whole ounce of meat*, including bone; but he will be expected to make no bones about it, should he be unfortunate enough to receive a portion with no meat at all in it. The good soldier always tries to remember that if he were engaged in a campaign in a perfectly desert country, and if all the Commissariat and baggage animals had been killed for food a month before, he might conceivably be called upon to bear privations almost as great; and it is the constant object of the War Office to aid the soldier in realising this particular feature of actual warfare. Two ounces of potatoes are also to be allowed, but these must be weighed before being pared, and—if possible—directly they are taken from the ground, when a good deal of earth is likely to be attached to them. Bread, made of finest alum and bone-dust "middlings," to the extent of an ounce per man, to be also allowed. A tea-spoonful of grated cheese on Thursdays. Suet-puddings on alternate Sundays.

*Third Meal.*—Takes place at 4·30, when, having recently dined, men are not likely to be hungry, and so to waste the national resources. Pint of tepid tea, with *three* slices of bread and margarine.

*Fourth Meal.*—Supper. Should the Contractor announce that he does not feel able to supply a fourth meal at the figure for which he has tendered, the Authorities will desire to leave the matter in his hands, feeling certain that he has the highest interests of the Army at heart. If they are called upon to choose between starving the Exchequer and feeding the soldier, or starving the soldier and feeding the Exchequer, they feel bound to select the patriotic alternative.

The above highly liberal and generous scale has been decided upon after consultation with some of the leading Medical officers at Reformatories and Workhouses. It is confidently hoped that it will lead to a great increase in the flesh, bone, and sinew of our recruits; if, however, it should be found that *too much* adipose tissue results, the meals can easily be reduced in quantity, or quality, or both.

Soldiers of a peculiarly ravenous disposition, who really feel that they could eat something more between 4·30 in the afternoon and the following morning, will be allowed—after medical examination—to still the pangs of appetite, by obtaining at the canteen, before going to bed, two or three drops of a powerful and inexpensive sleeping draught, which will carry them safely through to next morning's breakfast. Or, if they choose, they can "recruit" outside in the nearest dram-shop.

## A NATIONAL MUDDLE; OR, THE INVENTOR AVENGED.

(*Government Drama in Active Rehearsal.*)

ACT I.—*A Room in the Permanent Sleepy Department.* Half-awake Official *discovered dozing at desk. Enter a* Sanguine Inventor.

*Half-awake Official* (*rousing himself*). Ah! Mr. What's-your-name? Come about that new gun of yours, eh?

*Sanguine Inventor.* Yes, and this is the twenty-fifth time I've called about it. Surely, the Authorities can make up their minds. Come: what do they mean to do about it?

*H. O.* Well, you see it was to carry twenty miles——?

*S. I.* Yes, and go through thirty-six inches of steel plating.

*H. O.* Just so. Well, come, you know, that's too much for us. We don't care about such distances and figures.

*S. I.* "Don't care?" I don't understand you. Why, it's an entirely new departure!

*H. O.* Yes, but this Department doesn't care about new departures. It sticks to the old lines.

*S. I.* But the army that first adopts my gun, will revolutionise all the conditions of warfare.

*H. O.* That's just why the Department wouldn't touch it. It doesn't want to revolutionise anything. It has got its own principles and ideas to work out, and it has quite enough to do to keep pace with them, I can tell you.

*S. I.* Will you purchase it, or not? You shall have it for £1000.

*H. O.* Quite out of the question at that figure. But the fact is, we don't want it at any price. You had better take it elsewhere.

*S. I.* As you will. I shall certainly take it—to the Continent.

*H. O.* So do. And now good morning.

[*Bows him out, and falls asleep, while* Sanguine Inventor *proceeds to carry out his threat as Act Drop descends.*

ACT II.—*Tableau, representing an interval of ten years, during which* Sanguine Inventor *applies to the Foreign European Governments, and disposes of his invention to several of them on highly advantageous terms. His new gun being pronounced on all hands the "weapon of the future," its merits are freely discussed in scientific Continental military circles; and the rumour of its various excellences at length reaching the Officials of the Permanent Sleepy Department, they lethargically appoint a Committee of Inquiry to investigate its merits, as the Act Drop descends.*

ACT III.—*A Room in the Permanent Sleepy Department.* Half-awake Official *discovered, engaged in an interview with* The Representative of the Firm of Messrs. MIDDLEMAN & Co.

*Half-awake Official.* You see, there is a public clamour got up about the gun, and so, I suppose, we must have it. What's your figure?

*The Representative of Messrs. Middleman.* A million and a half; not a penny under.

*H. O.* Oh! but come, that's sticking it on rather too stiff. Why, ten years ago we could have had it for £1000!

*The R. of M. M.* Very possibly. And you were great fools not to purchase at the price. But we have since managed to secure the patent for a pretty penny, and you don't think we are going to do business without making a tidy profit? A million and a half is our lowest figure. So you may like it or leave it, just as you choose.

*H. O.* If it wasn't for the clamour, we would soon let you know which we would do. However, we've no choice; so, I suppose, you must have your price.

[*Proceeds to make arrangements for the payment of the purchase-money for a ten-years' old invention as the Act Drop descends.*

ACT IV.—*Tableau representing the* Sanguine Inventor, *who has now patented a Gun that will carry forty miles, and penetrate 6 feet of steel plating, offering its refusal to the Permanent Sleepy Department. He has an interview with the* Half-awake Official, *who, informing him that the Department has just paid a million and a-half for his previous invention, points out that they are not prepared to negotiate any further for the purchase of any improvements.* The Sanguine Inventor *thereupon straightway disposes of his new secret to further foreign European Governments, who, adopting it with enthusiasm, utilise it with the greatest success, as the Act Drop descends.*

ACT V.—*Represents the Interior of the Permanent Sleepy Department after the Declaration of War by several Continental Powers, one of the* Sanguine Inventor's *Patent Shells fired by the Enemy having just blown the entire Office into the air.* The Half-awake Official *is discovered slowly emerging from the* débris.

*Half-awake Official* (*rubbing his eyes*). Dear me, this is very awkward. I suppose we ought to have purchased that fellow's Invention, after all. However (*coming forward*), if our kind friends in front are only satisfied, we can't deny that we have brought about a precious "National Muddle"——

*Sanguine Inventor* (*taking his hand*). And have seen the Sanguine Inventor at last "avenged." [*They embrace as the Curtain falls.*

## OUR BOOKING-OFFICE.

CAPITAL number of the *Fortnightly*; that is, as much as I've read of it. "*Imprisonment for Debt,*" by Judge CHALMERS, should be studied by everyone who wants to get into debt and keep himself out of prison. I gather from this article that imprisonment for debt isn't quite the pleasantest way of spending a few days in a recess. But in his next, perhaps, Judge CHALMERS will tell us exactly how the prisoners are treated? Why should not a caged prisoner, who can but won't pay, be made to pay by setting him to some work which will bring in sufficient money to satisfy the creditor and the expenses of his detention?

"Where was the Baron when the light went out?"

The literary critic who writes so trenchantly on the *Fall of Fiction*, in the same number, ought by this time to have read *Rhedah's Revenge*, wherein I finished off the mighty RITERAGGARD himself with the stock-in-trade of his entertainment. Let Mr. RIDER HAGGARD get a new set of puppets, and learn some fresh tunes on his pipe to which they can dance.

Before changing the subject, I may mention that one of "The Friendlies" informs me that, in *Rhedah's Revenge*, I was wrong in making "Rhinoceri" the plural of Rhinoceros. I thought I was. I ought to have written, as he says, "Rhinocerotes," or "Rhinocerosses;" but then, you see, it occurred to me that "Rhinoceri," having no existence, were just the very animals that RIDER HAGGARD would have pledged his veracity as a Romancer that his mighty hunters had shot. When I come across such solemn affidavits, "I say pooh-pooh to him," and my nose, having in it more of the antique Roman than the Greek, becomes "rhinocerical." (For which word, see Dixon's Johnsonary Lathomised.)

The four volumes of *Weird Tales* have continued to delight me. There's one by Mr. EDMUND YATES, called *The Skeleton in the House*, written, a foot-note confidentially informs us, "while he was still in his twenties,"—which sounds like the British Workman "coming in his thousands." First-rate vintage "The Twenties,"—wish I had a lot of them; and this weird tale of Moi Même's is so racily told, and with such conviction, that I am heartily sorry he has seen only one ghost in his life. Or perhaps he has seen a lot of them, and won't tell. Please E. Y. give us another ghost, there's a good haunted man, do! I've tried all sorts of spirits without effect. Nowadays I am trying to get one skeleton at all events into my house by conjurations of ANDREW CLARKE, ROOSE, THOMPSON, and BANTING, by spells of dry toast, no butter, no white of eggs, no sugar, no starch (great deprivation this—I was *so* fond of shirt-fronts fresh from the wash—quite a glutton at them), no fat, no potatoes, no pudding, no sweets, no nothing in fact, and yet the skeleton still weighs fourteen stone with the flesh on. Would fright do it? I shall go on with these *Weird Tales*—one every night at bedtime—and then, "Out, out, brief candle!" and under the clothes disappears the head of the

BRAVE BARON DE BOOK WORMS.

## ADVERTISEMENT GRATIS.

*À PROPOS* of some allusion to *Pepita*, now playing at TOOLE's Theatre, we have received a letter purporting to be written by one of the Managers of this Operatic Company, informing us that "The B. P. know"—what, he doesn't say—"and" (we quote *verbatim*) "their verdict is taken, not a silly paper, and, I am glad to say, we refuse money nightly." Very magnanimous conduct on the part of "We." Refuse money nightly! We wish we—"*nous autres*"—had the chance. Would we avail ourselves of it? Ahem! Well, we must at once visit TOOLE's, and, *pro formâ*, tender our coin? Will it be refused? or, shall we be let in? And if the latter, shall we be let in for something good? *Nous verrons*, "*nous autres.*"

## GENEROUS OFFER.

*Buyer (who having had a legacy of £30, invests in 6 screws for Cab-proprietor's business).* "YOU MIGHT GIVE US A SOVEREIGN FOR LUCK; I'VE DONE FAIRISH BUSINESS."

*Seller.* "WELL, I CAN'T DO THAT. TELL YER WHAT THOUGH, I'LL CHUCK YER THIS OTHER 'OSS IN."

## THE DIARY OF A NOBODY.

*August* 22.—Home sweet Home again. CARRIE bought some pretty blue wool mats to stand vases on. FRIPPS, JANUS & Co. write to say they are sorry they have no vacancy among their staff of clerks for LUPIN.

*Aug.* 23.—I bought a pair of stags'-heads made of Plaster of Paris and coloured brown. They will look just the thing for our little hall and give it style; the heads are excellent imitations. POOLERS AND SMITH are sorry they have nothing to offer LUPIN.

*Aug.* 24.—Simply to please LUPIN, and make things cheerful for him, as he is a little down, CARRIE invited Mrs. JAMES to come up from Sutton and spend two or three days with us. We have not said a word to LUPIN, but mean to keep it as a surprise.

*Aug.* 25.—Mrs. JAMES arrived in the afternoon, bringing with her an enormous bunch of wild-flowers. The more I see of Mrs. JAMES the nicer I think she is, and she is devoted to CARRIE. She went into CARRIE's room to take off her bonnet and remained there nearly an hour talking about dress. LUPIN said he was not a bit surprised at Mrs. JAMES's visit, but was surprised at her.

*Aug.* 26, *Sunday.*—Nearly late for church, Mrs. JAMES having talked considerably about what to wear all the morning. LUPIN does not seem to get on very well with Mrs. JAMES. I am afraid we shall have some trouble with our next-door neighbours who came in last Wednesday. Several of their friends, who drive up in dog-carts, have already made themselves objectionable. An evening or two ago I had put on a white waistcoat for coolness, and while walking past with my thumbs in my waistcoat pockets (a habit I have), one man, seated in the cart, and looking like an American, commenced singing some vulgar nonsense about, "*I had thirteen dollars in my waistcoat pocket.*" I fancied it was meant for me, and my suspicions were confirmed; for, while walking round the garden in my tall hat this afternoon a "throw-down" cracker was deliberately aimed at my hat and exploded on it like a percussion cap. I turned sharply, and am positive I saw the man who was in the cart retreating from one of the bed-room windows.

*Aug.* 27.—CARRIE and Mrs. JAMES went off shopping, and had not returned when I came back from the office. Judging from the subsequent conversation, I am afraid Mrs. JAMES is filling CARRIE's head with a lot of nonsense about dress. I walked over to GOWING's, and asked him to drop in to supper, and make things pleasant. CARRIE prepared a little extemporised supper, consisting of the remainder of the cold joint, a small piece of salmon (which I was to refuse, in case there was not enough to go round), and a blanc-mange and custards. There was also a decanter of port and some jam puffs on the sideboard. Mrs. JAMES made us play rather a good game with cards, called "Muggins." To my surprise—in fact, disgust—LUPIN got up in the middle, and in a most sarcastic tone said, "Pardon me, this sort of thing is too fast for me. I shall go and enjoy a quiet game of marbles in the back garden." Things might have become rather disagreeable but for GOWING (who seems to have taken to LUPIN) suggesting they should invent games. LUPIN said, "Let's play Monkeys." He then led GOWING all round the room, and brought him in front of the looking-glass. I must confess I laughed heartily at this. I was a little vexed at everybody subsequently laughing at some joke which they did not explain, and it was only on going to bed I discovered I must have been walking about all the evening with an antimacassar on one button of my coat-tails.

*Aug.* 28.—Found a large brick in the middle bed of geraniums, evidently come from next door. PATTLES AND PATTLES can't find a place for LUPIN.

*Aug.* 29.—Mrs. JAMES is making a positive fool of CARRIE. CARRIE appeared in a new dress like a smock-frock. She said "Smocking" was all the rage. I replied it put me in a rage. She also had on a hat as big as a kitchen coal-scuttle, and the same shape. Mrs. JAMES went home, and both LUPIN and I were somewhat pleased—the first time we have agreed on a single subject since his return. MERKINS AND SON write they have no vacancy for LUPIN.

---

**Motto for the Gaiety Adapters of "She."**

"IF we do prove him Haggard,
Though that his Jesses were our dear heart-strings,
We'd whistle him off."

(*Joe Knight's Shakspeare, Revised Version. Othello,* Act III., sc. 3.)

DERISION.

*Bagnidge* (*to his Friend's Keeper*). "Tut-t-t-t—dear me! Woodruff, I'm afraid I've shot that Dog

*Keeper.* "Oh no, Sir, I think he's all right, Sir. He mostly drop down like that if anybody Misses!!"

## BEAUTIFUL TAR.

Song of an Enthusiastic Scientist.

Air—"*Beautiful Star.*"

Beautiful Tar, the outcome bright
Of the black coal and the yellow gas-light,
Of modern products most wondrous far,
Tar of the gas-works, beautiful Tar!
Tar of the Gas-works, &c.

In fancy's ear thou seem'st to say,
"Follow me close, I am bound to pay.
On me experiments freely try;
For if there's a *multum in parvo*, 'tis I."
Tar of the Gas-works, &c.

Men told us once, with a cheek quite calm,
Of the things that the Arabs could get from the palm;
But that fraud botanic is distanced far
By the modern marvel, the black Coal-tar.
Tar of the Gas-works, &c.

House and garments, victuals and drink,
The nomad got from the palm, I think;
But as source of beauty, and bliss, and balm,
Coal-tar from the palm-tree must bear the palm. Tar of the Gas-works, &c.

Protoplasm? Oh, that's played out;
The true protoplasm is Tar, no doubt.
As "promise and potency," Tar must take
What vulgar sciolists call "the cake:"
Tar of the Gas-works, &c.

There's hardly a thing that a man may name
Of use or beauty in life's small game,
But you can extract in alembic or jar
From the "physical basis" of black Coal-tar.
Tar of the Gas-works, &c.

Oil, and ointment, and wax, and wine,
And the lovely colours called aniline;
You can make *anything*, from a salve to a star,
If you only know how to, from black Coal-tar. Tar of the Gas-works, &c.

'Tis found the basis of all things sweet;
Sugar is settled, and beet is beat;
The western root and the eastern cane
With ubiquitous Coal-tar contend in vain.
Tar of the Gas-works, &c.

You can carry the stuff in your pocket or hat,
And it will not hurt you, or make you fat;
Of saccharine matters the wholesomest far
Is the stuff extracted from black Coal-tar,
Tar of the Gas-works, &c.

The very bees mistake it for honey!
'Tis a fount of pleasure, a mine of money;
And the Bounty question without a jar
Will soon be settled by black Coal-tar,
Tar of the Gas-works, &c.

Triumph, O Tar! Stuff half divine!
The world's whole interests soon will twine
Around thine essence the subtlest far,
Tar of the Gas-works, black Coal-tar—
Tar of the Gas-works, black Coal-tar!

---

A Person of Light and Leading.—Will o' the Wisp.

## *NOUS* AT NEWNHAM.

(*By a "Babbler in the Land."*)

[Miss Helen Gladstone says that when she was a student at Newnham, a motion was brought before the Debating Society there, and carried by a large majority, that life without gossip was not worth living.]

Excellent, Miss Helen Gladstone!
That is not the frump or "fad's" tone.
Girlhood without Gossip? Dreadful!
Fancy Fanny with a head full
Of *on dits* and tittle-tattle
Sworn against all pretty prattle!
Vowed to theorems and theses!
No, the little talking teases
*Could* not care for Mind or Matter,
Art or Science, without Chatter.
*Mr. Punch*, though gabbling cad you hate,
You'll applaud the "sweet girl graduate"
Who, howe'er chockfull of knowledge
Holds that girlhood, e'en at College,
Still may without blame or loss sip
Talk's essential nectar—Gossip,
Only scorned by peevish quizdom;
For as Wit to heavy Wisdom,
Banter gay to bitter brooding,
*Soufflé* light to suet pudding,
So is Gossip bright and blameless,
As unspiteful as 'tis aimless,
To the heavy altercation
Pompous prigs call Conversation!
Life without it worth the candle?
No, dear *Punch*. Dull spite and scandal
Very properly you tackle,
But you will *not* "cut the cackle."

## DUE NORTH.

*Tower—Obstruction—Berths—Problem—Information—Weather—Passengers—Steward—Picturesque—Uncertainties.*

To the Tower—in a cab! Visions of CRUIKSHANK, HARRISON AINSWORTH, *Maugher of the Axe*, *Xit*, the Giants, the Torture-room, *Cicely* being dragged down-stairs, and Mephistophelian *Simon Renard*. Suppose a shell or two would knock the old place all to smithereens,—to W. H. Smithereens,—*à propos* of HARRISON AINSWORTH.

"We're going to have a very fine Passage!"

The Tower is not a *Tour de force*. Down a dirty lane occupied by vans, carts, and crowds of men,—dockyard labourers waiting for work towards St. Katherine's wharf. Glad to know that I have arrived half an hour before the boat starts, as, if an intending passenger were at all late, and if there were but one waggon more in this dirty narrow lane, and one cab coming up the street when mine is going down, to reach the wharf itself in time to catch the boat would be simply impossible. Not a policeman visible, no official of any sort at hand to regulate the traffic and clear a way to and from the point of departure. How the exports and imports ever get out of these narrow thoroughfares without smashing and jamming, and loss of life, or damage to limb, and how the passengers —especially the female passengers—for the various steamboats ever reach their destination in safety is a marvel to me.

*Happy Thought.*—Yet this stoppage of traffic is appropriate to the locality. The Tower and "the block!"

I meet HOBSON at the entrance to the wharf. He assures me, as his dear friend, that he is as annoyed as I am about the obstruction, and especially annoyed on *my* account. "But look here!" he exclaims abruptly, adroitly changing the subject, "we've got the best berths in the ship!" and he leads the way to the steamer, almost skipping with delight at his own craftiness in securing these exceptional berths.

*Happy Thought.*—The Skipper and his craft.

We have: so much is evident: but two other passengers are to occupy the two other berths in the same cabin.

"Perhaps they won't come," I say, with a glimmer of hope, and relying on the probable obstacles in the narrow approach.

"They're here already," says HOBSON, with an air of genial hospitality, pointing out their overcoats and bags, which I thought were his own.

"I've taken the two upper berths," continues HOBSON, still congratulating himself on his acuteness. "Plenty of air, you see"—here he opens the port-hole—"and the other chaps are very quiet fellows. I've seen them. It will be all right, I'm sure you'll like it."

"Shall I?" I return, doubtfully looking at my berth, which is as high up and about as roomy as the top shelf of the linen-cupboard in an old-fashioned housekeeper's room.

*Problem.* How to get there? Not being a bird, I can't fly up. Not being a gymnast, I can't jump up. If there's no ladder, I must evidently climb up. I mention "ladder" to one of the officials of the steamer who looks in at the cabin casually,—ship's officers I think they're called,—and ship's officer only laughs and goes away again. Clearly a ladder is out of the question; it certainly was out of the answer, as far as the merry but uncommunicative ship's officer is concerned. Consequently, as I put it to HOBSON (who can get into his own berth as easily as possible by merely stepping on to the top of the fixed washing-stand when closed, and crawling in at the foot of the bed), the problem developes itself into two parts. *First:* How to climb without grazing my knees and doing myself some serious internal injury from the effects of which I may never recover. *Secondly:* How to climb up without considerably inconveniencing the man on the shelf below, by kicking him on the head, stamping on his nose, putting my foot on his mouth, or otherwise so alarming him, that, if asleep, he may wake suddenly, forget where he is, think that I am a burglar, and incontinently seize me by the leg and bring me down to the floor, when, unless I am stunned and with both arms and legs broken, there must ensue a combat of two in which the other couple must inevitably join.

"You'll find it very comfortable," says HOBSON; "the ship is lighted by electricity,"—as if this would help me to climb up into my jam-cupboard shelf, or send me to sleep when I get there,—"and the whole place is deliciously clean and comfortable. Let's go on deck," he says, in a persuasive voice, and I follow him as he skips up the companion.

We come upon a communicative passenger, who seems to be an acquaintance of HOBSON'S. He informs us that, "This isn't the Company's new boat. The new boat's much better than this."

"This is a very good boat," protests HOBSON, as if it were his own.

"Oh, she's good enough, and fast enough," says the communicative acquaintance; "but she's old. She's fast, though," he repeats, as if being "old and fast" were a recommendation to anybody.

"Ah! she's a first-rate vessel," says HOBSON, standing to his guns, on my account, I am sure, otherwise, I fancy, he would agree with his communicative acquaintance.

The latter continues, "She's still a good seagoing boat," resumes the communicative acquaintance, "but she's no breadth of beam. She'll roll"—[will she, O dear!]—"she'll roll, if there's any sea on," he repeats, emphatically, as if he were drawing our attention to an inspired prophecy, "she'll roll."

HOBSON observes with equal certainty, "But there will be no sea on." All on my account, I'm sure. I'm afraid his forecast would honestly be in favour of there being "a sea on."

"You should have gone by the new boat," says his acquaintance.

I cannot help asking him how it is that if the new boat is so perfect, he, himself, didn't go by it?

"I *am* going by it, next Saturday," he replies, "I'm only here to see a friend off." And time being up, he bids us good-bye, and in another ten minutes he is on the quay, waving his hat, and pitying us.

Observing me somewhat depressed by this information, HOBSON is careful to assure me that, in his opinion, we shall have a capital passage. True, we are beginning well; but then this is only the river; dirty, but interesting. We have a considerable number of passengers. There are three horse-artillerymen, with swords and spurs, who seem rather out of place on board. There are a few persons, young men and young women, with sticks, rugs, waterproofs, umbrellas, maps, guide-books, and hand-bags; a reserved person in an ulster, with opera-glasses; and three awkward youths of the superior 'Arry type, two of whom are in a state of perpetual admiration of the third, who is a repulsively larky young fellow, in a yachting cap, a dirty-looking flannel shirt, false collars, and probably false cuffs, with a crimson tie, evidently their leader and model in waggery; a staid and very stout old Darby and Joan, who seem glued to their seats, and nudge one another from time to time when they are passing anything that seems to either of them worthy of notice; these, with a few more middle-aged quiet couples, a very English-looking person deeply interested in a French novel with the familiar yellow cover, and a High Church clergyman with a moustache, represent the tourist element. All the others, both fore and aft, seem to be attired in the ordinary top-hat and black coat of London respectability, as if they had strolled down to the wharf, come on board by merest accident, and been carried off before they knew where they were.

Most of these persons at once contract with the Steward for their meals at so much a head for the voyage, and, should the weather prove favourable, they take twice of everything on principle. On a rough passage I suppose the Steward has the best of the bargain. And he certainly plays his cards well, as the time fixed for the dinner on board is two o'clock, just as the ship is off Southend, when bidding farewell to the river, we enter on the real sea-passage.

*Happy Thought.*—If you want to know what sort of passage it is going to be, ascertain the number of passengers contracting at so much a head for their meals, and then *watch the Steward's face after Erith*. If you see the Steward smiling, beware,—if he chuckles and rubs his hands gleefully, prepare for squalls—and if he laughs outright, disappear to your berth, and make such arrangements as your past experience may suggest.

HOBSON is a capital companion. He is most anxious that nothing should even have the appearance of any likelihood to go wrong. He never attempts forced jollity, but, naturally enthusiastic, he has cultivated enthusiasm; and naturally sympathetic, he has cultivated the art of sympathising. I confess to being very soon depressed, especially with the probability of nasty weather in view.

The sky appears lowering.

"We shall have a storm, I think," is my melancholy foreboding.

"Oh, no," replies HOBSON, cheerily. "That dark appearance is due to London smoke." And then he dilates on the subjects of smoke consumption, fogs, chimneys, gas, storage of force, and so forth. In the meantime, I am watching the clouds.

"It's raining, I think," I say, not liking to be certain, and still hoping against hope, as I see the marks of heavy drops falling, as if nails had been driven into the deck at equal distances.

"Rain!" exclaims HOBSON, putting on his glasses, and looking about him with an air of the utmost incredulity at the bare idea of the possibility of such a thing. "Rain? No. I think it's the spray from the engine." And he looks round with a chirpy and perfectly satisfied smile (being much pleased with his own ingenious explanation), just as a heavy rain-drop as big as a pea hits him sharply on the tip of his nose. He looks up with an expression of childlike surprise, as if this were some part in a funny juvenile game, and he had to turn round twice and find out who had touched him on the nose.

"There's more where that came from," I say, seizing the campstool and making for cover under the awning. There is: it comes down heavily.

He follows me with his campstool, and his waterproof buttoned up—for in spite of the sanguine tone of his consolation to others, he himself is never without a handy and really serviceable Mackintosh—and looking round on the people all huddled together like sheep in a storm, he says beamingly, as if he took rather a pride in this downpour, "Ah! that's something like a shower!"

Then he continues:—

"You'll see, this will clear the air; it's just what was wanted—not by *us*," he puts in, finely anticipating the general objection, "but by the atmosphere, and it will be for our benefit, as we shall have a lovely passage. Wind S. by S.W.!" he exclaims, in an ecstasy of delight, turning in that direction; "couldn't be better, dear friend; couldn't be better!"

"The rain makes the deck so sloppy; that's the worst of it," I grumble.

"That *is* the worst of it," returns HOBSON, triumphantly; "I quite agree with you, that *is* the worst of it; but there's no mud, as there would be ashore, and in five minutes the sun will come out and the Captain will send a man with a mop, and the deck will be as dry as a bone. Look, it's stopped now. And there's a dry place right in the middle of the vessel, where you will scarcely feel motion at all."

We enjoy sunshine for a while. But the wily man with the mop does not make his appearance as the clouds are once more gathering.

"Looks threatening," I observe; and I mean it.

"Oh, no," HOBSON replies, rubbing his hands gleefully; "when it begins like this, it's always fine afterwards."

"Rather misty," I say, pointing ahead to a dense grey mist into which we are rapidly steaming.

"Yes, *rather* misty," he returns, for the fact is undeniable; but as he has a good word even for a river-fog, he at once adds cheerfully, "But what a wonderful effect! Look at that boat emerging from the mist like a spectre!"

"Subject for Mistler,—I mean WHISTLER," I observe, gloomily.

"Exactly, dear friend, exactly," he replies, delighted to find me willing to enter into his artistic views of this arrangement in fog and smoke. Then he points towards the dense mass of grey vapour which we are now approaching, and exclaims, "Look!" After which he throws back his head and folds his arms with the air of a connoisseur regarding some great masterpiece of Art, and says, "There! *There* are wonderful effects! Wonderful! wonderful!" And, as a wandering black barge slowly emerges from the fog, he repeats to himself, *sotto voce*, "Wonderful! Beautiful!" in a subdued tone of the most intense admiration. His tone of unqualified approbation reminds me of the old Herr VON JOEL, who used to go about at PADDY GREEN'S selling twopenny cigars for sixpence apiece, and exclaiming, "Pewtiful! Pewtiful!" Then, as the clouds gather thicker and thicker, and the fog becomes more and more dense, he turns towards me, smiling brightly, and says with an air of conviction that deceives nobody, "Ah! dear friend, we shall have a very fine passage."

Hardly are the words out of his mouth than down comes the rain in bucketsful. "*Thunder*," as the stage-directions have it, "*is heard in the distance, and the scene is illuminated with vivid flashes of lightning.*" We descend below.

"If it's going on like this——" I begin, grumbling.

"It won't," HOBSON assures me. "The effects of this storm will be to make the sea perfectly calm, and with the wind in a rather rainy quarter, we shall have a splendid passage. You'll see. It will be beautiful! beautiful! You won't feel even a qualm."

And if I did, he would tell me that the qualm I felt was the best qualm in the world, and that a calm would follow on a qualm, and then, if I were very unwell, he would prove to me scientifically that nothing could be more beneficial to my general health than this short sharp attack of *mal de mer*.

We are steaming down the Thames, with every now and then a stoppage (the signal "Stop her!" being given by a sharp bell and a gruff voice, as it appears to me,—a similar method being used to indicate "Go ahead again!"), in order to allow time for various huge unwieldy barges,—laden or empty, which are generally in charge of an inadequate crew, consisting of a dirty man clinging to a prodigiously long pole, with which he is stirring up the mud, a barking dog very angry with our steamer, and an unkempt indolent boy,—to get out of our way and save themselves from being run down or swamped; and we are rapidly passing landmarks familiar to Londoners who dine at Greenwich, and many more quite unfamiliar even to them. I am beginning to feel hungry. Good or bad sign? "First-rate sign, dear friend," replies HOBSON, enthusiastically. "First-rate! Shows it's agreeing with you." Glad to hear it, but I have my doubts.

## OVENLY!

A CORRESPONDENT, signing himself "A HAUGHTY CULTURIST," sends us this cutting from *The Garden*, which we at once proceed to plant within our own borders:—

Bedded Out; or, "Cometh up as a Flower!"

IMPROVER.—A lady highly recommends a youth, age 17; three years' good general experience under glass in her garden.

Three years under glass! The lady doesn't mention his height, nor his temperament, which must be somewhat of a hot nature associated with the Sunny South.

## THE SYSTEM.

"Lord CHARLES BERESFORD says, indeed, that the fault is not theirs, but that of the system."—*Times*.

WHAT is it, when the Country facts appal,
And men for explanation loudly call,
Delays, impedes, and paralyses all?
The System!

What is it makes our training course effete,
And leaves us, should a foreign foe we meet,
To face him with a makeshift patched-up fleet?
The System!

What, spite the ample millions it obtains,
The public clamour scornfully disdains,
And takes good care the Navy nothing gains?
The System!

What is it hoards up useless stores by tons,
What falsifies on measured mile the runs,
And turns out fighting ships without their guns?
The System!

And what, if peace to war by chance give place,
And bring us and our dangers face to face,
Would launch on us a national disgrace?
The System!

So what should Englishmen, without a doubt,
While yet they've time to know what they're about,
Destroy, tread under foot, smash, trample out?
The System!

"HOMBURGING THEM."—Last season H.R.H. the Prince of WALES found that all the American Dudes at Homburg were sincerely flattering him by closely imitating his costume, whatever it might be. But a genuinely happy thought occurred to H.R.H. He arrayed himself, so the *Liverpool Post* informs us, in hideous attire, the like of which was never seen in Tweed or out of it. The Dudes were done, and H.R.H. bears the distinguished title of the Prince of Wiles.

## OUT OF TOWN.

(UNFASHIONABLE INTELLIGENCE.)

*Visitor.* "What a roaring Trade the Hotels will be doing, with all these Holiday Folk!"

*Head Waiter at The George.* "Lor bless yer, Sir, no! They all bring their Nosebags with 'em!"

## THE "IRREPRESSIBLE CHINEE"!

(*An expansion and new application of the neatest of American Nursery Rhymes.*)

Ping-Wing, the Pieman's Son,
Was a troublesome chap from far Canton.
Wander he would, and wherever he went
He raised up ructions and discontent.
Like little Ah Sid, with his "yukakan!"
He "velly much bothered um Melican man."

Ping-Wing, like little Ah Sid,
Was a cute little yellow-faced Chinee kid;
And, like his compatriot, sly Ah Sin,
He had tricks that are dark and an eye to the tin:
To scrape and store it afar he'd roam,
But he always wanted to *spend* it at home.

Ping-Wing he could "terribly toil,"
A sleek-faced slave—till he'd sacked the spoil.
Then Ping-Wing, the Pieman's Son,
Would hook it homeward to far Canton,
And live in comfort and cut a dash
At the West's expense with the West's hard cash.

Ping-Wing, with his saffron face,
Played it rather low down on the Western race;
For he worked so cheap and he worked so quick,
And never resented the snub or kick;
And the West conceived it could play and rest
Whilst Ping-Wing worked for it. Innocent West!

Ping-Wing he would wash and scrub,
Whilst the Western male abhors the tub,
He would slave and save, and live upon rice,
Which to Western molars is not so nice.
So the wise West chortled, and argued thus:—
"This yaller Nigger's a useful cuss!"

But the Western wiseacres didn't quite see
The whole of the game of the Heathen Chinee;
And *when* they twigged Ping-Wing his plan,
It fearfully flustered the "Melican man,"
And raised no end of a hullaballoo
In the land of the bounding kangaroo.

Ah Sid, when a bee by mistake he got,
Found "um Melican butterfly velly much hot,"
So the Melican man and the Cornstalk bold
Soon found Ping-Wing was too hot to hold,
And, despite his patience and power of work,
Ping-Wing isn't wanted too near New York.

The Congress found that the Pieman's Son
Had much better keep to his own Canton;
That his shifty fingers and saffron skin
Might suit Hong-Kong or might fit Pekin,
Or any abode near the Chinese Wall;
But were not wanted in 'Frisco at all.

Though Ping-Wing toiled, and was meek and mild,
Chinese cheap labourers domiciled
'Twixt the Pacific and the Atlantic
Were quickly driving the Yankee frantic.
Diplomacy saw it were clearly best
To speed Ping-Wing as a parting guest.

But Ping-Wing, the Pieman's Son,
Is a dogged critter not easily done.
The wild West wanted his neck in the noose
Of "Heads I win, (pig) tails you lose."
But the Treaty shaped that wish to gratify,
Celestial cuteness refused to ratify.

So Senator Scott he ups, and he,
Like Bill Nye, "goes for that Heathen Chinee."
The Western World for the issue waits,
But all about the Pacific Coast States
You may hear men singing of Chinese crime
To this newest shape of a Nursery Rhyme:—

"Ping-Wing, the Pieman's Son,
Was a troublesome cuss from far Canton.
He laboured hard, and he lived on rice,
But his tricks were dark, and his tastes not nice.
He burnt the Convention, and then said he,
'Me wonder whar dat Treaty be!'"

## "DOUBLING."

In the case of Woodworth *v.* Sugden, reported last Saturday, Mr. Justice Denman is reported to have asked—

"Is Mr. Sugden advertised to appear at both Theatres to-morrow night?
*Mr. Bramwell Davis.* Yes."

What a wonderful man! What a marvellous being in whose weird existence the laws of time and space are annihilated, and the powers of the Chancery Division have actually to be invoked in order to restrain Mr. Sugden from appearing in two places at once!

# THE "IRREPRESSIBLE CHINEE"!

"PING-WING, THE PIEMAN'S SON,
WAS A TROUBLESOME CUSS FROM FAR CANTON.
HE LABOURED HARD, AND HE LIVED ON RICE,
BUT HIS TRICKS WERE DARK, AND HIS TASTES NOT NICE.
HE BURNT THE CONVENTION, AND THEN SAID HE,
'ME WONDER WHAR DAT TREATY BE!'"—*American Nursery Rhyme revised.*

## PLAY-TIME AT THE HAYMARKET.

NOT by any means a model of construction, conventional in its dialogue and action, with scarcely a line worth remembering, with only a glimmer of comedy-humour here and there in the characters of *Lady Betty* and old *Seabrook*, and with one strong dash of misplaced burlesque melodrama in the character of the Demon Butler, whose part is considerably damaged by the absence of topical song and dance, *à la* LESLIE, as *Jonathan Wild*—with all these defects, and in spite of them, *Captain Swift* is, in itself, a Drama of powerful dramatic interest, and so admirably acted all round, that it holds an audience enthralled from the rise to the fall of the Curtain. The story is clearly told, and the acting is excellent—herein is the open secret of its success, for success it must have already achieved.

Dance of the Victim Master and Demon Butler, as (it ought to be) performed at the T.R. Haymarket.

Occasionally marred by some conventional melodramatic starts—false starts—which with melodramatic asides of the old-fashioned "Ha! that face!" or, "Ha! that voice!" "Strange!" "'Tis he!" pattern,—wrongly supposed to be necessary for emphasising "a situation,"—Mr. BEERBOHM TREE'S *Wilding, alias Captain Swift*, is a very fine performance. Certainly, the touching and impressive scene of the farewell in the last Act could not possibly be better rendered than it is by Mr. and Mrs. BEERBOHM TREE; indeed, the latter I have never yet seen to so great advantage. I do not think Mrs. TREE ever succeeds in her "make-up" for the stage,—too white, I should say. But to find fault is easy, to suggest the improvement is difficult. There is a great natural charm in Mrs. TREE'S impersonation of the otherwise conventional character of a love-sick, romantic young lady. The faults of this part are the author's; its virtues the actress's.

LADY MONCKTON is heart and soul in the very trying part of *Mrs. Seabrook*. She seems to be oblivious of the audience, and actually to be the character she impersonates. The art is less completely concealed than in that exceptionally finished performance of hers as the wife of *Jim the Penman*. But this again is the author's fault.

As I consider it all round, I must own that I do not remember ever having seen a piece so lifted above the commonplace and conventional by the talent of the actors, as is this play of *Captain Swift*. There is a jarring note in the scene in Act III., between *Wilding* and *Mrs. Seabrook*, and it is this:—the audience share with *Mrs. Seabrook* the knowledge that she is *Wilding's* mother. *Wilding* is in ignorance of the fact; so that when *Mrs. Seabrook* makes affectionate advances towards him, the unscrupulous Bushranger would see in this what *Captain Hawksley* saw in *Mrs. Sternhold's* affection for him; that is, additional profit and safety out of this middle-aged woman's vanity. The audience, undoubtedly, must take this view of the scene, and so, when *Mrs. Seabrook* sits on the sofa, and says, in a comparatively light and airy tone, "Come and sit beside me," there is a titter through the house just at a critical moment when the scene, which requires the most delicate handling by the actors, without any help from the author, can least bear it. I fancy both Mr. TREE and Lady MONCKTON will agree with me on this point.

Melodramatic music played throughout the dialogue of this same great scene in Act III. is, emphatically, a mistake; it interrupts the action, and distracts the attention, tires the audience, and hence it happens that the charming song of Mrs. TREE'S, subsequently "heard without," which should be so effective, becomes an anti-climax. This Act should have ended with the exit of *Wilding*, which should have been simultaneous with the last note of the song, and the fall of the Curtain. The letter-reading is another anti-climax.

Miss LECLERCQ attempts too much with the very common-place and, for her, very poor and uncongenial part of *Lady Staunton*, who, after all, is a mere type of the "*confidante*," or "Charles his friend," in petticoats. In make-up, Mr. TREE, Mr. MACKLIN, and Mr. KEMBLE are perfect.

Having naturally alluded to *Captain Hawksley*, I would ask why adapt the well-worn business of the cigar-lighting from *Still Waters run Deep?* It was highly effective in the scene between *John Mildmay* and *Captain Hawksley*; it is singularly pointless in an analogous scene between *Mr. Gardiner* and *Captain Swift*.

Since Mr. TOOLE made *The Butler* a popular character on the stage, there has been a run on butlers. Nowadays, no piece is perfect without a butler in it of some sort, comic, tragic, melodramatic, or demoniac. It is this last type that Mr. CHARLES HADDON has selected for his play of *Captain Swift*. Mr. HADDON must have had butler on the brain,—can he affirm that he Haddon't?—as the grotesque demoniac character has so little to do with the essence of the plot, that he may be at once set down as superfluous. This Superfluous Demon Butler, as impersonated by Mr. BROOKFIELD with genuine burlesque melodramatic humour, just gives the necessary comic relief to the play. When *Captain Swift* is heard making a bag of himself in September by blowing out his brains off the stage, it is a pity that the comic countryman Detective (new type, created and patented by Mr. CHARLES ALLAN), and the helpless old Foozle, capitally represented by Mr. KEMBLE (another version of *Brother Potter*, also from *Still Waters*), should not have descended all together by a trap licensed to hold three comfortably, with the Superfluous Demon Butler standing over them; and perhaps, if there were room in the trap for four, I should add *Lady Betty* to the group.

The Demon Butler, who is made up rather after one of the acrobatic GIRARDS, disappoints every one by not sliding over the tables and chairs as a genuine GIRARD would certainly have done. He is, as I have said, Superfluous; all the use he can be put to is to help the Detective, and, as far as that goes, the Detective, "from information received," could get on just as well, even better, without him. Unless the Demon Butler has a prologue, an *entr'acte* topical song and dance, and an epilogue, with final disappearance down a trap-door, he will always be "superfluous" as long as *Captain Swift* shall run, which ought to be, and I sincerely hope will be, for many hundred nights. When the inevitable Country Company go on tour with *Captain Swift*, the superfluous Demon Butler might be played without words by a clever pantomimist, and called the "Dumb Waiter." This would be at once economical and effective. Every lover of good acting should go and see *Captain Swift*, on the recommendation of JACK IN THE PRIVATE BOX.

## ALDERMANO ITALIANO.

*At the Guildhall. Prosecution by the National Vigilance Society for publishing Boccaccio's "Decameron."*

"'The book,' said Mr. AVORY for the defence, 'had been in publication for over 400 years, and at the present time there were three copies of the work in the English language in the Guildhall Library, and about 200 in the British Museum.' Mr. Alderman PHILLIPS, who had previously mentioned that he had read *The Decameron*, both in Italian and English, said he did not intend to send this case for trial, because he did not for a moment believe that a jury would convict. The case was then dismissed."—*Daily Telegraph.*

Rather a change from what would probably have happened some forty years ago, in the good old days of JOHN LEECH'S and DICKY DOYLE'S Aldermen, when there were Corporations within the Great Corporation; when no Alderman could have been alluded to physically as a No-body, when Wenison was their Wittles, and Tuttle was their only soup, and like *Sir John Falstaff*, they "babbled," not of "green fields," but of "green fat." In those good old days, had this case come before Mr. Alderman and Sheriff GUZZLER (of the firm of BOOZER, SWILLY AND GUZZLER, Portsoken Ward), the report might have been on this wise:—

*Alderman.* Eh? D. CAMERON? DONALD CAMERON, of course.

*Counsel* (*explaining*). The *Decameron* of BOCCACCIO, your Worship.

*Alderman.* Ah! I didn't catch his title—DONALD CAMERON of Bock—what was it? There's a CAMERON of Loch Something, and there's a CAMERON in the Ward, a most respectable Councillor and Vintner.

*Counsel* (*further explaining*). No, Mr. Alderman, this is a Book.

*Alderman.* A Book?—eh? Oh, not Bock. Book? DONALD CAMERON, of Bookcadgers, did you say?

And so forth. And then the publisher would have been fined, and the editions confiscated. And now, "*on a changé tout cela*," as the Belgian LORD MAYOR would say, and be immediately understood by more than one decorated Deputy. Did the prosecution of the ZOLA translations come before Alderman PHILLIPS? No doubt he has put his knowledge of the French language to as good a purpose as he has his proficiency in Italian. Pity that he didn't have the opportunity of saying, "I've read all these in the—ahem—in the original French (*applause in Court, immediately suppressed by the usher*), and I really do not think that a jury, who couldn't possibly possess my educational advantages, ought to have a chance of convicting,—as I am sure they will, if I send the case for trial."

That's the sort of Alderman and Sheriff. "Sheriff thou art, and shalt be more hereafter!" All hail, Future Lord Mayor! The expiring Mayoralty wants a few little Italian olives, just to give it some fillips.

MARRIAGE EVIDENTLY NOT A FAILURE.

*Joan* (*to Darby, who is getting stout*). "LET ME TIE IT FOR YOU, DARLING."

## A SERIOUS QUESTION.

Is it not within the bounds of probability that to the highly-coloured pictorial advertisements to be seen on almost all the hoardings in London, vividly representing sensational scenes of murder, exhibited as "the great attractions" of certain dramas, the public may be to a certain extent indebted for the horrible crimes in Whitechapel? We say it most seriously;—imagine the effect of these gigantic pictures of violence and assassination by knife and pistol on the morbid imagination of unbalanced minds. These hideous picture-posters are a blot on our civilisation, and a disgrace to the Drama.

## LEGISLATIVE WORK AND WAGES.

IN proof that the "Payment of Members," if now legalised, would be no novelty, "SCACCARIUS" sends the *Times* the subjoined extract from the Exchequer records during the period of the "Long Parliament":—

"Received by mee, JOHN MERRICK, Knt. of THOMAS FFAULCONBRIDGE, Esq., Receiver Genl. of the Revenue, the some of fiftie twoe for my weekly allowance of fower pounds as a Member of the Comone House of Parliamnt due for one quarter of a yeere ended at Michas. last 1645. By warrant from the Committee dated 25th of October 1645. I say received £52. "JO. MEYRICK."

It were superfluous to observe that Mr. MEYRICK could not even spell his own name, merely because he appears to have spelt it in different ways. Even the Divine WILLIAMS himself did that. But suppose the Legislature were in these days to decree the award of pay to Honourable Members of the House of Commons for their attendance in Parliament, and required them to give a receipt for the money, wouldn't it be more than possible that some of the "Representatives of Labour" (to whom wages might be an object) would pretty nearly reproduce the deviations from the Dictionary remarkable in the foregoing transcript? A man's a man for a' that. Of course, a good deal depends on how much "a' that" might be. And an able but unlettered politician would need hardly declare, as the principal character in some old farce, when taxed with his orthography, used to say,—"It isn't the orthography that I care about, but it's that dashed spelling."

REPORTED BY G. OSB-RNE M-RG-N OR "THE OTHER G. O. M."—"MR. G." has enjoyed some uncommonly deep-sea-fishing sport in the recess, with Sprats to catch Wales.

"SOCIALISM AND TIGHT-LACING" are incompatible, morally. For the Socialist theory tends to the loosening of all bonds.

## THE WOLF AT OUR DOOR.

*A Morality from Norse Mythology.*

[In the Norse Mythology, the Wolf Fenris (Crime), rages for food in the precincts of Asgard. Ultimately, the Sword-god Tyr, loaded Fenris with the chain Gleipner, and thrust a sharp sword into his mouth, to prevent him biting more. Thus, says the legend, is Crime, which threatens to corrupt the human race, bound by the apparently slight fetters of Law, and as the power of the Wolf was broken by the Sword, that of Crime is kept under by the awards of Justice.]

WANTED a Gleipner! 'Tis very plain
That the Wolf 's abroad and has slipped his chain;
For the ruthless red-fanged savage,
In square, in street, and in sordid slum,
Strikes Justice helpless, and terror dumb
With his cruel unchecked ravage.
Law and Order? The catch-word slips
With ease complacent from canting lips.
The Law that Labour's last mite exacts,
The Order that silence for sorrow enacts,
These claim the world's solicitude;
For Property 's timorous, Wealth would tread
In peace and quiet its wine-press red,
And Culture shrinks with a querulous dread
From violence and vicissitude;
But Law alert at the poor man's hest
And Order that giveth the humblest rest,
Are these high matters the soul to vex
Of Statesman Y Z, or Policeman X.?

Could Tyr the Sword-god from Asgard come
To a West-end waste or an East-end slum,
Could he take a stroll when the night falls dark
Through Poverty's pleasaunce or People's park,
What would the Norse-god say? Why this.
"It is fearsomely clear that the Wolf Fenris,
As erst in Asgard olden,
Is 'waked by the moon and wants something to eat!'"
True the Law, in blue, is about on his beat,
But the echo far of his falling feet
At the distant end of the dusky street,
The Wolf doth but embolden.
His jaws are wide, and his teeth are white,
His eye is watchful, his tread is light,
The keen curst creature, a hideous sight!
Alone, or hungrily herded.
His play his death, and his life is prey.
Nay, bold from custom he braves the day,
In the silent waste or the narrow way,
And snatches sudden whate'er may stray
Beyond reach of the weapon wherewith—they say—
Law's vigilant guard is girded.
That Wolf, in faith, hath a shifting face:
Hunger and lust you may ever trace,
And blood-greed red and ruthless.
But now 'tis a visage of youth; anon
The brute-boy's beetling scowl is gone,
And you shudder and shrink as you look upon
Hag-age, hell-eyed, and toothless.
Nothing of harpy or gruesome ghoul,
That fiction shapes in its visions foul,
Naught of fiendish in form or glance
Dreamed in the broodings of wild romance,
Ever took horror of eviller shape.
Gorgon's rival, Chimæra's ape,
This Protean wolf-maw'd creature.
Sullen and sinister ruffian now,
Anon with a wanton yet womanly brow,
Again the monster doth mop and mow
With childish form and feature;
Yet wolfish ever, and wolf all through,
This new Fenris of an Asgard new.
But in sage in ermine, or man in blue,
We scarce discover the Sword-god true,
Our Wolf to seize and shackle.
The "Underground People,"—so it is said,—
Prepared a chain for their Thing of Dread,
Which, "small and slight as a silken thread,"
Was strong as steel, and heavy as lead,
Which gagged the maw, and which stayed the tread
Of the Fenris Wolf. Wake Tyr from the dead,
Our lupine foe to tackle!
Our "Underground People," whom we expect
To—Tyr would laugh at the word!—"detect,"

## OUR JAPANNERIES. No. 15.

CROSSING THE CHANNEL.

For all their mystery, somehow fail
To follow the slot, or to track the trail
Of the Protean Wolf, or his steps restrain
With the slight but terrible Gleipner chain;
Or, to thrust athwart his merciless maw,
The sharp, strong sword of unfailing Law.

---

THE COMING WINTER.—We hope no City Speculator has yet come across this advertisement in the *York Herald* of Sept. 4, 1888:—"TO LET, 8 Acres of FOG, to be eaten with Sheep." We have to swallow quite enough Fog already without being forced to accept as a daily dish, "Cold Shoulder of Mutton with Fog Sauce!" Boat stewards could vary their *menu* with "Chops of the Channel and Sea-fog pie."

---

### NEW NURSERY RHYME.

(Not *Sung at the late Eisteddfod.*)

TAFFY was a Welshman,
GLADDY was a chief;
GLADDY went to TAFFY's house,
To give his tongue relief.
GLADDY, when in TAFFY's house,
Thought himself at home;
But TAFFY, fearing party rouse,
With him picked a bone.
GLADDY went to TAFFY's house,
And his say he said;
But oh! he needed all his *nous*,
*Two* zealotries to wed.

## "SHE-THAT-OUGHT-NOT-TO-BE-PLAYED!"

*A Story of Gloomy Gaiety.*

Part I.—*Led by the Nose.*

I have agreed to write down my terrible experiences. A will stronger than my own desires it. I can but obey. If I could, I would refuse. For I had hoped to have done for ever with the novelist who revels in gore. Moreover, I have quite forgotten the incidents of the particular book that has been "dramatised by permission," and then "re-written and adapted" by an author, a stage

"She-that-must-be-obeyed."

manager, and a lady with the sometimes frequently-reiterated name of Clo. My memory is a blank, save that I have a feeling of gentle pain, as I indistinctly recall a prosy leader-spouting sorceress, who, to the best of my recollection, before dying turned into a monkey, and a man who was called Holly, to give opportunities for the perpetration of mild puns upon his name, and a terrible bore, called Job. Ah, yes, I remember the last! A nightmare, a horrible nightmare! —feebly humorous, insipid beyond conception, stupid to the last degree! And was I to see all this? Oh, horror! Led by the nose!

Part II.—*Heard through the Years.*

Let me quickly get through my task. I was in the Temple of the Drama devoted to this fearsome work. I saw around me faces that I had seen before. In a large box, apparently inconveniently crowded, sat, or rather perambulated, a pale person in a *pince-nez*, who seemed to take the greatest possible interest in the proceedings. This pale person in the *pince-nez* fairly fascinated me, and, when I was weary of looking at the stage (and I confess I was often, very often weary), I fixed my gaze upon him. And then a wonderful thing happened. Whenever I glanced at him, whatever might have been the provocation—however dull and prosaic and profitless may have been the dialogue,—I never found him asleep!

But to my task,—a bitter one. I saw before me the interior of a Palace, that somehow recalled to me *Nitocris* at Drury Lane. There was one striking article of furniture, a modern reading-desk, that seemingly had become petrified into stone for the occasion. Then I noticed a man called the Keeper of the Queen's Records, and those Records I discovered were three Deeds, looking with their seals about two thousand years younger than they were represented to be. Then a portly person appeared, dressed as an ancient Greek, save that his arms were tattooed after a decidedly modern fashion. Then came a gorgeously apparelled dame, who, from her proneness to spout without danger of interruption (in a tone that might mean a fortune to a curate reading the funeral service) what seemed to me to be lengthy leading articles on more or less interesting subjects, and from her fondness for, and power of keeping well in the limelight, I recognised as "the One who must be obeyed." And the lady in the limelight stabbed the ancient Greek with the modernly tattooed arms, and the Curtain fell for the first time. It would have been better for my peace of mind if the Curtain (so far as that evening was concerned) had fallen for ever! But no; I had to suffer for hours longer! Suffering to be heard through the years—heard through the years!

Part III.—*Seen by the Eyes.*

I was in Holly's Rooms at Cambridge. Holly, I found, wearing a maroon-hued velvet coat, and puce-coloured black-striped trousers! And then came the infliction of inflictions! Job, the would-be comic servant! Oh, how hard it was to bear! How hard! Even now, I shiver and turn cold when I think of him! They were joined, these strange ones, by the ancient and portly Greek with the modernly tattooed arms. This last was now dressed in a rather horsey costume of the nineteenth century; and then a strange thing happened. Without contradiction he declared, in spite of his portliness and other appearances distinctly arguing to the contrary that he was only five-and-twenty! Then this trio examined a box, and in the boredom that followed, a feeble glimmer of recollection of having read something somewhere like it before floated through my weary mind. Then the trio got on a Dhow of peculiar construction, and there was a mutiny and the stage became very dark. Then a strange thing happened. The crew, seemingly with considerable exertion, pulled the ship to pieces, and then drew a carpet over the remains. And the carpet was violently agitated, and the trio reappeared in a boat, and in the distance was the painting of the head of a comic negro! And a sense of deep relief filled my soul as the Curtain descended and allowed me to see no more! Oh, the weariness of that which had been seen by the eyes—seen by the eyes!

Part IV.—*Caught on the Cheek.*

Then came several hours in the land of Kor. I have a recollection of a lady wearing white muslin and a serpent, who wandered about always, always, in the limelight. I fancy she must have spoken for a very long while. And the ancient and portly Greek in the horsey clothes and tattooed arms, he, too, seems to have had a great deal to say. And I recall to mind an old man who got a laugh by calling the person in the puce-coloured and black-striped trousers "a baboon." And I have a vision too of some mild dancing by a small and select *corps de ballet*. And then I have standing out distinctly in my mind the black shadow of the greatest bore of them all. Job! Job! Job! Oh, the feeble "jokes," oh, the melancholy "wheezes!" And I know that there must have been several scenes, even if there were but little action. Stay, did I not see Holly dangling in mid air, supported by an iron wire attached to a hook? But my mind seems to have partly slumbered until I came to "The Cavern of the Fire of Life." Ah, I remember it well. It was an unusual cavern, and now and again there was a whistle that somehow or other recalled to me the joint forms of the stage-manager and the prompter, and then followed a rumbling noise attended by a puff of steam, that suggested to me a suburban laundry on a slack washing-day. And at length the lady (who, I gathered, had lived for more than two thousand years in the limelight), divested herself of most of her white muslin and all of her serpent, and disappeared in the fumes of the suburban laundry. And immediately there was some shouting, and a pleasantly-fat person in grey rags and a white wig staggered in from the wings and fell on the stage, and was soon hidden from view by the distinctly welcome Curtain. And there was applause. Then a young lady in a costume of masculine cut, walked across the stage, accompanied by an elderly gentleman. And more applause followed, and various members of the cast crossed the stage, inclusive of the lady of the limelight. And then a strange thing happened. The pale person in a *pince-nez*, in the apparently inconveniently crowded private-box, suddenly appeared in the front of the *loge* alone, and began to address us. He told us that he believed the piece we had just sat out with so much weary patience would "make, with a few alterations, an exceedingly fine play," and said something complimentary about the performance of the lady in the limelight. And this was the great comic effect of the evening! The speaker who thus praised the story I was told was the author of the story himself! Caught on the cheek! Caught on the cheek! "Caught on"—the *cheek!*

### Doctrine v. Deed.

"*Laissez-faire!*" cries caustic Bramwell.
He can scourge a sumph or sham well;
But one law at least is there:
He *can't* yield to,—*Laissez-faire!*

☞ **NOTICE.—Rejected Communications or Contributions, whether MS., Printed Matter, Drawings, or Pictures of any description, will in no case be returned, not even when accompanied by a Stamped and Addressed Envelope, Cover, or Wrapper. To this rule**

## B. & S.

*(Extracts from a Diary of Travel.)*

B. & S. are nothing to drink. So WILFRID LAWSON needn't "rise to order" any. B. is a rising town on one side of the Estuary of the Rubble. S. is a rising town on the other. B. looks down on S. S. loftily ignores B. Remember in days of earlier travel spending some time in town of St. Louis, U.S.A. Whiled away breakfast hour by reading what Kansas papers said of St. Louis, and what St. Louis journals said of Kansas. Month, September; flies abundant. Coloured gentleman told off with big fan to every couple in coffee room; fan always going in one hand, brushing off flies, whilst dishes served and removed with other. Newspaper controversy of the day turned on subject of flies. Kansas papers denounced St. Louis as fly-blown. When coloured gentleman temporarily removed flies from surface of St. Louis local journal, I read dignified deprecation of distinction thrust upon the city. "We do not," wrote the editor, "deny an occasional fly in St. Louis; but there are times when the outlines of objects in the domestic economy of Kansas are literally obliterated by the pest. Recently, a citizen of St. Louis entered the principal hotel in Kansas, intending to take his breakfast. 'What have you got a black cloth on the table for?' he asked the boy. 'That's not a cloth,' said the boy, whisking his fan. '*That's flies.*' And so it was."

"I rise to Order."

B. & S. do not indulge in open recrimination like St. L. and K. But they think the more.

The favours of the Estuary unequally divided. B. gets all the water; S. all the sand. B. has high tide twice a day; S. once a fortnight. S. says there's nothing like sand. "Water for me," says B. S. rigs up boats on wheels, and careers madly over the dunes. B. puts to sea in pleasure-boats, stepping right off its own sea-wall, and smiles with aggravating insolence at S.'s argosies. B. has a park facing the sea, enclosed within jealously guarded gates, accessible only to lordly residents. The sun arranges matters so that it sets full in sight of the park. Only Ireland between B. and the boundless Atlantic.

"Ireland in the way, as usual," said CLAUD HAMILTON, who, when Member for Liverpool, sometimes visited B.

But when it comes to the seasons, S. has the pull over B. B. has a summer season. So has S., and a winter season into the bargain. At B., people lodge. In S. they dwell. "Good Americans when they die, go to Paris." In the manufacturing districts of Lancashire, good general dealers when they retire, go to S. It is the very paradise of the *bourgeoisie*. Always looks as if it had just had its hands and face washed.

Late of Liverpool.

WHITLEY, another cheap tripper from Liverpool, with hands behind his back and smile on his face, says it reminds him of

> ". . . . the rose just washed in a shower
> Which MARY to ANNA conveyed."

(COWPER was the poet of WHITLEY's childhood; clings to him still.)

B. is an agglomeration of lodging-houses; S. is a congeries of residences. In new part of the town, every house is detached; everyone has a peaked roof; everyone is built of red brick; everyone has a grass plot in front; everyone has a little garden behind; everyone is prim and clean, and passing rich on the savings of a well spent life.

Also of Liverpool.

S., though it rather looks down on the summer, since B. shares its attractions and its advantages, is not above entertaining the day-trippers. They come in thousands, every day from July through September. Oldham, Manchester, Wigan, Preston, Liverpool, Bolton, Blackburn, Stockport, pour in their tens of thousands from the teeming mills. Those that land at B., presently take steamer, cross over to S., and return, grievously ill all the way. Those that land at S., journey in the same way to B. Four hours they spend at either side, on sand or sea-wall. A pleasant sight to see. All dressed in their best. Mother and father, sons and daughters, and babies innumerable. As different from Margate as East from West. Quaint in speech, odd in manner, amazing in dress; all honest pale-faced working men and women, sniffing the fresh air and gazing on the unaccustomed scene with infinite gusto. S. knows 'ARRY not, nor is B. acquainted with 'ARRIET.

"Like to see this, dear TOBY," said W. F. LAWRENCE, bowing gracefully to cheap trippers, who looked as if they might possibly be electors of the Abercromby division of Liverpool. "Quite a change from Salisbury Plain, which I am more accustomed to frequent."

At B. came unexpectedly upon ADDISON, Q.C., of Ashton-under-Lyne. Adds the last touch of genial attractiveness to the place. Pretty to see him standing on marge of Ocean, regarding its going and coming with friendly glance. Just the same here as in House of Commons. ADDISON, Q.C., walks up floor, beaming impartially on crowded benches right and left. House smiles back on him, and, before he reaches appointed place, and his portly person sinks into seat, murmur of welcoming cheer goes round. So it is at B. ADDISON, Q.C., standing with hands in trousers' pockets, and feet far apart, strides and smiles on the Irish Channel. Irish Channel returns friendly gleam of recognition; ADDISON breaks into ripple of happy laughter; and the sea roars back a delighted guffaw.

"A Constituent, I presume!"

Why this should be I don't know, any more than why ADDISON, Q.C., and House of Commons should always be smiling at each other. But so it is. B. and S. still divided by Estuary of Rubble, are momentarily united in happy effervescence while ADDISON, Q.C., standing on the prim sea-wall, looks across the Rubble at the yellow sands.

---

## TYPICAL TOPICAL STORIES FOR THE DEAD SEASON.

### REMARKABLE INCIDENT IN PALL MALL.

THE United Service Club (called by the Members of the Junior United Service Club "The Senior") was closed for repairs. Taking pity upon their miserable position—cold and coffee-room-less—the Committee of the Athenæum had asked the Members of the Senior to become for the nonce honorary guests of the more literary Club. The invitation had been accepted with avidity, and the staid-looking mansion standing at the south-west corner of Waterloo Place was crowded with elderly warriors belonging both to the Army and the Navy. As everyone knows, the Athenæum prides itself upon its Bishops. The Primate is, so to speak, the *spécialité de la maison*. But it was September, and few, very few, of the ordinary Members of the Athenæum were in Town. On the other hand, the invited warriors were present in abundance.

It was in the Coffee Room. An exciting scene was being acted. A waiter had produced an imperfectly cooked chop. The Generals and the Admirals were very wrath, and the use of the capital "D" had become most fashionable. It was then that the Bishop of —— entered the Coffee Room, and, listlessly seating himself at a table, ordered a chop. He was composing a sermon, and was unconscious of the noise around him. At length the should-be succulent viand was placed before him. He thrust his fork into it, and found that it was imperfectly cooked. He was about to utter an exclamation of anger when the steward interposed.

"Nay, my Lord. Curb your profane tongue. See those innocents. Not before the (Naval and Military) boys!"

And suppressing an oath the good Bishop gave his blessing to the warlike throng, who sank on their knees to receive it. And it was at this point I awakened from my slumbers, and found that what I had witnessed was only a dream!

---

APPROPRIATE CANTATA FOR THE NEXT "FESTIVAL OF THE THREE QUIRES."—*The Jackdaw of Reams.*

# WOOING THE AFRICAN VENUS.

*(Some way after Homer's Hymn to Aphrodite.)*

[A Charter has just been granted to the Imperial British East Africa Company. This Company will now administer and develop a territory with an estimated area of about 50,000 square miles, including some of the most fertile and salubrious regions of Eastern Africa.]

THE force, O Muse, and functions now unfold
Of Afric's Venus, graced with mines of gold;
Who e'en in BISMARCK lights love's furious fire,
And makes all men woo her with hot desire.
From all earth's nations, Frenchman, Portuguese,
From Yankee shores and from all Europe's [seas,
Adventurous patriots crowd to seek and share
Love of the Libyan Venus. Three there are
Whose minds are mainly set upon that love:
The Briton, proud as Ægis-bearing Jove,
Who deems her indevirginate, her eyes
Being black and burning, like her own fierce skies.

He for her preference will do all he can,
Who never faltered in the face of man.
Shunning not strife, or Mars his warlike banes,
But much preferring Trade; his artizans
Taught all earth's countries all the Arts that are
Associate with things vehicular.
The Teuton next, a stalwart suitor he,
A trifle truculent, a mite too free,
Holding all things in war and wooing fair,
Hoping tomato cheeks and orange hair,
By force of contrast, may avail to win
The dusky Aphrodite—and her "tin."
Thirdly, the broad Batavian, scant of grace,
Who trusts a lucky "start" in the love-chase
Gives him such lead that they who run from scratch
The lumpy "limit-man" may fail to catch.
Others—the Frank, the Belgian—too there be,
But just as Paris had the choice of three,
So the Black Venus seems confronted now
By three chief suitors.
Swart yet stately brow
To which one wilt thou bend in coy selection?
O coal-black Charmer, all thy swart perfection
Of ebon-moulded limb and sable hair
To the hot winds of torrid Libya bare,
Witches the world as once, in style the same,
"The all-of-gold-made-laughter-loving-dame"—
As Chapman after Homer calls her—did
At odorous Cyprus. Lifting languorous lid,
Late late in the world's history thou dost draw,
As did the Paphian when her form men saw,
Snow-white and rose-tinct from the waves arise.
Thou art not snow and rose-leaf to our eyes,
But "tawny-fronted," like the Egyptian Queen;
Yet what strange Cleopatra charms are seen
In thy most opulent blackness, that bewitch
All modern men who would be loved—and rich.
Homer—and Chapman—speak in diction bold
Of "Cyprian Venus, graced with mines of gold."
They write of one—but then 'twas not a man—
"Whom all the gold of Venus never can
Tempt to affect her pacts with god or man."
Well, that was not John Bull, but priggish Pallas—
What man unto thy golden charm is callous,
O ebon-skin'd, yet aureate Aphrodite?
But stay! Poetic flights should not be flighty
That deal with themes like goddesses and gold.
Who is the new Anchises, kingly bold,
Whom rich-crown'd Afric Venus will approve,
And dower with her profitable love?
Anchises with the Paphian had the pull,
Shall it be so to-day with brave John Bull?
It looks a little like it. See him stand,
Love in his eyes, a Charter in his hand!
Such strenuous wooing is most apt to win
Women of mortal or immortal kin.
The swarthy Siren whom all men desire
Looks on him coyly, yet with eyes of fire.
Teuton, Batavian, Frank will Venus shunt?
Well, Bull at least is fairly to the front.

## PLAY-TIME AT THE COMEDY THEATRE.

What the plot of *Uncles and Aunts* may be, I have only the vaguest idea. Everybody pretends to be somebody else, nobody is anybody in particular, but the girls, Miss Cissy Grahame and Miss Vane Featherston—she isn't in the least vain, I'm sure—are very pretty and lively. Mr. Penley, with his wonderful make-up and his quaint silliness, is immensely funny, but the fun is distinctly limited to Mr. Penley; and, with the exception of the scene between Miss Maria Daly and Mr. Penley in the Second Act, the situations of the piece contribute very little towards the amusement of the audience. There is one perfect piece of acting in it, unexaggerated, simple, un-selfconscious, thoroughly artistic both in breadth and in detail, and this is Mr. W. F. Hawtrey as *Bates*. And who is *Bates?* Well, before answering my own question, let me refer to what I said last week about a sudden run on Butlers among our most modern *dramatis personæ*. "Kettle began it"—Mr. J. L. Toole began it, and every one knows what Toole's Butler was. He was, *per se*, unique, inimitable. He was a Butler who, as a matter of fact, could only have been tolerated as an old, attached, and very

HEBREW MELODIES.

Says Aaron to Moses, "A Garden of Roses!" | Says Moses to Aaron, "All Roses of Sharon!"

eccentric servant, retained on account of long-valued service; as *rara avis* as *Sam Weller*. But Mr. Hawtrey's Butler is all of the modern time, irreproachable in costume, quiet, and unobtrusive, speaking when spoken to, and only volunteering remarks when he is quite sure of the sort of audience he has got to appreciate them. Even then he flatters the vain, empty-headed, middle-aged Uncle, one of the family, by deferentially laughing at the latter's stupid jokes. To see him carefully and systematically clear away the breakfast things, fold the cloth, and walk out with the tray, is a study for all young Actors whose chance for the future may lie in taking subordinate parts. Nothing is omitted; nothing is over-elaborated. Watch him when he comes in suddenly and finds his master in a most compromising situation with two young ladies. His bearing at the trying moment is not only a study for young Actors, but a lesson to Butlers of all ages.

Mr. W. F. Hawtrey does not make a grinning idiot of his Butler,—*pas si Bates*. And let not only Pa' see *Bates*, but Ma' too, and the rest of the family, is the recommendation of Jack in the Private Box.

## A DETECTIVE'S DIARY À LA MODE.

*Monday.*—Papers full of the latest tragedy. One of them suggested that the assassin was a man who wore a blue coat. Arrested three blue-coat wearers on suspicion.

*Tuesday.*—The blue coats proved innocent. Released. Evening journal threw out a hint that deed might have been perpetrated by a soldier. Found a small drummer-boy drunk and incapable. Conveyed him to the Station-house.

*Wednesday.*—Drummer-boy released. Letter of anonymous correspondent to daily journal declaring that the outrage could only have been committed by a sailor. Decoyed petty officer of Penny Steamboat on shore, and suddenly arrested him.

*Thursday.*—Petty officer allowed to go. Hint thrown out in the Correspondence columns that the crime might be traceable to a lunatic. Noticed an old gentleman purchasing a copy of *Maiwa's Revenge*. Seized him.

*Friday.*—Lunatic dispatched to an asylum. Anonymous letter received, denouncing local clergyman as the criminal. Took the reverend gentleman into custody.

*Saturday.*—Eminent ecclesiastic set at liberty with an apology. Ascertain in a periodical that it is thought just possible that the Police may have committed the crime themselves. At the call of duty, finished the week by arresting myself!

## DUE NORTH.

*Fellow Passengers—Discussions—Information—Diversion—'Arry—New Coinage—Dinner—Contentment—Whist—All's Well—Retirement.*

THERE is a Positive Man on board, with a quiet wife and a "pocket telescope." The Positive Man is full of information as to every object of interest on the banks, and is invariably wrong.

"That's Rosherville, 'the place to spend a happy day,'" he tells his wife, in a waggish vein, pointing out a pier, some trees and houses.

"No, Sir," says a trim-looking fellow-passenger, with an insinuating manner, "that's Greenwich. Rosherville is farther down."

"Oh—ah—yes," says the Positive Man, as he takes a good look at

Mist again! By an Impressionist.

Greenwich, and then exclaims, as if he now recognised it perfectly, "Of course it is. I meant Greenwich when I said Rosherville." Then, turning to his wife,—"That's Greenwich, where the Chelsea Pensioners are." And again he is corrected by the Trim Man, who has in his hand DICKENS's *Dictionary of the Thames*, which he invariably consults before volunteering any information.

HOBSON, in his kindliest humour, confides to me that he is deeply interested in an elderly Gentleman, evidently travelling alone, who has not spoken to anyone, and is always taking a few hurried steps from one side of the vessel to the other, and nervously examining the banks on both sides through his field-glasses, as though he were expecting a friend from shore to come out in a boat and join him. The friend doesn't come, and the lonely traveller—(there used to be a piece called *The Lonely Man of the Ocean*. Can this be its hero?)—becomes more and more restless every minute.

"It is not easy to distinguish objects along the shore," observes HOBSON, approaching the subject delicately.

The Restless Passenger, still looking anxiously through the field-glasses, replies slowly,—

"No, it isn't. But," he continues, in a plaintive tone, "I can't—see—where—the Royal Albert Docks are?"

"No?" returns HOBSON, with an air of cheerful surprise, and then, out of sheer good-nature, he begins looking about everywhere for the Royal Albert Docks, with the evident purpose, should he find them, of at once presenting them to the Restless Passenger.

"Ah, surely!" exclaims the Restless Man, "those are the Royal Albert Docks"—and he focuses a block of buildings, and the tops of a crowd of masts, which he can just see in the distance.

"That's Erith," says the Positive Man.

"Is it?" says HOBSON, ready to agree with him, for the sake of making things pleasant all round.

"No—that's not Erith," says the Trim Passenger, fresh from a surreptitious dip into his Guide-book, "that's Tilbury Fort."

"There's the Arsenal," says the Positive Man, after a short pause.

"What Arsenal, dear?" asks his wife.

"Why, Woolwich Arsenal, of course," he answers, with an air of superior knowledge.

"No, that's not Woolwich Arsenal," says the Trim Passenger, with a short apologetic cough just to break the intelligence gently to the Positive Man, "that's Gravesend."

"Gravesend!" repeats the Positive Man, scornfully.

"I don't think it *can* be Woolwich Arsenal, dear," objects his wife, timidly, "or why should 'Rosherville' be written up in large letters?"

This is a facer for the Positive Man, who growls out "Umph! Very odd!" and seems by his manner to imply that some one has been tampering with the names of the localities just to spite him personally. Subsequently regaining confidence, from the fact that, in the absence of the man with the Guide-book, on two occasions his statements have passed unchallenged, he points out Limestone Works as the Royal Albert Docks, and is immediately contradicted by a chorus of bystanders, who, unfortunately for him, see "Limestone Works" as clearly written up as his wife had previously seen "Rosherville." The Positive Man, defeated, shuts up his pocket telescope with a sharp click, like the Duke of WELLINGTON on a totally dissimilar occasion, and walks away. *Happy Thought.*—He and his telescope both shut up.

With the laudable desire of diverting the Restless Man from his monomania about the Albert Docks, HOBSON remarks, with an air of lively interest, "Where are the great Sewage Works? I don't see them."

"Your nose will be of more use to you than your eyes when you come within two miles of them," drily observes a little withered-up, wiry man, like an elderly Scotch terrier. The ladies eye the last speaker with a look of intense disgust, and the little wiry man's observation would be passed over in pitying silence by the company generally, as if they forgave him this once, and wouldn't say anything about it if he didn't do it again, but for the youthful leader of the 'Arries, in grey flannel shirt with sham collars and cuffs, who comes out with a loud laugh, which is immediately echoed by his admiring companions, and exclaims,—

larly,—"Yes, that *was* rather thick."

"Yes, that *was* rather thick."

It is the first time I've come across the word "thick." It bothers me. I don't see its immediate application.

The little old wiry Scotch-terrier man evidently understands what "thick" means, as he takes it in a complimentary sense, and forthwith fraternises with 'ARRY and his band.

"Come and 'ave some lotion, old man," says 'ARRY the First, patronisingly, to his new acquaintance, who must be forty years his senior. The sun-dried old chip of a very old block, with wiry iron-grey hair, replies that "he doesn't mind if he does take a lotion." Whereupon, all the 'Arry band shout with laughter, and their leader declares openly that in his opinion the little withered-up old man is "a thick 'un—a regular thick 'un"; and "this is the verdict of them all," as following their foreman, the jury of 'Arries descend the companion, and disappear with their new acquaintance.

"Dinner at two," says the Steward, "when we're off Southend. You can have anything *now*, if you like, Sir?"

Ominous question. *Now*—or never? No; I'll wait till two, and chance it.

A tall, languid person, in a deerstalker and an ulster, whom I have noticed for some time standing near us, and who, I fancy, is waiting patiently for the reversion of my campstool,—which he won't obtain, as I carry it with me wherever I go,—observes, in the patronising tone of a man who wishes it to be understood that he is accustomed to frequent only the "hupper suckles" of Society,—

"Rather an absurd hour for dinner,—two?"

"Except," I say, "when you're hungry, and then any hour is a good hour for dinner."

"And," he continues, without noticing my reservation, and speaking severely at me, as if the hours for meals were of my choosing, "I suppose, tea at seven, and a heavy breakfast at eight in the morning. All this sort of thing upsets the digestion. It's impossible to feed at such a ridiculous hour."

"Ten to two!" exclaims HOBSON joyfully, and I am grateful for the interruption as the languid man is inclined to adopt a bullying tone towards me. "This *is* doing you good, eh? Didn't I say so?"

Then as I follow him in his blithesome skip towards the companion, he pauses, and, as if he had a rare treat in store for me, whispers, with a confidential chuckle, "I've secured the two best seats at the head of the table next to the Captain! Aha!" And elated beyond measure with the success of this last instance of his forethought—all on *my* account I am convinced, and not the least on his own—he trips down the stairs, and in another five minutes the bell announces feeding time, and the passengers troop in and take their places on either side of a long table at the head of which is the Captain, a fine upstanding middle-aged man in a nautical uniform, who bows reverently over a huge steaming joint of boiled beef rising out of a sea of pale turnipy gravy, says grace, in which all those who have contracted with the steward for their meals heartily join,—and then he sets to work to carve for his hungry family of sixty persons, and appears as Captain CARVER, playing the part to perfection until further notice, which is given by himself only when he is thoroughly exhausted.

*Dinner.*—Saloon cool. No smell to speak of. Motion of ship rather more perceptible here than on deck; but hunger is a sharp thorn.

*Happy Thought.*—The test of qualmishness has arrived. If I can stand this, the "biled mutton and bilious sauce," and the strange manners and customs of some of my immediate neighbours, who evidently are of opinion that fingers were made, not only before forks, but before toothpicks, I can stand anything. I do; and what is more, enjoy the dinner and the Captain's conversation—but not the manners and customs aforesaid—immensely.

As a precaution, and to make assurance doubly sure, HOBSON proposes a bottle of champage. Why, certainly: quite a Happy Thought.

I notice that the languid person who thinks two o'clock a preposterous and absurd hour for dinner, is doing remarkably well in spite of the absurdity of the idea. As for the "high contracting parties," the Steward must be a loser to-day, as they take twice of everything. 'ARRY, from somewhere about the middle of the table calls out, "'Ere, Waiter!"—this causes a laugh among his admirers—"tell the Captain I'll trouble him again." To which the

Captain Carver in his celebrated Saloon Entertainment.

Captain, who, poor man, is only just commencing his own dinner, mutters knowingly, "No, I'm hanged if you do!" as with a smile he beckons to an under-steward to remove the joint and carve it at the side-board.

"It's not like this when it's rough," says Captain CARVER, slily to us, alluding to the run on the joint. I assent to his remark, with an Old Saltish sort of sea-dog wag of the head; but I do not confide to him that "*I* am not like this when it's rough." HOBSON pledges him cheerily in a glass of dry Pommery, and he acknowledges the toast, being a teetotaller, in a brimmer of gingerade.

After dinner, a sudden shower of rain compels us to seek refuge in a small cabin, facetiously termed "the Smoking-Room," where the atmosphere is, to use 'ARRY'S expression, "rather thick."

Here 'ARRY and his party are in great force, playing a rubber.

"O Jee-roo-salum!" cries 'ARRY, when he loses a trick, whereupon his admirers roar with laughter.

'ARRY has not been giving his best attention to the game, and on his partner, an elderly, business-like looking man, warning him of the consequences, 'ARRY gives a wink at his companions, and says, "Steady yerself, EMILY!" which witticism sends them into convulsions.

The wiry old Scotch-terrier-like man is also here, pulling at the stump of a cigar, closely watching the game, with difficulty refraining from offering advice, but consoling himself by telling the lookers-on in whispers what he would have done if he had been in the last player's place, and by significant shrugs and grunts expressive of his disapprobation of the style of play generally. 'ARRY takes a trick with great delight, in spite of some mistake of his partner's.

"Ah," says 'ARRY to the latter, "you're not too thick, you ain't."

"Thick" puzzles me. Presently the wiry old man offers to make him a bet.

"No, old boy," replies the knowing and suspicious 'ARRY, "you're too thick for me." And his companions shout with laughter.

When one of his opponents at whist is rather slower than usual in dealing, 'ARRY calls out "Time!" and subsequently requests him, if he has dealt himself a good hand, to "Walk round and show his muscle." Fortune favours 'ARRY with first-rate trumps,—and ARRY triumphantly coming down with his Ace says:

"'Ow's that for kitchen soup?"

Immense delight of the 'Arry Gallery, which is raised to the highest pitch when he throws down the Queen of Trumps, and in a sort of tune sings:—

"That's a *Beau*-ty! that's a *Beau*-ty!"

When he and his partner ultimately win the game, he leads a chorus in which all his companions heartily join, and the purport of which, as far as I can catch the words, seems to be a tuneful expression of a wish, addressed to some imaginary butcher by an intending customer, to be informed as to the market price of liver, and a further demand of a like nature as to the current quotation of kidneys.

There being no more rain, this is the last I see of 'ARRY and his comrades, until next morning when they complain of headache and evince an inordinate passion for kippered herrings, and boiling hot tea.

We are standing well out to sea. Daylight and the coast-line are disappearing.

"Now!" cries HOBSON, who is in ecstasies at the verification of all his prophecies about the state of my health, and the excellence of the passage. "Now!" he cries, extending his right arm towards the horizon, and then turning towards me as if the supreme moment had arrived when he must unburden himself of a tremendous secret, "Now, dear friend, *there is absolutely nothing between you*"—he emphasises this with his left hand—"*and the North Pole!*" Whereupon he takes one step back, folds his arms, and interrogates me with a searching regard, as if he were suspicious of my still concealing something from him, and so by my reticence compelling him to believe that *there is something between me and the North Pole!*

It's a fearful charge,—worse than being accused of disrespect for the Equator,—and I assure him that as far as I know, there is nothing whatever between me and the North Pole. And so we sit on deck, chatting, and congratulating ourselves on its being one of the most lovely nights we've seen for a very long time.

HOBSON delighted. Didn't he tell me it would be a perfect passage? The lights ashore become few, and far between, and gradually disappear entirely. Mysterious lights, now green, now red, approach us, and the Look-out Man, and the Captain, and the Man at the Wheel, keep up a trio of an hour's duration, led always by the first-mentioned as tenor, followed up by the Captain as baritone, and finished by the steersman as *basso-profondo*.

It must be very annoying for the Look-out Man, who never announces any discovery of his, such as "Light on the port bow!" "Light on the starboard!" or whatever it may be without the Captain immediately replying "Aye, aye!" in a tone which certainly conveys that he has seen this danger a-head ever so long ago, and is perfectly aware of it. Very satisfactory to the passengers to know they have such a Captain as Captain CARVER, whom nothing can escape, but still rather disheartening for the Look-out Man, who seems to be perfectly incapable of giving the Captain any information which the latter does not already possess.

Begin to feel drowsy.

"This is doing you good!" exclaims HOBSON, surveying me with pride.

"All right up to now," I say, cautiously. "But suppose it should change to stormy in the night?"

"Not a chance of it," replies HOBSON. And we descend to our Cabin, which, fortunately, is at present unoccupied.

Now, how to climb up to my nest?

## AN OPPORTUNITY.

LONDON is always a nice place for equestrian exercise, but just now, in the "dead season," if you ask "What's up?" the answer must be, "Roads, pavements, streets, boards, red flags, &c."

Quite right, of course, and just the time of year for it. Only, as there are workmen digging into the soil of Kensington Gardens and the Parks, *Mr. Punch*, in the interest of Equestrians generally, would again beg to inquire why on earth there cannot be—

*First*,—A ride under the trees from Kensington to Bayswater through Kensington Gardens.

*Secondly*,—Another ride across Hyde Park, as a trifling variation on the monotony of Rotten Row and the dreariness of the ride between the Marble Arch, which is now being "restored," though no one ever had the audacity to remove it.

*Thirdly*. *À propos* of "restoration," why not restore at once the soft ride all round the Park?

*Fourthly*. And why not do the same in Regent's Park, where the only chance for Equestrians is about half a mile of "the soft" in the Inner Circle?

*Fifthly*. Why not open up two or three rides in Regent's Park? Who objects? There's room, and to spare, for everyone, Pedestrians and Equestrians alike, and plenty of space for amusements of all sorts.

Surely GEORGE RANGER, our Ædiles, and the Police Commissioners, might hit on some plan between them for the benefit of the Liver Brigades of Light and Heavy Cavalry.

SOMETHING TO BE THANKFUL FOR.—Our dear old friend, Mrs. RAM, just saved herself from a nasty fall the other day coming down-stairs. "I should have broken my leg or worse," she said, "if I hadn't put out my hand and caught hold of the barristers."

MONOTONOUS.—While the Sacred Lamp of Burlesque was alight at the Gaiety, there was a variety of tunes all through the entertainment. Now, there is only one Eyre.

RINGOAL.

A NEW AND CHARMING GAME. AS IT IS, HOWEVER, RATHER APT TO DECAPITATE THE LOOKERS-ON, IT IS WELL FOR THESE TO PROVIDE THEMSELVES WITH SHIELDS, IN THE SHAPE OF SUNSHADES, UMBRELLAS, LAWN-TENNIS BATS, &C.

## BLIND-MAN'S BUFF.

A STRANGE mad game to play in such a place!
The monster City's maze, whose paths to trace
Might tax another Theseus, the resort
Of worse than Minotaurs, for blindfold sport
Would seem the most unfitting of all scenes;
What is it there such solemn fooling means?

Means? Ask purblind Municipal Muddledom
The true significance of the City Slum.
Ask, but expect no answer more exact
Than blundering palterers with truth and fact
Range in their pigeon-holes in order neat,
The awkward questionings of sense to meet,
And, meeting, blandly baffle. Lurking crime
Haunts from of old these dens of darksome slime.
There, where well-armed Authority fears to tread,
Murder and outrage rear audacious head,
Unscanned, untracked. As the swift-sliding snake
Slips to the covert of the swamp's foul brake,
Fearless of following where no foot may find
Firm resting, where the fœtid fumes that blind,
The reeking mists that palsy, guard its lair;
So Crime sneaks to the Slum's seclusion. There
Revealing light, the foe of all things ill,
With no intrusive ray floods in to fill
Those hideous alleys, and those noisome nooks,
With health and safety. Flush with limpid brooks
The slime-fouled gutters of the Ghetto, drive
Plinlimmon's breeze through Labour's choking hive,
But let not light into the loathsome den
Where hags called women, ghouls in guise of men
Live on death-dealing, feed a loathly life,
On the chance profits of the furtive knife.
The robber's mountain haunt, the outlaw's cave,
Guarded by rocks or sheltered by the wave
From feet intrusive, furnish no such lair
For desperate villany or dull despair,
As this obscene Alsatia of the Slums.
Town's carrion-hordes flock hither; hither comes
The haggard harpy of the pavement, she
The victim's victim, whose delirious glee
Makes mirth a crackling horror; hither slink
The waifs of passion and the wrecks of drink.
Multiform wretchedness in rags and grime,
Hopeless of good and ripe for every crime;
A seething mass of misery and of vice,
These grim but secret-guarding haunts entice.
Look at those walls; they reek with dirt and damp, [tramp
But in their shadows crouched the homeless
May huddle undisturbed the black night through.
Those narrow winding courts—in thought—pursue. [wife,
No light there breaks upon the bludgeoned
No flash of day arrests the lifted knife,
There shrieks arouse not, nor do groans affright.
These are but normal noises of the night
In this obscure Gehenna.
Must it be
That the black slum shall furnish sanctuary
To all light-shunning creatures of the slime,
Vermin of vice, carnivora of crime?
Must it be here that Mammon finds its tilth,
And harvests gold from haunts of festering filth? [stricken dumb,
How long? The voice of sense seems
What time the sordid Spectre of the Slum,
Ruthless red-handed Murder sways the scene,
Mocking of glance, and merciless of mien.
Mocking? Ah, yes! At Law the ghoul may laugh,
The sword is here as harmless as the staff
Of crippled age; its sleuthhounds are at fault,
Justice appears not only blind but halt.
It seems to play a merely blinkered game,
Blundering about without a settled aim,
Like boys at Blind-Man's Buff. A pretty sport
For Law's sworn guards in rascaldom's resort!
The bland official formula to-day
Seems borrowed from the tag of Nursery play,
"Turn round three times," upon no settled plan,
Flounder and fumble, and "catch whom you can!"

---

THE DANGER OF DROWSINESS.—A Railway accident is not uncommonly attributable to a sleeper having given way. Considering the lengthened hours of exhaustive exertion to which signalmen and other overworked servitors attendant on railways are commonly subject, one wonders that terrible accidents do not occur even still more frequently than usual through the somnolence of railway sleepers.

---

AN historic name that may always be introduced "*à propos de bottes*"—BUNYAN.

# BLIND-MAN'S BUFF.

*(As played by the Police.)*

"TURN ROUND THREE TIMES,
AND CATCH WHOM YOU MAY!"

*Mossoo—cheerfully* (*he has just blown a hole through the Squire's hat*). "AHA, MON AMI! VOILÀ COMMENT DES ACCIDENTS ARRIVENT!"

## A DITTY FOR DINARD.

AT fair Dinard to-day
You can flirt, dance, and play,
As at most of such French places we know;
You can bathe at your ease,
In what costume you please,
On the beach near the little Casino.

There 's a sea very blue,
And the sky's azure too,
And the air may be held to be bracing;
But the nymphs we see there,
With their stays *dans la mer*,
Counteract its effects by tight-lacing.

You will find at the Club
Men quite game for a "rub,"
Or for Poker, when daylight is ended;
You may lose, if you go
To the *Petits Chevaux*,
Or to Baccarat,—not recommended.

No one Tennis forgets,
And they work at their "setts"
With an ardour that 's simply astounding;
From the morning till night
ATALANTA flies light,
And the balls o'er the court go rebounding.

Thus we live by the side
Of the fast-flowing tide,
An improvement in health the great gain is;
While no river in France
Can compare with the Rance
Near Dinard, which in Ille-et-Vilaine is.

## "MAKING A BRITISH HOLIDAY."

MY DEAREST BLANCHE, 1276, *Park Lane, Sept.* 14, 1888.

In spite of being in Town in the middle of September, I have had *such* a good time of it! Oh! I do *so* wish you had been with us last Thursday. Well, you must know, dear, that CHARLEY (who has his long leave just now) persuaded Mamma to allow FLORENCE and myself to go with him to the Alexandra Palace to see Professor BALDWIN take his sensational leap. As CHARLEY said, "it was absolutely rippin'!" It *was*, really! Mamma would not come, because, she said, "he might get killed!" "Why, of course he might," replied CHARLEY; "but that's half the fun of it." He appealed to us; and although, of course, we were not "cruel," or anything of that sort, yet we were forced to confess that the jump would have been *rather* insipid if taken without risk of danger. "Just so," replied Mamma—she can be awfully disagreeable at times. "Then you really go to see Professor BALDWIN on the chance of being present at his immolation."

Well, reasonably enough, this made us both *very* angry with Mamma for saying such dreadful things, and all the more determined to go, so when CHARLEY called for us the next morning, he found us ready waiting, and impatient to be off. We were both dressed in white, with "picture" hats and long pompadour parasols. We first tried getting down to the Alexandra by rail. But it was *too* awful! Every carriage was filled with *three times* as many travellers as it should have naturally contained! You can fancy, dear, what a terrible crush there was! So then CHARLEY very wisely got a Hansom, which I confess was a little small for three, but still *much* better than the railway. And so we drove down, enjoying the fun *immensely*, and CHARLEY making us laugh by telling us how nearly the Professor was run over by a steam-engine on one occasion. So ridiculous, you know, dear, not to be able to guide the parachute, but to be *forced* to come down in all *sorts* of absurd places! And then FLORENCE (who, you know, dear, *entre nous*, makes rather a parade of her sensibility), said she hoped we should not go *too* near—not where there was any chance of coming across anything disagreeable. "Oh," said CHARLEY, "if he *does* fall, I fancy he will bury himself in the earth in the tidiest manner possible. So you need be under no apprehension of seeing anything ghastly." And at this moment the Hansom cabman put his head at the hole in the roof and told us that he had heard it strike six, and he thought it would be better if he pulled up on the brow of a hill we had just reached. So CHARLEY bundled out and helped us girls to descend.

We had scarcely taken our seats on a rug that CHARLEY had spread for us on the grass, when up went the balloon with the Professor dangling to it. "Oh, I am *so* glad!" cried FLORENCE. "They said he might back out of it by pretending that the wind was in the wrong quarter, or something silly of that sort! Now I *do* hope he goes up two miles! It won't be the least bit of fun unless he goes up *quite* the two miles!" Well, I must confess, my dear, I was never so excited in all my life! Up went the balloon, and we saw the Professor getting smaller and smaller until he looked quite like a funny little doll! "By Jove, he's going to jump!" said CHARLEY, who had been watching the whole affair through a field-glass. And jump he did! For a moment my heart stood still. He came down like a stone. "Smash, I think," observed CHARLEY, quietly, and I thought I would not have missed it for anything, as we should have seen all the affair without any of the unpleasant details. All of a sudden, CHARLEY said the parachute was opening and he was safe so far.

Of course we girls thought that now all the fun was over. Not at all. The excitement was next, to see how long he would hold on. "Bet you a pair of gloves he comes down safely!" shouted CHARLEY. "Very well," I replied, "I will bet he doesn't!" And of course I was now doubly interested, as my gloves depended on it. Provoking! I lost, and CHARLEY was triumphant!

And now, dear, as I hear the bell ringing for dressing, I must put down my pen. I hope you will get up to Town in time to see the Professor take one of his *wonderful* leaps. Good-bye!

Your own loving friend, MAUD.

P.S.—We went to see the Roman Sports at the Italian Exhibition the other day. One thing was *very* absurd. When a gladiator is to be killed, they appeal to the Vestal Virgins to know if his life may be spared. And then the Vestal Virgins point to the earth with their thumbs to say "No." So absurd! As if anyone would like to see a man killed before her very eyes!

### To a Lively Authoress.

O FRISKY Matron, writing in the *U-*
*-niversal* or Quilterian *Review*,
Calling to mind in these still lively latter days
The telling touches in those brilliant *Saturdays*,
Say what is your "Philosophy of Marriage?" [parage?
Do you the Cotyledonous dis-
Or would you send to hermitage and holler-tree
Marital victim to his Gynœcolatry?
Better do this than drown dull care, feel chippy,
And live Socratically with XANTIPPE. [that's risky!
Is this the moral! Let's do all
In Cyprian bowers let us live "all frisky"!

"PURSUIT OF KNOWLEDGE."

*Son and Heir (whose Inquiring Turn of Mind is occasionally a nuisance).* "I SAY 'PA, WHAT'S A V'CAB'LARY?"
*Father.* "A VOCABULARY, MY BOY—WHAT D'YOU WANT TO KNOW THAT FOR?"
*Son.* "'CAUSE I HEARD 'MA SAY SHE'D NO IDEA WHAT A TREMENJIOUS V'CAB'LARY YOU'D GOT, TILL YOU MISSED THE TRAIN ON SATURDAY!"

## OUR BOOKING-OFFICE.

GOOD novel *Hartas Maturin*, by H. F. LESTER. So excitingly interesting. The character of *Hartas* himself is finely drawn, and that of the visionary *Bastian* might have been imagined and described by Lord LYTTON in such a work as *Zanoni*, or *A Strange Story*. I hope there are not many Bastians about, as his theories would do away with all moral responsibility, and necessitate the building of Public Lunatic Asylums on an extensive scale, and a consequent increase of burden on the unhappy ratepayer. But Mr. LESTER is "only purtendin'," and "there ain't no such person." I am sorry that Mr. LESTER'S heroine should be troubled with a profusion of golden hair; I should have cut that hair, or dye'd it; and I do not think that the lighted end of a cigar put into the pocket of a damp coat would set a house on fire, particularly such a house as the author has previously been at no little pains to describe. But these are mere details. The idea of the story is decidedly original, and to lighten the tragedy of the tale there are many touches of genuine humour.

I have just seen Messrs. BARRAUD'S eighth number of *Men and Women of the Day*, wherein a portrait of HELEN MATHERS, Mrs. REEVES, looking as if she were trying to imitate the American *Siffleuse*, is between those of Dr. W. G. GRACE, the Cricketer, and Lord Justice COTTON, with a wig which, were he LORD CHANCELLOR, would be suggestive of the Cotton-Woolsack, but, as he isn't, it is evidently only an old wig that doesn't fit him. HELEN MATHERS, the charming Novelist, couldn't be in better company than appearing thus with GRACE and COTTON, typical at once of her literary and personal charms on the one hand, and of her devoted domesticity on the other. Well selected.

Also the September Number of *Our Celebrities*. There is about WALERY'S Photographs a soft tone that I've rarely, if ever, seen equalled. The portrait of Sir MORELL MACKENZIE this month is perfect as a print, and lifelike as a portrait. The great merit of this positive likeness is a "negative" one; I mean the absence of the stereotyped background, in which, as in a cold ancestral hall, with only one chair in it, to which he fondly clings, stands Lord STANLEY of Preston. The fault of background, in my humble judgment, produces a theatrical effect in the otherwise striking reproduction of Lady LINDSAY'S living presentment. Here we have the same baronial hall, the same urn of ancestor's ashes, perhaps, in the distance, only the chair is different, and there is some drapery introduced with a property cushion for the lady's foot, a Wardour Street table, and a property vase and book. The entertaining and interesting monographs, by L. ENGEL are drawn from his usual well of pure and undefiled ENGEL-ish.

*Tracked Out*, by Mr. ARTHUR À BECKETT, is, I am informed, having a perfectly unprecedented sale. It is indeed a weird story. Yet there is nothing quite new under the sun, as, I think, the weird author will himself be the first to acknowledge when he reads *A Tale of Wonder*, by WILLIAM MAKEPEACE THACKERAY, now republished by ELLIOT STOCK, in a collection of the Novelist's early writings, compiled by C. PLUMPTRE JOHNSON, in which *the decapitated Head tells its own decapitated tale, and the criminal is discovered!!* How's this for High, inquires THE SAGACIOUS BARON DE BOOK-WORMS.

## PASTORAL TO THE "BOY BISHOP."

[The *World* says of Dr. JAYNE, the new Bishop of Chester:—"He cannot be said to have made any mark there (*i.e.*, at Leeds)." . . . . "In person, he hardly realises one's idea of a Bishop: he enjoys a fair, fresh, ingenuous boy-like aspect, and owns an engaging frank demeanour." . . . . "and he will be, by far, the youngest Bishop on the Bench."]

AIR—*Refrain of "My Pretty Jane."*

MY fairish JAYNE, my boylike JAYNE,
Oh, never look so shy;
But come, oh come, and go a Bishoping,
While the bloom is 'neath your eye.

*Chorus (everybody at Keble College):—*

My fairish JAYNE, my boylike JAYNE,
Oh, never look so shy; &c., *da capo.*

CANDID OPINION.—Coal Tar Sugar can't be Beet.

## OUR JAPANNERIES. No. 16.

**FIRST MEETING OF THE PARNELL COMMISSION.**

*Toby, M.P., Q.C., with a brief to watch the case for the Public, presents Lika Joko, who watches the case for Japan, to the Three Commissioners.*

"A SERIOUS QUESTION."—We are glad to learn from several Correspondents that the question we asked last week as to the murderous theatrical picture-posters is likely to lead to beneficial results. We agree with the *St. James's Gazette*, that legislation on the matter is an imperative necessity. These "colourable imitations" of crime are a disgrace to our civilisation, our Literature, and our Drama. And *à propos* of advertisements not pictorial, isn't it bad taste on the part of the Lyceum management to use a line from St. Paul's Episple as an advertisement for the play of *Hyde and Jekyll?* Is it to show that *Hyde* can quote Scripture to his purpose?

A COSY BUT NOT COSSEY CHURCH.—A Correspondent writing to the *Spectator*, says that in Whitby Parish Church, "The old three-decker," consisting of Clerk's desk below, reading desk in the middle, and pulpit atop, still exists. What spot more appropriate for a "three-decker," than the marine locality, Whitby-on-the-Sea. *Vive* "three-decker!" and may it be long ere it gives way to other decker-ations.

"O MY PROPHETIC SOUL! MY UNCLE!"—Why didn't the Duke of AOSTA pay a visit to Monaco? Because he preferred Nice.

## "OH, DON'T HE LOVE HIS MUMMER!"

IN Mr. HARRY QUILTER'S *Universal Review* for September, Mr. GEORGE MOORE runs a-muck against "Mummer Worship." The well-worn theme of "the *status* of the Actor" is to the author of that

"But MORE of More Hall,
With nothing at all,
He slew the Dragon of Wantley!"

strong Zola-esque novel, *The Mummer's Wife,*—in which, by the way, while spades are called something more than spades, there is much unpalatable truth,—like the proverbial red rag to the bull, or the ankles of the timid stranger to GEORGE MEREDITH'S "distraught goose."

All that Mr. GEORGE MOORE has to say about the "Stage as a profession" has been said, without mincing matters, long ago in Mr. EDMUND YATES'S *Time* (a Magazine), and in the *Fortnightly Review*, in Mr. ESCOTT'S time. Mr. MOORE wanders away from his text of *Mummer-worship*, and needlessly and inconsequently attacks Mr. CHARLES WYNDHAM and Miss MARY MOORE for their Continental tour with *David Garrick*. That Actor and Actress should be received into "Society" at all "does make him so wild." Well, he needn't meet them. He can keep aloof from Society, and the loss will, of course, be Society's.

"Because I have cakes and ale," Mr. MOORE seems to say to the Actors, "therefore *you* shan't be virtuous." And "you shan't even be respectable, if I can help it," is his implied determination; forgetting that "respectability is the homage paid by vice to virtue," with which cynical definition Mr. MOORE should be satisfied, as covering all his ground of complaint.

The artistic temperament is innately Bohemian, and it feels itself ridiculous when attempting to shine with the veneer of *bourgeois* respectability. But the ostentatious Bohemianism which Mr. GEORGE MOORE considers the proper colour for the Actors to live and die in, with its inordinate vanity, vulgar self-consciousness, affected *bonhomie*, and flippant profanity, is more repulsively snobbish and revoltingly caddish, than the best silk-hatted, frock-coated Respectability can ever be.

The craze of Actor-worship is rapidly passing away. BUFFALO BILL'S popularity with "Society" hit the histrion a serious blow; so did the momentary success of the athlete. The fault is in the Worshippers, not in the object of their adoration. Mr. GEORGE GROSSMITH laughs pleasantly at the craze in his amusing shillingsworth, entitled, *The Clown in Society*.

Let the Actor enjoy himself with his Dukes and Duchesses, his supper and champagne, and do you, Mr. MOORE, enjoy yourself too, with your "couple of Princesses and a Duchess" (which is your own modest allowance for yourself "in perspective"), but you needn't throw stones through the window panes, merely because you catch sight of Comedians in the Duke's drawing-room.

If the Actor's vanity hungrily craves for recognition in what is termed "Society," then, like the little boy in the bath, "he won't be happy till he gets it." And if that makes him happy, Mr. GEORGE MOORE, "happy man be his dole." But why envy him? Why blame *him?* Blame Society,—and your task is futile and endless.

---

THE *Morning Post*, last Wednesday, mentioned a "Firework Drama," by Mr. BROCK, at the Crystal Palace. Of course the leading Lady was Miss CATHERINE WHEEL. There must have been several Stars. Probably the show concluded with a political Squib. The next novelty in the Pyrotechnic Theatrical line will be an adaptation of one of PLANCHÉ'S old Fairy-tale Extravaganzas, to be entitled, *Rocket with the Tuft*.

## A TALE OF ONE HUNDRED CIGARS.

SIR,—The ordinary Englishman may fondly imagine that he can pass his cherished Havannas, up to, say, one hundred, through that remarkable institution known in France as the Douane. That's where he's wrong. He can't! At all events, he can't, if he tries to be honest, as I did, and disclose the fact that his *paquet* contains Havanna cigars. As is well known, the French Government is a paternal one, and in its infinite wisdom does not permit anything but cabbage, *choux*, to be smoked in La Belle France. Real tobacco is considered deadly. However, let me at once proceed to the recital of the One Hundred Cigars.

First week of August I wrote, enclosing cheque, to the Army and Navy Stores, from Royat-les-Bains, to order one hundred of the forbidden fruit, I should say, weeds. By return I get receipt from Stores, and note to say that "the goods shall be forwarded with all practicable dispatch." So far, so good. Four days after this I receive from Monsieur le Chef de Gare du Nord at Paris the following most bewildering communication:—

*Grande Vitesse* 1. *Trafic International. Paris.*

MONSIEUR,—J'ai l'honneur de vous informer qu'il est arrivé à votre adresse, en grande vitesse [observe the sarcasm], dans les magasins du douane, à la Gare du Nord, expédiés par M. Army Navy (*sic*), à Londres, les colis ci-après designés: 100 cigarres.

Vous devrez signer l'une des deux formules ci-dessous, selon que vous prendrez livraison en gare ou que vous préférez vous faire livrer la marchandise à domicile par le camionage de la Compagnie.

I do so. Sign the "*formule*" which permits, apparently, the delivery of our one hundred *chez nous*. Alas! how little I knew of the ways, and means, of the Douane. Daily we (myself and expectant friends) journey down to the Gare de Royat, "*pour demander si les cigarres* [why two r's?] *de Monsieur sont arrivés.*" "*Non, Monsieur, pas de paquet pour vous.*" *Quoi faire? Nous attendons.* On a Wednesday in August we receive a *billet-doux* from the *Chef de Gare*, as follows:—

"Nous avons reçu votre lettre. Les cigarres étant prohibés, veuillez adresser une demande d'autorisation d'entrée sur papier timbré à M. le Directeur de la Douane pour obtenir l'entrée des cigarres conformément aux instructions, jointes à notre avis 338 du 11 courant."

I fly—always with my friends, who are now beginning to doubt whether I ever ordered any cigars at all, and are rather less generous with their own towards me than they were—to the post-office to purchase the cherished "*papier timbré.*" We are told, "*Vous trouvez ça chez le marchand de tabac.*" Thither we wend our weary way, to learn that "*Il n'y en a pas ici. C'est à Clermont* (town twenty minutes by carriage from Royat) *que vous trouvez ça. Rue Saint Esprit.*"

My friends will not quit me, so we all go together. Arrived at Clermont, we find the *marchand de tabac*, Rue Saint Esprit, and are, on payment of *soixante centimes*, armed with the formidable *papier timbré*. So off we walk to the nearest *café*, demand ink and pen, and indite in our most classic French a humble petition to the *Directeur de la Gare du Nord, à Paris*. In five minutes more it is in the letter-box, and we are wending our way back to the iron waters of Royat. We feel we require tonics. This ends our labours on Thursday. *Allons! du courage! Enfin c'est toujours possible que M. le Directeur de la Douane finira par nous envoyer nos pauvres cigarres.*

Seated at dinner on the following Saturday evening, we learn, to our dismay (a heavy rain-storm is at the moment doing its best to wash the town away), that the ill-fated cigars have at length arrived at the hotel, but the well-meaning though officious Concierge has sent them away, because he did not know if Monsieur (meaning the humble individual who now addresses you, "*moi qui parle*") was prepared to pay the trifling sum of thirty-six francs duty on one hundred cigars! Having explained that I was ready to pay double, he secured the cigars; and thus, after much time, labour, journeying, lamenting, and heart-ache, I was rewarded by the receipt of my One Hundred Cigars! How sweet was the first one (slightly damp, it is true), but *real* tobacco! All's well that ends well.

*Moral.*—When endeavouring to pass a cigar through the Douane, allow at least a fortnight for the function. Ah! *Mr. Punch*, I know *you* smoke, like myself, *good* cigars, and I feel that, in your kind heart, I shall find some of that sympathy which may soothe my shattered nerves. *Vale, amice!* Yours, A MERE BACCA TELL.

---

"QUITE ENGLISH, YOU KNOW!"—We see a new Opera announced for the 25th at the Crystal Palace. It is an English Opera, *Libretto* by an Englishman, C. BRADBERRY (never seen it spelt like this before—"put it down a 'u,' my Lord"), and the music by another Englishman, Mr. GEORGE FOX. The subject is *The Corsican Brothers*. Mr. FOX ought to play *Château-Renard*. Of course he can, Brothers, if he pleases. With the usual white face, corked eyebrows, and Mephistophelian moustache, he might come out as a sort of Guy Fox. Success to the English Composer.

## THE PARNELL COMMISSION.

(*Special Report.*)

"*Monday, September* 1.—Mr. Justice HANNEN, Mr. Justice DAY, and Mr. Justice SMITH, sitting in the Probate Division of the Royal Courts of Justice, met to-day to hear the matters at issue between the *Times* and Mr. PARNELL. Sir CHARLES RUSSELL, M.P., Q.C., represented Mr. PARNELL and the other Irish Members concerned. Mr. GRAHAM appeared for Mr. WALTER and Another. TOBY, M.P., Q.C.* (instructed by Mr. GEORGE LEWIS, of Ely Place, Holborn, W.C.), watched the case for the Public."—*Morning Paper.*

CUT this out of morning paper; great deal more; columns of it; but don't suppose there'll be room to print it. Yet a most interesting case. My first brief. Fancy I have started pretty well. Feel the wig rather hot, and always blushing to find gown nearly slipping off. Observe that CHARLES RUSSELL keeps *his* gown well over his shoulders, whereas GRAHAM, when addressing Court, generally has the collar somewhere in neighbourhood of small of his back. Suppose they begin that way, working gown up to the shoulders as they advance towards CHARLES RUSSELL's *status.*

"Knocking at the door."

Everything very agreeable. Wondered, when I went in, what the Judges would say. "Is the old min friendly?" I said to myself, looking up at HANNEN. Found he was, very. When I said I appeared for the public, he made me a little bow, and observed, "The case of the public is in excellent hands." Very nice that. Felt quite encouraged. Determined to justify good opinion. Opening presented early in case. When GRAHAM was asked whom he represented, he replied, "My Lud, I appear, with my learned friend the ATTORNEY-GENERAL, for the defendants in the case of *O'Donnell* v. *Walter.*"

Here was my chance. Seized it with alacrity.

"My Lud," I said, hitching my gown over left shoulder, and cocking back my wig, as I have observed another eminent Q.C. do, "interposing as *amicus curiæ*, I may observe that my learned friend is a little inaccurate. He says he appears *with* the ATTORNEY-GENERAL. May I point out, my Lud, that it would be more accurate to say 'he appears *without* the ATTORNEY-GENERAL?'"

"Silence!" shouted a person in gown, who, I subsequently ascertained, was called the Usher.

Have a good look at the Judges. HANNEN in the middle, sitting in the chair he usually fills as President of the Divorce Court. A plump pleasant-featured man.

"Looks," says CHARLES RUSSELL, "as if he was able to bear with equanimity the failure of other people's marriages."

On the left SMITH, a quiet keen-faced man, who says very little, but evidently thinks a good deal. On the right DAY. DAY simply delicious. Haven't seen anything so lovely for years. Never get tired of watching him. Splendid figure-head for a ship. Widely opened, stonily-staring eyes; uplifted eyebrows wrinkling the massive forehead; lips slightly parted; moves head slowly from side to side gazing round Court with air of perpetual surprise. Sometimes looks up at ceiling, as if wondering what it could be for. Then gaze slowly lowered to desk, marvelling how the deuce it got there. Again, slowly surveys Court. Think I hear him whispering to himself, "Dear me! What a lot of reporters!" Looks as if he'd never attempted a joke in his life, or understood one. What a prize mute he'd make at a first-class funeral!

Case grows interesting as it goes on. CHARLES RUSSELL portentously bland. Never loses his temper for a moment. Is so amiable; must be winning hand over hand. Argues for disclosure of documents, specification of charges. "Let-us-know-what-we-have-to-meet," and all that sort of thing. Fancy I've heard all before in the House of Commons; nothing came of it there except occasional beating in Division Lobby. Now HANNEN gravely listens. SMITH (not OLD MORALITY) twinkles with attention. DAY solemnly nods his head with curious rhythmical action of the mechanical Mandarin. Seems to be something in it, after all. GRAHAM drops his gown half an inch lower down the length of his spine, and says the things the ATTORNEY-GENERAL and EDWARD CLARKE used to say in House of Commons. But HANNEN swoops down on him like a falcon; rather paralyses him. GRAHAM wriggles and wrestles, falters and stumbles. His face settles into stony pallor, pitiful to see. Quite sorry for him. Think I'll give him a lift. Nothing like a word of sympathy in times like this. Write on slip of paper,—

"*Threaten to move for a writ of fi. fa.*"

Haven't clear idea what writ of *fi. fa.* is. Fancy it's a sort of protest, as who should say, "*Fi. fa.* shame!" Pass the slip of paper on to GRAHAM. Eagerly opens it. Reads, and looks back at me. I nod to him cheerily.

"Try that, old fellow," I say.

GRAHAM evidently doesn't catch on. Paleness deepens. Stares at me angrily. Put open hand to side of mouth, and loudly whisper, "*Fieri facias!*"

"Silence!" says the Usher.

Presently GRAHAM cites at large from case of *Brown* v. *Watkin*, also case of *Dike* v. *Stephen;* drifts gently to *Shaw* v. *Smith*. Time seems opportune for creating little diversion.

"My Lud," I say, addressing President, "as our time is valuable, perhaps your Ludship, whilst my learned friend proceeds with his citations, would favour the Court with your views on the question, 'Is Marriage a Failure?' Your Ludship's remarkable opportunities for——"

*The Usher.* "Silence!"

I thought he'd say that.

At half-past one, adjourned for luncheon. A little late in returning to Court. Found the O'GORMAN MAHON, with *facias* nearly as *fieri* as GRAHAM's. Seems he wanted to get in without ticket. Messenger declined to admit him.

"There's my cyard," said The MAHON, pressing pasteboard on acceptance of trembling minion. "A frind will call upon ye this evening."

Inside Court Judges got on a long way. In fact, a few minutes after, the whole thing seemed to come to an end. RUSSELL got all he asked for, and, there being nothing more to do, adjournment proposed.

*The President.* "We have all spent a very comfortable afternoon."

*Toby, M.P., Q.C.* (*interposing as* amicus curiæ). "As your Ludship pleases."

*Usher.* "Silence!"

Then we picked up our briefs and went out. My learned friend ASQUITH's brief lying close to mine, I picked that up too. Has an overwhelming effect in walking through the crowd, to carry from Court a good armful of papers.

* The Dog has taken silk, and never told his oldest and best friend!—*Punch.*

---

## A WHITEHEAD TORPEDO FOR THE CITY.

SATURDAY next, Michaelmas Day. Also City elects new Lord Mayor. Hail, JAMES WHITEHEAD, Alderman that is, Lord Mayor

Michaelmas Day in the City. Turtles electing a Lord Mayor.

that shall be! There is nothing suggestive of the Torpedo about him but his name. A capable, courtly man, who will do honour to the high position he is called to, and will, with peculiar fitness, inaugurate the new era of City administration in conjunction with the working of a Radical Local Government Act passed by a Conservative Ministry.

---

### Morality at a Tennis-Match.

(*By a Buffer.*)

To prophesy our downfall is not rash,
Now all our boys—and girls—seem "going to *smash!*"

"TELL-TALE TIT!"

(*Middle o' September!*)

*Bagnidge* (*having made sure with both barrels*). "ANOTHER BIR——"

*The Keeper* (*aghast*). "BIRD!—NOT A BIT OF IT! 'DON'T KNOW WHAT MASTER 'LL SAY WHEN I TELL HIM! WH', YOU 'VE SHOT A PHEASANT!"

## OUR BOOKING-OFFICE.

A MOST amusing and companionable little book is Mr. GEORGE GROSSMITH'S *Society Clown*. The "Snobbish Chapter" is, in idea, at least, quite Thackerayan. "G. G." thoroughly enjoys a story that tells against himself. The love-letter from the lady who had "a Sunday out," is delicious. What became of this poor Columbine our gay Clown doesn't tell us. Inspired to drop into poetry,—to the air of "*The Fine Old English Gentleman*"—I joyously sing,—

The Clown in Society.

I like to read GEORGE GROSSMITH'S tales of everywhere he goes,
Of Princes, Dukes, and Duchesses, and all the swells he knows.
I revel in the thought that I can see him on the stage,
And sit in front without a smile, and put him in a rage.
*Chorus*—This Clown of High Society, all of the modern time.

I like to read the in-vi-ta-tion sent him by the Prince,
To dine with H.R.H. abroad,—but has he had one since?
I like to think that I can go into the Galleree,
And chuck an apple at his head,—which he can't do to me.
*Chorus*—This Clown of High Society, all of the modern time.

To call himself "a clown," I think, is hard—on HARRY PAYNE,
Who always comes at Christmas Time with "Here we are again!"
Who 'll soon bring out his memoirs of tip-top Societee,
Where he never had the pleasure of encountering G. G.
*Chorus*—This Clown of High Society, all of the modern time.

If you're going a long journey by train, buy *The Society Clown*. The time will pass so quickly with this book in your hands, that the station where you ought to have got out will have escaped your notice, and you'll wake up at the terminus with the prospect of having the book still to amuse you on the return journey.

From gay to grave, I am still going quietly, very quietly, through Mr. HAWKINS'S most carefully compiled and entertainingly written two Volumes, entitled, *The French Stage in the Eighteenth Century*. He has stated the case of the disabilities of the French Comedians, on the whole, very fairly, considering that he candidly avows himself a warm partisan, whose bias has prevented him from admitting that the other side has any case at all. His book, as far as I am able to judge from the first volume, ought to be a standard work of reference for students of the French stage in the Eighteenth Century.

Several Correspondents write to me, asking, where can we procure those *Weird Tales* which you have twice recommended? Well, unfortunately, there was a rush upon them by friends who promised faithfully to return them; but instead of keeping their word, they've kept my books. In the meantime I can only say that they are pocket volumes, adapted to anybody's pocket,—evidently, by the disappearance of my little lot,—consisting of a collection of very old ghost stories, English, Scotch, American, Irish, familiar, it may be, to most readers over fifty, but refreshing even to them, and accepted with delight by the second and third generation. I am fond of old friends, and was delighted to welcome them again. Some of them, however, I had never read before. They are published by BLACKWOOD, and are so portable that I wish they weren't, as I shall never see them more.

"THESE ENGLISH ARE SHREWDLY OUT OF BEEF!"

*Henry the Fifth*, Act III., Sc. 7.

*Lord Wolseley* (*to Tommy Atkins*). "Why, bless me! you look half starved! What'll you take!"

*À propos* of "refreshing," I have just dipped into Dr. Hueffer's *Correspondence of Wagner and Liszt.* Letter-writing is to some of us nuisance enough: letter-reading is worse. But in this case—

"Richard and Francis were two clever men;
Clever at music and clever with pen."

These two geniuses wrote their thoughts impulsively to each other. Their letters are really the conversation of two earnest men, at one in Art, but at issue over the great problems of life. Here and there, as naturally as possible, crop up business and domesticity. Of the two "Special Correspondents," I prefer Liszt, who writes in a tone of conviction, which, except as regards music, is absent from the letters of Richard Wagner.——*Strange Story of a Manuscript found in a Copper Cylinder.* Ought to have been left there. It is advertised as a Jules-Verne-like story, might be called a Verne-and-Vater story. It is childish: and its improbabilities are rendered still more improbable by some of the pantomimic illustrations. Long way down-hill after Verne. "*Facilis descensus a Verne-o,*" says the ever classical and always happily grammatical

Learned Baron De Book-Worms.

---

"Fine weather," said Mrs. Ram; "but these East winds are very dangerous. My Nephew is laid up with an influential cold."

## DUE NORTH.

*Other Climbs—Night—Lodgers—Early Rising—First Meal—Contraction — Expansion — Arrival — Separation — Balmorality — Anticipation—Alteration—"Strangers yet."*

HOBSON, with the agility of a Harlequin, has disappeared by the shortest and quickest route over the washing-stand into his berth. With his back turned to me, he murmurs, drowsily, but consoling to the last,—

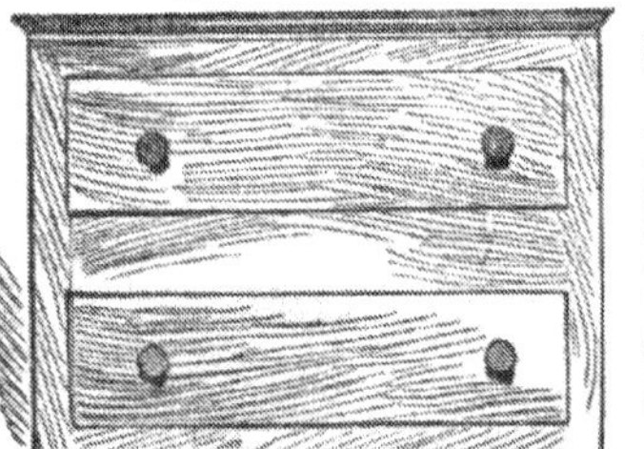

The Cabinit Berth chest of drawers.

"You'll like your berth. It's deliciously comfortable,—tip top! It's the height of luxury." Then he adds, in a gradually descending scale,—*tonus peregrinus*—as he snuggles into his pillow, "Good night, dear friend!"

"Good night!" I return, as I stand dubiously looking up towards the elevated jam-cupboard shelf in which I have to repose, if I can.

"The height of luxury!—tip-top!'" I mutter to myself. "It *is*. How can I get there?"

Economy of space in a small House.

*Happy Thought.*—Necessity, being the mother of invention, ought to give me a tip about a berth. Necessity's tip is the employment of travelling-bags and campstools as aids towards getting into this berth. Necessity may have an extra tip in store for me—a tip over. While arranging my plan of campaign, I find myself humming involuntarily the air from the *Bohemian Girl*, "My berth is noble, and unstained my crest." But, if I come a cropper over this attempt, my crest won't be unstained.

One struggle for life . . . a clutch . . . a kick (if there were anyone in the berth beneath, how wild he would be—and very naturally—with my toe within an inch of his nose—but, thank goodness, there's nobody there) . . . a gasp . . . a momentary spasm, as if a sinew had cracked somewhere—(didn't *Hamlet's* sinews crack, or didn't he appeal to them to "Bear him up?"—yes—that's what I say now, "And you, my sinews, bear me strongly up!")—whoop!—and I sink breathless, a confused heap of "dishabilly," on the jam-cupboard shelf, the bed-clothes disarranged, and the floor littered with bags and campstools, which the next man who comes in will have to clear away.

As to re-arranging the pocket-handkerchief which does duty for a sheet, or doing anything with the strip of flannel meant to represent a blanket, I give it up in despair. Stretching is impossible; so is sitting up: even turning requires the most careful attention.

How did this Lady manage to get into any berth, specially a top one?

No—certainly a berth on board a steamer is *not* the place where "the weary are at rest," nor am I at all sure that it is the place "where the wicked cease from troubling," as one of our fellow-passengers, entering in the dark, and, stumbling over the campstools and bags, swears horribly.

*Happy Thought.*—Pretend to be fast asleep. No connection with bags and campstools. Oh no! "Confound them! Who could have put them there? Infernally idiotic!" Quite so. Good night!

Fellow lodger, who subsequently occupies what I may term the ground floor under HOBSON'S apartment, switches on the electric light, not altogether, as I fancy from his manner, unmaliciously, though it produces no effect on either myself or HOBSON, who are both, like Brer Fox, "layin' low and sayin' nuffin'. After some puffing and wrestling with luggage,—his own, I hope,—our Fellow-lodger switches off the light, crawls into his hole, and subsides. We are all quiet,—playing at being asleep,—when the fourth lodger enters, and uses more bad language in the dark. The effect of the darkness is demoralising. Then he makes grabs at everybody's luggage, tumbling about as if he were playing Blind-man's Buff, until the first fellow lodger (on the ground floor at HOBSON'S) growls out, "Why don't you switch on the electric light?" Whereupon the latest arrival, who has brought into the cabin a curiously blended aroma of tobacco and whisky, guides himself up to the switch by laying hold of the side of my berth, which causes me to give a warning kick in the direction of where I think either his nose or his eye may be, just as a quiet hint that he had better not rouse the sleeping lion in the jam-cupboard. "Switch-back" amusement. Once more the full electric light is switched on, and our friend commences his preparations for retiring, humming the "*Boulanger March*," with variations from other sources, and interrupted by occasional ejaculatory anathemas on everybody else's luggage, and especially on the bags and campstools, which latter, after barking his shins severely with them, he chucks violently into the saloon, exclaiming, "Out you go, dash you!" and I feel that the campstools so addressed are myself in effigy. At last he, too, crawls, like a wounded rabbit, into the hole in the tree (as it were) underneath my nest, where I distinctly hear him groaning and rubbing his ancle. Then, as he has forgotten to switch off the light, in a few minutes' time a deep voice from below—it is the voice of HOBSON'S ground-floor lodger—asks me, if I "won't mind switching it off, as it's nearest me." My first idea is to continue my pretence of being asleep; but, on second thoughts, as there is less chance than ever of getting any sleep with this light glaring right in my eye, I uncurl myself very cautiously, somehow, lift myself up without hitting my head, and extend my arm without falling out, and once more we are in comparative darkness, and I am having a final struggle with the bed-clothes.

*Morning.*—Dear friend HOBSON up very early. Wish Dear Friend would stop in bed. He says he wants to see the sun rise. Evidently he has never seen it before. He is delighted that I have slept so well. I am obliged to admit that I have slept. Gradually fellow-passengers reappear. The majority look as if they had slept in their clothes. With many of them a penknife is a substitute for the particularities of the toilette.

The First Day.

The same, *next morning*, after a night at Sea.

How the ladies must regret their curling-irons! I quite understand the objection of some ladies to a voyage by steamboat.

*Breakfast.*—Marvellous solo performances on fish, eggs, chops, bread and butter, toast, coffee, marmalade. Poor Steward! HOBSON beams on me when I take a chop. "It's doing you good," he says cheerily. I hope so, I'm sure. All the contractors being in great form at breakfast, take twice and even three times of everything.

*Happy Thought (except for Steward).*—They contract, but they also expand.

We disembark at Granton. I part with dear friend HOBSON, whom I thank heartily for the pleasant trip, giving him the credit for the fine weather and everything, whereat he repeats, "I told you it would be all right." and is uncommonly pleased that I am pleased. Off he goes to his destination, and as the boat has just conveniently missed the only train that would have taken me to Lochglennie, I am in Edinbro' alone. Title for novel, *Alone in Edinbro'!* Remember to have heard of an eight o'clock *table d'hôte* at the Balmoral Hotel.

*At the Balmoral.*—I like the name of Balmoral. So proper. A Balmasky Hotel would attract a class of customers who preferred a "Bal" without the "moral." Willing and obliging Hall Porter, with beaming smile, as if he had been expecting me ever so long and is so glad to see me at last, fetches my luggage out of fly. Pleasant and affable young ladies at the *bureau*. None of your stuck-up minxes with somebody else's hair piled up on the top of their heads. Oh, no! nothing of that sort. Agreeable, affable; probably "Scotch lassies." Old gentleman of florid complexion, with fierce white moustache, and of an upright carriage suggestive of retired Indian Colonel (on the stage in a farce with Mr. TOOLE), or the Master of a Ring, and wearing a peculiar hat with a brim so crisply curled up at the sides that, with a few strings and a rosette, it might suit a Junior Dean, is standing in hall. Know his face: recognise his ferocious white moustache. He is the *beau idéal* of *Sergeant Bouncer* in *Cox and Box*. Being alone in the world just now, I am glad to initiate a conversation with the Veteran. I am commencing when pleasant young lady, beaming gracefully across counter of *bureau*, informs me in her pleasantest manner, with just a flattering tinge of regret in her tone—(and without any brogue, so she isn't "a Scotch lassie,")—that the hotel is full; whereupon, the Hall Porter, still with

THE DIVIDED SKIRT.

beaming smile which has not yet faded away, promptly picks up my luggage, and is off with it to the fly. His rule is, "Welcome the coming 'Guest,'" and "speed the parting." The "*parting*" guest, to him as a rule, must be the more valuable, and more to be smiled at. Where am I to go? More alone in Edinbro' than ever! On the chance of some suggestion being made, I address the gallant Bouncer.

The Veteran replies cheerily in broad Scotch,—The McBouncer,—and I gather his meaning to be, that, if they haven't a bedroom here, they (the Balmoral Hotel, that is) can get me one elsewhere.

"Ye'll just taylaphone," says the McBouncer, turning to one of the pleasant young ladies, and, on hearing this, she at once sounds a bell to bespeak somebody's attention. The Veteran evidently possesses some local influence. The Hall Porter pauses, and the smile, which had almost died out with the removal of the third bag, begins to beam again gradually. Song to Hall Porter, "*O smile as thou wert wont to smile Before that weight of care,*" &c. Substitute "luggage" for "care," and there's the ballad complete so far. Shining "Boots"—quite an "Upper leather"—assists cheerfully.

The McTaylaphone replies that he places the best bedroom at my disposal, and I accept. I am "bedded out" like a plant, but return to the Balmoral at feeding time, 8 P.M.

*Balmorality Dinner.*—Large room. Small tables, so that one can dine quietly alone, or with three strangers at most. It being just the end of August, of course Grouse will be on the *menu*, and of course, this being Scotland, we shall have dishes peculiar to the country. I don't know what the dishes are, except Scotch broth, collops, and haggis—("The Midnight haggis" mentioned by *Macbeth*),—but every country has its *spécialités*. Let's see. Here's the McMenu. "*Potage*"—that's French, not Scotch; perhaps they mean "*Porridge*"—no —"*Consommé au Profitrol*" (what on earth's that?) and "*Purée aux Navets.*" "*Navets*" not Scotch. I read on: all French, nothing Scotch:—"*Sole au gratin, Merlan frit sauce Tartare—Croquettes—Compôte—Bœuf Rôti—Agneau, Salade,*"—excellent dinner, *but* no Grouse!

I protest to German Waiter, who doesn't clearly comprehend. English Waiter, lively and attentive, recognises the justice of the protest. He, too, is Alone in Edinbro', for the other Waiters are foreigners. He returns, delighted to be able to inform me that I can have Grouse, "instead of" Beef. I think the stipulation somewhat severe, but I accept the terms, though I am not treated precisely on "the most favoured nation" (or ration) principle, as I have to pay half-a-crown extra. The Grouse being excellent, and the whole dinner good, I am content. Everything satisfactory at the Balmoral Hotel on this occasion, but, on my return visit, only the following week, when I am leaving Scotland, I couldn't imagine that it was the same Hotel.

I entered with a smile of recognition for everyone, as it seemed only yesterday since I had quitted the place. But "a change had come over the spirit of their dream." There was no beaming Hall Porter, only a McSulky, who growled out something, and disappeared. The genial and courteous Veteran McBouncer was nowhere to be seen. The affable and sympathetic Fairies of the *bureau* were no longer there, though I fancy I spied one of them with her pleasant face bent over the ledger, not daring to look up and smile, for fear of the other three, who, I remark, are severe, stiff, and unapproachable. Here was I, once more "Alone in Edinbro'," with a bag and great-coat.

"Can I leave my things here?" I ask of a Boots, who, instead of answering, dives head-foremost down a dark passage, and is lost to view. Not the Boots of a week ago,—New Boots; never did like New Boots; no longer the polished Boots.

One of the young ladies from the *bureau* has come out into the Hall, and is standing with her back to me. I repeat my question, timidly, I admit, but if I am wrong in addressing her on the subject, she will, I trust, graciously correct me. Not a bit of it. "Can I leave my things here?" I ask, with the utmost deference.

The unapproachable young lady deigns no response, but walks slowly towards the other side of the Hall. Her distant manner chills and repels me. It seems to me as if I had proposed to her and been indignantly rejected. I cannot, I dare not ask her another question. I fancy I catch a sympathetic glance from the eye of the pleasant girl at the ledger. I feel that, with all the will in the world to be affable and nice-spoken, she can't do it as at present situated.

The Head Waiter comes down the stairs. I try *him*. "Can I leave my——"; but before the words are out of my mouth he too has vanished with a whisk of the napkin, and is seen no more.

At last, by going up-stairs to the *salle à manger*, I procure some attention from a startled chambermaid, who eyes me suspiciously, but who kindly allows me the use of soap and water and a jack-towel in a bath-room, there being, apparently, no properly appointed lavatory. What has come over them all? Is this a bad day with the Balmoralities?

The dinner at 8 is good enough (no Grouse), but the Waiters bring and take away the dishes in a violent hurry, as if they had backed themselves against time to make so many people swallow five or six courses and have everything cleared away in half an hour from the moment of starting. So swiftly do the dishes come and go that when I am at the second course two undersized German Waiters are hovering about me with the pudding.

Not out of greediness, nor from any inordinate craving of the appetite, but simply to show them that I will not be bullied, and that I positively refuse to do a serious injury to my digestion merely because they have a match against time, I determine to take or at least, to order, twice of everything except the soup.

"*Saumon sauce Genevoise*, or *Merlan frit?*" asks a German Waiter, bending over me insinuatingly, giving me the choice of two platefuls. I reply sternly, I will take *Saumon* first, AND the *Merlan frit* afterwards.

The German Waiter almost collapses. He cannot believe his ears. But I mean what I say; and I do take both. This happens with all the other courses. I pull up at the *Entremets*, of which there are four varieties.

Long before I have finished, all the unprotesting *table d'hôters*, who yield in a spiritless manner to the tyranny of their oppressors, have stuffed themselves in a hurry and been cleared away.

* * * * *

I have anticipated my journey back so as to avoid a second visit to Edinbro'. At present I am intending to start to-morrow morning, having wired to that effect to "D. B.," at Lochglennie.

---

APPROPRIATE LOCALITY FOR MILITARY MANŒUVRES.—In Styria, where the Chamois shooting is going on. [See? *Sham War*. Aha! Yours ever, The Hanlam of Bedwell. Locked up again! Under Colney Hatches.]

---

WHAT WOULD BE LEFT OF IT?—If one of ZOLA's latest works—say, for example, *La Terre*—were Bowdlerised for the English public, the book would probably come out in the form of a clearly printed four-paged pamphlet.

## A CHAPTER ON FAME.

*The Actor.* "AH! IT'S ALL VERY WELL FOR YOU FELLOWS TO TALK ABOUT MY BEING THE PET OF THE PUBLIC, THE IDOL OF THE ARISTOCRACY, THE SPOILT CHILD OF ROYALTY ITSELF! I ADMIT ALL THAT; BUT REMEMBER THAT MY ART DIES WITH ME—WHEREAS YOUR PICTURES, YOUR POEMS, YOUR SPEECHES REMAIN TO SHOW THE TWENTIETH CENTURY WHAT—A—WHAT——"

*The Painter.* "WHAT OVERRATED DUFFERS WE WERE IN THE NINETEENTH, EH? WHEREAS YOU'LL NEVER BE FOUND OUT, OLD MAN. SO YOU SCORE AGAIN!" *The Statesman and the Poet.* "HEAR! HEAR!"

## THE NEMESIS OF NEGLECT.

"Just as long as the dwellings of this race continue in their present condition, their whole surroundings a sort of warren of foul alleys garnished with the flaring lamps of the gin-shops, and offering to all sorts of lodgers, for all conceivable wicked purposes, every possible accommodation to further brutalise, we shall have still to go on—affecting astonishment that in such a state of things we have outbreaks, from time to time, of the horrors of the present day."—*"S. G. O.," in Times of 18th September, in his Letter entitled, "At Last."*

THERE is no light along those winding ways
Other than lurid gleams like marsh-fires fleeting;
Thither the sunniest of summer days
Sends scarce one golden shaft of gladsome greeting.
June noonday has no power upon its gloom
More than the murky fog-flare of December;
A Stygian darkness seems its settled doom;
Life, like a flickering ember,
There smoulders dimly on in deathly wise,
Like sleep-dulled glitter in a serpent's eyes.

Yet as that sullen sinister cold gleam
At sight of prey to a fierce flame shall quicken,
So the dull life that lurks in this dread scene,
By the sharp goad of greed or hatred stricken,
Flares into hideous force and fierceness foul,
Swift as the snake to spring and strong to capture.
Here the sole joys are those of the man-ghoul,
Thirst-thrill and ravin-rapture.
Held DANTE's Circles such a dwelling-place?
Did primal sludge e'er harbour such a race?

It is not Hades, nor that world of slime
Where dragons tare and man-shaped monsters fought.
Civilisation's festering heart of crime
Is here, and here some loathly glimpse is caught
Of its barbaric beating, pulsing through
Fair limbs and flaunting garb wherewith 'tis hidden.
Mere human sewage? True, O Sage! most true!
Society's kitchen-midden!
But hither crowd the ills which are our bane:
And thence in viler shape creep forth again.

Whence? Foulness filters here from honest homes
And thievish dens, town-rookery, rural village.
Vice to be nursed to violence hither comes,
Nurture unnatural, abhorrent tillage!
What sin soever amidst luxury springs,
Here amidst poverty finds full fruition.
There is no name for the unsexed foul things
Plunged to their last perdition
In this dark Malebolge, ours—which yet
We build, and populate, and then—forget!

It will not be forgotten; it will find
A voice, like the volcano, and will scatter
Such hideous wreck among us, deaf and blind,
As all our sheltering shams shall rend and shatter.
The den is dark, secluded, it may yield
To Belial a haunt, to Mammon profit;
But we shall reap the tillage of that field
In harvest meet for Tophet.
Slum-farming knaves suck shameful wealth from sin,
But a dread Nemesis abides therein.

Dank roofs, dark entries, closely-clustered walls,
Murder-inviting nooks, death-reeking gutters,
A boding voice from your foul chaos calls,
When will men heed the warning that it utters?
There floats a phantom on the slum's foul air,
Shaping, to eyes which have the gift of seeing,
Into the Spectre of that loathly lair.
Face it—for vain is fleeing!
Red-handed, ruthless, furtive, unerect,
'Tis murderous Crime—the Nemesis of Neglect!

---

THE STRIKES IN PARIS.—This Tower of Eiffel being built by an Eiffel-utin' gentleman seems to be productive of nearly as much discord as its prototype of Babel. A lunatic project, at best, but the only sensible person to appeal to in the present difficulties is, luckily, "The Sane Prefect."

# THE NEMESIS OF NEGLECT.

"THERE FLOATS A PHANTOM ON THE SLUM'S FOUL AIR,
SHAPING, TO EYES WHICH HAVE THE GIFT OF SEEING,
INTO THE SPECTRE OF THAT LOATHLY LAIR.
FACE IT—FOR VAIN IS FLEEING!
RED-HANDED, RUTHLESS, FURTIVE, UNERECT,
'TIS MURDEROUS CRIME—THE NEMESIS OF NEGLECT!"

## THE (POLITICAL) PLEASURES OF MEMORY.

WE want, indeed, another SAMUEL ROGERS,
(The dullest, sure, of all poetic codgers!)
To sing in sounding verse, as once did he,
The *Pleasures of* (Political) *Memory*.
Oh, joy—if you're a Statesman—just to cast
A retrospective glance upon the past,
The pamphlets written in your fiery youth,
And then be told you are not speaking truth;
To chat about the Cabinets you have known,
And then to have this charge against you thrown,
That your remarks are disingenuous riddles,
In fact, that you are telling taradiddles!
O Memory, friend of philosophic age!
You seem to put our Statesmen in a rage.
Memory, of course, may be a boon, but then
There seem as many memories as men;
And no two of those memories accord
More than their owners do, which seems absurd.
They won't agree in style at all exact
About the shortest speech or simplest fact,
Be't yesterday, or twenty years ago;
One vows 'twas thus, another swears 'twas so,
And, though in speech as bland as a sweet-briar,
Each calls the other an egregious—story-teller.
*Pleasures of Memory?* At the phrase one smiles;
Pleasures of wrangling tabbies on the tiles,
Of scuffling crows over some carrion scrap!
No, ROGERS, you need *not* return, old chap!

### "Is Marriage a Failure?"

AH me, my dear, my dear *Mr. Punch*, I am afraid it is! I've done my best; but no, the Thanes fly from me, and I am, in the language of Lawn Tennison,

"LOVE FIFTY"—*alias* CAN'T-MARI-ANY IN THE MOATED GRANGE.

DEAR SIR,—Marriage *is* a failure, at least in my case. I've been rejected again to-day. "This is the third time of asking."

TIM IDLEIGH.

## HAPPY HAWARDEN.

*Mr. Gl-dst-ne sings to the Mahdi Ali, at Hawarden, to the Air of "Marlbrook."*

AND SO YOU HAVE COME FROM THE NIZAM!
PRAY TELL HIM HOW I GOOD AND WISE AM,
THOUGH AT TIMES TROUBLED MUCH I BY FLIES
I STILL AM THE GRAND OLD MAN. [AM,
SAY, I LOVE THE MA-HOM-ME-DAN—

(*Aside.*) TELL ANOTHER LIKE THAT I CAN.
(*Aloud.*) NOW SIT YE BENEATH MY UMBRELLA,
AND CHUCKLE LIKE OLD *MISTER WELLER*,
WHEN *AXE'D* IF YOU E'ER SAW A *FELLAH*
LIKE ME. I'M THE GRAND OLD MAN!

## THE LONDON BLACKS.

MOORE'S Melodies at the St. James's Hall are nowadays those played by the evergreen and ever black-faced Moore and Burgess Minstrels. The Minstrel Boy never goes to the wars, as he never performs out of St. James's Hall,—at least such was once the tradition. It is now exploded. They have, we believe, played out of the Hall, and a cataclysm has not arrived. On their programme the title "Christy Minstrels" is not to be found. Why is this thus? Are they no longer Christy'uns? Perish the thought!

Professor Blackie who never performs out of St. James's Hall.

On the inauguration of their Twenty-fourth consecutive Season, Mr. EUGENE STRATTON sang "*The Whistling Coon*" for the 1135th time, and the audience, who had not heard it one thousand one hundred and thirty-five times, encored vociferously, but the strict rules of the primitive Christy'uns do not admit of encores being taken. Excellent rule. They should call themselves "The Burgess and No-More Minstrels." *A propos*, where was BURGESS on this memorable occasion? Does Mr. MOORE sing for self and partner? Perhaps BURGESS is keeping himself in reserve, and will burst forth upon us all when the Entertainment achieves its quarter of a century. Still there must ever be a slight cloud of sadness passing over the happy faces of the audience at the thought, that while MOORE is working like a Nigger, BURGESS is—doing what? Careering about, enjoying himself? Or also working? Where *is* BURGESS? Tell me, Shepherds, have you seen my BURGESS pass this way? Depend upon it that when they want a real novelty to attract all London, they'll announce

GREAT NIGHT WITH THE MOORE AND BURGESS MINSTRELS!
FIRST APPEARANCE OF BURGESS!!!

They are welcome to this suggestion; but the curiosity of the public is aroused, and will not be satisfied, except by BURGESS. "Plenty of Burgesses in the City of London," Mr. MOORE will reply; but this won't do for us. Loud calls for BURGESS! BURGESS! and No MOORE at present from Yours truly,

BLACK JACK IN THE PRIVATE BOX.

## A LITTLE "CUTTING."

HERE is an advertisement from the first sheet of the *Times*, September 21, which will please Mrs. LYNN LINTON, who, "touched with the spirit of Christianity," is so hard in the *Fortnightly Review* on the dear "*petits abbés*" of the Eighteenth Century:—

TO NOBLEMEN and others.—A young Clergyman, fond of riding, driving, shooting, hunting, cricket, and all outdoor sports, would be glad to hear of a good LIVING.

Quite the sort of cleric for a Rural Deanery. There's life—sporting life, at all events—in the old Established Church yet. We hope the Rev. Yoicks Tallyho won't be long without a living in a good-going grass country. We drink to him a Stirrup Cup.

### "A SERIOUS CHARGE."

SIR,—Three-and-threepence for one dozen of the best natives at my Club!! I've backed my bill, and sign myself,

*Grotto Club.* SOLVITUR DANDO.

MR. SLIBLOTES WAS THINKING HE WANTED A LITTLE CHANGE, AND WHETHER HE AND FLARROP MIGHTN'T RUN OVER FOR A COUPLE O' DAYS TO SPA OR WIESBAD——

*Mrs. S. (who had been reading "the Papers" too).* "OH, AH! AND THERE'S GOING TO BE A BEAUTY SHOW THERE! OH, I SHOULD SO LIKE——I'LL GO WITH YOU, DEAR!"

[*But he didn't go, and the Beauty Show was a failure.*

## VOCES POPULI.

### AT A HIGHLAND CATTLE AUCTION.

SCENE—*A Yard. In the open space between the rows of pens the* Auctioneer *is trying to dispose of some horses which are trotted out one by one in the usual fashion.*

*The Auctioneer (spectacled, red-bearded, canny, slightly Arcadian touch imparted by straw hat, and a sprig of heather in his button-hole).* What 'll I say for this noo? (*A horse of a meditative mien is just brought in.*) Here's a beast, and a very good beast, from Lochaber! (*The bystanders remain unmoved.*) He was bred by Meester MACFARLANE, o' Drumtappit, and ye 'll all ha' haird on him as the biggest breeder in these pairts. (*Heads are shaken, so much as to intimate that this particular animal does not do* Mr. MACFARLANE *justice.*) Trot him up an' doon a bit, boy, and show his action—stan' away back there! (*With affected concern.*) Don't curb him so tight—be careful now, or ye'll do meeschief to yourself an' others! (*As the horse trots past them, several critics slap it disrespectfully on the hind-quarters—a liberty which it bears with meekness.*) There's a pace for ye—he's a guid woorker, a gran' beast—hoo much shall we say for him? (*Nobody seems able to express his appreciation of the grand beast in figures.*) Just to stairt ye then—twenty poon! (*Even the animal himself appears slightly staggered by this sum; bystanders are quietly derisive; Auctioneer climbs rapidly down without interruption till he reaches six pounds, when he receives his first bid.*) Sex poon' is bed for 'm—is there ony advance on sex poon? (*Someone in the background:—* "Fifteen shellin'!") Sex-fefteen—noo, Meester MCROBBIE, wull ye no luik this way? (Mr. McR. *responds by a decided negative.*) Ye won't? Ah, I never got ony guid from ye—'cept when I didn't meet ye. (*This piece of Scotch "wut" raises a laugh at* Mr. McR.*'s expense, but does not affect the bidding, which still languishes.*) Then, he's going at sex-fifteen—for the last time. Whaur's my bedder at sex-fifteen? (*Repentance or modesty prevents the bidder from coming forward, and the* Auctioneer *continues, more in grief than anger.*) Eh, this is too bad noo—I'll thank no man for making me a bed, 'cept those that are meant in airnest. No one bed onything for a beast like this! Then I hae to tell ye ye've not bed near up to the resairve price on it. (*Suddenly becomes weary of the animal.*) Tak' it awa'. (*The next horse is led in.*) Now, here's a beast that's well-known, I'm thenkin'. (*The general expression signifies that its reputation is not altogether to its credit.*) There's a well-bred mare—open up, and let her show hersel'. (*The mare is shown, but fails to excite competition.*) Ah, ye'll ony buy screws to-day, an' not the nice things at a'—tak' her away. (*The mare is taken out ignominiously;* Auctioneer, *followed by crowd, leads the way to where a pony and trap are standing harnessed*). Noo, I'm gaun to pit up the pony an van—just show them hoo she goes in hairness, boy. (*To intrusive collie.*) Out of the way, dug, in case ye get your feet smashed. (*Trap starts off, and is driven out of sight.*) Whaur's the laddie gaun ta? Thenks he'll show himsel' at Nairn, maybe! Ah, here she comes. (*Trap returns at a modest pace.*) Stan' back noo, all of ye; give her room. I'll sell the mare first, and a beauty she is—what shell we say? Ten poons—and she's a nice one! Well, stairt her at five, she may get up. (*Bidding gets up to ten pounds, where it stops.*) Then she goes at ten, and I'm very glad she's gaun to a gude auld friend o' mine—Meester MCKENZIE, o' Glenbannock. Wull ye say five mair, and take the hairness, Meester MCKENZIE? It's *richt* hairness! (Mr. McK. *declines to be tempted.*) Well, I'm sorry ye wull na, I'd ha liked (*sentimentally, as if it had been the dream of his life*) for the mare an' the hairness to go togither and no to pairt them—but as 'tis, it canna be helped. We'll pass on to the pegs, if you please. (*Passes to a row of pens containing pigs, and mounts some planks placed along the top.*) Now, these are some proper pegs. (*A rush is made for the rails enclosing the pigs, which instantly become self-conscious and redouble their grunts*). Noo, laddies, laddies, it's no fair o' ye taking up a' the room i' that way. I'm quite sure there's a lot o' ye in front that's no buying pegs—ye hanna the luik o' pairsons that buy pegs. Stan' by for shame, and don't keep them that comes to buy, where they canna see sae much as a tail. Hoo much apiece for these palefaced pegs? Ye've an awfu' guid view o' them then, Meester FERGUSON—luik this way once again for forrty an' threepence. (*Persuasively.*) It'll soun' better wi' the threepence. Gaun' for forty an' three. (*The owner of the pigs calls out* "No!") I thocht I made a law here that people having pegs should gie me the resairve at the time—see what ye do now, PETER MACPHAIRSON, make a fule of the buyers and a fule o' mysel'!—but (*with tolerant contempt*) PETER is not a strong man, we must no be haird on PETER. (*Roar from crowd; disappearance of* Mr. MACPH.) I'll cancel no more sales that way, however, as I eentimate to ye once for a'.

*'Arry (on tour from Town—to his admiring friend).* I say, CHARLEY, what d'yer bet I don't talk to some of these chaps in their own lingo?

*Charley.* What a fellow you are! Mind what you are about, that's all.

*'Arry (going up to an elderly person in the only Scotch cap visible).* Hech, Sair, but yon's a braw bonnie wee bit piggie fur a body to tak' a richt gude wullie waucht wi' gin ye meet him comin' thro' the rye!

*The Person in the Scotch cap (who happens to be a retired Colonel in a Highland Regiment, who is somewhat careless in his attire).* I think you will find that sort of thing better appreciated after you've got home.

['ARRY *returns to* CHARLEY, *feeling much smaller than he allows his friend to perceive.*

### A LIBERAL-UNIONIST BIRD.

THE writer of an interesting article on "Birds of London," in last week's *Saturday Review*, quoting the late FRANK BUCKLAND, says that the thrush "does actually sing the following words,—'Knee deep, knee deep, knee deep; cherry du, cherry du, cherry du, cherry du; white hat, white hat; pretty Joey, pretty Joey, pretty Joey.'" Is this bird to be heard in the neighbourhood of Prince's Gardens, South Kensington? or, if he ever performs out of London, was he down at Bradford the other day, singing, with very slight variation, "Knee deep, cheery too, cheery too, white hat, pretty Joey!" If the London Thrush did this, wasn't it a Lark!

## OUR JAPANNERIES. No. 17.

LIKA JOKO'S PIC-NIC

### The Plaint of a Patriot.

"The great majority of London Waiters are foreigners."—*Globe.*

WE licked 'em all in the tented field,
And now at the tablecloth are we to yield?
If so it is clear—and a thundering shame—
That foreigners win by "a *waiting* game."

"MERRY WIVES" AT THE CRYSTAL PALACE.—The second appearance of Mr. BEERBOHME TREE as *False-stuff* has not yet been announced.

APPROPRIATE TO THE SEASON.—*Q.* What is double as good a game as Fives?—*A.* (*evident.*) Tennis.

### Thought for the Close of the Cricket Season.

'TWIXT *belle* and batsman there's some difference small;
One likes, the other doesn't, "a good ball."
*Belle* hopes for, batsman doesn't, "a rare catch,"
With her 'twill win, with him 't may lose the "Match."

"FROM what I hear of Mister ZOLA's works," observed Mrs. RAM, indignantly, "I wouldn't read five lines of his cleverest writings unless all the horrible disgusting stuff were first illuminated out of them."

SHAKSPEARE FOR SENSATIONAL ADVERTISERS.

HANG out our horrors on the City walls;
The cry is, still "*They come!*"

## 'ARRY ON MARRIAGE.

DEAR CHARLIE,

YOUR larst *wos* a lark; gave me fits and no error, old pal.
You 've 'eard 'ARRY was 'ooked after all, and engaged to old SUDDLEWIG's gal?

Come now! who are yer gettin' at, carnt yer? *Me* make up to Carroty MEG?
Are you on the mug-lumbering lay, or has someone bin pulling *your* leg?

Who give you *that* orfice, dear boy? It is wonderful rum, swelp me bob,
'Ow these ere sort o' things get about. Fact is, CHARLIE, I'm fair on the job,
As you know, with the ladies all round; carnt resist me, the sweet little dears;
But 'ook on to one? Not me, CHARLIE; leastways, I should 'ope not for years.

Run in blinkers at my time of life? Try the tandem with *me* in the shafts?
Not likely! I likes a short run with the trimmest of tight little crafts;
But one consort all over the course like, is not 'ARRY's form by a lump;
'Ow could you imagine, dear boy, as yours truly 'ad gone off his chump?

Is Marriage a failure, my pippin? "Oh, ask me another," sez you;
"That kibosh 'as 'ad a long innings, and wants yorking out." Werry true!
The *D. T.* is a regular mug-trap, there isn't a doubt about that,
But you must ha' bin reading it, CHARLIE, to go and book *me* for a flat.

"Is Marriage a failure?" old mivvies are asking. Of course that depends;
But a dashing young feller like me, with good looks, and good 'ealth, and good friends, [and nice,
Knows a trick that's worth two on it, CHARLIE. While life goes on nutty
And the ochre slings in pooty slick, it is blooming bad bizness to splice.

Look at swells! *They* ain't in no dashed 'urry to church themselves out of good fun;
And wy? Clear as mud, my dear feller! The cash keeps 'em fair on the run.
When they do get stone-broke prematoor like, as 'appen it may to the best,
Then they looks for a Missus with money, and rucks in along o' the rest.

But the ruck is no place for a racer as hasn't yet parted with pace,
Ain't aged, nor yet turned a roarer, but still 'as a chance of the race.
While a hoss can find backers, dear boy, it will run if it's got any blood,
And when *no* 'andicapping won't land it, it's time then to go to the stud.

I mean 'aving a run for my money; no 'arness and nosebag for me;
Leastways not at present, my pippin; I like to feel rorty and free,
And the gals likes it too, I can tell yer; lor' bless yer, if I did a splice
D'yer think I should be so much sought for, or found arf as jolly and nice?

Wot mucks me, old man, is the manner in which a chap gets the off-shunt
As soon as he's labelled "engaged," and so 'eld to be out of the 'unt.
He may be jest as nice as Jemimer, all flare-up, and everythink fly,
But when once he gits wot's called *feeonsay*, the gals jolly soon do a guy!

If this 'ere tommy-rot got about, mate—I mean my engagement to MEG,—
It 'ud spile 'ARRY's game with the gals wus than fits or a dashed wooden leg.
No; it's "I'd be a butterfly," CHARLIE, with me, for a long time to come;
Married life may be ticketed honey, but I know it's more of a hum.

"Spoons" is proper; the best barney out, mate; but marriage—that brings knife-and-fork.
Fancy carving for five, plus the Missus! I tell you, old pal, it means *work*.
You remember BOB BINKS—a rare dasher! fair filberts he wos on a spree,
Now he 'as to grub seven, all told, and he ain't five year older than me.

Met him yesterday, CHARLIE. "Well BOBBIE, 'ow trots it, my topper?" sez I.
"Trot, 'ARRY," sez he, "ain't the word; 'ardly runs to the crawl of a fly."
He'd a *hapron* on, CHARLIE, and kicksies as must ha' been out by his wife,
Him as used to sport KING's best dittos *on week days!* And that's married life!

"Wot, *is* Marriage a failure?" I chuckles. "Oh, cheese it, old feller!" sez BOB,
And—he swore 'twas a cold in the 'ead, but I'm blowed if it wasn't a sob.
"Seven mouths, and six weeks out of work, mate! In Queer Street, and cleared of the quids!
I should just make a 'ole in the water, if 'tworn't for the wife and the kids."

I stood him a lotion, poor beggar; he'd stood me a lot in his time,
For I was jest fresh on the war-path when BOBBIE was fair in his prime.
Great Scott, wot a patter he 'ad, and a mouth on 'im, ah! like the doose;
And now he wears old 'ome-made bags, and can 'ardly say bo to a goose.

"The kids is the *crux* of the question," says Mrs. LYNN LINTON. In course!
BOBBIE BINKS could ha' told her that, CHARLIE, and put it with dollops more
She's a-teaching 'er grandmother, she is, although she's a littery swell, [force.
And as to "the State" steppin' in, yah! the State knows its book fur too well.

If the country took care of the kids, and diworce was made easy all round,
Wy, *I'd* marry, mate, early and often, and so would lots more, I'll be bound.
But, oh my, wot a mix, my dear CHARLIE! Free Love and Free Contract? Oh, yus!
The Guvment as Grandmother's dear, mate, but wot would it cost as a Nuss?

In one thing, old pal, I go pairs, with this Mrs. LYNN LINTON exact.
She sez it's a—let'see, wot is it?—a "physiological fact"
That some chaps who're fair flamers as lovers, are failures as 'usbands. That's me!
So I mean spooning round like permiskus, and Mrs. L. L. would agree.

Whether man's poly—wot's it?—by nature, I'm blowed if I know, my dear boy,
But a man, if he isn't a juggins, makes fair for one mark—to *enjoy*.
If I was a Toff and 'ad tin, I should do as the Toffs do, no doubt.
Yank on to one gal, a fair screamer, and yet keep my ogles about.

That's wot I call genuine yum-yum, fair rations all round, and no kid;
But it's doosed expensive, dear boy, and not done on a couple of quid.
Ah! a lot of highflyers is spiked for the want of the ochre, wus luck!
Wot's the good of a way with the women all round, when a cove's got the chuck?

No, CHARLIE, the dowdy-domestic, pap-bowls, p'ramberlators, and that
Is not *my* idea of the rosy, so MEG don't 'ook *me* for a flat.
If it ever *should* run to a Wife, and—well, trimmings, perhaps I may marry,
But till I can splice *ah lah* Toff, CHARLIE, no double-'arness for 'ARRY.

---

"THE ELIZABETHAN DRAMA REVIVED" AT THE CRITERION.—See Mr. MALTBY as the Tutor. First-rate acting. Also LOTTIE VENN's *Betsy*. All good: rattling through three Acts in two hours in splendid fashion. The Author, being present one night, thought he would take a leaf out of Mr. RIDER HAGGARD's latest book, and mark his approbation of the performance in a speech from his private box. Fortunately he only thought.

---

## AN ADMIRALTY BALLAD.

(*Lately Sung, with far too much success, by the First Lord.*)

You tell me that the lately gathered fleet
Reflects no credit on the British Navy,—
That, formed of ships of types grown obsolete,
It well may set alarmists crying "*Cave!*"
You point to bursting guns, defective speed,
To priming boilers, and insist 'tis funny
That I of all these things should take no heed.
"No heed," forsooth! 'Tis that I have no money!
For, let the angered country fume or frown,
You see, I'm bound *to keep expenses down.*

So if to-morrow, by some grave mischance,
These piping times of peace should know infraction,
And war declared with our good neighbour, France,
Should see us worsted in some naval action,
And if our food-supply should halt,—then cease,
And famine force us in capitulation
To sue upon our bended knees for peace,
And bite the dust in our humiliation,
I still should glory, though they sacked the town,
That in my day *I kept expenses down!*

---

WELL BEFORE THE TIME.—No, no! We cannot stand this! Just as the summer is beginning—September 18,—but better late than never, I find, placed on my study table, with the compiler's compliments, a copy of LETTS's Diary of 1889!!! Out, LETTS!

## PLAY-TIME IN COURT AND LANE.

*The Court.*—To start her new Court Theatre, Mrs. John Wood has achieved a fair success with *Mamma*. To this success Mr. Grundy, the ingenuous but not obtrusively brilliant translator, has contributed very little, as it is obtained by a combination of conscientious acting with a cleverly-contrived farcical plot, the construction of which, however, is not without its faults. The First Act is disappointing. The fun of the Second Act is rapidly developed by scene after scene of ingenious *équivoque*. No one could play the odious, unprincipled Mother-in-law with greater humour than Mrs. Wood, but she has scarcely a good line to say, and the part is against the sympathies of the audience; and indeed this is true of all the characters in the piece. Mr. Hare is not well suited, but his exhibition of abject terror on unexpectedly encountering his terrible Mother-in-law is absurdly, though painfully, real.

"Is Marriage a Failure?" Ask Mamma at the Court Theatre.

Mr. Arthur Cecil's friends will be pleased to see him "taking his whack" with the same gusto he used to exhibit at the breakfast-table in *Friends or Foes*, only in different way. Mr. Groves, with his genial manner, is the embodiment of The Groves of Blarney. The scene between Mr. Eric Lewis and Mr. Hare, in the last Act, is one of the best played in the piece. The climax of each Act is unsatisfactory,—more markedly so in the translation than in the original. A gentleman striking a lady is unpleasant, and besides this there is another smack, a smack of stale Divorce Court garlick; and this, if only as a mere *soupçon* breathed over the farcical ingredients of the comic salad, is just enough to impair the thorough heartiness of the merriment with which a piece of genuine though extravagant fun should be received. It is the irony of fate that anyone bearing the proverbial name of Grundy should be responsible for the English *rechauffé* of this essentially French dish.

*The Lane.*—The Armada is a difficult subject to tackle dramatically. Druriolanus and Hamiltonius have tackled it. The play is a series of stirring pictures of life and character in the sixteenth century,

Druriolanus blowing away his Audience to the Refreshment-Rooms. Entr'acte for a few bars' rest.

and Queen Bess was never so correct as is Miss Ada Neilson in her impersonation of her. I am sorry we did not see the elderly Virgin Queen—vergin' on fifty-eight—riding, like the Old Lady of Banbury, on a white horse at Tilbury Fort.

Mr. Leonard Boyne is gay and gallant as the naval hero, though the authors have made a grave mistake in not giving to him the line spoken by *Lord Burleigh* or *Sir Francis Walsingham*, who in reply to a patriotic speech from *Elizabeth*, exclaims, "'Tis yourself that speaks!" This with "Sure," to begin with, and "bedad" to finish with, would have brought down the house. Mr. Boyne's speech at Old Cheering Cross is capitally given.

Mr. Leonard Boyne asserts the right of public meeting at Cheering Cross, close to Trafalgar Square.

That thorough Elizabethan Actor, Mr. Harry Nicholls, who is never so much at home as in Shakspearian characters, perfectly revels in the part of a Cockney of the sixteenth century. His song on board ship is a specimen of real racy Elizabethan humour. I regret he did not give us a solo version of the duet in the Pantomime, "*Marry come up! Forsooth! Go to!*" which he might have sung in the presence of the Grand Inquisitor. There is a good Servant in Act II., who intrudes upon his master, Mr. Luigi Lablache, as Don Somebody or other (Don Qui?) at an awkward moment, and announces pleasantly enough, as a couple of ordinary visitors, "Two Familiars of the Holy Inquisition," all in black—quite "the wholly Inky-sition"—who have just dropped in, in quite a friendly way, to make a morning call. However, as their arrival is the signal for the Scene to finish, they are welcome.

If I were Druriolanus, I should cut out the lines concerning "Sons of burnt fathers"—(I didn't quite catch it, and I've mislaid the playbill)—written in Shakspearian blank verse and spoken by Milton; I should say, well spoken by Miss Milton. The lines go for very little, and as to the *tableau* representing Seymour Lucas's picture, I do not know what the original went for, but the *replica* goes for nothing. Instead of Seymour Lucas, see less Lucas.

Altogether a splendid spectacle. Ships wonderful. Sorry Harry Nicholls isn't in the sea-fight. When the fireships appear, he might have come down to the flote, and recited "*The Boy stood on the burning Deck,*" after which, quick Curtain.

Miss Winifred Emery is a charming Actress, creating a great effect on everybody except the Black Ink-quisitor, who orders her off to be cremated; from which shocking fate she is rescued by British Tars, who rob the Spanish Stake-and-Onionists of their choice morsel just when "they'd made their little pile." Miss Emery sometimes becomes quite Terry-fied in action and utterance, as, for example, when she jerks out with a pause between each syllable. "Not—the—tears—of—all—the—An—gels" would do something or other, I forget what, but, *à propos* of this sentence, I feel pretty certain that, if the Recording Angel, whose tear blotted out *Uncle Toby's* warm-hearted, impulsive oath, were to visit our theatres just now, he would find his charitable sympathy considerably exercised, and might possibly refuse to obliterate the score against some actors who commit a breach of the Third Commandment every night, *emphasis gratiâ*, that is merely for the sake of intensifying the reality of a dramatic situation. If only as a matter of questionable taste, this growing habit, which is about on a par with Mr. Mansfield's using a line from St. Paul's Epistles as an attractive advertisement for his recent nightmare Drama at the Lyceum, should be corrected. This is not a case of the Frenchman's "*Mon Dieu!*" which is simply equivalent to our "Heavens!" or "Goodness me!" I am inclined to neither Puritanism nor Profanity. *Odi profanum*, says everyone's truly,

A Familiar of "The Wholly Inky-sition."

Jack in the Box.

## MONU-MENTAL SUFFERING.

*Poor Old Mon.* "Oh dear, I do feel so Chippy! I'm afraid there's something wrong with my Head! It's on Fire!"

[*Sings dolefully, "Ah che la Mortar."*]

*Dr. Stonemason* (*aside*). "Ah, *very Cracky!*"

## VOCES POPULI.

### ON A TRIP TO STAFFA AND IONA.

Scene—*Oban Pier. Deck of the "Grenadier." Time,* 7·50 a.m. *Excursionists embark, wearing the air of chilly depression or unnatural liveliness common to people who have got up too early in the morning. The knowing ones select chairs in comfortable corners.*

*The Timid Tourist* (*to Hearty Ditto*). I suppose we shall not have much more motion than this anywhere to-day, Sir?

*Hearty T.* Oh, *this?* This is nothing; we're shut in here, you see. When we get out of the Sound of Mull, and meet the Atlantic, we shall get shaken up a bit, and a good thing too! We don't want a *mill-pond*, eh?

*The Timid T.* (*who would much prefer a mill-pond*). No, no—of course not.

[*Considers seriously whether he cares so very much about going to Iona after all. Steamer starts. The knowing Passengers discover that they have chosen seats facing the wind, and change. Well-read Tourists quote the "Lord of the Isles," out of their guide-books, to people who have none. After rounding Ardmore Point, the steamer becomes decidedly lively.*

*The Hearty T.* Now for it—here it comes!—*Now* she catches it! There's a beauty!

[*Repeats this before and after each wave, until a silence falls upon him.*

*Attentive Husband* (*to Wife, who is "enjoying it immensely," but does not seem inclined to talk*). Now *do* notice the play of light and shade on the mountains over there, darling.

*The Wife (faintly).* Lovely, dear, lovely!

*Att. Husb.* But you're not looking—you really oughtn't to miss this, it's magnificent! Turn round and look; it's exactly behind you.

*Wife (with feeble irritation).* I know, dear—but I can see it *quite* well where I am, *really* I can!

NEARING STAFFA.

*Excursionist (with his hat tied round his ears by a handkerchief—to a Haughty Tourist).* Can you tell me, Mister, if that's the Dutchman's 'At over there?

*The Haughty T.* Can't say, I'm sure—you'd better ask him.

*An Enthusiastic Excursionist (in a tall hat secured under his chin with string).* To think of landing on Staffa and seeing those wonderful caves with our own eyes—it seems like a dream, Sir, a beautiful dream! I suppose the jetty's at the *back* of the island, eh?

*Well-informed Person.* Oh, there's no jetty—we shall be landed in boats; and roughish landing it is, as a rule.

*The E. E. (cooling).* Is that so? Well, I'm not sure, after all, that one doesn't get a better idea of things by not going too near them.

*The Wife (who has come entirely to oblige her Husband).* Oh, don't mind *me*, don't stay behind on *my* account—there's no reason why *you* shouldn't go on the island, if you want to. Only, don't ask me to come with you—because I shan't. I've done enough in coming as far as I have, *I* think.

*Her Husb.* Yes, you stay quietly on the steamer; that'll be the best thing for you.

*The Wife.* If you go, *I* shall go. I'm not going to be left all alone here, so don't think it, though *why* you can't be contented to see Staffa from where you are, without going poking your nose into every hole on the island, I'm sure *I* don't know!

ON STAFFA.

*In Fingal's Cave.*

*Excursionist with an eye to effect.* Fine big place, you see; but they don't make 'arf enough of it. They ought to light it up with coloured fires, ready for when we come.

*Another Exc.* Did the 'Arp and Concertina come ashore, d'ye know? Because we might get them to give us a tune inside here if they have.

*On the Boulders.*

*A Young Wife (who has been prostrate for the greater part of the trip).* HARRY, I can't go back on board that horrid steamer again. You mustn't ask me; promise me you won't!

*Harry.* But, my dear love, what are we to do?

*His Wife.* Why, *live* at Staffa. You always say you hate fashionable places and *(persuasively)* I'm sure this is nice and quiet, HARRY!

ON RETURNING TO THE STEAMER.

*A Tourist who has stayed behind (to a Tourist who has gone).* Well, was it *worth* it? [*Rather patronisingly.*

*The Tourist who has gone.* Oh, marvellous—grand!
[*Gives an elaborate description.*

*The T. who has stayed behind.* Well, I had half a mind to go myself—thing you don't see twice in a lifetime, and all that—but *(candidly)* the fact is, the ship seemed steadier, and it struck me as a good opportunity to go below and get some lunch—and a capital lunch I *had*—there was roast beef, corned beef——
[*Describes lunch vividly.*

ON IONA.

*The Tourists land, and are welcomed by a chorus of Native Children, chanting, "Shells a penni, necklace twopence, seaweed a penni, sea archid twopence." Tourists follow the Guide with the sheeplike submission peculiar to them; one Excursionist observes that it is "hallowed ground," to which his neighbour, without exactly knowing why, assents, and becomes depressed. Gradually, however, the modern spirit begins to assert itself in the majority.*

*A Sceptical T. (gazing at the Tomb of the Kings).* For anything *we* know, they may be all bogus, every one of them, eh? Fancy us staring solemnly, as if they were perfectly genuine—that's a good joke, that is!

*Frivolous T. (turning to the tombs of the MACLEANS).* 'Ullo, 'ere's a fine old feller with his sword be'ind 'im!

"NOUVELLES COUCHES SOCIALES!"

"I SAY, UNCLE, THAT WAS YOUNG BALDOCK THAT WENT BY,—WILMINGTON BALDOCK, YOU KNOW——!"

"WHO THE DICKENS IS *HE*?"

"WHAT! HAVEN'T YOU HEARD OF HIM? HANG IT! HE'S MAKING HIMSELF A VERY FIRST-RATE POSITION IN THE *LAWN-TENNIS* WORLD, I CAN *TELL* YOU!"

*Guide (long-sufferingly).* That is MACLEAN of Duart.

*Friv. T. (pointing to effigy of armed Chieftain).* And is that his good lady next him?

[*Spirits of party revive; the inevitable Funny Man comes out with great success, and a little Tourist of comic exterior who trots up breathless at every halt, and asks a serious question, is hailed with delight, and treated as a Humorist of the finest water.*

LEAVING IONA.

*Young Lady.* Oh, do you know, it was *such* a pity! I was down in the Saloon, reading up all about Iona in the Guide-book, and I never noticed we were there till it was too late to land. Still I can say I've *seen* it, you know—can't I?

ON THE WAY HOME.

*The Officious T. (to a Lady, who is beginning to think she has got over the worst of it now).* You'll excuse me, Ma'am, but wouldn't you feel more comfortable if you had your chair the other way? You see, where you are is just in front of the Cook's Galley, and there's a warm smell of burnt mutton-chops coming up that——

[*The Lady moves, and—much to the surprise and indignation of the Officious T.—"does not say so much as thank you."*

*Steamer nears Oban; the Comic T. illustrates the steps of the Highland Fling, till he falls over a campstool. Small stout men, who have been invisible till now, emerge, and point out scenery. The man who plays the Concertina collects subscriptions in a saucer, being careful to weed out every copper coin as it is contributed.*

*Final Verdict (by a Lady who has passed the entire day on a deck-chair, with her head in a shawl).* Well, there was less to see than I expected!

---

"THE FOUR GEORGES."—GEORGE RANGER (of the Parks), GEORGE JOKIN' (of the Exchequer), GEORGE GROSSMITH (of the House of Savoy), GEORGE LEWIS (of Ely Place).

---

NEW VERSION.—Call no man happy until you know he has not written a diary.

## DUE NORTH.

*Arrival—Welcome—Introductions.*

FOUR hours from Edinbro' to Lochglennie, changing several times, and stopping at Dunblane for the sole purpose, apparently, of listening to a pertinacious fiddler. "Trains may come and trains may go, but he fiddles on for ever." Twenty minutes with a deaf Scotch fiddler! Away! Farewell, Dunblane!

*Lochglennie Station.*—In answer to a porter at the gist of whose question I can only hazard a guess, I say, "Yes, I'm going to Mr. BUDD." Whereupon he immediately returns—

"Eh, then the mash-sheen's here."

The "mash-sheen" (which sounds as if I had come all the way

"The Mash-sheen."

down here to bathe on the sands) is an open car, outside the station, guarded by a small sprightly man in a respectable Sunday suit, top-hat included, who might be anything from a small bootmaker's assistant to a sheriff's officer in good country practice. Not in the least like an ideal stalwart Highlander in the national costume. Odd. Nowhere do I see, or have I seen, the national costume. All trousers, or knickerbockers, and gaiters. *Happy Thought.*—The national costume is evidently "more honoured in the breech than in the observance." Self and bags bestowed in car, which is, I should say, set on what may be called "*Very-rough-Sea-springs.*" *Happy Thought.*—Capital exercise for one of the Livery of the City of London.

*At last! Lochglennie Lodge. Little* (*!!*) Shooting-Box. Big Shooting Portmanteau, Grand Shooting Trunk! *Little!* It may have been little once—as we all were—but it has grown, and the population of visitors has overflowed into an *Annexe* about a hundred yards from the house.

It has been raining all the morning. It has been raining ever since I arrived yesterday in Edinburgh, but at this moment there is a cloudless blue sky. A beautiful view of plain, valley, river, and heather-covered hills. Not a soul about. Driver is down taking out bags, and an elderly servant has appeared (no stalwart Highlander in kilt as yet. Where are they?—all "kilt entirely?"), a bell has sounded, and as if this were a cue on the stage, or a preconcerted signal, as I have reason subsequently for believing that it is, JOHNNIE BUDD appears out of a small side-door, a stately Lady walks on to the chief doorstep, somebody passes her and descends to the garden, one man with a gun comes out of the *Annexe*, a third with a fishing-rod from out of a shrubbery (why in a shrubbery with a fishing-rod?), and lastly, before I have time to take it all in, or they all to take me in, DAVID BAIRD, D. B., suddenly looks out of a top window, and, clapping his hands, cries "Now, boys! One—two—three—all together!"... and all together they shout out, "How *are* you?"

Then they all disappear (including startled horse with cart at a gallop and little man running after it) as suddenly as they have appeared, like mechanical figures, except D. B., who romps down an outside staircase (such as are common to Swiss chalets), jumps on to the path, and delighted beyond measure at the success of this well-rehearsed *coup de théâtre*, grasps me by the hand, and once more exclaims, "How *are* you?" Then, in an earnest tone, as if for one moment he would drop joking, and exhibit the deepest interest in the state of my health, he says, "But——" he pauses, and no other way of framing his inquiry suggesting itself, he is compelled to repeat, only slightly varying the emphasis to suit the seriousness of the occasion, "*How* are you? But really,"—here he taps me with two fingers of his right hand on my chest—a mode of salutation, he explains, customary between "'The Two Macs' before the row begins," and once more he inquires—"*How* are you?"

Before I have time to reply, he continues pleasantly, "You know my uncle, the Laird," and therewith D. B., introduces me to my host, a square-built broad-shouldered man of middle height, with healthy brown complexion, and good working shooting-suit of same colour to match, with leather over the shoulders, which is more suggestive to the Cockney mind (my own at the moment) of a Metropolitan Turncock than a Scotch sportsman. JOHNNIE BUDD has an encouraging smile, but a somewhat nervous manner, as if a trifle uncertain as to how the new arrival would take this kind of hearty reception improvised by "D. B."

The Laird.

Finding that I quite enter into the spirit of the thing—(it's safest for a comparative stranger to do this at once, as if the "way of the house," whatever it may be, is just exactly what you had expected all along, and what you wouldn't have had altered, *no*, not on any account)—he shakes hands, a second time, warmly.

"Delightful place you have here, Mr. BUDD," I say.

"He's not Mr. BUDD here—he's 'the Laird,'" cries D. B. "Everything here is 'by order of the Laird.'" And as he says this, he strikes an attitude, and takes off his cap reverentially, as I have seen a Russian official do (on the stage) whenever he has had to bring in the Czar's name authoritatively.

"The air of Scotland agrees with your nephew," I observe.

The Laird smiles. D. B. chuckles. I look from one to the other. What is the matter with both of them?

"How *are* you?" exclaims D. B. He can't help it. He must start any communication of importance with this preface, and finish with it too. "How *are* you?" Then confidentially, "The Laird's not my uncle, and I'm not his nephew. See?" Here he taps my chest in "The Two Macs" fashion—"I call him Uncle, but he doesn't call me Nephew. At least he does sometimes. He's only an uncle on the mother's great first cousin's grandmother's side. See?" Two Macs entertainment again—"No real relation." Then he turns to JOHNNIE BUDD, as if for corroboration—"Are you, Laird?" To which the Laird, who has been nervously smiling all the time, and is still rather uncertain as to how I am going to take it all, replies hesitatingly, as if he hadn't quite made up his mind on the subject of D B.'s affinity to him, "No,—we're not near relations. And he impresses the fact on me by adding, "No, we're really not."

"No," continues D. B., seriously. "You see I never had any uncles and aunts to speak of, and so I—your little D. B.—got 'em as he wanted 'em. When I found someone I liked, I made him an Uncle, or an Aunt, as the case may be. See?" Two Macs again. "Hullo!" he exclaims—"here's another of 'em!" And, as the very handsome upright Lady, with powdered grey hair, and a mantilla gracefully thrown over her head, whom I have already seen at the door, advances towards us, D. B. says, "Here's the Good Aunt. Allow me to present you. Laird's guest, Good Aunt!" and he bows between us much as the Clown does when he is apologising for having run full tilt into the Swell's lowest waistcoat button, and swears he "didn't mean it, 'pon his word of honour!" Whereupon the stately Lady, with the sweetest smile imaginable, welcomes me to Lochglennie, and is about to ask me some question, when a quiet, very thin, aristocratic-looking gentleman, with grey whiskers, greyish face, and grey suit to match (very odd: all the men, I subsequently notice, have suits to match their complexions, or complexions to match their suits,—*Happy Thought*—so as not to frighten the grouse with too much colour), walks out, with the puzzled air of a man who has come suddenly out of a cellar into the broad light of day, blinking like one of the prisoners released from the Bastille. Before the grey Man from the Bastille has quite grasped the meaning of the scene before him, D. B. shouts out,—

"Here's another of 'em! *How* are you?" Whereupon the grey thin man rubs his eyes,—he must have been shut up in a cupboard—(Can it be the skeleton brought out to meet me?),—and not being prepared with an immediate and telling repartee, which, I admit, is difficult to find, smiles good-naturedly at me, and putting out his hand, as if he were feeling his way along, but really intending me to shake it, which I do, he says, "Ah! delighted to see you—um—how dee do?"

"This," says D. B., holding the skeleton from the cupboard by the elbow, and explaining him as if he were a figure in a show; "this is the Wicked Uncle, husband of the Good Aunt. His name is Norval on the Grampian Hills, and one of his ancestors, the MCCOLLOP of Collop, had something to do with the murder of MARY Queen of Squats, and he's never been the same man since." All this in a breath; then he shakes hands with the Wicked Uncle, kisses the Good Aunt's hand ("Or the hand of the Good Aunt," he says, winking at me aside, "OLLENDORFF!"), and beaming on everyone all round, he votes that "the question be now put," which is—"How are you?"

CÆSARISM

# A WISE WARNING.

*(Founded on the first part of an old Fable, the Sequel of which Mr. Punch trusts may never apply.)*

DÆDALUS BISMARCK (*Political Parent of* WILHELM ICARUS).

"MY SON, OBSERVE THE MIDDLE PATH TO FLY,
AND FEAR TO SINK TOO LOW, OR RISE TOO HIGH.
HERE THE SUN MELTS, THERE VAPOURS DAMP YOUR FORCE,
BETWEEN THE TWO EXTREMES DIRECT YOUR COURSE.

"NOR ON THE BEAR, NOR ON BOÖTES GAZE,
NOR ON SWORD-ARM'D ORION'S DANGEROUS RAYS:
BUT FOLLOW ME, THY GUIDE, WITH WATCHFUL SIGHT,
AND AS I STEER, DIRECT THY CAUTIOUS FLIGHT."

OVID, "*Metamorphoses,*" *Book VIII., Fable III.*

It now strikes the Good Aunt that I must be hungry, and simultaneously it occurs to the Laird that luncheon will be ready in ten minutes, and that he will show me to my room in the *Annexe*, where I am to be chummed with two other sportsmen. Evidently large party.

"Where's DOLLY?" asks the Good Aunt.

"DOLLY?" replies the Wicked Uncle, trying to wake himself up by taking off his Scotch cap and gently stirring his hair, which is what theatrical wig-makers term 'sparse,' "DOLLY's out with the Baron, shooting." DOLLY and the Baron! Then there are young ladies here, and a foreign nobleman. Large party. Fashionable one too. Thought I was coming to a rough-and-ready little shooting-box.

"I haven't seen NELL all the morning," says the Laird, in a tone of regret.

"She went with DUNCAN," D. B. answers, "when he was off to see to the pits."

Aha! all sporting—the young ladies evidently. DOLLY has gone out shooting, NELL has gone to see about the pits.

"Shall we wait for GRANNIE to come in to lunch?" asks the Laird of the Good Aunt, with an air of hesitation.

"I don't think it's much use," replies the Good Aunt. "GRANNIE went out driving——"

"Oh, no!" interposes the Laird, anxiously; "surely they never were going to drive this morning—I told MALCOLM——"

"Ah!" interrupts D. B., "then GRANNIE's gone out fishing a long way down the stream."

"Alone?" asks the Laird, who, as I see, is naturally anxious about the old lady—his grandmother, I presume—who must be a more determined sporting character than "Mr. MANTON."

"Alone?" returns D. B. "Oh no,—I saw the boy and Ross carrying the nets and lines."

"Oh, that's all right," says the Laird, quite satisfied as to his elderly relative's safety. "I'm glad GRANNIE didn't take the canoe. It's not safe to fish out of."

"Safe! A canoe for an old lady!" I cannot help exclaiming.

This remark of mine causes considerable amusement. Even the Laird's quiet smile develops into a genuine laugh. The Skeleton from the cupboard is tickled too, and repeats to himself, "Old lady! Aha! that's good!" W. B.'s hand comes down with a slap on my shoulder as he gives his war-cry of "How *are* you?"

It is uttered in such a tone of triumph, and the laughter is so genuine, that I perceive I've made a mistake as to Grannie. At this moment a herculean young fellow, six feet two if he's an inch, with a comparatively small head—quite in keeping with the herculean character—on the top of which is a deer-stalker stuck all over with flies, hooks, and bits of line, as if he had just escaped from a Lunatic Fishing Asylum, where they would put hooks and flies in the hair instead of straws, joins our party. He wears large melodramatic piratical boots, carries a huge fishing-rod, and is hung about with straps, leather cases, and baskets, as if he were a pedlar with a lot of things to sell, and is introduced by D. B. to me as GRANVILLE BLUNT, known as "Grannie." Then D. B. surveys the circle formed by the Good Aunt, the Wicked Uncle, the Laird, Grannie, D. B. himself, and the boy; and as if it were the cue for curtain and end of First Act, he laughs all over his face, and exclaims, "How *are* you?" which at once disperses the group.

The Laird shows me a deliciously comfortable bed-room and a sitting-room in the *Annexe* which are at my disposal, "commanding," as the advertisements say, "beautiful and extensive views." Then the Laird departs to see about the lunch.

*Happy Thought.*—Put myself *au courant* with the company in the house. "Who are the girls?" I ask. "Girls?" repeats D. B., surprised, "what girls?" Then, with an air of mistrust, "You're joking—you're trying to get at me—oh, yes"—and he puts himself on the defensive by resorting to his magic phrase, "How *are* you?" He is just off when I stop him, and assure him I'm serious. "Who is 'Nell,' they were talking of, who has gone out with DUNCAN to the pits." More laughter. D. B. nearly has a fit, but relieves his feelings by snapping his fingers, crying "Who-whoop!" and dancing a few more steps of the Highland Fling; after which performance he stops to explain that "Nell's the Retriever, and DUNCAN's the Keeper."

"And what's Dolly? A dog or a cat?" I ask.

"DOLLY? Oh, don't you know him? Capital chap—he has the next room to you. DOLLY WHITE, in the Guards. How are you, DOLLY?" he cries, out, rapping at the partition; to which summons the immediate response, in a defiant tone, comes back, "How are you?" "The other chap," he continues—"he's not in now—is the Baron." Why Baron? "Don't know—always call him 'The Baron.' Rather think it's because he once went down a coal mine. There's the luncheon-bell." He pauses at the door, however, as if he has forgotten to say something of the utmost importance, and then exclaims, "How are you!"

"QUITE WELL, THANK YOU!" I roar back at him, and he disappears as if I had broken the spell by this happy and truly original repartee. But somehow, the air is full of, "How are you?" and as, brush in hand, I survey myself in the glass, I stop myself in the act of saying to my own reflection, "How *are* you?" This is catching.

## ROBERT'S LONG WACATION.

SUTTEN suckumstances, incloodin a most unnesessary abundence of rain, combined with a rayther onusual detishency of the currant coins of the realm—as the loryers terms what I shoud call a werry near aproach to stumptupedness—indooced me and my fare Partner to give up our ushal long wacation, this here yeer, of a hole week at the See Side, or on the River, and spend it in jolly old Lundon, the land of my Birth and the 'ome of my blooming manhood.

And upon the hole, I don't reelly think as either me nor my Partner has werry much regretted it. In fact there's so many wunderfool things to be seen here, if one only has the time, without not nothink to pay, and so many bewtifool plaices to wisit, on the same werry libberal terms, that a week dewoted to 'em flies away like one a clock, which, as we all knows, don't take so werry long to do; besides, if one's bound to be wet thru for a hole week, it's far better to have it at ome than a broad. Fust and foremost, then, I wisited High Park, and with the xception as there wasn't not nobody there xcept me and three other gennelmen and one man on a horse, it was jest as bewtifool as ever, and the flower-gardens was that splendid and tidy as did great credit to Feeld Marshall "GEORGE," as has the care on 'em, and sines his onered name on all the boards as is stuck up at all the gates.

It was a bewtifool morning when I started, after a rayther late Brekfest, and I had jest got to about the werry middle of the Park, when, without the werry least notice or warning, down came sitch a storm of rain as I has werry seldom bin drenshed by. I stood up under a littel tree as was near me; but tho' I bleeve as it tried its werry best to keep me a dry place under its bows, it was all in wane, and by the time as the storm was over, and the sun cum out agane, I was wet through to my werry skin, and the heat of the sun shining on my wet close had the singler affect of making 'em all smoke, and a rayther imperent-looking boy acshally arsked me weather I knowed as all my steam was a blowing off, and weather I was afeard of busting my Biler! Oh, them London Boys! What little respec they has ewen for an Hed Waiter! In coorse I allers treats 'em with the most horty contemt.

Well, my fust day's holliday being rayther a failure, I spent the nex one, which was one long down pore, in the buzzum of my famly; and though I bort no less than three halfpenny Papers, and red 'em all rite through, yet I must confess that it was about the werry longest day as I amost ewer remembers. Praps the two singler suckemstances that my fare Partner had a bad tooth ake, and gave me nothink but the cold sholder for lunch, and dinner, and supper, may have had sumthink to do with it. But so it was, and I sort my downy couch at a most unnateral hurly our.

What append next day I'll tell you next week. ROBERT.

---

'AVE A NEW CHAPLAIN.—We knew Mr. ARTHUR ROBERTS had not been in London for some time, having, as we believed, marched with the Avenue *Old Guard* to take the provinces by storm; but certainly we were not prepared for an announcement, in a daily paper, occurring in the course of a short paragraph, to the effect that "the Rev. ARTHUR ROBERTS, M.A.," did something or other as "Chaplain to the Prince of WALES." "A loss to the Stage," we said to ourselves, resignedly, "but a gain to the Church. And then what an entertaining Chaplain he will be for H.R.H., if he is only anything like as amusing as he was as *The Vicar of Wideawakefield.*" But our train of thought on this line was rudely run off the rails by the almost immediate discovery, on comparing this paragraph with similar ones in other contemporaries, that the "Rev. ARTHUR ROBERTS" was a misprint for "the Rev. ARTHUR ROBINS." Really printers should not trifle with our tenderest feelings in this flippant manner; but, on reconsideration, we congratulate H.R.H., the Church, and the Stage, on things being *in statu quo* Avenue.

Church and Stage.—"The Vicar of Wideawakefield."

---

NEW ILLUSTRATION OF AN OLD ÆSOP'S FABLE.—On the first night of the successful Opera *Carina* at the Opéra Comique, the audience cried "WOOLF!" so often, that when a young lady appeared in answer to this summons for the Composer, they wouldn't believe that she was really the WOOLF in question.

*First City Man.* "Edication, oh, rubbish! There—I've only 'ad 'alf a Year's Schoolin' all my Life!"

*Second City Man.* "Oh, I say! You must 'a' wasted that time most awfully, old Fellow. He-he-he!"

## THE COMING DOG.

(*By a Comfort-loving Cynic.*)

A New Dog is coming! the more, Ma'am, the merrier,
You think. The new tyke is a "Tartar fox-terrier."
He's silky and splendidly smooth, so 'tis said;
His manners are mild and his colour is red.
A lady's dog quite! How your heart will be struck.
Well, well, my dear Madam, here's wishing him luck!
But permit me to hope, when he reaches your lap,
That the new dog won't whimper, or snivel, or yap;
Not, like the Toy-terrier, shiver with dread,
Nor, Pug-fashion, grunt with a cold in his head;
Nor look, like the Dogs of that queer Dachshund breed,
As though two additional legs were his need:
Nor, like the Fox-terrier, chevy the cat,
Nor, like a King Charles, get abnormally fat: [them?)
Nor like shaggy Skyes (Ma'am, what *is* there to pet in
Have very weak eyes and long hair that *will* get in them.
Whatsoever his colour, red, yellow, or green,
I'm sure if he's quiet and decently clean,
Not given *too* greatly to pant, snort, and snuffle,
Nor always involving your guests in a scuffle;
If he isn't unpleasant to any one sense,
And *doesn't want worshipping*; then, Ma'am, immense
The relief of your friends will, I'm sure, be all round,
To think that *one* bearable pet you have found!

Forthcoming Interesting Publication.—Mrs. Ram is informed that the next book of Aristocratic Reminiscences will be by Lord Howard, of Gossip. "This," the old lady thinks, "ought to be most entertaining."

### Lucifer's Latest.

[Another explosive, called "Ekrasite," has been invented in Austria. Its effect is expected to be "something unprecedented."]

Satan, in Milton, flamed at Heaven defiance,
And railed at earth with rhetoric corrosive.
Now, posing as mild friend of Man and Science,
He'd probably invent a new explosive!
To verbally "blow up" mankind's mere pother;
Far better help them to blow up each other.

New Work by Archdeacon Farrar.—*The Veget-Arians of the Fourth Century.*

## THE TOAD'S DIARY.

Commenced B.C. 20,000.

Not half a bad sort of place this Prehistoric World. Rather too much commotion going on, though, to please me. Don't care about these "Periods." Precious cold, too, this *Glacial* one. Shouldn't wonder if there wasn't a change coming. One never knows what to expect next. Halloa! what on earth's this? Just what I said. Blest if there isn't a great big bed of clay let loose, and swooping down on me. No escape. Smothered! Well, this is pleasant! Goodness only knows when I shall get out again. And what can a toad do with himself, buried away like this? Ruminate? Yes—but how long? 'Pon my word, I'm afraid this will be precious slow.

• • • • • • •

I said once I thought this would be "slow." That must have been ever so many thousand years ago, and here I am still. "Slow" isn't the word for it. It's *deadly dull*, that's what it is. Then it's so horribly damp. Wish I had got boxed up in a bed of coal. Those Mastodons seem to have stopped thundering about up above. Kept it up no end of a time, but they're quiet at last, so I suppose they've become extinct. Made room for an inferior animal. As I'm alive, it's Primæval Man! I can hear him loafing about all over the place. Well, I don't think *he's* good for much. Does nothing but hang about his caves. Then he's such an uninventive beggar, *he'll* never dig me out. Dare say he'll last though five or six thousand years. What a prospect! And I feel I'm getting limp. Bother Primæval Man,—and the clay!

• • • • • • •

Thank goodness, that awful fraud, Primæval Man, has disappeared at last. World seems waking up a bit, though nothing very much going on. Great Pyramid just finished. Babylon going it. Troy taken. The Chinese inventing gunpowder. Wish they would blow up this clay bed. Feel I'm getting awfully weak in the legs. Nothing going on here but savages walking about in blue paint. Wonder how many more thousand years I'm to be smothered up here. Really it gets slower and slower every century.

• • • • • • •

Things brightened up considerably since my last entry. Roman Invasion. William the Conqueror over. Charles the First's head cut off. Battle of Waterloo. Exhibition of '51. Jubilee. Jot these down as occurring to me as happening in the course of the last eighteen hundred years. Not that they've affected me. I'm still bedded up. Believe my memory's going. If I don't soon get out of this, feel I shall end up by being fossilised.

Halloa! Surely that must be the sound of a pick. And they are coming this way. Yes, it is! Hooray! Liberty at last! Bless the Railway Cutting, and the Contractor! They've dug me out. I'm free! That is, comparatively speaking, for I've fallen into the hands of Mr. T. L. Patterson, of Greenock, and have been mentioned in the *Times*. He says, I "seem to have no bones," and my legs "bend any way," and that I have "two beautiful eyes," but don't "seem to see." Perhaps not. I should like to know what his eyes would feel like, or, for the matter of that, his legs either, after being clayed up for twenty thousand years. However, give me time, and I shall soon pull together again. Meanwhile, all I ask is, that he won't send me off anywhere by Parcels Post.

### Impromptu at a Theatre.

(*By a Victim of the Prevailing Fashion of Feminine Head-gear.*)

This pile before me—I know not its *nomen*—
Hides all the actors, and half the flats.
"The higher Education of Women,"
Applies not so much to their heads as their *hats!*

The Teuton Oliver Twist.—Bismarck asking for *Samoa.* (Mem. Kindly pronounce it as much like *Some more* as possible.)

### Shakspeare Applied.

(*By a Stout Gentleman who objects to foreign climes and climbing.*)

Better bear the *hills* we have,
Than fly to others that we know not of.

FINIS!

(THE END OF THE SEASON.)

## THE LAST (JURY) MAN.

(*A Long way after Campbell.*)

*The British Constitution's doom*
*Is Chaos and Old Nox,*
*When you can't get twelve honest men*
*Into the Jury Box!*

I HAD a vision in my sleep,
My fancy took a tidy sweep
Adown the gulf of Time!
I saw Old England, and behold,
Owing to idleness and gold,
'Twas given up to Crime!

The Judge's eyes did wildly glare
Where, white with age and wan,
There stood within the Box, else bare,
A lonely Jury Man.
Some were exempt by "tips"—the brand
Of bribery stained the Briton's hand,—
From "urgent business" some;
Some swore they couldn't leave their bed,
Some that their Mothers-in-law were dead,
And so they could not come.

Yet, martyr-like, that lone one stood
Before the Beak's dread eye.
He said, "My Lud, it ain't no good;
There's only you and I.
Men don't find Jurying good fun;
They're all 'exempt;' I'm the last one
To turn up, dontcher know.
A thousand 'cases' wait us here—
'Twill take us all our time, I fear.
*I'm* game—so on we go!

"What though the officer go forth?
Britons have now such skill
In 'getting off,' that 'tisn't worth
His while to hunt 'em still;
*We*'ll have to do it; fire away!
A dozen cases in a day
Will be enough for *us.*
It's no use getting in a fury!
At least, you're certain that the Jury
Will be unanimous.

"You will not fill this Box—'tis small—
With the old dozen men.
No; those who've once escaped its thrall
Will not return again.
Lor', *do* you fancy they'll come back
To these hard seats, that cramp and rack,
In these chill draughts to writhe?
You made the Jury-Box abhorred
By dull discomfort, good, my Lord,
*I* once was brisk and lithe;

"Now you perceive my erst bright eyes
Have lost their ancient fire,
I've suffered untold agonies.
To shiver or perspire,
To faint with heat, to gasp for breath,
Are not nice things, but till my death
It shall be my one boast,
That I ne'er slunk at Duty's call.
I've but one fear, 'tis that I shall
Return here—as a ghost!

"Oh, should my spirit, by fate's whim,
Or destiny's last lark,
Come back unto this Court so dim
Into this Box so dark!
No! I should *then* evade the summons
By such excuses—they are rum 'uns—
As "City Magnates" use,
And brothers of the brush or pen,
And lots of selfish idle men,
Who Duty's task refuse.

"Go on! Whilst pluck can hold me up
In this void Box's waste,
I'll sit, although the bitter cup
Is little to my taste;
When to the wall I turn my face,
The last of the old Jury race,
Our Senators, who nod
Over our laws, and fog, and twist 'em,
May *modify the Jury system:*
Or, if they don't, it's odd."

## THE CORRECT CARDIFF.

AT the Autumn Meeting of the Associated Chamber of Commerce at Cardiff, Sir JACOB BEHREN spoke in favour of the formation of a Commercial Party, independent of party politics, in the House of Commons. The President opposed the proposal, the Resolution was negatived, and subsequently Sir MICHAEL HICKS-BEACH, in expressing his agreement with the dissentient majority, declared that there was already a superabundance of such parties. We should think so, indeed! The multiplication of "parties," ostensibly "independent of party," will make the House as parti-coloured (or, which is much the same thing, *party*-coloured), as JOSEPH's coat itself. Why, every interest, opinion, or fad, might organise its own knot of supporters into an "independent party," and Parliament become, indeed, a "fortuitous concourse of atoms," without cohesion, which means Chaos come again. The Cardiff assembly was quite right in refusing to be a party to this party-proposal.

The world's a stage, where each man plays his part,
But "companies" must combine in union hearty.
'Twill be, as old dames say, "a pretty start,"
When "person" (as in Cockneyese) means "party."

## SUMMONED FOR RATES.

(*Notes from a Diary in the Recess.*)

*Tuesday.*—Spent a pleasant morning in Sessions House, Broad Sanctuary, Westminster. Outside, summer suddenly returned; Raining in torrents. Inside, a collection of men and women—chiefly women—all steaming wet. Behind a desk, two Magistrates and a clerk; in front, the Rate Collector. The rest, ratepayers—or to be more precise, people who hadn't paid their rates. Summoned to show cause why. Cause varied; result the same; can't pay. Out of work some; sick others; sad all. A pitiful story, and a purposeless gathering. Magistrates apparently can do nothing.

"We are machines!" said the Chairman, smiling genially upon depressed elderly gentleman, whose rates are horribly in arrear. "You must pay by the 8th of October. Next case!"

Depressed elderly gentleman falls into the rear without word of protest. Always been falling into the rear since he was born. Movement quite natural to him.

Middle-aged lady in an apron and seething mental condition comes up next. Has prepared for Magistrate some autobiographical data. Her story graphic, rather than succinct. Magistrate tries to get in his *formula* about "Adjourned-till-9th-of-October-must-pay-on-the-8th." Middle-aged lady branches out into statement of her troubles prior to last year but one, when MARY ANN was run over by a 'bus.

"Adjourned-till-9th-of-October," says the Magistrate, as if it were an incantation warranted to shut any woman up.

Twelve years she's lived in the house; always paid rates up to two years ago. (Watching opportunity, machine grinds out refrain, "Must-pay-on-the-8th-of-October.") MARY ANN was in hospital for six weeks; hardly been of any use since; Mrs. MOGGINS would bear testimony to extraordinary expenses consequent upon calamity.

Stone-Deaf.

"Adjourned-till-9th-of-October," the machine wearily warbles. "Call-the-next-case."

Next case is that of ARTHUR WILLIAM CLUFF. "ARTHUR WILLIAM CLUFF!" loudly called. No response. Old gentleman with wonderful waste of woollen comforter round his neck stares steadily into space. He is the party who came in just now; tried to get point of his dripping umbrella into my boot; only partially succeeded.

"This is him," said a faded woman in a shawl, thrusting him forward by the shoulder; "he lives in our street and is stone-deaf."

This said with smile of pride. ARTHUR WILLIAM CLUFF, by his supernatural deafness, evidently sheds lustre on his immediate neighbourhood. In pride of association faded woman in shawl momentarily forgets the unpaid rates. ARTHUR WILLIAM with difficulty brought up to the Bench, making dashes with his dripping umbrella at other people's boots. Magistrate, lifting up his voice, asks his name. ARTHUR WILLIAM makes no responsive sign. Rate Collector, standing by, bellows in his right ear,

"Are you ARTHUR WILLIAM CLUFF?" That seems to be wrong ear. Old gentleman obligingly turns round the other. Rate Collector shouts down it. ARTHUR WILLIAM, catching the whisper, nods assent.

"Have you paid your rates?" Collector, prompted by Magistrate, halloas. ARTHUR WILLIAM frankly admits he hasn't.

"Adjourned-till-9th-of-October," says the Magistrate.

"Adjourned till the 9th of October," reiterates Collector, standing on tip-toe, the better to command ARTHUR WILLIAM's accessory ear. ARTHUR WILLIAM raises no objection to that, but does not seem to see relevancy of remark.

"Tell him he must pay on the 8th of October," says the Magistrate, bellowing at the Rate Collector as if he, too, were deaf.

"You must pay on the 8th," the Collector, goaded to desperation, roars with all his might.

"Well, I will, if I can," says ARTHUR WILLIAM, with a cheerfulness that suffused itself all over the damp Court. His umbrella having now dripped itself dry over Rate Collector's boots, ARTHUR WILLIAM goes out to get it wet again. Cases by the score, and the dozen. Doesn't seem money anywhere to pay the rates. But it does seem that the rates must be paid, and by the 8th of October, too.

The forlorn, damp, and penniless crowd having cleared out, each comforted with the inevitable prospect of the "9th of October," our turn comes. Half-a-dozen of us. Not here on account of rates, but in connection with jury lists. A blow struck at British Constitution by attempt to include name of TOBY, M.P., upon jury list. Peers and Members of Parliament always exempted. Why should Barkshire suffer in its privileges? Not if its senior Member can, at whatever personal inconvenience, assert them. Proceedings not unduly extended. Considerable list of exemptions settled by Act of Parliament. List worth considering by anxious parents about to select avocations for promising sons. You can't, for example, be summoned on a jury if you're a coroner, or an apothecary, or a Member of the Mersey Docks and Harbour Board, or a pilot, or a bailiff. Also exempted if you happen to be a gaoler, or if you keep a public lunatic asylum. Moreover, if you've been attainted of any treason or felony, or are an outlaw, you can snap your fingers at "Church Wardens and overseers of the parish, when preparing the jury lists." That's how it came to pass that *Friar Tuck* was never on a jury, and how *Robin Hood* always avoided this peremptory interruption of his avocations. Members of Parliament bracketted for jury-list purposes with outlaws and keepers of lunatic asylums. TOBY, M.P. for Barks, was, of course, exempted, and left the Sessions Court without a stain on his character.

---

## OUR BOOKING-OFFICE.

IT is certain that *Thoth, A Romance* (W. BLACKWOOD AND SON), would never have been written if Mr. RIDER HAGGARD had not published his most famous book. *Thoth* is a sort of male *She*, and might as well have been called *He*. Unlike *She*, who lived continuously through a couple of thousand years, *Thoth's* forefathers come to life only occasionally. But that is quite enough when there are a good many of them. *Thoth* himself is a remarkable personage, with a touch of Professor BALDWIN in his character. He improves on the Professor's machinery, since he dispenses with the parachute, and, when he goes up in a balloon fashioned in the shape of a bird, is able to bring the whole boiling down wherever he pleases. The kingdom *Thoth* rules is an island in some unnamed sea, where the residents are brought up deeply rooted in the heresy of woman-hatred. This being carried to extremes, the consequences are natural and inevitable. Part of the population is drowned in the sea, and the remainder are buried in the sands of the desert. The book makes encouraging reading for members of the Women's Rights Association, only I hope it won't be dramatised.

"You Thothy Perthon!"

Number 4 of *Our Celebrities* (SWAN, SONNENSCHEIN & Co.) is just out. Excellent portrait of Sir PHILIP CUNLIFFE OWEN, and LOUIS ENGEL's list of the numerous orders Sir PHILIP has received from the Crowned Heads of Europe, is astonishing. Theatrical Orders are not included in the collection. Sir PHILIP's appearance at a foreign Court seems to have been the signal for decorating him at once; the cue was, "Give your orders—Sir PHILIP's in the room." The second portrait represents Sir CHARLES RUSSELL, apparently trying on a new Q. C.'s wig, and trying to look as unlike himself as possible. The striped trousers quite out of character with the dignity of the upper portion of the forensic costume, and must have offended the artistic eye of Count WALERY, the eminent Photographer, who should have induced him to put on knee breeches and buckles for the occasion. But it is difficult to induce any man of Sir CHARLES's determination of character to change his habits at a moment's notice; still, as "Standing Counsel to the Jockey Club," he might, at least, have worn breeches and boots, and have a whip in his hand. But where is his most characteristic snuff-box? Capital monograph about him by L. E.

Lastly there is the living presentment of Mr. EDMUND YATES, "*Edmundus Ed. Mundi*," whom "L. E." naturally treats with respectful admiration. The likeness is excellent. But what could WALERY have been about to pose EDMUNDUS thus? He has a book in one hand with his finger marking a place for reference, and having decided what he is going to say in his criticism on it, he is evidently thinking what on earth has become of his own writing-table, his editorial seat, his pens, ink, and paper, and why these obtrusively theatrical "stage properties," including the chair in which he is seated, have been substituted for the real articles? He should have been up-standing, self-supporting, for he surely has no need of "props." It is a speaking likeness, not a writing one.

## A SHOW OF "SAVOY FARE."

IF SHAKSPEARE as *librettist*, and MOZART as composer, had both come to life again and written the most marvellous opera ever heard by mortal ears, the Press generally, with the solitary exception of the musical critic of the *Times*, could not have gushed more rapturously, in larger type, and at greater length over such a work, than they did over the latest comic opera by GILBERT and SULLIVAN at the Savoy. Judging by the crisp and epigrammatic title, *The Yeomen of the Guard; or, The Merryman and his Maid* (you pay your money, and you take your choice of alternative titles) the *librettist* seems, up to the last moment, to have been undecided as to what he should call his new and original infant. In "the book of the words" he does not describe it as either serious or comic, simply as an opera, which is wise. I have always contended that "new and original" need not mean new *to everybody*, and *quite* original, and I am pleased to see that at last the critics, in dealing with this *libretto*, are inclined to favour my opinion. But had the opera been at the Saveloy Theatre instead of the Savoy Theatre, and written by two unknown *collaborateurs*, say SULBERT and GILLIVAN, instead of GILBERT and SULLIVAN, wouldn't the virtuously-indignant critics have been down on the librettist for not informing the public that the plot was founded on that of *Maritana*? The timid novice SULBERT might, perhaps, have attempted to disarm criticism by calling his new and original opera *The Beefeater's Bride; or, The Merryman and his Maritana*, and would have humbly admitted his indebtedness to Mr. W. S. GILBERT for the use he had made of the latter's genuinely humorous Bab Ballad *Jester James*. The stern critics would promptly have pointed out that in good old FITZBALL-and-WALLACE'S *Maritana, Don César* is in prison and condemned to die, and so is *Colonel Fairfax* in *The Beefeater's Bride*; that the *Don* is married in prison to a veiled gipsy dancer, *Maritana*, and, the *Colonel* is married in prison to a veiled gipsy dancer, *Elsie Maynard*. "*Maynard*," the critics would have bitterly exclaimed, "is but a poor English rendering of *Maritana!*" With scathing irony they would have shown how, in the old opera, *Don César* escapes being shot, and returns "all alive O;" while in the new and original work *Colonel Fairfax* escapes being decapitated, and also reappears on the scene. *Don César* enters disguised as a monk; *Colonel Fairfax* comes in as a Beefeater. *Don César* and *Maritana* subsequently fall in love with each other: so do *Colonel Fairfax* and *Elsie Maynard*. *Don César* is pardoned by the King for a very good reason: the *Colonel* is reprieved for no reason at all, except to finish the opera, "a reason," the satirical critic would have added, "sufficiently satisfactory to the audience."

"I have a song to sing O!"

Then some erudite critic would have pointed out to the unfortunate SULBERT that an unknown librettist must not rashly tamper with history in a work intended to be serious, and would have lectured him on the utter improbability of a gipsy girl in all the bravery of an Esmeralda costume (whether accompanied by *Point* as *Gringoire* or not) daring to come rattling her tambourine and singing, within the precincts of the terrible Tower in the reign of Bluff King HAL, when Gipsies were harassed, persecuted, hunted out of the kingdom, or strung up on the readiest made gibbet; and directly it was known that the gallant officer who, as a sorcerer, had been languishing in gaol, on being liberated, had married a heathen gipsy (supposing a priest had been found rash enough to commit such a sacrilege), the pair of them would have had short shrift and been burnt as witches; and as *Colonel Fairfax*, had already escaped decapitation, the professional Merryman might then have observed, "Mark you, the Colonel did but exchange his chop for a stake. A pretty conceit."

Beyond the above points, there is absolutely no resemblance between the two plots, and though poor SULBERT (without GILLIVAN) would thus have suffered at the hands of the Critical Faculty for daring to claim novelty and originality for his story, yet for Mr. GILBERT, of the firm of GILBERT and SULLIVAN, the critics have nothing but obsequious compliments and good-natured excuses. As to the music, even the sharpest and most hostile ear could not detect a trace of WALLACE in the latest composition of Sir ARTHUR SULLIVAN. He, at all events, is guiltless of any intrigue with *Maritana*. It is genuine SULLIVAN, and charming throughout, though not, at first hearing, very catching,—which must always be the public test,—with the exception of the duet, repeated with chorus as *finale*, "*I have a song to sing, O*," the first phrase of which I did manage to carry away with me, but while humming it on my road home, I found myself imperceptibly wandering into the "*Lullaby*" in *Cox and Box*, where I very nearly lost it altogether.

*Dame Carruthers'* first song, "*When our gallant Norman Foes*" is most effective, and might be in serious opera, were it not for the chorus of Beefeaters. Mr. COURTICE POUNDS is a simpering effeminate *Fairfax*, but sings prettily a ballad about "Moon" and "June," after the Yeomen in a previous "number" have already chorussed about "Noon" and "June." But of course the subject of the weather is inexhaustible, and there are plenty of rhymes still left to "Joon." The part of the *Jester* is a capital skit upon *Touchstone* and the Shakspearian clowns generally, and, with subtle cynicism, Mr. W. S. GILBERT shows how wearisome is the most excellent fooling of these mediæval drolls to the playgoer of to-day. The notion of the *Jester* in search of a place, and being examined by an intending employer as to his capabilities ("My *caper*-bilities" *he* would say, and might have executed a short dance as a specimen), struck me as exquisitely humorous when I first read it some years ago (Was it among a second series of *Bab Ballads* in a magazine, or was it a short Christmas story by the same author?), but the idea seems to lose something of its humour on the Stage.

In a week or two, no doubt, *Jester* GEORGE will introduce some of his gaggery-waggery, and when, *à propos* of *Colonel Fairfax* making love to *Elsie*, he has to say something about "lying close as a maggot in a nut," he will add, "But, ifakins, what careth she for a 'nut,' now that she hath the 'Kernel'? A pretty wit!"

Mr. DENNY, as the Gaoler, is very much Mr. DENNY as the rural Policeman in *Dandy Dick*, only with music, and without the dialect. When *Phœbe* (Miss JESSIE BOND, who is, before all, the life and soul of the opera) introduces to him first her lover as her brother, and then afterwards her real brother, and Mr. DENNY exclaims, "Another brother! Are there any more of them?" one really expects him to add, "It's a nice lot of ac-quain-tances you're inter-doosing me to," or something much to that effect, which he used, in similar circumstances, to say to his wife in PINERO'S Comedy.

In the book, Mr. GILBERT has carefully pointed out, using capital letters for the purpose, that the first stanza of his *finale* is written in "ELEGIACS." This is very considerate, as it directs the critics' attention to a fact that might otherwise have escaped their notice. In old days, the jokes in the books of every Burlesque used to be printed in italics. There was no possibility of anybody passing over a pun. The motive in both cases is much the same.

The fault in the representation is that, with the occasional exception of Miss JESSIE BOND and Miss BRANDRAM—none of the actors play with conviction. They seem uncertain as to the character of the piece,—is it serious, or isn't it? And if it isn't, are they to keep the joke to themselves, or to let the audience into the secret? Mr. GROSSMITH, with an occasional sly wink at the house, seems to incline to the latter view, and no doubt when he has exaggerated his dances, developed his comic business, and made the part quite his own, it will go with roars, especially his contradictory duet with Mr. DENNY, which is clearly founded on the model of the well-known comic song, where the wife pertinaciously insists that something can only be cut with scissors, when the husband obstinately sticks to it that a knife must be used:—

> "Cut it with a knife,
> Said he.
> Cut it with the scissors,
> Said she.
> (*He*) Knife, (*She*) scissors, (*He*) knife, (*She*) scissors, &c., &c."

Only that, in this duet, the quarrel is between Mr. DENNY and Mr. GROSSMITH first as to whether somebody was creeping or crawling.

> "He was creeping,
> He was crawling,
> (*D.*) Creeping, (*G.*) crawling, &c., &c., &c."

And then they differ as to how the man sank in the moat,—Mr. DENNY says, "like a stone;" Mr. GROSSMITH says, "like a heavy lump of lead;" and then they alternate "lead," "stone," and so forth, which will work up, with comic business, into something very funny, and probably be the hit of the piece. The best serio-comic song, as far as words go, is, to my thinking, the first one sung by the *Jester*. The scenery and the costumes are excellent.

My summary is this:—Cut at least twenty minutes out of the First Act; take a quarter of an hour out of the Second Act, so as to finish by eleven; never let the Beefeaters go off without a dance; induce Mr. TEMPLE to abandon all attempt at playing his part seriously; in fact give every one of them *carte blanche* ("a very D'Oyly-Carte task," as the *Jester* would say) to go in for the old larks of *Mikado & Co.*, and the Savoyards will feel themselves once more at home, and their kind friends in front will be satisfied with everybody generally at the House of Savoy.

JACK IN THE STALL.

## HORRIBLE LONDON: OR, THE PANDEMONIUM OF POSTERS.

THE Demon set forth in a novel disguise
(All methods of mischief the master-fiend tries)
Quoth he, "There 's much ill to be wrought through the eyes.
I think, without being a boaster,
I can give their most 'cute Advertisers a start,
And beat them all round at the Bill-sticker's art.
I will set up in business in Babylon's mart,
As the new Pandemonium Poster!"
So he roved the huge city with wallet at waist,
With a brush, and a stick, and a pot full of paste,
And there wasn't a wall or a hoarding,
A space in a slum, or a blank on a fence,
A spare square of brick in a neighbourhood dense,
Or a bit of unoccupied boarding,
But there the new poster, who didn't much care
For the menacing legend, "Bill-stickers beware!"
Right soon was tremendously busy
With placards portentous in purple and blue,
Of horrible subject and hideous hue,
Enough to bemuddle an aëronaut's view,
And turn the best steeple-Jack dizzy.
Oh, the flamboyant flare of those fiendish designs,
With their sanguine paint-splashes and sinister lines!
Gehenna seemed visibly glaring
In paint from those villanous daubs. There were men
At murderous work in malodorous den,
And ghoul-woman gruesomely staring.
The whole sordid drama of murder and guilt,
The steel that strikes home, and the blood that is spilt,
Was pictured in realist colours,
With emphasis strong on the black and the red,
The fear of the stricken, the glare of the dead;
All dreads and disasters and dolours
That haunt poor Humanity's dismallest state,
The horrors of crime and the terrors of fate,
As conceived by the crudest of fancies,
Were limned on these posters in terrible tints,
In the style of the vilest sensational prints
Or the vulgarest penny romances.

That Bill-sticker paused in his work with a look
Which betrayed the black demon, and gleesomely shook
His sides in a spasm of laughter.
Quoth he, with a sinister wag of his head,
"By my horns, the good artist has lavished the red!
This home of coarse horror—this house of the dead
Looks crimson from basement to rafter.
How strange that a civilised City—ho! ho!
'Tis their fatuous dream to consider it so!—
Which is nothing too lovely at best, should bestow
Such a liberal licence on spoilers!
These mural monstrosities, reeking of crime,
Flaring horridly forth amidst squalor and grime,
Must have an effect which will tell in good time
Upon legions of dull-witted toilers.

Taken in through the eyes such suggestions of sin
A sympathy morbid and monstrous must win
From the grovelling victims of gloom and bad gin,
Who gapingly gaze on them daily;
A fine picture-gallery this for the People!
Oh, while this endures, spite of School Board and Steeple,
*My* work must be going on gaily!"

## A ROYAL APPARITION.

LAST Friday the *Times* Correspondent at Bucharest, writing about the entertainments given in honour of the Prince of WALES, said—

"In the evening there will be a series of *tableaux vivants* representing scenes from SHAKSPEARE'S works. These have been carefully rehearsed under the superintendence of Queen ELIZABETH."

What better person could they have had as an authority except SHAKSPEARE himself? But how did they get her? Were Spiritualists employed? If this be possible, then it is not unlikely that DRURIOLANUS is already shaking in his shoes lest Her Majesty, more ruffled than ever, should pay him an unexpected visit at Drury Lane, and insist on superintending a night revival of the *Armada*, with ghostly scenery, costumes, and appointments, and a phantom cast. Only thus would her *manes* be satisfied, and then she herself might be re-hearsed, and conveyed in state to Westminster Abbey, DRURIOLANUS superintending.

### In Statu Pupillari.

YOUNG Master BALFOUR, without an apology,
Speaks on philosophy, also theology.
To listen his Grandmother will not be loth,
When ARTHUR has learnt just a little of both.

"OLD TOM."—HOLMES at Home, the HOLMES of our Ancestors, in last week's *World*, must have been to a considerable number of persons one of the most interesting of the series. A person, whom the veteran octogenarian TOM HOLMES knew, was acquainted with another person who had received an account of the Great Fire of London from an eye-witness! Fancy that! Such evidence at hand would simplify a large portion of the Historian's labour! A cordial welcome to Old TOM. Plenty of spirit in him yet. His health!

A NEW AND AGREEABLE TOY.—THE PARACHUTE.

YOU TIE A BIG STONE TO THE FOUR CORNERS OF A POCKET-HANDKERCHIEF, AND FLING IT AS HIGH AS YOU CAN. SOMETIMES THE HANDKERCHIEF EXPANDS AND RETARDS THE FALL OF THE STONE—SOMETIMES IT DOESN'T.

## GOOD-BYE TO THE (CRICKETING) SEASON.

(*A Fond Farewell, something in the style of Praed, composed at the Oval in October by our Own Old Enthusiast.*)

GOOD-BYE to the Season!—'Tis over!
Pavilions no longer are gay;
Bat, bowler, and leal Cricket-lover,
Are scattered like M.P.'s away.

The Last Ball of the Season.

WALTER READ bobs no longer his brown end
At point, watching BANNERMAN'S "shape;"
GILBERT GRACE has gone home to dear Downend,
BOB ABEL is bound for the Cape.
For want of a fuller enjoyment,
Till Bat, Ball, and Stumps, can come out,
At Football a few find employment,
But Cricket is done, beyond doubt.

Good-bye to the Season!—The weather
Has bowed at the shrine of St. Gamp;
Wet wickets have sodden the leather,
And stumps have been pitched in a swamp.
Chill deluges, varied with thunders,
The Cricket-crack's "average" queer.
Bad hits and bad misses are blunders
Scarce blamed in so beastly a year.
There are all sorts of excellent reasons
All round for the prevalent "duck;"
So, Good-bye to this wettest of Seasons!
Its memories are mainly of muck.

Good-bye to the Season!—The chances
That filled even champions with gloom;
The rascally tricks and rare dances
Devised by the demon of doom.
The "bad hits" that should have been "beauties,"
The good ones so palpably "flukes";
The fielders so slack in their duties,
The Captains so tart in rebukes;
The cocksures who dropped bobs and tanners
On matches like Surrey *v.* Notts;
The consequent breaches of manners;
The subsequent downfall of "pots."

Good-bye to the Season!—the rages
When second-rate teams came out strong;
When ABEL—for *one*—stayed in ages,
Or READ missed his tip and went wrong;
When clever and "champion" Surrey
The Cornstalks thrice tackled in vain—
Lost twice by bad fortune and flurry,
And missed winning once through the rain;
Whilst Gloucester, whom Surrey could swallow,
And Leicester whom Gloucester could eat,
Both licked the Australians hollow.
"Good old Surrey" wound up with defeat.

Good-bye to the Season!—the "Terror"
Who put such a break on the ball;
Yes, TURNER *can* bowl, "and no error,"
And FERRIS makes many sing small.
But England has no need to fluster;
She is not deficient in "stars";
Still, when her best men she can muster,
She wins in these willowy wars. [killing!
There's LOHMANN, how straight and how
He'll "hold up our end," please the pigs;
And slashing MCDONNELL'S scarce willing
To stand many overs of BRIGGS!

Good-bye to the Season!—A wetter 'un
Seldom spoiled "place," "pitch," and
But here's to our evergreen veteran ["pace";
Still to the front—GILBERT GRACE!
"The Doctor" stands nominal second,
But who plays so often as he?
Still W. G. must be reckoned
As virtual top of the tree.
The theme of all Cricket-feed speeches,
The pet of pavilion and field,
His pre-eminence no one impeaches,
To none need our "Champion" yield.

Good-bye to the Season!—Another
Will come with the coming of May;
Though the new county boundaries bother,
The cry of the boys will be "Play!"
Will it come like *this* terrible "tryer?"
Or come very much the reverse?
Will its scorings be lower or higher?
Will its weather be better or worse?
Will it favour the bowler or batter?
Will it come with dry turf and clear sky,
Or washy and squashy?—No matter:—
Good-bye to the Season—good-bye!

## DUE NORTH.

*Shakspearian—Household—Luncheon—Family Party—Mysterious—Pony—Another—Perilous—Down again—Rest—Thankful.*

**FROM** what I hear of the names of the servants inside and outside the house, such as DUNCAN, DONALD, ROSS, DONALDBLAIN, it appears that, with the exception of *Macduff, Banquo*, and the Three Witches, we have pretty nearly the entire cast of *Macbeth*. The part of *Macbeth* is filled by the chief housemaid and housekeeper, whose name is MACBETH. Whether she is MARY, or JENNIE, or EFFIE, I do not know,—and, by the way, what was *Lady Macbeth's* Christian name? Her husband never mentions it, and the only term of endearment by which he addresses her is, "dearest chuck." Why "chuck"? Our MACBETH at the shooting-lodge — a tall, good-looking lass, about thirty or so, a strapping wench with an elegant figure,—would forcibly resent being called a "chuck" by anyone, even if there were a male MACBETH on the premises who had acquired a right to do so. She can walk with the swing of a man, pull stroke or bow in a boat, or scull it single-handed across the lake, if need be; is a good shot with a rifle, can do tailoring or cobblering to perfection,—"odd jobs executed at the shortest possible notice,"—and has a ready eye to the wants and comforts of all the visitors in both departments—the House and the Annexe—of the establishment over which she presides. She is invaluable: and though in the Annexe we do not see much of her, yet it is to her that we have to make known our wants, which, once mentioned, are immediately supplied. In the House itself, on a busy evening, when the sportsmen have come in late, and everybody is, more or less, hurrying up in their dressing for dinner, and everybody has mislaid something, and no one can find anything, then down the passages, from the bachelors' quarters, and from the rooms where the young ladies are, come the reiterated cries, as if they were uttered by the Apparitions that rise out of the Witches' cauldron, of "MACBETH! MACBETH!! MACBETH!!!" And instead of losing her presence of mind, and exclaiming, flurriedly, "Had I three ears, I'd hear thee!" she pleasantly replies, in her strong Scotch brogue, "All right, Sir, I'm coming directly!"—and come she does to everybody in turn, and everybody in turn is more than satisfied. A wonderful woman.

"How dee do?"

There are three young ladies under the care, apparently, of the Good Aunt. I am not introduced, but they all say, as the Wicked Uncle did, "How dee do" to me, at lunch time, and address one another by their Christian names, MILLIE, EVELYN, and the youngest and smallest is MADGE. Who they are, what their surnames may be, whether they are sisters, wives, or cousins belonging to the other guests, I haven't the slightest idea. It seems to be taken for granted in this present company, which is, to all intents and purposes, a family party, that there is no such being as a stranger in existence within these four walls.

"You should have gone out fishing this morning, MILLIE," says the Baron to the young lady.

"She couldn't," replies EVELYN, "as I wanted her to walk out with me."

"Good Aunt," says D. B., "how are you? MADGE, you'll have to march out with the five o'clock tea, if we drive."

"If you're going to drive, I'd rather walk, if I may," says Miss MADGE, appealing to the Laird, "the trap shakes so!"

Whereat there's a laugh all round, and the very young lady colours up and looks frightened. The Laird hastens to the rescue.

"It's not 'driving' in a trap," he explains, smilingly, "the grouse are driven by beaters, while we stand behind butts. I'll show you the butts; you can see them from the window with a good glass."

"How on earth should MADGE know your sporting terms?" says the Good Aunt interposing. "It's her first day up here!"

On careful and separate inquiry, I find that none of the party have ever met one another before last week, and the young ladies only arrived yesterday. The people who brought them went away at once. They are "left here till called for."

The talk is all sport: either shooting or fishing. Everyone explains to everyone else why some particularly easy shot "didn't come off," and some one is always saying, "Ah, I oughtn't to have missed *that!*"

GRANNIE, the fisherman, who, out-of-doors walks about with flies and hooks stuck all over his head, has seen fish rising in every direction. But it appears that, unfortunately, the fish have seen *him*, and so, though he kept on changing his flies every half hour, and waded up to his middle, yet,

"He did not catch that trout,
Brave Boys!
He did not catch that trout!"

And so he will give the trout a holiday, and go out shooting this afternoon.

It has been pouring with rain. It is pouring now, "And," says the Laird, "we shall have showers all the afternoon."

"Showers" here are, I find, pelting storms which wet you through in a couple of minutes.

"In this rain," says the Baron, walking to the window, "we're sure to put up something on that hill yonder."

*Happy Thought.*—If I go with them, I'm sure to "put up something,"—my umbrella.

"You can have the pony, if you like to ride up to where we're driving," says the Laird to me. On consideration, being fond of air and exercise, I accept. The pony is ordered, and I anticipate a good gallop over the hills and far away, two or three hours' exercise, happy return home, rub down, bath, change, and splendid appetite for dinner.

They start, all the party, except the ladies, and disappear. The ladies melt away and become invisible. I am to join the sportsmen as soon as I like. Of course mounted, I shall easily catch up the infantry, so I tell the youthful gillie, DUNCAN, who comes to inform me "the pony's ready saddled," that I'll start in a quarter of an hour.

I follow the boy to where the pony is. Pony! it is a rough-looking sort of cart-horse, over fifteen hands, with an old saddle, loose girths, and a single snaffle rein that looks as if it would break with the slightest strain. However, I said I would go: and perhaps the "pony" is better than he looks.

In less than five minutes I find he isn't. His pace is a quick slouching walk with rather a nautical roll in it. His head droops heavily, as if he were sadly weary of this sort of life. He is led by the lad DUNCAN, who carries a switch, as if he were a donkey-boy and I was having sixpennorth on the sands: and we are ignominiously following another "pony," which is being personally conducted by an elder gillie. This other pony is also over fifteen hands, and across its back are swung panniers for game, baskets holding five o'clock tea and other provisions, and such a lot of wraps and waterproofs as to suggest the idea of the baggage pony being a "clothes horse." I have no one to say this to, so keep it to myself and appreciate it dismally. It is just as if the sportsmen were the army on active service, and I had been classed among the *impedimenta*. Perhaps, I think to myself, things will be better presently as we go uphill.

*Happy Thought.*—"Speculate for the rise."

Nothing of the sort. The ground gets worse and worse. Each fresh bog is boggier than the last, and the higher we get, the steeper is the climbing, and the more perilous my situation. The elder gillie plods on his way, morose and taciturn. The younger, my Donkey-boy, blithe, but silent. It is a melancholy party; quite funereal. The coats and wraps, slung across first horse, are suggestive of the lifeless body of some one whom we have shot, and whom we are going to bury up in the hills, and I, mounted, am either a prisoner or chief mourner, it doesn't much matter which. The boy gives up leading the cart-horse-pony, and strolls on with the taciturn gillie. I try to engage the elder gillie, from a distance, in conversation, but he won't be engaged. I want to interest him in my own personal safety, so that if anything happened, by which I mean if my horse fell head-foremost into a bog or tumbled down sideways over a narrow ledge,—my knees shudder at the thought,—he, being on friendly terms with me, and living in dim hopes of half-a-crown, would rush to my assistance.

*Happy Thought (of the gillie).* "Speculating for the fall." (*My* fall.) But gillie senior refuses to be interested; he won't talk, not even of the weather. The youthful gillie, DUNCAN, follows his example so closely that he won't be communicative even to the extent of informing me what sort of day it was yesterday, and what amount of sport they had had the day before that. WILSON BARRETT, with his favourite "How long!" flashes across my mind at several critical moments. "How long" will this saddle remain on the horse? and "How long" shall I remain on the saddle? Till accident us do part.

Elder and younger gillie silent, as if overcome by some great grief, or groaning in spirit against their Saxon oppressors, trudge on, jumping without effort from rock to rock, the elder one jerking the horse's leading-rein, encouraging it to land on sharp projections, and to founder desperately through morasses. I watch the proceedings with fearful interest, knowing that whatever happens to the horse in front of me must, it is ten to one, happen to mine. But the horse in front carries only waterproofs, empty bags, and materials for five o'clock tea, while mine carries *me*. As we cross a torrent, my horse balancing itself on the pointed tops of rocks which just peep out of the damp moss, and where a slip from any given point must precipitate us into the depths below, I am inclined to whisper nervously in the horse's ear, with a view to inspiring him with confidence, "Remember you carry CÆSAR and his fortunes!" and I heartily wish CÆSAR were anywhere else at this moment.

It is no sort of use attempting to guide the beast. I try to comfort myself with the reflection that the horse knows the country, and must have been up here any number of times. The circumstances on former occasions may have been totally different, and one circumstance certainly is quite different now, and that is, that *this is the first time he has ever travelled across these hills with me on his back,—and,* I add to myself most fervently,—*it will be the last!*

I rode up here for exercise, anticipating an increase of temperature, skin-acting, and everything beneficial for a person with certain gouty tendencies. But here we are, creeping up the mountain's side ("We wandered *up* the mountain's side"), and I am feeling colder and colder. I would get off and walk if my boots were not too thin for the slosh, and I foresee catching a severe cold. After an hour and a half of this amusement, and catching sight of the shooters only for a moment when they were all too occupied to talk—especially the Wicked Uncle, who is craftily lying in wait for a grouse behind a butt built of peat, like a brigand looking out for the solitary traveller,—I come to the determination that, directly I see anything resembling a road, I will descend and run down it as hard as I can, at the risk of dislocating my ankles, in order to circulate my blood, which must have gone down nearly to zero.

Hoorah! "*Thalatta! Thalatta!*" I mean The Road! The Road! "Let us take to the Road, Boys!" Highwayman's song in *The Beggar's Opera*. It is not exactly a road, but, when the winter is over, and it is no longer a water-course, it is evidently used as a road by the natives, who must be very easily satisfied. Small rates ought to have been charged for mending this road, and the biggest rate ever known on it is the pace at which I am going down when once fairly started.

To the astonishment of the taciturn gillie and the dismay of DUNCAN the Donkey-boy who had charge of me, I slide off the horse on to the ground, and run. They halloa to me. No—not back again—I wave my hand. They are dumfounded. I feel like a prisoner escaping; and they, as I glance back at them, look as the guardians must have looked, to whose care the historical Royal Personage was entrusted, when he said, "Good-day, Gentlemen!" and their horses being blown, galloped away in the direction of England, Home, and Beauty!

Free! Free! Free! Never again on the fifteen-hand cart-horse-pony for me. Free! Free! Free! Splash—dash—slash—dash—into the ruck, into the muck, into the water, over the stones, whack, crack, not "down on my back," but going as if I were wearing the seven-leagued boots, until the grand perspiration effect is produced. I hear the Donkey-boy pursuing. He has been sent after me by the Laird, who, he shouts to me, breathlessly, is very angry with him for leaving me to find my way alone. But, for all his holloaing, I won't stop, and he catches me up by a short cut, and on we go together, panting, until I come to a dead stop in the valley, and am anxious to know the shortest cut to the Lodge, as the rain, which has been threatening proceedings for some time past, is beginning to fall, and, if I get wet in this fever-heat, I tremble for the consequences. The youthful gillie points out the road,—over the meadow, round by the swing-bridge. He will go there by another and a shorter route. *Allez!* On we goes again! He his way, I mine. The big rain-drops become bigger. "Speed thee on, my bonnie Shanks's mare, I have trusted thee many a time before, and will again!"

"Here we are again!"

The last mile is always the longest. Then the swing-bridge—a narrow plank hung on wires—a miniature suspension Hammersmith, swaying like a slack rope as I cross it cautiously. BLONDIN for ever! The opposite bank of the river is gained! Saved! saved! The rain! "Let it come down." And, as I quote *Macbeth*, MACBETH herself, the ever-vigilant housekeeper, sees me flying past the front-door ("You should see my coat-tails flying!"), and calls out, "Ye'll just be soaked through. I'll send you your hot water,"—and so she does; and in another half-hour I am comfortably seated in an arm-chair before the fire in the smoking-room, with a pipe and the first book I can lay my hand on, just to enjoy a quiet read and rest in the two hours that remain to me before dinner. The library here is not a large one. There are two shilling novels, *Jorrocks's Jaunts*, BRADSHAW's latest publication, and *The New Newgate Calendar*, illustrated, in two volumes. It is one of these last-mentioned that is now in my hand; and it is this that, an hour afterwards, drops with a bang on the floor, as I wake up and see D. B.'s face at the window, as he cries out,

"Here we are again! How *are* you?"

## OUR BOOKING-OFFICE.

I HAVE just finished *Mapleson's Memoirs*. Poor dear Colonel! An "old soldier" of course and yet how ill-used he must have been by everyone. His stories are told with touching simplicity, and many would be highly amusing if the reader could only get rid of the feeling that he is listening to the lamb bleating out how he was shorn, and how the wind, always so difficult to raise, was rarely if ever tempered to his poor back.

Skipping over several Pages.

Pity the sorrows of a poor old Man-
-ager, whom Opera brought down to the floor,
Who means to come up smiling when he can,
And is but looking for just one chance more.

It's a wicked and ungrateful world with which the guileless Colonel has had to deal. He cherishes the tenderest memories of his collaborator and whilom principal, the late E. T. SMITH, who was not Policeman X., but an ex-policeman, afterwards Operatic Manager, and perfectly adores the generous and sympathetic *Diva*, formerly La Marquise DE CAUX, now Mme. NICOLINI, and known to all the world as PATTI. If her agreements with other Managers are similar to the one published in Vol. II. of the shorn *Impresario's* Memoirs, then I pity the Operatic Managers. Of course a *Diva* has a natural and inalienable right to do the best for herself she can. There will always be somebody to take up a *Diva* like PATTI, as long as the public, generally but not always, as has been recently proved, will pay high prices to hear a brilliant singer unsupported, in preference to giving a reasonable amount for a good all-round performance. It would be worth while to compare with the Maplesonian Memoirs WILLERT BEALE's recollections, published, I think, some years ago, which told of a time when Operatic artists were a trifle more Bohemian, but infinitely more genial and obliging to their employers.

The Fourth Volume of the MARSHALL and IRVING *Shakespeare* is out. Messrs. MARSHALL and IRVING have constituted themselves into a sort of Editorial Committee, "with power to add to their number;" and consequently several collaborators now appear on the scene whose names were not in the original cast. The notes are useful and interesting, as far as I've been able to dip into them. I anticipate much amusement from the two volumes of *Edmund Kean*, by FITZGERALD MOLLOY; also from the Autobiography of SIMS REEVES, compiled by him from his own notes. Sitting down as Author! This is full change for a Tenor! I've another Music-Book on my desk, *Musical Memories*, by Dr. SPARK. This ought to be very light reading. I shall leave the gay SPARK for a while. If the SPARK flickers, he may be revived by a slight puff.

Littery and Artistic.

*The Emperor's Diary*, edited by H. W. LUCY, is just out, price one shilling, which isn't much for the Diary of an Emperor. Not the least interesting part of this pocket-volume is the Editor's introductory remarks on the policy of Prince BISMARCK, at the same time that he sympathises with Dr. GEFFKEN, the literary and journalistic gentleman who is now in prison on the charge of having brought the Diary to light. There is a similarity between Herr WON LUCY and Prince BISMARCK, inasmuch as both have taken up a German subject, but in very different style. As BISMARCK has his spies everywhere, I should recommend Herr WON LUCY "to lay low and say nuffin" for some little time, never to go out after dusk, and in the daytime to be carefully and artistically disguised as somebody else, as LIKA JOKO for example. BISMARCK is reckless and resolute, and would think nothing of kidnapping Herr WON LUCY and incarcerating him in a dungeon quite near to Dr. GEFFKEN, beneath the Castle Moat.

Eye Opener.

So Mote-n't it
Be, says the Potentate

Who now has the honour of subscribing himself everybody's most sincerely, the Musical-Political-Artistic-and-Literary

BARON DE BOOK WORMS.

## A FLAGRANT INJUSTICE.

(*The "United Service Unemployed" Club Smoking-Room. Noon.*)

BEHOLD A DOZEN HONEST, ENLIGHTENED, AND ABLE-BODIED BRITONS—RETIRED GENERALS AND ADMIRALS, HALF-PAY COLONELS, SUPERANNUATED MAJORS AND CAPTAINS, NOT TO MENTION LEISURED YOUNG GUARDSMEN, ALL IN THE FULL POSSESSION OF THEIR FACULTIES—ALL BORED TO EXTINCTION (EXCEPT THOSE WHO ARE SO FORTUNATE AS TO BE FAST ASLEEP), AND ALL CRUELLY DEBARRED FROM THE PRIVILEGE OF SERVING ON A JURY OF THEIR COUNTRYMEN! WHY?

## LITTLE JEM'S DOOM;

### OR, THE PROVIDENT PARENTS' RESOURCE.

(*Brief Low-Life Tragedy, produced lately with only too much success on the stage of the Great Metropolitan Theatre.*)

ACT I.—*A London Slum.* Rival Insurance Touts *discovered, recommending the advantages of their respective enterprises to the notice of two* Provident Parents.

*First Rival Tout* (*summing up*). Well, there you are. You pays a mere pittance monthly, and, if anything happens to the little one, why you has him buried respectable, with a regular first-class funeral, as should be a comfort to the feelings of a decent couple of parents like you, and quite reconcile you, so to speak, to the loss of him.

*Second Rival Tout.* And if you put into our concern, mind you, the money you gets more than covers the expenses. When all 's paid, you 'll find you 've got a tidy bit over for yourselves. You might make about two pound out of it, and that ought to console you. It does most of 'em.

*First Rival Tout.* But we don't ask no nasty questions, you know, if so happens you have to put in your claim.

*Second Rival Tout.* No. If you pays your first premium to-day, and comes next week for the burial-money, we stumps up like men, we do, and don't make no fuss.

*First Rival Tout.* I tell you what: our concern has been a real blessin' to thousands, that it has.

*Provident Male Parent* (*convinced*). Well, there 's summat in what you chaps say, and I don't mind tryin' it on Little JEM here. (*Addressing* Provident Female Parent.) What do you say, Missus? JEM has been a ailin' lately, and if he means goin', I 'd like to see him shoved away proper; 'specially when there 's that two pound over to be got out of the job. (*His "Missus" nods assent.*) All right, Mate, then. I'm game. Make out the ticket.

[First Rival Tout "*makes out the ticket,*" *and* Little JEM's *life is forthwith insured in the "General Cosmopolitan Infants' Coffin Supply Association" as Act-drop descends.*

ACT II.—*A Coroner's Court. An Inquest has just been held on the body of* Little JEM, *who has recently died under somewhat suspicious circumstances. The fact that he has for some time past been gradually sinking in an ill-ventilated back room, purposely neglected by his* Provident Parents, *has not come out in evidence; nor has it transpired that they have familiarised themselves with the idea of his decease, and, seeing it will not only relieve them of the cost of his maintenance, but also put some ready-money into their pockets, have come to regard it as a consummation devoutly to be desired. So it has come about that though* Little JEM *has been deliberately done to death by his businesslike natural protectors, the verdict has not been one of Murder, or even of Manslaughter, but of "Death from Natural causes." The Coroner, however, assuring the Jury that he will see that their recommendation, that the Government should take some steps to legislate for the protection of infant life from the baneful influence of such Societies as the "General Cosmopolitan Infants' Coffin Supply Association," shall be forwarded to the proper quarter, the Scene closes.*

*Provident Male Parent* (*who has received the burial-money, and is returning from the funeral, addressing his "Missus."*) Well, that's done, though we ain't made quite two pound by it. Still one pound sixteen ain't bad, with little JEM out of the way, and all. (*Confidentially.*) I tell you what it is, Missus, I votes we take out a ticket for our SAL and lanky JOE. When times is black, it ain't half a bad resource. I 'll just look up that Insurance chap again.

[*Is left meditating "murder" as Curtain descends.*

"A 'PLEASURE-HORSE' used to do double duty in former days," observed MRS. RAM; "and for my part I regret that Wives no longer ride on pillories behind their Husbands."

# WHITECHAPEL, 1888.

First Member of "Criminal Class." "FINE BODY O' MEN, THE PER-LEECE!"
Second Ditto. "UNCOMMON FINE!—IT'S LUCKY FOR HUS AS THERE'S SECH A BLOOMIN' FEW ON 'EM!!!"

"I have to observe that the Metropolitan Police have not large reserves doing nothing and ready to meet emergencies; but every man has his duty assigned to him, and I can only strengthen the Whitechapel district by drawing men from duty in other parts of the Metropolis."—*Sir Charles Warren's Statement.* "There is one Policeman to every seven hundred persons."—*Vide Recent Statistics.*

OUR NEW M.F.H.

*Kennel Huntsman.* "A MAN BROUGHT THIS HERE LAST NIGHT, BUT HE DIDN'T LEAVE NO MESSAGE TO SAY IF IT WERE FOR RIDIN' OR BILIN'." [*Delight of our new M.F.H., Mr. Popple, who has given £40 for it to carry a Whip.*

## ROBERT'S LONG WACATION.

LARST weak I told you I'd kontinuew in my nex. This is my nex and I rekummense. The nex day, it looking raything inclined to be fine, as if the rain was beginning to get rayther ashamed of itself for doing its werry best to spile all the crops, and all surten peepel's tempers, and other peepel's best close, I perswaded my wife to go with me for a wark on the bewtifool Tems Embankment, and there we strolled about in the lovely gardins for a nour or two, and I wentured to say, as the tooth ake was much better, that the nice looking surroundins, with the River a flowing by, reminded me of that appy day in Grinnidge Park, when I arsked her to share my umbel fortunes for wheel or for wo. She was ewidently pleased, and a smile lited up her ample feeters, when, as ill-luck woud have it, jest at that werry moment, down came one of them orful downpores as seems to have bin trying all this summer to beat the record, and allers succeeding.

Well, after that day's xperience, I must confess that, bewtifool as is the well kep Gardens, and the floing River, and the nice cumferal seats, the Tems Embankment is not a conwenient plaice to seleck to be cort with your best Beloved, with jest the remanes of a bad toothake, in a drenching storm of rain and thunder and litening, and with her best dress on. So we have not repeated that xperiment. The nex day we spent at the Great British Mewseum, and we both agreed that it seemed a great pitty that the Country was so werry pore that they coudn't afford to have the Stattys mended. There was several of the most bewtifoollest of 'em all as had either a harm, or a leg, or an and or two, broke rite off, and one of 'em had his nose nocked rite off, and, aperiently, no attemp being maid to mend any on 'em. Them as is without heds of coarse represents peeple as was beheded afore their warious deaths, so the same fault cannot farely be found with them. We coudn't, neether on us, at all hunderstand why so many on 'em was not allowed to dress theirselves propperly afore they had their stattys taken. Mrs. ROBERT ewen going so far as to say as she thort as sum on 'em, speshally the ladies, ort to have bin ashamed of thereselves, let alone the chance of catching werry bad colds.

Of course it rained pretty hard before we got home; but we had not werry far to go, so we did not git so werry wet this time, fortnitly. The day after was much like the day afore, so, as I coudn't go out, I purtended to be a reading, and slep a good deal of the time; but, when night came, we went to the Theater, so as to have a nice evening's emusement, to cheer us both hup. Ah, that was a nice evening's emusement that was!

I went carefully through the warious statements in the Noosepapers, and picked out a Play that as the *Times* said "thrilled the House!" and, as the *Adwertiser* said, "would attract all playgoers;" and, as the *Daily Noose* said, "held the audience breathless." So off we went to the "Liesee' em," and there we sat for a hole hower a seeing sitch a xhibishun of disgusting orrers as we neether of us never seed afore and fondly opes as we shall never see no more. We coudn't stand no more of it, but went out in the middel of the werry wust part, feeling quite hill, and warked home a grumbling and a growling all the way at being so shamefoolly deseaved by the jockular papers, and wundring how any man coud have taken sitch a lot of trubbel to both look and hact more like a wild beest than a man.

However, a nice little bankwet that my partner had prepaird as a surprise, and a partickler nice glass of ot Rum and water, enabled us to sup full of hoysters insted of "full of orrors," as sumbody says, and we was abel to bannish 'em from our thorts and to sleep the sleep of the hinnercent. ROBERT.

---

THE COLD WEATHER HAS SET IN!—How to warm yourself. Sit near our FURNISS, when he is giving his lecture on Portrait-painting. As suitable to a wintry entertainment, the lecture is illustrated by "Slides." In spite of being near the FURNISS, the views are not dissolving; in fact our artist has positively declared that he sees no reason for changing his views.

---

AN IRISH DELICACY.—The Parnellite Members are declared by a contemporary to give themselves the airs of exceptional education, and delicacy of constitution. Let them, then, be so careful of their constitution, as closely to confine the pursuit of their aims and ends to constitutional methods.

---

INTERESTING TO GEOLOGICAL AND MEDICAL STUDENTS.—In future, no one will be eligible for the Swiney Lectureship who has not gone through a regular course of BACON.

## REALISTIC.

*Amateur Stage Manager* (*in black hat*). "WE'VE SETTLED IT. WE'RE GOING TO PLAY '*THE TICKET OF LEAVE MAN*,' AND I'VE CAST YOU FOR *MELTER MOSS*—YOU KNOW, THE OLD JEW. SPLENDID PART!"

*Second Amateur* (*in white hat*). "OH, I COULDN'T DO IT, MY BOY—I SHOULD HAVE TO WEAR A FALSE NOSE!"

## TWO VIEWS OF BOULOGNE.

(*A Page from a Diary kept at Monte Carlo Minor.*)

*Monday.*—Arrived by the *Mary Beatrice*, one of the best boats of the South-Eastern Railway Company. Really delightful. Breakfast in London at 8·30, catch the 9·40 Express, and be in Boulogne in time for luncheon! Everything so fresh and foreign. Glad to see the red trousers of the soldiers; and the place itself so cheery. The Casino admirable. Capital Band. Theatre, too, very amusing. Light Opera, nicely sung. Remarkably good. Seen worse things in Paris. And then the *Chemin de fer!* Of course object to gambling, on principle; but what possible harm can there be in risking a few francs? I did, and won ten by embarking my fortunes on the *blanc*.

*Tuesday.*—Greatly disappointed. Boulogne is not at all like what it used to be. "So English, you know." Too English, in fact, and not good English either. More like bad Bayswater. The French soldiers, too, are all undersized, and the place itself desolation in its most desolate form. Hotels closed, and houses to be let or sold everywhere. The Casino has certainly deteriorated. Band small, and not particularly skilful. Theatre pitiful. Saw some dreadful piece, in five Acts, that apparently was being played by amateurs. Most feeble performance I have ever witnessed. And then the *Chemin de fer!* I repeat, I object to gambling on principle; but granted that it is *not* wrong, what possible good can there be in risking a few francs? I did, and lost twenty by embarking my fortunes on the *rouge*.

*Wednesday.*—Really Boulogne improves on acquaintance. I am not surprised that some people call it "Beautiful Boulogne," the air is certainly delightful—I think finer than Brighton or Folkestone. I know others say that the place has fallen off terribly since the establishment of the so-called gambling at the Casino. This is absolute rubbish. I can recall no prettier sight than the toy engine, with its model carriages, running round the track, with its piece of spring wire striking against the brass bars, and stopping now at Brussels, now at Vienna—at one moment near the red, at the next close to the white. It is so simple, that even a child might play at it. So different from Monte Carlo. Everyone knows what *that* is like. There fortunes are really lost, and suicides are of common occurrence. But at Boulogne it is merely an amusing distraction. I don't pretend to play myself, but I certainly won five francs by showing a partiality to "*Londres.*"

*Thursday.*—I am not at all surprised that some people call this place "Beastly Boulogne." It certainly deserves the name. The port at low tide is absolutely awful. No; if you want bracing air, go to Brighton or Folkestone. I am told that interested persons declare that Boulogne is growing, and owes much of its prosperity to the establishment of gambling at the Casino. This is absolute rubbish. I know of no more painful sight than to watch the eager faces of the players as the monotonous model train clicks with its wire against the brass rails. The time has arrived for writing plainly. The gambling is the curse of the place. Stories are heard on all sides of money squandered and lost. The mode of playing is so simple that even a poor innocent child can risk and lose as high a stake as five francs. It is so different from Monte Carlo. Everyone knows what *that* is like. There you can avoid playing if you wish, and may enjoy life at one of the loveliest watering-places in the world. But Boulogne is vastly different. A two-penny-halfpenny place, that only a few years ago was the refuge of the fraudulent bankrupt! Boulogne, indeed! And the gambling too is a hard business. It is no idle distraction. You see, day after day, men, women and children standing round the baize table losing all they have! It is a dreadful sight! A really dreadful sight! I don't pretend to play myself, but I certainly lost five-and-twenty francs by plunging blindly on "*Bruxelles.*"

*Friday.*—Most amusing. Spent a day in looking about. Went up to the Mairie to see a civil marriage. Very fine affair. Carriages aud carpets. The bride a good-looking young lady, and the bridegroom decidedly *distingué*. Evidently persons of good position. People lunching at the hotel also interesting. One gentleman's face I recognised. Sure I have seen him somewhere before and under pleasant circumstances. I do not think he can be a parson, and yet he would adorn a pulpit; and that reminds me,—I wonder why the clergy fight shy of the Casino. They might do much good, I think, if they visited it more frequently. Now, for instance, they might dance occasionally at a *Bal de Famille*. Quite a nice set, some people in evening dress, and one or two wearing gloves. Had heard that the riff-raff from the fast hotels congregated at these gatherings. Not at all. I don't think so. And the games of chance. Really nothing at all. Merely a pretence at baccarat. Could not hurt anyone. As for the *Chemin de fer*, well, I can only say that I have cleared thirty francs from first to last. I am thinking of taking a deck-cabin on the *Louise Dagmar* (excellent boat, always punctual) for my passage back.

*Saturday.*—Well, really it is too much! Just discovered that the bride at whose civil marriage I assisted yesterday was a scullery-maid from a local restaurant! And the gentleman of prepossessing appearance who lunched at the same table with me, and who I at a first glance took for a parson, turns out to be a *croupier!* I should not have been in the least surprised to have seen him dancing at the *Bal de Famille*, if his duties had not required his attendance elsewhere. Such a *Bal de Famille!* Fishermen dancing with fisherwomen; and on my word they seemed the "best set." The rest of the company reminded me of a dull evening at the Hall-by-the-Sea. And the gambling! People writing to the papers about Monte Carlo when Boulogne is ten times as bad! Baccarat played every night and ruining scores, hundreds! As for the *Chemin de fer*, well—I can only say that I lost three hundred francs at a single sitting! I am going home at once by that nightmare of my childhood, the all-the-way-by-sea-and-river London Boat!

### French Rosycrucians.

UNDER the exalted patronage of the Comtesse DE PARIS, the "Rose of France" has been adopted by the Royalists as their distinctive flower, and they have instituted among themselves a new Society, entitled, the "League of the Rose." An apt addition of the rose to the *fleur-de-lys*—a new alliance of lilies and roses. The "League of the Rose" may be considered the French counterpart of the British Primrose League. Revolutions, we know, are not made with rose-water; but the rose appears to have been appropriated to serve the purpose of a Legitimist reaction. By wearing it in their button-holes and displaying it on their banners, the confederates of the Rose League appear to have persuaded themselves that their prospects are *couleur-de-rose*.

## OUR JAPANNERIES. No. 18.

ON THE STUMP.

CHURCH AND STAGE.—Strictly speaking, the word "Mummer" cannot be applied to an Actor, and both in the title *Mummer's Wife* and in the recent article "Mummer Worship," with which Mr. IRVING "did well," though perhaps not wisely, "to be angry," the word "Mummer" is used contemptuously of the regular professional Actor. But such application shows ignorance. "*Momerie*" is defined in the best French theatrical dictionary as, "*Mascarade, bouffonnerie, déguisement de gens masqués pour aller danser, jouer, se réjouir.*" And the first Mummer was Momus, the professional jester, the Merry Andrew, the Tom Fool of the Court of King Jove "in the air, Of the skies Lord Mayor." Let those whom the Mummer's cap fits, wear it, but most certainly neither Mr. IRVING nor Mr. WYNDHAM need be hurt by anything written against Mummers and mumming. Can it be true that HENRY IRVING refused to speak at the Church Congress simply because he would have been brought in contact with Momerie in any shape? If so, it is a pity, as Momerie in his own shape at the Congress was in excellent form; and though with Momerie "Mum's the word," yet on this occasion he spoke out strongly, and did his best with "Pessimism." The Church Congress, owing to the abstention of the leading Tragedian (his health in a glass of "Pommery," which rhymes to "Momerie!"), felt some delicacy in dealing with the subject of IRVING and the Irvingites, and so let it alone. But—aha!—a time will come!

## ODE TO THAT TOAD.

[A letter in the *Times* gave an account of a Toad found in a bed of clay, and supposed to have lived there since the Glacial period.]

"Owed to a Creditor."

BLAMELESS Batrachian, whom poetic fancy
Dowers with evil gifts and powers sinister,
Optics of glance malefic, labial orifice,
Sputtering poison!

Could not thy kindred *gobemouches* (far less sensible)
Leave thee alone a bit, refrain from ranking
Thee with the frog-shower, fish-fall, huge sea-serpent,
And great gooseberry?

Thirty thousand years in clay? Ridiculous!
Fie on the fudge about times prehistoric!
You a survival faint from epochs glacial?
*Credat Judæus!*

Bet them a bob that *you* are no Toad-TANNER,
Foolish enough to practise secular fasting,
Cramped in a clay-cleft without worms, or nourishment
Entomological!

Man is a clayey creature, O Batrachian!
He it is who, caved in his crass credulity,
Lives through the ages a purblind existence—
Toad-in-the-hole-y!

## VOCES POPULI.

### AT TABLE D'HÔTE IN THE HIGHLANDS.

SCENE—*A long dinner-table, garnished with spiky plants languishing in their native pots. Visitors discovered consulting Wine-list, which they do with knitted brows for some minutes, and then order whiskey and soda. German Waiters get in one another's way, and quarrel in whispers. Late comers enter, either sneakingly, as if inclined to apologise to the Head-waiter, or swaggering, as if they didn't care particularly about dining, but had just looked in. Conversation is conducted in a low and decorous tone.*

*The Diffident Diner* (*to Neighbour, politely*). Might I trouble you for the—ah—Mennu?

*The Neighbour.* Eh?

*The D. D.* Would you kindly pass the—er—(*changes his mind about the pronunciation*)—May-nu?

*The Neighbour* (*blankly*). I'm not seein' ony of it aboot here.

*The D. D.* I was only asking you if you could reach the—(*decides to alter it once more*)—M'noo?

*The Neighbour.* Will I rax ye the *hwhat?*

*The D. D.* (*meekly*). The Bill of Fare, please.

*The Old Maid* (*to Elderly Bachelor*). And what have *you* been doing to-day?

*The Elderly Bachelor.* Well, I took the train to Tay—Tay something or other—and on by coach through Glen—Glen—(*gives it up*)—foozle-um, to Loch—bless my soul, I shall forget my own name next!—and by the Falls of Glare? falls of Bower? (*I can't remember all their confounded names!*), and back by the Pass at the other end of the loch, y' know.

*The O. M.* A charming trip! I'm quite *longing* to do it myself!

*Provincial Paterfamilias* (*across the table, to Friend*). Oh, yes, I've got all my youngsters here; they like the knocking about from coach to steamer and that. I dunno that they notice the scenery much, but (*tolerantly*) it does 'em no '*arm!*

*A Pretty Sister* (*to Plain Ditto*). JENNY, don't look that way—there's that man who sat next to us at Oban, don't you remember? I don't want to have to bow to him!

*The Plain Sister.* Why, FLORRIE, I thought you rather liked him! I'm sure you talked ever so much to him that evening.

*The Pretty S.* I know; but I shouldn't have if I'd known he was going to turn up again in this ridiculous way.

*The Grumbler* (*who dines early when he is at home—generally on chops*). I give you my word I've not tasted salmon, grouse, or venison, not once all the time I've been in Scotland!

*A Stout Man* (*sympathetically*). Nor have I, Sir! That is—at the Skinflint Hotel they did give us what they were pleased to call a "Salmi of Grouse"; but what d'ye think it was, Sir?—four backs as bare as my hand—and the rest of it rabbit!

*German Waiter.* Vill you dake frite fish or whide fish?

*The Grumbler.* Oh, whichever you like! (*To the Stout Man.*) They put it down as "Whiting," and "Fillet of Sole," and all that—but it's never anything but fried 'addock all the time!

*The Stout Man.* I'll tell you a thing that happened to me at the Haggisburgh Hotel—I asked for some marmalade at breakfast, and—you'll never guess what they brought me—*treacle*, Sir—as I'm a living man, they brought me treacle! [*And so on ad. lib.*

*The Gushing Visitor.* What charming *Menus*—with pictures on them, too! And see, what's printed on the top: "A Gift to the Guest." I *do* call that *so* nice of them, GEORGE, don't you?

*George.* I do indeed, my dear. I should feel uneasy at profiting by such reckless and almost oriental hospitality, if I was not reassured by observing an advertisement of somebody's beef-tea on the back.

*The Newly-Married Wife* (*to Husband*). JACK!

*Jack.* Well?

*N. M. W.* Wasn't it idiotic of me to go and leave my umbrella behind like that?

*Jack* (*tenderly*). Not a bit.

*N. M. W.* JACK, I won't have you saying I'm not idiotic when I know I was. Now say I was idiotic, like a good boy.

*Jack.* Shan't!

*The N. M. W.* Then you shan't have any melted butter till you do! [*Dispute lasts throughout meal, and is in danger of culminating in a serious misunderstanding, until* JACK *finally admits, in a very handsome manner, that perhaps she* had *acted rather idiotically.*

*An Impressionable Tourist* (*to himself*). What a lovely girl that is next to me—how superior she seems to all these other people! No wonder she is so silent! I must speak to her, if only to hear her voice. I'll try it—she can but snub me. (*Aloud, to Fair Neighbour.*) What a wonderful view you get here of——

*Waiter* (*suddenly interposing with dishes*). Gudlet or Hash Muddon?

[*The Divinity appears, in the business of choosing, to have forgotten that she has been addressed; the* Impressionable Tourist *feels that the golden moment has flown for the present, and bides his time till the sweets appear, when she opens her lips for the first time.*

*The Divinity* (*to her Mother, a Glasgow lady*). Mammaw, aw'm say'n—they've pit tae much sugar in th' Semolina pudd'n!

[*The dream fades; Impressionable Tourist decides to spend his evening in the Billiard Room as usual.*

## PICTURE-GALLERIES FOR THE PEOPLE.

*Picturæ idiotarum libri sunt;* but there are idiots and idiots—the simply illiterate and the imbecile. The latter have been provided with an abundance of pictures, which, adapted to their capacities, serve them instead of books; namely, the numberless pictorial advertisements on the walls and hoardings which they can run and read. Most of these posters are calculated merely to catch the idiots' pence, but many appeal to their propensities, particularly cartoons representing scenes from revolting stories and execrable dramas. Go where they will, creatures of vile impulses and weak intellect are gratified by figures, chiefly female, falling stabbed or shot, or the victims of savage and brutal assaults and outrages, sprawling on the ground.

Is it really true that the works of High Art collected in National Galleries, and other pictorial Exhibitions of the better class, exercise an elevating influence on the minds of the people who contemplate them? Because, then it may reasonably be supposed to follow that a degrading influence is exerted by illustrations of robbery with violence, and ferocious homicide, upon beholders of the baser sort. Idiots of that description need give themselves no trouble whatever to go and see those hideous productions of the pot-boiler's paint-brush, the puffs of abominable novels and atrocious plays. The peculiar picture-galleries established to attract the multitude, stare them everywhere in the face—exhibitions on view from morning to night every day of the week, and all of them open on Sundays, when the others credited with improving the minds and cultivating the taste of the masses, are mostly closed. Supplied as the idiots are with a profusion of pictures which cannot fail to afford them diabolical suggestions, what wonder when some of them are occasioned to reduce those horrible imaginings to practice?

TO THE CITY OF LONDON (AFTER THE RECENT ACCIDENT).—"*Si Monumentum requiris, circumspice!*" Free translation—"If you still want the Monument, look out!"

## THROUGH HIS PACES.

*Small Talk from Scotland Yard.*

*Chief Commissioner* (*blandly*). So you want to enter the Detective Department. Well, what are your qualifications. (*Briskly, as if springing a mine on him.*) What can you do? [*Eyes him attentively.*

Brought to book.

*Candidate* (*taken aback*). Well, I can do almost anything. (*Considering.*) Leastways—anything that ain't much out of the common. (*Tentatively.*) I can ventriloquise a bit.

*Chief Commissioner* (*impressed*). Ha! What can you imitate?

*Candidate.* Well, I can do a man's voice up a chimbley, and cocks and hens, and a cove a-sawing of a beam—(*with increasing confidence*) and I can do JOE in the Copper.

*Chief Commissioner* (*encouragingly*). I see—a character part; and I suppose you have had some experience at Private Theatricals?

*Candidate* (*feeling he is getting on*). Bless you, yes, Sir, I should rather think I had. I've played *Box*, the Armed Head in *Macbeth*, and the Third Officer in the *Lady of Lyons*, and (*generalising vaguely*) a lot more of that kind. I'm a splendid hand at "making up," I am.

*Chief Commissioner.* And could no doubt undertake a Variety Entertainment. You know what I mean, don't you? You bob down behind a table every minute, change your costume, and come up as somebody else. You think you could embody various characters?

*Candidate* (*reflectively*). Well, Sir, I think I could,—most of 'em. Anyhow I'd try.

*Chief Commissioner.* Just so. (*Pauses a minute—then suddenly, as if just struck with the idea.*) By the way, are you accustomed to the management of bloodhounds?

*Candidate* (*hesitating*). Well, I can't say as how I've ever had much to do with *them*. But (*with confidence*), I knows all about beagles. But, bless you, Sir (*smiling as if at the* Commissioner's *fears*), I ain't afraid of the 'ounds. I'm very fond of dogs, and should soon get into their ways.

*Chief Commissioner.* Quite so. (*Summing up.*) Well, I don't think there's anything else. (*Struck by an afterthought.*) Wait a moment, though, I forgot. You are able to march? Know your drill, eh?

*Candidate.* Yes, Sir.

*Chief Commissioner.* Have served in the Force?

*Candidate.* Yes, Sir.

*Chief Commissioner.* Are well known to all the Constables?

*Candidate.* Yes, Sir.

*Chief Commissioner.* And (*coming anxiously to the point*) to *all the thieves, pickpockets, and burglars?*

*Candidate* (*with alacrity*). To every man Jack of 'em, Sir.

*Chief Commissioner* (*eagerly*). Are you sure?

*Candidate* (*triumphantly*). Cock sure, Sir.

*Chief Commissioner* (*with enthusiasm*). Then that settles it. You'll do. [*Passes him, rejoicing, into Detective Department, as scene closes.*

## VOCES POPULI.

### AT SOME HIGHLAND SPORTS.

SCENE—*A Glen in the North. On a rock above, the non-paying Public are perched, as a Poet present remarks, "like sea-birds." Below, an enclosure surrounded by rough seats, Local Magnates in waggonettes and dog-carts, &c. On a platform a Piper is seen strutting round, performing, with infinite satisfaction to himself, upon his instrument, while a Jury of three take notes solemnly in a tent. In an adjoining field a small party are playing football, with an ostentatious unconsciousness of any rival attraction, that is possibly due to some private pique. The Piper ceases with the weird suddenness with which he began, and marches off; a Rival Piper, in the dead silence that ensues, calls out, "Very well played,* LACHLAN MACKINNON!" *At which* MR. MACKINNON *seems to be inwardly confounding his friend's impudence. Another Piper mounts the platform, and performs apparently the same air. Other Pipers criticise, and compare notes.*

*First Piper.* JOHN MACPHAIRSON played that "*Shaoil a Bhiodh*" ferry well, but he was mekking one or two slips. He went wrong here and there—he did that.

*Second Piper.* Aye, he didna bring out the drone eno', to my thinking. Hoo d'ye play the "*Masther o' Mar o' Shean*," KENNETH MACRAE?

*First P.* Oo, ah, I must be thinking. (*After a silence.*) *I* begin it this way (*hums in* Second Piper's *ear, confidentially*): "Dum-dee-ee-eee-ah-ee; ah-oo, di-doo, di-de-ee." That is how *I* play "*The Masther*," ANGUS.

*Second P.* I do not tek it the same way—this is mine. (*Buzzes in* First Piper's *ear.*) "Dee-ee, eeee, ee-ah, a-a-ah, di-doo."

*First P.* (*after giving the buzz careful consideration*). Yes, that iss a good way, but I wass thinking there will be more of the music in mine.

*Third P.* At Tobbermorry I gained first prize—I do not care who hears me—though it was only the second medal I wass getting whateffer!

*Fourth P.* It iss true—I was quite ashamed of the chudging myself.

*Third P.* Mirover, they told me I was to play anything but "*Gnaillibh a chéile*," my favourite tune.

*Fourth P.* It is ill chudging when the Pipers will no be playing all the sem tune.

*A Chronic Cockney* (*patronising one of the Pipers*). So you 'aven't got your great man down 'ere this time—the *Champion* Piper, you know!

*Piper* (*who considers himself second to none on his instrument*). And who wass he?

*The C. C.* Why, SHAMUS MCRANNOCH—they tell me he got all the medals at Inverness last year.

*Piper* (*loftily*). Did SHAMUS play the pipes? I wass not hearing of it; he puts the stone, yes, a little—and the caber, he can toss the caber, too; but I wass not effer hearing that he played the pipes.

*The C. C.* D'yer know 'oo's winnin' now among you pipers, eh? I suppose they give the medal to the feller who kills the most old cows. Shouldn't care about being on the Jury myself, yer know. I'd rather be set down to class the tom-cats in my back-garden at 'ome.

*Piper* (*politely*). You will be understanding more about the tom-cats and such things.

*The C. C.* I've 'eard, though, that the sound of the bag-pipes will call a dead 'Ighlander back to life—either that or the smell of whiskey—*whusky*, *you* call it, you know. But, between you and me now, you don't call that beastly row you make *music*, do yer—honour bright now? (*Finds the Piper has turned away; the* C. C. *tells a friend that he has* "Just 'ad a very pleasant conversation with one of these fellows—very intelligent chap—I like going among the natives yer know, and gettin' to understand them and that.")

*The Sports proceed; the Hammer is hurled, and on one occasion causes infinite amusement to the "Sea-birds," by just missing one of the Judges. The Spectators nearest the Enclosure show a less keen sense of humour. The Caber—a rough fir-trunk, 21 feet long—is tossed, that is, is lifted by six men, set on end, and placed in the hands of the Athlete, who, after looking at it doubtfully for a time, poises it, raises it a foot or two, and runs several yards with it, after which he jerks it forward by a mighty effort so as to pitch on the thicker end, and fall over in the direction furthest from him.*

*A Lady Spectator* (*disappointedly, after a Competitor has at length succeeded in accomplishing this difficult feat*). Don't they toss it any further than *that?*

*A Native.* Oh, aye, Mem. I hef tossed it three hundred feet and more myself.

*The Lady.* Have you, indeed—and where was that?

*Native* (*modestly*). Over a cliff—from the top right down to the bottom.

*The "Egg and Spoon race"—a contest peculiarly characteristic of the Hardy North—is about to be run; the Competitors assemble in line, each dauntless youth holding a spoon in which an egg reposes.*

*Simple Little Wife.* But tell me, ALFRED, what happens if one of them drops the egg?

*Afred* (*readily*). Oh, he has to sit down and eat it instantly with the spoon.

*Simple Little W.* How curious these old Highland customs are!

*The Athletic part of the Sports are over by about 4·30* P.M., *and the reels and sword-dances begin. Four reels have been danced, and six sword-dances.*

*Mrs. Campbell, of Loch Gorrie* (*to* MR. SENTERBORD, *who, finding that it is nearly six, and there are eight more people waiting to dance the sword-dance in turn—is retreating quietly*). You really ought *not* to miss the Highland Fling—it comes next on the programme.

*Mr. Senterbord* (*departing*). Oh, I *won't*—I'll drop in to-morrow, after the Regatta.

*Dancing continues; fourteen separate sword-dances and fifteen entries for the Fling. Local Magnates, who are not compelled by their position to remain, drive off yawning, and commending the quality of the bag-pipe playing. Magnates whose Pipers have won a medal receive congratulations suspiciously from London friends. Outside the grounds, other fine old Highland Sports "Putting the Cocoa-Nut," "Glass bottle and Steamed Egg stalking," and "Trying the Weight," are now in full swing. Highlanders "left Sporting."*

## AGRICULTURE'S LATEST RÔLE.

*(A Bucolic Ballad, with a Borrowed Refrain, Dedicated to the British Dairy Farmers' Association.)*

"WHERE are you going to, my pretty Maid?"
  *(Butter, and eggs, and a pound of cheese!)*
"I'm going a-milking, Sir;" she said;
  *(Butter, and eggs, and a pound of cheese!)*
"For times are bad, and the farm don't pay.
'Tis Pasture *v.* Arable, so men say,
If still I'd be prosperous *this* is the way.
  *(Butter, and eggs, and a pound of cheese!)*

"I'm tired of corn-growing that brings little cash,
  *(Butter, and eggs, and a pound of cheese!)*
The old business of Ceres seems going to smash.
  *(Butter, and eggs, and a pound of cheese!)*
Free Trade and the Yankee have finished her clean.
From furrow and sheaf there seems little to glean,
From ploughed land to pasture I'm changing the scene.
  *(Butter, and eggs, and a pound of cheese!)*

"I hope you'll allow I look fetching like this,
  *(Butter, and eggs, and a pound of cheese!)*
A Dairymaid's dress suits me sweetly, I wis.
  *(Butter, and eggs, and a pound of cheese!)*
Just twig my short petticoats, look at my pail!
The bards are all ready a Milkmaid to hail!
I mean making prettiness *pay*,—shall I fail?
  *(Butter, and eggs, and a pound of cheese!)*

"You've been to the Dairy Show, Sir, have you not?
  *(Butter, and eggs, and a pound of cheese!)*
Those churners competitive *were* a sweet lot.
  *(Butter, and eggs, and a pound of cheese!)*

## IS DETECTION A FAILURE?

*In the interests of the Gutter Gazette and of the Criminal Classes, the Sensational Interviewer dogs the Detective's footsteps, and throws the strong light of publicity on his work. Under these circumstances, it is not surprising that Detection should prove a failure.*

Miss HOLMES, and Miss KEEL, and Miss BARRON, who won,
Seemed not a bit fagged when the business was done.
I'm sure Butter-making *looks* capital fun.
(*Butter, and eggs, and a pound of cheese!*)

"Then Cheese! Good old Cheshire and Cheddar, I hope,
(*Butter, and eggs, and a pound of cheese!*)
With Gruyère and Camembert shortly will cope,
(*Butter, and eggs, and a pound of cheese!*)
Why, why should the foreigner be all the go?
No, Cheshire and Wiltshire will struggle, I know;
I'll back them to beat GORGONZOLA & Co.!
(*Butter, and eggs, and a pound of cheese!*)

"In addition to these, there be poultry and eggs;
(*Butter, and eggs, and a pound of cheese!*)
They will set Agriculture again on her legs;
(*Butter, and eggs, and a pound of cheese!*)
But "Milk from the Cow" is the thing that will pay
(Ask the Marquis of BRISTOL, and Earl GALLOWAY),
And *that's* why I'm going a-milking to-day."
(*Butter, and eggs, and a pound of cheese!*)

---

SONGS WITHOUT WORDS.—From *The Musical World* (whose critic by the way politely observes that it would be "ungracious to quarrel" with the Savoy *librettist* for calling his plot "new and original" after taking its essence from *Maritana*,—but would it have been "ungracious to quarrel" with SULBERT had the Opera been by two writers called SULBERT and GILLIVAN?) we learn that SULLIVAN'S *Mikado* is now being performed daily at a Danish Circus at Stockholm. "No words are given," but it is "*acted and danced.*" Of course it is unprecedentedly successful. Why not try this plan on alternate nights with the *Beefeater's Bride; or W. S. Merryman and his Merrytana?* The arrangement would draw enormous houses, consisting of those who, having once heard the words and music together, would like to hear again and again Sir ARTHUR'S charming melodies alone, and see the pretty dresses and the *mise en scène.*

## PLAY-TIME IN THREE PLACES.

BEFORE this appears, M. MAYER will have commenced his season of French plays at the Royalty Theatre. Those who know HALÉVY'S delightful book *L'Abbé Constantin*, will be curious to see what kind of a play it makes. Certainly, if closely adapted, and if the actors enter into the spirit of the original work, it should be an exception to the majority of French pieces, which are forbidden fruit to the "young person," and can only be thoroughly enjoyed by those who can honestly adopt CHARLES LAMB'S view of the Comic dramatists and the actors of the Restoration. M. HALÉVY has done much to atone for the brutal materialism of Zola-esque literature with his perfectly pure and thoroughly natural characters in the story of *L'Abbé Constantin.* The best specimen of M. HALÉVY'S cynical humour is his *M. et Mme. Cardinal.* In his tenderness, his human sympathies, his searching analysis of character, his sarcasm, and his cynicism, M. HALÉVY seems to me to approach nearer to THACKERAY than any other French author I can call to mind. He has the advantage over THACKERAY in being also a dramatic author, though I think his most successful pieces have been in collaboration with M. MEILHAC and others, as it usually takes from two to five French authors to make a play of any sort, even an ordinary farce. In this instance, M. LUDOVIC HALÉVY'S story has been dramatised by MM. CRÉMIEUX et P. DECOURCELLES.

"*The Jodrell (late Novelty) Theatre*" was announced to open this evening. *The Jodrell (late Novelty)* is not a good title for a Theatre. When a Novelty is late, it is no longer a novelty. This theatre ought soon to be in vogue as curiosity may at first be aroused by some one at a dinner-party inquiring of a friend across the table, "Are you going to *The Jodrell* to-night?" or "Come to *The Jodrell!*" or "Shall we *Jodrell* together this evening?" *Jodrell* is a good word, and may be used as a verb, as the Germans use "jödel."

Fancy a theatre called after the excellent Earl of SHAFTESBURY! A new meeting-house, a novel Exeter Hall, yes;—but a theatre! I should as readily have imagined a French Theatre called after BOSSUET, or an English one after JEREMY COLLIER. But as some one has somewhere said before, and more than once, I believe, "What's in a name?"

JACK IN THE BOX.

## OUR BOOKING-OFFICE.

At a time when more or less nonsense is talked and written about the status of the Actor,—recently rather Moore than less,—Mr. Fitzgerald Molloy's *Life and Adventures of Edmund Kean* will interest a large number of readers on and off the stage. I should be inclined to say that Edmund Kean was the greatest histrionic genius the English Stage ever saw, not excepting David Garrick. There seems to have been no single department of his art in which he did not excel. He had a strong sense of humour (in which the Kembles were deficient), he could execute acrobatic feats, was an excellent mimic, could play pantomime, could burlesque tragedy, could sing, play, dance, fence, excite laughter, inspire terror, draw tears, and extort enthusiastic applause from most unsympathetic and occasionally antagonistic audiences. He conquered all along the line. As for "social status," he could have been whatever he liked to be, a peer among peers, had that been his desire; but he was what he chose to be, and what at last he despised himself for being.

"Social Status," forsooth! What is "Status"? The answer will be found in *Whitaker's Almanack*, where you will learn the status of everybody, from the highest rank down to a cab-rank. "'Tis in ourselves that we are thus and thus." Conventionality is the sworn foe of genius. Real Genius cannot rest satisfied with humdrum middle-class respectability. Poor Kean! A staunch loyal friend, a wilful man of generous impulses, lavish with boon companions, but mean where love and duty demanded generosity, the self-indulgent victim of a designing woman and her highly respectable husband, pelted, hooted, broken by disease and intemperance,—what a finish to a brilliant career!

Mr. Fitzgerald Molloy is an impartial biographer, neither uselessly blaming, nor needlessly moralising, but writing with charitable sympathy for the human errors of the man, and with honest scorn for the Pecksniffian Pharisee, who cannot understand genius, and is quite as unable to imagine, as he is unwilling to make allowances for, the dangers which beset the path of any public favourite, especially that of an extraordinary histrionic genius. "Alas, poor King of shreds and patches!" Baron de Book Worms.

## DUE NORTH.

*Excursion to a Waterfall—The Wicked Uncle's Strange Story.*

*Next Morning.*—Rain, and occasionally half-hours with the best sunshine. Good Aunt and young ladies have driven off to pay a few neighbourly calls within a radius of fifteen miles or so, do a little shopping,—no matter how bare the village, where there are ladies there is always shopping—and lunch out. Wicked Uncle feeling a bit rheumatic, says that as I am not accompanying the shooters, he will show me a beautiful Waterfall, not a very great distance off. It is so damp and cold that I propose taking the least drop possible of whiskey before we start. Wicked Uncle negatives the proposal with prompt decision. I agree with him, and totally abstain. We start, carrying macintoshes and umbrellas. From talking about sport we get to scenery: from scenery to the extent of the Laird's property: from this to a comparison with other big properties: and finally, by a very easy and natural transition, we arrive at the vast estates of which the Wicked Uncle would now be the proud possessor, as I understand him, but for the machinations of the Machiavelli in petticoats, whom I have heard "D. B." irreverently term "Mary Queen of Squats." For this unfortunate sovereign the Wicked Uncle cannot find epithets sufficiently insulting. Hitherto I have imagined myself pretty well posted up in the history of this ill-used lady, whom I have always championed as a victim, if not a martyr. But the Wicked Uncle throws an entirely new side-light on Mary's character. He speaks with the conviction of a contemporary who had known her personally, and who had suffered a great wrong at her hands, which he is in a position to prove up to the hilt. It is curious too, that in his narrative he brings in scarcely one well-known historical name. I listen with momentarily increasing interest to the commencement of his story when the Wicked Uncle suddenly stops near a small inn, and observes that he is not quite sure if there isn't a shorter cut to the Waterfall than the road we are taking. He will "inquire within." We enter.

"Mornin'," he says, addressing a very youthful bar-maiden, who smilingly returns, "Good morning, Mr. Fraser," and immediately pours out a small measure of whiskey, empties it into a tumbler, and pushes the water towards the Wicked Uncle. "Will *you?*" he asks, hesitatingly. It is my turn to decline with thanks. He drinks it off, observes that this will make him feel a little less chilly, and adds that he was wrong to have refused it at starting. Then as he is leaving I remind him that he hasn't asked the shortest way to the Waterfall.

"Oh," he replies, "I think I remember it."

And as we resume our walk, I ask him to go on with his narrative, in which I am already deeply interested, not so much on his behalf, as for the sake of the good name and reputation of Mary Queen of Squats.

"My ancestor," the Wicked Uncle recommences in a gloomily-confidential manner, his countenance flushing slightly with the air and exercise; "my ancestor was Sir Werdie Fraser, of Kantork, the Master of the Sentences in the Scotch Chancellerie, you know—he was *the* Fraser, you may remember, who threw himself across the doormat, and declared that if they wanted to get at the Queen, it must be over his body—you recollect, of course——"

I have a vague recollection of some incident of this sort, and so reply, "Yes, yes," and he continues, "Well, he was the descendant of Werdie of the Whirlpool."

"Why Whirlpool?" I ask.

"Because," answers the Wicked Uncle, somewhat testily, as if annoyed at my ignorance, "he lived in a castle where no one could get at him without crossing a whirlpool"—(I am satisfied)—"and he refused to pay the Queen a road collop."

I do not like to irritate him by inquiring what a "road collop" may be, and so nod my head as a sign of intelligent assent which seems to relieve his mind of some considerable load as he quickens his step, and proceeds with his narrative in a more cheerful tone.

"A road collop, to which she was no more entitled than you are. So from that minute she hated him. Mary never forgave, you know"—(I was not aware of this, but I think it safer not to dispute the assertion)—"and she was determined to take it out of him somehow; and, by Jove, she did. And," he adds, bitterly, "our family lost about a hundred thousand pounds by it."

"How?" I ask, stopping to put on my macintosh, as the rain is beginning again.

"How!" returns the Wicked Uncle, sarcastically; and then, suddenly changing his tone, he says, "It's such a nuisance walking in macintoshes. We'd better take shelter in here." And I follow him up a narrow path to a small cottage, over which there is a board with the intimation that Mrs. M'Clean is licensed to sell spirits. "Mornin', Ma'am," says the Uncle, politely.

"It's a wee bit moist," observes the dame, returning his salutation, and forthwith produces a whiskey-bottle, two glasses, and a jug of water. I sip mine. The Uncle, complaining of rheumatism in the left arm, which he can scarcely lift, he says, and which is evidently quite different to the other, which he can lift easily, disposes of his "wee drappit" at a draught; and, as I walk to the window to watch the weather, I fancy he repeats the dose. The rain ceases, and once more we are on our road.

"Are we near the Waterfall?" I ask him.

"The Waterfowl?" he asks; and for the moment he appears quite oblivious of the main object of our walk. Then, as if suddenly recalling it, he answers somewhat indistinctly, "Oh, yes,—we're quite near now,—there's a short cut somewhere off this road."

"Good," I return, not feeling such perfect confidence in the Wicked Uncle's topographical knowledge as I did at starting. "And now, what had Mary Queen of Scots to do with your losing the property?"

He walks a little slower, and regards me fixedly, as if failing to comprehend the exact bearing of my question. I repeat it, and remind him at the same time at what point of his story he had arrived.

"Ah!" he says, "Yes!"—as if the whole narrative were once more coming back to him more vividly than ever. Then he mutters vindictively, "Mary was a bad 'un,—a regular right down bad 'un."

"But," I ask, being unwilling to contradict him until I have heard what ground he has for the assertion, "what did she do to Werdie of the Whirlpool?"

"What!" he exclaims, hotly. "She fascinated him. He fell in love with her, deserted his wife and children, made over all his estates to her. She gammoned him into a marriage. They were privately married in Scoop Castle——"

"Oh, my dear fellow!" I cannot help protesting, "what proof can there be of this?"

"Proof!" he exclaims, stopping still. "Proofs! We have the documents in our family. There are whole roomfuls of old papers. When the wretched creature had got all she wanted out of him, she was afraid of his betraying her, and so she had the poor devil stabbed in several places at once, and when he was on his death-bed some old abbot or monk wrote down the story as it came from the dying man's lips, when the whole truth came out."

"What became of the document?" I ask, intensely interested.

"We've got it somewhere. I remember my father and grandfather talking about it. It's in an old house belonging to our family——" Here he stops and stretches out his stick as if making a point. "The Waterfall 's up there," and he indicates a path through the garden of a pretty little hostelrie which calls itself "The Falls Hotel."

A tidy landlady appears at the door.

"Mornin', Mrs. BRAITHWAITE!" says the Wicked Uncle.

"We've still got some of that old whiskey you used to be so fond of, Sir," says the tidy landlady, by way of reply.

"Have you?" he returns. "Ah—well," he says, looking at me, "we must taste that. It's no use trying to get to the Waterfall to-day," he says, looking at his watch; "Must back t' Lunch," and he takes down the nip with real relish. We bid the tidy landlady good-bye. When we are about a hundred yards down the road the Uncle discovers that he has left his umbrella behind. He won't be a minute; only just back to Mrs. BRAITHWAITE's. In something under a quarter of an hour he returns. He seems to walk with some difficulty. This he attributes to rheumatism.

On our way home he is less communicative than he was. He seems to regret having confided to me his family grievance. I ask him why he doesn't publish the family documents? I remind him of the existence of the Old Manuscripts Commission, and point out how valuable these documents in the possession of his family would be. "Think," I say to him, "of the new light these papers would throw on the controversy as to the truth about MARY Queen of Scots." But the Wicked Uncle preserves a dogged silence. Once he mutters bitterly, "What's—doose—use—now?" After a time he uses strong language about MARY Queen of Scots, then he relapses into silence, and, with his head bent, he either seems to be carefully watching his feet, or to be walking in his sleep.

We walk on, but our pace is delayed by the Wicked Uncle, who insists on carefully picking his way so as to avoid the slosh and mud, in which, however, he is not signally successful, as any effort to keep clear of a puddle on his right sends him into another on his left. On every occasion he exclaims, in the most good-natured tone possible, "Bless the Queen!" a formula which he uses as a substitute for more forcible language. Whether he is blessing MARY Queen of Scots, or our own Gracious Sovereign, I haven't an idea, but he is no longer stern and vindictive; and when I try to introduce afresh the subject of "road collops," WERDIE's last dying speech and confession, the Old Manuscript Commission, and the search into his historical papers, he only stares at me with a blank expression, shuts his eyes, opens them, and says in a tone of helpless resignation, "What's—doose—use?"

We reach the house. Long after luncheon time. The Wicked Uncle begs me to "'scuse him a minute as must write a port'nt ler." Neither ladies nor shooters have returned. The attentive butler has kept luncheon hot for anyone who may come in. No sign of Wicked Uncle. I finish lunch. In the library (not the bookshelves in the smoking-room where the literature is limited to the *New Newgate Calendar, Illustrated*, and one or two other books already specified), I find *Robertson's Scotland* in ten volumes. I examine the index, and retire to our bachelors' quarters in the Annexe with several of them. Now I will read up the subject, and refute the story I've heard this morning. I sit down with note-book, pens, ink, and paper. Light pipe. Storm. Afternoon becoming darker. Candles necessary: I am still at work on the subject (not having yet come across any mention, even in the earliest history, of WERDIE of the Whirlpool), when I hear a loud shout, much laughter, then the watch-cry of the Lochglennie Clan, "How are you?" and my door is opened by D. B., who exclaims:

"How *are* you? What have you been doing with the Wicked Uncle?"

"Nothing," I protest. "Why?"

"Because," says the Laird, with a quiet chuckle, "when the housemaid went to light the fire in the smoking-room, she found him fast asleep in the waste-paper basket."

"I know," says D. B. to me, "he's been telling you all about WERDIE and MARY Queen of Squats, and he always finishes like that. He's all right now. How *are* you?" and off they go to their dressing-rooms.

I read no more of *Robertson's Scotland*, and shall not write to the Secretary of the Old Manuscripts Commission.

---

"OH, MY DEAR MUMMY!"—In last September's Number of *The Universal Review* there was an article on "Mummer Worship," and in the October issue there is a graceful and witty poem by Sir EDWIN ARNOLD, which might be called *Mummery Worship*, as it is addressed to a pair of old slippers in the Egyptian Exhibition. Perhaps they were CLEOPATRA's. *Certes*, Sir EDWIN, that female sarpint was a slippery sort of person. The pictures, signed "J. B. P.," possess more than artistic merit, as they exactly illustrate the poem without departing one iota—or rather one "Delta"—from this dream of Old Nile.

## IMMORTALITY INDEED!

LORD RONALD GOWER, it is said, "has been at work for twelve years" on a statue of SHAKSPEARE, which has now been presented to the town of Stratford-on-Avon.

Lika Joko's idea of the Gower Shakspearian statue after reading the *Times* report.

SHAKSPEARE, says the description of it in the *Times*, "is here represented as seated, with a quill in his right hand." How original! how clever! in his right hand! not behind his ear, or in his mouth, but absolutely in his right hand, as he must have actually used it, unless he were left-handed. And to think that the renowned sculptor was only twelve years over this great design!! Well, well!! Wonders of genius will never cease.

The description goes on—"his left carelessly thrown over the back of a chair"—how graceful! how natural! "Carelessly," you'll observe—"and holding a roll of manuscript." Now, who but a born genius would ever have dreamt of representing SHAKSPEARE in such an attitude, and with these properties, "a pen in his right hand," and a "roll of manuscript in his left." What perfect symbolism! "Beneath him," continues the description——but there, what matters what is "beneath him?" Suffice it that there are figures of *Lady Macbeth, Falstaff, Hamlet, and Prince Hal.* Then there are "comic and tragic masks"—here's original symbolism for you!—and there are "pilaster angles," and "astragal entablature." We wouldn't have had it without these last not for worlds. Then there are "emblematical plants, fruit, and flowers cast in bronze."

"The monument," says the reporter, proudly, "has been presented to the Shakspeare Memorial Association by Lord RONALD GOWER, *and its value is estimated at several thousand pounds.*" Crafty reporter! "Estimated," indeed! By whom? By Lord RONALD? At how much? "*Several thousand pounds.*" Nonsense! —much under the mark—say "millions." But then, why millions? "A thing of Beauty is a joy for ever"—and is priceless. After the luncheon, that Past Master of post-prandial oratory, and himself no mean sculptor, Mr. GEORGE AUGUSTUS SALA, in his happiest vein, proposed "The Immortal Memory of SHAKSPEARE," but *not* (at least according to the report), "coupled with the name of the eminent Sculptor, Lord RONALD GOWER." As Parisians now possess a statue of the "Divine WILLIAMS," can anything more be done to prevent Englishmen forgetting SHAKSPEARE? No. The Bard has been chiselled by Lord RONALD GOWER, and his Immortality is at last assured.

---

### TO THE MAORI FOOTBALL TEAM.

YOU'VE come then, brother Maoris,
At us to have a shy,
And if we'd guard our glories,
We'll have to mind our eye.
Our camp you seem to flurry,
And stir its calm content;
You've flabbergasted Surrey,
And scrumplicated Kent!

Your kicking, brother Maoris,
Has given *us* the kick;
You're well matched all, well "on the ball,"
And strong, and straight, and quick.
By Jove, this *is* a rum age,
When a New Zealand team
Licks BULL at goal and scrummage!
It beats MACAULAY's dream.

You're welcome, brother Maoris,
Here's wishing you good luck!
With you there pace and power is,
And skill, and lots of pluck.
A trifle "rough." Why, just so!
But that you'll mend, no doubt,
And win, all Sportsmen trust so,
In many a friendly bout.

WISE IN HIS GENERATION.

The reason Jones doesn't Marry (so he says) is not that he lacks either the Means or the Opportunity—it is because he is of an extremely *Domesticated* Nature, and likes to Spend his Evenings *at Home*.

## WAITING HIS "TURN."

*Boulanger, "the Café Chantant St. Arnaud," at the wings, loquitur :—*

All very well, *mon vieux!* Congratulations
Shower upon you from the house all round.
You fancy this the finest of ovations,
And feel a thrill of triumph, I'll be bound.
But stay awhile! I dog you like grim fate;
And all things come to him who will but wait.

Bow! bow! The *bouquets* and "*Bis! bis!*" seem glorious,
E'en when they come from rustic hands and throats:
Your well-drilled *claque* is getting quite uproarious;
Vociferations though are not *quite* votes.
This hurricane of *bravas!* wild and windy,
What is it but what coarse John Bull calls "shindy."

Mere *charivari*, very little meaning,
*Cher "Faute-de-mieux"!* A truly happy *nomen*,
In which, though your conceit is overweening,
You must, methinks, detect a fateful omen.
You're but a stop-gap Star, man, after all;
And when *I* rise upon them, *you* will fall.

Your Song! Mere clap-trap smooth and noisy clatter;
In a good house it scarce would get a hand.
And as for your stale "business" and poor "patter,"
Those who applaud them do not understand.
Oh yes, bow, smirk, my Carnot, swallow praise
Whilst you can get it; 'tis a passing craze.

My "turn" will come, and my new song, "*Revision*,"
Will bring the house down in a sort of style
Shall make you a mere memory of derision;
So at your fleeting triumph I can smile.
Why, in its fullest flush my presence stings;
*I* caught that furtive look towards the wings!

I am your *atra cura*, and you know it.
Ask Floquet! Such tame trash invites its doom.
You want a *chic* composer and a poet,
Whose verse can make the People thrill—Bim! Boom!
I know the trick of it, I'll make them burn,
Flare, flame, explode! I only wait my "turn"!

## MOST UNWARRENTABLE!

The attack on Sir Charles Warren. Those who join in blood-hounding him down must be interested in renewing the scenes of riot and disorder in Trafalgar Square with which Sir Charles dealt most effectively. The Police Force requires strengthening, and Sir Charles is perfectly alive to the fact. What on earth can it matter if, in number, our Police compare favourably with the Police force at Constantinople, or St. Petersburgh, or Vienna, or Jericho, if we have not sufficient Police to protect life and property in the Metropolis? The Londoner may say,—

"What care I what force there be
In Jerusalum or Amerikee,
If there aren't enough for me
In London?"

Socialistic sensational Journalists and rowdy demagogues would like to see the Police Force reduced to one in every two thousand, until they fell to fighting among themselves, when they would be the first to yell out "Police!" and scream for the intervention of the enfeebled arm of the law.

## Nursery Rhyme for Young Italy, Oct. 12.

The King in the Quirinal,
Feeling very funny;
The Kaiser in a parlour,
Tired after journey.

The Pope was in the Vatican,
Looking at his shoe;
Up comes the Emperor,
And says, "How d'ye do?"

"Savoy Fare."—*Couplets à la Gilbert sauce Sullivan.* N. B.—At this House of Call for the Public, the dinners are always *à la Carte*.

# WAITING HIS "TURN."

The "Café Chantant St. Arnaud." "ALL VERY WELL—'FAUTE DE MIEUX'!—BUT WAIT TILL THEY HEAR MY NEW TOPICAL SONG, '*REVISION*.' *THAT*'LL FETCH 'EM!!"

## METROPOLITAN IMPROVEMENTS.

A SHORT ACT OF PARLIAMENT IS PASSED, PROVIDING THAT NO MAN SHALL BE ALLOWED TO OCCUPY THE INSIDE OF AN OMNIBUS UNTIL EVERY LADY IS SEATED.

SIR MORELL MACKENZIE, in his "Reply," has performed an eminently successful operation on the German "Doctor Wasps." He has taken the sting out of their tales.

## CALLING TO MIND AN OMISSION.

AN evening paper, last week, filled several columns of its pages with a list of the robberies that have taken place of late in various parts of London. One entry was to the effect that twelve months back, a bottle of lozenges was stolen from the shop of a chemist, and there were other announcements of equally startling importance. Strange to say there was no reference to the disappearance of brains some years ago from the office of the paper in question—from the Editor's room—brains that seemingly have not since been recovered.

### Conundrums.

No. 1.—Of what use was VINCENT HOWARD in the Detective Department?

No. 2.—Of what use is he anywhere?

⁂ *A prize will be given for a moderately satisfactory solution of either of the above conundrums.*

HEIGHO, BACCHE!—In the *Times*, last Friday, its Correspondent at Vienna wrote, under the heading, "AUSTRIA-HUNGARY:"—

> "The vintage has begun all over the Empire, but the wine will be everywhere poor in quality, and not much in quality. There never was within living memory such a bad year for vines."

This is bad for Austria-Hung'ry, but it's worse for Austria-Thirsty.

"WHAT IS WORN" is the title of an article on Fashion in the *Daily News*. "I can answer the question, 'What is Worn,'" writes a Constant Non-subscriber, signing "IMPY Q-NIOUS." "My last two winters' overcoat is worn—very much worn. So much so, that I can't wear it *out*."

## THE DETECTIVE'S RESCUE.

*Brief Libretto of the Day, recently set to Popular Music.*

*The Scene represents an Enchanted Hall in the Palace of the Demon of Sensationalism.* A Dismayed Detective *discovered, hotly pursued by a miscellaneous crowd of Sensation-mongers, Prominent Members of the Criminal Classes, Sub-Editors of Daily Papers, Anonymous Correspondents, Loafers, Idlers, and others. On the Curtain rising he cowers before them, as they crowd round him, threateningly singing the following chorus—*

CHORUS.

MISCREANT! Caitiff! thus around thee
Closing, glibly we confound thee!
Thou must feed the morbid hunger
Of the grim Sensation-monger.
Tell us then what thou art doing,
What and whom art thou pursuing?
Quick! Give details! No delay!
Answer our persistent bray.

DISMAYED DETECTIVE.

Good people, surely you'll reflect
My work is simply to detect.
And how can I my object gain
If I my methods must explain?
It certainly would not be wise
To tell my plans,—drop my disguise.

A PROMINENT MEMBER OF THE CRIMINAL CLASSES (*con fuoco*).

What! Would you gag the Daily Papers,
That tip us your Detective capers?
Why! how could coves like us find out,
Without 'em, just what you're about?

AN ANONYMOUS CORRESPONDENT.

And how could I my fancies air,
And help to feed the daily scare?
How pen my rubbish without stint,
And see myself set up in print?

A SUB-EDITOR OF A DAILY PAPER.

And how could I material waste
Which tickles so the public taste?
(*Advancing on Dismayed Detective.*)
So tell me what you mean to do,
What course you purpose to pursue.
I care not how the wind I raise
So that I feed the public craze!

CHORUS (*threateningly*):

Answer! Give the information
We are craving for sensation.
Quick! The details! No delay!
Answer our persistent bray.

DISMAYED DETECTIVE.

And they would force me to reveal
The very facts I should conceal!
There's no escape. Else would I fly!
Will no one give me help?
[*Enter a Chief Commissioner.*

CHIEF COMMISSIONER.

Yes, I?

CHORUS (*falling back*).

Sir CHARLES himself! What can he have to say?

CHIEF COMMISSIONER.

Attend! I'll sing you my official lay.

*Song.*

When tracking some terrible crime,
For a moment the force seems at fault,
And Justice appears for a time
To be baffled, and beaten, and halt.
When no clue on the surface is seen,
And the trail is obscure and effaced,
Do you think the Detective's so green
As to let you know all he has traced.
Surely, goodness alone knows what next you'll expect!
You forget a Detective is meant to *detect.*
So it isn't by showing his hand,
Or supplying the needs of the Press
With a sketch of the scheme he has plann'd,
That his efforts he'll crown with success;
But by keeping the threads that he's got
To himself, careful no chance to miss.
Well, he tracked out the dynamite plot—
Ten to one he'll make something of this!
But that you'll share his confidence, pray don't expect.
Bear in mind a Detective is meant to *detect!*

CHORUS.

We like not your official lay,
And heed no word of what you say.
Fit but, with your blockhead Force,
Crowds to drive from Charing Cross.
Military Martinet,
We'll be even with you yet!
Thus your *dictum* we oppose.
(*They seize the* Dismayed Detective.)
What you're up to, quick, disclose!

CHIEF COMMISSIONER.

Release him! (*Waves truncheon.*) For I summon thus a power
Beneath whose gaze a crew like you will [cower!

[*The Scene opens at back, and reveals the* Goddess of Luke-warm Public Opinion *surrounded by a halo of moderate light. She extends her wand, when all the* Chorus *shrink back dazed, leaving the* Dismayed Detective, *who approaches her gratefully, in the centre of the Stage.*

CHORUS (*shuddering as they retreat*).

Baffled! who will feed the hunger
Of the balked Sensation-monger?
Still, whate'er the world may say,
We'll keep up our blatant bray!

[*They cower lower and lower slinking away, while the* Goddess of Luke-warm Public Opinion *smiles faintly on the* Chief Commissioner *and the* Dismayed Detective *as the Curtain slowly descends.*

## ANTICIPATIONS OF NEXT LORD MAYOR'S SHOW.

["The Lord Mayor Elect wishes the Procession to be worthy of the occasion, and the Corporation of London. He is opposed to the introduction of the Circus element and allegorical display, which accord neither with his own taste, nor, in his opinion, with the dignity of the City."—*Vide the Papers.*]

THE Fathers of the City were seated in the Council Chamber, engaged in a deep consultation. It was within measurable distance of the Ninth of November, and consequently the Lord Mayor shortly was to proceed in state from London to Westminster.

"This is a more than usually interesting occasion," observed one of the Fathers, gravely. "It is possible that we may never have another Lord Mayor,—leastways, not the likes of them as we have had."

"'Ear, 'ear!" murmured an Alderman of the old school, who had passed the chair.

"And this being so," continued the other, "I hope, I do hope, that the Show will be worthy of the event. For instance, I trust, I do trust, that the City Marshal will be seen a-riding in front of it all, a-mounted on horseback?"

"My objection to the Circus element has become historical," returned the Lord Mayor Elect, with considerable dignity.

"And I do beg," continued the Alderman, ignoring the interruption, "that we shall have the men-in-armour. I may say that without the men-in-armour the day would go for nothing. The Missus—I should say my Lady wife—and the young 'uns like to see the ancient knights, and without them the day would go for nothing."

"Don't say that," remonstrated an Alderman, thin and smart, with a *pince-nez*, of the new school. "You are forgetting the banquet. You can't say a day which gives you a fair *menu* goes for nothing. *C'est blague, mon cher*; or, as we used to say at the dear old 'Varsity, *garrula lingua nocet!*"

Then came a chorus of the discontented. They followed one another like a chime of bells.

"Yes, but how about the ancient knights—are we to have any men-in-armour?"

"And surely we are not to be cut out of our banners?"

"And the fire-engines—ain't we to have any of them?"

"And I do like to see a Life-boat. It gives such a benevolent air to it all, you know."

"And the Rangers—them with the guns—what about them?"

"The procession will worthily represent the dignity of the City of London," replied the Lord Mayor Elect, evasively.

"Yes, we know all that," observed another Alderman, rather coarsely, "and that the surplus saved out of the Show is to be given to a charity. But what is the Show to be like? Ain't we going to have any gals in tights seated on globes as Britannia, and all that sort of thing?"

"I am not very fond of the allegorical."

"Oh, gammon!" continued the critical Corporationist. "Let the young 'uns have a chance. If it ain't too late, why not have a giraffe or a couple of elephants from the Zoological Gardens?"

"Gentlemen," returned the Lord Mayor Elect, with dignity, "believe me, I am not unmindful of the importance of the Metropolis of the World. I believe you will find that the Procession will uphold by its magnificence the best traditions of this great centre of civilisation."

And amidst some sounds of dissatisfaction, the meeting dissolved.

When he was alone, the future Chief Magistrate of the City of London knitted his brow in the profoundest thought.

"What shall I do?" he murmured. "They are never satisfied! Have I not selected a West-End Coachmaker? Have I not contrived a card of invitation that should provoke the admiration of the whole of the civilised world? What more would they have? May I not give up the cumbersome Beadles, the useless Commissionaires? And forsooth, the Procession—the real Procession—with myself in a brougham, and the City Marshal on the box—is not sufficiently ornate for them! Well, I must contrive something better—something that by its splendour shall catch the fancy of the groundlings."

And so late into the night and far into the early morning the Lord Mayor Elect pondered. Day was breaking when, with a shout of triumphant joy, he jumped to his feet.

"I have it!" he exclaimed, "I have it! Splendour without vulgarity! Comfort and dignity! I have found the happy mean."

A fortnight later all London was anxiously waiting the approach of the annual Procession. It came. But to describe it the pen fails. And that being the case (as will be seen by the sketch above) resort has been had to the Artist's pencil.

"NUMBER ONE!"

*The Squire* (*to Northern Farmer*). "The Day doesn't look very promising, Hutchinson. What does your Weather-glass say this Morning?" *Mr. H.* "I've no lookit at the Glass to-day, Sir. I got all my Hay in Yesterday!"

## CAVE CANEM!

(*A Page from a Diary kept in the Neighbourhood of Whitehall.*)

8 a.m.—Up early to visit Hyde Park, where I want to test the value of some bloodhounds as applied to the discovery of crime. Make the acquaintance of two full-grown brutes, who examine my boots with suspicion. I am glad on the whole that they are under restraint. It is suggested that they should hunt me. Cannot very well refuse, but would far rather have left that sort of thing to an Assistant-Commissioner. However, not to be done. Half of them recently resigned, remainder (lazy people!) no doubt still comfortable in bed. Never can teach my subordinates the value of early rising!

9 a.m.—Just reached the Powder Magazine. Had to run for my life. For the moment have distanced the bloodhounds. Inspected the sentry, and got him to give me over his orders. Quite right; no smoking to be allowed within ten yards of the gunpowder—very proper precaution. A careless smoker, throwing away a lighted lucifer, might set the place on fire. Bricks and stones ignite so very easily. Obliged to be off again at the double, as I can hear the snarls of the bloodhounds, who are once more on my track. Hope they will spend a few minutes with the sentry before they follow me.

10. a.m.—Brutes still pursuing me. Concealed myself in the Park-keeper's Lodge, and was nearly arrested on suspicion of being a distant relative of "Leather Apron." That's the worst of offering a reward! It causes so many innocent people to be taken up for nothing. No time for more. Just squared Park-keeper, and am off again. Trust the brutes will have a bad quarter of an hour with the custodian of the gardens before they resume their pursuit of me.

11 a.m.—Just escaped. Not a moment too soon. Hadn't reached the Marble Arch a minute before the hounds sighted me, and made for my boots. Only time to jump into a Hansom, and drive to my Club.

12, Noon.—Finished my lunch, and enjoying a few minutes' rest in the smoking-room. Early edition (2nd) of the evening newspapers, just arrived. Why won't they leave me alone? Several suggestions that I should resign. Half a mind to—would if those horrid beasts, who I can hear barking outside, would only understand that I had given up the Police. Committee just sent polite note, presenting their compliments, and calling my attention to the rule forbidding the admission of dogs into the Club-house. Appears that the bloodhounds have rushed into the hall and eaten my hat and umbrella. Committee are under the impression that the hounds belong to me!

1 p.m.—Occupying my room in Whitehall Place. Got away from the Club, without my hat and umbrella, by a back entrance. Will give strict orders that I am not to be disturbed. Have called down the tube, and can get no answer. Have just remembered that I have sent the entire Staff (disguised as washerwomen) to Whitechapel, to look about them. Don't much like to be alone with those brutes on my track.

2 p.m.—Just as I expected! They have traced me, and I can hear them on the staircase. Wish I had a revolver. Great nuisance that the lock of my door is out of repair. They are sure to come in! As I am a man of ready resource, have hidden myself on a shelf over a water-bottle. Have always heard that water destroys the scent. I can hear the bloodhounds sniffing outside! Most annoying to be all alone. Wish I was back at the Soudan!

3 a.m.—Have been for the last hour on the shelf. The dogs have made my room their own. Have watched them from under a pile of newspapers. Fortunately, they have preferred devouring my despatches to searching for me. Boy just brought in my tea. Before I could speak to him they had begun to hunt him! For a moment I am alone.

4 p.m.—Back again on my shelf. The intelligent beasts (far too intelligent!) after disposing of the tea and muffin-boy, have returned to hunt me. I am safe for the moment, as they are devouring my cocked hat, sword, and top-boots. A great nuisance as they (the cocked hat, &c.), form an effective portion of my favourite costume. Cat's meat man outside. Can hear his cry. The bloodhounds have heard it too, and have disappeared to hunt him. Saved for the present!

5 p.m.—Brutes back again. They have discovered me! I am keeping them off with a poker and a bag of biscuits. My shouts should be heard. Really, these people obey my orders too literally.

### A STRAIGHT TIP.

"Can't say I quite like the Cut of that Suit of yours, Governor!"
"What! Why, confound it, Sir, my Tailor's the Best in London!"
"Ah, dessay; but you should try our Chap down at Eton—*he*'s the man! And you might just mention my Name, you know!"

When I said that everybody was to be off to Whitechapel, I did not mean, of course, that Whitehall Place was to be deserted. Wish I could induce the bloodhounds to go opposite to pay a visit to the Commissioners in Lunacy. Not that they would find *them* (as they are always from town inspecting outlying asylums), but they might have a little fun with the Secretary, who is a fixture.

6 p.m.—Still on my shelf. The bloodhounds are engaged at this moment in eating some dog-muzzles and my box of decorations. And now they are ready for a spring! Well, I will make a good fight of it!

7 p.m.—Saved! Six perfect strangers have rushed into the room. The brutes are seized and handed over to the proprietor. The bloodhounds in handcuffs (applied to their legs) are now being carried off in triumph. Very grateful to my rescuers. It appears that the six perfect strangers are prisoners who have been arrested on suspicion. As they have done me such a signal service, I can but release them. I have less compunction in giving them their freedom, as I find that they have all been staying for the last three months in a boarding-house at Margate. From this I fancy it is improbable that they could have been concerned in the sad affair at Whitechapel.

8 p.m.—The staff of the office have just come back. They have returned, having arrested, by mistake, one another. This is most satisfactory, as it is proof that they must have been admirably disguised. Am on the eve of leaving the office for home, having just issued an order that the use of bloodhounds by the Police will be suspended until further orders.

## TRANSYLVANIAN SPORT.

*(From Our Special Sportsman with their H.R.H.'s.)*

Last week the Prince of Wales and the Crown Prince went outto shoot bears. The bears behaved in their usual bearish manner—they are regular beasts—and refused to meet their Royal Highnesses. Beaters—in their beautiful old gold-beater-skin costume, still worn here (and by the bye, the Court Plasterers also stick to their ancient dress in this Conservative State)—went into the woods and forests with the Gold Sticks in Waiting, and made noise enough to wake the sleepiest grizzly. But Bruin wouldn't show himself, and though we waited in the plains below for hours, yet we saw nothing. The scouts came up, and in broken English, which they've learnt out of compliment to our Prince, reported, "All bear!" so, thinking they meant that "All the bears were coming," or that "the bears were everywhere," we got ready, presented, but didn't fire. *L'Ours—voilà l'ennemi!* But there was no *Ours*.

One of the Half-Crown Princes out with us (any number of them about—plenty of change), tried to make an international joke about "waiting *hours* for an *ours*," but he was hushed down by both the Princes, and I had to tell him afterwards, that as he really couldn't pronounce either French or English properly, he had better keep his jokes in those languages to himself. Poor dear Half-Crown! he was so sorry, but he soon laughed it off when I called him "Young Two-and-Sixpence," which set the whole party in a roar just when the only bear that has been seen all day showed its nose round a corner.

If we hadn't been convulsed, that bear would never have lived to tell the tale, but as it was, bang went all our barrels, and when the smoke cleared off, all I saw was the Half-Crown Prince going head over heels backwards down the rocks, owing to the violent recoil of the gun when he was laughing, and three of the *chasseurs* jumping about, chucking their plumed hats in the air, and shrieking with pain, though, being courtiers, they had to pretend it was their way of expressing excessive annoyance at the disappointment their Royal Master and his distinguished guest had suffered. "Mark, Bear!" shouted a Styrian Count in pink tights, green and gold coat, and leather boots with spurs. But it was a false alarm.

No more at present, as the Royal Currier is just leaving, and he'll have nothing to curry if I don't send this despatch. We're all well. Don't talk of making a place "a regular Bear-garden." This is one, and as quiet as the Great Desert on a Sunday night.

* * * * *

P.S.—I re-open this to say that I've hit on a plan which has met with the approbation of everyone. I kept it dark till now! My fortune's made!! *I brought out a bag of buns from England, the very same sort that they give to the bears at the Zoological.* I am now going out baiting traps and tops of trees * * * * Sure of sport!!! I expect nothing less than a Marquisate for this, with a *château*, and any number of thousands a year, to keep up the Bears in this district. . . . . Expect more by wire, road, or rail, from

Your own Noble Sportsman,
Rudolph the Rifleman.

## THE DUEL OF DIGESTION.

[M. Alexandre Dumas describes French duels as a mere appetite-provoking preliminary to a good breakfast, enjoyed by principals and seconds together.]

When Alphonse and Jacques
Go out to attack
Each other, and try the *duello*,
Their friends gather round,
With emotion profound,
Admiring each daring young fellow.

And both look so fierce,
In "carte" and in "tierce,"
They posture and lunge, 'tis quite thrilling;
You'd think that a life
Must be ta'en in the strife,
And each man is bent upon killing.

But, bless your heart, no;
It never is so:
A scratch or a touch, and it's ended.
No man comes to harm
With a prick on his arm—
Thus honour and safety are blended.

They go back to town,
They win cheap renown
In *cafés* where friends are assembled:
As heroes to-day
They describe all the fray,
As if e'en the solid earth trembled.

The *déjeuner*'s there;
The bloodthirsty pair,
With seconds, go back and do credit
To dishes and wine:
So Dumas doth opine
Such duels are shams, and has said it!

Women as Poor-Law Guardians.—Guardian Angels

## A BEAR IDEA.

AIR—"*The Whale.*" *To be set and sung to an Accompaniment of Hungarian Gipsy Music, to be composed by Archduke Joseph, and Dedicated to H.R.H. the P. of W.*

'TWAS in October's month,
Brave Boys,
With RUDOLPH we did repair,
And we all went away
To Transyl-va-ni-a,
We went for to shoot a bear,
Brave Boys,
We went for to shoot a bear.

I took three guns,
My deadliest ones,
For partridge, grouse, or hare,
With cartridge and ball,
Both great and small,
Wherewith to shoot that bear,
Brave Boys,
Wherewith to shoot that bear.

When H.R.H.
Was making a spache
At luncheon—(sumpshus fare!)—
A Keeper so cute
Says, with a salute,
"I think as I've tracked a bear,
Brave Boys,
I think as I've tracked a bear!"

I was showing RUDOLPH
The rules of golf,
For which he doesn't care,
When up comes ELLIS,
And what he's got to tell is,
That "someone has heard a bear,
Brave Boys,
That someone has heard a bear!"

An Aide-de-camp
Was singing a song,
And I was joining in the air,
When RUDOLPH cries out,
With a very loud shout,
"My eyes! there is such a bear,
Brave Boys.
My eyes! there is such a bear!"

Trim ESZTERHAZY,
Who was getting rather lazy,
Jumped up, and cried out,
"Where?"
And gay Count BREDA,
As bold as a Crusader,
Cries, "Let me shoot that bear,
Brave Boys!"
Cries, "Let me shoot that bear!"

Says I, "Crown Prince,
I'll never wince,
And on my head my hair
Will not with fright
Stand bolt upright,
Whenever I see that bear,
Brave Boy,
Whenever I see that bear!"

I seized my gun,
With a bound and a run,
The danger I longed to share;
When just behind a tree,
A-looking at me,
I saw that grisly bear,
Brave Boys,
I saw that grisly bear!

He was rubbing his eyes
With some surprise—
He'd just awoke from his lair.
I aimed—he ran—
Bang! flash!—in the pan!
So I did not kill that bear,
Brave Boys,
I did not kill that bear!

## TALKING IT OVER UNDER DIFFICULTIES.

"On the occasion of the Emperor WILLIAM's visit to the Vatican, his Majesty evaded the repeated attempts of the POPE to discuss the question of the temporal power of the Papacy."—*Daily Paper.*

IN the absence of any more direct information on the subject, the following brief dramatic version may be confidently regarded as an authentic account of the termination of the rather embarrassing interview to which the above paragraph refers:—

SCENE—*An Audience Chamber in the Vatican. The* POPE *discovered according a private interview to the* Emperor of GERMANY, *in the course of which he has made several attempts to introduce the question of the "Temporal Power," but has been successfully foiled by his Imperial visitor, who, by keeping up a rattling fire of conversation on any and every subject, from the weather downwards, has managed, during the fifteen minutes the interview has already lasted, as yet completely to evade the introduction of the, to him, unwelcome topic. The* POPE, *feeling that the time is slipping away, and that it is no good beating about the bush any longer, at length determines, at all hazards, to take the bull by the horns, and bring matters to an issue.*

*The Pope* (*cutting the* EMPEROR *short in a humorous account of the failure of the* Prince of WALES, *in his recent expedition, to get a shot at a single bear*). Ah! very droll, your Majesty; very droll. But I wish to speak to you about a very different matter (*coming to the point*)—the Temporal Power, you know——

*The Emperor* (*quickly*). Ah! The Temporal Power. Just so. Of course (*airily changing the subject as he approaches the window*). Dear me! (*looking out*) I had no idea, your Holiness' was so well off here. What a capital garden!

*The Pope* (*continuing*). You know, it is necessary——

*The Emperor* (*brightly, misunderstanding him*). Of course, it is necessary. Pegged up, as you are, here, it must be quite a resource to you (*again looking out*), and there seems a good lot of it.

*The Pope* (*ignoring his misinterpretation*). I mean it is necessary to the exercise——

*The Emperor* (*cutting in briskly*). Of course it is necessary for exercise; and, I'm sure, I'm very glad your Holiness is able to get it. I doubt if you would be able to get on without it.

*The Pope* (*still holding on*). To the exercise of my spiritual functions, and so its restoration——

*The Emperor* (*catching at the word glibly*). Restoration! To be sure. That's going on everywhere. All over the place, in fact. Quite a rage for it. Such lots of new *Boulevards*. I'm sure I don't know what they won't restore next.

*The Pope* (*determined to get it out*). And its restoration is the only sure guarantee for the security of European Peace.

*The Emperor* (*flying off at a tangent gaily*). Peace! Ha! Of course—The League of Peace. Just been cementing that over the way at the Quirinal. Fancy, too, it looks like certain success.

*The Pope* (*still sticking to his guns*). Your Majesty, there is only one thing certain, and that is that Rome must come back.

*The Emperor* (*merrily*). Come back? From what I have seen, I should say it was more inclined to go forward. (*With a good-humoured wink.*) But, of course, your Holiness knows best.

*The Pope* (*nothing daunted*). It must become Papal Rome once more.

*The Emperor.* Ha! hum! exactly. Quite so. (*Feeling things are getting hot and changing front, with sudden effusion.*) But, by the way, what a delightful afternoon it seems to be turning out. Quite pleasant, I declare. And that reminds me. (*Jumping at Happy Thought.*) I really must be going.

*The Pope.* What, going without settling anything?

*The Emperor.* Settling anything? Why, yes, everything is rather unsettled, isn't it? (*Beating a retreat.*) Hum! Yes! Precisely. Just so. Of course! (*Taking his leave respectfully.*) Anyhow, it is so kind of your Holiness to have received me. Enjoyed our talk so much, you know. 'Pon my word, I have.

[*Bows himself out, and joining his suite with "evident signs of deep emotion" depicted on his countenance, leaves the* POPE *shaking his head, conscious that he has had a not very satisfactory interview with a remarkably unmanageable and troublesome young man.*

## ROYAL VISIT TO HIS OWN CAPITAL.

ON Wednesday last London was brilliantly lighted to honour the arrival of King FOG, who paid his first state visit of the season to his own capital. He entered the City on the East, and proceeded in triumphal procession towards the West. On reaching Kensington he returned. His Majesty also visited the suburbs. The royal progress was celebrated by grand fantasias on A Thousand Respiratory Organs, Baron BRONCHITIS was out with his Bandannas borne by four hoarse-men. The Actors of London, with bad colds, were represented by Mr. HERMANN WHEEZIN, and in the train of King FOG followed the celebrated General DE PRESSION, with deputations from the various states of Ill-health and Indi-gestion. The rear was brought up by bands of Roughs, Burglars, and Policemen at a respectful distance. His Majesty has been taking a slight rest during the last few days but he has no intention of quitting the Metropolis for some time to come.

## OLD KING COAL.

### SONG OF AN ANTI-SCIENTIST.

*King Coal (roused out of his slumber).* "OH, WHAT A BORE!"
*London (to Science).* "TAKE MY ADVICE, AND DON'T HAVE ANYTHING TO DO WITH HIM. HE'S A GREAT DEAL TOO DEEP FOR US."

"'Is there Coal under London?' We sincerely trust there is not, and that, if there is, it will never be discovered. The prospect of a colliery district at Streatham, with an eventual revival of the iron industries of Surrey, Kent, and Sussex, is enough to make every Londoner despair.'"—*Times.*

YES, Old King Coal is a merry old soul,
 And a merry old soul is he;
  But we shall all be undone
  If they find him under London;
 So we trust *that* is fiddlededee.
Oh! the plague and the pother, Oh! the shindy and the smother

That in all suburban districts we should see!
So Old King Coal we'll trouble you
To disturb not the S.W.,
And let us live on easy in E.C.

For though Old King Coal is a useful old soul
Whom generally men are glad to see,
Yet we all shall be despondent,
If the "Thunderer's" Correspondent
Correct in this affair should prove to be.
Fancy carrying the drill to the foot of Streatham Hill,
Or filling Hampstead Heath with reek and roar!
No, prithee, Madam Science,
Stay your hand with this appliance,
For a "bore" at Richmond Hill *would* be a bore.

It may be as you say, that below the London Clay,
At Tottenham and eke at Kentish Town,
You, by boring a big hole,
May arrive at last at Coal,
That is if you dig very deeply down.
Yet spite of any treasures that might come from the Coal Measures,
And the "Wealden denudations," and all that,
The Metropolitan zone
You had better leave alone,
The game's not worth the candle, Ma'am, that's flat!

*Punch's* heart is hard as steel against WHITAKER's appeal
For sub-Jurassic borings and such stuff.
Wealth-grabbing is our time's tone,
But below the London limestone
Is no place for Dives' delving,—that's enough.
Cut your scientific cackle, bring no more Contractor's tackle
To mar our grim Metropolis still more:
For though Old King Coal
Is a merry old soul,
We do not want his mirth near Thames's shore.

## OUR BOOKING-OFFICE.

FOR those whose musical memories are well stored, Dr. SPARK's *Musical Memories* have not much novelty to offer. All the professional people of his acquaintance seem to have been as nearly morally and socially perfect as may be. He is quite a "good GRIFFITH," (not the safe man with an "s," but the oral biographer of Cardinal WOLSEY) in his reminiscences, and thereon is much to be commended. *De mortuis nil nisi bonum.* But how interpret "*bonum?*" I should say in a biography let us translate it as "a good thing" about so-and-so. Well, he has some "good things" in this sense, and he tells them in a sufficiently lively manner to warrant me in alluding to him as "The Vital Spark." He tells very naïvely of dinner-parties at PATTI's on "off nights"—which seem to have been rather "'On' nights"—when "at the invitation of STRAKOSCH he had an opportunity of dining with the family party"—he means the family PATTI—("sometimes strengthened," he goes on, whispering in brackets, "by two or three influential critics) at their charming house, Rossini Villa, Clapham Park. These indeed, were delightful times," &c., &c. Clapham rather discounts the "Rossini" of the Villa. On the whole, very nearly, Vital SPARK's book is chatty and amusing for any half-hour unoccupied.

The Autobiography of SIMS REEVES is a thrilling Romance. It opens with a sensational murder, and the book, like *Prospero's* Island, is "full of strange noises." There is not enough about SIMS REEVES himself, details of his studies, and so forth.

People are going about laughing—all business is suspended—chuckling and nudging is the order of the day. No more coughs and colds. Try *Toole's Reminiscences.* The Booksellers are all making jokes over the sale of BOSWELL HATTON's TOOLE's Reminiscences. A person went to one in Hatton Garden, and asked if he had one of TOOLE's reminiscences. "No, he Hatton't," was the reply. And then the office-boys danced and cheered, and one who had previously rushed out with five-and-twenty copies under his arm, returned with, "Sold again!" I read bits of it here and there in the *Sunday Times*, but must sit down to it quietly, and be strapped into my arm-chair. A Physician will be at hand, to prevent me dyin' o' larfin'.

One MOORE book, called *Spring Days.* Even the *Pall Mall Gazette* describes it as "a nasty dish," and can scarcely find a chapter without some "flagrantly bad taste." This being so, perhaps its author will change its title to *Spring Onions.* This is a matter of taste for perfumery. Spring! Spring! beautiful Spring! Loveliest Onion of the Year! sings the Lady of Shalot (at a distance) to her own BARON DE BOOK WORMS.

"'ANDICAPPED!"

*Gaol-Bird* (*having just picked "Landlord's" pocket*). "AMERIKIN WATCH! SHABBY OLD 'UMBUG!—AND 'IM A MAN O' PROPERTY TOO! UGH! WHAT 'ITH DOWNRIGHT FRAUD LIKE THIS 'ERE, AN' COERCION, AN' WHAT NOT, A POOR MAN HA'N'T GOT A CHANCE!!"

## CHURCH AND STAGE; OR, ST. JAMES'S THEATRE.

*The Dean's Daughter* is an unwholesome, unpleasant, poorly-constructed play, with here and there some sharp, flashy writing, which is more acrimonious than amusing.

M. Lafontaine in the street of the Dean, Soho. "Perfectly Abbé!"

The Very Rev. Rutland Barrington in the dress of the Dean of St. James's. "J'y dine; J'y reste!"

As novel-readers know, *The Dean's Daughter* is by the author of *Ariane* and *As in a Looking Glass*, which last was the novel that made Mr. PHILIPS'S reputation. *Ariane* dramatised was a repulsively realistic, but decidedly powerful drama. In it virtue was not rewarded, as there was none to reward; but vice was punished, and the existence of all the unprincipled, godless *dramatis personæ* was shown to be thoroughly miserable. But in this play at the St. James's the Divorce Court, like "the Waverley Pen," comes "like a boon and a blessing to men," and women, too, and such small virtue as there is in the piece, or what the authors would have us accept as a substitute for virtue, is rewarded by Messrs. GRUNDY and PHILIPS by giving the divorced woman in marriage to the nominal co-respondent (after he has shot another would-be co-respondent, his rival), who clasps her to his manly breast in the presence of her former husband (whom the divorce has freed in order to continue a *liaison* with somebody else), and of a third lover—a mere boy who might as well have been in Eton jacket and turn-down collars, with apples and sweets in his pocket,—whose hand and fortune this injured innocent, introduced into Society under an assumed name, has just accepted. On this "heroine of the Divorce Court," before or after her marriage, an audience cannot waste its sympathy, as before marriage she is not in love with anybody,—though she foresees the probability of her being so with somebody after marrying the wrong person,—and, with her eyes open very wide indeed, she allows herself to be induced by her reprobate father, whom she despises, and her odious companion, *Mrs. Fortescue*, to marry a fortune and a title.

*Miriam St. Aubyn* is an ungrateful part, prettily and cleverly, if not brilliantly, played by Miss OLGA NETHERSOLE, who is possessed of considerable emotional power, can rise to dignity of action, and has the true touch of pathos in her voice. She comes from the Adelphi to play the daughter of the Dean, and her place in *The Union Jack* is taken by another of the DEAN family,—DOROTHY DENE. Another coincidence is, that the Christian name of *Lady Ashwell* in the piece is DOROTHEA, and as she is to marry the *Rev. Augustus St. Aubyn*, she also will be a DOROTHY DEAN.

I suppose the somewhat scrappy dialogue is mainly taken from the novel, and of this Miss HILL has all the telling lines, which, intended to be the comic relief of the piece, she delivers as though she were once more *Cynisca*, in modern costume, impersonating a sort of vixenish chorus, making a running commentary on the action. Does Miss HILL correctly interpret the Authors?

*Sir Henry Craven* is one of the line of old diplomatists that commenced, I fancy, with *Baron Stein*. Here, he is a dummy *Sir Peter Teazle*, who marries a young girl in the country, and then reminds her of what she was before she became his wife. This *Sir Peter* should have been stuffed full of good things, and killed in the *entr'acte* after Act III., when he would have died deeply regretted by a numerous Dress Circle. As it is, he has little to do, nothing worth hearing to say, and reappears inopportunely as Lord Anticlimax in Act IV., just in time to spoil a fairly effective dramatic situation.

Miss ADRIENNE DAIROLLES, as the French Maid, is uncommonly good. How she would suit that wicked French part in *Bleak House!* *Prince Balanikoff*, the would-be co-respondent of foreign extraction, looks like a melancholy Polish Jew, and his walk reminded me of the little mechanical tin-toy man drawing the cart, of whom we've seen so much recently, taking his exercise in the streets. Miss HILL says "Ta, Ta, Prince," to him. This exactly describes him. When the Russian is scratched, you find the Tar-Tar Prince underneath, and his violent scene is his best, melodramatic though it must necessarily be. Last, but certainly not least, comes the Very Revd. RUTLAND BARRINGTON, Dean of St. James's. He looks the Dean as well as did the late JOHN CLAYTON, but he is so intimately associated with Mr. GILBERT'S Vicar, who wore much the same costume in *The Sorcerer*, that any audience would never be surprised were he to step forward and, to Mr. ARMBRUSTER'S excellent accompaniment, sing, "Ah me, I was a pale young Curate *then*." Perhaps Jester GEORGE will provide him with lyrics describing his regret at having quitted that company with the refrain, "Ah me, I was a stout young Actor *then!*" But, pooh, bah! He is Manager now and Comedy actor. He has to play a part in which there is little wit and no finesse; it is the *Reverend Mr. Pecksniff* and *Lady Ashwell* is his *Mrs. Todgers*. But *Pecksniff*, sober or inebriated, was amusing, and then in the end, he failed in his villany, and was only let off with a sound thrashing. The Dean is unpunished, for the possible loss of *Lady Todgers'* hand and fortune wouldn't affect him very much. The best-played scene, which does not owe much to the writing, is the one between Mr. LEWIS WALLER and Miss NETHERSOLE, when the heavy haberdashery-young-man kind of lover tells *Miriam* that her wishes are his commands, and says farewell for ever—only to reappear in the same place five minutes afterwards.

The play is preceded by a One-Act Comedy called *A Patron Saint*. At present the St. James's Management must be contented with one Saint as a Patron for the evil Dean's doings. I fancy the patronage will not be considerable, either of saints or sinners.

To come from such exceptionally unwholesome "home produce" as *The Dean's Daughter* to so exceptionally wholesome a French piece as *L'Abbé Constantin*, is as refreshing as escaping from an infected atmosphere into the pure air. M. LEFONTAINE is perfect as the Abbé, a genuine French type. The delicacy of his art is a study, but there is no call upon him for any strongly emotional acting. The two young men's parts are fairly acted. Miss JANE MAY, "My Pretty JANE," is not seen to advantage, and the piece, though pretty and simple enough, is deficient in any real dramatic interest. On Thursday, M. LEFONTAINE is to appear in *Le Fils de Famille*, and *M. L'Abbé* should be reserved for occasional *Matinées*. JACK-IN-THE-BOX.

## DUE NORTH.

*Evenings at Lochglennie—Weather Notes—Finale.*

OUR evenings are lively. Miss MILLIE plays the piano, Miss EVELYN is a violonist, and Miss MADGE a banjoist. They all know each other's music, and can play from memory almost any song or air that may be "inquired for."

D. B. is a proficient on the penny whistle, and DOLLY WHITE is a master of a small, peculiar-shaped instrument, of Italian nationality, called, I think, the *occarina*, which, when placed close to the performer's lips, makes him look as if he were doing a conjuring trick, and pretending to swallow a baby's shoe. GRANNIE plays a *mirloton*, which he has brought from Paris. The Baron's instrument is the cornet-à-pistons, but, as the Good Aunt, who is our sole audience, declares she cannot possibly stay in the room with that noise, we insist on the Baron performing with a pocket-handkerchief stuffed into the cornet, the effect of which is very much as if he were playing it under the bedclothes. The Laird has made a life-long study of the side-drum. From his earliest years he was always attached to it, and it was attached to him,—by a string. Now his performance on it is that of a Professor. He is a Master of the Rolls.

"Very few people," he says, when he finds you are inclined to talk seriously on the subject, "very few people know what there is to be got out of a drum. It is not all noise. How effective it is at military funerals, muffled!"

This seems rather a gloomy view to take of it. When an invitation is sent to the Laird to attend a funeral, do they add on his particular card, "and bring your drum, muffled"? I don't like to ask this, and he continues, "it is the universal instrument. All nations have the drum."

"And chickens have drumsticks," puts in D. B. And by way of showing us that his remark was not meant seriously, he nods at me and says, "How are you?"

The Laird insists on my being provided with an instrument. The Wicked Uncle refuses to resign the triangle, which, he protests pathetically, he has played since the second night he came here, and wants to know why I shouldn't have the fire-irons, as *he* had when he first arrived? This proposition seems to be considered as fair and just, and so GRANNIE hands me the poker and shovel, with which I have to serve my apprenticeship as it were, with the reversion of the triangle, on the departure of the Wicked Uncle. We are all in our places, with Miss MILLIE at the piano. The orchestra is wonderfully successful. Perhaps the most effective of the *morceaux* is a song sung by D. B., entitled "*The Man that struck O'Hara,*" which offers peculiarly fine opportunities for the side-drum and the fire-irons. There is one part—a pause—where the chorus leaves off, and only the side-drum and the fire-irons come in with one tremendous crash, illustrating the force with which "the man that struck

O'HARA" was floored by the latter's friends, who, to avenge his injuries, dragged his assailant—

"Down the passage, down the stairs,
Over tables, over chairs,—
Scarcely time to say his prayers——"

Then, I think, in the awful pause that follows, comes the whack of the drum, together with the crash of the fire-irons—a most dramatic effect—as the chorus immediately bursts forth with savage exultation,

"Rags and bones were all they left
Of the man that struck O'HARA."

This so delights us all, that we play it over several times, on each repetition finding some new beauty in it, and finally finishing it with almost barbaric intensity.

The Good Aunt looks at her watch. "Half-past ten. '*God Save the Queen*,' if you please, Gentlemen," she says, and, in compliance with the request of our audience, we give the National Anthem with full orchestration.

Then comes the last ceremony of the evening. Every lady who retires at ten is entitled to "Musical Honours"—that is, "By Order of the Laird," each lady is escorted down the passages to her room by the male contingent of the orchestra, in full marching order. So GRANNIE, as drum-major, walks first; then come the ladies with bed-chamber candles; then the band, at quick march, playing "*Boulanger's March*," alternated with the "*British Grenadiers*," as we call at the different rooms, and, having seen all the ladies to their apartments, we right-about-face, and march briskly back to the appropriate and inspiriting air of "*The Girl I Left Behind Me*," until we reach the Smoking-room, where we are disbanded, and go from labour to refreshment.

*Next Day, and Day after, and several Days after that.*—Rain persistently. Waterproofs and umbrellas required, if only to walk about the garden. It sounds paradoxical, but it's true, or ought to be, that, when it's wet, it is fine for fishing. Plenty of fish in the river, but they remain there. I go on the moors, when they're driving, and catch a severe cold.

Next day stay in, and see the sport from window, as the shooters are visible to the naked eye as they go up the hill.

*Happy Thought* (*as I see them in the distance*).—"How happy could I be with heather"—if it were only dry, and not such a trouble to walk through.

*At my Window.*—They're having good sport, judging from the reports I hear. Reports becoming more and more distant, and only miniature mechanical toy-men and puffs of smoke can be seen through glasses. "*Lookers on see most of the game.*" Quite untrue at this distance, as I see most of the men and nothing whatever of the game.

GRANNIE, the fisherman, returns, despondently. He has lost his best fly, which has been taken by a prodigious fish. "So," says he, "I was spoof'd over that." He thinks it rather hard to be "spoof'd." But he has had no luck. "Are the flies," I ask, —meaning a whole pocket-book full of them such as he has got— "expensive?" "Yes," he replies, "they cost a goodish bit; but," he adds, in the tone of a disappointed man, "so does all sport. What's the use of climbing over moors, or wading up to your neck in water, merely to be spoof'd in the end?" I admit that this does sound hard. We talk sport generally, and I obtain some valuable information. Has he been lucky in horse-racing? "No," he replies —"lost." Then he adds, with playful irony, "It's 'osses makes the 'oof to fly." This, I presume, is a new sporting proverb. Play on the words, "'osses" and "'oof," by dropping the "h." "No," he explains, "'oof' means coin." *Unde derivatur "Oof"?*

I keep private Meteorological Notes. We begin with,—

*Any Day.*—10 A.M.—Rain. Everything wet—turf, garden-seats, &c., &c.

10·30.—Sun. Everything dry.

11.—Scorching. Must change things to summer suit.

11·30.—Am in summer suit. Deluge of rain. Change again. Gaiters, goloshes, thickest boots, umbrella, sou'wester.

12·30.—Sun suddenly brilliant. Heat tropical,—moist heat, like vapour-bath. Birds singing. Open all windows. In-doors unbearable. Gnats, flies, wasps, bees. Hang up waterproof, get rid of gaiters, goloshes, &c. Return to summer clothing. Go in to lunch. Doors and windows open. Iced drinks. At lunch arrange for walk, going out in canoe, under shady trees, on river's bank. Lawn tennis, if not too sultry, or sit under trees, in American chairs, reading.

2·30.—Transformation scene! Quick change! Torrent of rain. Driving wind from S.E. Rush for waterproofs. Chilly. Arctic cold.

3.—In-doors, putting on winter things. Lighting fires. Shutting all windows. Sit down to be comfortable.

4·15.—Suddenly, sun, tropical heat again—let fires go out—go out ourselves—going to be fine? No—weather suddenly (every change in Scotland is sudden,—the people are cautious, but the weather is impulsive) becomes mixed, and, to express it musically, we have no longer a solo of sun, or of rain, or of wind, nor do we have a duet of rain and wind; but we have a wonderful trio of sun, rain and wind, in unison!!

It is a Grand Meteorological Opera. A magnificent symphony, or cantata,—water-cantata,—might be written entitled *The Weather*, which idea I hereby offer to Sir ARTHUR SULLIVAN or Mr. GORING THOMAS or Dr. MACKENZIE, with my compliments, and "no fees." All that is required to-day, as the shades of evening gather round us, is that the First Act of the New Meteorological Scotch Opera should end with a magnificent *ensemble* of rain, hail, thunder, lightning, snow, all this to the "sun's setting," and with fine "passages for the wind." These last can be found in the house and outbuildings. As somebody sings, "*So the Story goes*," and so it goes on for ten days,—and then, *on the first fine day, I go off!*

No help for it; I've made all my arrangements. Must depart. There's no doubt about it. This is the first fine day, and bid farewell I must to Lochglennie, and the last words that salute my ear as the train moves off come from D. B., who rushes to the corner of the platform, and just as the train is getting up its speed shouts, "How *are* you?" To which, the remembrance of GRANNIE's ill luck flashing across my mind at the moment, I have only time to reply "Spoof'd!"

And "spoof'd" I am by the weather. And now "Bock agen!" And so ends my ten days' holiday Due North.

## DIVINE SHAKSPEARE AND THE GREAT SCOTT.

IMMORTAL Dramatist and Novelist! Spell Scot with a single "t," and it will stand for Lord RONALD of the Sculptor's chisel. This coincidence has struck a student of SCOTT's *Border Minstrelsy*, and, though too late for last week's issue, some verses have arrived from "AN OLD PARLOUR-BORDER MINSTREL," which he says he has adapted from a familiar old Scotch ballad to the occasion of Lord RONALD GOWER's presenting a statue of SHAKSPEARE to the people of Stratford-on-Avon, which event we chronicled last week.

Chiselled by a canny Scot.

AIR (*Old Scotch, like the Whiskey*)—"*What gat ye for Supper, Lord Ronald, my son?*"

I.

Where gat ye your statue, Lord RONALD, my son?
It's as white as a spectre, my handsome young man.—
Oh, I made it in France, mither,—mak my bed soon,
And I've gi'en it to Stratford, and fain would lie doon.

II.

Will ye do one for London, Lord RONALD, my son,
Now that SHAKSPEARE's in Paris, my handsome young man?—
Oh, London saw mine, mither,—mak my bed soon,
And in Paris *c'est connu*, so let me lie doon.

III.

Why not MOLIÈRE for London, Lord RONALD, my son?
'Twould be but politeness, my handsome young man.—
Oh, I'm weary of Paris, mither,—mak my bed soon;
The Bard took twelve years there,—so let me lie doon.

The "OLD PARLOUR-BORDER MINSTREL" adds that "this, with the drone of the pipes, will enchant all hearers." For the sake of metre, he wishes "Paris" in the penultimate line to be pronounced "Parrs," as one syllable; that is, if we see no objection—and we don't.

IMPORTANT PORTENT!—Mr. IRVING, who is always making good speeches, made a telling one at Bolton, which, as reported, seems to have consisted principally of one lengthy but most appropriate quotation. But what was really remarkable was that, from beginning to end, he never once mentioned "Friend TOOLE." How's this? Where was JOSEPH BOSWELL HATTON to note the portentous omission? JOHN LAWRENCE will address "Friend Irving" with the words of the song that Miss GRACE DAMIEN sings so charmingly, "*Can You Forget?*"

"OLD FOLKS AT HOME."—Mr. BAILEY has written an interesting book, called *Modern Methusalehs*. The Author must be henceforth known as "The Old Bailey."

SOCIAL AGONIES.

*Angelina.* "LOOK, EDWIN! MR. AND MRS. DEDLEIGH BOREHAM! I'M QUITE ASHAMED TO MEET THEM! THEY'RE ALWAYS ASKING US TO DINNER, AND WE'VE NEVER EVEN ASKED THEM INSIDE OUR HOUSE! WE REALLY *MUST* MAKE *SOME* RETURN!"

*Edwin.* "SOME *RETURN!* WHY, CONFOUND IT! ONCE WE ACTUALLY *DID* DINE WITH THEM! WHAT *MORE* CAN THEY EXPECT!"

## "THE SISTERS THREE;"

OR, THE LEAGUE OF PEACE.

*A Modern Bismarckian Version of an Ancient Classical Myth.*

"THEN must he suffer what the Fates ordain;
For Fate has wove the thread of life with pain!"
So mild ALCINOÜS, great Phæacia's King,
If one may trust what POPE and HOMER sing.
ALCINOÜS though was not a Teuton; no;—
And I am scarcely "mild," to friend or foe.
On German ears such gentle accents jar.
Who was it said that Man is his own Star,
"Commands all time, all influence, all fate.
Nothing for him falls early or too late"?
I like that better! Parcæ of my own,
Each crowned, each seated on a radiant throne,
With robes star-spangled,—docile each to Me,
As the Fates were, 'tis said, to Destiny!—
That's more like my ideal. Come, let's limn!—
Clotho, the distaff-bearer; she looks grim,
Deep-eyed, contemplative, with glance afar,
As one who scans the serried ranks of war
From some plain-dominating pinnacle.
Yes, that's a master-piece: stands clear, looks well.
Germania calmly spins the web of Peace;
Her grip upon the spindle shall not cease
Whilst *I* am Cloud-compeller. Blessed PAX!
That distaff, well "replenished with smooth flax,"
As smooth CATULLUS—is it not so?—sings,
Must, in the present shaky state of things,
Be firmly handled, or sedition's shocks
Will send us back to Erebus and Nox.
Better their dismal daughters! Iron might
Alone may war with Chaos and old Night.
Scruple that shirks, and pity that will pule,
May please the poets, but they cannot rule.
The "Fatal Sisters" knew not change nor ruth.
Those old Greek singers had an eye for truth;
And that is something more than one can say
For sentimental twanglers of to-day.

Then Lachesis! Yes—that's the style of head
For her who, under guidance, spins the thread
Of Policy—which is a kingdom's life.
Lachesis knows the woe of inner strife,
For all her haughty Hapsburg lip. Spin out
The long thread lightly; veil that look of doubt
Which on the face of Clotho dwells and lingers.
'Tis yours to "make it pliant 'twixt the fingers,"
And "equalise" ('tis no light task!) "the tissues."
Spin on; I have an eye upon the issues.
Your Crown looms shadowy; with that dual blur
Of lamp-lights when—(a thing that will occur)—
A man hath wined not wisely, but too well.
A Fate, remember, must be firm and fell.

And Atropos? Aha! This Fate looks steady,
The shears firm-gripping, and to use them ready.
A crown of lesser height but firmer poise.
Could Fates be glad, one might conceive she joys,
Like some young pard, in her life-slitting function,
Which she would exercise without compunction.
But Fates, like suns, must neither lag nor haste,
Not theirs to husband and not theirs to waste
The thread attenuate, but to twirl, spin, slit,
As what e'en they obey may order it.

And that, the higher overmastering source
At once of web and shears, of fate and force?
Well, the wise ancients left that agent vague;
And so will I. It is the petty plague
Of little minds to pry.
My picture! So!
It does not follow MICHAEL ANGELO
With any servile closeness, I admit. He
Painted those pitiless hags that in the Pitti
Freeze all men's marrow with their stony glare.
The gazer who can front those orbs might dare
To meet Medusa's petrifying glance.
But times must change, creeds shift, and Art advance.
Masters may differ. This is my design
For the Three Modern Fates; much less malign
Than massive MICHAEL'S, yet prepared to act
With iron promptness. A political pact
Like this should bid all war and tumult cease,
Since the Three Fates form now a League of Peace!

---

MRS. RAMSBOTHAM, being told of the "Pastels' Exhibition," observed, "Let me see, who is PASTEL? Isn't he a doctor who cured mad dogs? It must be a most interesting show. Where is it—at the Crystal Palace, where the Cat Show was?"

Atropos. Lachesis. Clotho.

"THE SISTERS THREE;" OR, THE TRIPLE ALLIANCE.

## OUR NEW M.F.H.

MR. TOPPLE, OUR NEW M.F.H., HAS DECIDED TO HUNT THE HOUNDS HIMSELF; BUT FINDING IT IMPOSSIBLE TO REMEMBER THEIR NAMES, HE HAS ADOPTED THE ABOVE CAPITAL PLAN.

## ROBERT'S ESTONISHMENT.

I HAVE lived to see the day wen a Cheerman of a Copperashun Cummittee has publickly dared,—without a blush, as far as I coud see, and I fixt my egle gaze upon him as he spoke,—to xclaim to an estonished crowd, "Water, brite Water for me! and give your wine to the trembling Debbawshe!" How the three or four ancient Deputys as herd him liked the strange words of course I don't know, but this I do know, that when a few ours arterwards the Cummittee was all seated cumferally together at their faverite Gildhall Tavern and me a waiting on 'em, as ushal, they all drunk the plucky Cheerman's good helth together, and chaffed him most tremenjusly about his watery speech. But he bore it all chearfully, like a man and a brother, and tossed off a bumper of fine old Port after thanking them for their kyind wishes.

So I needn't have bin so werry grately alarmed at the Cheerman's xtrornary speech, but he ewen did wuss then that on another simmyler ocashun, as I will now perceed to relate.

It seams as the Copperashun, not kontent with setting up the best Skools, and the best Libery, and the best Markets, and the best Bridges in all the hole City, has lately gorn into the Parks and Open Spaces line, and after spendin about a quarter of a millyun of money in buying Epping Forrest, as I herd the Cheerman of the Cummittee say ony a few weeks ago, has quite lately took charge of Highget Woods, and wen sumbody arsked leave to put up a Fountane there, so that the pore littel boys and gals as goes there coud wash there hands, and setterer, the Copperashun not ony allowd it, but sent down a Cummittee to see as it was all rite, and to take charge of it, and it was on this ocashun that the Cheerman made the owdacious speech I have menshuned. I was there, and I herd what was a going on, and I scarcely xpects to be beleeved when I says that sum of the pore littel children, dreckly as the Cheerman's back was turned, acshally went up and drunk sum of the werry cold water, pore littel things! The Cummittee might have let it run ginger beer just for wunce. But wuss remanes behind. For ony larst week the same Cheerman took down the werry same Cummittee to take over another Fountane, as another liberal minded Gent—tho' he is a blooming Conserwativ—had offered to give for the Queen's Park at Killburn, which is another of their good worx.

It was a bitter cold day, so the bizziness was got thro' raything more quicker than afore, and wen the liberal conserwatif Gent had made his nice little speech and anded over his nice littel Fountane, the Cheerman stood forrard, and I coud see a wisibel shudder run through the elderly members of the Cummittee for fear as he shood commit hisself as afore. But no, he awoided the dellicate subjick alltogether, and made one of them bewtifool littel speeches as only Cheermen can make, and the Cummittee was ewidently much releeved in their minds speshally the old uns. But, wunderfool to relate, insted of dessending from his stony pedestal of glory and retiring gracefoolly amid the peeple's cheers, he acshally filled a pewter cup to the brim and quaffed it off without a shudder, and called upon his Committee to boldly stand forward and do likewise! Oh, the grim smiles upon their countynancys was a sight to see! One ancient Deputy endevourd in wane to conceal his disgust, while another had the pluck to boldly announce what all the others dowtless thort, namely, that he shood prefer it with jest a leetle drop of old Skotch whiskey in it!

And now jest one word of frendly warnin to my kynd Patrons.

It's trew, as I'm told, that the Board of Warks, having failed to give sattisfaction by living on nothink but Work and Water, is about to give place to another Board with a different name, but with the same hutterly himpossibel condishuns, and you may be thinkin of haltering your old successful, becoz libberal, plan of hopperashuns, to catch a little fleating poppylarity. But it will be a orful mistake, for while it will chill and disappint your frends it will ony excite the contemt of your foes.

ROBERT.

## WHAT'S-HIS-NAME AND THE SATURDAY REVIEW.

IN answer to numerous Correspondents, we beg to state, on more than undoubted authority, that,—

1. *The "Saturday Review" will* not *in future appear every Tuesday.* 2. *That it will be edited by its Editor in London, and* not *in a Cottage near the "Merrie Green Wood."* 3. *That its Editor is* NOT *going to undertake the chief direction of the Detective and Private Inquiry Department of the Police under the sobriquet of* "POLLOCKY." 4. *That neither Mr. What's-his-name nor Mr. What-you-may-call-um is engaged on the paper.* 5. *That every report put about by Thingummy Bob when he was rather Thingummy Tight is hereby emphatically contradicted.*

PRIMITIVE ARITHMETIC.

*New Mistress.* "And what Wages do you expect?"

*New Cook.* "Well, Mum, it depends on the Style you live in. If I'm to do the Dining-room, Entrance 'all and Doorstep, as well as the Cooking, like in a Middle Class 'ouse—Twenty Pounds a year. But if I'm to have a Kitchen-maid to 'elp, and nothing but the Cooking to attend to, like in a *Gentleman's 'ouse*, I shall require Forty!"

## HISTORY AND MYSTERY.

[At Liverpool, Queen Patience, *æt.* 19, wife of the deposed King Ja-Ja, was highly charmed with the railways and the electric light, but imputed both to the inventive genius of the "debble," "as man have no sabbey do dem tings."—*Evening Paper.*]

Old English worthies never saw
  The Railway or Electric Light,
Which, seen but unexplained, with awe
  And wonder would have dazed their sight;
Such marvels, *certès*, they 'd have thought,
Could be by warlocks only wrought.

Witchcraft, not very long ago,
  Stood on the code of actual crimes;
Most things whose causes none could know
  Were magic in the good times.
Whate'er they didn't understand,
To solve the "debble" was at hand.

Grave doctors, lawyers, and divines,
  Regarded, from their point of view,
As portents, prodigies, and signs,
  And cantrips, to his action due,
Each new discovery science made.
Invented by the "debble's" aid.

In her philosophy, to-day,
  Queen Patience, not above a child,
Is just about as wise as they,
  When faggots were for witches piled.
The learned need not boast, a pebble
They care no longer for the "debble."

A Last Flare-up!—The flickering Lord Mayor, who will be extinguished on the Ninth of November, has been writing to the papers, indignantly denying that when in Belgium he ever made the "ridiculous statements" or expressed the "contemptible opinions" about London (*e.g.*, its being "the cesspool of Europe") that have been attributed to him. Neither *Mr. Punch*, nor any other sensible citizen, ever for one moment believed that the now flickering and sputtering Civic Light could have "said such a tings." The idea of a Lord Mayor of London fouling his own Mayor's nest! Why, it would be enough to make Whittington "turn again" in his grave. Farewell, brave Polydore! Here comes the Ninth of November, with the Extinguisher, and the next Lord Mayor's banquet will be your "blow out!"

## SEEN YOUR CRISPI?

Signor Crispi, the Italian Premier, having recently been interviewed by an English Journalist, a representative from 85, Fleet Street, was despatched to Rome to see him. The following is the report that has been received from our Correspondent, which is published with all rights reserved, but not necessarily as a guarantee of good faith.

I must say I was a little surprised to find that instead of being "a short compactly-built Italian," as I expected to see him, from the description furnished by my journalistic colleague, Signor Crispi was decidedly podgy, not to say stout. He received me with great courtesy, seating himself gracefully on the only chair there was in the room, and apologising profusely for not being able to offer me one too.

"You have seen, no doubt," he said, with a smile, "that your predecessor, in interviewing me, 'had not exchanged half-a-dozen sentences with me ere he recognised in me a man to whom waste of time and verbal banalities were assuredly little less than intolerable.' He was right. And now what can I do for you?"

"Lend me half-a-crown," I replied, from force of habit.

To my surprise he produced the coin, and, for a moment, I thought he was about to present it to me. However, the shrewd common sense of the man conquered, and he replaced it in his waistcoat pocket.

"You will pardon me, but, to please a dear little niece of mine, aged five, I promised never to put my name on a bill of exchange, and never to lend a sixpence to any one. I am unwilling to deceive her."

"Well, if you will not do me this trifling favour," I replied, a little vexed, "perhaps you will reveal the secret of your future policy."

"With pleasure," returned Signor Crispi, promptly; "but I must rely on your discretion *to tell no one save the readers of your paper*. If you cannot give me that assurance, I must be, as we say in Italy, as dumb as a plum-pudding, and as reticent as a mince pie."

I gave the required assurance.

"Now I can tell you what I propose to do. As you are aware, we have a secret treaty with Russia (the Emperor William brought it from St. Petersburg, as a present for me, in his portmanteau) and relying upon this we shall insult France next month so grossly that we are sure to be nicely at war with her by Christmas. Consequently I would advise you *to sell for the fall*."

"Most interesting," I murmured, "and now tell me about England. I think you were in London?"

"Only for a short time—six months. But I admired your city. Your Vauxhall Bridge Road was magnificent!"

"Did you see any of the buildings,—monuments?"

"Why, certainly, yes. Your Victoria Station was not then built, but your Lambeth Suspension Bridge was splendid!"

"Where did you lunch?"

"At a baker's. I used to buy a crumpet, soak it well in water, and eat it. It was really excellent!"

"Yes—and could you speak the language?"

"Only a few words. 'Cabman, you are a thief—I will not pay you your fare!' This sentence was electric, and, thanks to the teaching of the Cabmen, I soon learned good, strong, forcible

## OUR JAPANNERIES. No. 19.

THE GRAND OLD STUMPER AND HIS OFFSHOOTS.

English. For instance, I thoroughly understand the value of the termination of Amsterdam. I also acquired from them the rudiments of boxing."

"Do you take any interest in our country, now that you have so much to do in your own Parliament?" I asked.

"Assuredly, yes," he replied. "When your journalistic colleague called, I showed him Mr. RITCHIE's Local Government Bill, which had been sent to me, I fancy, as a practical joke. However, I have determined to understand it, and have procured to assist me in that endeavour this beautifully illustrated work, which I am told is your standard authority on all matters of law."

The Italian Premier then produced the latest edition of the *Comic Blackstone*, which I assured him would indeed be of infinite service to him.

"And now I must leave you, as the King has been waiting for me for the last hour and a half. You will forgive me for locking up the side-board, but it contains not only spirits, but some valuable plate."

And thus the interview ended. Two minutes later I was in the street, carrying with me a strange umbrella, that I had secretly secured as a memento of my very interesting visit. I have retained that umbrella ever since!

"CUM GRANO SALIS."

Old Method for Catching a very Old Bird—the Goose that Lays the Golden Eggs.

PRAYER-BOOK REVISION.—Mr. ROBERT FOWLER will probably be invited to join this Committee. His department will be to bring out a new Psalter.

*PRINCE KARL*, at the Lyceum, seems to be a puzzle to such playgoers as have seen it. An incoherent and grotesque sort of American farce with a part in the broken Dutch dialect that RIP VAN JEFFERSON once made so popular here at the Adelphi. It might be termed a "What-you-may-Karl-it" sort of piece.

## THE GORDON MONUMENT AND ITS MESSAGE.

[On October 16, at 11·30, the Gordon Monument in Trafalgar Square was unveiled by Mr. PLUNKET, the First Commissioner of Works, without speech or formality of any kind.]

IN silence! Somewhere in the wild Soudan
Lies, silent too, the calm heroic man,
Whom none of English blood henceforth may name
Without a thrill of pride shot through with shame.
And here's his statue! Slain afar, alone!
Memory needs no memorial of stone
To speak of GORDON, or awake a thought
Of the pure paladin who toiled and fought
For England, and Humanity, and Heaven;
The record of whose life should be a leaven
Of quickening greatness in a factious age
Of petty jealousies and Party rage.
Fortitude, Faith, and Justice; noble three,
Linked by the gentle bond of Charity,
These deck his statue as they graced his life.
England, with pride and shame so much at strife
In every proud and patriotic breast,
What speech avails? Silence perchance is best.
But there's a work of his, memorial high
At once of GORDON and of Charity,
Which we, without o'ermuch of empty speech,
May carry on. To save, to help, to teach
The young of England was our hero's aim.
To let his death destroy his work were shame.
GORDON'S Boys' Home! There speaks a strong appeal,
Which every heart of British make should feel.
It cries for aid; response should not be slow;
For hearty help thereto, right well we know,
Would fill the hero's heart with more content
Than glowing praise or glorious monument.

## AN APPEAL TO THE PUBLIC.

LAST Thursday Sir ARTHUR SULLIVAN gave an amusing and instructive lecture at the Birmingham and Midland Institute on Music. Why on Music? How perverse! Why there are a number of subjects of which he is utterly ignorant, and on which, therefore, he could have lectured with far more benefit to himself at all events. But Sir ARTHUR is unselfish, and so he told them how, in the course of his cramming at the British Museum, he had come across a picture dated 866 A.D. of "a concert consisting of a six-string harp, a four-string fiddle, a trumpet, and a crooked horn. Curiously enough," continued Sir ARTHUR, triumphantly, "this is, with the exception of the horn, exactly the same combination of instruments that we see nearly every Saturday night playing outside a London public-house." Ahem! "*We* see." Who are "*we*"? The three Savoyards, Witty S. G., D'OYLY CARTEY of Killaloe, and the eminent lecturer? *Not* "every Saturday night," but "nearly every Saturday night." "Playing outside;" then "we" see them on coming out, eh? This is the consequence of an admission, a free admission. A hearty vote of thanks was accorded to Sir ARTHUR for his address, in which he gave sound advice to his hearers, and had a kind and generous word for everybody of note in the musical profession.

## RECKLESS WRECKERS.

ON the first night of the re-opening of the St. James's Theatre, under the management of the Rev. Mr. RUTLAND BARRINGTON, there seems to have been a row. Some unprofessional critics in the gallery objected to something that Mr. CLEMENT SCOTT, the able critic, attached deeply to the *Daily Telegraph*, had written about "Wreckers on a First Night," and to prove how unprejudiced they were, and how quietly they could behave, the Wreckers in the gallery, who resented the Critic's accusation, determined to give the In-CLEMENT SCOTT D. T. fits; and so the Gods yelled at him from above, and though guarded by a chivalrous Knight, Sir JOSEPH the Erudite of the order of Minerva, these rowdies followed him, threatening personal violence. It was more than ten to one against Mr. SCOTT coming off scot-free. But he did. Only—where were the police? or where was *a* policeman to act as a Coast-guardsman, and rout or arrest the reckless "Wreckers"? If they begin this with Critics what will they do with Editors!! Guilty Cinnas will tremble if violent mob-lawlessness is to supersede comfortable criticism. So, down with *premières* altogether! Let's have a solemn critic's night with the critics arranged on their benches, "a terrible show," no disturbing "wreckers" present, and smoking allowed in every part of the house.

"This must be stopped."

## J. M. Levy.

BORN, 1812. DIED, OCT. 12, 1888.

A NAME that fame will link with the Cheap Press!
He seized the moment and he snatched success.
The proletariat pence he found would build
A fortune for the shrewd and the strong-willed,
As well and swiftly as patrician pounds.
Keenness that measures, kindness that abounds,
Are not the worst equipment for that strife
Of loves and interests which men call Life.
With him 'tis o'er, and many known to fame
Have left less good and less-enduring name.

## THE PASTELLIST OF THE PAVEMENT.

MR. SALA—it could have been no one else—in a lively and instructive article on "Pastels" in last Saturday's *Daily Telegraph*, describes the art and artist thus:—

"It holds a middle rank between drawing and painting. The draughtsman, strictly so called, executes his designs with the lead pencil, the pen, or the chalk crayon. With the last he may work on a tinted ground, he may even use brown chalks, also he may employ red." . . . . "The worker in pastel is essentially a worker 'in the dry.' Moisture is the greatest foe he has to fear." . . . . "Instead of palette and brushes, the pastellist needs only a long box, the compartments of which are filled with coloured crayons," &c., &c.

After reading this, put a penny in your pocket, and go and watch the method of the Pastellist of the Pavement, who brings his chalks in the morning, and walks his chalks off in the evening. He is indeed a "*worker in the dry*," and "*moisture is the greatest foe he has to fear*," for a shower of rain causes him and his colours to run together. The only brush he is likely to have is one with the police, but this is very rare, as the Pastellist of the Pavement is inoffensive and industrious. The Art is, from the nature of the case, low, but when the Pastellist of the Pavement has arrived at a certain pitch—a good one in a respectably frequented thoroughfare—there he sticks, and never gets beyond it.

"COOL AS A CUCUMBER."—In the *Times* of last Thursday, Mr. JOHN FINUCANE wrote a letter indignantly denying that in a speech at "Windygap"—(number of blusterous speeches made at many Windygaps all over the country and by men of all sorts and conditions of parties)—he had told the blacksmiths to shoe the landgrabbers' horses and "drive the nails into the quick." He wrote at a white heat from "*Coole House, Caherelly, County Limerick.*" But if anyone's residence should be styled "Coole House," it should be that of the Irish Secretary, who is "cool as a cucumber." How some of the Nationalist "Coolies" would like to give Cucumber BALFOUR a dressing with a taste of his own vinegar and plenty of pepper!

**AN UNSELFISH MAN.**

*Colonel Slyboots, M.P.* "SO SORRY TO LEAVE YOU ALL ALONE AT MUDBORO', MY LOVE; BUT DUTY WILL COMPEL ME TO BE AT MY POST AT WESTMINSTER FOR THE AUTUMN SESSION, YOU KNOW. SO DULL IN TOWN WITHOUT YOU, TOO."

*Mrs. S.* "POOR DEAR! THEN I'LL ACCOMPANY YOU, MY ANGEL!"

*Colonel S.* "OH, ON NO ACCOUNT. WOULDN'T HEAR OF IT!"

## CATCHING THE EARLY BOAT.

*In Bed; at the Highland Hotel, Oban.*—What an extraordinary thing is the mechanism of the human mind! Went to sleep last night impressed with vital importance of waking at six, to catch early steamer to Gairloch. And here I am—broad awake—at exactly 5·55! Is it automatic action, or what? Like setting clockwork for explosive machine. When the time comes, I blow up—I mean, *get* up. Think out this simile—rather a good one . . . Need not have been so particular in telling Boots to call me, after all. Shall I get up *before* he comes? He'll be rather surprised when he knocks at the door, and hears me singing inside like a lark. But, on reflection, isn't it rather *petty* to wish to astonish an Hotel Boots? And why on earth should I get up myself, when I've tipped another fellow to get me up? But suppose he forgets to call me. I've no right, as yet, to *assume* that he will. To get up now would argue want of confidence in him—might hurt his feelings. I will give him another five minutes, poor fellow . . .

*Getting Up.*—No actual necessity to get up yet, but, to make assurance doubly—something or other, forget what—I will . . . I do. Portmanteau rather refractory; retreats under bed—quite ten minutes before I can coax it out . . . When I have, it won't let me pack it. That's the worst of this breed of brown portmanteaus—they're always nasty-tempered. However, I am getting a few things into it now, by degrees. Very annoying—as fast as I put them in, this confounded portmanteau shoots them out again! If I've put in that pair of red and white striped pyjamas once, I've done it twenty times—and they always come twisting and rolling out at the back, somehow. Fortunate I left myself ample time.

Man next door to me is running it rather fine. *He* has to catch the boat, too, and he's not up yet! Hear the Boots hammering away at his door. How *can* a fellow, just for the sake of a few more minutes in bed—which he won't even know he's *had!*—go and risk losing his steamer in that way? I'll do him a good turn—knock at the wall myself. "Hi! get up, you lazy beggar. Look sharp—you'll be late!" He thanks me, in a muffled tone, through the wall. He is a remarkably quick dresser, he tells me—it won't take him thirty-five seconds to pack, dress, pay his bill, and get on board. If that's the case, I don't see why *I* should hurry. I've got much more than that *already*.

*At the Quay.*—People in Oban stare a good deal. Can't quite make out reason, unless they're surprised to find me up so early. Explain that I got up without having even been called. Oban populace mildly surprised, and offer me neckties—*Why?*

Fine steamer this; has a paddle-wheel at *both* ends—"because," the Captain explains, "she has not only to *go* to Gairloch—but come back as well."

First-rate navigator, the Captain; he has written my weight, the date of my last birthday, and the number of the house I live in, down in a sort of ledger he keeps. He does this with all his passengers, he tells me, reduces the figures to logarithms, and works out the ship's course in decimals. No idea there was so much science in modern seamanship.

*On Board.*—Great advantage of being so early is that you can breakfast quietly on deck before starting. Have mine on bridge of steamer, under awning; everything very good—ham-méringues *excellent*. No coffee, but, instead, a capital brand of dry sparkling marmalade, served, sailor-fashion, in small pomatum-pots.

What a small world we live in! Of all people in the world, who should be sitting next to me but my Aunt MARIA! I was always under the impression that she had died in my infancy. Don't like to mention this, because if I am *wrong*, she might be offended. But if she *did* die when I was a child, she ought to be a much older woman than she looks. I *do* tell her this—because it is really a compliment.

My Aunt evidently an experienced traveller, never travels, she informs me, without a pair of globes and a lawn-mower. She offers, very kindly, to lend me the Celestial globe, if the weather is at all windy. This is behaving *like* an Aunt!

We are taking in live-stock; curious-looking creatures, like spotted pug-dogs (only bigger and woollier, of course) and without horns. Somebody leaning over the rail, next to me (I *think* he is the Public Prosecutor, but am not quite sure), tells me they are "Scotch Shortbreads." Agreeable man, but rather given to staring.

Didn't observe it before, but my Aunt is really amazingly like GLADSTONE. Ask her to explain this. She is much distressed that I have noticed it; says she has felt it coming on for some time; it is not, as she justly complains, as if she took any interest in politics either. She has consulted every doctor in London, and they all tell her it is simply weakness, and she will outgrow it with care. Singular case—must find out (delicately) whether it's catching.

We ought to be starting soon; feel quite fresh and lively, in spite of having got up so early. Mention this to Captain. Wish he and the Public Prosecutor wouldn't stare at me so. Just as if there was something singular in my appearance!

They're embarking my portmanteau now. Knew they would have a lively time of it! It takes, at least, four sailors, in kilts, to manage it. Ought I to step ashore and quiet it down? Stay where I am. Don't know why, but feel a little afraid of it when it's like this. Shall exchange it for a quiet hand-bag when I get home.

Captain busy hammering at a hole in the funnel—dangerous place to spring a leak in—hope he is making it watertight. The hammering reminds me of that poor devil in the bedroom next to mine at the Hotel. *He* won't catch the boat now—he *can't!* My Aunt (who has left off looking like Mr. GLADSTONE) asks me why I am laughing. I tell her about that unfortunate man and his "thirty-five seconds." She screams with laughter. Very humorous woman, my Aunt.

Deck crowded with passengers now: all pointing and staring . . . at whom? Ask Aunt MARIA. She declines to tell me: says, severely, that, "If I don't know, I ought to."

Great Heavens! it's at *me* they're staring! And no wonder—in the hurry I was in, I must have packed *everything* up! . . . I've come away just as I was! *Now* I understand why someone offered me a necktie. Where shall I go and hide myself? Shall I ever persuade that beast of a portmanteau to give me out one or two things to put on—because I really *can't* go about like this! Captain still hammering at funnel—but he can't wake that sleepy-headed idiot in the next room. "Louder—knock *louder*, or the boat will go without him! Tell him there isn't another for two days. He's said good-bye to everybody he knows at Oban—he will look such an ass if he doesn't go, after all!" . . . Not the least use! Wonder what his name is. My Aunt says *she* knows, only she won't tell me—she'll whisper it, as a great secret. She is just about to disclose the name, which, somehow, I am extremely curious to know—when . . . .

Where am I? Haven't they got that unhappy fellow up *yet?* Why the dickens are they knocking at *my* door? I've been on board the steamer for hours, I tell you! Eh? *what?* Five minutes to eight! And the Gairloch boat? "Sailed at usual time—seven. Tried to make you hear—but couldn't." . . . . Confound it all! Good mind not to get up all day—now!

BARBARIANS AT PLAY.

*John Bull.* "PLAY FOOTBALL, BY ALL MEANS, MY BOY—BUT DON'T LET IT BE THIS BRUTAL SORT OF THING!"

## A NATIONAL GAME;

*Or, What it seems likely to be coming to.*

MIDLAND YAHOOS *v.* NORTH COUNTRY SAVAGES.

THESE two formidable and ferocious teams were both powerfully represented yesterday in the first match of the season that came off at the Subscription Grounds under the Thugby Association Rules, when, owing to their well-known deadly tactics, the afternoon's play was expected to be more than usually prolific in the fatalities and accidents now commonly considered inseparable from any well contested match, and the takings for gate-money were enormous. The Strangers had the kick off, and upon SMITH, for the Home team, securing the ball, and making a very pretty run with it down the centre, he encountered JONES, who, taking a well-timed and vigorous spring, mounted on his neck, when by an adroit twist, cracking his spine, he obliged him to relinquish it. The ball was then dribbled rapidly towards the Strangers' goal, where a spirited scrimmage ensuing, BROWN and ROBINSON, the half-backs, speedily had their thighs dislocated amidst a general breaking of arms and crackling of ribs.

Some brilliant combinations now followed on the part of the Home team. PARKINSON, who had already had his jaw broken, and a blood-vessel ruptured, being, however, obliged to use his hands, a proceeding which instantly brought JONES into his neighbourhood,

"A WORD IN SEASON," &c.

"NEVER MIND, MEASTER!—UP YE GETS AGEN. YOU WOR WERRY NIGH OFF *THAT* TIME!"

who, once more successfully repeating his famous leap, again cracked the spine, and left his second man dead upon the field. It being now only within a few minutes of the calling of time, and thirteen of the Home team being, more or less, seriously disabled, while only four of the Strangers were left to limp to their places, the Umpire decided that the game was over for the day, and the majority of the injured men were forthwith removed to the local Hospital from the ground on stretchers. A riot among the betting fraternity, who were attending the match in great numbers, that at one moment seriously threatened to imperil the peace of the locality, was eventually quelled by the Police.

## THROUGH AN IMPERIAL HORSE-COLLAR.

IT appears that during the German Emperor's visit to Naples a Newspaper Correspondent, disguised as a waiter (what would our own "ROBERT" say to such a freak?), was present at an Imperial luncheon. It seems that King HUMBERT was kept on the broad grin by the KAISER's witticisms and practical jokes. Amongst the latter was the admirable jest of preventing Prince HENRY of Prussia from seeing a passing torpedo-boat by pushing him back into his seat. This mirth-provoking *plaisanterie*, according to the journalistic *garçon*, caused His Majesty of Italy to explode with laughter. Fortunately for the world, a record of some of the other quaint conceits of WILLIAM THE SECOND has been preserved, from which the following short paragraphs are extracted:—

*A Rather Fishy Remark.*—Prince HENRY having cut his finger in attempting to eat peas with a carving-knife (after the German fashion) his Illustrious Brother thrust a couple of inches of sea-snake over the wounded part. "What have you done that for?" asked His Royal Highness. "I want to make it 'eel!'" was the witty reply. Count HERBERT VON BISMARCK (who was in attendance) yelled with merriment for more than an hour.

*Consommé-ate Wit.*—The King of ITALY was taking some soup, when by suddenly jogging His Majesty's arm the German Emperor caused some of the savoury liquid to trace a pattern upon the Royal shirtfront. "What did you do that for? Do you know what you have done?" inquired the Italian Monarch, rather hotly. "I owes the soup," replied the German Emperor, in excellent English. "I *soup owes!*" Count VON BISMARCK (who was in attendance) had to swallow a table-cloth to suppress smiling.

*Butter and Butter.*—Before leaving Naples the Emperor got up early, and, running to the apartments reserved for his Royal host, plastered the passage in their immediate neighbourhood with butter. The Crown Prince, slipping down, sprained his ankle, and smilingly declared that he did not like butter-slides so early in the morning. "I see," responded WILLIAM THE SECOND, "butter late than never!" Count VON BISMARCK (who was in attendance) commenced dancing a saraband to conceal his merriment.

*Grimaldi Outdone.*—At the Review at Rome the German Emperor rode rather a restive charger. His Majesty, being an indifferent horseman, was soon thrown into the midst of the Italian Royal Family, occupying a barouche. Immediately recovering his composure, he made a grimace, and exclaimed, using the Imperial Plural, "Here We are again!" Count VON BISMARCK (who was in attendance) stood upon his head, as a token of silent sympathy.

From the above it will be seen that, should it be considered advisable to produce a Pantomime in Berlin next Christmas, at the Imperial Court, there will be no difficulty in procuring a thoroughly efficient amateur Clown.

"SOLVITUR STEAMENDO."—Ten days ago Sir EDW-RD W-TK-N sailed for India in the P. & O. *Arcadia*. In Arcadia there is much to be learnt, and the Great Railway Arcadian is anxious, we hear, to ascertain by personal inspection how it happens that the Mails are carried distances up to 12,000 miles, and, such is the excessive punctuality, always delivered *before*, not after, time by the "P. & O., Weather or no" (as one of their own P. and Oets sings), with a view of applying the same system on the S. E. R. Yes, S. E. R. No more late trains!

A PROTEST.—Our "ROBERT" wishes it to be publicly known that his surname is not ELSMERE. "This HELSMERE," he writes, "is, as I ear, a clergyman, and I may ave bin mistook for im, on account of simmerlarrity of kostoom, wich is a kumplerment to the revvrunt gent in henny case."

MR. J. L. T-LE, LORD R. G-W-R, LORD MAYOR TORPEDO (ELECT), AND MR. OSC-R W-L-DE, ADOPT THE NEW STYLE, AND LEAD THE FASHION ON NOV. 5TH.

"MEN'S DRESS.—If it be true, as announced, that men are going to wear embroidered trousers this season, the first step will be taken towards a further embellishment of masculine attire."—*Daily News.*

## A PLAYGOER'S PROTEST.

DEAR MR. PUNCH,

I am nobody,—not even a Critic. Still less am I a dramatist or a librettist. I am simply a playgoer, and a reader of criticisms upon plays. And there are some matters concerning both the plays and the criticisms which puzzle me exceedingly.

So far as I can gather, certain Critics seem to have two ways of dealing with a man who has made a shining, and especially a sudden, success. The one is to "slate" him with unmeasured maliciousness, the other to beslaver him with indiscriminate praise. It is rather difficult to decide which is the more offensive, the splenetic slaughtering, or the fulsome gush.

I am a lover of all sorts and conditions of music, "from gay to grave, from lively to severe," I may almost say from the sublime to the ridiculous. I am also a great admirer of Mr. GILBERT'S peculiar humour, especially when it is wedded to Sir ARTHUR SULLIVAN'S music. You may imagine, therefore, that I anticipate with immense pleasure the production of a new piece at the Savoy. I do not go to First Nights, but I eagerly scan the Press notices of the new piece, with a view of tasting, as it were, in advance the quintessential flavour of the treat in store for me. And if I can obtain a copy of the Opera before seeing the performance itself, I do so, and read it carefully.

Of course, therefore, I promptly perused the Press Criticisms of the *Yeomen of the Guard.* What a promising consensus of praise! GILBERT at his best, SULLIVAN better than ever! The music was almost bound to be good; in the libretto I should have expected a choice literary banquet,—if the admiring Critics had not made the mistake of quoting. Then—well, then, I began to have my doubts.

One Critic in a Sunday paper, for instance, was generally laudatory. Coming to particulars, he quoted with approbation the lines:—

> "The rose's sigh
> Were *as a carrion's cry*
> To lullaby
> Such as I'd sing to thee,
> Were I thy bride!"

If this is not nonsense, I am a Dutchman. But I am not a Dutchman. It *may* be that Mr. GILBERT here is the victim of a printer's error. But the Critic praised the lines *as they are printed!*

Another Critic, in a weekly review, quoted in brackets the words "*she* be," as though they constituted a marvellously original and humorous rhyme to "PHŒBE." He might almost as well have praised the novel coupling of "love" and "dove," or the selection (by a post-Ingoldsby poet) of "Greenwich" as perfectly antiphonetic to "spinach." A third congratulates Sir ARTHUR on his good fortune in having such lyrics as these to set to music. Such lyrics as *these?* Here be specimens:—

> "Here's a man of jollity,
> Gibe, joke, jollify!
> Give us of your quality
> Come fool, follify!
>
> "River none can mollify;—
> Into it we throw
> Fool who doesn't follify,
> Cock who doesn't crow!"

If this be not the merest doggerel with rhymes as forced as they are feeble, what in the name of metre gone mad *is* it?

Again:—

> "*1st Yeoman.* Did'st thou not, oh, LEONARD MERYLL!
> Standard lost in last campaign,
> Rescue it at deadly peril—
> Bear it bravely back again?
> *Chorus*—LEONARD MERYLL, at his peril
> Bore it bravely back again!"

Is this so *very* much above the level of the celebrated "eagle" who "played with" (and attempted to rhyme to) "the sea-gull!" Is it anything like as good as the old nursery jingle—

> "There was a little girl
> Who had a little curl
> Which hung down the middle of her forehead,
> And when she was good
> She was very, very good;
> But when she was bad, she was horrid!"

Mr. GILBERT as a lyrist is not altogether unlike that illustrious young lady. At any rate, when he is good—as in most of the *Bab Ballads* and many of his Operas—he is *very, very* good. Like his own *Point,* he has "a pretty wit," but in this piece at least seems very chary of exercising it. He doubtless *can* "jest you, jibe you, quip you, crank you," only he *doesn't;* though he *does* "wrack you" with bad verse, and "riddle you" with forced rhymes, *e.g.*:—

> "Joyful, joyful!
> When virginity
> Seeks, all *coyful*
> Man's affinity;
>
> "Fate all flowery
> Bright and bowery
> Is her dowery!
> Joyful, joyful!"

But, after all, it is not Mr. GILBERT whom I, as a playgoer, have to pick a bone with, but his fulsome "Critics." Mr. GILBERT must, long ago, have cynically laughed in his jester's sleeve at these adulatory notices of his work. One can imagine what a brilliantly bitter *Bab Ballad* he could make of it all.

The work, we were told in advance, with a considerable flourish of critical trumpets, was to be "a new departure." It is certainly a departure from the land of Topsy-turvy wherein GILBERT and SULLIVAN have so long disported themselves, and wherein they worked so harmoniously, and with so much success. But what is it? Serio-comic romantic Opera? Possibly. But if so, the "departure" cannot appropriately be called "new." I agree with your "JACK IN THE BOX" that, had any other writer announced the libretto as "new and original," the Critics to a man would have been down upon him for filching the essence of *Maritana.* As it was, they very mildly accused, profusely excused, and extravagantly "enthused." However, we are transferred from imaginary Topsy-turvydom to the historical Tudor period. There is not very much of the Tudor style about the dialogue; there is even less about the lyrics:—

> "Tower warders
> Under orders
> Gallant pikemen, valiant swordors!
> Brave in bearing
> Foemen scaring
> In their bygone deeds of daring,
>
> "Ne'er a stranger
> There to danger—
> Each was o'er the world a ranger:
> To the story
> Of our glory
> Each a bold contributory!"

Somehow this does not smack *very* strongly of the days of bluff King HAL, does it? That, perhaps, would not much matter, were it flowing or funny; but it isn't.

Enough. I have not yet seen the piece. I have no doubt that when I do, I shall enjoy the music and be pleased with the *ensemble.* But dealing with the libretto as a production for which the Critics have claimed considerable literary merit, what *is* one to think—of the Critics? Yours, &c. PLAYGOER.

MAGIC AND MYSTERY.—The following extraordinary circumstance is vouched for by several eye-witnesses of unimpeachable veracity. A tall man of respectable exterior, with a pale face, dark moustache, and a peculiarly saturnine cast of countenance, was observed walking down a street leading out of the Strand. For obvious reasons we suppress the name of the street pending further inquiry. Stopping for a minute in close proximity to a lamp-post, he plunged both hands into his trousers' pockets. A sudden gleam was seen to illuminate his countenance; he was heard to mutter some words, which were probably cabalistic, and then *suddenly turned into a public-house!* The Psychological Society has been communicated with, and M. B. DE KOLTA, the inventor of the Vanishing Lady and the Pavilion Cocoon, has undertaken to find out how this marvellously rapid and complete transformation was effected. AUGUSTUS DRURIOLANUS hopes to purchase the patent for his Christmas Pantomime.

UP AND DOWN.—The *Times* calls public attention to the fact that Land which is "going down" in England is "going up" in Australia. Well, there *are* places in the world where Land seems to be continually "going up," such as Japan and other volcanic districts; but whether many speculators would be eager to invest in the consequent "ground rents" is another question.

# Captain Gleadall, of the "White Star" Line.

## IN MEMORIAM.

"Many an old voyager across the herring-pond will be sorry to hear of the awfully sudden death of that staunch veteran shipmaster, Captain GLEADALL, of the 'White Star' Line, who for ten years had the *Celtic*, and later commanded that favourite ship the *Germanic*. Captain GLEADALL died at the post of duty: he was found seated in the *Germanic's* chart-room when the ship was running through a fog, his face prone on the open chart he had been studying when the life had suddenly gone out of him. During his long and worthy sailor life he had rescued a great number of lives, and had received recognitions of his courage and humanity from almost every maritime nation of Europe and America."—*The World, Oct.* 23, 1888.

SUDDEN, yet splendid too! What fitter end
Can fancy fashion for the brave old tar,
All his long life with wind and wave at war,
The Ocean-crosser's trusty guide and friend,
Keen-eyed to mark, stout-hearted to contend,
With every danger of the treacherous deep?
So might we all, who life's long watch must keep,
Fronting its perils our last moments spend:
Like gallant GLEADALL, playing well our part
To the last pulse within, not of our fate
But of the great ship's course considerate;
Humanity's loyal servants, high of heart,
Content the great dismissal to await,
And fall at last—face forward on the chart!

## PLAY-TIME WITH FRENCH ROYALTY.

ON Thursday last I went to see *Le Fils de Famille*, in order to compare M. LAFONTAINE as the *Abbé Constantin* with Mr. LAFONTAINE as *Alphonse Deshayes*, Colonel of a regiment of Lancers. He does not appear till the Second Act, and then he comes *en bourgeois* to a ball. Not a trace of the kindly genial simple old Abbé about this stiff-backed elderly martinet, who is every inch a soldier, and whose bearing is that of a man who has risen from the ranks, and who is nothing if not a soldier. I may be wrong in supposing that he has risen from the ranks, but certainly his comparatively uneasy bearing in "Society," his awkward compromise between a gracious bow and a short, sharp, military nod, and his hearty grasp of the hand when he wishes to express his cordial agreement with *M. François*, the Artist, gave me this impression; and the sentiments the authors have put into his mouth concerning the well-born prodigals, "*ces enfants mal élevés*," who put on a uniform as a disguise, and then wish to take it off again as though it were *un costume de Carnaval*, confirm me in my view of the character.

Dean's Treat, Soho.

In this Second Act M. LAFONTAINE is perfect; with the exception of exaggerating and repeating the business of his characteristic bow, merely for the sake of obtaining a laugh from the feather-headed.

In the Third Act M. LAFONTAINE, with great judgment, shows the old soldier quite at home in undress and in full uniform. The awkwardness has entirely disappeared, not a trace of his forced "society manner" exists, and here and there we get a hint of that natural kindliness common to the good hearts of the Colonel and the Curé. Occasionally a mannerism of utterance reminded me of the Abbé, but it was only a momentary family resemblance, which I was on the look-out to detect. I hope, before his departure, that on one night he will give us an Act of *L'Abbé Constantin*, followed by the Second Act of *Le Fils de Famille*.

Mlle. JANE MAY is lacking in the quality of earnestness that alone could make the girl's part interesting. She seems to consider *Emmeline* as a heroine of Opéra-Comique, and that the authors themselves have not got much beyond this I am not prepared to deny, but it is just one of those parts that the pathetic power of an actress should lift above itself. M. SCHEY gives a broadly humorous sketch of a French *maréchal de logis*. He is rather inclined to exaggerate, as if he were playing *Valentine* in *Le Petit Faust*, but there is true low comedy in his impersonation of the type.

In M. LAFONTAINE's impersonations of the Abbé and the Colonel is to be seen a very near approach to the perfection of the comedian's art: and on the same stage may be also seen glaring examples of the worst fault of the French school of acting, viz., the actor insisting on points by addressing his speeches point-blank at the audience.

Now that M. SCHEY has arrived, couldn't we have *Tricoche et Cacolet* again? CHAUMONT and NOBLET are coming with *Divorçons*. *En attendant*, M. LAFONTAINE is announced to appear in *Le Gentilhomme Pauvre*. It ought to be a very fine performance.

JEAN DANS LE LOGE.

## OUR BOOKING-OFFICE.

PUBLISHED by WHITTAKER & Co., with two "t's,"—not that benefactor of society, WHITAKER, the Almanack Maker and universal intelligence provider,—is a small volume, well got up and clearly printed, of the selected poems and songs of CHARLES MACKAY, "the British Béranger," as DOUGLAS JERROLD styled him. It was only lately that some one was recalling to the public mind, in aid of a MACKAY Fund, that JERROLD'S "B. B." is the author of "*Cheer, Boys, Cheer!*" "*There's a Good Time coming, Boys!*" "*To the West!*" "*Far, far upon the Sea!*" which were all associated with the name of HENRY RUSSELL, whose music gave them an immense popularity. Unfortunately, Mr. Words goes for very little where Mr. Music steps in, and Mr. Music gets all the credit which should be divided between Messrs. Words and Music. Certainly this class of songs would not have obtained their success without such music as HENRY RUSSELL composed for them. And then the Composer, who was a capital entertainer and pianist, sang them himself, with no voice to speak of, but, all the same, most heartily, and with great dramatic skill. But CHARLES MACKAY has written songs that require no singing to recommend them, and ballads that suggest their own music; as for instance, "*Geraldine*," "*The Angel and the Mourners*," "*The Wayside Spring*," "*The Dream of the Reveller*," "*The Fair Serpent*," "*I Love my Love*," "*I lay in Sorrow*," which doesn't seem a very good stock to "lay in,"—but read the two verses. Get the book. He is not a TENNYSON nor a BROWNING; it is all simple versification; nothing abstruse, subtle, or obscure; yet plenty of food for thought, and much that will "catch on" and be remembered, says the BARON DE BOOK WORMS.

Based on solid principles.

## A CIGAR CASE.

"Miss MAGGIE LOCKHEAD WATSON brought an action for £500 against Mr. WILLIAM KIRKLAND, because he failed to marry her. KIRKLAND, who was a smoker, received a letter from his sweetheart, the plaintiff, in which she stated, 'You must choose between me and a cigar.' He selected a cigar instead of Miss WATSON, and hence the action. The Sheriff Substitute decided in KIRKLAND's favour, and yesterday the Sheriff Principal upheld that judgment."—*Daily News.*

DON'T you consider, sweet Miss MAGGIE LOCKHEAD
WATSON, that some one showed himself a blockhead
For choosing thus? If this be true we read,
It must have been a choice cigar indeed;
And the cigar, now, was it new and green
And soft? Was it Imperial or Queen?
For if it was all these, then he won't thank
His lucky stars, for "his offence was rank."
Did it look light, seductive to the lip,
Or was it very rich, with a fine tip?
So, was it rank or wealth that this choice weed
Embodied? Well, the parties are both freed.
Let 's trust that this Cigar no heart hath broke,
Not new that sanguine hopes should end in smoke.

WHISPER FROM THE GAIETY.—"In the time of CHARLES THE SECOND," wrote a *D. T.* leader on Dress last Saturday, "it was a disgrace for a man of fashion to wear a suit too long." Observed S-MS to P-TT-TT, in the absence of their tyrannical Stage Manager, "It isn't considered a digrace in the time of CHARLES THE THIRD for burlesque actresses to wear a suit too short." "Hush!" said his partner, "he comes! We must dissemble!" [*They dissemble accordingly.*

PRO BOHNO PUBLICO.—Our friend BORROWDALE, whose library is composed exclusively of books which have been lent to him at various times during his long and honourable career, humorously calls them "Bone's Editions."

THE Duke of WESTMINSTER, one of London's greatest landlords, is now created a tenant, in fact the only Lord Left Tenant of the County of London, by the Local Government Act.

**SOCIAL AGONIES.**

*(Exit awful Bore, after protracted Visit.)*

"OH, WILLIAM! HOW *UNGENIALLY* YOU SAID 'HOW D'Y DO?' TO POOR PROFESSOR BLOKER!"
"YES, INDEED, PAPA! AND OH, HOW EFFUSIVELY YOU BADE HIM *GOOD-BYE!*"

## THE MENACING MONSTER.

*A Dream of the Day After To-morrow.*

"The formation of the great Association for a monopoly in salt is likely to have imitators, and it is now said that the formation of a gigantic monopoly in coal, with a capital of eighty millions, is under consideration. This will probably be followed by similar combinations to control iron, cotton, woollen, and other manufactures. Hitherto it has been fondly believed that the growth and progress of English trade was chiefly due to a wholesome competition. . . . All this, it seems, is to come to an end, and the American system of monopolies is to take the place of the English system of competition."—*Standard.*

THE Day of Big Things was approaching its noon;—
(Its dawn had first glimmered across the Atlantic)—
Each trade had swelled out like a Monster Balloon,
And nothing was noticed that was not Gigantic,
Things seemed to hark back to the morning of time,
When Monsters and Mud were Creation's chief features.
When sixty-foot saurians revelled in slime,
With Mastodons, Mammoths, and other huge creatures.
The Mammoth, indeed, seemed the type of the age,
Which was ruled by the love of the simply colossal.
To have a Big Boom was the general rage,
And every man's dream was to "run" or to "boss" all.
There *were* some who were silly enough to inquire
The probable goal of this curious tendency;
But most were contented to share—or admire—
The Day of Big Things in its blazing resplendency.
And as for the Small Things—*they* went to the wall,
For people or plans not extremely Titanic
Were calmly considered "not in it at all,"
And snubbed with a scorn which was ultra-Germanic.

Ah me, the Big Booms! That got bigger each day,
The monopolist "Rings," like the circles in water,
Grew wider, and swallowed up all in their way,
Of shops and small firms there was general slaughter.
The millions of Naboths had never a chance,
Against the few Ahabs, whose numbers still dwindled;
The "Trusts" piped the tune, and the victims must dance;
They had nothing to do but to stare and be swindled.
*That* was not the word that was used, to be sure,
To prig on so spanking a scale is *not* prigging,
But—well, say "financing" with motives quite pure,
Or controlling the market by ringing or rigging.
Conspiracy? Nay, *that* is not quite the word
That only applies to malign combinations
Against—well, say Rent,—which are wrong and absurd;
But to keep up high prices by smart "operations"
In salt or in iron, in coal or in wool,
Is plainly legitimate pulling together.
For who would protest, save a poor well-plucked fool,
Against the snug flocking of birds of a feather?

"Strikes? Well, they were rascally ruinous things,
For they kept down fortunes by keeping up wages.
'Twixt Labour's Trade Unions and Capital's Rings
The fight was prolonged, but no longer it rages."
So chuckled Monopoly, cock of the walk
Once more on the death of that plague, Competition.
The new Mammoth, Mammon, with saurian stalk,
The Colossus of Cash in plethoric condition,
Like dragons primeval, were lords of the time;
They battened and browsed on the best: as to others,
For them 'twas enough to be trampled to slime,
In poverty equal, in death only brothers.

O glorious epoch! O outcome divine
Of that Spirit of Trade which sublimes our humanity!
Its heaven the Market; the Loom and the Mine
Its ladders to opulence; all else is vanity.
To paddle one's own poor canoe might seem fun
In Trade's earlier days of competitive rivalry.
But oh! when the Many give place to the One,
Competition must go, like good-feeling and chivalry.

THE OCTOPUS OF "MONOPOLY."

Monopoly was not content very long
  With sharing its millions in narrow community
Between the mere few who were clever and strong,
  Its natural issue was *Absolute Unity*.
The One at the top, and the Many below!—
  That must be the Monster's ideal, the goal of it.
To get the World's trade in one "Ring" at a blow,
  With one bloated Moloch of cash in control of it,
That, that was the notion, and that was the aim;
  But just as that "Trust" comprehensive, colossal,
Was reared, Mammon's victims grew tired of his game,
  And Demos with Dives played mad pitch-and-toss all.

A dream! Ah, perhaps; but some visions unveil
  A meaning from wide-awake vigilance hidden.
The Day of Big Things means a scourge and a flail
  For the myriad small ones to Life's banquet bidden.
The Epoch of Monsters once more to revive,
  In Creation or Commerce, is sheer retrogression.
The Thunderer would rule, and the Titans would strive,
  But freedom and peace are poor man's best possession.
"These Little Ones" also have places and claims.
  The many-armed Monster, Monopoly, subtle
Of motion as greedy of maw, has the aims
  Of the cruel, all-grabbing, all-palsying Cuttle.
Beware of it, Trade! 'Tis a creature to dread,
  To fight to the death, as St. George did the dragon.
Call Law to your aid—let her strike *at its head*—
  And the menacing Monster will drop dead as Dagon!

## GOOD DAY'S WORK.

DEAR MR. PUNCH.—It is stated that "in view of the serious dangers that attend upon even a temporary stoppage of a great artery of traffic in London, the Corporation are considering the expediency of carrying on the forthcoming repairs of Blackfriars Bridge, not only night and day, but on Sunday, as well as week day." As yet, however, they have not therefore been charged, by agitators for the enforcement of the observance of Sunday as a Judaic Sabbath, with proposing to employ me as an instrument wherewithal to deprive the working classes of their day of rest. Now then, I suppose, it will no longer be pretended that I am designed to serve that purpose in the hands of good people allied to promote the opening of Museums and Picture Galleries on Sundays, and consequently, in time past, accused of trying to insert the thin end of your ancient friend THE WEDGE.

"SO ENGLISH, YOU KNOW!"

*Anatole.* "TIENS! BONJOUR, ISIDOR! YOU SPICK ENGLEESH? BIEN! I GO TO PLAY AT ZE FOOTBALL-TENNIS-CRICKETTS? COME YOU?"

*Isidor.* "NOT AT PRESENT. BUT I VILL GO TO FIND YOU VEN I SHALL 'AV PASSED AT ZE BUREAU TO PAY MY INCOMESTAXES!"

## AN ARM FROM THE ARMADA.

(*Fragment from a Romance of* 15 + 18 + 88.)

IT matters not how I came to be living three hundred years after the great fight off Plymouth Hoe. That is my affair, and no one else's. Suffice it to say that I came up by a train, and took an omnibus to Catherine Street, and entered the National Theatre, where I found Mr. AUGUSTUS HARRIS, surrounded by a number of articles I immediately recognised as relics of the battle in which I had taken part in 1588. I remember the day perfectly. Sir FRANCIS DRAKE, Sir MARTIN FROBISHER, Lord HOWARD of Effingham, a few others, and myself, were aboard the *Capitana*—no, we took *that* during the action, so I think it must have been the *Lively Polly*. Yes, now I call it to mind, it *was* the *Lively Polly*. And yet, on referring to a Catalogue furnished by the courteous Lessee of Drury Lane, I am not at all sure but it was the *Ark Raleigh*, or the *Ark Royal*. I have all the greater confidence in the latter suggestion, as I see that that capital vessel was the flag-ship of the British Fleet.

"Have a pinch of snuff, TOMMY?" said DRAKE (he always called me TOMMY, although my real name was MARMADUKE)—"have a pinch of snuff?"

And then good old FRANCO—(I always called Sir FRANCIS "FRANCO," because we had been at school together)—produced a Horn Tobacco Box.

I mentioned this to one of the erudite assistants of the joint-author of *The Armada*.

"We have the very identical box here," replied the assistant. "It is No. 247 in the Catalogue, and bears the name and arms of Sir FRANCIS DRAKE."

And to be sure there it was! Then I came upon a chair which I immediately recognised as one that used to stand in the study of Sir WALTER RALEIGH. He used to invite me to occupy it while reading his *History of the World* to me.

"What is No. 318?" I asked, with some curiosity.

"That," returned my courteous informant, "is a Spanish torture chair. You will observe here is a steel waistband for fixing the octagonal stake with various screws. Here is a double manacle with triangular padlock. Yonder a gag with rack action for opening mouth, grasping and drawing out tongue. There a steel dilator for lower part of body. Here——"

"Oh! yes," I interrupted; "I know the whole bag of tricks. Dear old WALLY used to say that he was obliged to apply them all to keep me from falling asleep."

"It is, we fancy, nearly a hundred years later than the date of the Armada," continued my guide; "but it shows, to quote the Catalogue, 'what would have occurred in nearly every English town *if the Armada had been successful*.'"

"There," I replied, "I think you are wrong. My friend, Sir WALTER RALEIGH, told me that it was given to him by a Spaniard—he was called Don QUAY—in return for a pouch of tobacco. But still it is a most interesting relic."

Then I saw a large number of helmets, swords, pictures, seals, and engravings that I quite remember noticing during the pauses of the glorious combat. I was particularly struck with an etching reproduction of "the Armada in sight," by SEYMOUR LUCAS, R.A.

"Most lifelike," I observed. "I recognise FENTON, and ST. LEGER, SOUTHWELL and MANNINGTON, GEORGE JENNER, COOK, and, of course, dear old DICK HAWKINS."

"Were you there?" asked a bystander.

"Was I there!" I exclaimed, indignantly. "Of course I was, and got a seat for Mr. SEYMOUR LUCAS, who was painting it. The original was sent, shortly afterwards, to Australia."

At this moment a theatre-loving descendant of my dear old friend, Sir MARTIN FROBISHER, seized me by the arm, and with him I hurried off to see the admirable spectacular Drama that through the kindness of Messrs. HAMILTON and HARRIS, had been provided for our delectation. And thus, seated in the Stalls, I fought my battle over again.

(*Signed*) A SURVIVOR OF THE SPANISH ARMADA.

TRANSLATION OF "EQUINOX."—A Night-Mare.

"THAT NASTY ORANGE-PEEL!"

*Gallant Old Gentleman (rushing to her assistance).* "I'M AFRAID, MA'AM, YOU'VE HAD A FALL—I HOPE——"
*Short-tempered Old Lady (snappishly).* "WHY, YOU DON'T S'PPOSE I'D SIT DOWN HERE, YOU OLD STUP——!"
[*He helps her up, and makes off hastily.*

## A NEW "SPEAKER'S COMMENTARY."

(*Intended as a few hints to budding Orators, in addition to the very excellent advice which Mr. Bright has recently given them.*)

DON'T let your audience know what is coming next. Cultivate the art of oratorical surprises. Should your hearers also cultivate surprises, and welcome you with an outburst of hisses, allude playfully to the geese that once saved the Capitol. This *may* disarm hostility. It may also do the reverse.

If any member of your audience should be so ill-mannered or so destitute of appreciation as to go away in the middle of your oration, remember that this invariably happens to the best speakers in the House of Commons. Try and wither the offender with a glance. This requires practice. Should this fail, you might put your audience in a good temper by inquiring, "Why is our friend who is leaving like a barn-door fowl? Because he is looking for an egg-sit." This will direct amused attention to the out-goer, and make others less willing to follow his example.

N. B.—At the end of the meeting, leave, if possible, by a side-door. People have been known to resent humour of the above description.

If you cannot comfortably accommodate all the leading points of your speech on your shirt-cuff, pin them (on a piece of paper) to your handkerchief, which you can occasionally dangle before your face in a graceful and unpremeditated manner.

Make friends with the Reporters. An amiable Reporter explains away a multitude of brickbats.

When interrupted, never lose your own temper—or you may find somebody else's!

When working up to a joke, it will be advisable to wreathe your face beforehand with a seductive smile. Practise well before a looking-glass.

Though argument is popularly supposed to have something to do with proof, recollect that certain people are quite proof against argument. Humour them. Appeal to their feelings, not their heads. Try the "Three B's"—blarney, blather, and bunkum.

People who don't see a joke always think there is something profane in it. Don't be too witty. This is a fault which you will probably find no difficulty in avoiding.

Perhaps the very best way to "bring down the house," is to bring down a lot of particular friends who will "make a house" for you.

---

"SLATIN BEY."—The *Times* Correspondent, writing from Vienna, reported last week that "SLATIN BEY asks his friends to send him a few newspapers." We are glad to be able to announce, in the interests of the higher criticism in Art, Literature, and the Drama, that SLATIN BEY is coming over to England, and has been engaged as Literary and Dramatic Critic on *Mr. Punch's* Staff. All those who have anything to fear from SLATIN,—look out!

---

SOME impulsive Americans wanted his title to be changed to "Lord Get-the-Sackville."

## A SPORTSMAN'S SONG.

*Arranged for the Suburban Deer-Stalker.*

SING ho! for the bang of the Verderer's gun,
As from his third-class stepping,
He starts for his annual bit of fun
In the sylvan glades of Epping.
He isn't a very good shot, is he:
But his aim is wild and his range is free,
And, whether he hit or miss his mark,
He knows that he is out for a lark.
So ho! sing ho! for the Verderer's sport,
At Epping he'll show you the proper sort.
Give him his gun, and he'll blaze away,
Nor care a rap what the public say.

Sing ho! for the Verderer's random shot
As he sees the herd advancing,
And he takes his sight and covers the lot,
The risk of a bad one chancing.
So ho! but the Verderer has his luck,
For he breaks the leg of a harmless buck,
That limps away with its shatter'd bone
To linger for days, then die alone.
So ho! Sing ho! for his glorious sport,
At Epping he'll show you the right good sort;
And will—till the Public shall have their say,
And he and his gun both get blazed away!

---

ATHLETIC SPORTS IN INDIA.—Lord COLIN CAMPBELL has gone out to practise at the bar in Bombay. Capital exercise.

---

"YOU'RE having a high old time of it," as the Currant-jelly said to the Venison, which had been hanging for three weeks.

## OUR JAPANNERIES. No. 20.

## PARNELL COMMISSION.

*(Special Report.)*

[Yesterday the Commission of Judges resumed their sittings in the Parnell Case. The Judges were Sir JAMES HANNEN, Mr. Justice DAY, and Mr. Justice SMITH. For the *Times* there appeared the ATTORNEY-GENERAL, Sir HENRY JAMES, Mr. W. MURPHY, Mr. W. GRAHAM, of the English Bar, and Mr. J. ATKINSON and Mr. RONAN of the Irish Bar. For Mr. PARNELL and other Members Sir CHARLES RUSSELL appeared, and with him Mr. ASQUITH, Mr. REID, Mr. LOCKWOOD, Mr. LIONEL HART, Mr. ARTHUR RUSSELL, of the English Bar, Mr. ARTHUR O'CONNOR and Mr. HARRINGTON of the Irish Bar. TOBY, M.P., Q.C., instructed by Mr. GEORGE LEWIS (of Ely Place, Holborn, W.C.), again held a watching brief for the Public.—*Morning Paper.*]

*Monday, October 22.*—Cut this out of morning paper. Plenty more where it came from. If the Editor liked to have it all, and leave out pictures, would make quite interesting series of numbers. Suppose there would be objections on part of artists. Some people are so narrow-minded. So have boiled down account of proceedings. Observed considerable addition to strength of Bar. On opening day only CHARLES RUSSELL and ASQUITH on one side, GRAHAM on the other. Now two benches full of wig and gown. Room for us of the Inner Bar, but terrible crush behind.

"All on account of you," GEORGE LEWIS whispers. "Very well to begin with. But when they saw you were engaged, found it necessary to muster in larger force."

Pleasant to have one's position so early and strikingly recognised. Must keep up dignity. Shall begin with Usher. If he interrupts again, shall have him *mandamus'd.*

Eleven o'clock. Curtain rises; discloses Judges standing in doorways like three figures in weather-box, which tell you whether it's going to be wet or shine. Bar rises and bows. Three figures bob, advance a step, and take seats. (Evidently going to be either wet or shine.) Attorney-General opens case for prosecution. Goes back to prodigious speech delivered by him in case of *O'Donnell* v. *Walter*. Quotes whole batches of it. Remember how Coleridge, L.C.J., softly slumbered through it. Our President wide awake. Smith quietly observant. Day beginning to get over novelty of situation; gives up staring stonily round; makes occasional note. President begins with old protest about knowing nothing. Fancy he's heard the name of Parnell and Davitt—or is it Dayvit? Something in the City, aren't they? Attorney-General, therefore, bound to go into full detail. Grinds along till one o'clock, when President capitulates: falteringly admits that he has not only read the whole of *Parnellism and Crime*, but has a minute index.

"Why didn't he say so at first?" growled familiar voice from back of Court. It was Joseph Gillis, and in female society! Stout lady, in black, with large hat and plumage borrowed from a hearse, seated in Press Gallery; said to be representative of *Wandering Woman*, weekly illustrated. Joseph's eagle eye, surveying Court, perceived her. Sidled up, appropriating next seat. Happened to be that of representative of *Potsdam Press*, temporarily absent. *Potsdam Press* returning, protests. Joseph Gillis ignores him. Comfortable seat; female society; good view of Judges; will stop. Does.

"Remember Mitchelstown?" says Joseph, winking at me.

"Remember Paris!" I say, sternly, not relishing this familiarity. Joey B. smiles. But the shot goes home. Observe that, after luncheon, he finds quarters remote from the charmer.

*Tuesday.*—Joseph Gillis arrives, brisk, and early. Proposes to take his seat on benches reserved for us. Usher interposes. Warns him off. Usher not such a bad fellow, after all. Joey B. then drops into bench reserved for Solicitors in charge of cases. Something evidently up. Turns out to be Joey B. himself. Thrusts thumb in arm-hole of waistcoat. Holds out left hand, peremptorily signalling President. Catches his eye. Calls him "Sir," and announces that he is going to conduct his own case. President stares inquisitively at him. Smith regards him with bland smile. Day, withdrawing gaze from ceiling, where he was almost certain he'd seen a fly, turns animated visage full upon Joseph Gillis. Never saw anything like this before. Eyes widely open; lips slowly part; regards him as if fascinated. Joey B. takes no notice of sensation created; makes his application as if moving for unopposed return, and sits down to listen to Attorney-General.

Mr. Attorney paces along by the hour. Monotonous; uninteresting; stale stories of ancient outrage; "thrice-boiled colewort," as Carlyle said. Flounders hopelessly amongst Irish names. Calls Davitt, Dayvit, and Parnell, Parnell. Charles Russell diligently follows, taking notes.

"What date is it?" he casually asks. The Attorney-General turns round and glares upon the benevolent downcast visage.

"I was careful at the commencement to mention the date," he hisses through clenched teeth, "if my learned friend would only listen. Tenth of March!"

"Ah!" says Charles Russell, going on writing. Attorney-General discovers fresh outrage.

"What date?" Russell asks, in a low voice, going on writing, and not looking up. Mr. Attorney turns upon him like baited bull; glares and fumes and gives date.

"Ah!" says Charles Russell, writing it down. These the only flashes of thunder and lightning to vary the monotonous peppering on the window-panes of the Attorney-General's incessant small talk.

*Wednesday.*—Not sure I would have taken silk if I had known how dull it is to sit here day by day and listen to Mr. Attorney. Much livelier in the House of Commons. Always something turning up there. Nothing here but Attorney-General, humdrumming round familiar facts, reciting *Parnellism and Crime* by the page, and, when things getting too exciting, dropping back into memories of his speech in *Walter* v. *O'Donnell*. Wonderful how Judges on Bench keep awake. Perhaps they wouldn't if President would only give way. Pretty to see Brother Smith furtively turning to see if Brother Hannen has dropped off. If he had, might be chance for another honest person. But Brother Hannen positively enjoying himself. Leans over desk so as not to miss single phrase of Mr. Attorney's honeyed eloquence. Mr. Attorney, what with difficulties about pronunciation of Irish names, and what with constant occasion for snapping at Charles Russell, sometimes gets wrong in date or other detail of intricate statement. Hannen down on him in a minute.

"He may have known nothing about the case when he took his seat on the Bench," says Lockwood, just finishing another sketch of Brother Day, "but he knows more now than us all put together. Probably the only man in Court who could stand examination on Webster's narrative."

As the days wear on, our Day takes on added stolidity. Only time when he displays momentary animation is when he, too, turns to see if Brother Hannen has not dropped off, and meets his particularly wide-awake gaze. Torquemada's guilty start when he finds he's observed is delightful. Stares straight up at the ceiling, slowly gazes round the Court, deliberately makes a note, and says nothing. Never does say anything.

"What do they call him Talkee-meeda for?" Joseph Gillis whispered to Michael Davitt.

"Don't know," said Davitt, "unless it's because he never says anything."

*Thursday.*—"Box A!" said Brother Hannen, entering Court this morning, and plumping down on desk before him large tin box.

"Box B!" chimed in Brother Smith, plumping down another box on his desk.

"I C," said Brother Day, gloomily—and when we have a gloomy Day, it's dark indeed.

"Poor Day!" said Attorney-General, who, in spite of this fearful long speech inflicted upon us, is a kind-hearted man. "Must try and make up a box for him!"

"You could easily do that," said Charles Russell, dryly.

One of these two boxes contains the documents whose history is told in Soames's affidavit. Appears some person from America wrote to *Times* offering important documents incriminating Parnell; negotiations for purchase entered into; documents delivered; found

Wednesday's Sensation.—Lika Joko appears.

to be forgeries; so put them in two boxes, one marked A, the other B; locked them up and handed them into custody of Judges. Attorney-General more than hints that that great and good man, George Lewis, knows all about the plant. George Lewis, ever childlike and bland, looks straight before him as if he had not even heard the insinuation.

Judges never let boxes out of sight. Sleep with them under their pillows at night. Bring them into Court in the morning, take them away in afternoon. Nobody knows whether forgeries are in Box A or Box B, which deepens the mystery.

"What *is* in the Box?" Charles Russell thundered yesterday when subject first came up.

"Snuff!" said Attorney-General, snapping his fingers.

It is his way when angered. But Charles Russell gazed longingly at the Box, and drawing forth his Bandana, wistfully blew his nose.

What if it were true, and if, almost within reach, there were such boundless store of Black Rappee!

*Friday.*—At seven minutes past three this afternoon Attorney-General breathed his last sentence in Speech. Affecting scene. Sorry, after all, to part with Speech. Lived on it through a melancholy week. But self-preservation a powerful instinct. Another day of it and one of us must have succumbed. Just as well it should be the Speech.

Peacefully passed away in the still afternoon, aged twenty-two hours fifty-seven minutes. Omit flowers.

---

Belief in General Boulanger.—Hasty generalisation.

"LE SPORTMAN."

"HI!! HI!! STOP ZE CHASSE! I TOMBLE—I FALOFF! *STOP ZE FOX!!!*"

## AN EXPLANATION OF THE COCOON TRICK.

(*By One who has passed a Night with the Spirits.*)

I HAD determined to find out "how it was done." I had seen the placards showing me a lady with wings emerging from what seemed to me to be the skeleton of an egg cup, and I knew that this marvellous performance was repeated every night at a Music Hall. But how was it done? That was the point—how was it done? I was pondering over the matter in my study with a glass of whiskey and water beside me. For a while my mind, like SULLIVAN's organ-man, was "ill at ease," when all of a sudden a trance-like calm fell upon me. I was glad of this, for I knew that I was about to learn the secret. I learn most things after a trance-like calm has fallen upon me. For a while I could not exactly follow what I was doing. Then my brain became as clear as a bell—as crystal. I was standing with Mr. AUGUSTUS HARRIS among the Armada relics at Drury Lane, talking to the descendants of the Elizabethan heroes who had saved England from invasion three hundred years ago. They were loud in their praise of the Lessee of the National Theatre.

"Yes," returned the part-author of *The Armada*, "I certainly get as near truth and nature as possible. For instance, the scene of the Holy Inquisition was real. I got it at some reduction, as it is obsolete in Spain. You see before you real tormentors, real tortures, and real victims. The gentleman that is dropped through the trap-door at the commencement of the Act in a condition of some exhaustion I had to take as a fixture. He said he was accustomed to his rack, and could ill do without it. Yes, we do not only use real tortures, but sometimes discover real secrets."

"You do!" I exclaimed, "then do you think you could find out for me how the *Cocoon* trick is done at the Pavilion?"

The Lessee of the National Theatre nodded an assent, and led the way to the stage. When we arrived there we found the gentleman to whom reference has already been made, stretching himself at full length on the rack.

"Well, Sir," said the Lessee, "and how are you enjoying yourself?"

"Thoroughly," was the immediate reply, "they have been giving me an extra twist this morning, and I feel all the better for it. But now I think I am done to a turn."

He was taken from his apparently unconventionally-fashioned couch, and dropped through his usual trap, in his customary condition of exhaustion.

"And now, perhaps, we had better see the talented inventor of this marvellous trick," said the courteous Lessee, and a gentleman of evidently foreign extraction was introduced.

"Do you require my assistance?" asked the Chief Inquisitor, in a voice that reminded me of the palmy days of the Legitimate Drama, suddenly appearing at the wing.

"Thank you, No," returned the courteous Lessee. "I think we can get on without you."

The Chief Inquisitor bowed in a stately manner, and, with much dignity, withdrew. The gentleman of evidently foreign extraction was then invited to seat himself on a torture-chair that had been specially brought for him from the collection of Armada relics.

After a few minutes passed in cheerful preparation, the talented inventor said that he was then in a position to explain his secret, on the condition, however, "that it went no further."

"It is as simple as possible," he observed, smilingly, as he rose from the torture-chair. "It is done by swallowing a potion, similar in character but different in effect to that consumed by *Dr. Jekyll* and *Mr. Hyde*. But perhaps you would like to see it done."

I said I would, and, by a dexterous twist of the wrist (very neatly performed) both the Inventor and myself were "passed" into the Pavilion in an instant. The Hall was crowded, and I found myself behind the scenes. A beautiful young lady was standing beside me with a glass in her hand. I heard the Inventor speaking to the audience. I saw him hold up a sort of frame, covered with tissue-paper. I watched him as he drew, with admirable skill, a worm, and then a cocoon. Then I noticed that the frame and tissue paper had disappeared, and a sort of large walnut, made of silk, had taken their place.

"Now," said the Inventor, "I will place this Cocoon into this receptacle, and in a moment you will see what happens."

As he spoke, the young lady raised her glass to her lips. I immediately seized it and swallowed its contents myself. Then a strange thing happened. I found myself suddenly emerging from the Cocoon, to the surprise of both the Inventor and the audience.

"Done like that!" shouted LIKA JOKO, the well known Japanese Secret-discoverer, suddenly appearing on the stage. "Not at all! See now, I will show you how it *is* done!"

But at that moment the scene faded away, and I found myself in my own study with my head resting tranquilly in the coal-scuttle. How I got there—whether I was "passed" or not by the Inventor—is still a secret to me. But this was not the only thing that puzzled me. I could not understand the condition of the whiskey bottle. Before I left my study, I fancy, I say I *fancy*, it was nearly full—now, undoubtedly, it was *quite* empty!

---

### New Version.

(*By a Disgusted M.P.*)

REMEMBER, remember
The Sixth of November?
Of *course*, for it can't be forgot!

*I* know no reason
Why late in the Season [rot
We're mustered to rage and talk

---

"IS LIFE WORTH LIVING?"—PADDY LANE gave a bob to avoid a shot from the revolver. Only a bob! He got off cheaply. But, as he observed, "It's better to be a coward for five minutes than to be dead for the rest of your life." PADDY was right. Life is certainly worth living—at that price.

## THE CHALLENGE: OR. THE RIVAL CHANTICLEERS.

*Grand Old Chanticleer (fortissimo).*

Cock-a-doodle-do-o-o! Cock-a-doodle-do-o-o-o!!!
Gather round me, hen-birds all—pretty Partlet crew!

*Chorus of "Women's Liberal Federation" Hens.*

Cackle! cackle! Grand Old Bird! Where's the fowl dares tackle
Such prodigious spurs and beak? Cackle! Cackle! Cackle!

*Grand Old Chanticleer.*

Ladies, thanks for your response to my stirring clarion.
Fancy there's a business here I alone can carry on.
Fighting Cocks are plentiful, game birds some are terming 'em,
But I really think you need a change of breeds in Birmingham.
Kept a little mite too much to one stock and brood, I think.
Once you deprecated change, but you have changed your mood, I think.
"Crested Ch-mb-rl-ns" no doubt are a breed pugnacious;
Very valiant, vigorous, vehement, vivacious.
But one family of fowls may be *over*done, Ladies.
Mean to challenge 'em myself, think we'll have some fun, Ladies.
Want to rule the roost too much, the C. C.'s do. Monopoly
May do in screws, but not in fowl-runs—if I *must* talk shoppily.
JOEY C., as Cock o'the Walk, considerably plumes himself,
But when a bird backs all his brood, I rather think he dooms himself;

Crested Ch-mb-rl-ns *all* crow loud, strut with much show abdominal;
Some say that JOE's supremacy is little more than nominal,
Even in crow and strut; though these he carries to excess, he [JESSE.
Has rivals in his brood, who are not *all* as meek as
However, that's mere local cackle, though good K-NR-CK —come! a gem!—
Tells me that complaints of this are not confined to Brummagem. [RICHARD,
Still I'm here to fight Big JOE, not AUSTIN, nay, nor
I into him, he into me, are pretty sure to pitch hard,
When it *does* come to fighting. Ladies, I am game to tackle
On his own walk that Chanticleer!

*Chorus of "W. L. F." Hens (effusively).*

O lovely! Cackle! Cackle!!!

*Brummagem Bantam.*

Well, it's like his impudence! And on my own walk, too!
But I'll beat the Old Bird yet, and by a long chalk, too!
*He* talk of Monopoly? Well, that's really queer;
He who'd rule *all* roosts alone, Grand Old Chanticleer!
Well, I'll fight him! As for you, poor Partlet-Chorus—pooh!
They shall find that two can play at Cock-a-doodle-do-o-o! [*Makes ready.*

---

A NICE LOOK-OUT FOR LONDON.—The *Standard* is delighted that the Duke of WESTMINSTER has been appointed Lord Lieutenant of the County of London, because he will "bridge over the gulf between the old *régime* and the new." Let us hope that the new Westminster Bridge will prove a success—come up to the "Standard," in fact. But one Duke will not make a London County Council, and this "gulf," according to Mr. HAMER's letter in the *Times*, may be, after all, a bottomless pit of Bumbles and Blackmailers, wide and dark indeed, beyond even the possibilities of "filling up," suggested by the heroic self-sacrifice of a Ducal Curtius. *Mr. Punch* hopes that this HAMER hits wide as well as hard.

---

## "EDUCATION, OR STARVATION?"

[The poor child attended in Court herself, was fined two-and-sixpence for not having attended school when she was nursing her father, and then burst into tears, saying that the only money she had they wanted at home for bread.—*Vide Daily Telegraph Report, Nov.* 3.]

EDUCATION
Is vexation,
But Starvation's worse.
Can School-Board be
With fine and fee
Earning the poor man's curse?

---

## GETTING ALONG NICELY.

IN its Dramatic and Musical column, last Friday, the *Daily Telegraph* informed the world that Mr. WILSON BARRETT "without assistance, has both constructed and written a play called *Now-a-days*." W. B. is "getting a big boy now!" Fancy being able to write a play without assistance! And what was the "assistance" he received before this daring effort? Why, according to the same authority, it was Mr. HALL CAINE. So when he got free of this CAINE,—which has always been a tutor's assistance,—little Master WILSON BARRETT procured pens, ink, and paper, and wrote a play, all by himself! When little boys get hold of the pens and ink, they generally make a nice mess of it; but we are sure Master WILSON B. is a good boy, and *he* won't do anything of that sort, *will* he?

An Impressionist.

## FAMILY JARS.

*Joan.* "THE *IDEAR* OF SUSAN'S ASKIN' JOHN TO WILLIAM'S FUNERAL, AFTER THE WAY 'E'D BEHAVED! I SHOULDN'T CERTAINLY EVER *DREAM* OF ASKIN' 'IM TO *YOURS!*"

*Darby.* "*WHAT!* THEN ALL *I* CAN SAY IS, I SHOULD BE VERY MUCH OFFENDED IF YOU *DIDN'T!*"

---

## THE NEXT DIPLOMATIC INCIDENT.

*Letter from —— Smith, Esq., to British Minister.*

DEAR BRITISH MINISTER,—I AM an Englishman who has become an American, and want to know which way I ought to vote at the present crisis. I reckon I may take it that this change of front on the part of present Government is all bamboozle. That is so! Post me up on the right side of the rails. I calculate I can influence a lot of votes, to get them put, bedad, to the credit of the unspeakable Saxons! Hurroo! *Erin go bragh!* Yours respectfully,

(*Signed*) —— SMITH, ESQ.

*Telegram from British Minister to —— Smith, Esq.*

I think you ought to vote for the present Government, as I fancy that after the Election is over the good sense which has ever been the characteristic of the present President will once more become apparent. As you are personally unknown to me (although of course your name is perfectly familiar to me), I have taken the precaution to pay a small additional sum to have this telegraphed to you with the words "Strictly private" added to the message.

*Cablegram from Minister to Premier.*

Very awkward this telegram of Minister. Well-intentioned, but ill-timed. Please do something.

*Cablegram from Minister to Premier (an hour later).*

Have sent Minister his passports.

*Cablegram from President to Premier (an hour later).*

Have ordered Minister to be off at once.

*Cablegram from President to Premier (an hour later).*

Sending out declaration of war by next mail.

*Cablegram from President to Premier (an hour later).*

At Cabinet Council just held decreed the immediate annexation of Canada and Australia, and the speedy invasion of India.

*Cablegram from President to Premier (a week later).*

Election over. Pulled it through. Countermanded annexation and invasion. Sorry Minister has gone. Give him my kind regards. Calculate you may consider this incident at an end.

## "FAUST GAIETY."

On the third night of its existence I saw the new burlesque of *Faust* at the Gaiety. *Faust up to Date* is not *Faust up to Much*. Such as it is, it has taken two distinguished Adelphi melodramatists, Messrs. PETTITT and SIMS, to do it. Clearly the melodramatists are dissembling. The Extravagant Travesty plays two hours and three-quarters, and is therefore about two hours too long. Here and there the two dissembling melodramatists have made a conscientious attempt at burlesquing some of the principal situations in the Opera and drama. Occasionally there are some good lines, as there ought to be in the course of two hours and three-quarters, though, whether in dialogue or in song, it seemed to me that the utterance of only Miss ST. JOHN, Mr. LONNEN, and Mr. STONE was distinct.

*Patron of the Drama (to Box-office-keeper concealed within).* "I say, is the second act better than the first? *(Sadly.)* There's no dancing in it, don-cher-no."

There is nothing remarkably amusing in the First Act, which, however, is the better of the two; but in the Second Act, there is a dance of four girls, all alive and kicking, which is more effective from its eccentricity than its grace; and in the last scene there is the now inevitable Irish song for LONNEN, of which a Mr. MARTIN is announced as the writer and composer, the talented authors of the burlesque having, as I suppose, drawn the line at "a rival" and "ar-rival," or at "flying being a matter of a-pinion," and MEYER LUTZ, composer of the music of the extravaganza, being unwilling to enter for an Irish jig competition. Be this as it may, the Martin-Lonnen song, which is not brought in till just before the finish, as a *bonne bouche*, is not a patch upon "*Killaloe*;" but to see the chorus-men seriously marking the time on each other's heads with their shillelaghs, after the fashion of "The Two MACS," is very funny, and a hit, "or several hits," as the Dissemblers would say. The music is poor, and affords little opportunity for FLORENCE ST. JOHN or for anybody else. Mr. STONE, who appears as *Valentine*, may probably be—as the dissembling melodramatists nightly jointly observe—a precious Stone, only requiring a better setting to display his real brilliancy; but those who remember M. MILHER as the burlesque *Valentine* in *Le Petit Faust*,—an *opéra bouffe* full of fun and sparkling melody,—will be inclined to regret either that the English low comedian has never seen that performance, or, if he has, that he has not sufficiently profited by it.

By the time this notice appears, improvements may have been made in the piece. After the First Act, I overheard a Masher plaintively inquiring at the pigeon-hole of the Box-office, "Is the Second Act any better than the first?" What the invisible official's answer to this was I could not catch, but the complainant, in a deeply injured tone, went on, "Look here, there's no dancing in the First Act, don-cher-no." I suppose he received some comforting assurance on the subject from the hidden oracle, the veritable Jack-in-the-Box-Office, as further observation made he none, but with his hand on his swelling shirt-front, returned, struggling with suppressed emotion, to his stall. Gaiety Management ought to know how to cater for Gaiety Masherdom: "plenty of 'caper' sauce," as the dissembling Adelphian melodramatists would say, both together, of course.

Yet when that bright particular star of burlesque, the inimitable NELLIE FARREN, is absent from the Gaiety, the gaiety of its patrons seems to be eclipsed. What a "little *Dr. Faust*" she was, when TERRY was the *Mephistopheles*, and KATE VAUGHAN the elegant *Marguerite!* I hope, for the sake of Mashers and Management, it may not turn out that

> There's nae luck about the house,
> There's nae luck at 'a;
> There's nae luck about the house
> When our own NELL's awa'.

Yes, in her absence the Gaiety *Faust* seems but forced gaiety, after all, judging at least by the present effort, says, with incorrect pronunciation,

JACK-IN-THE BOX.

P.S.—In my criticism on the *Dean's Daughter*, a fortnight ago, I referred to Mr. F. C. PHILIPS as the Author of *Ariane*. Mrs. CAMPBELL PRAED wrote *Ariane*. But there is a strong similarity of character in the two heroines, with neither of whom should we feel any sympathy. As CHARLES JAMES FOX wrote,—"It has been thought dangerous to the morals of mankind, even in fiction and romance, to make us sympathise with characters whose general conduct is blameable." Hear! hear! And as I could not imagine anyone sympathising with *Ariane*, or with any of the *dramatis personæ*, so I did not consider that play as dangerous to morals. Thus, "the point of this here remark lays in the application of it," as I was comparing the moral effect of the two plays, and not their literary or dramatic merits.—J. I. T. B.

---

## VOCES POPULI.

### AT A NORTH BRITISH HYDROPATHIC.

SCENE—*An immense Drawing-room, lighted by numerous gas-burners, and furnished on a scale of imposing splendour. It is after dinner; tea and coffee have just been served in the corridor outside, and persons of more luxurious habits have brought in their cups to sip at leisure. On settees in the centre sit middle-aged Ladies in grey, red, and white woollen shawls, each politely admiring the other's work. Very young Ladies whisper and laugh in the window-seats, all about nothing, and exhibit the liveliest affection for one another. Others converse, not unconscious of the distinction, with the exceptional Young Men who have donned evening dress, and who glide about with an agreeable air of feeling perfectly at home. People who don't know anybody sit apart in chairs, perusing* "The Hotels of Europe," *or anything else they can get hold of, and wondering why other people are so unsociable. A stout old Lady in a corner is discoursing to a meek little old Maid, in a strong Yorkshire accent, which from time to time compels the unwilling attention of everybody in the room. The old Lady's husband endeavours in vain to catch her eye from the background, as her confidences threaten to become of an alarmingly intimate nature. In the foreground, two Visitors have just discovered a bond of sympathy in the fact that neither of them has found Scotch scenery quite what he expected.*

*First Visitor (delighted).* You weren't much impressed with the Kyles of Bute? You don't say so! Now that really is *very* curious—no more was I! Now, Loch Lomond is certainly rather pretty—(*as if he did not wish to turn its head*)—*bits* of it, you know. But the Trossachs—what are the Trossachs, after all?

*Second V.* Exactly. (*Feeling that this settles the Trossachs.*) What *are* they? And then some people tell you *Glencoe*'s so magnificent—I went through it in a pouring rain, and all I can say is—*I* couldn't see anything in the place! and look at Staffa and Iona—why, to hear some people talk——

*First V. (in a large-minded way).* Well, I didn't think Iona was so bad myself, I must say——

*Second V.* Ah, perhaps you're a good sailor, now I'm always ill on any steamer——

*The Yorkshire Lady (in a slow ruminating voice).* An' so ah said to ma husband, "Ah doan't loike to cloime oop on them 'cherry boonks,' as they cahl them, it may be vara noice," ah said, "when ya git oop, but if ah *was* oop, ah'd hev to coom daown agëan." An' ma husband sez to me, "Doan't ya be sooch a blethrin owd"——

[*Her Husband drops a book in the background.*

*A Young Lady who likes Excitement (to one of the agreeable Young Men in Evening Dress).* Oh, Mr. TORCKLER, don't they ever *do* anything here?

*Mr. Torckler.* Oh, yes, I'm going to ask that lady in the blue spectacles to sing in a minute, and there's somebody in the house somewhere, who will play the flute, if you go the right way to manage him.

*The Y. L. (pettishly).* Oh, I didn't mean *that*—I meant get *up* something.

*A Solitary Stranger (seizing the opportunity of speaking to somebody).* If you're fond of climbing, there's a very nice mountain in the vicinity—you can get up it easily in three hours, and it's only eight miles by road.

*The Y. L. (stiffly).* Oh, thank you very much. (*To* Mr. T.) I mean get up a dance, charades, *anything*!

*An Habituée.* Ah, you should have been here the week before last, when the house was full! There was something going on every evening in the Recreation Room—theatricals, dumb-crambo, thought reading, and I don't know *what* all—such *fun* we had!

*The Y. L. (coldly).* Really? (*To* Mr. T.) But *why* couldn't we dress up, or something? [*Vaguely.*

*Mr. T. (doubtfully).* Well, there's not much point in dressing-up unless you do something when you *are* dressed up, is there?

*The Y. L. (who would be quite satisfied with the mere dressing-up).* I suppose not. Well then, we might *dance*.

*Mr. T. (who doesn't dance, but would recite if anybody were to ask him).* Not enough men.

*The Y. L.* Oh, some of the girls—(*by which she means the other girls*)—can dance with one another. Do propose a dance.

*Mr. Torckler (diplomatically).* Er—well, I must find out what people think about it before proposing anything, you know. (*Circu*

## ESSENCE OF PARLIAMENT.

EXTRACTED FROM

### THE DIARY OF TOBY, M.P.

*House of Commons, Tuesday Morning, Nov. 6.*

DE *missa ad mensam;* from Probate Court to Westminster, which is quite another thing. Returned my brief in PARNELL case. All very well for young fellow like CHARLES RUSSELL to slave all day in Probate Court and toil all night at Westminster. But he hasn't been in collar since A.D. 1841.

Looked in at Speaker's Court this morning, to pay respects to SPEAKER. In excellent health and spirits; has had good rest, and ready for work. Found him, by way of rehearsal of business that opens this afternoon, blocking his own wig.

"The only measure—7½ in. × 11—one in my position *can* block," he said, gently touching one of the curls.

"Going to have a quiet time, Sir, do you think?" I asked.

"Well, that depends," he said, slowly. "We may and we may not." This very interesting. Nothing like going to head-quarters for information. Everybody asking how the Autumn Session is likely to turn out. Put simple question to SPEAKER; answers it at once; doesn't require notice, but gives a simple, absolutely safe answer. Shall know now what to say when anybody asks me.

## DOWN ON DONNELLY;

*Or, Crushing the Cryptogram.*

"The Sonnets present evidence for SHAKSPEARE's authorship like the links of chain-mail in an armour of proof. And the man who wrote the Sonnets must also have written the Poems and Plays. This can be established by those principles of scientific demonstration that have been applied to both in the present work. The *same unlearned man wrote both!* Then the secret history in the Sonnets is in agreement with the public history of the time, and both are in antipodal antagonism to the Great Cryptogram."—*Mr. Gerald Massey, in his new edition of "The Secret Drama of Shakspeare's Sonnets."*

A POET on *the* Poet! That should herald
A real Champion's advent. Go it, GERALD!
*Punch* puts it pleasantly in the vernacular,
For only owls and humbugs ape the oracular
IGNATIUS now, the "Moon-Raker" gone frantic,
Who hunts for mare's-nests under the Atlantic,
And SHAKSPEARE's text, is naturally stilted,
But under MASSEY's mace he must have wilted
Like the pricked bladder that he is. Yes, go it!
A poet, sure, should understand a poet.
You show 'twas SHAKSPEARE, he who sweetly sonneted,
Who wrote the Plays,—and DONNELLY is bonneted!
Your monumental book's a trifle bulky
(Five hundred pages turn *some* critics sulky,
My massive MASSEY), but 'tis full of "meat,"
And sown with Song as masculine as sweet.
Mellifluous echoes of the master-rhymes,
Whose music filled the Great Armada times,
Three centuries since, and still moves heart and brain
More than the pageantries of Drury Lane.
"Tush! none but minstrels' like of sonneting,"
Sings SHAKSPEARE's self with an ironic ring.
Minstrels at least will thank you; for the rest
Who have not time or heart for the Great Quest
After the Secret of the Sonnets, these
May dip and taste where there's so much to please
Both student bee and social butterfly;
Whilst *all* will track with grateful heart and eye
Your slaughtering of that colossal Sham
Egregious DONNELLY's Great Cryptogram!

*lates at as wide a radius from her as possible, while she endeavours to find out from the expression of those he addresses, their willingness to dance or otherwise—an object in which she might be more successful if he were mentioning the subject at all.)*

*The Yorkshire Lady* (*as before*). An' ah went straäight hoam, an' ah poot on a moostard pleäster, bahk an' front, an' next moarnin' boath ma legs wur ahl swelled oop loike—— [*An agonised expression in her hearer's face warned her to lower her voice at this point.*

*Another Young Man, in Evening Dress, approaches a group of Young Ladies.*

*All the Young Ladies* (*coquettishly*). Now you mustn't come here, Mr. PATTLE—you *are* such a dreadful tease! You must promise to behave if we let you stop. [*They make room for him with alacrity.*

*The Y. M.* (*taking a Novel, with an elegant carelessness*). Is this *very* pathetic?

*The Owner of the Novel.* I won't have you making fun of it—it's *lovely*. I've wept *pints* over it! I left off just at the most exciting part. I'm dying to know how it goes on—I should be reading it now if I didn't want to finish this sock. [*Knits calmly.*

*The Y. M.* (*to Vocalistic Young Lady*). Aren't we to have a song this evening?

*The Voc. Y. L.* How can you ask me? Why, you know how I broke down last night!

*The Y. M.* (*gallantly*). Well, I'd rather hear *you* break down than other people *finish*. I know that.

*Proud Mother* (*from Provinces*). There's my daughter here will be happy to sing if you like to ask her—she's had a first-rate teaching; and people who know what good singing *is*, tell me——

*The Daughter* (*in modest confusion*). How *can* you go on so, Mamma? You'll make the gentleman think I'm something wonderful! (*She is induced to consent to sing.*) Well, what will you have? I've got "*Only the Moon and Thee, Love!*" (*looking up under her eyelashes*)—some of my songs *are* rather soft—and there's "*Say but One Word, and I am Thine!*" (*archly*)—that's a hint to some of you young gentlemen! Will you have that? Or this is a pretty one—"*One Kiss, and then—we Part!*"

*The Y. M.* (*prudently, after looking through her music*). I think, if you wouldn't mind singing "*The Better Land*"——

[*She is disappointed, but sings it, without interrupting either the reading or the conversation.*

*The Yorkshire Lady* (*speaking through music*). So ah said to th' Doactor, "Doactor, ah want you to tell ma joost wheer it is ah'm sooffrin'—is it ma loongs," ah said, "or ma chest, or ma——"

*The Singer* (*with solemn feeling*). "Not there—not they-ere, my che-ild!" [*Song concludes amidst faint and absent-minded applause.*

*The Young Lady who likes Excitement* (*to herself*). *That's* over, thank Goodness! There's plenty of time for a dance still, if they only make haste. I'm sure I can hear some one playing a Waltz in the Recreation Room. What are they waiting for? (*Two Men enter, and look around inquiringly*). Have they come in to find partners? Then there *is* dancing! (*The two Men bring out a chess-board, and begin to play*) .... *Pigs!* (Mr. TORCKLER, *after conversing confidentially in various quarters, goes out with* Mr. PATTLE.) They're going to arrange about it at last! (*Waits hopefully for some time—the lively young Ladies collect their work, and go out too*). Oh, those girls are going now. I'd better *ask* someone, perhaps. (*Crossing to* Matron). Do you know where those gentlemen in evening dress have gone?

*Matron.* I heard them say something about a game of billiards, and a cigar.

*The Y. L.* (*blankly*). Oh (*hopefully*), but all those young ladies—where have *they* gone to?

*Matron.* The young ladies? Oh, *they*'ve gone to bed—we keep early hours here, you know.

*The Yorkshire Lady.* An' he gave ma a perscreepshun, ahl fooll o' things that ah wasn't to teäk. Ah moos'n't eät brëad, an' ah mooan't eät potëatoes, nor yet mooffins, nor tea-cäak, nor no pëastry nor swëats (*meditatively*)—boot ah niver *wur* a swëat eäter—ah niver wur thot! (*And so on.*) [*Drawing-room gradually empties, till the* Yorkshire Lady *is left alone with the little old Maid, who throws in an automatic "Yes" at intervals, and wonders if it will be rude to say she is rather tired.*

**OUR IMBECILES.**

*Elderly Masher* (*who can't see that his attentio is are unwelcome*). "I'M SURE YOU 'RE FOND OF *MUSIC!*
*Persecuted Fair One* (*pettishly*). "OH—YES—VERY—WHEN IT PUTS A STOP TO *CONVERSATION!*"

## THE AUTUMN MEET.

A HUNTING SONG FOR THE ST. STEPHEN'S SEASON.

AIR—"*A Southerly Wind and a Cloudy Sky.*"

M.F.H. *sings*:—

A NONDESCRIPT wind and November sky
Look queer for a hunting morning.
But the Meet is fixed, and away we hie,
Loved leisure and liberty scorning.
To horse, my lads, to horse, away!
The chase admits of no delay.
On horseback we 've got, together we 'll trot.
(Though if *I* see the need of it, may I be shot!)
More spouting forbear, see the cover appear!
(The pack 's a mixed lot, and the country is queer.)
Drag on him! Ah, wind him, my good, steady hounds!
(That sounds like full faith, but I fear with faint grounds.)

If only the cover and furze they will draw,
I'll envy not BARRY or MAYNELL;
But LABBY cares little for good canine law,
Wild WILL is the plague of the kennel.
When away we fly, some puppies may halt,
Some strike a false trail and the pack put at fault.
Will they cast round the Schoolhouse far out of our track?
To the old Shamrock Spinney essay to try back?
Shall we hear a hound challenge in Sackville Sedge,
Or take us full tilt o'er "Diplomacy" hedge?
"Hark forward! Hark forward!" Oh, bother the noise!
Keep 'em straight if you can, SMITH, *then* "at it, brave boys!"

A stormy sky surcharged with rain
The chance of good sport opposes.
In the mettle of some of the pack trust is vain,
And *I* haven't much faith in their noses.
Each moment now the sky grows worse;
Enough to make bland B-LF-R curse.
If they'll pick the ground we would take them through,
All 's well; but if not, there is mischief a-brew.
If we can but get on, we 'll make some of them quake.
Let us hear the hounds challenge, and in the right brake,
Tally ho! Tally ho! then, across the clear plain.
Tally ho! Tally ho, boys! Have at him again

We must ride, whip and spur, for, I hope, a short chase;
Our horses all panting and sobbing.
Young Madcap and Riot will soon want to race;
I fancy we 'll have some rare mobbing.
But hold,—alas! they 'll spoil our sport,
If they over-run or head him short.
Clap round him, dear BILL, and if some of the pack,
Like Random, go hotly, hark back! hark back!
Some will see a fresh quarry in every bush;
If you let 'em run wild, we shall ne'er get the brush.
Who-hoop! who-hoop! I'd give many a crown
If the fox we are after were fairly run down!

## CUTTINGS TRANSPLANTED.

THIS came out of the *Bristol Times and Mirror*, October 29:—

RESIDENCE, most centrally-situated, CLIFTON, to be LET, with a permanent Gentleman Lodger, who will remain if desired (or for SALE).

Rather hard on the Lodger, unless, like every other man "he has his price," and can pocket the proceeds for his own benefit.

This is idyllic, out of the *Stamford Mercury*:—

HOUSE-PARLOURMAID wanted. Must be thoroughly fitted and recommended, defty and debonair. Man-servant kept. Bachelor's house.

"Defty and debonair!" Quite Miltonian. Appropriate too in the pages of a Mercury interesting himself in looking out for a Hebe. "Bachelor's House." Alas! poor Bachelor!

NOTE BY LORD GOT-THE-SACKVILLE.—The American BAYARD may be "without fear," but he 's not "without reproach."

MRS. RAM says the fogs affect her severely, and she's afraid her cold will turn to comic Bronchitis.

# THE AUTUMN MEET.

HUNTSMAN. "MORNIN', M' LORD!"

HIS LORDSHIP. "MORNING! YOU'VE GOT A MIXED LOT IN THE PACK, SMITH,—AND A DIFFICULT COUNTRY;—HOPE YOU'LL KEEP 'EM WELL TOGETHER!"

## A PARTHIAN SHOT.

*Examiner.* "THANK YOU, MR. JONES! I'M AFRAID IT ISN'T NECESSARY TO TROUBLE YOU ANY FURTHER. GOOD MORNING."

*Plucked One (who has at all events read his Nineteenth Century).* "AH, IT'S ALL VERY WELL; BUT THEY'LL BE EXAMINING *YOU* PRESENTLY—*AND SEE HOW YOU'LL LIKE IT!* GOOD MORNING."

## ROBERT ON THE NEW LORD MAYOR'S SHO.

WELL, I suttenly did think that, ewen in these times of uniwersal mokery and irrewerence, there was jest a few things as might reesonably be xpected to remane sacred from the profain touch of the ribald gester, and fust and foremast among 'em was the hancient, the time-honnerd, the truly gorgeus festival of Lord Mare's Sho!

But no, I was rong for wunce, and I confesses it in sackcloth and hashes; that is to say, I am sure as I wood, if so be as I knowd how to get through that werry gritty an skrunching seremony. But then, of coarse, I did not make proper elowance for the ordassity of a Gent who combines in his own sollem person such a strange wariety of karacters as a Hem Pea, a Barrow Night, a Pollytishun, a Joker, and a Tea Toteller!

And what a hordience Sir WILLIAM LAWSON selecks to adress on so himportant and hinterestin a subjeck! What can a lot of mere Wesmorland Woters kno or care about Lord Mare's Sho? Why, less than even he does—and how much is that? Why he acshally tells his pore hignorant lisseners, and xpecs them to bleeve him, that it is the custom to have in the sacred Sho camels, and bufferlows, and ellefants, and jackasses, and men in armer, and tom-fools, a marching about! What a minglin of the subblime and the ridicklus! Elefants and Men in Armer on the one hand, and Jackasses and Tom Fools on the other! My curiossity is naterally xcited to kno who he could have meant by the jackasses and tom fools; but I naterally refranes from persuing the dellicate inquiry too fur.

Leaving his discripshun of the Sho, I passes on to his ludickrus acount of the werry grandest bankwet as takes place in the old City, as is so notorious for em. Woud it be bleeved that so wunderfool is his hutter hignorance on these himportant matters, that he acshally describes the Ero of the nite as being serrounded with Torys and Turtels! Torys and Turtels! What a singlar combinashun! Torys, the bo hideal of humane wisdom and wirtue, and Turtels, the bo hideal of skrumpshus and happytising food!

But only to think of the witty water-drinker's hutter hignorance of igh-class wittels, as well as of igh-class drinks. Why he acshally seams to fansy as that Turtels is brort on table at dinner, all hole, like Turbots, and such small dear! Ah, what a rewelashun it will be to him sum day when he fust tastes REEL TURTEL SOUP! I halmost henveys him his grand sensashun.

I admires his awdassity much more than his good taste as to the halterations he boldly ventures to suggest in the grand percesshun, and from what I ears, here and there, I don't think as there ain't werry much chance of there being adopted. What mere rubbish to have a picter of Mr. GOSCHEN hoffering Lord SORLSBERRY a blank check! Wot's the use of a blank check, I shood like to know, to Lord SORLSBERRY or to anyboddy helse? If the Chancesellor of the Xchecker had a bin shown a-hoffering of him a five pun note for hisself, there woud be sum sense in it, and in spite of his estonishment at a pressent from sitch a quarter, his Lordship woud probberly have accepted it with rapshure.

And then only fansy a doing away with the thrillin and awe-enspirin site of no less than six reel Men in Armer, all brort from the Tower of Lundun, by the speshal permission of H.R.H. the Dook of CAMEBRIDGE, to keep the mob in order, and substitootin for 'em Mr. WILKIE COLLINS a milkin a Cow in a werry large feeld! Why the thing's too ridickulus to ewen dream about, tho I confesses as I do have sum rayther rum uns sometimes, 'speshally after a werry scrumpshus bankwet. However, seeing, I spose, in what *Amlet* calls his mind-your-eyes, that, in a Persesshun in the werry richest City in the hole World, sumthink like splender woud be looked for, he proposes to have, next to the Cow-milking seen, a Gilded Carrage; all werry right and werry propper, says ewerybody of taste; but he must have a nice idear of the size of a Gilded Carrage, for it is to contane not ony Mr. JOE CHAMBERLING—as he werry irreverently calls the fashnable Member for Brummagem—but he is to have with him a lot of Dooks, and Dutchesses, and Publicans, and Archbishups, and Brewers!

Why, wot nonsense! Why, ewen a large penny Homnibus woodn't hold 'em! And wot a way in which to speak of the werry hiest horders of the Nobility, Dooks and Dutchesses, and Archbishups, and the most usefullest of all our Mannyfacterers, Brewers and Publicans; wiz., to tork about a *lot* of 'em, as if they was to be put up and nocked down at a Hoction!

But a truce to all this ribaldry and werry watery wit, at witch I confesses as I ceased to be surprized when wunce I learnt that its Orthur had never tasted reel Turtel Soup, on the one hand, and never now knowed wot it wos to drink a glass of generous old Port, or ewen jest a wee drop of reel Scotch Whiskey, on the other.

Poor old Gennelman! we must, of coarse, make ewery posserble alowance for him under the pecooliar circumstanses of his werry sad case. ROBERT.

### Mot by a Midlothian Unionist.

[Mr. GLADSTONE, writing to Mr. HOLMES IVORY, Hon. Sec. of the Midlothian Liberal Association, speaks hopefully of the prospects of Home Rule in the Constituencies] :—

IN such optimist dreams though you seem to believe,
To a Scholar like you is it needful to state,
My dear WILLIAM, that it is the dreams that *deceive*
Which pass through the *Ivory* gate?

NURSERY TALK.—A discussion has been going on as to what "a Nurse's position" should be. Doesn't her position depend on that of the patient, or the baby? "A PRIVATE NURSE" writes to *The Hospital* to ask—Is it a rule for a Private Nurse to take her meals in the kitchen? Certainly not, if the custom of *Mrs. Gamp* and *Betsy Prig* is still of any authority. But perhaps those good old days are gone for ever; but *Gamps* and *Prigs* never demeaned themselves by taking their meals in the kitchen.

### To Sir Polydore de Keyser.

WELL, "Every dog must have his day,"
And every Lord Mayor too;
But when his day is done, he may,
In all "the beauty of De-K.,"
Become a Knight, like you.

NEW SETTING OF AN OLD SAW.—You cannot touch "*La Terre*" without being Soil'd.

**PARLIAMENTARY.**

*Pedestrian (in a hurry).* "HI! 'GIVE YOU FIVE SHILLINGS TO GET ME TO WESTMINSTER BY TWELVE O'CLOCK."

*Cabby.* "OH, YOU MAY CORRUPT ME, SIR. JUMP IN. IF WE CAN ONLY SECURE THIS OLD HOSS'S VOTE, WE MAY CARRY IT!"

## OUR BOOKING-OFFICE.

A VOLUME of IBSEN'S Plays (belonging to "the Camelot Series," of whose existence I am hereby made aware) has been lent me by a simple trusting friend. The good simple soul has written his name in the fly-leaf, with a date; but there is sufficient space to write above his signature:—"*To my dear friend the Baron de Bookworms, from his sincerely attached*," and here will come in, quite neatly and appropriately, his own name in his own handwriting. I have only had time to read the first two plays, *The Pillars of Society*, and *Ghosts*. The first of these, until the middle of the Second Act, is troublesome reading, the dialogue being diffuse, commonplace, and the stage-directions ridiculous. But when the interest really commences, and the reader is on speaking terms with the various characters, then, as the story is gradually worked out, the plot proves to be as strong as the characters are original. Properly condensed and well acted, it ought to be a powerful play, for which able exponents should be found on the English stage. The translation is evidently truthful and very close, but the hand of a practical playwright is needed to put it into proper form. It is a pure-minded, manly-spirited, noble play, pointing a moral without any cant of goody-goodiness. Nor is it deficient in material for good low comedy or eccentric character, without which it is difficult for the best intentioned play to be anything but a burden to the most sympathetic and patient audience. The dramatic possibilities in *The Pillars of Society* are great, but the play as it stands certainly would not do for the stage, and the bald translation makes it a tedious study taken as literature.

As to *Ghosts*, the second play, the translation here given may be close, but the dialogue is even more diffuse than in *The Pillars*, and it is pointless, and irritatingly wearisome to read. Here and there a situation in the painfully repulsive story is undoubtedly dramatic, yet, as a play, whether for an English audience or any other, I sincerely hope its production is impossible. The subject could be powerfully treated in a Charles-Reade-ian novel; but it requires the touch of a master hand to adorn the pitiful tale, and point the moral. So, on consideration, I shall not inscribe my name on the fly-leaf, but shall return the book to my friend to prove to him that he has not shown misplaced confidence in his friend, and then he will perhaps lend another and more valuable book to the honest

BARON DE BOOK-WORMS.

## BALLADS OF TO-DAY.

### "ONE AT A TIME."

*By Bungham Down.*

HEAVILY through the Casino  
The fumes of the roses float;  
Heart of my heart! How could *he* know  
She had come by the tidal-boat?  
As stiff as a royal merino,  
Or the fur of the sea-side goat?

(*Andante hideoso.*)

And he danced on one and the other,  
He was far too ugly to care,  
And Beauty her shrieks would smother,  
And Valour forget to swear,  
For he was a famous Poet,  
And rich and debonair.

(*Tempo di Valse.*)

"*One at a time, love, one at a time!*  
*Ever he murmured the old sweet rime:*  
*One at a time, love; fair is fair,*  
*Haro! and motley's the only wear!*"

(*Puffo ma non troppo.*)

And he leaned from the lush Casino,  
And scanned the sounding sea;  
Like the salt of a fruitless Eno,  
It cream'd with a mocking glee,  
Or moaned like the Moning Congou  
At a foggy Five o'Clock Tea.

They play'd at the little horses,  
But little of them reck'd he,  
As he yearn'd for the stars in their courses  
And the moon in her crescentrie,  
And his pulses reserv'd their forces,  
For there in the dusk was She!

(*Twingiamente.*)

And the vacant space where his heart had [place  
Throbb'd with a fancied pain,  
As the phantom boot on a long-lost foot  
Wakes bygone griefs again.

(*Maestoso giocoso.*)

There's a lonely tomb where surges boom  
And the griddering pebbles grind,—  
But he dances on one and the other,  
He is far too ugly to mind.

"*One at a time, love, one at a time,*  
*Softly he murmurs the sweet, old rime:*  
*One at a time, love; fair is fair,*  
*Haro! and motley's the only wear.*"

## OUR JAPANNERIES. No. 21.

COURT UP FOR LUNCH.

## THE PARNELL COMMISSION.

(*Special Report.*)

*Tuesday.*—Joseph Gillis has taken somebody else's seat this morning. It's mine. Has "called" himself to the Inner Bar, and now sits with us. Suppose he'll be donning wig and gown presently. Here he sits all day. Pretty to see him, as the shadows lengthen, lay his head on Lockwood's broad shoulder and sweetly sleep. Something weighing on his mind. Moments of abstraction when he sits gazing afar. Once heard something like a sigh.

"Anything gone wrong?" I ask.

"Not yet," he says. "But I'm afeard. Do you think, when I get into the witness-box and they examine me about my visit to Paris in the spring of 1882—'in the spring, a young man's fancy,' don't you know—do you think anything will come out about private affairs?"

"Do you mean," I said, "will they want to know anything about that little affair with the widow, that let you in for the breach of promise case?"

"Well, you needn't put it quite that way, Toby; but that's somewhere about it. You know all about legal procedure. Will the Judges let the Attorney-General go into that matter?"

"I fancy they will," I said. "But I'll look up the authorities. Haven't got your *Coke upon Littleton* in your waistcoat pocket, have you?"

No, JOSEPH hadn't; and him to be sitting with us of the Inner Bar! TIM HEALY turned up, but not in wig and gown.

"No," said TIM, "not going to stand in the way of JOSEPH GILLIS. Since he's taken to the law, I take a back seat. He needs no assistance." So TIM sits on modest bench with the Solicitors, and presently tackles the Judges.

"I'm Mr. HEALY," he says, when making an application on order of business.

Brother HANNEN gravely nods, as if that didn't matter very much. JOSEPH GILLIS, who tried a fall with Brother HANNEN earlier in the proceedings, has been quiet for day or two. Encouraged by contiguity of TIM, he returns to attack. JOSEPH, pulling up his coat by back of collar, as he has seen HENRY JAMES do with his gown, argues that the whole of speeches should be read. Blandly hints that HENRY JAMES, in picking out particular paragraphs, was chiefly concerned to mislead the public who read the newspaper reports. Pretty to see HANNEN looking under his glasses at the future ERSKINE. A glance of mingled curiosity, impatience and growing anger. JOSEPH, wagging his forefinger as he has heard *Mr. Jaggers* used to do, lays down the law, and is himself promptly laid by the heels.

The Star.

"No, no, no!" says Brother HANNEN, testily turning away.

That's all; only a monosyllable reiterated. But, how eloquent with impatient disgust of JOSEPH's slightly incoherent and somewhat malignant suggestion! JOEY B. doesn't try to catch the President's eye again. Sits and ruminates.

"Tell you what, TOBY," he said, "when we reach Civil Service Estimates, shall move to reduce vote for law expenses by £5,000, salary of President of Probate Court. What does he mean with his 'No, no, no'? On the whole, I'd rather have dealings with the Speaker."

*Wednesday.*—Appearance of Court distinctly changed this morning. Chamber crowded. Bar in full attendance and plainly on the alert. PARNELL, who is methodically as late as HARTINGTON, is actually in his place. JOSEPH GILLIS, descended from high estate on Q.C. Bench, humbly seated in Solicitors' quarter.

"Not nearly such a homely place as the House of Commons, TOBY," he whispered, enviously eyeing my wig and gown. "Can do anything I like there; say what I please, at what length I like, and sit where I think proper. Remember the time when House was in Committee, and I sat in Speaker's Chair, behind COURTNEY? Be a pretty row here, I suppose, if, after luncheon, Judges came in and found me sitting in President's chair! But I will do it some day. JOEY B. is tough, dev'lish tough, as they 'll find to their cost."

Curtain drawn back. Judges enter; stand for a second in the doorway; Bar and audience rise with swift rustling noise; Judges bow, take their seats. Play about to begin; subdued buzz of excitement. "What is it?" I asked Sage of Queen Anne's Gate, who is looking on.

"*Cherchez la femme!*" he says.

Instinctively turn to look in direction of newspaper lady in black hat and hearse-plumes, forsaken by JOSEPH. On the way eye falls on familiar figure. It is he—I mean it's SHEA. (See Sage's joke now. Will laugh as soon as Court adjourns for luncheon. Daren't do it before. Brother HANNEN says he won't have anyone laughing in Court.)

O'SHEA in box all morning and far into afternoon. Doesn't seem to like it; shaved off whiskers in order the better to face ordeal. But no use. In unbroken line below him sit old familiar friends. PARNELL, pale-faced, haggard-looking, staring with reproachful eyes; DAVITT, taking notes; TIM HEALY, speechless with anger; and finally, JOSEPH GILLIS, smiling a ghastly smile, and thinking of the days that are no more, when he went down to Galway, and, in defiance of PARNELL, pulled O'SHEA's hair and scratched his face.

A trying ordeal for the once *débonnaire* but now decidedly damaged Captain. Some signs of quailing at first. Strong disinclination to meet the four pair of gleaming eyes on Solicitors' Bench. But, growing steadier under fire, the Captain fairly faces Sir CHARLES RUSSELL. Answers his searching, subtle questions, fully and frankly.

*Thursday.*—In the hands of the Police all day. Taken up by P. C. IRWIN as soon as O'SHEA had left the box. Subsequently handed over to custody of P. C. O'MALLEY. O'SHEA just looked in to bring document signed by some eminent politicians meeting in convenient public in Wardour Street, protesting against his exclusion from politics. O'SHEA told me all about it.

"MULQUEENY took me there," he said, "in four-wheeled cab, blindfolded. Engaged cab by the hour. Drove round by Clapham Common, I believe, and so reached Wardour Street. Took bandage off my eyes when I entered the room. Rum lot, seen through tobacco-smoke. Smell of lemon in whiskey. Somebody hit me on small of back with flat side of sword. Then I signed my name in red ink (they said it was blood). They all swore at PARNELL; said I ought to be Chief-Secretary. I paid for drinks, put protest in my pocket, and came away. Nothing particular ever came of it; still we—I mean they—had very pleasant evening. But I advise you to keep out of politics, TOBY. You never know what you'll be let in for."

Police Witnesses charming fellows, especially IRWIN. Best type of Irish peasant; good-looking, gentle-mannered, shrewd, smiling, slyly humorous, with delicious brogue. His conversation with CHARLES RUSSELL worth sitting a week in Court to hear. There was a wide world of eloquence in his way of saying "Sir CHARLES." Entreaty, expostulation, hesitation, alacrity, doubt, assent, certainty, contradiction, and above all, wheedling, each expressed in turn in rich mellifluous breathing of commonplace name. RUSSELL fretted and fumed under iteration. Snappishly protested.

"Oh, don't call me Sir CHARLES," he said.

"Very well, Sir CHARLES," said IRWIN, in softest cooing notes, as a nurse might soothe a restless infant.

Policeman to Policeman succeeded, as Amurath to Amurath. Interesting in its way, but finally soporific. Brother DAY began to take on a glassier stare as the afternoon shadows lengthened. Presently his chin sank on his breast, and he became profoundly engrossed in meditation on evidence.

The Close of Day.

"It's getting late," said LOCKWOOD. "This is what we call the close of DAY."

---

## THE IDEAL GYURL.

["Woman's work, what should it be but scrubbing furniture, dusting walls, sweeping floors, helping with the farm-work, or in the garden or dairy?"—*Professor Ruskin's last; and why doesn't he stick to his last?*]

"O MARY, go and scrub the drawing-room floor, [chairs,  
And dust the drawing-room  
And make the kitchen stairs  
As clean as clean can be!  
For so, Professor RUSKIN bids, whose word  
Is law to you and me."

She was a Girton maiden, and her brain  
Was crammed with learned lore,  
With culture to the core,  
And physiologee!  
But now she hoed potatoes, and at night  
Dead-tired home came she.

Oh, can this be the highest fruit of time,  
This bowed and wrinkled maid,  
This weather-beaten maid,—  
A gruesome sight to see?  
Was never horny-handed ploughboy yet  
Had such a hand as she!

They tried to find a mate for her, but man,  
But inconsiderate man,  
But beauty-loving man  
Preferred another She!  
And now that maiden may be heard to cuss  
Her RUSKIN heartilee!

---

PHŒBUS TO THE FORE.—With what object are letters in a disputed handwriting ordered to be photographed?—To bring their authorship to light.

---

FREE TRANSLATION.—*Quis custodiet ipsos custodes?* "Who shall examine the Examiners?"

**STUDIES IN EVOLUTION.**

ALDERMAN BROWNJONES SENIOR EXPLAINS TO HIS SON, ALDERMAN BROWNJONES JUNIOR, THAT THERE IS A LAMENTABLE FALLING-OFF SINCE *HIS* DAY, IN THE BREED OF ALDERMEN-SHERIFFS—NOT ONLY IN STYLE AND BEARING, BUT EVEN IN "HAPPETITE"!

## OUR BOOKING-OFFICE.

LET no one say that in the absence of LIKA JOKO from his own native village, there is no artistic talent left in Japan. Just look at the Japanese draughtsman's picture of MASÉ, one of the forty Ronins, drawing a bow as he points an arrow at the spectator, in No. 6 of *Artistic Japan* for last October.

I should like to have seen Mr. TOOLE's *Recollections told by Himself*, chronicled by JOSEPH HATTON, and published by Messrs. HURST AND BLACKETT, illustrated by a Japanese artist, though Messrs. BRYAN AND MARGETSON have done their work very well. It is a very amusing book without an unkind or ungenerous word in it about anyone in or connected with the theatrical profession, and this is saying a good deal for Mr. TOOLE's forbearance, seeing how easily and successfully he might have retaliated on those who of late years, under the flimsy pretence of criticism, have rarely missed an opportunity of venting their petty personal spite on the comedian whose well deserved popularity, and his numerous acts of generosity, must necessarily have made for him many enemies. Mr. HATTON in Boswelling JOHNNIE TOOLE has cleverly contrived to give the necessary "go" to most of the stories, which otherwise, owing to Mr. TOOLE's inimitable and original manner of oral narration would certainly have lost considerably when told in print.

There is one story about H. J. BYRON which Mr. TOOLE records as occurring a week or so before his death. The story is this: BYRON's coachman wrote to him to say that a mare in his stable in London was ill, and he wanted to know if he should give her a ball. To which BYRON replied, "Yes—only don't ask too many people." Now I, *moi qui parle*, myself heard BYRON say this, as he said it to me one morning at Ramsgate, where he was staying three or four years before his death. He was holding the coachman's letter in his hand as I entered the room, and was roaring with laughter. "My coachman writes," he said, chuckling, and pulling at his moustache, "to say that a mare of mine is ill, and asks me if he may give her a ball, as he wouldn't do it without permission. I was just saying to my wife that I think I shall write and say, 'Yes—give her a ball, only don't ask too many people'"—and then he laughed till he almost cried over it, so immensely was he tickled with the absurdity of the idea. There was a comparative stranger to him present, who did not see the joke immediately, and this made BYRON and myself laugh all the more. I've no doubt that so good a thing he repeated; but the fact of the coachman's letter having arrived that morning, is pretty clear proof that I was among the three first—the others were his wife and the unimpressionable stranger—who heard him say it.

In No. 4, Vol. I. of *The Salon* I find the name of the French actor, GIL PEREZ spelt "GILPRÉ." Was this his real name, or is it a misprint or an error in spelling, like "chawtle in his joy," instead of "chortle in his joy," which occurs in the same number? There should be no mistake about "chortle," which belongs to the classic English of the Victorian Era.

Christmas Books are well ahead of the time when they are due. I suppose all much the same as usual, but I shall make a dip in the lucky bag, and select. To anyone in want of indoor exercise, on a wet day, I strongly recommend the perusal of Mr. WALTER BESANT's *The Inner House* (ARROWSMITH's Christmas Annual), as affording plenty of opportunity for skipping. It may please Mr. BESANT's admirers, but it struck me as an uninteresting namby-pamby romance.

The best Christmas Book I've seen as yet, that is to say, really a book for Christmas time and the children, is *The Marvellous History of Jack the Giant-Killer*, by RICHARD DOYLE. It is a book for boys by a boy, for it was drawn by him in 1842, when he was in jackets and turn-down collars. It was before he signed his initials to his drawings, with or without the eccentric dicky-bird; but no signature is necessary to inform us who the artist was that "inventidit druit, et didit," when we see these quaint figures of dwarfs and giants, and funny little creatures climbing up or hanging on to the border of every page. To have kept the letter-press in fac-simile manuscript is the publisher's mistake, as some folks will find it difficult to decipher: but this is of less consequence, as each picture tells its own story, and is delightfully grotesque.

I gave JOSEPH HATTON's *Captured by Cannibals* to a big boy to read. He polished it off—I am not aware that Mr. HATTON's style requires this treatment—and returned it with thanks, informing me that he thought it would suit younger boys than himself admirably. I read the volatile Mr. G.'s article on ELIZABETH and the Establishment in the *Nineteenth Century*. Mr. G. must have his own private History of England and defies State Calendars. He should write an Elizabethan drama for AUGUSTUS DRURIOLANUS, who might put him right in some of his historical facts.

Reporters differ. Looking through *My Autobiography and Reminiscences*, by W. P. FRITH, R.A., with Notes (my own), I find that the modern HOGARTH gives an account of the banquet held in honour of MACREADY, on the occasion of that eminent tragedian's retirement from the Stage. Says he (after declaring that CHARLES DICKENS made an admirable speech), "and THACKERAY also spoke well and very humorously," to which I have added (in pencil in the margin), "This is news, indeed!!" Now, it happens, that Mr. JOHN COLEMAN was also present at this remarkable dinner, and according to *him* (he has it down in his book upon *Actors he has Known*, just published), the author of *Vanity Fair* made a mess of his speechification. To quote Mr. COLEMAN's own words, "THACKERAY, who had to propose the health of 'the Ladies,' would, I thought, have broken down every moment, not from the cause assigned by some 'd—d good-natured friend,' but from sheer nervousness." He moreover notes that BULWER LYTTON (who was in the chair), "seemed to him," to regard his rival novelist's "discomfiture with an amused and languid disdain which overlaid a somewhat deeper-rooted feeling." Again, the two historians adopt a distinctly different tone in referring to the speech of CHARLES KEMBLE. I give their impressions of the oration side by side:—

| *Charles Kemble's speech, according to Mr. Frith.* | *Charles Kemble's speech, according to Mr. Coleman.* |
|---|---|
| I was close to CHARLES KEMBLE, who spoke right well. * * * When the old man rose, feeble and bent, but with the old stately bearing, and in the sounding and dignified, though somewhat shrill voice peculiar to the KEMBLES, responded most happily to the toast, the *row* was deafening. | CHARLES KEMBLE, whom I saw for the first and last time on that occasion, made a somewhat irrelevant speech, in the midst of which he "dried up," and sat down. |

Really, when the two autobiographers have nothing better to do, they might read one another's "Recollections." I am sure that one or the other of them will find something that he *must* have forgotten!

*À propos* of the stage, Mr. W. DAVENPORT ADAMS (the well-known dramatic critic) has published a very readable little volume of essays, called *Byeways in Bookland*. It is pleasant to take a stroll through the leaves Mr. ADAMS has collected for us in these byeways. The leaves, although a study in "black and white," are full of charming colour.

THE BARON DE BOOK-WORMS & Co.

## "BEWARE!"

*Mr. Bull* (*to Miss America*). "Trust *him* not. He is Fooling thee!"

A doubtful Party's whispering thee,
Take care!
He can both false and friendly be,
Beware! Beware!
Trust him not,
He is fooling thee!

He has false eyes, their gleam means crime.
Take care!
He's playing tempter all the time;
Beware! Beware!
Trust him not,
He is fooling thee!

His hands in blood he'd fain imbrue;
Take care!
And what he whispers is not true.
Beware! Beware!
Trust him not,
He is fooling thee!

He has a lot of votes, of course:
Take care!
He is a fiend without remorse.
Beware! Beware!
Trust him not,
He is fooling thee!

He'll give those votes, and promise fair,
Take care!
A demon gift is but a snare.
Beware! Beware!
Trust him not,
He is fooling thee!

### A SAW ILL SET.

Mr. Punch,—The writer of a recent review of Dr. Marston's work on Actors, adduces the celebrated definition of "Genius" as "an infinite capacity of taking pains," and ascribes it to Lord Beaconsfield. As you know, it passes for Carlyle's. The house of the late Seer of Chelsea being tenanted by Spirit-rappers, who are said to have been invoking him—and Beaconsfield, too—at *séances*, the Mediums could easily set then to settle their respective claims to the above saying, if necromancers are not impostors, and if both the statesman and the philosopher would either of them care to be credited with a stupid observation. But it is unlikely that any ghost walks in Cheyne Walk.

Why, *Mr. Punch*, you, yourself, the greatest Genius living, must of course, well know that, so far from being a capacity for taking any pains at all, Genius is an endowment which enables anybody to do without effort marvels and prodigies which nobody else could achieve whatever pains they could possibly take. Only think of Handel and Mozart performing and composing music almost before they were out of their frocks and trousers! Of Pope, who "lisped in numbers, for the numbers came." Of BIDDER, and other calculating boys who similarly, when mere babies, could solve the most intricate arithmetical problems by a merely instinctive faculty. Don't you think, Sir, Genius had much better be defined a capacity of doing wonders, without taking any pains at all?

Wouldn't you say that you, in your own person, find an infinite capacity of taking pains a great auxiliary to genius indeed, and quite essential to success in its highest flights, but something as totally distinct from it as a watchmaker from a TENNYSON, or a BROWNING, or even from you?

As to Lord BEACONSFIELD's authorship of the account of Genius imputed to CARLYLE, don't you think that it might just as well have been set down to Mr. GLADSTONE; and that, if it had been, that right honourable gentleman would bo as much annoyed as you would be in case you were charged with having originated it yourself? Do help to withdraw from circulation a current misdescription of Genius altogether at variance with

COMMON SENSE.

## THE HOSPITAL FOR SICK CHILDREN.

"MRS. KEELEY in a new piece!" sounds startling as a bit of theatrical intelligence—nevertheless, it was a fact last Friday. This lively and accomplished young lady of eighty-three played to a crowded and enthusiastic house for the benefit of the Hospital for Sick Children in Great Ormond Street. Happy Charity to have such an advocate!—happy ASHBY-STERRY to have his lines so delightfully given! Not a point was lost, not a chance given away; the clever and experienced actress showed she had not forgotten a particle of her art—she had the same wondrous power over her audience that she possessed years ago.

At the conclusion of her address she said, with wondrous earnestness, in speaking of the children:—

"I crave for them your sympathy untold,
Your love, your help, your pity—and your gold!
The last I'm bound to have, for, you must know,
I played *Jack Sheppard* many years ago!
I've not forgot his impudence, his dash—
His rare persuasive power when seeking cash!
Stand and deliver—sovereigns, fifties, fives—
We want *your* money, for we want *their* lives!"

It is to be hoped that the eloquence and persuasive power of Mrs. KEELEY will have the effect of "sovereigns, fifties, and fives," being speedily delivered to the treasury of this excellent Institution, which is only waiting for money in order that its new wing may be built, and its sphere of usefulness substantially enlarged.

FELINE AMENITIES.

"MY DEAR SUSAN! I DECLARE YOU'RE GETTING MORE LIKE MARGARET EVERY DAY!"

"OH, COME NOW—YOU SAY THAT TO FLATTER ME!"

"*WHAT!* YOU DON'T MEAN TO SAY YOU *ADMIRE* HER!"

## A CASE OF SOUND MEDICINE.

"From the time when medical knowledge was first embodied in rules of practice, and probably from a much earlier period, Music has held a recognised place in the treatment of disease. . . . Lauded in connection, for example, with gout."—*Lancet.*

SCENE—*A Sick Chamber.* Invalid *discovered groaning on a sofa. Enter* Doctor, *briskly.*

*Doctor.* Well, and how are we to-day?

*Invalid.* Oh, very—very ill! Worse, Doctor—worse!

*Doctor.* Dear me! Surely you could not have taken the medicine I ordered.

*Invalid.* Oh, yes, indeed I did.

*Doctor.* Sure you did not swallow the embrocation and use the sleeping draught for a lotion?

*Invalid.* Oh, no, Doctor; I was very careful indeed! (*Sadly*). But they all have done me no good. I think I am worse than ever! Oh! [*Groans.*

*Doctor.* Dear me, that's bad! Let me see your tongue; and then you can tell me your symptoms.

*Invalid* (*after showing his tongue*). Well, Doctor, you see I have a pain here, and a pain there. [*Describes in detail his ailments.*

*Doctor.* You surprise me! But I fancy I can put you straight. Just sing "*She Wore a Wreath of Roses.*"

*Invalid.* I am sure I can't! I haven't sung for years.

*Doctor.* The greater the reason you should commence. Now, then, "*She Wore a Wreath of Roses.*" Come make an effort (*sings*)—"She wore a wreath ——". Now, then, go on.

*Invalid.* I am sure I can't. (*Sings feebly.*) "She wore——"

[*Gives the rest of the song with unconventional variations.*

*Doctor.* Come, now, don't you feel better already?

*Invalid.* Well, I don't know; still——

*Doctor.* Of course you are! And now for a dance. I fancy "*The Highland Schottische*" is about your figure. Come. (*Sings and dances.*) "Rumtum titiddy-ee, tiddy-ee, tiddy-eee; Rumtum tiddy-ee, Ri de foll de dolly de?" Surely you can dance to that?

*Invalid.* I will try it. Let me see. "Rumtum-titiddy-ee."

[*Sings and dances feebly.*

*Doctor.* That's right! (*Takes his hands, and dances about energetically.*) Never mind the twinges at first. They will go off by-and-by. (*After a few minutes of singing and dancing.*) There now! How do you feel?

*Invalid* (*sinking on a couch.*) I am much, much better.

*Doctor* (*heartily*). I knew you would be!

*Invalid.* And now, Doctor, that I am cured, do you mind telling me what was the matter with me?

*Doctor.* Certainly. I have treated you for a slight attack of gout! As you are not yet quite yourself, I will send you a Saraband to be danced before bed-time, and the music for a Polka-Mazourka, that you must run through two or three times before you have your breakfast to-morrow morning. And now good-bye, as I have to go and cure some children suffering from measles with a good wholesome dose of "*Sir Roger de Coverley.*" [*Exit.*

A NUT PARTIALLY CRACKED.—It was recently suggested in the *Times* that cocoa-fibre would be useful as material for lining our warships. This theory, though not solving the old problem about the presence of milk in the cocoa-nut, *does* account for the hair outside.

MORE OF A UNIONIST THAN EVER.—Mr. CHAMBERLAIN. Best wishes to "JOSEPH's Sweetheart."

## ROBERT ON LORD MARE'S DAY.

THE revells was all over on the hallowd Ninth. The three most himportantest persuns of the hole himportant City; wiz., the parst Lord Mare, the present Lord Mare, and the future Lord Mare, was all comferally sleepin in their downy beds of lucksery; the appy Gests was all fled; the careful Committee Men had carefully locked up all the cubbord fulls of broken wittels, includin hole quartz of reel Turtel Soop, and seweral hole ams and fouls, as was all to be give to the Poor nex mornin, and the tired and sleepy Waiters had taken care that none of the fine old Wine shood be wasted, and then sort their umbel omes; and the ony sound to be herd was the silent tread of the ever wakeful Watchman, who was, for some hours to come, the great City Surweyor. But why does he cum to a sudden paws in his silent rownd? why, after a close examination of it with his lighted dark lantern, does he xclaim, "Why, ROBERT, my toolip, what on airth are you dooin there?"

The part omitted from Torpedo's Show by order of the Royal George.

I was a sleepin the sleep of the onest but tired-out Waiter, under a Sofy in the Committee's priwet refreshment room, havin laid down jest for about 40 winks; and havin, in the dark, rapt a table-cloth around my manly figger, to keep out the cold, I must suttenly have out raythe a strange apairance to my frend the Watchman wen I stood up to my full hight before his estonished eyes!

It was all the frutes of hover work. It is, I bleeves, about the werry fust time in all my long life as I have hever been gilty of sitch a hact of dense stoopidity, and I shall take preshus good care as it's the last. But my xcuse must be that it was all dun from a good cause and with a nobel hobjeck. I had herd sitch alarmin roomers of what was to be done, and what was not to be done, as respecks the Sacred Sho, that I was deturmind to see for myself with my hone eyes, and hear for myself with my hone hears, and be reddy to ersist the pore Life Gards and the pore Huzzas if they shoud be atacked by the angry mob who was of coarse naterally disappinted at being deprived of their speshal darlings, the Men in Armer from the reel Tower of Lundon, and ROBBING HOOD's Merry Men from Hepping Forest, and Burnthem Beeches.

But I need not have bin alarmed. Why, the brave fellers played away on their drums and trumpits and orns and rumbones, all thru the shouting Mob, jest the same as if they'd a bin in High Park.

As I stood gazin at 'em with all the admirashun as I coud muster considerin how werry cruelly I was a being shoved about by the thortless and hignorant Mob, I begun for to wunder how on hearth they ewer manages to do all they've got to do when they gos into Battel. The genelman as has 2 drums to play on, in case I spose as one shoud brake, woud always have his too drumsticks with witch to defend hisself from the hinsolwent fo, as *Othello* wery propperly calls him, but how about the gent with the orn? Supposing as he's ordered to "up Gards and at 'em!" jest think what he's got for to do. He has to play his orn, to guide his galliant steed, and to fite the Fo, and all with ony 2 hands! It's quite bad enuff for me wen I has to carry a Tooreen of hot bilin Soup, and a cupple of wine-glasses, and a carving nife in my mowth, but I reelly thinks as his case must be wuss than ewen mine.

However, a trewse to these reffleckshuns, and let me purseed to state that, tho the "Royal GEORGE," the Commander-in-Cheef, did most unkindly refuse to let us have jest about ten or twenty thousend Wolunteers to pertect us all, in the habsence of the six Men in Harmer, I can conseenshusly declair, and wen I says that, I means it, that neether the Lord Mare's State Cocheman, nor his State Postilyun, nor ewen his three State Footmen, showd by their pail faces any fear of the shoutin mob as was a scrowgin around 'em. What they felt in their hinnermost buzzums, them alone can tell.

The scoffin and grinnin 'Sinnick dowtless grinned and scoffed more than ewer when he seed the rain a poring down in the hurly morning; but if he had had my xperience he woud have known that, on all sitch himportant occashuns as Lord Mare's Sho, "The clouds will pass if we've pashens to Wait;" and so it was on Friday.

I got back to Gildhall weary and worn, and rumpled to that xtent, that not nobody but them as know'd me well coud ever have took me for a hed Waiter; but a good wash and brush up, and a clean white coller and choker, and two glasses of old brown Sherry—the werry best rewiver as kindly natur ewer perwided for xhausted Umanity—set me to rites, at eny rate for a time.

ROBERT.

## HOE DEAR!

READ GLADSTONE's advice about fruit-farming, jam, cherries, apples, and all the rest of it, with great interest. Why *do* the poor congregate in big towns, instead of doing this sort of thing in the country? So improvident! Believe there's a fortune to be made out of growing fruit and vegetables for London market, and mean to try.

Have bought a small farm. Nice light soil. Owner (who seems very anxious to get away), describes it as a "pebbly loam." More pebbles than loam, apparently. "Scratch your loam, and you find pebbles." Owner shows me orchard, paddock, cart-shed, &c., and induces me to take over his live and dead stock at valuation.

Settle at farm. Twenty miles out of town. Nearest rail two and a half miles; cartage to railway costs more than I expected. Have to pay Gardener, too; pay *him* more (I fancy) than either of us expected. Buy some books on fruit-farming, and feel rather proud of my position. Shall talk (to friends who don't know much about me), of "my place in the country." Hope they won't come down and find me hoeing mangel-wurzels.

Rather disappointed with perusal of the books. Find apples don't like a "pebbly loam." Also only a few kinds of apples have any sale nowadays. Call in a horticultural expert, and ask him to inspect my orchard.

Expert comes. Condemns orchard root and branch. Says, "only thing to be done is to grub up these 'ere trees, and plant noo ones." Well, then, what advantage do I get out of the old trees? "None whatever," he replies; "might just as well have bought a bit of meadow." Depressed. I think of riddle—"What's the good of Acres when you can't get a Bob out of them?" Riddle depresses me still further.

Give up apples. Plant no end of cherries and gooseberries. Gardener says, "important for fruit to go off directly it's ripe." Mine goes off before it's ripe. Goes off altogether; boys steal it. Also plant cabbages and mushrooms. Gardener says, "a fine opening for mushrooms." Spend a month or two buying spawn, making beds, &c. What a lot of attention mushrooms do want! Call this "*small* culture," indeed! Find that the opening for mushrooms has closed when I come to sell them. Buyers offer a price which just about covers cost of carriage to town. I ask why? They explain that "public fancy has changed; mushrooms not in vogue—tomatoes are."

Try tomatoes. Try 'em out of doors, and get 'em nipped by frost. Try again under glass. Putting up glass very expensive. Gardener suggests grapes. After buying one or two choice varieties, find Gardener doesn't understand planting them! Buy book on Grape-culture. While book coming, put grape-plants in cellar. Cellar doesn't suit them, it seems. Finally, when book arrives, plants have to be thrown away. Result of first year's fruit-growing—loss of £300. Not making fortune yet.

"Can small farms be made to answer?" somebody wants to know. Yes, if you don't mind the answer being "No!"

This year try asparagus, in corner of large field. Very successful. Think of making a "corner" in asparagus in London vegetable market. Gardener falls in with idea, and we keep crop back for a time. Consequence is, when we offer it, nobody wants to buy! Have to eat most of it myself. Get perfectly sick of asparagus in a week. Sick of Gardener, too. Dismiss him. He tells me, just as he's going, that "them pertaters has the disease awful bad, and there ain't a cherry on the trees because of caterpillars." Winds up by saying, there's a bill coming in for "them sparrergrass beds."

There is indeed. Such a bill! Seems that nothing will grow on the "pebbly loam," but that first one has to "make" the soil, and afterwards grow things. Always thought farms had good soil to begin with. What's the good of the Creation, if the ground has to be made all over again?

Losses increasing. As last desperate resource try jam. Erect small jam-factory. Have one or two fields of strawberries. Find a man who says he understands all about jam-making. "Get equal quantities of jam and sugar, and boil 'em up together," he says. It sounds very simple. Sugar bill enormous. When jam made, it really does look and taste very nice indeed. Send it to London. Letter in a few days from agent to say he can't sell my jam at any price. Too pure. Public like it with more "flavour" in it. And this comes of making real home-made jam. What a fool the public must be! Sell my farm at fearful sacrifice, and live in a "flat"—rather a suitable residence. Turn Tory. Understand *now* why poor congregate in large towns. Wonder if *they've* all been fruit-farmers like me, and made as much out of it?

---

SUMMER IN WINTER.—Don't forget MRS. JEUNE this winter. She makes her usual benevolent appeal on behalf of the starving children. "One pound," says the *Standard*, "provides an ample dinner for one hundred and thirty-seven hungry little ones." There's a Sovereign remedy for starvation!

## THE CRAMMER'S LAMENT.

(*Song for the Times.*)

THERE's a stir in the air; there are straws on the wind
That with dismal forebodings are filling my mind!

One Result of Cramming.

'Tis whisper'd the public, that so long has slumber'd,
Is waking at last, and that my days are number'd.
Oh! say not 'tis true, for if fierce competition,
The secrets of which I have measured so neatly,
Is flung by the Powers that be to perdition,
Dismember'd, undone, and exploded completely,
Oh! I ask you, despairing, what future there'll be
For a poor shunted, unemployed Crammer like me?

For if they decide, in the service of truth,
To rescue the mind of intelligent youth
From a system that all its intelligence clearing
Clean right out of the way, ekes it out with veneering,
A showy acquaintance with facts but inducing,
And all solid knowledge away glibly casting,
Instead, in its place, its mere semblance producing,
And that for a fortnight, at most, only lasting!
Oh! I ask, if this happen, what future there'll be
For a poor shunted, unemployed Crammer like me?

## THE DIARY OF A NOBODY.

*October* 30.—I should very much like to know who has wilfully torn the last five or six weeks out of my diary. It is perfectly monstrous! Mine is a large scribbling diary with plenty of space for the record of my everyday events, and in keeping up that record I take (with much pride) a great deal of pains. I asked CARRIE if she knew anything about it? She replied it was my own fault for leaving the diary about with a charwoman cleaning, and the sweeps in the house. I said that was not an answer to my question. This retort of mine, which I thought extremely smart, would have been more effective had I not jogged my elbow against a vase on a table temporarily placed in the passage, knocked it over and smashed it. CARRIE was dreadfully upset at this disaster, for it was one of a pair of vases which cannot be matched, given to us on our wedding-day by Mrs. BURTSETT, an old friend of CARRIE's cousins, the POMMERTONS, late of Dalston. I called to SARAH and asked her about the diary. She said she had not been in the sitting-room at all; after the sweep had left, Mrs. BIRRELL (the charwoman) had cleaned the room and lighted the fire herself. Finding a burnt piece of paper in the grate, I examined it, and found it was a piece of my diary. So it was evident someone had torn my diary to light the fire. I requested Mrs. BIRRELL to be sent to me to-morrow.

*October* 31.—Received a letter from our principal, Mr. PERKUPP, saying that he thinks he knows of a place at last for our dear boy LUPIN. This, in a measure, consoles me for the loss of a portion of my diary, for I am bound to confess the last few weeks have been devoted to the record of disappointing answers received from people to whom I had applied for appointments, for LUPIN. Mrs. BIRRELL called, and in reply to me said, "She never *see* no book, much less take such a liberty as *touch it.*" I said I was determined to find out who did it, whereupon she said she would do her best to help me, but she remembered the sweep lighting the fire with a bit of the *Echo*. I requested the sweep to be sent to me to-morrow. I wish CARRIE had not given LUPIN a latch-key. We never seem to see anything of him. I sat up till past one for him, and then retired tired.

*November* 1.—My entry yesterday about "retired tired," which I did not notice at the time, is rather funny. If I were not so worried just now, I might have had a little joke about it. The sweep called, but had the audacity to come up to the hall-door, and lean his dirty bag of soot on the door-step. He, however, was so polite, I could not rebuke him. He said SARAH lighted the fire. Unfortunately SARAH heard this, for she was dusting the bannisters, and she ran down, and flew into a temper with the sweep, causing a row on the front door-steps, which I would not have had happen for anything. I ordered her about her business, and told the sweep I was sorry to have troubled him—and so I was, for the door-steps were covered with soot, in consequence of his visit. I would willingly give ten shillings to find out who tore my diary.

*November* 2.—I spent the evening quietly with CARRIE, of whose company I never tire. We had a most pleasant chat about the letters on "Is Marriage a Failure?" It has been no failure in our case. In talking over our own happy experiences, we never noticed that it was past midnight. We were startled by hearing the door slam violently. LUPIN had come in. He made no attempt to turn down the gas in the passage, or even to look into the room where we were, but went straight up to bed, making a terrible noise. I asked him to come down for a moment, and he begged to be excused, as he was "dead beat," an observation that was scarcely consistent with the fact that, for a quarter of an hour afterwards, he was positively dancing in his room, and shouting out, "See me dance the Polka!" or some such nonsense.

*November* 3.—Good news at last. Mr. PERKUPP has got an appointment for LUPIN, and he is to go and see about it on Monday. Oh, how my mind is relieved! I went to LUPIN's room to take the good news to him, but he was in bed, very seedy, so I resolved to keep it over till the evening. He said he had last night been elected a member of an Amateur Dramatic Club, called the "Holloway Comedians;" and, though it was a pleasant evening, he had sat in a draught, and got neuralgia in the head. He declined to have any breakfast, so I left him. In the evening I had up a special bottle of port, and, LUPIN being in, for a wonder, we filled our glasses, and I said,—"LUPIN, my boy, I have some good and unexpected news for you. Mr. PERKUPP has procured you an appointment." LUPIN said, "Good biz!" and we drained our glasses. LUPIN then said, "Fill up the glasses again, for I have some good and unexpected news for you." I had some slight misgivings, and so evidently had CARRIE, for she said, "I hope we shall think it good news." LUPIN said, "Oh, it's all right. *I'm engaged to be married.*"

## THE VADE-MECUM OF A CHIEF MAGISTRATE.

*Question.* When is reference first made to you by the Press?

*Answer.* In the early autumn of the year, when paragraphs appear in the City papers briefly alluding to my antecedents, and noting my probable election.

*Q.* Have you then an opportunity of further advertising yourself?

*A.* Certainly. If I am energetic, I can let it be known that I object to something or other favoured by my predecessor.

*Q.* Can you do more than this in the same direction?

*A.* Well, there is no reason why I should not, in advance of the time fixed for my appearance in my official residence, notify the funds I purpose founding there.

*Q.* Is this not encroaching on the prerogative of your predecessor?

*A.* Not seriously; as when I do this he, from an official point of view, will be moribund.

*Q.* Then I presume you consider yourself well advertised by the banquet itself?

*A.* I consider it practically my entrance into public life; for in the papers next day my speeches, which hitherto have received little attention, will be reported at a length only second to that reserved for the utterances of the Prime Minister.

*Q.* Before attaining your exalted rank are your opinions considered of any value?

*A.* No, of very little value, and probably on my retirement the store set upon them will sink to the original standard.

*Q.* Do you not during your tenure of power obtain many advantages?

*A.* Certainly. *Ex officio* I am a member of the Privy Council, and in certain emergencies, this may confer upon me the performance of duties of the highest dignity. I have the precedence of an Earl outside the City, and when I dine in state can call upon the Sheriffs (or as in the future it will be—the Sheriff), to attend upon me.

*Q.* Have you not omitted something which adds to your pomp?

*A.* I presume you refer to my custom of marching about in the company of two persons, carrying respectively, a gigantic sword and a huge mace.

*Q.* Do not these persons, with their comic weapons, introduce what may be termed, the "pantomimic element" into your progresses?

*A.* Possibly, but their existence is sanctioned by long usage.

*Q.* You have too, have you not, a wardrobe full of official costumes?

*A.* Certainly. Some of the robes are extremely gorgeous, both in colouring and material.

*Q.* And generally, during your term of office, do you not receive very marked attention?

*A.* I do. My letters to the papers are printed in the leader page, in leaded type, my movements are reported with regularity and accuracy, and my presence in even the highest quarters is regarded with satisfaction rather than astonishment.

*Q.* And this deference is paid to you for a year?

*A.* Or rather, for eleven months, as my doings during the last twenty or thirty days of my tenure of power are considered of less moment than the proceedings of my successor during the same period.

*Q.* And at the end of your year of office what will happen to you?

*A.* If I am lucky I shall retire with a Knighthood into the dense obscurity of City private life.

*Q.* Will you, after your retirement ever re-attract public attention?

*A.* To judge from precedents, I do not think I ever shall.

**UGH!**

*Little Darling.* "THAT WAS A *WHITE* SUGAR-ALMOND I GAVE OO, MR. SQUEAMS. DOES OO LIKE IT?"
*Crusty Old Bachelor (who is trying hard to swallow the dainty in question).* "VERY MUCH INDEED, THANK YOU!"
*Little Darling.* "IT WAS *PINK—ONCE!*"

## THE GERMAN FOX AND THE BRITISH LION.

(*A Fable after the fashion of La Fontaine.*)

A CERTAIN Lion, whose re-echoing roar
Had long been heard on Afric's eastern shore,
Had hard thereby a den convenient, spacious.
Leo was vigilant, not *too* pugnacious,
Yet always ready,
With strength exceptional and ardour steady,
To help maintain, even on that wild border,
His leonine ideas of Law and Order.
The King of Beasts, like other royal bodies
Who're not quite *fainéant* noddies,
Loved not the anarchical and the chaotic.
In fact his foes declared him too despotic,
Too apt to bring down his prodigious paw,
And call *that* Law.
At any rate our Lion autocratical
Was down tremendously on the piratical.
Now in that torrid region
Dwelt certain lesser beasts—their name was legion—
Whose sole idea of kingship was sheer knavery
Built up on Slavery.
Leo with tooth and claw was prompt to drop
Upon these robber-bands. He strove to stop
The grisly game to which the ghouls were given,
And long had striven
Almost alone indeed and single-handed;
For, though the other brutes he'd fain have banded
Against these common curses of their kind,
He somehow seldom found them in the mind.
Greed, fear, and faction,
With brutes as men, are foes to common action.

There came into that region, rather later,
A certain Fox. No beast had shrewdness greater;
And, adding lupine strength to vulpine cunning,
He rather fancied he was in the running
For the reversion
Of Leo's sovereignty; indeed *some* said,
To share the Lion's skin ere he was dead,
Was an idea running in his head;
Perhaps 'twas an aspersion;
But anyhow Reynard, with all his tricks,
Found himself shortly in a sort of fix.
He hardly prospered as he deemed he ought to,
And sedulously sought to.
He was not trusted somehow, which seemed funny.
When deeds of iron follow words of honey,
Faith fails. That queerest seems of paradoxes—
To Foxes.
So *rusé* Reynard thought that he would try on
A sort of Confidence Trick with the old Lion.
He rigged himself in proper pilgrim guise,
With palmer-hat that flopped o'er his sly eyes,
With staff, and scrip, and scallop all complete,
And a long gaberdine that reached his feet,
Properly girdled; one in fact might term it
*The* costume for a new Peter the Hermit.
Togged in this manner,
He bore in hand a big emblazoned banner,
Whereon was written in much broidered bravery,
"Down, down with Slavery!!!"
Thus robed, our Reynard Leo thus addressed:
"Leo, my friend, I'm really quite distressed
At the black deeds that shame this region torrid;
They're truly horrid!
As for one cruel and kidnapping band,
*They* ought to be put down with a strong hand.
You who're so noble, generous, and strong,
Must feel, I'm sure, that it is really wrong
To give free licence to this bad black trade.
Shall we not join, then, in a New Crusade?
You always were a bit of a knight-errant,
I've quite a fit of missionary zeal;
United, I am sure that you will feel
Our influence on this sin will be deterrent.
And—though *that* is, of course, the merest trifle—
Help any doubts of our good faith to stifle
(I've found such doubts a little in my way).
Come, Leo, what d'ye say?"

Leo said little, but he looked a deal,
For, hanging at the back of Mr. Fox,
Girt to his body by a chain of steel,
He spied a certain box,
Savouring to Leo, who could spot a trader,
More of the bagman than of the Crusader.
"Reynard," he mused, "whence is this new-born passion
For the knight-errantry not much *your* fashion?
Can it, oh! can it be a mere pretence
To gain prestige—and trade—at my expense?
True, it might task all
Our banded strength to crush the desert rascal,
The battener on blood, whom I, 'tis true,
Have hunted long, with little aid from you.
If—if indeed
You meant it in good faith, his cursèd breed
We'd quickly banish from this tropic shore.
But—*is* there nothing more

# THE GERMAN FOX AND THE BRITISH LION.

Fox. "ACH! YOU ZAT ZO NOPLE ARE—ZO SCHDRONG—ZO MACNÂNIMISCH!—LET US IN ZIS ZO HOLY GRUSADE TOGEZZER CHOIN! YA?" The Lion. "HUMPH!!!"

OUR NEW M.F.H.

"WARE 'HARE!" SHOUTED MR. TOPPLE, TRYING TO CRACK HIS WHIP,—AND THIS WAS THE RESULT.

Behind—like that black box—my foxy friend?
And is it like to happen in the end
That my good name will make yours brightly
Or you spoil mine?" [shine,

All this was muttered in the Lion's mane.
"Ah!" cried the Fox, "I see 'tis very plain
That you, so noble, so magnanimous,
So truly one of *us*,
Help in our new Crusade *cannot* refuse!"
(Aside he chuckled, "Ah, my little ruse
Has fairly fetched him then, the blind old
Leo said—"Humph!" [sumph!")

*Moral.*

When Fox with Lion hunts, one would be sorry
To say who gains—until they've shared the quarry!

## STOPPING THE STRAND.

(*A Church Catechism.*)

*Question.* Is the church (of St. Mary-le-Strand) worth preserving?

*Answer.* The Rector naturally replies, "Yes;" so do the verger, the pew-opener, the clerk, the bell-ringers, and the lay-helperess who brushes the dust from the floor on to the prayer-books, and from the prayer-books back again on to the floor, once a week.

*Q.* How much money is required in order to prevent the whole place tumbling on to the heads of wayfarers along the Strand?

*A.* Three thousand pounds.

*Q.* What is the feeling of Londoners as to the request for this sum lately published by the Rector in the newspapers.

*A.* They wish he may get it.

*Q.* What is the chief complaint against the edifice?

*A.* That, besides being ugly and unsafe, it is an intolerable obstruction. That, just where the Strand ought to widen into a really noble thoroughfare, it is cramped up into the dimensions of a narrow lane by this building, leaving barely space for two vehicles abreast, the foot pavement being reduced in like ratio.

*Q.* What is the remedy suggested for this ecclesiastical obstructionist?

*A.* The Clôture—shutting it up, and then pulling it down.

*Q.* Is not the church one of striking architectural beauty, so as to warrant its preservation on that score?

*A.* Not at all. On the contrary, it is a bad specimen of debased "Queen Anne."

*Q.* Would not its demolition deprive a large and important congregation of a place of worship?

*A.* It would distribute a congregation averaging about twenty or thirty among the multitude of other half-empty churches existing in the immediate neighbourhood.

*Q.* Would not the widening of the Strand sweep away some old and venerable specimens of London Street architecture?

*A.* Yes, it would mean the removal of the venerable thoroughfare known as Holywell Street, with its high-class shops and noble literary associations.

*Q.* What then is wanted?

*A.* That the new London County Council should take the matter up, and knock the church down, with what speed it may.

---

ON "ALL FOURS."—British Protectorate in Borneo,—"Hugh Low (Union) Jack, and the game." Other Protectorates generally suggest another game,—Cribbage. But of course this doesn't apply to *us*.

## FRUITS FROM THE TREE OF KNOWLEDGE.

BOARD Schools are not all paid for out of rates;
Nor *gratis*, quite, crammed Board School children's pates,
Parents have still the cost in part to bear—
Not much, yet more than most of them can spare;

Their tributary pence required to send
For children forced instruction to attend:
But, what with rates and fees for mental "feed,"
Those youngsters get, however, taught to read.

That knowledge they are mostly apt to use;
Fictitious literature in general choose:
Tales of adventure, villany, and crime,
Horrors and vices, which their minds begrime.

'Twas hoped that education would avail
To elevate them in the social scale.
What profit may accrue from learning, see;
The Penny Dreadful for the Penny Fee!

---

FROM STRATFORD-ON-AVON.—Was *Banquo* a sculptor? Shakspearian commentators are unable to answer this question with absolute certainty, but they are quite sure that he had a Ghost.

---

ACADEMICAL.—"Messrs. C. V. STANFORD and A. C. MACKENZIE, to be made Doctors of Music, *honoris causâ*," at Cambridge. The *libretto* of the solemn ceremony will of course be "*Cantabile.*"

---

HISTORICAL NOTE.—In mediæval times the rich Abbots of a sporting turn used to keep hounds. Over the kennels was inscribed *Pax*.

**EXCLUSION.**

*Policeman (at the Law Courts).* "STRICT ORDERS TO-DAY, M'M. NO ONE TO BE ADMITTED UNLESS THEY 'RE IN WIG AN'—THAT IS—BEG PARDON, M'M—BARRISTERS, M'M—ONLY BARRISTERS!"

## HAND AND FOOT AT HANDOUB;

*Or, What the Latest Intelligence is coming to.*

SUAKIM, *Nov.* 12.—The enemy again continued last night their shelling operations against the Water Forts, making excellent practice, and succeeding in sending six shots in succession through the top of the General's tent, the final one being specially well-aimed, and going clean through his moderator, which it effectually extinguished. On lights being fetched, and an examination made of the ammunition used, much enthusiastic satisfaction was expressed by all the officers present on its being ascertained as a fact that it had been supplied by a well-known British firm. Its destructive capabilities having just been conclusively demonstrated, a high and flattering opinion was expressed on all hands at the circumstance.

This morning the long-expected reinforcements, consisting of five mounted infantry, one gun, and two artillerymen, having arrived from Egypt, the General determined to make a reconnoitring movement in the direction of Handoub, for the purpose, if possible, of ascertaining the strength of the enemy. This they were not long in disclosing, for they instantly threw out a thoroughly disciplined and well-equipped force of cavalry, about five hundred strong, which, sweeping at a charge down on the little contingent, capturing the gun, and sabring its defenders, much to his surprise, obliged the General to take to flight, and pursued him up to the fortifications, which he barely reached in safety, followed by a perfect hail of bullets.

It is understood that after this experience he will probably endeavour to impress on the authorities at Cairo the necessity of their taking vigorous measures, and despatching further reinforcements to enable him to cope with the situation, which he describes as "threatening."

This evening there is a rumour of telegraphic communication from headquarters, acknowledging the receipt of the General's application and promising the despatch of "five more mounted infantry, another gun, and two more artillerymen, in the course of a month or so," which they think will "meet the requirements of the situation."

As the mail is leaving, the Dervishes, who have just mounted twelve Armstrong guns in a position thoroughly commanding the Citadel and the Water Forts, appear to be massing in large numbers close up to the fortifications, as if meditating a determined night-attack. Her Majesty's cruiser, *Bouncer*, which is our only defensive resource in any emergency, seems, unfortunately, somehow to have disappeared on the horizon. The General, who has apparently noted this incident with regret, seems uneasy, and is inquiring about cellar accommodation in the suburbs. Altogether the outlook is gloomy.

## THE ALMIGHTY *HALF*-DOLLAR.

A SONG BY A SUFFERER.

"*Facit indignatio versum,*"
Florins are a nuisance—curse 'em!

CONFOUNDED coin, whose prevalence confounds
Finance domestic more than any other,
Why thus beset me on my daily rounds
With constant bother!

The Mint was mad the day it fashioned you,
And sowed you broadcast on enslaved society.
What man knows not the mischiefs that you brew
In vile variety?

You were not wanted; you are awkward, odd,
A coin which trade's arrangements do not follow;
And yet, beshrew you! you, like Aaron's rod,
All others swallow.

A shilling is the price for heaps of things,
A sixpence purchases at least as many;
And every moment from the pocket brings,
The useful penny.

Even the odd Half-crown may have its use,
But why bring *you*, you poor superfluous bore in?
What mortal ever wants, save to abuse,
The fruitless Florin?

And yet you crowd my pocket, fill my purse,
To the exclusion of brave "bobs" and "tanners."
I lose my cash through you, and—what is more
Perhaps—my manners!

Say, that a cab I call, the distance, say,
Is half a mile, the fare—of course, a shilling.
The tariff-rate, arranged, the which to pay
I'm not unwilling.

My hand in all my pockets wild may range,
But not one sixpence or one shilling collars.
(For if you change a sovereign now, your change
Is *all* "Half-dollars").

Cabby has none—cabbies are far too "wide"—
So, after lots of hunting, and much "bobbery,"
I pay two shillings for a half-mile ride!
*I* call it robbery!

Two shillings or four sixpences fulfil
The Florin's every duty, and *their own too.*
Why then the Florin, which of purse and till
A plague has grown to?

Silver I scarce can get, save in its form;
I've seven in my pocket at this moment!
Can such a curse—excuse my language warm!—
Need further comment?

Why flood the circulation with these coins,
Which rile the testy, and which rob the thrifty,
And only serve the servant who purloins—
The Cabman shifty?

I'm sure they rob me of ten pounds a year,
(I gravely doubt if 'tis not nearer twenty),
Which I might save were "bobs" less scarce, and dear
Old "tanners" plenty.

I've suffered long: at last my plaint's in print.
*My* plan—most men, I'm certain, will agree to it—
Is, call the Florin in! I hope the Mint
Will kindly see to it!

MOTTO FOR LORD MAYOR TORPEDO'S BANNER.—"*Pas Grand' Shows.*"

MOTTO FOR EX-LORD MAYOR SIR POLYDORE'S BANNER.—"The Period of D.K.," and "After me The Torpedo."

PHENOMENAL SUNLIGHT AT NIGHT.—Of course our "London particular" atmosphere prevents us, at this time of year, from seeing a real English sun, so we adapt from the French, and the playgoer has only to visit the Royalty in Dean Street, Soho, in order to enjoy *Clara Soleil*, which, as the title implies, is a piece of a very light character.

# ESSENCE OF PARLIAMENT

EXTRACTED FROM THE DIARY OF TOBY, M.P.

*Tuesday.*—Pretty fair attendance in both Houses, considering. G. O. M. and most of his merry men down at Birmingham, making speeches by the furlong. House of Commons plays second fiddle. Still, we've a few left at Westminster. The Curse of Camborne back again in full blast. Pops up suddenly at question time. Quietly floored by Speaker, but up again.

"They think they did a good thing in suspending me in July," says he. "Got rid of me for a week or two. But I'll make it up now. You'll see."

Jesse Collings here too, and with Birmingham ablaze!

"How's this?" I ask. "You in London when Birmingham's keeping political holiday?"

"Is it?" he asked, with look of innocent surprise. "Now you mention it, I *did* hear something about it; under the auspices of what is left of Liberal Association, wasn't it? And Gladstone was to be there. Yes, yes, I remember. They asked me to meet him in the Mayor's parlour; but I declined. Sorry to do it. Pained to hurt feelings of estimable person. But it wouldn't do. If I had accepted invitation, Gladstone would have been sure to have imposed upon concession. Too much would have been made of it: and I plumply but regretfully said 'No.' Did you hear whether the proposed gathering was abandoned?" Grandolph here, enthroned in corner seat.

"Sorry to hear you've been ill, and are going to throw up the sponge," I say; for, though he's a trifle cantankerous, and apt to turn upon his friends unless they will consent to be his adulators, I like Grandolph.

"You dear, credulous Toby!" he cried. "Have you, too, been taken in by that *blague?* I'm pretty well, thank you. All the better for a rest; all the readier for work when opportunity comes. Perhaps it would please some people if it were true that I had broken down, and would not trouble them any more. But, with every natural disposition to oblige, can't please everybody. So I'm pretty well, thank you. Keep my eyes open, and my hand ready to strike."

A quiet night, with Harcourt softly purring to himself on Front Opposition Bench, and Old Morality thinking how pleasantly the mice may play when the cat's away. (*Vide* Copy-book.)

Grand Cross looks down from Peers' Gallery on the familiar scene and thinks of days that are no more. Another Cross (not yet grand) appears on the scene, walking up to take the Oath. It is W. H., Member for West Derby.

"Do you think, TOBY," said Grand CROSS, "he'll ever make the same position in the House that his father did?"

"I hope not; indeed, I hope not." I say fervently

Grand CROSS stared. Think afterwards wasn't quite the thing to say; might have put it in another way. But a little hurried, and was thinking of something else.

*Business done.*—Supply.

"Grand Cross stared."

*Thursday.* — Reminded of our loss by little incident that took place at opening of sitting. STORMOUTH DARLING took seat for St. Andrew's University. LORD-ADVOCATE used to represent St. Andrew's. Certainly, hard for anyone to take a seat when *he's* in it. But, alas! he's out, vanished with the snows of yesteryear. Made something in the City of Edinburgh, with a fat salary and a noble title.

Room for Scotch Members to breathe now. Early effect seen in debate on alleged malversation of Crown Lands and Waters in Scotland. Someone been selling the fishing rights on an Invernesshire loch, and turning banks and braes into deer-forests. Not a new thing; didn't happen during the recess; why wasn't it brought up before? Simply because the burly LORD-ADVOCATE was at hand, and Scots-wha-hae shrewdly thought they'd suffered enough in times past without wantonly incurring fresh danger. The MACDONALD's place scarcely filled up when FRASER MACKINTOSH, in his animated and picturesque style, clamours about fishing rights and talks treason about deer-forests.

OLD MORALITY turns uneasily on the bench, and looks wistfully towards the corner-post against which the departed LORD-ADVOCATE's back was wont to rest with temporary impunity. Sorry for O. M. Tell him a little secret. Amongst messengers on duty at Lobby-door, is one who bears singularly close resemblance to the departed chief. About the same height, perhaps a trifle less burly, but with the same capability of extended shirt-front, the same pose of head, the same striking profile, and the same expanse of beardless countenance.

"If, old friend," I say to First Lord, "you could double his wages, practise him in the cultivation of infinite scorn of Scotch Members, dress him in a suit of the Chieftain's clothes, and prop him up with his back against the post at the end of Treasury Bench, you'd hear no more of FRASER MACKINTOSH."

"Thank you, TOBY," said O. M., pressing my paw. "That's a very valuable suggestion. I'll see if something can't be done in the matter before Scotch Votes come on next week. 'To be Forearmed is to be Forewarned,' as we used to write in fair round hand."

In the meanwhile ROBERTSON goes a step higher, and fills a section of the LORD-ADVOCATE's place, whilst STORMOUTH DARLING comes in as Solicitor-General for Scotland.

"CHARLIE used to be my DARLING," said OLD MORALITY, turning round to gaze at the venerable figure of the Member for Deptford; "now it's STORMOUTH. Life is full of change. Here to-day, we're gone to-morrow."

*Business done.*—Committee of Supply.

*Friday.*—House more than ever empty to-night. Great counter-attraction at Guildhall. Her Majesty's Ministers dining with LORD MAYOR.

"Some of them," GORST says, snappishly, "and some, if you please, not so. All of us asked; all accepted. Then screw is put upon all under Cabinet rank to make them stop here to help to keep a House."

Gloom and depression all over House. Quite a different scene at Guildhall, where the Aldermen go wild over ARTHUR BALFOUR, and the Alderwomen openly murmur, "What a nice-looking young man!" The Marquis sonorously eloquent. The LORD MAYOR looked well, and spoke well. Excellent beginning for what promises to be memorable year in the City.

*Business done.* — Junior Ministers kept in. Education Vote agreed to.

---

ADVICE TO A GOOD SERVANT.—Always keep your place.

## "WHAT IT MAY COME TO,"

*Now that Royal Residences are put up to Let.*

SCENE—*Interior of the Government Auction and Estate Office. Plans of Castles, &c., on the walls.* Official *discovered asleep over an early edition of an evening paper.*

*Successful Australian (sharply).* Now then, you Sir—wake up!

*Official (coming to his senses).* I beg pardon—what can I do for you, Sir?

*Suc. Aus.* Well, I want to find some little property in London to settle down in during my stay in the Mother Country—a leasehold for twenty or thirty years, you know.

*Official.* We do not usually let anything under ninety-nine years, Sir.

*Suc. Aus.* Oh, I dare say we shall not quarrel about a month or two. But what have you got? How about Windsor Castle?

*Official.* Not in the market, Sir. It is in the occupation of the family.

*Suc. Aus. (in a disappointed tone).* Never mind; I am not particularly sweet upon it. Too far off. Anything Hampton way?

*Official (referring to ledger).* The Court, Sir, has been recently taken by Sir WILLIAM HARCOURT, who has got rid of his holding in the New Forest (which some say was not a good bargain) to a Native Prince just arrived from India.

*Suc. Aus. (after a moment's reflection).* Well, wasn't there a rather nice building in red-brick, Kensington way?

*Official (smiling).* I presume, Sir, you refer to Kensington Palace. I am sorry to say, Sir, I cannot do anything for you there. The Palace is let out in flats, and tenanted at present by Mr. HENRY LABOUCHERE, Mr. BRADLAUGH, Sir CHARLES WARREN, Professor BALDWIN, Canon FARRAR, Mr. DAVITT, Mr. ARTHUR ROBERTS, and Sir RICHARD WEBSTER, the Attorney-General.

*Suc. Aus. (in a tone of annoyance).* Dear me, there seems to be nothing you can let me have.

*Official. (hesitatingly).* Well, there is one property, certainly, in the market, but we can only let it to a *very* careful tenant.

*Suc. Aus.* I will be careful enough if it only suits me. What is it?

*Official.* Buckingham Palace, Sir. It has been recently in the occupation of—— *(Murmurs a well-known name.)*

*Suc. Aus. (impressed).* Indeed! But why did he leave? Nothing wrong with the drainage, or anything of that sort?

*Official (promptly).* Oh dear no, Sir. The fact is he *would* cut down all the trees in the back garden, and we were reluctantly obliged to——

*Suc. Aus.* I see! Well, put it down to me—I will take it.

[*Scene closes, upon the preparation of a lease for* 999 *years.*

---

## ANSWERS TO CORRESPONDENTS.

DOMESTIC PETS. — If the Lawn-Tennis Net, spread, as you describe, over the top of your Area, is not considered by your neighbours a sufficient restraint for your two full-grown Bengal Tigers, why not keep them in the coal-cellar? You could then feed them conveniently with the tinned salmon you mention, through the aperture in the pavement in front of your premises. There being a Board School opposite, you cannot, of course, very well give them an airing in the day-time, but between two and three o'clock, A.M., in the small hours of the morning, when the streets are more or less deserted, you could, with the aid of nine or ten policemen, armed with red-hot pincers and crowbars, easily manage it. Anyhow you could do no harm in trying the experiment. With regard to the Kangaroo, having succeeded in getting it there, by all means keep it in the linen cupboard. If it show signs of growing obstreperous, give it chloral with its dog-biscuit.

CARDS. — There is an infallible method of securing all the four honours in your own hand at whist; but, by playing with prepared packs, providing yourself with "advantage" cuffs and "expansion" sleeves, and dealing with a New York "luck manipulator," you may be tolerably sure of holding good cards. It would be as well, however, to be cautious in having recourse to these artificial aids, as your frequent detection in their use at any well-known West End Club might possibly lead to some slight unpleasantness with the Committee.

COUNTRY HOUSE.—If your servants are all giving you warning, because, as you say, the mansion you are renting for the summer months is "haunted," why not take the bull by the horns, and lay the Ghost yourself. You have only got to conceal yourself in the Picture Gallery, where the Knight in Armour comes along groaning every night as the clock strikes twelve, and waiting his appearance, hit him full in the chest with the warming-pan—and the thing is done. Try this. The celebrated Crusader of Bitson Abbey was met three nights running in this fashion, and he vanished eventually with an unearthly oath, and has never been heard of since.

"The University of Giessen has made BISMARCK a Doctor of Divinity."—*Times, Nov.* 13.

## MR. BULL AND MYNHEER.

"On the 17th November Dutchmen are preparing to celebrate the seventy-fifth anniversary of the liberation of the Netherlands from French domination, and the re-establishment of national independence."—*Times.*

"It is just two centuries to-day (November 5) since modern English political history began with the landing of WILLIAM of Orange at Brixham Harbour, Torbay."—*Mrs. Lynn Linton, in "St. James's Gazette."*

*Mr. Bull.* Your health, Mynheer, in a genuine Dutchman's draught! You know, perhaps, what the rousing chorus of the popular glee says:—

"It's oh! that a Dutchman's draught should be
As deep as the rolling Zuyder Zee!"

*Mynheer.* Verily, Mr. BULL, VAN DUNK's powers of potation were less typical than some shouters of that roystering chorus seem to suppose:—

"Mynheer VAN DUNK,
Though he never got drunk,
Sipped brandy-and-water gaily;
And he quenched his thirst
With two quarts of the first
To a pint of the latter daily."

'Tisn't a legion of bibulous VAN DUNKS, my friend, who would have snatched Holland from the ocean sand-flats, or fought PHILIP of Spain. But for once, and, in response to your hearty challenge, I'll not shirk even what you call a Dutchman's draught. This schnapps is no bad stingo, as mellow as old Irish, and as toothsome as "right Nantz."

*Mr. Bull.* Well, Mynheer, we have been linked in many ways in history. We have fought yard-arm to yard-arm, with no great discredit to either. If we have given you a licking, occasionally, in return you have given us a king. That trims the balance, I reckon,—not to name VAN TROMP and his broom! But the toast I now propose is, "Liberty, and our Lasting Friendship!" In connection wherewith accept my hearty congratulations on your glorious anniversary.

*Mynheer.* Thanks, my friend! In return accept *mine* upon *yours*. Seventy-five years or two centuries, they both represent the same thing, the thing we have both fought for and laboured for, the very breath of the nostrils of both Hollander and Anglo-Saxon—Liberty! [*They drink deeply.*

*Mr. Bull.* By the way, Mynheer, there is likely to be yet another link between us. If I may trust the *Cambridge Review*, you are adopting, under whatever difficulties, our national game. I understand there are more than a hundred cricket-clubs in Holland! I hope we shall see you and your Batavian batsmen and bowlers at Lords and the Oval yet. You *ought* to be handy at "the willow," Mynheer.

*Mynheer.* Why, yes, willows we have in plenty, but in circumscribed, sandy, dyke-divided Holland, good cricket-grounds are scarce, and good wickets not so easy to get as in your own grassy Isle. But difficulties notwithstanding, my boys have been going it at the Malibaan, and many "een zeer leelijken bal"—what you call a "shooter"—has flown from a Dutch fist during the last few seasons.

*Mr. Bull.* Hooray! If we once fight on the cricket-field we shall hardly want to fight elsewhere, Mynheer—even in Africa, I hope.

"In matters of Commerce, the fault of the Dutch,
Is giving too little and asking too much."

You know the old metrical sneer. Suppose we alter it to:—

"In matters of bowling the fault of the Dutch,
Is changing too little, 'long-hopping' too much."

That takes all the sting out of it, Mynheer. And you'll soon alter all that, with a few wrinkles from our GRACES, LOHMANNS, and STEELS. Already, I'm told you are rattling wicket-keepers, and no muffs at a catch.

*Mynheer.* You do me proud, Mr. BULL. And if I also may venture upon doggerel in a language which is not mine own, I would add:—

And when we're a little bit more of "dry bobs,"
We shall not be such "passive victims of lobs."

as your *Daily News* says we are at present. Perhaps with mole-hills in the out field, and a public right-of-way between the wickets, even your own champion would find his scores dwindling, and his average suffering.

*Mr. Bull.* Probably. But pretty soon I expect we shall hear of a "Batavian GRACE," in a sense quite other than that of DISRAELI's celebrated back-hander to poor BERESFORD HOPE.

*Mynheer.* I hope so, I'm sure. But, of course, in—

A land that rides at anchor and is moored,
In which they do not live, but go aboard,

as another of your satirical rhymesters has it, our willow-wielders are at a disadvantage. Still *this* sounds business-like, Mr. BULL:—

"*F. Lelyveld en Suermondt top scorers waren. Nu volg de een batting performance, zooals maar zelden hier in Holland gezien wordt. Terwijl Nolet heel kalm blockt, sloeg v. Haeften er lustig op los.*"

*Mr. Bull.* Business-like? It sounds quite international and Volapük-ish, Mynheer. By Jove, I seem to see my way to a rattling song for a Cricket Supper,—"*The Hit to Leg,*" to the tune of "*The Cork Leg,*" you know.

(*Sings.*) I'll tell you a tale without any flam,
Of a Slogger named Mynheer VON CLAM.
Who every morning said, "I am
The hardest hitter in Rotterdam."
Ri-tooral-looral, &c.

One day he'd been having a turn at the keg,
And he stood at the wickets as stiff as a peg.
He feared he should hardly "break his egg,"
But he fluked a most wonderful hit to leg.

The fine hit gave Mynheer delight,
He had timed it well, and he caught it right.
It soared and soared to an awful height,
And in less than a moment was out of sight.

The batsmen ran a regular race,
Till each was perspiring and purple of face;
Still that ball went on at a pelting pace,
And the fieldsmen still kept up the chase.

They added a hundred and one to the score,
Then they stopped, perspiring at every pore;
They had won the match, midst a general roar,
*But they never got sight of that ball any more!*

My tale I've told, both plain and free,
Of the hardest slogger that could be,
He never was out at all, d'ye see
From that wonderful hit to L. E. G.,
Ri-tooral-looral-looral-looral,
Ri-to-looral lay!

*Mynheer.* Ha! ha! ha! Another bumper, Mr. BULL! Here's a health to Britons, Batavians, and Batsmen!!! [*Left drinking.*

AT HYDE PARK CORNER, NOV. 16.

## THAT EVENING PIPE.

[The Recreative Evening School Association has asked for the use of the halls in the new Board Schools, and begs the School Board to permit the evening pipe to the working-men, in the hope of attracting them from the Public-house. Mr. WILKS and the Rev. C. BROOKE, of the Board, opposed this, on the ground that smoking was most injurious.]

THAT evening pipe, that evening pipe!
C. BROOKE and WILKS, with wisdom ripe,
Would put it out, would stop its puff.
How can such Sages talk such stuff?
Wiseacre WILKS and Reverend BROOKE
The working-man "had cut a snook"
At JAMES himself if, Royal quack, he
Had tried to rob them of their 'baccy;
And think you then they will be fast
To heed *your* baby Counterblast?
Take *Punch's* tip, my reverend blokes,
Let the poor man enjoy his smokes;
Don't from his programme strive to wipe
The pleasure of that evening pipe;
'Tis one of the few things that charm,
And do him no especial harm;
At all philanthropy he'll sniff,
That starts by cutting off his whiff.
If you've so strange a nose indeed,
As cannot stand the fragrant weed,
Don't into poor men's pleasures poke it!
There!—put *that* in your pipes, and smoke it!

## THE OLD GUIDE

*(A New Reading.)*

"TRY NOT TO PASS"—THE OLD MAN SAID—
"YOUR BILL. I'LL POINT THE ROAD INSTEAD.
YOU'LL FIND THE END IS—MUCH THE SAME."
"I KNOW," THE YOUNG MAN CRIED, "YOUR GAME,—
'ALTERNATIVE!'"

### A SPECIAL CHRISTMAS APPEAL.

FATHER DAMIEN, the heroic priest who is voluntarily undergoing slow martyrdom by leprosy in the Island of Molokai, appealed some months ago for a thousand pounds to gratify "the only wish that still remained in his mind," which was "to provide a suitable church for his lepers." Only half of this sum has been forthcoming, five hundred pounds are still wanted, and the brave Father DAMIEN, dying by inches of a dread disease, is "disappointed." *Is* this right? Those who think it is *not*, can help to alter it, and to make up the sum by December 1, "so that it may be sent out as a Christmas present to Father DAMIEN." Christmas is at hand; if there is any worthier way in which the great Season of Gifts could be celebrated, *Mr. Punch* would like to hear of it. Now then, Ladies and Gentlemen:—

"Christmas comes but once a year,
And when it comes it brings good cheer."

Let it bring cheer, before it is too late, to Father DAMIEN, the heroic martyr of Molokai, from Father Christmas.

The Hon. Treasurer is the Rev. H. B. CHAPMAN, 177, Camden Grove North, Peckham, to whom all letters should be addressed. Mr. CHAPMAN will acknowledge all subscriptions immediately. He would be much obliged if subscribers would write "DAMIEN Fund" on the envelope of their letters.

Let *Mr. Punch* once more have reason to be proud of his readers

## RUBY.

(NEW VERSION.) A SONG OF A SYNDICATE.

(*Sung by Captain P-tt-n.*)

I SPOTTED the chance of a "boom" last year,
But now I perceive that we 're all done brown;
Our Syndicate 's out in the cold, I fear,
And the India Office has let us down.
'Twas a Burmah Spec, that seemed bound to succeed,
For the Chief Commissioner did not decline,
Lord DUFFERIN smiled, and they all agreed
That *we* were to boss the big Ruby Mine.
'Tis a memory sad, and our hopes fast fleet,
For lost seems the chance of that fat five years;
The Concession is cancelled; what use to treat,
If GORST steps in, and our bargain "queers"?

Once more to the market it open lies,
That grand Concession. You must agree
That there is cause for immense surprise,
And the passionate pleadings that break from me,
Oh, Ruby Mine, darling, that opening grand
We greeted with joy may be never our own,
Perchance, it may pass to another hand,
Though the STREETER Syndicate loudly groan.
The Concession I settled seems mere dead leaves;
May Parliament list to our earnest prayer!
Oh, GORSTY, whose conduct our bosom grieves,
We pine for the hour of our meeting there!

## MUSIC OF THE FUTURE.

THE NOVELLO Series of Oratorios will commence early in Dec., under the conductorship of Dr. A. C. MACKENZIE. As the name NOVELLO implies, there are plenty of Novelloties in the programme. We hear that someone has re-written "*Jubal's Lyre*," and that Dr. MACKENZIE has re-set it. Not having as yet received the score from Our Own Special Musical Critic, we can only give the public a specimen of the librettist's adaptation. Here is a verse:—

"O had I JUBAL'S Lyre,
I'd punch his wicked head,
And teach him (by desire)
To tell the truth instead."

The musical setting to this is, we are informed, well worthy of the inspiration to which we owe these magnificent words. Dr. MACKENZIE—not Sir MORELL, but the still more Musical Doctor—is, of course, the composer, and the Morell of the lines lies in the application of them.

**COMPORTMENT.**

*First Tailor.* "DO YOU BOW TO YOUR CUSTOMERS WHEN YOU MEET THEM IN THE STREETS?"

*Second Ditto.* "WELL, AS A RULE I DO, BUT I ALWAYS CUT MY MISFITS!"

## ROBERT ON THE TURTEL FAMINE!

PRAPS one of the werry wust sines of the low wulgarity and hutter habsense of respek for other peeple's feelings, as marks the present low levelling times, is to be seen in the missplaced and crewel jokes with which the sad intelligense has been reseaved of the probbabel "famine of Turtel" with which the werry hiest horders of the dining-out world is now threttened!

That the pore hungry *can-oil*, as the French werry propperly calls the mere mob, who of coarse never has tasted, and is never likely to taste, the most xquizzet dellycasy of the werry grandest of *menus*, shood rejoice at the hawful prospek of a hutter failure of this werry grandest of crops, is but materal and ony conformabel to their gelous natur. But that hedhitters of respectabel noosepapers, who are themselvs sumtimes allowd to partake of this expensiv lucksury, shood jine in the ribbold jeer, is, I confess a staggerer, and has, I also confesses, touched me deeply.

Can any one of these ginerally respectabel Gents have ellowed hisself to reflekt, carmly and seryously, upon the degree of sumthink werry near aproaching to hagony with which the great Firm of BRING AND RIMER must have seed aproaching the possybillity of a Lord Mare's Banqwet on the sacred 9th without no Turtel Soup! I am appy to say as the dredful secret of the possibel cumming Famine was not rewealed to me until the nex day, or I werry much dowt weather I cood have gorn thro my heavy dooties with my customery sucksess.

There's jest one little suckemstance, of so nobel and ginerous a charackter, that I feels it my dooty to reweal it for the hadmirashun of posteryty. In spite of the tremenjus wallue of Turtel Soop at that time, and its posserbly fabbylus wally when the dredded famine has reeched our shoars, no differens, I am hinformed, was made in the cusstomary derangements, but the hole of the left Soop on the Friday's Bankwet was given to the Pore, as ushal, on the follering morning!

Whether it woodn't have been more keanly apreeshiated had it have been distribooted among the noble Army of Waiters, as made the Bankwet so great a sucksess, it is not for me to say, and I dismisses the ongenerus thort with a si.

I hundestand as sewerel of the great Liwery Cumpanys have patriotically resolwed to adjurn sum of theyr most skrumpshus Bankwets for the presint, in hopes the Famine may blow over, and however much me and my class may lament our terrybel losses, I am obliged to confess as they are rite, for how could they posserbly hask a Royal Prince, or ewen a Royal Dook, to theyr Alls of Ospitalerty without the customery lushus lucksery to which they has so long bin acustomed.

Why the West Ingy Plainters, who cultiwates Turtels the same as our Farmers cultiwates Bullocks, shood suddenly be so werry short of 'em, of coarse I am quite hunabel to say, but it suttenly does look rather suspishus that it shood have append at jist the werry busy time when the demand for 'em is so werry owerpowering.

The base ellusions to Conger Eels and Wales, I treat with the utter contemp they deserve. Sumbody says in the play sumwhere, that sumthink or other is "werry like a Wale," but he would be a bold man indead as wood say as a Wale was "werry like a Turtel!"

No thank ye, that woodn't do for a hexpert with the werry slitest xperience, and suttenly not for ROBERT.

WHAT WILL THEY DO TO THEM?—MURPHY and BRANNAGAN have obtained the QUEEN'S pardon—for what? For having been in penal servitude for nine years? Surely the QUEEN'S pardon in such a case should mean something more than "I beg your pardon, and I grant you grace," and should be accompanied by a provision for life, subscribed by witnesses, judge, and jury. We hope it has already taken this form, and that those who are now convinced of the great wrong done to these two men may have "The courage of *their* conviction," and speak up boldly in behalf of MURPHY and BRANNAGAN.

## OUR BOOKING-OFFICE.

A DELIGHTFULLY told romance is *The Countess Eve*, by J. H. SHORTHOUSE. An additional charm is, that it is in one volume. No wanderings, as in *John Inglesant*. One of the heroes is an Actor. I should like to hear what Mr. IRVING would have to say about the truth of this character to nature. Mr. SHORTHOUSE'S Stage is an ideal one; but then the story is as fancifully conceived and nearly as weird as that of *Le Juif Polonais*. The triumph of good over evil is strikingly worked out. The scene is laid in France, and the characters are all French. This being so, why introduce little bits of French? For example, why suddenly style the Superioress of a Convent, whom he has hitherto spoken of as The Abbess, as *La Mère Abbesse*? Why make an old servant ask the two Gentlemen, "Would *les Messieurs* partake of *déjeûner* before returning to the City?" Are *les Messieurs* and "*déjeûner*" untranslatable? By what authority does Mr. SHORTHOUSE use a *circonflexe* in *déjeuner*? One of the most subtly conceived and cleverly drawn characters in the book is the little chattering Vicomte. But no more, or as Mr. SHORTHOUSE would say, not a word *de plus*. Those *qui* like *les romans*, I *fortement* recommend *à lire* this *livre*. *C'est* published *par Les Messieurs* MACMILLAN.

Bow-wowing him out.

I've carried a Walker's pocket-book wherever I've walked during this year, and am quite sorry to part with it. Still I must in favour of another Walker—No. 7—a size larger, but slimmer and more pocketable. Walker's No. 4, I recommend for ladies who have pockets. The varieties might suit Wagnerites who could speak of the Walker pocket-books as "the *Walkerie*."

What a magnificent Christmas present would be the HARRY FURNISS'S collection of his Artistic Jokes, splendidly bound in one volume, containing photographs of every picture in his Bond Street show, which made such a hit last year, and drew crowds to see his rare burlesque treatment of the works of the Royal Academicians. This book, of which he is compiler, printer, and publisher, and part author with "E. J. M.," would be, indeed, a rare gift, as the issue is limited to about a hundred and fifty copies, and it is becoming rarer every day. "Get it," says THE BARON DE BOOK-WORMS.

## VOCES POPULI.

### AT EDINBURGH CASTLE.

SCENE—*Entrance to the Castle. A small* Party of Sightseers *have just retained the services of an* Official Guide.

*Guide (in a mellifluous tone and without any stops whatever, fixing his eyes on vacancy, having apparently committed his discourse to memory).* Before commencing our round of the Castle Lady and Gentlemen I will ask your attention to a few remarks upon the trench below the drawbridge where we now stand most parties are apt to run away with the erroneous impression of its being the ancient moat which a moment's reflection will show us how absurd this is being more than one 'undred feet above the base of the solid rock before us is the exercise ground formerly the scene of countless burnings 'angings and other revolting spectacles common to that barbarious age now appily for ever past from us!

*First Sightseer (desirous to gratify the* Guide, *and display his Military knowledge).* You could hold this place against any odds, eh? Practically impregnable, I suppose?

*Guide (blandly).* Well, Sir, as a fortress, it is quite obslete, being commanded by Arthur's Seat.

*A "Stoopid" S.* Who did you say commands the Castle?

[*Discovers that he is cut off from* Guide *by a body of soldiers marching down to drill. By time he comes up with him again,* Guide *is already explaining something else, and question allowed to drop.*

*Guide.* Above the same-eye Gothic arch under which we are now about to pass you will observe the Scots arms carved above with the motto *Nemo me impugn lacessit* no one provokes me with impunity.

*The Stoopid S. (in a whisper). What* did he say provoked him?

*Guide (continuing).* In the chamber above the last and innermost gate making seven in all and lighted by a single grating it formed the place of confinement for the luckless ARGYLL previous to his execution there the original study was made by WARD for his picture the "*Last Sleep of Argyll*" now in the 'Ouses of Parliament.

*Sightseers (who have never seen the Westminster frescoes).* Really? painted *there*, was it! [*They regard the grating with dawning interest.*

*The S. S.* Singular thing to do—sending an artist to paint him asleep before they cut his head off, curious days, those, Sir, curious days! [*Moralises on the past.*

*Guide.* The portion above is modern having been re-erected in recent times in the latest baronial style on your left as you go forward Lady and Gentlemen you will observe a flight of steps formerly at once the route for persons of royal and noble blood and the only means of access from the condemned cells to the place of execution a striking contrast thus we see afforded between the two sides misery and splendour the 'ighest and the lowest. (*Halts in an impressive manner. Sightseers prepare, in limp attitudes, to receive information.*) You follow the direction of my staff to the furthest corner of the ramparts where the turret projects it was there that a rather romantic——

*An Old Lady (arriving hurriedly).* Are you the Guide? Can you explain the Castle?

*Guide.* Yes, Ma'am, that is what I am here to do—(*placidly*)—it was there that a rather romantic but strictly——

*The Old Lady.* Wait a minute. I want my friend to hear this. I'll fetch her. [*Starts in search of friend, who is drifting aimlessly about amongst the cannon, and comes under protest.*

*Guide (proceeding)*—a rather romantic but strictly according to our historical records a curious coincident took place the manner in which the Castle was taken by surprise by RANDOLPH with only thirty picked men ascending the well-nigh precipitous rock the checkwatch or as we now call it the patrol was at that moment being relieved and the sentinel in mere wantonness or pure folly seizing one of the stones with which in those days for purposes of defence the rampart was then encumbered and shouting "Away!" I see ye well urled it over the rampart upon the 'elmets of the crouching escalade!

*The S. S.* The crouching *which*?

*Guide (repeating with relish).* The crouching escalade fortunately without injury to any of the scaling-party which waiting till the checkwatch had gone by clutching the ivy in their garntletted 'ands they reached the summit overpowering the sentinel and taking the Castle by surprise the feat being counted as one of the most daring stratagems known to 'istry!

*The S. S. (admiringly).* And were *you* there?

*Guide.* No, Sir; it took place in thirteen 'undred and *twelve*, Sir—(*impassively*)—before I was born, Sir. (*Continuing as before.*) In yonder building now the Armry the ruthless CRICHTON entertained the DOUGLASES at a banquet the cover being removed revealed the black bull's 'ed symptom of violent and immediate death struck with 'orror at the sight they begged for their lives being brutally refused and slain on the spot the iron tank on your right as you ascend is comparatively modern and constructed to 'old water in the event of a siege to provide against the garrison being reduced by thirst the water is forced up into the tank each day by gravitation from the Pentland 'Ills. I may here mention that the piece of ordnance we are now passing is the famous Mons Meg. Ladies and Gentlemen it is unnecessary for me to explain the cannon the inscriptions on the carriage being its 'istry.

*The S. S.* Is that the gun they fire every day by electricity?

*Guide.* It was last fired in 1682, Sir, being burst by the discharge and consequently now obslete, even for peaceful purposes. [*The party pass into the quadrangle and face the Royal Apartments.*

*Guide.* The wing on your right was set apart for the Court and Royal Suite in front stands the ancient Banqueting 'All here ARGYLL feasted and connived with CROMWELL at the death of CHARLES the FIRST that doorway leads you to Queen MARY'S Room the birthplace of JAMES THE SIXTH afterwards JAMES THE FIRST of Scotland. Ladies and Gentlemen—(*mysteriously*)—I am now going to explain something which you will find in none of the authorised guide-books or 'istorical records will you all remain kindly where you now are for a few minutes, and keep your eye fixed on me? [*Walks slowly to a doorway, and touches a stone above it with his stick, sightseers look on, apparently in expectation of some startling conjuring trick.*

*Guide (returning with subdued importance).* A curious discovery never yet cleared up was made some years ago in the exact spot which you saw me touch with my stick some workmen making alterations came upon a coffin of oak which being opened proved to contain the skeleton of an infant of great auntiquity——

*The S. S. How* old did you say the infant was?

*Guide.* Its exact age is unknown, but it was of a great auntiquity and enveloped in a covering wrought with two initials, one of them an I being distinctly visible being reported to Major-General THACKERY then in command of the Royal Engineers he gave orders for the skeleton to be replaced and the aperture sealed up which accordingly was done though what or 'oo the infant was it is a mystery—(*solemnly*)—probly will ever remain a mystery but that is where the infant was found and where it now is.

*The S. S.* Did you say that JAMES THE FIRST was born in there?

*Guide.* Yes, Sir, we have 'istorical record of that being so.

*The S. S.* Very *well*—(*triumphantly*)—your mystery 's accounted for at once! [*Looks round to discover effect, and perceives that his theory does not seem to be generally understood, and realises for the first time that he does not understand it himself.*

*Guide (declining to pursue the subject).* Here Ladies and Gentlemen my duties terminate you will now inspect at your leisure for there is no occasions to hurry taking your own time about it the Crown Room the Birthplace St. Margaret's Chapel Mons Meg and the view from the Castle ramparts the official charge I may here remind you is sixpence each person. Thank you, Sir, I am much obliged to you. [*Scene closes on* Sightseers, *trooping up staircase in varying states of contented vagueness as to what they are going to see when they get up.*

## THE DIARY OF A NOBODY.

*Sunday, November* 4.—CARRIE and I troubled about that mere boy LUPIN getting engaged to be married without consulting us or anything. After dinner he told us all about it. He said the lady's name was DAISY MUTLAR, and she was the nicest, prettiest, and most accomplished girl he ever met. He loved her the moment he saw her, and if he had to wait fifty years he would wait, and he knew she would wait for him. LUPIN further said, with much warmth, that the world was a different world to him now,—it was a world worth living in. He lived with an object now, and that was to make DAISY MUTLAR—DAISY POOTER, and he would guarantee she would not disgrace the family of the POOTERS. CARRIE here burst out crying, and threw her arms round his neck, and in doing so, upset the glass of port he held in his hands all over his new light trousers. I said I had no doubt we should like Miss MUTLAR when we saw her, but CARRIE said she loved her already. I thought this rather premature, but held my tongue. DAISY MUTLAR was the sole topic of conversation for the remainder of the day. I asked LUPIN who her people were, and he replied, "Oh, you know MUTLAR, WILLIAMS AND WATTS." I did not know, but refrained from asking further questions, at present, for fear of irritating LUPIN.

Portrait of Nobody, by Himself.

*November* 5.—LUPIN went with me to the office, and had a long conversation with Mr. PERKUPP, our principal, the result of which was that he accepted a clerkship in the firm of JOB CLEANANDS AND Co., Stock and Sharebrokers. LUPIN told me, privately, it was an advertising firm, and he did not think much of it. I replied, "Beggars should not be choosers;" and I will do LUPIN the justice to say, he looked rather ashamed of himself. In the evening we went round to the CUMMINGS', to have a few fireworks. It began to rain, and I thought it rather dull. One of my squibs would not go off, and GOWING said, "Hit it on your boot, boy; it will go off then." I gave it a few knocks on the end of my boot, and it went off with one loud explosion, and burnt my fingers rather badly. I gave the rest of my squibs to the little CUMMINGS' boy, to let off. Another unfortunate thing happened, which brought a heap of abuse on my head. CUMMINGS fastened a large wheel set-piece on a stake in the ground by way of a grand finale. He made a great fuss about it; said it cost seven shillings. There was a little difficulty in getting it alight. At last it went off, but, after a couple of slow revolutions, it stopped. I had my stick with me, so I gave it a tap to send it round, and, unfortunately, it fell off the stake on to the grass. Anybody would have thought I had set the house on fire from the way in which they stormed at me. I will never join in any more firework parties. It is a ridiculous waste of time and money.

*November* 6.—LUPIN asked CARRIE to call on Mrs. MUTLAR, but CARRIE said she thought Mrs. MUTLAR ought to call on her first. I agreed with CARRIE, and this led to an argument. However, the matter was settled by CARRIE saying she could not find any visiting-cards, and we must get some more printed, and when they were finished would be quite time enough to discuss the etiquette of calling.

*November* 7.—I ordered some of our cards at BLACK'S, the Stationers. I ordered twenty-five of each, which will last us for a good long time. In the evening, LUPIN brought in HARRY MUTLAR, Miss MUTLAR'S brother. He was rather a gawky youth, and LUPIN said he was the most popular and best amateur in the Club, referring to the "Holloway Comedians." LUPIN whispered to us that if we could only "draw out" HARRY a bit, he would make us roar with laughter. At supper, young MUTLAR did several amusing things. He took up a knife, and with the flat part of it, played a tune on his cheek in a wonderful manner. He also gave an imitation of an old man with no teeth, smoking a big cigar. The way he kept dropping the cigar sent CARRIE into fits. In the course of conversation, DAISY'S name cropped up, and young MUTLAR said he would bring his sister round to us one evening—his parents being rather old-fashioned, and not going out much. CARRIE said we would get up a little special party. As young MUTLAR showed no inclination to go, and it was approaching eleven o'clock, as a hint I reminded LUPIN that he had to be up early to-morrow. Instead of taking the hint, MUTLAR began a series of comic imitations. He went on for an hour without cessation. Poor CARRIE could scarcely keep her eyes open. At last she made an excuse, and said "Good-night." MUTLAR then left, and I heard him and LUPIN whispering in the hall something about the "Holloway Comedians," and to my disgust, although it was past midnight, LUPIN put on his hat and coat, and went out with his new companion.

## GUIDES, PHILOSOPHERS, AND FRIENDS-IN-NEED.

THE ladies and gentlemen interested in floating the "Lady Guide Association," appear not only to have discovered a new social want, but to be, moreover, confident that they have hit on an excellent method of meeting it. The following extract, however, from a little pamphlet they have recently published furnishes the best explanation of the objects they have in view, which are:—

The Guide who "knows her way about."

"1st.—To supply efficient Guides, who shall be ladies by birth and education, for the services of strangers, foreigners, and visitors of their own sex, to the Metropolis and its Environs.

"2nd.—To provide remunerative employment for intelligent gentlewomen, who from the present overcrowded labour markets, are now debarred from earning a livelihood.

"3rd.—To assist all new comers, by giving information upon every subject connected with their visit, aiding them in every way, in a manner which shall relieve them of all trouble, spare them imposition, and ensure their comfort.

"4th.—To advise Visitors as to the several ways of seeing and enjoying this Country, at given prices, and to save the time and money of such visitors."

And to the above, by way of a sort of happy after-thought, they subjoin the following foot-note:—

"N.B.—The Guides will be prepared to attend mixed parties of ladies and gentlemen, families and children, and those other than gentlemen travelling *en garçon*."

It appears from the foregoing brief schedule of some of her proposed requirements that the finished "Lady Guide" will have to be a very formidably accomplished person, possessing all the highest moral, social, and intellectual attributes, imbued with a spirit of the profoundest philosophy, and combining all this with the advantages of the most perfect walking encyclopædia. It is not surprising, therefore, to find the Association hinting at the necessity of candidates wishing to offer their services as "Lady Guides," having to pass some slight "preliminary examination." Unfortunately, they do not furnish a specimen test-paper, but that deficiency has been met by the publication of the following list of questions:—

1. A four-wheeled cab, containing five inside passengers, two children on the box, and seven trunks on the roof, is taken from Liverpool Street Station to the extreme end of Hammersmith, and the Lady who has secured your services as guide, after having made the cabman carry the seven trunks up to third storey offers him, as his fare, two-and-ninepence, which he indignantly refuses. On his subsequently claiming thirteen and sixpence, and taking off his coat and offering to fight the gentleman of the party for that amount on the steps of the house in the presence of a sympathising crowd, what speedy measures, if any, should you adopt to effect a compromise?

2. You are commissioned by a Lady, who is desirous of giving an afternoon house-warming at her new Mansion in North Bayswater, to provide some suitable entertainment for her friends. How would you set about this? Would you, if you wished to secure the services either of Mr. CORNEY GRAIN or Mr. GEORGE GROSSMITH, call on one or both of those gentlemen, and ask them to give you a little specimen of their respective *répertoires* as a preliminary to engagement? Do you think they would oblige you by doing this? Or do you think they would resent it, and that the matter would fall through? Supposing it were to, would you be prepared to take a cab, and hunt up all the Music Halls in turn, in the hope of securing some suitable talent?

3. You are engaged to conduct an intelligent, scientific, and inquiring party of sixteen people over Windsor Castle, the Mary-le-bone Workhouse, the Thames Tunnel, Hanwell Lunatic Asylum, the National Gallery, the British Museum, and the London Docks. Do you think that your thorough knowledge of English history, your acquaintance with the working of the Poor Laws, your grasp of the progress of European Art, and your general familiarity with all the great political, commercial, engineering, economic, and other problems of the hour are such as to warrant you in facing the coming ordeal with a jaunty confidence?

4. You are required by an economical Duke to provide a cheap wedding for his only daughter, and he has stipulated that the breakfast shall not, at the outside, cost more than ninepence a head. With a four-and-sixpenny bridal cake, and a sound champagne that must not exceed fifteen shillings a dozen, how do you propose to make the thing go off with *éclat*?

"HERE WE (DON'T) GO UP, UP, UP!"—Last Saturday night the Curtain of the Shaftesbury Theatre would not go up at any price. Wasn't there a *lever du rideau* in the bill? If so, why wasn't it used?

THE CHILD OF THE PERIOD.

*Aunt Betsy.* "I REALLY WONDER AT YOUR HAVING SO MANY FRENCH BOOKS IN YOUR LIBRARY, JAMES, WITH ALL YOUR DAUGHTERS GROWING UP!"

*Eva (who has overheard).* "FRENCH BOOKS, INDEED! THE IDEA! WHY, WE SHOULD *NEVER* THINK OF READING A FRENCH BOOK, IF WE COULD HELP IT—*NOT EVEN IF PAPA WERE TO FORBID US TO!*"

## EXTREMES MEET.

(*An Ancient Story with a Modern Moral.*)

THERE was (of course it *must* have been long since—
The present would regard with lofty pity
Men who such civic folly could evince)—
But, whensoe'er it was, there was a City;
A populous City, of colossal size,
Over some hundreds of square miles extending,
Its palaces the marvel of all eyes,
Its serpentining maze of streets unending.
And it was wealthy, was that City wide,
The opulence of Ophir were a trifle
To what was stored in it on every side.
Its banks to sack, its palaces to rifle,
Might tempt such stoics as LYCURGUS taught,
Much more mere ruffianly back-street banditti;
So that if Wealth's position e'er was fraught
With desperate danger, it was in that City.

And Power there had fashioned a Police
To safeguard Wealth, and keep poor rascals quiet;
To bid the worrying wail of misery cease,
And check all impulse to rapine and riot.
Most wise, most provident in Power, of course;
Where Lazarus and Dives are close neighbours,
It needs the presence of well-ordered force
To keep Wealth safe, and Work-thralls at their labours.

"Force is no remedy." This doctrine mad
Was held by some of Liberty's loud zealots.
"How save by force is Order to be had
'Midst a mixed horde of millionnaires and helots?"
So Power very pertinently asked;
And Law, in Power's hands, supplied the answer,
And held that to have bettered it had tasked
The skill of an Utopian necromancer.

There came a time—(of course, 'twas long ago)—
When Power and its Police began to wrangle.
Now, Music won't maintain its magic flow
When even the performers jar and jangle.
If the Big Drum belabours the Trombone,
And the Bass Viol pummels the First Fiddle,
Good-bye to harmony! Time, tune, and tone
Will be chaotic as a madman's riddle.
Well, the Police appeared to lose its head,
And Power its heart; a serious disaster!
They seemed demented by some strange new dread,
And doubtings as to which of them was master.
A Democratic Spectre startled some
As a new avatar of Demogorgon.
Others opined that this was all a hum,
That the loud mouth was merely Freedom's organ,
Not Anarchy's red maw, or Robbery's gorge,
Gaping for prey, and avid after plunder;
'Twas merely an excuse for Power to forge
Fresh chains for Freedom and keep Labour under.

Hence chiding and cross purposes, and hence
Much heated fuss that needed sense refrigerant.
You cannot quite depend on the Defence
When the Defenders are themselves belligerent.
One Chief was sacked because he let the clutch
Of Anarchy come close, and did too little.
Another one because he did too much,
Or so some said. "Nay, not a jot or tittle!"
Others retorted. That he *said* a lot
Was very certain, and, no doubt, a pity.
Meanwhile, with wills at war and tempers hot,
The prospect was not pleasant for that City.

The bearings of this ancient legend be
In their contemporary application.
If such be visible to Wisdom's eye,
Wisdom should promptly change the situation.
Power may at the implication chafe;
Police may fume at the implied comparison;
But *is* the Citadel entirely safe
Whilst there is angry strife amidst the garrison?

### A Distinction.

A CORRESPONDENT wants to know if an Editor of a satirical and humorous Magazine ought not himself to be an exceptionally brilliant wit? Our reply is, "Not necessarily; but it is absolutely essential that he should have all his wits about him,—on the staff."

# EXTREMES MEET.

SIR EDMUND. "MY DEAR WARREN, YOU DID TOO MUCH!" SIR CHARLES. "AND YOU, MY DEAR HENDERSON, DID TOO LITTLE!!"

MR. PUNCH (*sotto voce*). "H'M!—SORRY FOR THE *NEW MAN!!*"

## ENDICOTT'S LEGACY.

[The first of the ENDICOTTS, ancestor of the Miss ENDICOTT whom Mr. JOSEPH CHAMBERLAIN has just married at Washington, introduced into America the English Daisy which in Massachusetts is still called "Endicott's Legacy."]

ALL men of British blood are kin,
However far they range.
Both JOHN and JONATHAN must win
By floral interchange.
Two centuries and a half ago
JOHN ENDICOTT, we're told,
First bade the British Daisy blow
In Massachusetts old.
Now JOSEPH's luckiest of lots
Is to bring home—(Hurroo!!!)—
The flower of the ENDICOTTS
From Massachusetts new!
Sure Flora on the match must smile!
Fortunate JOSEPH C.
Thus to bring back to the Old Isle
ENDICOTT'S Legacy!
'Twixt England, Old and New, fresh link!
Arrah, now, PAT, be aisy!
You'll surely join us as we drink
"The Orchid and the Daisy!"

## THE DRAMA—MAJOR AND MINOR.

*Dr. Birch's Academy for Young Gentlemen.*

MY DEAR MR. PUNCH,

YOU know, when I grow up to be a big man, like my father, I want to be a great writer of plays—a Dramatist, don't you call it? I have already a stage, which cost seven-and-sixpence, inclusive of a very interesting piece, called *The Miller and his Men*, which is in Five Acts, and is printed in about eight pages. Now, as a very great treat, my father took me, the other night—when I came up to Town to visit the dentist—to see *Hands Across the Sea*, at the Princess's Theatre; and, from the papers, I learn that all the critics think it is a model drama. If *Hands Across the Sea* is a model Melodrama, I think *The Miller and his Men* must have been one too, as *Hands Across the Sea* can be played just as easily in my toy Theatre. Here is my version, and I don't think I have left out anything of importance.

Mellow Drammer.

### HANDS ACROSS THE SEA.

*(Adapted to the Stage of the Theatre Royal Seven-and-Sixpence.)*

ACT I.—*Farm in Devonshire.*

French Villain *and* Young Villain *come on.*

*French Villain.* You must marry the young girl, and get some money and come with me to the most beautiful woman in Paris. But first pay me all you owe me.

*Young Villain.* I can't. I have no money. I cannot pay.

*Young Villain's Father (coming in).* But I can for you. (*Gives lots of money to* French Villain, *who bows and goes off*). And now propose to the young girl.

*Young Villain.* I will. (Young Villain's Father *goes off, and* Young Girl *comes on.*) You must marry me!

*Young Girl.* I can't, because I want to marry——

*Young Farmer (coming on).* Me!

*Young Villain's Father (coming on).* She shan't; she shall only marry my young villain of a son. Her father left me power to make her marry whom I like. No one can stop me!

*Young Girl's Father (coming on).* Oh, yes—I can. I am her Papa!
[*Tableau. Curtain.*

ACT II.—*In Paris.* Girl's Friend *and* Comic Sort of Man *laughing.*

*Girl's Friend.* Why don't you marry me?

*Comic Sort of Man.* Because I don't understand you.
[*They go off.*

*Young Girl (coming on).* I don't like Another French Villain.

*Another French Villain (coming on through the window).* I love you!

*Young Farmer (coming on).* You mustn't! (*Scene changes to another part of Paris, where play is going on.*) You are a scoundrel!
[*Hits him.*

*Another French Villain.* Liar!

*Female Fiend from France.* Get me some money!

*French Villain and Young Villain (coming on).* We will! (*Scene changes to another part of Paris.*) Die!
[*They stab* Another French Villain, *and go off.*

*Young English Farmer (coming on).* Why, here's Another French Villain dead—murdered!

*Everybody (coming on).* You did it! You know you did!
[*Tableau and Curtain.*

ACT III.—*Condemned Cell in Paris.*

*Young Farmer.* I must escape.
[*Does escape and is pursued by Soldiers, &c., who point their guns at him.*

*Young Girl (coming on).* Don't shoot him! I have got a reprieve!
[*Everybody presents arms to her. Tableau. Curtain.*

ACT IV.—*At Sea.* Young Girl, Girl's Friend, Comic Sort of Man, *and* Young Villain, *on board ship.*

*Girl's Friend.* Why don't you marry me?

*Comic Sort of Man.* Never thought of that before.

*Girl's Friend.* Then you must be a stupid! [*They go off.*

*Young Farmer (coming on).* I have escaped from New Caledonia, and everybody thinks I am a sailor.

*Young Girl.* I would kiss you, only there are so many people about.

*French Officer (coming on).* I shall take you prisoner.

*Young Farmer.* What for? I am an English sailor.

*Young Villain.* No, you aren't. You are a murderer!

*French Officer (to his men).* Seize him!

*English Captain (to everybody).* Hearts of oak! Rule, Britannia! Three cheers for the red, white, and blue!

*French Officer (to his men).* Seize him, I say!

*English Captain (to everybody).* I am naughty-worded if you shall!
[*Tableau. Curtain.*

ACT V.—*In Australia. Everybody present except the* Young Villain's Father, Another French Villain, *and a* Female Fiend *from France.*

*French Villain.* The Young Villain murdered Another French Villain! I did see him do it!

*Everybody but the Young Villain.* Seize him!
[Young Villain *is seized.*

*Young Farmer.* Joy! and what shall we do next?

*Young Girl.* Why, marry, to be sure, and so will my Friend, and the Comic Sort of Man.

*Young Farmer (to her).* We will! (*To everybody.*) Faint heart never won fair lady! It is never too late to mend. "A stitch in time saves nine!" And thus we live for ever with "Hands Across the Sea!"
[*Tableau. Curtain. The End.*

There! I think that will do? Come and see it played.

Your affectionate young Friend, my dear *Mr. Punch*,
CHARLIE, *surnamed (at School)* THE PIECE-MAKER.

## OUR IN-DEPENDENCIES.

*Telegram from Prime Minister of South-West Cariboo to Secretary of State for the Colonies.*

HEAR you've appointed Sir MICHAEL TITMARSH as Governor. Don't send him out. Won't do at any price. Try another.

*From Colonial Secretary to Prime Minister of South-West Cariboo.*

Anything to oblige. Just told Sir MICHAEL he would not do. He seemed surprised, and asked why. Would you mind kindly saying why. Don't doubt your judgment, but it would look better to give a reason. Reply prepaid.

*From Cariboo Prime Minister to Colonial Secretary.*

We don't want him. Isn't that enough? I may, however, inform you confidentially, that somebody out here once saw a man like Sir M. riding on outside of a City Omnibus, reading a halfpenny newspaper. Mind and let us know whom you think of for his substitute.

*From Colonial Secretary to Cariboo Premier.*

Don't think of anybody. Leave you to suggest.

*From Cariboo Premier to Colonial Secretary.*

Glad you've adopted so sensible a course. Will wire names of acceptable persons for you to choose from in day or two.

*Colonial Secretary to Cariboo Premier.*

Received your names. LORD S. says he would be delighted, but thinks it would be difficult to find tenant for Hatfield House during his absence. Have sounded MR. G. also, who is much flattered, but thinks he's hardly good enough for the post. HOME SECRETARY here will probably be quitting the position soon; what do you say to him? Or, perhaps, SIR W. HARCOURT might think of place, and we could spare him.

*Cariboo Prime Minister to Secretary of State for the Colonies.*

Your last most insulting. We consider ourselves a cut above Home Secretaries, past or present. Surprised that S. and G. don't care to come. Have decided to fill up vacancy ourselves, and will let you know result in a month or two by letter. Meanwhile, try and remember that we are a Self-Governing Colony.

## A SLAVE OF FASHION.

*Lady (who has just paid a Month's subscription to the Circulating Library).* "WHAT KIND OF BOOKS ARE READ THIS SEASON?"

## THE VISIBLE PRINCE.—(A Story of Magic and Mystery.)

"How I should like to do all this?" I murmured to myself. I had been reading an account of the journey of an Illustrious Personage, and the passage had deeply impressed me.

"If you mean what you say," replied someone by my side, "I think I can manage it for you. All you have to do is to wear this, and express a wish to follow H.R.H. But I warn you that, until you return it to me, you will be able to follow no one else, and will remain a fixture until a new wish moves you on," and I found myself receiving an old opera-hat in the Coffee-room of my Club from a member I had not seen before.

"Do you mean to say that if I put this on it will carry me anywhere?" I asked, in a tone of astonishment. The strange member nodded.

I put the old opera-hat on my head, and wishing myself near the Illustrious Personage in question, suddenly found myself in Bulgaria. Immediately I formed part of a group that would have given an excellent subject to the Travelling Artist of the *Graphic* or the *Illustrated London News*. There was the Illustrious Personage, sure enough; and, so far as I could see, he was taking a hurried shot at a bird. He fired successfully, and then looked at his watch. Then he shook hands with some one in attendance, and was gone. I had mechanically removed my hat on finding myself in his presence, and at once found that, uncovered, I was helpless—could move neither hand nor foot. The companions of the Illustrious Personage retired, and I was left alone—in splendid scenery, but still alone. I put on my hat, and uttered a wish. In a moment I was in Hungary, inspecting a cavalry regiment. The Colonel of the regiment was complimenting his men on their smart appearance. Wearing my hat (for I had already found that my *chapeau* rendered me invisible), I approached nearer, and discovered that the Commanding Officer who was so complimentary was no less a person than the heir to an Illustrious Throne. I heard him ask for the time (his uniform fitted closely to his figure, and had no pocket), and, on learning the hour, he bade his men a hurried adieu, and hastily departed. Pressing my hat firmly on my brow, I uttered a wish, and immediately was in Russia. I recognised the voice of the Illustrious Personage. He was bidding the CZAR farewell. In another second he was gone!

Again, I found myself alone; and, perforce, had to resume my rapid travelling. It would be wearisome to recount the story of my wanderings. Suffice it to say that I visited in turn Athens, Berlin, Homburg, Monte Carlo, and Copenhagen. Although I had the advantage of my travelling opera-hat which conveyed me instantly from place to place without effort, I felt that I was wearing myself out, while the Illustrious Personage in whose wake I was forced to follow, seemed to me never to experience fatigue. He was always courteous, always cheerful, but always looking at his watch.

"Now," I murmured to myself, when I found myself in Paris, "I shall have a short pause before I recommence my wanderings." I was mistaken. Before I knew where I was, I found myself in Yorkshire, Wales, Glasgow, and the Isle of Wight. I felt that my magic opera-hat was less than a blessing—that it was nearer a curse!

"What *shall* I do?" I said, piteously, as I found myself alone at the bottom of a coal-mine, which I, in Illustrious company, had recently been inspecting. "What *shall* I do?" The echo offering no satisfactory reply, I once more wished my wish, and, *hi presto!* was back in London in my own Club. "Have you had enough of it?"

I turned round sharply, and found my fellow member of the morning seated beside me.

"Thank you," I replied, returning the gibus, "but pleasant as travelling may be, I honestly believe there is only one man in the world who is equal to the strain that you put upon me." And I glanced at the Illustrious Personage, who, I noticed, had just taken out his watch and was looking at it.

## THE MRS. HARRIS OF THE TREASURY.

"'BRING me my boots,' said the Baron." "Bring me the Last of the Barons," quoth *Mr. Punch*. And he was brought. "What saidst thou, my Lord, the other day, about the Public Prosecutor?" asked *Mr. P.*

"Sir," replied the Last of the Barons, "*Je vous dirai* —I mean, I will tell you. I said, in making certain observations on the case, I had been hearing"——

"Which you were thoroughly justified, Sir Last One, in making," interrupted *Mr. Punch*, approvingly. "But proceed."

The Last of the Barons blushed, and bowed, and then resumed—"I regretted that in this country there should be no Public Prosecutor."

"What!" exclaimed *Mr. P.*

"To quote the learned precedent of a certain *Prig*," said the Last One, "'I don't believe there ain't no sich person.' *Mr. Punch* clapped his hands. A thousand of his own pages appeared on the instant.

"Bring me *Whitaker's Almanack*," he commanded. At once it was handed to him. "Now, let us see," muttered *Mr. Punch*, turning over the leaves—"Government Offices—Treasury—Solicitor's Department—here we are—read." And the Last of the Barons read out—

"Solicitor and Public Prosecutor, Sir AUGUSTUS K. STEPHENSON, K.C.B., £3000."

"Well!" said *Mr. Punch*, "explain!"

"I can't," replied the Last of the Barons, sinking down in a chair, and pressing his hand to his brow, "I can't. There ought to be a Public Prosecutor—there *is* a Public Prosecutor—somewhere."

"And yet you regretted that, in this country, there should be *no* Public Prosecutor. How's that?" asked *Mr. Punch.*

"He is an impalpable official . . . no—I don't understand," murmured the Last of the Barons.

"Nor does any one else," returned *Mr. Punch.* "As you have hinted the Public Prosecutor is a *Mrs. Harris*. Only the £3000 per annum is real enough. Thank you, Last One, for again calling our attention to the fact. Glad to see the Last so well and so vigorous."

"Why not say Wig-orous?" whispered the Last of the Barons, as glancing timidly towards *Mr. P.*, he made hastily for the door.

"Good morning," said *Mr. P.* gravely, and the Last One returned to the Count of Queen's Bench.

"NOT THERE, NOT THERE, MY CHILD!"—On Friday night the intelligence that H.R.H. had preferred hearing *Nadgy* to being present at the opening ceremony of the Lyric Club, caused a Nadgytation from which the Committee are still suffering.

## ESSENCE OF PARLIAMENT. (EXTRACTED FROM THE DIARY OF TOBY, M.P.)

"Reducing the figures very small"

*House of Commons, Monday Night, November* 12.—House looked like old times at Question Hour. Benches full; great expectation; volleys of Questions. Particular inquiries about Wheel and Van Tax. GOSCHEN judiciously absent.

"No, TOBY," he said, nervously brushing his hat the wrong way. "If you don't mind, I'll just stop here in my own room till Questions are over. I know some one will ask whether it's true I have abandoned the Wheel and Van Tax. I can't, at present, bring myself to speak on the subject. I'm very much attached to the measure, as they say parents often are to the least thriving of their offspring. I have cherished it for months against assaults from all sides, and I cannot face the thought of abandoning it. Life would not be worth living without my Wheel and Van Tax. There's something soothing in the very name."

"Come, come," I said, not liking to see man of mirth like JOKEM thus broken down. "You've done your best; you can't help results. Besides, if you like the sound of name, and they won't let you have the Wheel and Van Tax, why not try a Weal and 'Am Tax? Anything to turn an honest penny!"

"TOBY," he said, springing up, and shaking me warmly by the paw, "You've saved me. A Weal and 'Am Tax is surely unobjectionable; repeated briskly, sounds much like the other; daresay, in time, I'll be able to transfer my affections. Excuse me, I must go and get up a few statistics, and see how it will work out. 'Weal and 'Am Tax;' good!"

Told HENRY JAMES about this. But so full of his own project, hadn't word of sympathy for GOSCHEN.

"Going to have such larks with WEBSTER," he said; "DICK

getting a little uppish since he's been ATTORNEY-GENERAL and Leading Counsel for *Times* in Probate Court. Rather inclined to snub me. But you stop till Vote comes on for Salary of Law Officers of Crown, and see what happens!"

Waited accordingly. SYDNEY BUXTON, having moved to reduce ATTORNEY-GENERAL'S salary, HENRY JAMES got up; cut ATTORNEY-GENERAL dead. To great delight of Opposition, argued with irresistible force against ATTORNEY-GENERAL taking private practice. Proved to demonstration, that, supposing by chance ATTORNEY-GENERAL were engaged in great case that demanded his presence in Probate or other Court from day to day, it would be impossible for him to discharge his duties to nation. ATTORNEY-GENERAL could hardly believe his eyes and ears. Wasn't this the learned gentleman who held a brief with him in a great case, who sat with him in Court in the morning, and indicted him at night in the House of Commons?

As for JOSEPH GILLIS, his delight threatened to deepen into uproar. His shrill "Hear! hear!" resounded through crowded and amused House. His eyes gleamed with delight as they watched the ATTORNEY-GENERAL. Smile on his face extended beyond all precedent.

"Must be down early to the Court in the morning," he said, "and see what WEBSTER says to JAMES when they take their seats together." *Business done.*—Supply.

*Tuesday.*—GRANDOLPH and JENNINGS on the job. SAGE of Queen Anne's Gate, and others, speaking disrespectfully of LORD CHANCELLOR. House seems to have heard something before of HALSBURY'S great merits as family man; but, never in such disrespectful detail. Appears, according to witnesses testifying upon their Parliamentary Oath, that LORD CHANCELLOR sort of farms out offices of State, first providing for those of his own family, and next for his family's friends.

"There never was such a jobber," says the SAGE, amid cheers and laughter. Filled up a certain office of Official Referee declared by Secretary to Treasury and CHANCELLOR of the EXCHEQUER to be unnecessary.

In the Heat of Argument.

"Filled it up," cried GRANDOLPH, "in the teeth of the opinion of the Treasury."

"Quite a dental operation, you see," said DUFF, giving his moustache that final twirl which GRANDOLPH affects to despise, but secretly envies. No one to say a good word for the Lord High Jobber, his far-reaching family, or his family's friends.

At very moment, as it happened, Lord High Jobber on his feet in Lords, perched on highest pedestal of loftiest morality, protesting against the Oaths Bill. Standing aside from the Woolsack, his svelt figure draped in graceful folds of flowing gown, his intellectual face shadowed under framework of massive wig, he spoke more in sorrow than in anger. All very well for Markiss to stand aside; for Bishop of CARLISLE actually to support Bill; for SPENCER, GRANVILLE, and DERBY, to declare in its favour. The purer nature, the more spotless integrity, of Lord High Jobber would have neither part nor lot with the accursed thing.

A beautiful sight! A touching spectacle! and all the while, at this very moment, separated only by the length of the corridor and breadth of the lobby, rude persons were prating about the good man's jobbery, and denouncing his dealings with unprotected public purse.

"Such is Life!" as OLD MORALITY profoundly remarked when he heard the story. *Business done.*—Supply voted.

*Thursday.* Decks cleared for action to-night. Been plodding along for ten days in Supply. Occasional explosions, like fog-signals on railway; but nothing serious. Now trumpet sounds; forces marshal in battle array. OLD MORALITY sounded trumpet, though not his own. Too modest for that. Anxious chiefly to get business through. Always ready to efface himself with that object.

"Tell you what, TOBY," G. O. M. said to me the other day, "some of you fellows laugh at SMITH, but he gets through his work uncommonly well; makes no fuss; always courteous; a thorough man of business; hasn't an enemy in the House unless it be GRANDOLPH; on the whole, in position of peculiar difficulty, does better than any-one else they could put there."

G. O. M. right as usual. House getting to like OLD MORALITY, something in the way it used to be attached to STAFFORD NORTHCOTE. Laughs at him now and then, but always good-humouredly. Really anxious to make things as smooth for him as possible. But line must be drawn somewhere. When to-night he announces introduction of new Land Purchase Act, shout of defiance goes up from Opposition ranks. Grand Old Man steps into front, waves the Grand Old Flag; next week there'll be a Grand Old Row.

Meanwhile HOME SECRETARY having a bad time. Peppered on all sides; adversaries in front of him, enemies to right of him. JOHNSTON at back of him. MATTHEWS in heat of argument momentarily turns back on SPEAKER, addressing Member below the Gangway. JOHNSTON discovers in this indication of design to undermine position of QUEEN as Head of Church. Hotly protests; MATTHEWS humbly apologises. *Business done.*—Supply.

*Friday.*—Met PSHAW-LEFEVRE in Library just now with hat tilted further than ever from lofty brow. Oddly enough, that's his way of indicating deeper depression.

"What's the matter?" I asked. "BALFOUR still refuse to put you on a plank bed?"

Haldane, *vincit!*

"No," he said, wearily, "I'm used to that exercise of tyranny. It's the SAGE of Queen Anne's Gate that weighs me down. You know all about my scheme for adding Mortuary Chapel to Westminster Abbey? Splendid idea; quite practicable; illustrated with maps. Talking about it to SAGE, told him how there were two houses close by Abbey, to be bought on easy terms, furnishing site for chapel. SAGE deeply interested. Much flattered by his attention; enlarged upon theme; said he thought it capital. Week after surprised to hear one of the houses been sold. 'Who bought it?' I asked agent. 'Mr. LABOUCHERE,' said he. Looked up SAGE. Expected to discover him deeply abased; found him rather radiant than otherwise. 'Capital investment for me,' says he. 'If site is compulsorily taken, you must pay me at least fifteen per cent. on my outlay. Meantime I shall live there. Nice situation; improving neighbourhood; close to House of Commons.' 'But you don't mean to spend any money on it?' I cried. 'Certainly,' said he, lighting another cigarette. 'Shall spend a good deal of money on it. Make the place quite comfortable; when you buy it, you must pay fifteen per cent. on all improvements.' There's a man for you!" says PSHAW-LEFEVRE, groaning his way out of Library. At work all night in Supply. Only three Votes passed. After Midnight HALDANE, by great stroke of luck gets a private Bill through Committee. Rare distinction in these times, which justifies air of triumph with which HALDANE walks homeward across lobby. *Business done.*—Supply.

## HEIGHO 'BACCY!

*(Ode on an Empty Pipe. By a Hard-up Smoker.)*

PLEASANT pipe, companionable clay!
Empty—like thy luckless master's pocket,

Fireless as Care's candle burned away,
Long ere daybreak, to the very socket!
When a cove is penniless and dry,
Having whiffed the last of his small whack, he
Can do nought but pouch his pipe, and cry,
*Heigho 'Baccy!*

Heigho 'Baccy! I can understand
How the "lag" in lonely cell longs for thee;
How the storm-tost sailor, far from land,
Yearns in night's long watch to "blow" or "chor" thee.

Comfortable weed! Out on the churls,
Scientific prigs, and sawbones quacky,
Who find mischief in thy fragrant whirls,
*Heigho 'Baccy!*

When the tinless toiler draws his belt
With a trembling hand a trifle tighter
To compress that vacuum each has felt
Who with poverty has been a fighter,
If his lips may but caress his clay,
Though cash will not run to glass or snack, he,
With recovered pluck can peg away.
*Heigho 'Baccy!*

When cold Care confronts one in life's road,
When bereavement chills the lonely ingle,
When sharp disappointment wields its goad,
When a chap is seedy, stumped, sad, single,
Then, however sage ones chide or croak,
Spite of doctor harsh, fanatic cracky,
There *is* comfort in a quiet smoke!
*Heigho 'Baccy!*

## ANSWERS TO CORRESPONDENTS.

CRICKETING VENTURE.—By all means carry out your plan of bringing over an Eleven of *Caggerwee* Cannibal Islanders to play a series of Matches with the leading County Clubs next season. Your idea of accustoming them to the game by letting them do their bowling, in the first instance, with a human head, and their batting with an adult thigh-bone, is excellent. Be careful, when you get them on to the field, that they do not eat the Wicket-keeper's gloves, and Longstops' pads, or want to roast the Umpire, as they invariably do in their own national game of *Balagoo*, after the first innings. You could convey them safely to the Oval in any Police omnibus. Spectators, of course, would have to look out for themselves.

DRESS CIRCLE.—It would have been better had you not, on being removed from the theatre, offered to fight the three Box-keepers with your left hand, and knocked the Acting Manager's hat over his eyes. Still your assailant had no right to obstruct your view of the stage by sitting on his great-coat, and then throw you over into the pit when you complained. Try a cross-summons.

CHESS.—You cannot move your Queen like a Knight, unless you get a safe opportunity, when your opponent is not looking. If you are getting the worst of a game when playing for a shilling, certainly knock the board over. This is frequently done in International contests and counts as a draw.

SPORTING.—You will be certainly right in entering your Four-wheeler cab-horse for the next Derby. Never mind the condition of his knees, but stick to your determination to ride the horse yourself, and you may yet pull off the race with him. There is a slight entrance fee; but you can get any further particulars from any one of the Stewards of the Jockey Club.

ETIQUETTE.—It is not exactly a breach of good manners at a fashionable dinner party to ask five times for soup, but it would be more *comme il faut* to be contented with three helpings. A blue satin tie and a buff waistcoat are not generally accepted as correct evening dress in the best society, but carried off with a little effrontery, they might pass muster. By all means try them at the Race Ball to which you refer, for if the worst comes to the worst, you can but be kicked out by the Stewards. Certainly, after the circumstances you mention, buttonhole the Duke, and if he resent the familiarity, slap him sharply on the back, and say, "I told you so, old fellow!" If this does not quiet him, repeat it.

## 'ARRY ON COMPETITIVE EXAMINATION.

DEAR CHARLIE,—I'm down on my luck, fairly chucked, and no error this go.
I was in for a slap-up new crib, and I thought I should come out top row;
And would you believe it, old pal, though I did do a bit of a cram,
I was bunnicked slap out of the 'unt all along of a bloomin' Exam!

*Me*, CHARLIE! and beated at last by a lantern-jaw'd son of a gun,
A ginger-'aired juggins in gig-lamps, who romped in before me like fun.
Mugged a lot about Parley Voo, histry, and grammar, and Latin, and stuff,
But no more in the know *as a man*, than a monkey—the tow-'eaded muff!

And this is wot Cramming has brought us to, CHARLIE! *Him* give me the
Becos he can spell a bit better, and me sech a scorcher? Wot muck! [chuck,
Hedgercation 's a fraud, my dear boy, as they shovel it into us now,
And I'm glad as some toffs as 'ave twigged it are raisin' a bit of a row.

Them there *Nineteenth Century* nobs knows their book, my dear boy, and no kid.
Wish they'd asked me to tip 'em *my* notions; I wouldn't ha' charged arf a quid,
I'm that fair on the bile, mate, about it. Competitive System? No doubt!
They may give it fine names like be blowed, but *I* call it a blooming Knock-Out.

It plays into the 'ands of the mugs and the mivvies, the saps and the sneaks,
That's wot this dashed "System" does, CHARLIE. A goose may be stuffed in six weeks,
Fit to cackle slap through an Exam, but it's all blessed fiddlededee
To suppose that competitive cram ever turns out sech sparklers as Me.

We are on the wrong lay, that's a moral; the duffers are 'aving the pull.
Jest look at the Germans, dear boy, how *they're* stealing a march on JOHN BULL.
Your sandy-topped Sausage in specs is a copping our cribs and our tin,
Whilst becos *we* carn't creak in six languages—bust 'em!—we've not a look in.

It's like this, old pal. Hedgercation is all very well in its way,
But it isn't the lingo as does it. A party may 'ave lots of say,
And yet when it comes to true smartness he simply mayn't be in the 'unt,
And it is jest these 'ere pattering prigs as is giving us snide 'uns the shunt.

Book-learning, dear boy, is like ochre, you don't want to spread it *too* fur;
If we'd all hedgercation and oof there would soon be a pooty fine stir.
Teach all the poor kids 'ow to patter hitalian, and play upon flutes,
And who'd sweep our chimbleys and sewers, or polish our winders and boots?

It's much too dashed levelling, CHARLIE. The few as has bullion or brains
Is meant for topsawyers as certain as mountains is higher than plains.
Yus; Life is a 'andicap, CHARLIE; it *would* be a blessed fine catch,
If yer trained all the duffers free gratis, and made all the pots start from scratch!

No privilege, CHARLIE, no patronage? Yah! that's all radical rot;
It's 'ad a long innings and wot's the result? Things is going to pot.
The swells 'as to sweat, and that spiles 'em, the commoners cram and go queer,
Whilst 'ARRY 's cut out by a mug with a head like a dashed pot o' beer.

Pooty nice state of things and no error! "Life's jest a long scramble," sez HARRISON,
"Of pot-hunting." Yus, and he's right, and 'as 'it on a O. K. comparison.
Blarmed noosance, yer know, if a feller can't nobble a crib and a screw
Without being crammed with more kibosh than CLIVE or Lord WELLINGTON knew.

WALTER WREN takes the tother side. Jest so! He lives up that street, dontcher
He's the crammiest crammer of all; wish he'd taken a turn, mate, at *me*; [see,
He'd ha' shoved me through somehow, you bet; he's a long-headed, 'ard 'itting
But a gent as is really a gent doesn't want to be *kep* on the shove. [cove,

Sez WREN, "Would you bring old jobbery?" WALTER, dear boy, that may do
For a slasher in QUILTER's new monthly, the flaming "Flamingo Review."
Nepo—wot's it?—sounds nobby, no doubt, but remember that there Board o' Works!
Human Nature is still Human Nature, and all on us cottons to perks.

We wants it made easy for right 'uns, and nice for the nobs—and wot 'arm?
There ain't enough nests to go round, let the few keep 'em cosy and warm.
That may not be highpolite morals, or wirtue on stilts, but I'll trouble you
To say if it isn't the way of the world, my dear W. W.?

To be worried 'arf out of our senses—us dashers—by dollops of cram;
And then spiked like a juggins at last by an eye-bunger called an Exam;
Great Scott, it's a jiggered fine joke. I'm with FREEMAN; Exams are
And if we don't bosh up that bizness Old England will go to the devil. [*all* evil,

Appointment by patronage! Ah! that's yer sort, mate, I freeze onto that.
Wot patron of sense would pluck *me* 'cos I 'adn't got grammar quite pat?
I'm fly, know each game on the board; yet becos facts and dates I carn't carry,
That tow-'eaded mug cops the crib, and I'm chucked!

Yours disgustedly, 'ARRY.

## CRITICAL MOMENT.

HITCH IN THE MACHINERY OF THE GOSCHEN PATENT "WEEL AND WAN" TOY. LEADER OF THE HOUSE APPEALS TO HERCULES FOR ASSISTANCE TO MAKE THE FIGURE WORK.

### "SO ENGLISH."

WHEN that scare took place in Whitechapel last week, the supposed criminal was pursued by Policemen and five Detectives. Everybody knew them! Here they come, all at once, jumped up from dinner perhaps; down with the knives and forks, and on with their hats, and off they rush all together, these five Detectives. How mysterious! How subtle! And the fugitive escaped, after all, without any difficulty!! What nonsense about an Englishman's objection to detection as a "spy system." Doesn't the Englishman enjoy the Detective in an exciting novel, and applaud *Hawkshaw* in the disguise of a navvy in the *Ticket of Leave Man?* Why, of course. The Executive and the Detective Departments should be as distinct as the left hand from the right, ready to assist each other, and under the direction of one responsible Head. As Chief of the Detective Department, we should select Mr. WILKIE COLLINS, assisted by Miss BRADDON and L. B. FARJEON. This would be the nucleus of an intelligent staff, to begin with.

"THE OTHER WAY ABOUT."

*Irate Passenger (as Train is moving off).* "WHY THE —— DIDN'T YOU PUT MY LUGGAGE IN AS I TOLD YOU—YOU OLD——'
*Porter.* "E—H, MAN! YER BAGGAGE ES NA SIC A FULE AS YERSEL. YE 'RE I' THE WRANG TRAIN!"

## HOW TO WRITE A CHRISTMAS STORY.

(*By One who has Done It.*)

THE room was full of shadows! Visions of his past life rose before him! He saw his boyhood, which, as he glanced at the MS. on his desk, gave such an excellent scope for illustration. Could he not picture to himself the arrival of the old-fashioned mail-coach in the Midlands; and had not this been actually done by one of the artistic staff attached to the periodical for which he was working? Was not the proof actually before him? Did he not see the cheery coachman, and the red-coated guard? And beside this picture was there not lying a weird representation of some dark arches?

"What does it mean?" he murmured for the third time as he placed the drawing well under the lamp that was standing on his writing-table—"what does it mean?"

He was a desperate man, and he felt that something must be done with it. It could not be wasted! No, it could not be wasted! It had come to him from across the sea—from an artist who had sought relief from pressing pecuniary embarrassment in the soft air of Spain. But it had to be introduced—it had to be written in.

"Ah!" he exclaimed at length, "I have it. This is a drawing of the Adelphi Arches. *Mary* must dream that therein she meets the slimy villain of my simple tale, *Dr. Uttercadson*, he of the too portly presence and the flowing moustache. The Adelphi Arches will be just the spot to meet him face to face and denounce him." And the plodding author continued his weary toil, sending away slip after slip of paper upwards. And now and again would he glance at a pile of engravings and smile sadly as one by one he knocked them off.

"Come!" he said, speaking to himself—it was a favourite habit, "I am doing famously. I have worked in 'the Wreck off Boulogne Harbour,' and 'the Grand Stand at Sandown.' For a moment a duel to the death between two gentlemen in the costume of CHARLES THE SECOND perplexed me—I confess it—perplexed me! But I have surmounted the difficulty by bringing it in under the title of 'the verdict is hotly discussed after the *Bal Masqué*,' and writing up to it! But I must not pause! What have we here? A Child playing with a White Vulture and the Emperor of GERMANY opening in state the Reichstag. Well, I must introduce both subjects into my weird tale—and what is this?—two men descending in a balloon at midnight in a forest? Hem! What shall I do? Ah, I have it! I can write up to that block, so that it may bear the appropriate label, 'The Lunacy Commissioners visit the grounds of Colney Hatch by Moonlight unexpectedly.' Still, I must confess that the subjects of the pictures handed out to me, although varied, are certainly confusing. I wish my task were done!"

And again he returned to his pen, ink, and paper. The room grew darker and darker, and nought was heard save the constant scratching of the pen and the occasional footsteps of the lad who carried away the sheets of paper. It grew darker and darker, and gloomier and gloomier. Suddenly there was the sound of a deep grave voice.

"Pause! Write no more!"

The Author looked up angrily, and then nearly swooned with terror; his hair stood on end, and his white lips trembled. There was a figure in white standing before him! A figure, a gruesome figure, with bare arms and dishevelled locks.

But the Author was a man of business, and, although every nerve in his body was quivering with emotion, he confronted the spectre, and gasped out, "'Write no more'! Why not?"

Then came the answer. It sounded like the knell of doom! The Author knew it was all over, and that his occupation was gone—if not for ever, for a long, long year!

"Why must you write no more?" said the spectral figure, explanatorily; "because we are full up; and because the rest of the space in the number will be required for advertisements!"

And trying to read over what he had already written, the Author fell into a deep, deep slumber!

---

THEY'RE beginning to "manage these things better in France." Edict of Prefect of Police banishing sandwichmen and advertising vans from principal Boulevards, has just been issued. Fancy costumes for sandwichmen prohibited! We should like to see Mural Decorative Art taxed heavily, and to put up murderous picture-posters made an indictable offence.

THIS IS AN ENGLISH DETECTIVE. YOU MAY KNOW HIM ANYWHERE BY HIS REGULATION BOOTS.

## THE DIARY OF A NOBODY.

*November* 8.—My endeavours to discover who tore the sheets out of my Diary still fruitless. LUPIN has DAISY MUTLAR on the brain, so we see little of him, except that he invariably turns up at meal times. CUMMINGS dropped in.

Nobody Nose.

*November* 9.—LUPIN seems to like his new berth—that's a comfort. DAISY MUTLAR the sole topic of conversation during tea. CARRIE almost as full of it as LUPIN. LUPIN informs me, to my disgust, that he has been persuaded to take part in the forthcoming performance of the "Holloway Comedians." He says he is to play *Bob Britches* in the farce, *Gone to my Uncle's*; FRANK MUTLAR is going to play *Old Musty*. I told LUPIN pretty plainly I was not in the least degree interested in the matter, and totally disapproved of amateur theatricals. GOWING came in the evening.

*November* 10.—Returned home to find the house in a most disgraceful uproar. CARRIE, who appeared very frightened, was standing outside her bed-room, while SARAH was excited and crying. Mrs. BIRRELL (the charwoman), who had evidently been drinking, was shouting at the top of her voice that "she was no thief, that she was a respectable woman, who had to work hard for her living, and she would smack anyone's face who put lies into her mouth." LUPIN, whose back was towards me, did not hear me come in. He was standing between the two women, and, I regret to say, in his endeavour to act as peacemaker, he made use of rather strong language in the presence of his mother; and I was just in time to hear him say, "And all this fuss about the loss of a few pages from a rotten Diary that wouldn't fetch three halfpence a pound." I said, quietly, "Pardon me, LUPIN—that is a matter of opinion; and as I am master of this house, perhaps you will allow me to take the reins."

I ascertained that the cause of the row was, that SARAH had accused Mrs. BIRRELL of tearing the pages out of my Diary to wrap up some kitchen fat and leavings which she had taken out of the house last week. Mrs. BIRRELL had slapped SARAH's face, and said she had taken nothing out of the place, as there was "never no leavings to take." I ordered SARAH back to her work, and requested Mrs. BIRRELL to go home. When I entered the parlour LUPIN was kicking his legs in the air, and roaring with laughter.

*November* 11 (*Sunday*).—Coming home from church CARRIE and I met LUPIN, DAISY MUTLAR, and her brother. DAISY was introduced to us, and we walked home together, CARRIE walking on with Miss MUTLAR. We asked them in for a few minutes, and I had a good look at my future daughter-in-law. My heart quite sank. She is a big young woman, and I should think at least eight years older than LUPIN. I did not even think her good-looking. CARRIE asked her if she conld come in on Wednesday next with her brother to meet a few friends. She replied that she would only be too pleased.

*November* 12.—CARRIE sent out invitations to GOWING, the CUMMINGS', to Mr. and Mrs. JAMES (of Sutton), and Mr. STILLBROOK. I wrote a note to Mr. FRANCHING, of Peckham. CARRIE said we may as well make it a nice affair, and why not ask our principal, Mr. PERKUPP. I said, I feared we were not quite grand enough for him. CARRIE said there was "no offence in asking him." I said, "Certainly not," and I wrote him a letter. CARRIE confessed she was a little disappointed with DAISY MUTLAR's appearance, but thought she seemed a nice girl.

*November* 13.—Everybody so far has accepted for our quite grand little party for to-morrow. Mr. PERKUPP, in a nice letter, which I shall keep, wrote that he was dining in Kensington, but if he could get away, he would come up to Holloway for an hour. CARRIE was busy all day, making little cakes and open jam puffs and jellies. She said she felt quite nervous about her responsibilities to-morrow evening. We decided to have some light things on the table, such as sandwiches, cold chicken and ham, and some sweets, and on the sideboard a nice piece of cold beef, for the more hungry ones to peg into if they liked. GOWING called to know if he was to put on "swallow-tails" to-morrow. CARRIE said he had better dress, especially as Mr. FRANCHING was coming, and there was a possibility of Mr. PERKUPP also putting in an appearance. GOWING said, "Oh, I only wanted to know; for I have not worn my dress-coat for some time, and I must send it to have the creases pressed out." After GOWING left LUPIN came in, and in his anxiety to please DAISY MUTLAR, carped at and criticised the arrangements, and, in fact, disapproved of everything, including our having asked our old friend, CUMMINGS, who, he said, would look in evening-dress like a greengrocer engaged to wait, and who must not be surprised if DAISY took him for one. I fairly lost my temper, and I said, "LUPIN, allow me to tell you Miss DAISY MUTLAR is not the Queen of England. I gave you credit for more wisdom than to allow yourself to be inveigled into an engagement with a woman considerably older than yourself. I advise you to think of earning your living before entangling yourself with a wife whom you will have to support, and, in all probability, her brother also, who appeared to be nothing but a loafer." Instead of receiving this advice in a sensible manner, LUPIN jumped up and said, "If you insult the lady I am engaged to, you insult me. I will leave the house and never darken your doors again." He went out of the house, slamming the hall-door. But it was all right. He came back to supper, and we played *bézique* till nearly 12 o'clock.

## THE TREASURY *MRS. HARRIS* AGAIN.

Is there, or is there not, a Public Prosecutor? Last week we recorded how the Last of the Barons regretted the non-existence of such an official in this country, and *Mr. Punch* brought forward the evidence of *Whitaker* and the Salary List to establish the fact of the P. P.'s existence. This week, in the Central Criminal, we find Mr. PURCELL saying, that the case in which he was engaged was one that the Public Prosecutor ought to have taken up. Whereupon Mr. POLAND requested Mr. PURCELL (what a lot of P.'s in this!) "not to attack an absent official;" and Mr. Justice HAWKINS observed (this was Justice to POLAND) that in his opinion "the Public Prosecutor was quite right."

Now, what have we got? *First*, that beyond possibility of doubt, the Public Prosecutor exists. *Secondly*, that he is "an absent official." *Thirdly*, that he was, at the time of speaking, "quite right." The last piece of evidence is important, and the Last of the Barons will now only have to regret that this official was "absent," but will rejoice that on occasion he should be "quite right." He is probably never absent on or about quarter-day, as *Whitaker* gives the salary of *Solicitor and Public Prosecutor*, *i.e.*, two single gentlemen rolled into one, in the person of Sir AUGUSTUS K. STEPHENSON, K.C.B., at £3000 per annum—and very kind of *Whitaker* to give it. Only—what's done with it?

ENGLISH COOKERY.—We're always hoisting the British flag, and we've done it again lately on Cook's Islands in the South Pacific. Great rejoicings at COOK's Tourist's Offices all over the world. Islands now added to the list of the Cookeries on which the sun never sets.

## THE "RIGHT TO KNOW."

IT is an axiom with the Press—no argument it needs to show—
That, "Other people's busi-ness the Public has a right to know."

Each blemish in a Hero's life—of yesterday or long ago—
His *real* relations with his wife, the Public has a right to know.

New works which all the world surprise are "stolen straight from So-and-so,"
That "all who please it plagiarise," the Public has a right to know.

Celebrities are interviewed, and all that, under torture slow,
From their reluctant lips is screwed, the Public has a right to know.

On deeds of ghastliness or gore a lurid light the Press must throw;
Details (as has been said before) the Public has a right to know.

To publish "clues" may serve to prime the criminal that's lying low;
But—every step in tracking crime the Public has a right to know.

State secrets to disseminate may harm a friend and help a foe;
The Cabinet may feel irate—the Public has a right to know.

When scandals come before the Court that force a hardened cheek to glow,
The whole unsavoury report the Public has a right to know.

And still the journalistic dredge seeks new impurities below,
Of which (ah, precious privilege!) the Public has the right to know.

Yet *Punch* at times is fain to doubt if it were folly to forego,
Or hard to learn to do without, *some* news we have the right to know!

## OUR BOOKING-OFFICE.

MR. F. C. PHILIPS has scored again with his *Little Mrs. Murray*, though he has not obtained the full marks entitling him to a special prize. The reader who takes up *Little Mrs. Murray* will be loth to part with her, as he will be always curious to learn what on earth this erratic person is going to do next. As a matter of fact, she goes to a variety of places, but does nothing—absolutely nothing, and nothing is done to her. She's not bad, she's not good—she's ordinary; and I suppose in this fact lies the real interest. It is, as it were, another version of *Nobody's Diary*, only that in this case the Nobody is a young widow who, wishing without visible means of subsistence, to make herself independent, takes to the stage, then to lady-companionship, then to Millinery, then to some sort of East-End Anglican Sisterhood, and then to the Matronship of a Private Lunatic Asylum; and, last scene of all, to marriage. There is no plot as there was (and a strong one, too) in *As in a Looking Glass*. The sketches seem to be from real life, and I should like to know the originals of the Manager of the Jollity Theatre, and of the *Reverend Simon Heady*, Superior of Saint Cunegonda's Sisterhood. The little woman is an excellent companion for an hour or so,—sprightly, interesting, and amusing.

I am choosing some Christmas Books and Cards, as, what the lawyers call, "these presents," and am puzzled between the charming "Photographic Opals," the original and tasteful designs of Messrs. HILDESHEIMER and FAULKNER, and the artistic reproductions of well-known pictures, and the delightful booklets of that publisher who rejoices in the truly Italian artistic Christian name of RAPHAEL, coupled with the truly English surname of TUCK. TUCK in again at Christmas-time.

To help me in running through these Christmas Books I'm compelled to engage a "Co."—the Christmas reading firm is BARON DE BOOK-WORMS & Co.—and as far as "Co." has gone I am informed that Miss ROSA MULHOLLAND has written *Gianetta*, a girl's story for a girl—quite an upper story. That Mr. HENTY, who has written plenty, is up to his best form in *Captain Bayley's Heir*—(young BAYLEY, we're not interested in the old 'un)—which is all about California, and published by BLACKIE. Then "Co." says that ROUTLEDGE's *Pied Piper*, illustrated by KATE GREENAWAY, is exceptionally pretty. "Now welcome KATE!"—which is *not* quoted from *Taming of the Shrew*. Mr. HOGG, the publisher, makes a hit with a collection of old fairy tales called *Children's Evergreens*. Nice dish at Christmas, ask for *Hogg and Evergreens*. Books marked WARNE are brand new, yet are "WARNE out!" My "Co." recommends WARNE's *Rosebud Annual* for the little ones.

Here's one by CHARLES F. RIDEAL, illustrated by HARRY PARKES. Nothing very startling: and author and artist seem to have got on well together, except in one instance, where they quarrelled over "*Mrs. Mashemall*," whom the author has described as "a smart spicy little body (blonde hair)," and the artist has depicted as a decidedly big body with very dark hair. *Our Farm*, told by PATTENDEN, and drawn by WAIN, rather funny, but not the work of a WAIN of original humour. Good sixpenn'orth, anyhow. *Flora's Feast*, published by CASSELL & Co., Limited, is a quaint Burne-Jonesian kind of book by WALTER CRANE. It comes out with the Christmas Books, and is about as Christmassy as the Sunflowerest æsthete could possibly desire. If I could select one picture above another, which would take the public, it would be the poppy-heads which are likely to be poppylar. "Co." is exhausted.

I've just seen the Christmas number of the *Penny Illustrated*, price fourpence, which means that this is equal to four ordinary numbers. The cover is the pink of perfection. The central picture in colours, of a child in bed, asking a kitten to come under the mistletoe, might have been termed Scratch Company. The child, whose teeth are not as white as could be wished, ought to have been in a "Cat's-cradle." The chief story, "Diamonds' led," by J. LATEY, Junior, shows that he was quite right to lead diamonds as Mr. W. MACKAY has followed suit with a melodrama on a similar plot in verse. *Diamonds Led*, is a three-volume novel essenced into five pages; and there is also a very funny notion for a new kind of advertisement in the story about *The Australian Parrot*. Several other good things in it; but that it is among the first to appear and comes out early, its motto might be, "Better Latey than never."

"Co." comes up again smiling. For a first-class piece of harmless nonsense commend me to *A Publisher's Playground*, a small (not too small) volume of poems produced by KEGAN, PAUL, FRENCH & Co., and presumably written by one of the Firm. If my presumption is correct, the Author's partners must be persons blessed with a sense of humour, which makes them ready at all times to sacrifice business considerations for the sake of a practical joke.

Mr. ANDREW LANG contributes to the Christmas store specimens of the "Grass of Parnassus." Being a collection of poems already published, it is not intended to be grass fresh cut, but for the matter of that, the bundle has all the sweetness of New Mown Hay, or if a scent is on my lips and under my very nose let me name, appropriately, "Y Lang Y Lang."

The old songs published by CASTELL BROTHERS are to be found in the daintiest little books. Each miniature volume can be had "for a mere song."

MARCUS WARD & Co.'s *Little Boy Blue*, and other old nursery rhymes, will be to the taste of the children young and old. *Oranges and Lemons*, and *Wee Willie Winkle*, are charmingly illustrated. Exit "Co."

*By the Sea* is a short collection of Poems, commencing with LONGFELLOW's *The Secret of the Sea*, the title of which would be a capital advertisement for an anti-mal-de-mer remedy. Illustrations not startling. But MARCUS WARD & Co. can afford to have a few not quite up to the mark when giving us such a dainty work as *Young Maids and Old China*, though old maids and old china go better together, as, from my experience, young maids play the very deuce with the old china in attempting to wash up. "Yes, your wash-up, it blew out of my hand, and broke all to nothing." That's how it happens with young maids, says the Baron.

I've just seen MARCUS WARD's *Christmas Cheque Book*. It's capital! I only wish it were just that capital that would dismiss satisfactorily all my other Christmas Books. Those of the Butcher, the Baker, and the Candlestick Maker, &c. No matter. We may be happy yet. Christmas comes but once a year. If it came twice I should be broke entirely, says your own Reviewer, THE BARON DE BOOK-WORMS.

## With a Mayer Maying.

| | |
|---|---|
| YOU ought to go and see<br>*Le Monde où l'on s'ennuie*,<br>Played at the Royaltee<br>Some night or *Matinée*, | "My Pretty JANE" is there.<br>November, you'll declare,<br>Is banished by this fair<br>And most refreshing MAY. |

SANDER *v.* THE DUCHESS OF MONTORCHID (*new style*).—What "Mr. MANTON" said of the cross-examining Counsel, "He did ask such orchid questions." And when Her Grace heard herself so ungracefully alluded to as "the old girl" in her Head Gardener's letter, Mr. MANTON is reported to have exclaimed, "Head Gardener, indeed! I'd like to give him some top-dressing!"

METEOROLOGICAL REPORT FROM THE SPECIAL COMMISSION COURT BY MR. E. HARRINGTON.—"Wednesday, November 21. Fine."

## THE NEW SOCIETY CRAZE.

*The New Governess (through her pretty nose).* "WAALL—I COME RIGHT SLICK AWAY FROM NE'YORK CITY, AN' I AIN'T HAD MUCH TIME FOR FOOLIN' AROUND IN EUROPE—YOU BET! SO I CAN'T FIX UP YOUR GALS IN THE EU-RÔPEAN LANGUAGES, NO-HOW!"

*Belgravian Mamma (who knows there's a Duke or two still left in the Matrimonial Market).* "OH, THAT'S OF NO CONSEQUENCE. I WANT MY DAUGHTERS TO ACQUIRE THE AMERICAN ACCENT IN ALL ITS PURITY—AND THE IDIOMS, AND ALL THAT. NOW I'M SURE *YOU* WILL DO *ADMIRABLY!*"

## CRAMMING VERSUS "CLEMMING"!

*A Plain Word in Season to the New School Board.*

GOOD Gentlemen,—wise men, or wiseacres, pundits, philanthropists,
Zealots of all of the Churches, fanatics of all of the Schools,— [fools,
*Mr. Punch* has a word for the ears of each one of your muster, a word
Men may strive to ignore or hush down, but which sounds, and will have to be heard! [work;
*Mr. Punch* is at one with your general aim, feels a pride in your
For instructing our People's a duty which none but a noodle would shirk. [sin,
And the young human creature untaught is a shame and a promise of
And the race of our strenuous day it is not the incult who will win.
Teach, teach!—'tis the task of the Age, the imperative call of the
Which whoso ignores is a vassal to folly, a pander to crime. [time,
Manly wisdom cries fie on the bigots, the bigots of dogma or doubt,
Who babble and fight at the portal whilst ignorance lingers without,
Kept back from the threshold thrice blest of the Temple where none should dispute, [brute.
The Temple of Knowledge humane, which upraises the man from the
The Creeds and the No-creeds contend, and negation and nescience cry
In as angry a chorus of hate as the dogmatists' furious fry,
Or the credulous bigots of Ephesus. Silence the wranglers all round,
The niggards who fume at the penny, the zealots who squander the pound!
And look to it likewise in time, oh ye busy Bigwigs of the Board,
That the hungry, ubiquitous Jobber, whose eye is on everyone's hoard, [trust.
Dip not grasping fingers *too* deep in the purse that ye hold but in
That new Laidly Worm of Corruption trails lately in London's foul dust [time
In a manner the idlest must mark. It were well to take warning in
By the fate of another big Board which has sunk in the Laidly One's slime.
But grant you all safe in your seats, hushed all partisan splutter and spleen, [clean:
With your sapient heads pretty cool, and your strenuous hands fairly
What then? There's a question confronts you that will not be shelved or set by, [honestly try.
Which will tax your good will and best skill, e'en supposing you
A pedagogue,—not of *your* sort, he preceded all Boards by some years,—
Said "Nature's a rum 'un!" Perhaps you're inclined to say ditto to *Squeers;*
But Nature will not be evicted, as you, with old HORACE, will find,
And Nature has given the urchin a *body* as well as a mind! [*sap.!*
You won't fill the latter, be sure, whilst the former is empty. *Verb.*
Stuff a half-starving "nipper" with isms and ologies? Poor little chap! [by force
Empty stomachs mean heads non-receptive, and cramming the latter
Means cruelty! Yes, and humanity bids you to halt on *that* course,
With an emphasis none can mistake. No, *it simply won't do,* that is flat. [not stand *that.*
Public conscience is callous sometimes; but it's stirred, and it will
The vision of BILLY and BETSY, bedraggled, and shoeless, and worn,
Without bite or sup in their stomachs, dragged in on a cold winter's morn [precious "three R.'s,"
From the streets, and all chance of "a job," to grind hours at those
Rises black on humanity's sight, and it jars, my dear Bigwigs, it jars.
If *'tis* Cramming *v.* "Clemming," my masters, then Cramming will go to the wall,
But *Punch* does not put it to-day as a hopeless dilemma at all.
Only two things have got to be reconciled,—*how* is a question for you,—
Instruction and common humanity. Teaching by Torture won't do!

---

MRS. RAM, speaking of Maréchal MACMAHON, informed her Niece that he was born an Irishman, but was subsequently neutralised as a Frenchman.

# CRAMMING VERSUS "CLEMMING"!

Board-School Master. "NOW THEN, BOYS, WE MUST GET TO WORK AGAIN!"

Advanced Scholar. "PLEASE, SIR,—MAYN'T WE HAVE SOMETHIN' TO RELIEVE THE CRAVINS OF 'UNGER FUST?"

"ADDING INSULT TO INJURY."

*Irate Old Gentleman in Garden* (*to Stranger, who suddenly drops from the other side of the boundary hedge*). "WHAT THE DOOSE D'YOU MEAN, SIR, BY COMING HERE IN THAT ABRUPT AND UNCEREMONIOUS MANNER? 'A MISTAKE,' 'VERY SORRY,' 'HOUNDS RUNNING!' BOSH! STUFF O' NONSENSE!" &c., &c.

## LESSONS IN JUSTICE.

(IN TWO TONGUES.)

*The French Method, reported in a Paris Paper. Close of the Thirteenth Day.*

THE Prisoner was admitted. He was self-possessed, grand, mysterious. He glanced round him with an air of disdain, and jeeringly bowed to the President who regarded him with hatred. Then the President put questions to him.

*The President.* You are a thief, a scoundrel, an assassin! You know you committed the crime of which you are accused. You are a villain!

*The Prisoner.* And you—polite. [*General assent.*

*The President* (*with indignation*). I will not have you say so! I tell you that I know you entered the room with the pistol. I know that you fired at the deceased. You know you did! Tell me, did you not kill the deceased?

*The Prisoner.* Why should I tell you? Is not your head of wood, M'sieu le Président? [*General laughter.*

*The President* (*with anger*). You shall pay dearly for this! You have insulted me—you have insulted the son of my mother—and insulting her son, you have also insulted my mother!

[*A deep murmur.*

*The Prisoner* (*shuddering*). Oh, no! I deny it! I am not so base!

*The President.* But I tell you you are! I tell you that there is no more wicked man in the world than yourself! You are a poltroon! [*Murmurs.*

*The Prisoner.* And you call the father of my innocent child a poltroon? It is an outrage! [*General assent.*

*The President.* Your appeal to your innocent babe will avail you nothing. Your innocent babe would be better without such a father! (*General shuddering.*) Yes, I mean what I say—you are a craven!

*The Prisoner.* This is too much! I am no craven! I love my country as a mother loves her son. [*General assent.*

*M. le Président.* You insult France when you call yourself her son! You insult the Republic. [*Loud murmurs.*

*The Prisoner.* It is not for you to judge! I know you, M'sieur le Président. Forty years ago you were in the service of the King!

*M. le Président* (*with a cry*). You shall be gagged if you utter such calumnies! You are a knave, a vagabond, a cut-throat! And now it is for the Jury to decide. Have you anything to say in your defence?

*The Prisoner* (*to the Jury*). I have nothing to say, save that I brand this man as a traitor! As for me I ask for liberty in the name of my infant—in the name of my child! I confess I am no saint, and if I *have* murdered, why in the name of my innocent babe I beg of you to stretch out your hands to me and save me from the scaffold. I wish to return to the world to watch by the side of a cradle!

The Jury, who were deeply affected, then retired, and, after two hours' absence, returned a verdict of Guilty.

*The English Method, reported in a London Paper. End of the First Day.*

The Prisoner, who was ably represented by Counsel, appeared to be deeply sensible of his position. He kept his eyes on the Jury during the brief summing up.

His Lordship said that he trusted the Jury would give the benefit of any doubt they might feel in the Prisoner's favour. In so serious a case they must not convict unless they were convinced of his guilt. The facts had been carefully laid before them, and he would not say a word to bias them either one way or the other. He entreated them to remember that the life of a fellow creature was at stake, and to let that recollection make them desirous to record only what was proper and just. The Jury then retired, and, after five minutes' absence, returned a verdict of Guilty.

---

"THE GREAT UNPAID."—Mr. E. HARRINGTON'S Fine—at present, November 23.

"A LITTLE KNOWLEDGE IS A DANGEROUS THING."

"And what's the little Darling's Name?"

"Well—you see he's our Eighth Child—so we've had him christened 'Octopus'!"

## SWEETS TO THE SWEET.

Dear Master Punch,

Answering to the note of the Oof bird, I planked down my ten toes in the Stalls, and was placed in the Strand Theatre last week as ever was. I found them all there, and was knocked by most of them. You bet they hit them! Those Sportsmen who expected to have some fun for their shiners must have made the welkin ring with their cries of anguish! There were some hoary-headed old chesnuts in the dialogue, and as for the music, it made me rush away in search of a loosen and a soda divided! You brown to what I mean? The jokes were of ancient date, and when some mummers appeared as Johnnies of the Jockey Club, the bet was declared O.U.G.H. It was a near touch that those who weighed in were not buried 'neath the pavement outside the Roman!

Yours, who has laid an even thick 'un that it won't run,

A Critic in Pink Spectacles.

P.S.—Pardon the above. I have seen *Atalanta*, the new piece at the Strand Theatre, and witness the result! I have not the least notion what I mean by the above slangy criticism, but then I could not make out what on earth Mr. Hawtrey meant by his equally slangy burlesque!

Summary.—In the "shooting-at-*Times*-Witness case," the revolver and the prisoner were both discharged.

## FOREIGN INTELLIGENCE.

As It is.—The Emperor of Germany yesterday distributed certificates of honour to the students in the Berlin Theological Seminary, appearing in the full uniform of a Pomeranian Grenadier. His Majesty expressed the pleasure it would have given him if he had been addressing soldiers instead of mere civilian nincompoops (*tölpels*), and rattled his sabre several times in a threatening manner. This is considered decidedly ominous in well-informed circles.

From Vienna it is announced that the Russian Government has, in the last few days, écheloned half a million of men along the Galician frontier. The official *St. Petersburg Gazette* explains the occurrence by saying that, "at this convenient season of the year, the troops are always moved about for change of air and scenery." This explanation has caused a serious fall in securities on the Viennese and Berlin Bourses.

The latest "Frontier Incident" is reported from Belfort. It appears that a French peasant proprietor, while pruning a hedge, slipped into a ditch, which forms the dividing line at that point between Germany and France. He was at once shot through the body and scalped by a regiment of Uhlans concealed in the neighbourhood. On the same day a German balloonist made an ascent from Strasburg, and came down in his parachute on French territory. He has been heavily manacled, and sent to Paris for shipment to New Caledonia. Franco-German relations have become in consequence somewhat strained.

As It Might Be.—All the European States having agreed to a partial disarmament, every kind of security has gone up at least 100 per cent., and national rejoicings are taking place in all the European Capitals. Herr Krupp is reported to be suffering from deep depression.

Germany having now made up her quarrel with France by "splitting the difference"—keeping Alsace and giving back Lorraine—French and Germans are fraternising all along the frontier. The favourite air in the Paris Music Halls is now "*Die Wacht am Rhein*," while the Emperor William has given orders for the "*Marseillaise*" to be played twice a day "Unter den Linden" by the Band of the Imperial Guards' Regiment.

In accordance with the general spirit of international magnanimity now prevailing, the Sultan of Turkey has consented to remove himself into Asia Minor, and leave Constantinople to be dealt with by a Conference of the European Powers.

There being no further use for most of the soldiers now enrolled in the various European Armies, it is expected that an international expedition of one hundred thousand men will shortly be landed in Africa, which will take Khartoum, smash up the Mahdists, find Stanley, abolish the Slave Trade, and open up the Continent to civilisation and commerce.

## CRAM DE LA CRAM.

Dear Mr. Punch,

There is a great deal of truth in the position taken up by the opponents of the Competitive Examination system. No one who has ever mixed up his answers and cribbed from a friendly neighbour who was answering Paper B, while he, the cribber, was confronted with the problems of Paper A, can entertain a doubt as to the elemental folly of settling a young man's prospects by his statements about subjects on which he is but superficially informed. I have suffered myself, but thanks to a pleasing exterior, a diplomatic wife who is very well connected, a large house, and exorbitant charges, I am the proprietor of a crammery which is viewed, and justly, as the very cram de la cram of the profession.

Facts, Sir, are stubborn things, and if there be one quality less desirable than another in the young, it is surely stubbornness; and how a constant familiarity with stubborn things can fail to produce deplorable results on plastic minds, I confess that I am quite unable to understand. My plan is to temper facts with fancy. Even Greek accidence lends itself to this humane and philosophical plan. Thus. Among a number of the deadliest kind of Greek and Latin adjectives I insert *Panjandrum* to be declined. The boy with imagination—the future journalist or financier—at once drops to it, thus:—*Pas-jas-der: pasa-jasa-dra: pan-jan-drum*, whereby we get Greek and Latin at one fell swoop, and invest Mongolian metaphysics with a halo of accidence. Again, in our last history paper, I lightened the horrors of the feudal system and the genealogies of our early Sovereigns by asking, Why was the Curfew Law like a Calendar? No less than seven boys supplied the right answer: "Because it was a Norman Ac'." This, Sir, speaks for itself. Yours faithfully,

Markham Primmer.

P.S.—I enclose a Prospectus. A reduction if you take a quantity.

"I advise you, my dear, to take up Music as a study," said Mrs. Ram to her Niece, "and I am told that one of the best books on the subject is Ranke's *History of the Pope*."

# ESSENCE OF PARLIAMENT

## EXTRACTED FROM THE DIARY of TOBY, M.P.

Harry Furniss

*House of Commons, Monday, Nov.* 19.—Spectacle of GEORGE CURZON, fresh home from Central Asia, accusing GLADSTONE of "immorality," calculated to create emotion. But it passed off very quietly. GLADSTONE not there to hear indictment. HARCOURT, JOHN MORLEY, and one or two others among the faithful, on Front Bench; but, as OLD MORALITY says, "It's surprising with what equanimity we can hear others accused of iniquity."

The flatness of this particular incident typical of night's proceedings. Seemed in advance that it would be quite otherwise. Government brought in new Land Purchase Bill. GLADSTONE long ago gave notice that, if they did, he'd make it hot for 'em. To-night came down to move crushing Amendment. Urgent Whips out; House filled; excitement growing. Just before business reached, telegram passed along Front Opposition Bench evidently created profound sensation. GLADSTONE read it; hurriedly consulted HARCOURT and CHARLES RUSSELL. Plainly a legal point. Learned all about it afterwards. Telegram from TIM HEALY at Dublin. Been engaged in Dublin Exchequer Division, before LORD CHIEF BARON, Baron DOWSE, and Chief Justice ANDREWS. Applied for writ of Habeas Corpus in case of JEREMIAH SHEEHAN, M.P., at present confined in Tralee Gaol. Crime alleged against Hon. Member was that he had shouted, "Boo for BALFOUR!" Court decided that in such circumstances SHEEHAN very properly in gaol, and refused to release him.

"What do you think of it?" said G. O. M., nervously reading over telegram for fifth time.

"Well," said HARCOURT, stroking the place where his beard ought to grow, "the bearing of the observation lies in the application of it. In the eyes of the law geographical boundaries do not exist. What is one man's meat is not necessarily another man's poison. If you boo for BALFOUR, and go to prison in Ireland, can you boo for BALFOUR at Westminster, and go scot free? The Court thinks not.

Remove the prisoner—I mean—I beg your pardon; but you'd better be careful."

HARCOURT, so convincing, rather frightened G. O. M. "Took all the starch out of his collar," as ROBERT JARDINE said, resting his chin firmly on the buttress of his own. Quite mild in his references to CHIEF SECRETARY; example infectious; no booing for BALFOUR on any Bench; consequently a distinctly dull night.

Sir Robert.

*Business done.*—Land Purchase Bill brought in.

*Tuesday.*—In Upper House, Lord High rises to explain. Brings down lengthy epistle, which he reads very badly. Seems that he has appointed only two blood relations to fat places. One of them, he mentions (as if the result was unusual and unexpected), had proved himself fully qualified for the office. The second, already possessed of a benefice, he had transferred to another benefice, slightly better in point of emolument, and with the advantage of more genial climate.

"And how does the climate suit him?" asked CLANRICARDE, gracefully bending his benevolent head. Lord High took no notice; went on reading; gave many interesting particulars about administration of Chancery Division, Clerks in Central Offices, and elsewhere. Noble Lords strained their attention to hear when he was coming to the point dealing with specific charges levied against himself in other House. But had so much to say about reductions of redundant Clerks and other matters, couldn't find time to deal with these. Triumphantly wound up with declaration that though salaries amounted to pretty tidy sum, they did not come out of pocket of tax-payer, but out of purse of unfortunate suitors.

Lord High sat down, astonished at his own moderation. The MARKISS listened, but said never a word. GRANVILLE, feeling necessity of breaking awkward silence on Front Bench, observed that as no notice of intention to deal with the subject had been given, it was not necessary for him to say anything.

"He was awfully severe on you," I said to GRANDOLPH. "Positively 'declined to repeat the gross language used.'"

"That's very well; but he might have answered the specific charge I brought against him."

The Commons flogging away at already dead horse of Land Purchase Bill. Members brought up to vote, wouldn't remain to listen. EDWARD GREY, chip of old block, made capital speech at outset, and later on, at eve of Division, when MORLEY followed HARTINGTON, benches filled up; cheers and counter-cheers rung through the Chamber. But no reality in fight; everyone grateful when it was over.

An Irish Landlord.

"Might arrange these matters much more cleverly," said HERBERT GARDNER, dropping in after dinner. "Let us have the Division first, and the Debate after. Great convenience to fellows with important engagements. Wouldn't at all interfere with delights of those who hanker after speech-making."

*Business Done.*—GLADSTONE'S Amendment to Land Purchase Bill negatived by 330 against 246.

*Thursday.*—"I'm not aware," said the SAGE, "that we have in the National Portrait Gallery or elsewhere any engraving, photograph, chromo-lithograph, or other portrait of BALAK the son of ZIPPOR. But, looking now upon the countenance of OLD MORALITY, I fancy we realise something of the expression on the face of the King of the Moabites as he listened to the address of BALAAM upon a memorable occasion."

OLD MORALITY certainly in sore plight. Second Reading of Land Purchase Bill moved; PARNELL delivered weighty speech against it; GRANDOLPH followed, and as he rose expression of pleased content dispersed itself over Ministerial ranks. Only on Saturday GRANDOLPH had spoken most graciously of the Government. Speech then anxiously looked for, as situation critical, and opportunity for smiting his old friends tempting. But GRANDOLPH had come nobly out of the fire. Having so recently assumed attitude of friendliness, would now surely go a step further, pulverise PARNELL, and demolish GLADSTONE. OLD MORALITY, sitting just under his young friend, folded his arms, leaned back his head in listening attitude, prepared to enjoy himself.

GRANDOLPH couldn't resist this final temptation. Had certainly come down determined to vote for the Bill; was probably also prepared to support it. But looking round on expectant lines of Ministerialists, on the Opposition already on guard against his onslaught, and, above all, on the broad, placid, pleased face below him, good resolutions melted. Instead of supporting Bill, and confounding Opposition, he riddled the measure with bolts of irony and scorn, reserving his most highly poisoned shaft to accompany declaration that still he would vote for Second Reading.

Shocked at Grandolph.

"It's such a little Bill," he pleaded; "cannot do much harm; and so very bad, that no Government, not even this one, dare venture to introduce another anything like it."

"TOBY," said OLD MORALITY, in a husky voice, as I helped GOSCHEN to lead him out into the fresh air, "an you love me, get GRANDOLPH never to support us any more."

"Never mind," said JOKEM, "it's GRANDOLPH'S turn now. But ours will come. He'll find his speech to-night an uncommonly difficult one to answer on some future day."

This was the tragedy; roaring farce to follow. Just before fall of curtain, Motion made from Treasury Bench to withdraw Bill establishing Minister of Agriculture. CHAPLIN solemnly rose from corner seat below Gangway, looking unutterably solemn. Rapturous cheers from malicious Opposition. CHAPLIN, it was understood, was to be first Minister under the Act. GRANDOLPH—that "imp of Parliamentary mischief," as DALRYMPLE calls him—learning this, put down Motion to move rejection of Bill. This made it impossible to carry it this Session. OLD MORALITY privately promised to say something soothing to CHAPLIN if he gave him opening. CHAPLIN now up, with his part in arranged conversation ready. OLD MORALITY waiting his cue. But the House would do nothing but laugh and ironically cheer. What should have been dignified scene becomes screaming farce.

A Bad Sixpence.

*Business done.*—Land Purchase Bill read Second Time.

*Friday Night.*—SEXTON incidentally mentions that Melancholy and Coercion Bill have just marked seven Irish Members as their own. Wants to know whether blow may not be averted till after Prorogation, so that we may have the pleasure and advantage of their company in Committee. OLD MORALITY, always anxious to oblige, undertakes to see what can be done. Members, hastening to Reading-room, eagerly scan names of the seven. Several disappointments, but at least TANNER is among them.

"Yes, that's all very well," said SAUNDERSON. "But you see how they bungle it in BALFOUR'S absence. Why couldn't they wait till the beginning of the Session? A foolish waste of opportunity to put TANNER in prison during the recess." *Business done.*—In Committee on the Land Purchase Bill.

---

"HIGHER Education indeed! It's the Lower Education, as recommended by King SOLOMON, that is neglected nowadays," says Dr. BIRCH, of Swisherton Academy.

---

THE New Maidstone Bicyclist Club is going to call itself (when it comes into existence) "The Wheel'd of Kent."

---

AN eminent Vet thinks he has discovered a treatment for horses that "make a noise" when they go out of a trot. He ought to do "a roaring trade."

**LOST ILLUSION.**

"WHAT, IS *EVERYBODY* WICKED, MAMMA DEAR?"—"YES, BERTIE." "ARE YOU WICKED YOURSELF, MAMMA, DEAR?"—"NOT SO GOOD AS I OUGHT TO BE!" "AND—*THE POLICE!?*"

## WHO CHASED COCK WARREN?

*A Nursery Rhyme for the Times.*

WHO chased COCK WARREN?
"I," said the Home Sparrow,
"With my views cramped and narrow,
I chased COCK WARREN!"

And who'll fill his place?
"Why, I," said MONRO.
"I'm the right man, I know,
And I'll fill his place."

And who'll tie your hands?
"Oh, I!" said Routine,
"That my business has been;
So, I'll tie his hands."

Yet, who'll see fair play?
"Well, I," said JOHN BULL;
"For I'm not quite a fool.
Come, I'll see fair play."

---

POLITICAL EYESIGHT.—A contemporary observes, with reference to the Noble Laureate, that:—

"Lord TENNYSON is not quite an octogenarian, although he is on the verge of it, having been born in 1809, the year in which Mr. GLADSTONE first saw the light."

With regard to Home Rule, however, the venerable ex-Premier will probably acknowledge that he did not see the light until somewhere about the year 1886.

## MRS. KEELEY INTERVIEWED.

THE Babies were quite determined that the good fairy, Mrs. KEELEY, and the lazy Laureate, Mr. ASHBY-STERRY, should not have it *all* their own way, and when little folk become determined at the Hospital for Sick Children, in Great Ormond Street, their determination is something wonderful! The boys said they had no pretension to be poets, but, at any rate, they felt equal to writing an Address; the girls declared they never expected to be great Actresses, but they were quite sure on the present occasion, they knew how to act. They had heard how the good fairy, Mrs. KEELEY, had recited for them at the recent Festival—they had been told how eloquently she had pleaded for them, and how she had drawn tears from the eyes of her audience, and, what was more, golden sovereigns from their pockets. One or two of them had been charmed with the clear tones of her voice, and had listened to the marvellous alternation of humour and pathos in her speech, and had been almost frightened by the applause with which the good fairy was greeted. Several had seen her going round the wards, chatting pleasantly with the Nurses, and having a kindly word for each of the little invalids. They had all of them hoped Mrs. KEELEY would get the first prize at the Doll Show, for they, all of them, were quite sure she deserved it. She had done so much for their benefit, that they were anxious to do something for hers. And so they asked the kind Lady-Superintendent, Miss K. PHILLIPA HICKS, who was always so bright and merry—always so busy, but never so busy as to be unable to bestow a kind word on her little charges, and to give a willing ear to their smallest troubles. And she soon arranged the whole thing for them. She told them the good fairy would shortly attain the age of eighty-four, which is a mere trifle for a fairy, and on her birthday they should have the opportunity of showing her how she occupied so large a space in their grateful little hearts. The day came, they set off on their pilgrimage to Brompton. Not all of them. Oh, dear no! Supposing one hundred and forty-four had started? Why, the Police would have interfered, and the HOME SECRETARY would have been sore troubled, thinking there was a demonstration of Lilliputian Socialists. Besides many were too ill, some were sadly crippled, and others too young. So a Committee of Seven were selected, and these tiny mites, in charge of a kind Nurse, set forth on the appointed day, in a beautiful carriage, drawn by real horses, driven by a live coachman. In the middle of the carriage was a lovely and gigantic bouquet, which everyone tried to hold, and which once or twice fell down and nearly smothered two or three of the deputation. But O it was a fine time! The Council of Seven say they never will forget it as long as they live. Suddenly, as if by magic, the carriage stopped, and they were in the presence of the good fairy in her elegant fairy bower. The deputation could not find words to express its pleasure. So it was fortunate they had an address already written, which was presented along with the bouquet. The address was a model of terseness which it would be well if provincial Mayors and others would endeavour to imitate. It ran thus:—"To Mrs. KEELEY. With every good wish on her Birthday—from her grateful little friends in the 'Hospital for Sick Children,' Great Ormond Street." Then followed the signatures, touching in their childish caligraphy, and the trembling innocence of tiny fingers. Cheered by the sight of their good kind fairy, made happy with the pleasant words which fell from her lips, delighted with the sight of her magnificent Persian cat, with an Arabian Nights tail, who purred the warmest of welcomes, the baby-interviewers retired. And when the lights burned low that night in Great Ormond Street, when there was nothing to be heard but the faint wail of some tiny sufferer, the almost noiseless footfall and the sweet-toned whisper of some gentle watchful Nurse, one cannot help wondering what sunny dreams, what pleasant fancies, what a sense of supreme repose and restful gratitude to the good fairy haunted the slumbers of the Council of Seven!

---

## "MADGY."

(*À propos of quite a new and original lever du rideau, recently performed at Edinburgh.*)

MADGY KENDAL quite forgot her ordinary prudence
In coming out so strong before the Edinboro' Students;
And afterwards she told the world the cause of her oration;
'Twas not, as some might think of MADGE, all her imadgynation.
But 'twas as she in the *D. T.* explained the simple case,
"*Some one had thrown a paper ball, and hurt the Double Bass.*"
Whoever did this thing was wrong, for, were he boy or man,
'Tis evident he'd made a hit before the play began.
Whether he hit the instrument or player in the face,
The silence of the thrower made his conduct doubly base.
She should not publicly have shown—it argues want of *nous*—
Displeasure at there being any "paper" in the House.

---

JEW DE MOT.—L'élite de la haute société Parisienne,—L'Isra-élite.

**SONG FOR THE SCHOOL-BOARD MINSTRELS. (Who Never Perform Out of London.)**

AIR—"*Keep in de Middle ob de Road.*"

WHEN de School-Board was young, friend FORSTER would [say,
*Keep in de middle ob de road!*
Don't all try for corner-man,—that don't pay.
*Keep in de middle of de road!*

For you must be a dreffle fool,
If you quite forget de true purpose ob School,
But you 'll be all right if you stick to de rule,
*Keep in de middle ob de road!*

*Chorus*—Den, members, keep in de middle ob de road!
If you want to win de race,
You must go a mejium pace,
And keep in de middle ob de road!

Now, if you by chance seem short of cash,
*Keep in de middle ob de road!*
Don't tax de people heavily, or soon you'll go to smash.
*Keep in de middle ob de road!*
But, if dey hear you a-singing too small,
Dey're sure to say you are gwine to fall,
And do not know your business, and are no good at all.
*Keep in de middle ob de road!*
*Chorus.*

Don't be too fast at cramming, you'll find that is no go,
*Keep in de middle ob de road!*
But little chance you'll stand if you make the pace *too* slow.
*Keep in de middle ob de road!*
London will not care for a Board dat's all awry;
Den show you are tolerant, as well as smart and spry.
She'll chuck you, if to imitate the bad Old Ring you try.
*Keep in de middle ob de road!*
*Chorus.*

You corner-men, don't kick up too much shindy left and right,
*Keep in de middle ob de road!*
And, Mr. (DIGGLE) JOHNSON, do not hold de reins too tight,
*Keep in de middle ob de road!*
Or de trap may capsize, and de wheels be in de air,
Don't show sectarian temper, or tear agnostic hair,
For you are *not* put dere ober trifles for to swear.
*Keep in de middle ob de road!*

*Chorus.*

Den, Minstrels, keep in de middle ob de road!
You will bless de rising race
If you go a steady pace,
And keep in de middle ob de road!

## THE REAL GRIEVANCE OFFICE.

(*Before Lord Commissioner Punch.*)

*An* Efficient Volunteer *introduced.*

*Commissioner.* Well, Sir, what can I do for you?

*Efficient Volunteer* (*saluting*). Assist me to get a satisfactory substitute for Wimbledon.

*Com.* Surely you are in good hands. I read in the papers this week there is to be a meeting of representatives of the National Rifle Association to consider what is best to be done.

*Eff. Vol.* Not the first by many, my Lord. Meetings are always being held with the same object in view.

*Com.* Do you suggest that these meetings are useless?

*Eff. Vol.* Certainly, as two parties are pulling one against the other.

*Com.* How comes it there should be such an unfortunate situation?

*Eff. Vol.* I suppose, my Lord, because one party thinks more of soldiering than five-o'clock tea and picnics.

*Com.* Would you suggest that Wimbledon was used for either purpose?

*Eff. Vol.* I would. The Cottage was the *rendezvous* of the *crême de la crême* of Society—very good people in their way, but not likely to produce a Queen's Medallist.

*Com.* And you think consideration for these distinguished persons keeps the question of a new site an open one?

*Eff. Vol.* I do. The people who used to come to Wimbledon to lounge on the lawn and eat ices are not likely to be satisfied if the new Shooting-ground is situated beyond striking distance of town. No doubt some of them might come to us on the tops of coaches, but only at considerable inconvenience.

*Com.* Then what would you suggest?

*Eff. Vol.* That the Volunteers, and the Volunteers only, should be considered, and Lady DE VERE and Lord MANIKIN should be told that their place is preferable to their company. What we want is a place where business, and business only, must have a call upon our attention.

*Com.* How would Aldershot do?

*Eff. Vol.* Admirably; and here (*producing a list*) is a paper containing a number of equally excellent sites. What we want is to have the matter settled at once, without further shillyshallying.

*Com.* I will see that your reasonable request meets with immediate compliance.

[*The Witness thanked his Lordship, and retired.*

## THINGS ONE WOULD RATHER HAVE LEFT UNSAID.

*Miss Margaret.* "PRAY SIT DOWN. I'M *SO* SORRY MAMMA AND MY SISTERS ARE OUT!"
*Shy Curate* (*who has called on Parish business*). "OH, *PRAY* DON'T MENTION IT. *ONE* OF THE FAMILY IS *QUITE* ENOUGH!"

## A CLEAR STAGE AND NO FAVOUR.

LAST Friday Mr. BANDMANN appeared before Mr. Justice STIRLING in the Chancery Division, and undertook to continue his previous undertaking not to perform *Dr. Jekyll and Mr. Hyde* in the United Kingdom. If this example is followed, of what varied enjoyments the theatre-going public might be deprived, as for example,—

Mr. IRVING appeared before the Last of the Barons, and undertook not to make a speech about the Drama in any part of the United Kingdom.

Mrs. KENDAL undertook not to come before the Curtain and address the audience in any part of Great Britain and Ireland.

Mr. TOOLE appeared before the Lord Chief Justice, (who had never heard of the eminent Comedian, and asked who he was), and undertook not to tell JOSEPH HATTON any more stories, and never again to play in *Ici on Parle Français.*

Mr. W. F. HAWTREY promised never to appear again as a King in a classical burlesque.

Mr. TERRISS undertook not to perform the character of a genuine British Sailor, in London or the Provinces, after the termination of his present engagement.

Mr. FORBES ROBERTSON submitted to a perpetual injunction preventing him from ever playing in blank verse.

Mr. CHARLES COLLETTE undertook not to perform in Comic Opera within the United Kingdom.

Miss GRACE HAWTHORNE has undertaken to cease from appearing in *Matinées* within the jurisdiction of the Supreme Court.

Mr. WILSON BARRETT appeared before everybody, and took a solemn pledge not to play again in any part of the United Kingdom.

OLD STYLE MODERNISED.—The Exchange Club, as a name, sounds well. Motto over the umbrella stand, "Exchange—no Robbery!" Members will be bound to exchange salutations and compliments every day. If the grill is to be a feature, the name "Exchange Club" is apparently only a new form of the old "Chop-House."

## A LIFE-BOAT STORY.—In Three Acts.

A dozen of hearts! and a dozen of hands! and the courage of death!—'tis a Yorkshire boast;
It was all they asked, one November noon, when a hurricane blew on the Whitby coast!

For a cry came over the wailing sands, and spread to the village, and swept through the street—
There'll be widows to-morrow and fatherless bairns, for exposed to the storm is the fishermen's fleet!
There was not a minute to dream or to think: it was "Who's for the Life-boat?" and "Who's for the shore?"
Just a kissing of lips of the lasses they loved—just a sigh, and a cheer, and a grasp of the oar—
For the men out at sea were exposed to the storm; but they were not forgotten by "pals" on the land.
Whilst there's life there is hope—whilst there's strength there's a rope—the heart of a friend and the grasp of a hand.
Just picture the scene, O my brothers in town, with your petty annoyance and impotent strife;
In the midst of our city it's Worship of Self! on the fishermen's coast it is Rescue! and Life!

Who's for the Life-boat? Strain your eyes, and deaden your ears from the shrieking wind;
The Answer's there! on the crested waves, in the hearts of the women they've left behind;
See! the cobbles are riding in dire distress! Will they reach the fleet? You may lay your life
There isn't a Yorkshire lad at the oar, who will bring discredit to mother or wife;
For nobody knows who's at sea or on shore—just a wild supplication that nobody dies,
When a blinding sleet sweeps the sea and the sand, and darkens the scene from the wondering eyes.
Then a silence falls on the women who wait, and a cry rings out as they bend the knee—
For they drag two bodies half-drowned to land,—and the rest?—they are left in the raging sea!
Lost! when the moment of rescue came, lost! within sound of their loved and land.
So the night closed black on the Yorkshire coast, and a wail went over the lonely sand!

But the morning breaks, and the storm is past; and over the village, and into the street
The sun is shedding its wintry rays, on the scene where they fought for the fishermen's fleet;
And the sea is calm, and the sand is still, where they manned the boat and they went to death.
What's that?—out there in the Steamer's wake! Here, give us your glass! Then they held their breath,
And a beam of light shot out of the sky, and a cheer roared out of the Yorkshire throats
As they saw their Life-boat making Home with the rescued crews from the fishermen's boats!
"Never say die!" is the motto of men who fight to conquer and mean to win;
But it's well worth living to earn the tears that wept them out and that cheered them in!
So the tale is told! But there's something more, that can never be done by praise or pen,—
We must think of the sea when the tempests roar; and give of our gold to the Life-boat Men!

*** The National Life-Boat Institution is to be found in John Street, Adelphi.

## WALL-PAPER MONEY.

Not a bad idea, that of taxing certain kinds of mural posters, which was lately started in the House of Commons. The Chancellor of the Exchequer was advised to turn his attention to pictorial mural atrocities—not being pictures by Murillo—and so find a possible substitute for the Weal and 'Am Tax (since deceased). The name "Posters," it was observed, naturally suggested the idea of a *Stamp* being attached to them. George Jokim didn't see the exact force of the suggestion at first; required posting up in the details before approving; but admitted there might be something in it.

Here is a sort of Poster (not Postal) Tariff, which ought to find a place in any new edition of the old Stamp Act:—

For any Pictorial Advertisement of extra large size—a sort of four-poster—exhibited on any wall, hoarding, scaffolding, or other public place . . . . £5 0 0

Additional stamp required, if the design and colouring fail to meet with the enthusiastic approbation of the Lord Chamberlain, Professor Ruskin, and the President of the Royal Academy . . . . £10 0 0

For every Advertisement which, after careful examination by a Committee composed of leading "realistic" Novelists and Playwrights, with the assistance of a picked body of nervous invalids, is pronounced to be "distinctly blood-curdling." . . . 20 0 0

N.B.—Solitary confinement in a cell, the walls of which are papered with the posters, may, in the discretion of the Magistrate or Judge, be substituted for a pecuniary penalty.

## OUR BOOKING-OFFICE.

For size, show, type, interesting matter, and admirable illustrations, I haven't seen a better book this booky season than Macmillan's *Coaching Days and Coaching Ways*, charmingly illustrated by Herbert Railton and Hugh Thomson. The letter-press by Outram Tristram is not up to the excellence of the pictures. Nothing racy, nothing *Shandy*-an about this Tristram. Pretty Christmas picture-card to send to a bachelor is that of the "Prize Babies." It can be purchased at Ackerman's. But of all the pictures that take my fancy as appropriate to the coming Christmas time is Raphael Tuck's wonderful reproduction of Raphael's (without the Tuck) "*The Madonna Sixtina*" in a frame closely copied from the one in which is the original at Dresden. An instance of the wonderful perfection attained by the chromo-lithographic process in reproducing a Master's work may be seen in the large chromo-lithograph of Sir John Millais' *Bubbles*, originally brought out by the *Illustrated London News*, and purchased as a decorative advertisement by the indefatigable Messrs. Pears—"sure such a Pears was never seen!"—which is now on view in the window of The Soaperies, New Oxford Street. This work of Young Chromo might deceive even Sir John himself. Now back to books again. I tried hard to fall in love with Lady Lindsay's *Caroline*, but couldn't manage it. I had to get out my skipping-rope, and then I went on by "leaps and bounds" to the finish. Perhaps if I were all alone on a wet day in a Scotch Inn, with only an out-of-date Guide-book, an ancient *Bradshaw*, and last week's local paper, I might find *Caroline* companionable.

My faithful "Co." utters a protest against *A Crown of Shame*, which, he says, is not very pleasant reading. Written by the daughter of Captain Marryat, it lacks the breezy wholesomenes of the works of the author of *Midshipman Easy*. The scene is laid in the tropics or thereabouts, and the sickly atmosphere of feeble vice is rather overpowering. He has also read a very clever pamphlet called the *Dawn of the Nineteenth Century*, which conjures up a vision of the British Empire on the 1st of January, 1901, that must satisfy every one. In this glorious prospect the great Colonial question is solved, and Ireland, without the assistance of a House of Commons sitting in Dublin, is tranquil. "Co." insists upon expressing his high appreciation of the *Happy Thoughts Birthday Book*, compiled by a young lady whose surname is very familiar to him. "Co." has found the quotations most apposite to the anniversaries of his friends and relations. He says that the lines selected for ladies' birthdays are (as they should be) invariably complimentary, so that he has had the satisfaction of soliciting the autographs of two Maiden Aunts (from whom he has expectations), without running the risk of forfeiting their favour. He adds that it is quite the book for a Christmas present—a present, he humorously continues, which will also record the past.

The Baron de Book-Worms & Co.

P.S.—Just seen latest number of *Our Celebrities*. Sir Arthur Sullivan's portrait is, as it ought to be, A. 1, for A. 1, or Arthur the First he is as a Composer and as a humorist in music. He is sandwiched between His Grace of Canterbury and the eminent surgeon-artist and *littérateur*, Sir Henry Thompson. Very appropriate the proximity of the latter to the Composer, as if Sir Arthur is ever hard up for a few notes, Sir Henry can give him one of his delightful "octaves."

B. de B.-W.

---

To Correspondents.—"When I made that note last week about the Gentleman who has devised a new treatment for 'roaring' horses, I did not mean anyone in particular.

(*Signed*) "Roary-up-the-Hills."

## OUR SPECIAL MUSICAL CRITIC (?).

THE great event of the week has, of course, been the production of DR. STEELING's much talked of Cantata, "*The Old Home Farm*," at the Northborough Festival. It was a happy idea on the part of Dr. STEELING to secure the combined choirs of Northumberland and Cumberland, but considering that the gifted Doctor has always conducted Northumberland, it was rather surprising that Cumberland led. The general arrangements were not altogether satisfactory. In the first place, the New Town Hall, like most public buildings, has been erected with a total disregard to acoustic properties; the combined chorus was indistinct; the town band entirely drowned the *soli*; and I was not supplied with a programme, nor could one be got for love or money. I am, therefore, somewhat hampered in giving my analysis of the work, especially as I; am unacquainted with the poem of "*The Old Home Farm;*" in fact, I never heard of it. Fortunately, I was seated next to a kind old gentleman who was well up in the subject, and said he had heard all the music before. The short overture, or rather prelude, to the Cantata was very effective. Avoiding the conventional crash "*tutti*," or the double *piano legato* strings, Dr. STEELING opens with the first and second horns thus:—

TWO OF "THE WORLD'S GREATEST WOMEN."
(*Not hitherto included in any List.*)

Mrs. Harris. Mrs. Gamp.

At intervals this is repeated very effectively. We are then introduced to the leading *motivo*:—

This is repeated *crescendo* until a sudden burst into the dominant with slight variation of the theme:—

There was a slight reminiscence of CZERNY's celebrated Op. 101, but the orchestral treatment was quite different. The opening chorus which my next-door neighbour informed me was entitled, "*Hail, Melancholy Chanticleer,*" was simply remarkable for the occasional Oboë *obbligato*:—

But the charms of the farmyard were more vividly before us in the following passage:—

VIOLINI PRIMO.

A duet, between *Elsie*, the milk-girl, and *Squire Dunrobin*, in which, as far as I could tell, he was questioning her as to where she was proceeding, and the amount of her fortune before offering her marriage, was one of the most original compositions in the work, and Dr. STEELING is much to be complimented. The great *tour de force*, however, was the grand chase by the farmer's dame after three small animals that had intruded themselves, without invitation, upon the premises. The fact that the animals were totally deprived of vision rendered the situation more poetic, and accordingly more dramatic. In these *soli* and chorus the Doctor has surpassed himself. It thus opens quietly on the strings:—

This is repeated three times, when the wood-wind follow thus:—

Added to these is a third phrase:—

And when all were played together, with the full strength of the orchestra, the audience rose *en masse*, and, after expressing their opinion, sat down again. The *finale* was also effective. There were to be (so I understood) festivities by moonlight. The theme, suggesting the rising of the moon, was quite characteristic of the gifted composer:—

In fact, the moon rose even higher, and nothing more suggestive of the rise of the moon has been heard since the song of *The Bedlamite* (with counter subject on the volovong and shoe-horn) in DR. STRAWS's *Water Cantata*, first performed at the Hanwell Festival. I thought the grand festival dance at the end slightly suggested an old tune—but I may be wrong; however the concluding bar were certainly original:—

THE ROYAL SOCIETY OF PAINTERS IN WATER COLOURS.—In these dull December days we should be grateful to Sir JOHN GILBERT and the clever Ladies and Gentlemen who give us glimpses of sunshine, of breezy country, of sea and forest, of foreign countries, and London streets, in their best aspect. All these you can enjoy without the expense of travel, or the inconvenience of wet weather. Just drop in at the pleasant Gallery in Pall-Mall, and you will be able to personally conduct yourself—you must conduct yourself, or you will be reprimanded by the Secretary—to all sorts of delightful places, for one shilling. The Gallery is just the right size to prevent weariness. You will go away refreshed—though you are not admitted by refreshment-ticket—instead of suffering from that most terrible of maladies, the "exhibition headache."

"Maxima debetur pueris."

## THE REAL MUSIC OF THE FUTURE.

SIGNOR FOGHORNI, THE GREAT HIBERNIAN BASSO-TENORE ROBUSTO-PROFONDO, IS SO DISGUSTED AT THE FRIVOLITY OF CONTEMPORARY MUSICAL TASTE (WHICH IS NOT RIPE ENOUGH TO APPRECIATE HIM), THAT HE GIVES UP ALL ATTEMPTS TO PLEASE THE PRESENT GENERATION: HE BUYS A *PHONOGRAPH* INSTEAD, AND DEVOTES HIS ENERGIES TO *SINGING FOR POSTERITY*. BY APPLYING HIS EAR TO THIS MARVELLOUS INSTRUMENT IMMEDIATELY AFTER SINGING INTO IT, HE NOT ONLY HEARS HIS SONG ECHOED BACK TO HIM OUT OF THE DIM FUTURE, BUT HE ALSO HEARS THE RAPTUROUS APPLAUSE OF UNBORN MILLIONS!

[*With Mr. Punch's compliments and apologies to Mr. Edison and Colonel Gouraud.*

## "FREE LANCES!"

[General BOULANGER has sent a letter to M. DÉROULÈDE, thanking the members of the League of Patriots for their sentiments of devotion to the cause of the National Party, which they know to be that of patriotic, honest, and sincerely Republican France.—*Times*.]

*First Free Lance* (*Boulanger*).

"MY good blade carves the casques of men,
My tough lance thrusteth sure,
My strength is as the strength of ten,
Because my heart is pure."
Ahem! No Tennysonian knight
Am I; yet 'twere not bad,
With matters in their present plight,
To pose as *Galahad*.

*Second Free Lance* (*Grandolph*).

Faith, how the swaggering Frenchman flaunts
His "stainless banner!" Bosh!
He'll find, for all his valorous vaunts,
That little game won't wash.
Fancy they hint the same of *me*,
The dolts whose shields I strike;
But anyhow my lance is free
To couch 'gainst whom I like.

*First Free Lance.*

Pst! Caracole, my coal-black steed!
The populace love prance,
To nodding plumes they give good heed;
At least 'tis so in France.
A Gallic *Galahad!* Yonder youth
Is of another strain,
Much less like *Lancelot*, in sooth,
Than *Gareth* or *Gawaine*.

*Second Free Lance.*

"How sweet are looks that ladies bend
On whom their favours fall!
For them I battle to the end
To save from shame and thrall."
Ah, limpid Laureate, Primrose Dames
Rain favours upon me;
But as to championing their claims
*À outrance!*—we shall see!

*First Free Lance.*

"When on my goodly charger borne
Through cheering towns I go,"
BLOWITZ my bounce and *blague* may scorn,
But *is* he "in the know?"
*Condottieri* sometimes come
Like SFORZA, to the front.
Yon springald whom some deem a hum
May still prove "in the hunt."

*Second Free Lance.*

"A maiden knight—to me is given
Such hope, I know not fear.
I yearn to breathe the airs of heaven
That often meet me here."
Humph! In or out I shall not blench,
But later I *may* find
The "heaven" of the Treasury Bench
A little to my mind.

*First Free Lance.*

I know my trade; with lance and blade
To fame I'll carve my way,
My foes are parlously afraid,
Whatever they may *say*.
Yon Briton is a *Puck*-like elf;
Seems out of it at present;
But he, like me, can make himself
Confoundedly unpleasant!

*Second Free Lance.*

Ho, there! Where go you, good my friend?
You fight—beneath whose flag?

*First Free Lance.*

I go for Glory! That's *my* end!

*Second Free Lance.*

And mine! May sound like brag.

*First Free Lance.*

Oh, not at all! We shall arrive!
But by what road,—who knows?
I'll show my friends that I'm alive!

*Second Free Lance.*

And I'll inform my foes!

[*Exeunt severally.*

**End of Anarchy!**

ORDER EVERYWHERE—*Mr. Punch's Almanack for* 1889.

## "FREE LANCES!"

FIRST FREE LANCE (BOULANGER). "AHA!—I GO TO DISTINGUISH MY-SELF!!" SECOND FREE LANCE (GRANDOLPH). "AHEM!—SO DO I!!" [*Exeunt severally.*

## VERY SIMPLE.

"Is there any way across this?"—"Do'naw." "Isn't there a Bridge anywhere?"—"Do'naw."
"Doesn't your Father go this way? How does he get across?"—"Gener'y Joomps it!"

## A CITY IDYL.

"There's a corner in pork, and a starling
Is building her nest in the corner;
And it's oh, (it is always oh) my darling,
There is hope in the heart of your City Jack Horner,
Who sits in the corner to pull out a plum
Then hey, for the bonny bright day that will come
For you and for me, my darling.

"Money was hard and your father was hard—
Yarely is piping the starling—
And we were depress'd as coffee or lard
But firm as copper, my darling.

"And your mother was brisk as inquiries for wheat—
Cotton is weak in the glooming—
For she thought that love's call we should fail to meet,
But like shard-borne beetles at twilight sweet
The Jan Van Beers went booming.

"And bacon closed with a steady tone,
Like choristers clearly quiring,
And hogs were ten points up, my own,
Like the solemn pine on the mountain lone,
Or pinnacles, cloud-aspiring.

"And closing prices, and stocks and shares
Are fair with a future pleasure,
As I wander, a victim to shocks and stares,
In my mooning hours of leisure,

"For tin is as quiet as eventide,
And ribs like the sun declining;
But rails rule firm as my winsome bride,
And love looks up like mining.

"And it's oh, my love, my love,
And it's oh, my dear, my dear,
I've done good work with the corner in pork,
And better with Jan Van Beer."

Thus sang the uncouth swain to the bulls and bears
While the still morn went out in shirtings grey;
He touch'd the tender stops of booms and scares,
With eager thought warbling his Mincing Lay.
He thought without alarm of settling day,
Nor jumped with panic fear when prices fell
Crashing, but every eve he took his way
To Tooting, all his tale of love to tell
While the stars rose, and wild swans left their haunts,
Stags sought the pools, and the grand elephants
Waved their Grand Trunks aloft, and all was well.

## POOH-BAH-RINGTON HALL, ST. JAMES'S.

Had *Brantingham Hall* been written by anybody else but Mr. W. S. Gilbert, how he, the author of *Engaged* and *Ruddigore*, would have chaffed it! How amateurish he would have considered the monotony of the stage-management, and how unmercifully he would have ridiculed the familiar melodramatic characters, with their old-fashioned melodramatic staginess of action and dialogue. "I would be alone!" exclaims the broken-hearted old nobleman. "Let me pass!" exclaims the heroine, addressing the villain, who is not opposing her progress, and, if he were, she has the door open immediately behind her by which she has just entered. The villain mutters curses as he gloomily seats himself at a table. There is the good old family solicitor, the lost heir turning up again, the mortgage to be foreclosed by the villain, who, of course, is ready to sell everybody up, if the persecuted heroine will not be his bride. There are a girl and boy, whose fun would be in keeping with the topsy-turvy eccentricities of a Savoy comic opera, but who are absurdly unnatural in the real life which the comedy is supposed to represent. Miss Neilson is young and pretty. As yet she cannot act, and the sooner she unlearns what she has evidently been taught to consider acting the better for her future histrionic career. Mr. Barrington is Mr. Barrington with a palpably sham scalp. Poor Pooh-Bah-rington! how he must regret having quitted the gay Savoyards! At the finish of the play Miss Neilson has to murmur, "Let us pray," or only the word "pray," apparently addressed to the audience, who, not having come to laugh, were unwilling to remain to pray, especially as at that moment the curtain was descending, and the piece was past praying for.

### A Most Happy Thought.

An admirable suggestion has been offered to the Chancellor of the Exchequer, namely, the proposal of "substituting for the Wheel-Tax a stamp duty on bills, posters, placards, and other mural advertisements." A very high amount of duty might be charged on those eyesores and nuisances without abating them, but in order to render it an alternative for the Wheel-Tax, the stamp must not be so heavy as to stamp them out.

Ecclesiastical Cæsarism.—*Julius* v. *the Bishop of Oxford.*

The Party of Boulanger.—Loafers.

## AN OPEN SECRET.

*Mendicant.* "PITY 'POOR BL——" *Gent.* "NO; I—AH—NEVAR——"
*Mendicant (forgetting himself).* "UGH! 'CAUSE YER 'VE GOT A SHINEY 'AT, AN' A HEYE-GLASS, AN' A 'REACH-ME-DOWN' HULSTER, AN' A NOBBY STICK, YER THINKS YERSELF SOMEBODY!"

## HOW TO SCORE AT FOOTBALL.

CONSIDERING the importation of sheer ruffianism into the Football Field of late, it is quite clear that the method of scoring the points in that game should be modified to meet this new state of things. "Goals" and "Tries," indeed! Why count such merely adventitious trifles? It is high time to recognise the fact that the aim of the players is (apart from the all-important question of gate-money), not so much to win the game as to pound and pummel, mutilate and maim, and, if necessary, kill each other. Let, therefore, the rules be adjusted to the facts. Then we shall be candidly informed, that in a match between—say, the Mudford Mutilators and the Thumpington Thugs, the former team, (or, what is the same thing, gang of roughs) won the game by two deaths, three broken collar-bones, and four injured spines, as against one death, seven smashed ribs, and fourteen minor maimings scored by the latter. This literal and honest way of scoring the game will frankly enlighten the public as to its real nature, and doubtless induce all who are not trained brutes and natural bullies to keep out of that scene of ignoble rowdyism known as the Football Field.

## THE WEARING OF THE GREEN.

(*New Society Version.*)

"There is almost a craze for green in the world of fashion."—*Daily News on "Evening Dress."*

*Belle of the Ball sings:—*

OH, some may bless the Emerald Isle,
Some count her as our foe,
For me, whilst Summer skies did smile,
Now Winter winds do blow,—
Whether in sunshine or in wet,
(Though loyal to my Queen,)
I kept and keep, without regret,
The Wearing of the Green.

Sweet tint! I love you passing well
With lilac at my breast,
Laburnum in my skirts' broad swell,
I look quite at my best.
I overheard Lord RONALD say
That I'm the Emerald Queen.
May failure banish not away
The Wearing of the Green!

Nay, MARIE, why that bitter sneer?
*Home Ruler?* Fiddle-de-dee!
I'm anti-Irish quite, my dear,
Like all Society.
I dote upon our brave BALFOUR,
PARNELL inspires my spleen;
But all the same I do adore
The Wearing of the Green!

Oh, I care not for the Thistle.
And I care not for the Rose;
But when the North winds whistle,
Or when June noonday glows,
Reds, blues, and pinks go friendless,
No gaudy tints are seen;
But I love with love that's endless
The Wearing of the Green!

O sea-green silk; O sea-weed stuff!
O verdant tintings all!
Ye suit my beauty well enough
At dinner, rout, or ball.
How long the fashion yet may live
Remaineth to be seen;
But while it lasts my heart I'll give
To the Wearing of the Green!

A MODEL MAN OF BUSINESS.—The HOLLINGSHEAD Testimonial List is open up to the end of the week. Apply to W. H. GRIFFITHS, Hon. Secretary, Shaftesbury Theatre. There never was a straighter and more trustworthy Manager of a Theatre than Practical JOHN at the Gaiety. His "No" meant "No," and his "Yes" meant "Yes." So no one could mistake his "Ayes" for his "Noes"; consequently there were no written agreements and no disagreements. Will he write his Reminiscences of the Gaiety as a new edition of the Chronicles of HOLLINGSHEAD (JOHN)?

## YANKEE DOODLE.

(*New Society Version.*)

YANKEE DOODLE comes to town,
Possessed of many a "pony";
Bringing his lovely daughter with
A view to Ma-tri-mo-ny.
Yankee doodle-doodle-doo!
The dollars come in handy,
Even to Dooks who have too few,
But know the *Ars Amandi.*

Yankee Doodle rails at rank,
That is for home consumption;
But at swell relatives the Yank
Don't kick,—he's too much gumption.
Yankee doodle-doodle-doo!
Love is sweet as candy,
His daughters "reckon" blood that's [blue
Scarce spoils the British dandy.

# ESSENCE OF PARLIAMENT
## EXTRACTED FROM THE DIARY OF TOBY, M.P.

*House of Commons, Monday Night, November* 26.—"TOBY, M.P., Sir," said JEREMIAH SULLIVAN, of the Irish Constabulary; "in my time I've made a good many arrests, but never before did I arrest the attention of the House of Commons; and bedad! if I can help it, I won't do it again."

A decent-looking man, JEREMIAH; a fine specimen of Irish Constabulary, but just now in rather limp condition.

"JEREMIAH," I said, "these Lamentations are natural enough on your part. You've got into a mess; but cheer up; BALFOUR will never desert you. In the meantime let this be a lesson to you. Beware of females; run not after them. She is bad, but SHEEHY you find is a syllable worse."

JEREMIAH a little puzzled with this simple impressive harangue; upset altogether with proceedings of evening. Told me all about it. Had summons handed to him to serve upon Member for South Galway. "Where'll I find him?" said SULLIVAN. "House of Commons only known address in London," says Superintendent. So JEREMIAH took train for London, and 'bus to Westminster. Found way into Octagon Hall; admired statues of Lord JOHN RUSSELL, and very big man with colossal legs and stupendous marble coat-flaps labelled, "IDDESLEIGH"; found two rows of people waiting at end of corridor leading to Commons.

"Is this the House of Commons?" says JEREMIAH, vainly looking for door-plate.

"It is," said a Polite Policeman.

"Well, I've called upon Mr. SHEEHY," say JEREMIAH. "Is there a knocker to the House-door, or d'ye ring a bell?"

"No," says the Policeman. "You send in your cyard."

JEREMIAH produced "cyard" with a flourish; handed it to Policeman between tips of thumb and finger, as he had seen the gentry do on the stage.

"Maybe," says JEREMIAH to himself, "if the master's not at home, they'll ask me into the kitchen, and give me a drop of something."

Waited quarter of an hour; then SHEEHY discovered sauntering down corridor.

"Who wants Mr. SHEEHY?" Polite Policeman bawled.

"Troth an' I do," said JEREMIAH.

"Then step inside," said the P.P.

JEREMIAH advanced. SHEEHY, thinking it was a constituent, warmly shook hands with him. JEREMIAH much touched at this friendliness; SHEEHY evidently going to make things pleasant; so JEREMIAH whispered in his ear,—

"I've got a little summons for you, Sorr. Would you step outside, and accept service?"

"What!" roared SHEEHY, and bolted into House.

"And wid that," said JEREMIAH, mopping his moist forehead, "I heard nothing more till I was taken before a lot o' gintlemen in a small room with nothing to drink and accused of undermining the British Constitution. It was a sore day when I left Limerick, and when I get back, begorrah, I'll go no more a visiting the gentry."

Sending in his Cyard.

*Business done.*—Land Purchase Bill in Committee. Very dull. SHEEHY suddenly bolts in; breathlessly declares he has had summons served on him in precincts of the House; uproar; confusion; Select Committee appointed to consider affair; Sitting suspended till Ten o'Clock; then Committee on Land Purchase Bill resumed. Continued at it till early morning, with pretty appearance of nothing particular having happened in meanwhile.

*Tuesday.*—DONALD CURRIE wants to know what's this about STUART-RENDELL and the G. O. M.? S. R. has placed his house at his disposal during stay in London; now making holiday arrangements for him in the winter; keeping open house at Naples with a back garden and property trees to cut down before breakfast.

"A gross infringement of my patent," says CURRIE. "I invented that at least four years ago. Who took him out touring round the coast in the *Grantully Castle*? Who gave him a cheap trip all round the Island? Who fetched his medicine, and who warmed his gruel? Who smoothed his pillow and looked after him generally?"

"Why you did," I said, entering warmly into his enthusiasm. "And when he got well he made you a Baronet. Now you've joined the other gentlemen of England, and try to thwart his policy."

"Just so; but that sort of thing ought to be protected by law, like any other invention. I don't mind being imitated. Have often heard OLD MORALITY say that the sincerest imitation is flattery. But let due acknowledgment be made. Let STUART RENDELL unto CURRIE the things that are DONALD'S." And the old gentleman, thrusting his hands into trousers' pockets, angrily strode off. Glad he went away just then. So angry that his conversation was getting a little mixed, and he was beginning to look at me as if *I* had been infringing his patent.

He strode away in anger.

Quiet night in House; much disappointment among Irish Members who know summonses are out against them. Found them wandering about the Corridor where valiant SHEEHY met JEREMIAH SULLIVAN; perambulating outer lobby; knocking up against any man who looks like member of Royal Irish Constabulary; draw a blank. Police wary after last night's scene. Positively decline to serve summonses, and SHEEHY left in sole possession of pre-eminence.

*Business done.*—Land Purchase Bill in Committee.

*Thursday.*—HOWORTH wants to know how about the Aged P.—not *Wemmick's* father, who lived in a little wooden cottage at Walworth surrounded by a moat, the object of tenderest solicitude on the part of his son. It was Aged Prelates HOWORTH was anxious about. Seems there are two in England and Wales over seventy-seven, and three whose years have reached fourscore. HOWORTH thinks it's time they should retire. If not, will OLD MORALITY bring in a Bill rendering retirement compulsory? Before he could answer, JOHNSTON, of Ballykilbeg, on his feet, his aggressive beard waving like blood-red flag.

"All very well," he shouted, "to talk about the Aged P., but what about the Aged G.? If some Bishops are seventy-seven and others eighty, how old is GLADSTONE?"

JOHNSTON has 'em there; sits down triumphantly. OLD MORALITY declines to do little sum. "Ha! ha!" says JOHNSTON, truculently waving his blood-red beard.

As for Aged P.'s, OLD MORALITY makes interesting statement that, "the more aged they get, the more active are they in the discharge of their duties and the fuller their possession of their mental faculties." House laughs riotously. But this nothing to its uproarious delight over OLD MORALITY'S summary of the Plan of Campaign at Suakim. British troops ordered to Suakim; storm of anxious questions from all parts of House as to what they are to do there, what will follow on new expedition, and who is to pay the cost?

Letter-writer to the *Times*. "Let me at him!"

"I wish," said OLD MORALITY, pulling out his stock of copy-book headings, "to be perfectly frank and candid with the House. A few battalions of troops are being moved from Cairo to Suakim, and they will be moved back again from Suakim to Cairo."

House roared with laughter. ABRAHAM (Glamorganshire, not Arabia), inflating his bosom, softly sings:—

"The gallant Duke of YORK! he had ten thousand men,
He marched them up to top of hill, and marched them down again."

OLD MORALITY began to feel uncomfortable. Surely hadn't made another joke like last week, when he dropped into declaration of Home Rule principles? Hurriedly turned over copy-book headings. No; there it was all right. Firmly repeated. "Troops are being moved from Cairo to Suakim, and would be moved back from Suakim to Cairo." House goes into shrieks of laughter. OLD MORALITY, gazing round with dumbly inquiring look, concludes he had better sit down, which he does.

"They're too much for me, sometimes, TOBY," he said wearily. "Suddenly break out laughing when I was never so serious in my life."

Pretty lively night all through till Half-past Eleven, when news comes from Holborn. Satisfaction impartially distributed. First it was said Liberal had got in; Opposition rose like one man and madly cheered; turned out that Conservative had kept the seat; Ministerialists up now, vociferously shouting. Each having had their turn, both went home.

*Business done.*—Land Purchase Bill read Third Time.

*Friday.*—A good long grind at Committee of Supply. Got many votes—one on behalf of distressed Spaniards, who rendered assistance to Great Britain in time of Peninsular War. Only five of these remarkably lusty persons living. Money cheerfully voted, in spite of nasty remarks from Irish Members.

"Must be getting on in life now," said HOWORTH. "Aged Prelates nothing to these Aged Peninsulars, who fought against BONAPARTE eighty-four years ago."

"There is nothing further from my intention than to hide anything from the House," said OLD MORALITY, who had recovered his spirits; "but Age is always Venerable." That settled it. Vote agreed to.

*Business done.*—In Committee of Supply.

## A GROVE OF BLARNEY.

Sir G. G., Director of the Royal College of Music, wrote last week to the *Times* a letter, complaining that nobody knows anything about the Scholarships of his Institution the R. C. M. The letter was evidently intended for a musical setting, and not having time at our disposal for this, we will just give one extract, with our idea of what it wants to make it half effective, so as to reach the masses.

Sir George Grove writing a long note.

He wrote thus:—"The Prince of Wales" (*Triumphal Hymn*—"*Bless the Prince*," *&c.*), "with great wisdom" (*Harps and trumpets; wind and string; obbligato pomposo*), "as it seems to me" (so 'umble! bless him! *Violin squirmoso* . . . But it is well to remind Sir G. G. that Sir A. S. has already used this very phrase in the great duet between *Bouncer* and *Cox*, in *Cox and Box*, "Or as it seems to me," "precisely," "quite so," "then we both agree," &c.), "ordained," (*full orchestra, fortissimo crasho, majestosissimo grandissimo*)—and then follows what the superior wisdom had ordained; namely, that throughout the length and breadth of the land the municipal bodies should make known the existence of these scholarships which are like the Waverley Pen "a boon and a blessing to men." So mote it be! After *Mr. Punch* has suggested the proper musical form of publicity, it ought not, at all events, to be Sir George Grove of Blarney's fault, if his ships, his well-found scholar-ships, are not duly manned.

---

## MR. PUNCH'S "CHRISTMAS ANNUAL" ALPHABET.

**A** is the Christmas Annual (so called, you may remember,
Because it's set-up in July, and published in September).

**B** is the Baby stealing jam—with pinafore and fist messy!
(This style of "Coloured Subject" is considered very Christmassy.)

**C** is the Carol, sung in snow. If anybody bets on it, [on it.
We'll wager there's a window-blind somewhere, with silhouettes

**D** is the Dancing in the Hall, where you'll a tiny flirt see
In rollicking "Sir Roger" make her Grandpapa a curtsey.

**E** is the Editorial, which explains each illustration.
(In many cases *not* a work of super-erogation!)

**F** is the Fun, which *we* should not—perhaps we're hyper-critical!—
At any other time of year particularly witty call.

**G** is the Girl with tennis-bat, inside a hammock sleeping,
Charming, and with the Season, too, so thoroughly in keeping!

**H** stands for Holly. Formerly some pretty maid with joy cut it,
If Artists brought in Holly *now*—the Editor would boycott it!

**I** is the Ice, of course, a crowd of merry school-boys skating on it—
But, as the subject's overdone, we need not be dilating on it.

**J** is the Jollity in which all hearts should join harmonic;
But Annuals "in the movement" take a point of view sardonic.

**K**'s Kissing 'neath the Mistletoe. Once *everyone* was doing it:
All high-class Illustrators now are rigidly tabooing it.

**L** is the Log they burnt at Yule. 'Tis long ago since *we* did it!
These patent gas-stoves possibly have somewhat superseded it.

**M** stands for Mistletoe—and here we *should* require apology,
Did we omit some mention of "Druidical Theology."

**N** is the Novelist whose tale is portioned 'mongst the pictures.
(As no one ever reads it, he is safe from any strictures.)

**O** is Originality—why hanker for a touch of it? [of it!
The Public's quite contented, though they mayn't be given much

**P**'s Pathos; if your eye is moist, be not ashamed to dab it!
It *is* a touching subject—"Child, with invalided rabbit."

**Q** is the Queen of Twelfth Night Feast, by drawing lots elected,
But that comes after Christmas, and may safely be neglected!

**R** stands for Robin. How upon his breast they used to dash on
The liberal crimson! now the bird is fallen out of fashion.

**S** is the Satire, harmless chaff on Persons in Society.
("Smart" Annuals supply it now in every variety.)

**T**'s a good Title: "Selkirk hears the distant church-bells chime."
Or—"Prehistoric Christmas, in the Tertiary Time."

**U** is the Undecided Man, who tries to choose an Annual, [new all!
From the dozens on the bookstall, where they look so spick and span

**V** is the Verse, which Editors o'er vacant spaces scatter,
It generally rhymes and scans—if not, it wouldn't matter!

**W**'s the Wrapper; as a work of Art, it is surprising,
And forms the best of mediums, too, for those who're advertising.

**X** is the Xtra Supplement. Subscribers who are slatterns,
May find their taste corrected by the "Gratis Sheet of Patterns."

**Y** stands for Yule—a term which makes some people rather restive,
But it means the same as "Christmas," and, in print, it looks more *festive!*

**Z** is the Zest with which (although there's little new or funny in 'em),
We pounce upon the Annuals, and invest our surplus money in 'em.

---

## ANSWERS TO CORRESPONDENTS.

A Mistaken Prescription.—You have totally misread our recipe. It was not three "pints" of Condy's Fluid that you were to have added to the basin of water which was to have served as a refreshing lotion for your face, but three *drops*. The result, of course, can only have been what you have described. We are not surprised to hear that your face has become a deep rich orange-brown. This is, of course, a little awkward, if you happen to be dining out. But you must not be impatient. It will possibly wear itself off in the course of a few months.

A Strengthening Regimen.—When you say that you feel at times "as if a steam-roller were going over you," you describe your symptoms, no doubt, accurately, but there is really nothing serious the matter with you. You had, however, perhaps, better take a tumbler of hot cod-liver oil, mixed with rum, before your meals, five times a day, and every half-hour a good wine-glass of Bloxter's Dyspeptic Elixir, alternating this, if you find the former pall a little upon you, with a quart of real turtle, water-gruel, or Fincher's Prepared Magnesia Paste. Keep to a generous diet, and eat as much pork, pastry, pickles, cheese, cucumbers, anchovies, and walnuts, as you can conveniently manage. Should the slight giddiness you mention continue, or even increase, after you have habituated yourself to this diet, endeavour to run a mile immediately after every meal, when no doubt it will pass off. A persistent effort in this direction for six months will make another man of you. By the bye, do not forget your hot mustard plunge-bath before going to bed every night.

Hunting Problem.—It is a pity that before inviting your sporting friends down to your new "place," and promising them a mount, you did not discover that not a pack of hounds met anywhere within twenty-five miles of it. However, you are evidently doing your best to remedy your mistake. Your sending off a cheque for ten pounds to the Battersea Home for Lost Dogs, with a request that the Manager would forward you "immediately by return" a miscellaneous dozen of them, and your opening negotiations with the local circus to which you refer, to get up something like a meet on your lawn on the morrow of your friends' arrival, were both happy inspirations. Perhaps the circus people might be able to supply you with a tame fox, or, if nothing better could be found, even a performing bear, which would almost complete your arrangements for your anticipated "run." If your friends are not very "keen," we dare say you will pull the thing through comfortably enough. Anyhow, we shall be glad to hear from you how it has gone off.

Economical Wedding Present.—We should certainly have thought that the young couple you mention would have been highly delighted with the three-and-sixpenny set of bedroom fire-irons with which you presented them, and would much have appreciated your kind offer to change them either for a black coal scuttle, metal gravy spoon, rolling-pin or kitchen umbrella if they would rather have preferred one of the above-named articles, and we cannot understand your having received no acknowledgment of your gift. As, however, the presents will probably be displayed at the wedding breakfast, and ticketed with the donor's names, perhaps you might find it more agreeable to be out of the way. We should advise you to absent yourself from the ceremony.

LATEST ADDITION TO THE ROYAL ACADEMY.

Delight of Moore on hearing that Burgess had been made an R.A.

## "APPLIED ART:" OR, HOW TO DIRECT PUBLIC TASTE.

*Moral (to Royal Academicians, from the President's Address).*—"IF YOU WANT A THING WELL DONE, DO IT YOURSELVES."

*Sir F. L-ght-n.* Good beys! The new Renaissance moves; Beauty's no more non-resident; [President!
And oh, the happiness it brings to an æsthetic *H-rs-l-y.* No doubt, for you, like me, dear boy, are nothing if not subtle,
I hope you'll find the "precious spark," Sir FREDERICK, in my scuttle.
What fitter place for "fire-germs"? *You*'re the new Prometheus, clearly,
And your language, well, you know, it's *merum nectar*—honey merely.

*T-d-ma.* "*Confectionery*," H-RS-L-Y! If you quote, man, do not garble.
But what d'ye think, Sir FREDERICK, of my hip-bath carved in marble?
Could Persia or Pompeii, aye, or even happy Preston,

Produce a thing it would more truly please your eye to rest on?
*Sir F. L-ght-n.* Most admirable, ALMA! When the chisel or the pencil [utensil,
Of the true Promethean artist shapes the humblest house-
Then the chill Philistine world will feel "the vital flame of beauty,"
A consummation we must aid. 'Tis clearly Art's first duty.
*M-rks.* Of course! A common kettle is a brutal bit of work;
But when 'tis no more "Sukey," but a penguin, crane, or stork,
With a handle like a pair of wings, a spout that's like a beak,
Then, by Jove! it knocks CELLINI to the middle of next week.
*Sir F. L-ght-n.* *Your* rhetoric, my M-RKS, is not too sugary or saccharine.
*M-rks.* Well, I don't mind something prettyish to put my beer or bacca in;
But as to pretty-pretty in my patter—that's all flummery.
*Sir F. L-ght-n.* Well, your kettle does you credit, though your style *is* somewhat summary.
The true receptive readiness, the growing malleability,
The definite intuition, the æsthetical agility,
That England lacks so sadly, will, no doubt, increase by culture,
And a fork that's like an eagle, or a spoon that apes a vulture,
Perchance *in time* will turn a guzzling Aldermanic ninny
Into a much more suitable companion for a PLINY.
Fancy Philistia civilised through the kitchen and the pantry
Pompeii left a blesseder bequest than—we'll say CHANTREY.
*Orch-rds-n.* From bluntness of perception there's no doubt the public suffers,
But this decorative candlestick, and these æsthetic snuffers,
I fancy ought to fetch it, and to make in its dull head room
For an adequate perception of Art-beauty in the bedroom.
*Sir F. L-ght-n.* I'm glad you take my cue, dear Q., and see that what I simply meant [plement.
Was this, that Art should permeate the humblest household im-
*M-ll-s.* *Simply!* Well, that's a twister. Though you're truly Ciceronian,
In exuberant verbosity you're transcendently Gladstonian,
I won't say meretricious, that would make your fine taste queasy,
But I'm hanged if you are simple, and I'm dashed if you are easy.
That "fire-germ of living beauty," in a lamp now, or a ladle,
In a spit, or in a pipkin, in a cauldron or a cradle,
What precisely *is* its meaning?
*G-d-ll.* Look at my Perambulator,
And I think you'll twig at once, JOHN. As Domestic Decorator
I conceive I've found my *métier*.
*P-ynt-r.* Then I hope you won't get out of it!
The Pap-Bowl is important in its way, there's not a doubt of it. [relish it
'Tis the Englishman's Palladium, but *do* you think he'll
A morsel more, if, with Minerva's owl, we chaps embellish it?
*Sir F. L-ght-n.* That precisely is the object of our latest Art evangel. [an angel."
*M-ll-s.* Well, upon the strings of eloquence you "fiddle like
But we are not now at Liverpool, nor with CELLINI toiling.
How can we banish Ugliness, yet keep our own pots boiling?
That's what I want to know, dear boy!
*Sir F. L-ght-n.* No longer worship Mammon!
*M-ll-s.* Humph! Coming from us fellows, don't you think that sounds like gammon?
*Sir F. L-ght-n.* Let's generate an atmosphere that does not reek of money;
Shun all that smacks of clap-trap, or is focussed to the funny.
Yes! Glittering gold should have no fascination for the Master, [plaster.
*His* aim should always be High Art, though clothed in vulgar
*M-ll-s.* Mine is in meerschaum, as you see, this time. But fancy smoking [joking.
My well-loved baccy in this thing! Sir FREDERICK, you are
Can we expect the public to develop "intuition"
Upon what's set before it at our Annual Exhibition,
Where the vulgar and the vapid, like the gazers, crush and jostle?
Of course, FRED, if a fellow *means* to be an Art Apostle
And *take his vows of poverty*——
*All.* Oh, hang it, that's not good enough!
*M-ll-s.* And toil enough, and stint enough, and o'er his labour brood enough, [and Fashion—
And shun the Swells, and cut the Clubs, and chuck up Fun
In fact pursue his mission with self-sacrificing passion;
He *may*, perchance, in time, assist in definitely moulding
That public taste which you have been so eloquently scolding.
But—*who is going to begin?* Mammon *must* be resisted,
If the best talent in the Cause of Beauty be enlisted.
Her cause is a most glorious one, we Artists should be leal to it;
But if we'd smash the Golden Calf, 'tis clear *we* [must not kneel to it!

## A CHOICE OF EVILS.

*Doctor.* "WELL, THERE'S ONLY ONE THING FOR YOU TO DO—YOU MUST GO *YACHTING* FOR NINE MONTHS!"

*Patient.* "OH! THAT COSTS SO MUCH MONEY—BESIDES I'M A BAD SAILOR—IS THERE NO ALTERNATIVE?"

*Doctor.* "WELL—YES—BY NO MEANS AN EXPENSIVE ONE—NOR ONE THAT WILL MAKE YOU SICK! *DON'T EAT SO MUCH!*" [*Patient chooses the Yacht.*

## OH (FOLK) LAW!

MR. ANDREW LANG, in his Presidential address to the members of the Folk Lore Society, alluded to modern slang expressions as belonging to a branch of popular etymology. He particularly alluded to the "Oof bird," which, he said, "he understood to refer in some way to the accumulation of wealth." He suggested that it might be argued that "Oof was a corruption of the French *œuf*, an egg, and that reference was made to the Goose with the Golden Eggs." Always ready to assist historical research, *Mr. Punch* gives a few ancient phrases, with their probable derivations:—

"*All Round my Hat!*" Evidently connected with the noble house of CECIL, who resided at Hatfield. Queen ELIZABETH once visited a SALISBURY at Hatfield, and, doubtless, asked to be taken "round."

"*Pop Goes the Weasel!*" Connected with the spending of money = "That's the way the money goes—*Pop goes the Weasel!*" To "pop" is a quaint expression for raising money on the security of personalty of an insignificant description. "Pop goes the Weasel" may be read, "the weasel goes pop—or popping," *i.e.*, visits a pawnbroker. Why a weasel should have been selected is unknown, unless the animal was the crest of some of the earlier Lombards. This is not impossible, as a weasel is described as a creature that can never be caught slumbering; denoting, therefore, a fund of extra intelligence.

"*Or any other Man.*" This catch-phrase was very popular some ten or twenty years (time passes so swiftly) ago. No doubt it should be "author man." An "author" man is, nine times out of ten, superior to any one else, and thus the saying, which was originated with a view to create attention, is calculated to carry out that object. It is said that it was invented in the time of CHARLES THE SECOND, but this may be because the first to use the phrase was a Christy Minstrel, who may have been a descendant of the guard that attended the dowry of Madras which the swarthy STEWART took on his marriage to his wife.

It need be scarcely added that *Mr. Punch* will be glad to receive any further information on the subject that any member of the Folk-Lore Society may be pleased to send to him. He would receive it for the sake of "Auld Lang Syne," as their President Merry ANDREW would say.

## PLAY-TIME ALL ROUND.

Arthur Roberts himself is as funny as ever in the new *opéra bouffe*, *Nadgy*, at the Avenue Theatre, though he has not been provided with sufficient material for his exuberant humour; that is, up to now. His lesson in deportment to the Ladies, especially when he shows them how to behave at a Linen-draper's, is capital fun. But I expect that, about Christmas-time, there will be something introduced into the Third Act, where the fun somewhat flags. The "*Zim zim zig-a-zig*" duet is amusing, and obtains as many *encores* as Arthur Roberts and his very talented assistant Mlle. Vanoni

The two Zig-a-Zigs showing a clean pair of heels to the Audience.

feel inclined to take. When they are exhausted, they shake the dust of the stage off their shoes at the wings, and, unfortunately, have no other scene together.

*Nadgy* has a good plot and some smart dialogue, and the Composer has hit upon some pretty melodies, of which the most taking, if not the best, is the tenor song, admirably given by the still "Jolly" party of the name of Tapley. Mr. Marsh has very little to sing or do, but he does that little well; and Miss Giulia Warwick looks every inch a Princess, and a little over, and she makes the most of the not very effective music that falls to her share. Mr. Dallas, as the gay old *Margrave*—(I wonder Arthur Roberts doesn't call him "Margate" by accident, and then make a mistake, and address him as "Ramsgate," and then as "Pegwell")—is just what I should imagine a gay old *Margrave* would be if he were Mr. Dallas. He has some funny lines to deliver, and now and then, like *Cox*, in *Box and Cox*, he "joins in a chorus," and, as an Irish witness from the Special Commission would say, "he occasionally takes his part in a solo."

Princess Giulia Warwick, "Oh! he's my Marsh!"

Miss Sallie Turner is one of the merriest sallies in the piece. Arthur Roberts, to whom I cannot help returning, as, after all, or before all, he is the principal attraction, is irresistibly comic in his sentimental speeches, which invariably terminate with a request that he may be allowed to explain a little puzzle.

*Nadgy* is bright and lively; dresses and scenes brilliant. Mons. Marius has put it on the stage in first-rate style. "A Mons a Mons for a' that!" as anybody may exclaim who has an *opéra bouffe* to produce, and is looking out for a Stage Manager. I suppose that, as the piece here owes all its success to Mr. Arthur Roberts, the audience on a first night don't call for "Author! Author!" but for "Arthur! Arthur!" Can anything of this sort be a failure with him in it? and Roberts + Vanoni = Certain Success. Q. E. D.

Plenty of stir in the Operatic World. *Dorothy* still running: has run over to the Lyric. *Paul Jones* coming to the Prince of Wales's.

Perhaps before Pooh-Bah-rington & Co. decide on the withdrawal of W. S. Gilbert's Pooh-Bah-rington Hall at the St. James's, Sir Arthur may be called in to introduce a duet between Miss Neilson, who, I hear, has a nice voice, and Pooh-Bah-rington, with a dance modelled on that of the Dancing Quakers or the P.-Bah and Jessie Bond's eccentric *pas de deux* in *Ruddigore*. The introduction might be too late to save the piece, but it would make a fine festive finish for the last night, and would draw one big house at all events, to speed the parting guest. In answer to numerous inquiries, the first initial in W. S. Gilbert's name does *stand* for William, but the second—the "S"—does *not* stand for Shakspeare.

Druriolanus is busy with his Pantomime. He does the thing thoroughly. Not a big head that he doesn't try on, not a trap on which he doesn't go down, or be shot up. Not a wire that is to carry a fairy that either he, or his indefatigable private secretary and literary adviser, does not fly across the stage upon, before allowing a *fée* or a *coryphée* to essay it. The flying fairies are so fond of their profession, that they soon become strongly attached to the wires that are to carry them. Fact. *The Babes in the Wood* is, as every one now knows, the subject. What are the odds against something being said about a "whine in the wood" in the course of the Pantomime? Last night of *Armada* on the 15th and abdication of Queen Elizabeth.

Private Box.

## VOCES POPULI.

### A GAME OF BILLIARDS.

Scene—*A Hotel Billiard-room—anywhere.* Mr. Balk *and* Mr. Footler *discovered about to begin a game.* Captain Hazard *and* Mr. Spottesbarde, *who have come in just too late to secure the table, seat themselves on bench, and look on. A* Friend *of* Mr. Footler's *is smoking in the background.*

*Capt. Hazard* (*in an undertone to Mr. S.*). They won't be long. We shall get a game before they close—it's only a quarter-past ten now.

*Mr. Footler* (*a weedy, limp man, with spectacles, and a mild expression*). It's ages since I've touched a cue—you ought to give me something, really.

*Mr. Balk* (*short, stout, and self-satisfied*). All right! How much?—will seventy do?

*Mr. F.* (*a little hurt*). Oh, I'm not so bad as all that—say twenty-five. [*Chooses a cue with great circumspection.*

*Mr. Footler's Friend.* I shall put a shilling on you, Freddy, my boy—so play up!

*Mr. Balk.* I'll break. I always make it a rule to play for safety. (*Makes a miss in baulk, but manages somehow to leave his ball near centre pocket*). Ah! (*with an air of reproaching somebody else*) too fine, too *fine!*

*Mr. F.* (*chalking his cue*). You've left me a chance there. Let me see—perhaps I'd better leave you where you are for the present, hit the red first, and come back to you afterwards? I think that's the better game.

*Capt. H.* (*aside, to Mr. S.*). Seems to think he's playing parlour croquet!

*Mr. F.* (*after shifting the position of his left hand several times, and agitating the end of his cue, misses red ball, and lands himself eventually in corner pocket*). I've let you off, you see! Now how the dickens did I do *that*, I wonder?

*Mr. B.* Can't say, I'm sure—that's three to me (*after playing*). Ha! I've left 'em for you again.

*Mr. F.* *I* can't do anything. . . . There, didn't I tell you so? But I've saved my miss, anyway!

*Mr. B.* (*walking round table*). I ought to do something here. Yes, I shall hit the red very fine, and go in off him into the left-hand top-pocket—that's the proper game (*plays*). Te-hee! Too much side on!

*Capt. H.* (*sotto voce*). He's right *there!*

*Mr. Footler* (*flurried*). My turn, is it? But—er—where's my ball—eh?

*Mr. Balk* (*good-humouredly*). Why, you see, you got into one of the pockets, old fellow, out of my way.

*Mr. F.* Ha! ha! So I did. I—I thought it was the best thing to do. What's the game, Marker?

*Marker.* Twenty-seven. Three.

*Mr. F.* I don't *like* potting my adversary's ball—but you leave me no choice. [*Plays.*

*Marker.* Three. Twenty-seven.

*Mr. Balk* (*encouragingly*). Very near, very near, Sir. Well, you haven't left *me* much.

*Mr. F.* (*laughing feebly*). No, I—I couldn't afford to. (Mr. Balk *makes an easy cannon*). Oh, good *shot!*

*Mr. B.* (*complacently*). Ah, I'm getting my eye in now. [*Strikes sharply, and sends ball off the table.*

*Capt. H.* (*aside*). (He'll be getting somebody's eye *out* presently!

*Mr. B.* (*receiving ball*). Thanks—much obliged. (*Explanatorily to* F.) I put rather too much screw on that time.

*Mr. F.* (*with pride*). That's another to me, Marker!

[*Makes a cannon.*

*Mr. B.* (*patronisingly*). There, you see, you can hit 'em when you take a little trouble. Not a bad stroke at all.

*Mr. F.* (*modestly*). I'm afraid it was a bit of a fluke. Oh, I go on playing, don't I? That's two to me, Marker—(*after playing again*) . . . and another to this gentleman.

*Mr. B.* (*plays, and makes another cannon*). I played for that. Creeping up to you, FOOTLER, eh!

[*Later.* Mr. FOOTLER'S *score is thirty-five* — Mr. BALK'S, *nineteen.* Mr. FOOTLER *is benignly patronising;* Mr. BALK *gloomy, and inclined to cavil.*

*Mr. F.* (*beaming with honest pleasure*). Five more to me, Marker! I hope you're keeping the score correctly?

*Mr. B.* Well, you aren't going to tell me you tried for that! . . . Two *more!* Come, I *say*—it's impossible to play against such flukes as that—you played to go in off the red.

*Mr. F.* Oh, n-not altogether . . . (*misses*). There, you can't say I didn't try for *that!*

*Mr. B.* (*scanning the cloth*). Um—don't like this at all . . . Shan't score *this* time. (*He doesn't*). Now you've *got* me! (*Gloomily*). [Mr. F. *plays, and makes three.*

*Mr. B.* (*disgustedly*). There, I never saw the balls run as they do for you in all my life!

*Mr. F.* (*generously*). Well, you're not in form to-night—I can see that.

*Mr. B.* Form! What good's form against such infernal fluking? There—*go* on—it's you to play!

*Mr. F.* I was just looking round the table, that's all. Well, I shall have a shot at the double event . . . Oh, hard *luck!*

*Mr. B.* (*growling*). Hard luck? Hard *stroke*, you mean! (*Plays.*) Was that a cannon, Marker?

*Marker* (*imperturbably*). No, Sir—nothing, Sir.

*Mr. B.* (*hopelessly*). It's no use—they won't run for me to-night!

*Mr. Footler.* Here, Marker, jigger, please. Is the red ball clear of the cushion?

*Marker* (*inspecting it*). Good half-inch, Sir!

*Mr. F.* Then that's *my* game. (*After playing.*) Phew! a mile off! You may beat me yet, old fellow.

*Mr. B.* Not to-night. *I* can't do anything. . . . There, ever see anything like that in your life?

*Capt. H.* (*in an undertone*). I'm hanged if *I* ever did! They ought to rent a table by the week if they want to play a game out!

*Mr. F.* Long game this! Tell you what, BALK, if you like to take that twenty-five back, I've no objection!

*Mr. F.'s Friend.* Oh, I say—and how about my shilling?

*Mr. B.* (*annoyed*). Don't be too confident, FOOTLER; I shall catch you up yet. I play a waiting game.

*Capt. H.* Jove—and so do we!

*Mr. B.* I wouldn't make too sure of that shilling, JONES, the game isn't over yet by a long way.

*Marker* (*confidentially*). Beg pardon, Gentlemen, but it's getting late, and those other Gentlemen are waiting to play—would you mind playing fifty instead of a hundred up? Makes a shorter game, Gentlemen.

*Mr. F.* Well, *I'm* quite willing.

*Mr. B.* Of course *you* are! But I never meant to give you twenty-five in fifty—I'd give nobody such long odds as that.

*Mr. F.* Then, look here, suppose we play fifty up, and you take twenty-five—that'll make you forty-six to my forty-seven.

*Mr. B.* (*brightening visibly*). That's fair enough—all right, Forty-six-forty-seven, Marker. I shall have a chance now. (*Lies on table and, in making stroke, kicks* Mr. F. *in waistcoat.*) Conf—FOOTLER, I shall have that stroke over again.

*Mr. F.* (*removing to a safe distance*). I shall take good care *I* don't!

*Mr. B.* (*after missing again*). Of course I knew I shouldn't bring a stroke like that off twice running—(*bitterly*)—you ought to run out easily, now!

*Mr. F.* (*trembling with excitement*). Oh, I'm not so sure about that. [*Aims jerkily.*

*Jones* (*his Friend*). Mind what you're about, old fellow—remember I've a shilling on you!

*Mr. F.* (*after missing*). Hang it, JONES! I wish you'd wait for the stroke—it's enough to put any fellow out!

*Mr. Balk.* Forty-seven all! (*Plays.*) Was that a kiss, Marker?

*Marker* (*impassively*). No, Sir; 'nother miss, Sir.

*Mr. Footler.* I'll make it safe this time. (*Plays.*) Pah, never got near it!

*Mr. Balk.* Now then—(*plays*)—tut-tut, not *legs* enough!

*Capt. H.* (*aside*). Legs! a centipede wouldn't have enough for *him!*

*Mr. Footler.* Forty-nine—forty-eight. This is getting devilish exciting! (*Plays.*) Oh, dear me, that's another to you—I *must* be careful now!

*Mr. Balk.* Oh, *you're* all right—I shan't get anything to-night.

*Mr. Footler* (*amiably, as* Mr. B. *is aiming*). Have some more chalk?

*Mr. B.* (*angrily*). Chalk! what the—there, it's all your . . . wait a bit—it's not going to be a miss, anyway . . . it's—hi! go on—go *on*, can't you! (*Ball wavers a few seconds, and drops into pocket.*) Game to me! (*Magnanimously.*) Well, FOOTLER, you play a finer game than I thought you did, but I fancy I should beat you by more than this on a better table, and then you *started* twenty-five to the good, you know! Capital exercise, billiards—the King of indoor games! [Mr. F. *puts on his coat sulkily.*

*Marker to Capt. H. and Mr. S.* (*who have risen eagerly*). Very sorry, Gentlemen, close on 'alfpast eleven, Gentlemen—closing time!

*Mr. F.* (*to Mr. Jones*). Well, old fellow, if I didn't quite pull it off, you'll admit you had a good run for your money!

[Mr. BALK *walks out with restored complacency.* Mr. FOOTLER *follows with* Mr. JONES *in a more resigned frame of mind. The Captain and his Friend reserve their remarks until they are alone. Lights extinguished as Scene closes.*

## OUR BOOKING-OFFICE.

"Co." draws attention to *Among the Turks*, by V. L. CAMERON, C.B., D.C.L., as a first-rate story of adventure by land and sea; also *In Palace and Faubourg*, by "C. J. G." (who is he?), which is very interesting, specially for youthful Marionettes—Co. begs pardon—*lapsus calami*—would have said, "Marie Antoinettes," —if considered as a Christmas book by the publishers, NELSON AND SONS. NELSON (AND SONS) expect every man this Christmas-time to do his duty. Has NELSON a column to himself in some paper, as his great namesake has in Trafalgar Square? But, *à propos* of Trafalgar Square, I must move on. "Next, please, Co."

*The Story-telling Album.* By WELLS, DARTON & Co. Co. cannot conscientiously encourage children in story-telling, but this is an exception, and to be recommended. Easy stories ("It is as easy as . . . story-telling"—*Hamlet* politely adapted), and bea—*u*—tiful pictures. Boys will like *That Bother of a Boy*, which is the story of an Imp, by GRACE STEBBING; and some amusement may be found in *The Moderate Man*, issued by publishers who have been Downey enough to get HARRY FURNISS to illustrate it.

Messrs. MACMILLAN are reproducing Miss YONGE'S and CHARLES KINGSLEY'S Books. They ought to be very popular; they were, once upon a time. But, personally speaking for myself, and not for "Co.," I never could read one of them, and can't now.

Mrs. MOLESWORTH'S "*Christmas Posy*" is first-rate, and entitles the authoress to be called Mother Bunch. Same MACMILLANS bring out double Christmas number of *English Illustrated Magazine*, which keeps up its literary and artistic *prestige*. The Quill Pen-elopes of *London Society* (Christmas number of course) are Mrs. LOVETT CAMERON (always pleasant reading), Mrs. CASHEL HOEY and Mrs. FLORENCE MARRYAT. When will these three meet again? Next Christmas probably. Good company these three ladies when you're training down to the country for Christmas.

My faithful "Co." reports that he has been reading with great delight a *Crack County*, by Mrs. E. KENNARD, which he fancies is either a hunting story, or the rough sketch for the *scenario* of a Christmas Pantomime. He inclines to the latter belief, as he finds such names as *Lord Littelbrain*, and *General Prosieboy*, which remind him of the customary lines in the play-bills,—"Cricketers—Messrs. GLOVES, STUMPS, BATS, and BALLS;" and "Lawyers—Messrs. COSTS, WRITS, and SUMMONS." If it *is* a hunting story, and only a hunting story, why then it is equally interesting, especially the earlier chapters of the first volume, in which is recorded a run after a fox in a fog! He, however, was sorry to notice that the fair Authoress is rather too fond of making her hunting-men use strong language. Had the novel been illustrated, no doubt it would have found a place in the Library of the late *Mr. Jorrocks.*

"Co." was under a misapprehension last week in putting down the pretty *Rosebud Annual* to Messrs. G. WARNE—it is published by JAMES CLARKE & Co. "Co." has been Warne'd. By the way, the *Australian Flowers Album*, with frames in the flowers for holding photographs, is, Co. thinks, very "tasty." There's humour in this idea of SMITH AND DOWNE'S, if you only select the right people to fill the spaces, as some faces set among the flowers do seem so appropriately placed. B. DE B.-W. & Co.

SOCIAL AGONIES.

*Mrs. de la Bore-Brown (to Jones, who, instead of listening to her Story, has been deeply interested in what young Smith is saying to Miss Robinson).* "AND NOW, TELL ME CANDIDLY—WHAT WOULD YOU HAVE DONE IN MY PLACE!"

## "REMEMBER!"

A WORD IN SEASON.

*Shade of Gordon, loquitur:—*

ONCE more into the Desert, once again
Treading the sands scarce free of the red stain
Left by your lost slain thousands? Back once more
To face the swarthy spearmen's rush and roar
With a mere handful? Can it really be?
Have you forgotten El Obeid—and Me?
Beware! What matter who your hosts may head,
That SALISBURY leads now where GLADSTONE led?
The doom of vacillation is the same,
Helpless confusion, failure, and disfame.
Yours to determine, lessoned by a past
At which your stoutest patriots stood aghast,
Yours to determine whether once again
The bravest English breasts should faint with pain,
With shame should sicken, at the piteous sight
Of Policy, the prey of Party fight.
Sinkat, Tokar, Khartoum! These names should teach
E'en slaves of purse-strings, dupes of flowing speech
How shambling statecraft may go blundering on,
Till, Valour paralysed, and Honour gone,
E'en the Exchequer finds how scant the gain
That comes from friends betrayed and heroes slain.

Remember! What you do, do well, at once!
He who, thrice schooled, forgets, is worse than dunce.
Yon is no region for the paltering pranks
Of trimmers tame from Party's rival ranks.
Withdraw your foot from out those treacherous sands,
Or plant it firmly there. The desert bands,
Their desperate valour in unequal fight,
The swift evasion of their trackless flight,
You know. Send no more knots of men to fall
In a lone waste or by a ruined wall.
Send them no more, I say, nor be content
To sit in sullen silence while they 're sent,
Pushed here and there like pawns, without an aim,
By bungling players of a blindfold game.
Yours the responsibility at last,
As yours the shame by such dishonour cast;
Be yours the resolution! Still Khartoum,
But named, clouds every English face with gloom.
'Twas there such fumbling policy as this
Found tragic issue. Can you—dare you—miss
The obvious moral? Caution is not crime,
But feebleness is guilt. Be warned in time!

## READ THIS! AN UNPARALLELED PRIZE!

*How to Get a Healthy Circulation in the Cold Weather.*

CHAMPION SQUIBS' UNPRECEDENTEDLY GENEROUS CHRISTMAS GIFT.

IN reply to our offer of one guinea for the best suggestion as to what would be at once the most popular and the most unique Prize for a successful answer sent in to our Christmas Conundrum, we (*Champion Illustrated Squibs*) have received bushels of answers, of which we print a few specimens.

"CONSTANT SUBSCRIBER" writes—"I think you couldn't do better than give one bound volume of your delightful paper to the successful Competitor. True, its market price is only about seven shillings, but *I* consider it worth ten times that sum, and so I am sure will all your other readers who, like me, have *no professional connection whatever* with your marvellous pennyworth."

"GENEROUS SOUL" says—"You do not state the limit of money value for the Christmas Prize. However, knowing how munificent you are, or wish to be thought, I fancy you could not do better than offer *two Special Private Pullman Cars*, one for meals, and the other for sleeping, such as the CZAR of RUSSIA uses, with a free pass for, say, twenty persons for one whole year, over all the railways of England and Scotland. This would get you a lot of readers among railway travellers."

"PALE STUDENT," who does not seem quite to have grasped what our design for Christmas is, writes as follows:—"I hear that you

## "REMEMBER!"

Shade of Gordon. "IF YOU MEAN TO SEND HELP, DO IT THOROUGHLY, AND—**DO IT AT ONCE!!**"

wish to do something *really surprising*. Well, what could be a greater surprise to your readers than if your Christmas Number were to simply contain, instead of the usual short stories and borrowed scraps, humorous and otherwise (especially otherwise), the *whole of* MILTON's '*Paradise Lost*,' printed '*in extenso*'? It might not largely increase your circulation, and in fact would probably ruin the paper, but think what an impetus it would give to the spread of a taste for high-class literature!"

"PRACTICAL" says:—"Why not make your prize something really Christmassy? I would suggest half a prize bullock for the most successful competitor, ten prime turkeys for second, a monster plum pudding for third, and so on through geese and fowls to a modest kippered herring. In this way you would share the advantages offered among a large number."

As none of the above suggestions are quite satisfactory, we have decided to keep the guinea for ourselves, and to select the following:—

UNPRECEDENTED YULE-TIDE OFFERING!

as our first prize (the only one) for the forthcoming festive season.

A Full-size African Rhinoceros will be despatched to the private residence of the person fortunate enough to give, in our judgment, the best answer to the conundrum which will be published in our next week's issue. In order to increase the pleasurable surprise when it arrives at the door, we shall give *no notice of its coming!* Thus, all our readers, successful or not, will share in the anxious expectancy consequent on the possible uncaging in their street of this truly noble quadruped. A special ship has been chartered to bring the animal over from the Congo; and we should advise the prize-taker to secure it in his back garden by a chain attached to the most solid thing in the neighbourhood. It is probable that cats will avoid the garden, and so a double advantage will be reaped by the fortunate owner.

N.B.—Should any difficulty be experienced with the animal, Messrs. CARTER, PATERSON & Co. would, if applied to, peremptorily *decline* to call for it with one of their vans. Our readers will admit that no such prize as this has ever before been offered by any English journal.

## THE DIARY OF A NOBODY.

*November* 14.—A red-letter day. Our first important party since we have been in this house. I got home early from the City. LUPIN insisted on having a hired waiter, and stood a half-dozen of champagne. I think this an unnecessary expense, but LUPIN said he had had a piece of luck, having made three pounds out of a private deal in the City. I hope he won't gamble in his new situation. The supper-room looked so nice, and CARRIE truly said, "We need not be ashamed of its being seen by Mr. PERKUPP, should he honour us by coming."

I dressed early in case people should arrive punctually at 8 o'clock, and was much vexed to find my new dress trousers much too short. LUPIN, who is getting beyond his position, found fault with my wearing ordinary boots instead of dress boots. I replied, satirically, "My dear son, I have lived to be above that sort of thing." LUPIN burst out laughing and said, "A man generally was above his boots." This may be funny or it may *not*, but I was gratified to find he had not discovered the coral had come off one of my studs. CARRIE looked a picture, wearing the dress she wore at the Mansion House. The arrangement of the drawing-room was excellent. CARRIE had hung muslin curtains over the folding-doors, and also over one of the entrances, for we had removed the door from its hinges. Mr. PETERS, the waiter, arrived in good time, and I gave him strict orders not to open another bottle of champagne until the previous one was empty. CARRIE arranged for some sherry and port wine to be placed on the drawing-room sideboard with some glasses. By the bye, our new enlarged and tinted photographs look very nice on the walls, especially as CARRIE has arranged some Liberty silk bows on the four corners of them.

The first arrival was GOWING, who with his usual taste greeted me with, "Hulloh, POOTER, why your trousers are too short!" I simply said, "Very likely, and you will find my temper '*short*' also." He said, "That won't make your trousers longer, Juggins. You should get your Missus to put a flounce on them." I wonder I waste my time entering his insulting observations in my diary. The next arrivals were Mr. and Mrs. CUMMINGS. The former said, "As you didn't say anything about dress, I have come 'half dress.'" He had on a black frock-coat and white tie. The JAMES', Mr. MERTON, and Mr. STILLBROOK arrived, but LUPIN was restless and unbearable till his DAISY MUTLAR and FRANK arrived. CARRIE and I were rather startled at DAISY's appearance. She had a bright crimson dress on, cut very low in the neck. I do not think such a style modest. She ought to have taken a lesson from CARRIE, and covered her shoulders with a little lace. WUMMINGS and his four daughters came, so did FRANCHING, and one or two of LUPIN's new friends, members of the "Holloway Comedians." We had some music, and LUPIN, who never left DAISY's side for a moment, raved over her singing of a new song called "*The Garden of Sleep*." It seemed a pretty song, but she made such grimaces, and sang to my mind so out of tune, I would not have asked her to sing again, but LUPIN made her sing four songs right off one after the other.

At ten o'clock we went down to supper, and, from the way GOWING and CUMMINGS eat, you would have thought they had not had a meal for a month. I told CARRIE to keep something back in case Mr. PERKUPP should come by mere chance. GOWING annoyed me very much by filling a large tumbler of champagne, and drinking it straight off. He repeated this action, and made me fear our half dozen of champagne would not last out. I tried to keep a bottle back, but LUPIN got hold of it, and took it to the side-table with DAISY and FRANK MUTLAR. We went upstairs, and the young fellows began skylarking. CARRIE put a stop to that at once. STILLBROOK amused us with a song, "*What Have You Done with your Cousin John?*" I did not notice that LUPIN and FRANK had disappeared. I asked Mr. WATSON, one of the Holloways where they were, and he said, "It's a case of 'Oh, what a surprise!'" We were directed to form a circle—which we did. WATSON then said, "I have much pleasure in introducing the celebrated Blondin Donkey." Frank and LUPIN then bounded into the room. LUPIN had whitened his face like a Clown, and FRANK had tied round his waist a large hearth-rug. He was supposed to be the donkey, and he looked it. They indulged in a very noisy Pantomime, and we were all shrieking with laughter. I turned round suddenly, and then I saw Mr. PERKUPP standing half-way in the door, he having arrived without our knowing it. I beckoned to CARRIE, and we went up to him at once. He would not come right into the room. I apologised for the foolery, but Mr. PERKUPP said, "Oh, it seems amusing." I could see he was not a bit amused. CARRIE and I took him down-stairs, but the table was a wreck. There was not a glass of champagne left—not even a sandwich. Mr. PERKUPP said he required nothing, but would like a glass of seltzer or soda water. The last syphon was empty. CARRIE said, "We have plenty of port wine left." Mr. PERKUPP said, with a smile, "No thank you. I really require nothing, but I am most pleased to see you and your husband in your own home. Good night, Mrs. POOTER—you will excuse my very short stay, I know." I went with him to his carriage, and he said, "Don't trouble to come to the office till twelve to-morrow." I felt despondent as I went back to the house, and I told CARRIE I thought the party was a failure. CARRIE said it was a great success, and I was only tired, and insisted on my having some port myself. I drank two glasses, and felt much better; and we went into the drawing-room, where they had commenced dancing. CARRIE and I had a little dance, which I said reminded me of the Mansion House. She said I was a spooney old thing.

## PUNCH AND "JUDITH" À LA MODE DE PARRY.

AN excellent performance of this, PARRY's Oratorio in London, at the St. James's Hall, last Thursday. One of the series of NOVELLO's Oratorio Concerts, with Dr. MACKENZIE prescribing—we should say, conducting. The boys made a great hit. Quite an Oratorio for holiday time, as there are so many children in it. It will, of course, be given again in the Christmas vacation. In his preface to the Book of the Words the Composer gives the reasons (quite unnecessary) for selecting this "Israelitish story," which he has illustrated with Israel-lightish music, as it is not in the least heavy or tedious. Its reception was enthusiastic; Mr. HUBERT PARRY and everybody was applauded, and Dr. MACKENZIE—now known as "the one MAC," to distinguish him from "the Two MACS"—beamed again as he "boo'd and boo'd" to the audience.

## Now and Then.

(*By one of the* 150 *Gladstonians who presented Mr. John Dillon with an Illuminated Address.*)

ONCE, I own, we looked upon JOHN DILLON
As a very wicked sort of villain.
Now a little touch of Party paint
Makes JOHN DILLON look almost a Saint.
Funny the effect of GLADSTONE's Bill on
Party points of view of Mr. DILLON!

**IDENTITY.**

*Enthusiastic Amateur (at the National Gallery).* "CAN YOU TELL ME WHERE I CAN FIND THE NEW 'CONSTABLE'?"

*Hibernian Officer.* "SHURE IT'S MESELF YE MUST MANE, SOR! I CAME ON JEWTEE HERE FOR THE FORST TOIME THIS WEEK, SOR!"

## TOO ADVANCED SHEETS; OR, SEASONABLE LITERATURE À LA MODE.

SCENE—*A Publisher's Sanctum. Time, December 1st,* 1888. *Head of the Firm discovered. To him enter* Author.

*Author.* I have called, as I promised I would, with a MS., which I believe to be suitable to your requirements.

*Publisher.* Most happy to receive it, my dear Sir, most happy. What is it about?

*Author.* It is a story intended for a Summer Number—for your next year's Summer Number.

*Publisher.* My dear Sir, *that* was distributed last November. But what is it about?

*Author.* I call it "May Day in India."

*Publisher.* Turn it into "Christmas Eve at the North Pole," and perhaps we may be able to find an opening for it.

*Author.* Well, the task is not impossible. I have carried out similar transformations. But what would you do with it in its amended form?

*Publisher.* Why, pop it into our *Christmas Annual for* 1889-90, which is now in a forward state of preparation.

*Author.* Surely you are a little early?

*Publisher.* Not at all—next year we shall produce our *Christmas Annual* in June! And now, my dear Sir, having settled our business, I am sure you will forgive me if I withdraw. Fact is, we are just now busy launching our Contemporary Magazine, which we have decided to call *The Twenty-First Century!* [*Exit hurriedly.*

## TO MY HAIRDRESSER.

*(Not to make Conversation.)*

You tell me that the day is fine,
You say my hair is getting thin,
Anon you proffer Smearoline,
Or comment on my tender skin;
Good friend, for goodness' sake forbear,
I prithee only cut my hair.

For think—a shy, retiring man,
I shun the toilet's public rite,
Until my Cousins—Cousins can—
Reproach me for a Perfect Fright.
And must I bear, too shy to snub,
The babble of your Toilet Club?

I know, for every day for years
I've scann'd the glass with careful eye,
Whether the heaven clouds or clears,
Whether the roads are wet or dry;
Indeed, indeed, I do not care
Whether you think it foul or fair.

And why observe, with honied zest,
What men by many phrases call,
That phase which must be dubb'd at best
Unduly intellectual?
What though my loftier temples shine,
That is no business of thine.

Think you, when, in your wrapper swathed,
I cower beneath the harrowing comb,
Or crouch, in creaming lather bathed,
Beneath the hose's numbing foam,
Or bear, while tears unbidden gush,
The rigours of your softest brush,—

Think you, at such a time as this,
I care to hear, with nerves unstrung,
The dirge of bygone days of bliss
Trip lightly from a stranger's tongue?
What if your victim stood at bay,
And told you *you* were bald or grey?

The head you handle like a block,
And brand with slighting comments cool,
Has bravely borne the battle's shock,
And starr'd the grey old walls at school;
Has sprained a Bishop's reverend wrist,
And badly bruised a Judge's fist.

They were not Judge and Bishop then,
But only chubby, scrubby boys;
And now they're grave and reverend men.
I value those remember'd joys,
And grieve that evil should be said
About my own, my only head.

Your politics are nought to me;
I'll keep my views about the weather:
I only wish we could agree
That I am neither wood nor leather.
Be gentle; 'tis the nobler plan,
And stint your chatter, if you can.

---

GOODY TEA-SHOES.—The latest fad in the way of fashion reported from the United States is the fancy of a fair novelist who has devised a sweet thing in shoes. Her own slippers, designed for display at afternoon tea, she has had made in the form of gloves, each of her ten toes provided with "a separate pocket of kid in which it rests like a finger in the elongated pouch of a glove." Evidently an æsthetic young lady this, with quite a peculiar conception of the τὸ καλόν.

# ESSENCE OF PARLIAMENT
## EXTRACTED FROM THE DIARY OF TOBY, M.P.

*House of Commons, Monday Night, December* 3.—"Monsignor!" I gasped, as familiar figure flitted down Corridor, making for House of Commons. "Is this you, or will the Conservative Party have the long-delayed pleasure of beholding your wraith?"

"It's me, or perhaps I should more correctly say, it is I," said the G. O. M., playfully making a lunge at my tail with his umbrella, as if he were lopping off a short but serviceable branch from a tree. "Suppose you thought I was down at Hawarden? So I was; went off about a week ago. Fancied I was tired; might leave Autumn Session to younger men. Did very well for first day or two; vigorously read lessons in Church; wrote letters by the dozen, post-cards by the score. Began an article for the *Twenty-first Century*. Read HOMER backwards; cut two old trees, and one early acquaintance; tried to make myself believe I was happy. But no use. Every morning papers came with Parliamentary Reports; BALFOUR back, in high spirits; Prorogation apparently as far off as ever; resisted temptation up to this morning. When papers arrived, containing columns of report of Saturday sitting, could stand it no longer. Irish Estimates on to-night; BALFOUR's salary to be voted; opportunity for going over everything from beginning. Couldn't face another week at Hawarden with business buzzing on at Westminster; so jumped into train, and here I am. Ta-ta. Just going to Boo for BALFOUR."

Booing for BALFOUR all round. ELLIS began it; HEALY took part in it; DILLON had his say; and TREVELYAN gave a brief history of SPENCER's administration. G. O. M. beat everybody in vigour and vivacity. Managed to say something new about Mitchelstown. BALFOUR swears that the shot which slew LONERGAN was a *ricochet*. Photographs taken on the spot show that LONERGAN was in direct line with barrack window when shot fired.

"Were the photographs taken by *ricochet?*" roared GLADSTONE, leaning half across the table, and literally glaring upon the pensive BALFOUR.

"Capital idea," said MAPLE-BLUNDELL. "Shall add a new wing to our Mammoth establishment, and advertise photographing by *ricochet*. Sure to take."

BALFOUR, as usual, best at bay; received no help; asked for none; up half a dozen times; agile, adroit, brilliant. Supposed to be on his defence, but ever on the offensive, slashing out right and left. No *ricochet* shots for *him*. *Business done.*—Irish Estimates in Supply.

*Tuesday.*—GLADSTONE yesterday, GRANDOLPH to-day.

"Which do you like best?" I asked OLD MORALITY.

"I'm past caring," he said, with a weary sigh. "You know what is written in the copy-book: '*The Crushed Worm doesn't ask which Wheel did it?*'"

Photographed by Ricochet.

GRANDOLPH's attack delivered by old familiar war-way of the Soudan. STANHOPE complains that it was an ambush. House ostensibly met to discuss salary and expenses of Chief Secretary. ELLIS has moved Amendment, cutting off BALFOUR's coals. "But, first of all," says TIM HEALY, "let's drag him over them." Process began last night, was to have been continued as soon as SPEAKER could be got out of Chair to-day; when GRANDOLPH suddenly and unexpectedly appears on scene; moves Adjournment, and attacks Government in rear; GLADSTONE, gladder than ever he came to town, holds them in check in front. Plan of Campaign carefully considered and laboriously worked out. Leading elements secrecy and surprise.

"House may not like this sort of thing, TOBY," GRANDOLPH said. "May talk about underhand proceedings, hitting below the belt, and all that; but if I can get my respected leaders in a hole, I don't mind what the gentlemen of England say about me. The MARKISS openly boasts that he can do without me. We shall see."

Surprise complete. Consternation profound; even danger of defeat in the division lobby. STANHOPE came out well; most difficult position and best speech since he's been a Minister. When he sat down, an awkward pause. No one quite ready to take sides either with GRANDOLPH or against. NOLAN obligingly rattled away.

GOLDSWORTHY, holding out his hat as if he were about to take up a subscription for the Sick and Wounded, besought the Government to "be firm." HARCOURT, with unusual timidity, felt the way; and finally the G. O. M., having had time to think matter over, and look at it all round, threw up his cap for GRANDOLPH. A big division; some anxious moments; a majority of forty-two for Government, and disappointment for GRANDOLPH.

"Drop in a sovereign!"

"I thought we should have run them closer than that," he said. "But it will serve. Only I wish we had the MARKISS in this House, instead of on the other side of the corridor. I suppose they told you of the message he sent me when I let him know he should hear from me shortly in the House of Commons? 'Dear RANDOLPH,' he wrote, 'I assure you you can't intimidate me by any amount of worrying of W. H. SMITH.' That's him: utterly selfish."

*Business done.* — RANDOLPH on the Rampage.

*Thursday.*—CURSE OF CAMBORNE muttering all over the House. Had spent some time in framing one of half a dozen questions; succeeded, after laborious effort, in making it what he thought attractive; handed it in at table; got up early this morning to enjoy sight of it in print and anticipation of putting it in House; found the SPEAKER had severely sub-edited it; taken out all the bad language, the innuendoes, insinuations, accusations. This is what the CURSE calls "emasculating" his question. Rises to make complaint; shows tendency to get behind SPEAKER's decision by reading out full terms of original composition. SPEAKER too quick for him. "Order! order!" he thundered, in a voice with which the CURSE is not unfamiliar. But he stumbled on. "I wish to explain——"

"Order! order! Put the Question!" says the SPEAKER.

"Shan't!" says the CURSE, and sits down pouting like spoiled child.

Business getting further in the rear than ever. Votes accumulate; opportunity of dealing with them decays. Time being shorter than ever, and business more pressing, SAGE of Queen Anne's Gate moves Adjournment, and proposes to discuss matter at length. The Grand Young GARDNER (where's his Wife?) smiles at the claims of OLD MORALITY to have conducted affairs on business principles. CHAPLIN, recovering from depression in which he was plunged by abandonment of Bill creating Minister of Agriculture, girds at the SAGE, and mounting high horse ambles round the House; sparkling speech of neatly written-out *impromptus*. But CHAPLIN has fallen on evil times. Present House doesn't care for his pompous periods and his antique mannerisms.

"Disraeli-and-Ditchwater."

"DISRAELI-and-Ditchwater," says Sir THOMAS ACLAND, retired Member, up on rare visit. Sat in House fifty years ago; remembers real and undiluted thing. HARCOURT—a sort of superior CHAPLIN — had his fling. Then OLD MORALITY trotted out references to "duty," "the country," "convenience of House," and so on. Said his say. Resolution withdrawn, and House got to work.

*Business done.*—Committee of Supply.

*Friday.* — "Why is the Hon. DADABHOI NAOROJI like the devil?" asks GEORGE ELLIOT, Junior, coming in after dinner ("GEORGE ELLIOT, Junior," says FOLKESTONE, "has inherited from GEORGE ELLIOT, *père*, a perennial after-dinner look, that grows a trifle accentuated towards eleven o'clock at night.")

"Order! Order!" I said, not, I trust, altogether without reminiscence of the deeper chest-notes and sterner manner of the SPEAKER. "It's all very well for the MARKISS, a master of flouts and jeers, to speak slightingly of our fellow-subjects from the far East. It is, I suppose, an outcome of Unionist principles. But obscure people, like you and me, dear GEORGE, must be very careful."

A Conundrummer.

"It isn't an insult—it's a conundrum."

"Oh, very well," I said, much mollified. "Then I give it up."

"Why is the Hon. DADABHOI NAOROJI like the devil? Because he's not so black as he's painted."

After this, proceedings in House seemed quite lively, although the business under discussion was none other than Employers' Liability Bill. Debated it till midnight. BRADLAUGH created some sensation by going over to Gentlemen of England.

"An early attachment, TOBY," he pleaded. "You remember how they used to clutch me on the way to the head of the stairs? They've got me now, and I never will desert them."

*Business done.*—Debate on Employers' Liability Bill.

## SIX OF ONE AND HALF-A-DOZEN OF THE OTHER.

(*Some little way after Mortimer Collins.*)

[It is stated that in Cornwall all sorts of flowers, from magnolia to mignonette, are still in full bloom in the open air, whilst another correspondent says that a hen "cut-throat" sparrow belonging to him has taken to laying eggs.]

OH, Summer said to Winter,
"Earth-lovers love me best;
For I flush the mead, and I fill the rill,
And the violet and the daffodil,
And the red, red rose o'er the world I spill;
And my dawns are cool, and my eves are chill;
And don't I run up the doctor's bill
For bronchitis and all the rest!"

But Winter said to Summer:
"Earth-lovers best love *me*:
For I now bring slop instead of snow, [so ;)
(Which comes in June, or mostly
And roses and noses at Christmas blow, [don't know,
And the birds their nesting-time
But lay in December—a pretty go!
And *your* azure skies, and your sunny glow
Are silly legends of long ago;
Whilst as to the Doctor's Bills, oho! [trow.
We are equally good at *them* I
Fact is, the difference 'twixt us two
Is the purest fiddle-de-dee!

AN ARTISTIC CHRISTMAS STORY.—The picture of "*The Violinist*"—a capital Storey—a good old Storey—(A.R.A.), presented by the Goldsmiths to the Guildhall Art Gallery.

## SCENE FROM GREAT CLASSICAL DRAMA.

*Sempronius Lessepsius.* "'Tis not in mortals to command success,——"
*Portius Gladstonius.* "But we'll do more, LESSEPSIUS. We'll deserve it!" [*Exeunt.*

## BARE-FACED TYRANNY.

IT is stated in an evening paper that "The Clerks in a well-known Bank in the Strand are not permitted to grow either moustache or beard." Let the Liberty and Property Defence League look to this gross infringement of personal freedom. If a man and a Clerk's hirsute adornments are not to be recognised as his own "property," and if he is not to have "liberty" to deal with them as he lists, then, indeed, ownership loses its last basis, and British freedom its last buttress. Let no shaven slave of draconic bureaucracy henceforth be tempted to render *Oberon's* lovely lines in *this* fashion:—

I know a Bank wherein no brave beards grow,
Where clean lips and shorn cheeks unwhiskered show;
Lips canopied with no moustachios fine,
Cheeks that know not the "mutton chop's" trim line.
There rules Autocracy, moved, as by spite,
To rob poor clerks of all hirsute delight;
Compelling each to shave, look cold and thin,
And, on chill winter mornings, cut his chin,
And to his desk come blue, with a sore heart—and skin;
This Bank's Bigwigs, kindly were they, and wise,
Would drop all such despotic fantasies.

A NEW CAST FOR DRURY LANE.—Last Saturday night that gay young buster, Lord RONALD GOWER, presented a gigantic plaster (of Paris) cast of SHAKESPEARE'S head and shoulders to DRURIOLANUS MAGNUS. The cast, which Lord RONALD has had in his eye, with this object in view, for some time past, is as white as a ghost, and at first it was supposed that it was intended as a likeness of Lord Mayor WHITEHEAD. DRURIOLANUS doesn't yet know what he shall do with it, but appeared much gratified on being presented by Mr. LEONARD BOYNE, on behalf of the Drury Lane Company, with a handsome silver flagon. The gift was full of signification, and yet there was nothing in it.

## SELECTION OF THE FITTEST.

THE expression, in certain quarters, of fears that at the forthcoming Election of Members for the newly constituted London County Council, there will, owing to the apathy and indifference of those nearly concerned, be a decided dearth of candidates of a desirable and acknowledged respectability, has suggested the publication of the subjoined brief paper of test questions. Anyone, therefore, anxious to save the new Council from the reproach of degenerating into a gigantic assembly of typical Vestrymen, cannot do better than scatter it among his friends. Candidates who find themselves able to answer it satisfactorily, may enter upon the contest with all confidence, assured that they are just the right sort of aspirants to fill the exalted office with distinction and dignity, and discharge its duties with ability and success.

1. With a view to a clear definition and establishment of your unquestioned social status, furnish your pedigree, in direct male descent, for not less than twelve generations, and state:—

A—Whether you are a Duke, Marquis, Earl, Viscount, or only an ordinary Baron;
B—If you have ever been Lord Chancellor, Archbishop of Canterbury, or Commander-in-Chief; or,
C—Have discharged the duties of Prime Minister, Chancellor of the Exchequer, Secretary of State for War, or of any other important post in which you are likely to have become so acquainted with the routine of official work as to guarantee in some measure, your fitness for undertaking the responsibilities attaching to the position of a London County Councillor.

2. If so, state all you know about a steam-roller. Draw a plan on a scale of 3 inches to a foot of "a Compton's twenty ton compound reversible granite-crusher," furnace and all, and explain.

A—What action the Parish is to take, if by some mischance it crashes through a shop-front and embeds itself in the basement, to get it out again, and
B—How you would propose to deal with it, with advantage to the Ratepayers' interests, when it is thoroughly worn out.

3. A generous and impulsive Master of a Workhouse takes all the paupers in his establishment to the Dress Circle at Drury Lane to witness an afternoon performance of the Christmas Pantomime, and further treats them to a champagne tea on their return from the entertainment. Should the expenses entailed by the above come out of the Ratepayers' pockets? If so, state why, and write a short essay exemplifying the broad distinction between the money-grabbing and cheese-paring instincts of the ordinary Vestryman and the philanthropic and large-hearted benevolence of the new County of London Councillor in their probable respective methods of dealing with the foregoing case.

4. How do you make gruel? If considered unpalatable and rejected by the inmates of the Union, would you be prepared to recommend that its place be supplied by Real Turtle, Liebig's Extract, Arrowroot, or by some other patent farinaceous and nutritive compound? If so, give your reasons why.

5. The tenant occupying No. 37 in a certain terrace writes to the Authorities complaining of the condition of the dust-bin of his neighbour, No. 38. The dust-cart is despatched forthwith, but the dustman, mistaking his instructions, only empties the dust-bins of Nos. 7 and 15. Meantime, the nuisance having become intolerable, the occupier of No. 37, much angered, insists on the intervention of the Sanitary Inspector, who, being nettled at the peremptory tone in which he has been addressed, says that he can detect nothing offensive in the condition of the dust-bin of No. 38, nor anything in the shape of a "nuisance" on which to report. The occupier of No. 37, now exasperated, is threatening the Authorities with proceedings, when typhoid fever breaks out suddenly and simultaneously at No. 4, 19, 25, 39, 40, and 52, and the occupier of No. 61 writes an indignant letter to the *Times*, giving a graphic history of the whole affair. Is anybody to blame? If so—who?

Work this out, and indicate the sort of course a County of London Councillor could pursue with dignity in dealing respectively with

A—The Dustman,
B—The Sanitary Inspector, and
C—The Tenant of No. 37.

6. Describe in a short poem, in blank verse, the doings of the London School Board, from its foundation up to the present date. Also analyse and examine the main features of the "Anti-Diggle-ite Reaction," define a "Progressionist," and give a short account of the earlier years of the life of Mr. MUNDELLA.

7. Finally, do you ride well on horseback, and make an imposing figure in the saddle? Answer this, and append a list of any other notably aristocratic characteristics with which you happen to be endowed and which, after you have answered the above technical questions, will, in your opinion, enable you with greater *aplomb* and presence, to discharge the exalted duties devolving on you in your distinguished position as a London County Councillor.

"THRIFT! THRIFT! HORATIO."—Lord Mayor TORPEDO has put off the Children's Fancy Ball and the *conversazione* in connection with the Home for Little Boys because of the state of the drainage at the Mansion House. While the Munching House is being deodorised, why can't Guildhall be utilised? No show, no ball, no *conversazione!* Soon there'll be no Lord Mayor. Torpid TORPEDO, this won't do.

## NOTICE TO QUIT.

"The City Lands Committee has decided to demolish Newgate Prison and the adjoining Old Bailey Sessions House. Trade will quickly exorcise the ghost of Newgate, as has Fashion the shade of the Tyburn gibbet; and the sooner the better."—*Times.*

AIR—"*Unfortunate Miss Bailey.*" *Newgate sings:*—

COMMITTEE bold, you'll drive us then from old-established quarters,
Near where the Smithfield carnifex the ox no longer slaughters.
Our wicked conscience smiteth us, we lose our stomach daily,
I near an unregretted end, and so do you, Old Bailey.
Oh! Old Bailey, unfortunate Old Bailey!

I recollect the days of wholesale hanging and gaol-fever,
When I was grim and you were gay; such times won't last for ever.
Like Pluto I drop iron tears, and your lank cheeks go palely;
No wonder! Ghosts around us glower; such horrid ghosts, Old Bailey!
Oh! Old Bailey, unfortunate Old Bailey!

Avaunt, JACK SHEPPARD, with black poll, and face so white and
Grim gallows-birds, don't gibber there, you use me ungenteelly, [mealy.
Avaunt, pale spectres of the hosts of victims slaughtered daily,
When men were hanged for stealing sheep, as well you know, Old
Bailey. Oh! Old Bailey, unfortunate Old Bailey!

Old friend, farewell! for you and I accounts must once for all close.
Ah me! how I regret the days of wigs and velvet small-clothes!
The days when body-snatching chaps the sexton jockeyed gaily;
How long will men remember me, or you, my poor Old Bailey?
Oh! Old Bailey, unfortunate Old Bailey!

Ah! when I think of MRS. FRY, and you of stout JOHN HOWARD,
I'm sure you feel remorseful, and I know I feel a coward.
My ancestor the Gordon rioters cremated gaily,
But ours is a worse fate, for it is final, poor Old Bailey.
Oh! Old Bailey, unfortunate Old Bailey!

Erect smart shops upon my site? You'd rather, so would I, burn,
To come back like the Phœnix. But we'll share the fate of Tyburn.
The times are most emasculate, they're waxing softer daily,
Soon they'll refuse to hang at all. Just think of *that*, Old Bailey!
Oh! Old Bailey, unfortunate Old Bailey!

Oh, bother Sir JAMES MACKINTOSH! Plague on Sir SAMUEL ROMILLY!!
They started this confounded game. Well, well, we've lived on chummily
For close upon a century; now we must say our *Vale!*
Humanity's too much at last for Newgate and Old Bailey. Oh! Old Bailey, unfortunate Old Bailey!

Now forth we fare, upon the night like *Sampson Brass* and *Sally*
In DICKENS's description; with *our* fate it seems to tally.
Old, hideous, unregretted, like twin spectres prowling palely,
Two shivering forms 'midst shades obscene, Old Newgate and Old Bailey.
Oh! Old Bailey, unfortunate Old Bailey!

*Moral.*

Ye callous selfish, warning take by this most sad example,
Beware how on humanity and pity's claims ye trample.
Remember bad old Newgate and the horrors done there daily,
And its kindred ghoul, the blundering and bullying Old Bailey. Oh! Old Bailey, detestable Old Bailey!

## QUITE UN-BAR-ABLE.

"The Hardwicke Society (consisting of Barristers and Law Students) has unanimously condemned the fusion of the two branches of the legal profession, 'having regard to the recently expressed opinion of the ATTORNEY-GENERAL that Barristers are at liberty, in non-contentious business, to deal direct with clients.' Several Barristers declared their intention of acting on the opinion so expressed."—*Daily Paper.*

SCENE—*Chamber in the Temple belonging to* Mr. P. T. LARSNY, *that "rising Junior." Time—Shortly after the Meeting above referred to.*

*Enter* Virago.

*Virago (taking a chair violently).* I know yer!

*Mr. Larsny (nervously).* Hem! I can't say I have the pleasure——

*Virago.* Oh, yes. Don't pertend as 'ow yer don't get coves off at the Ole Bailey. They calls *you* the Artful Dodger there.

*Mr. Larsny.* Highly gratifying, I'm sure. But may I ask what's the object of your visit?

*Virago.* I've bin pitching into that vixen, JEMIMA ANN TALBOYS, and now I'm *'ad up for it!* And I wants yer to defend me, o' course. (*Confidentially.*) Ain't I a *right* to knock 'er 'ead 'arf hoff when she calls me—(*repeats names with gusto*)? I wants yer to tell the Jedge and Jury that I 'ave a right; that's all.

*Mr. Larsny.* But you ought to have gone to a Solicitor, my good woman.

*Virago (rising threateningly).* Don't let me ketch you a-callin *me* a good woman again, young man!

*Mr. Larsny (getting behind a desk).* Oh no, certainly not. (*Aside.*) *Her* business certainly seems likely to be of a contentious character. Wonder what the ATTORNEY-GENERAL and the Bar Committee would like me to do under these circumstances. Wish some of them were here.

*Virago (slaps down six-and-eightpence on table viciously).* There's yer fee. Now, are ye a goin' to defend me or not?

*Mr. Larsny.* Hem! Rather a small fee. (*To Virago.*) I should be extremely pleased, I'm sure, to have such a client; but, you see, if I undertake this part of your case, I can't defend you in Court. I can *advise* you, and all that; but, as you're already summoned, if you want me to take up your case, you'll have to—consult a Solicitor.

*Virago (with contempt).* That's the law, is it, eh?

*Mr. Larsny.* Yes. Or, perhaps (*a happy idea striking him of paying off an old grudge*) you might call at this address at Lincoln's Inn—Mr. SNOOKS—he's a Chancery Barrister. I should like *him* to see you. I'm sure he'd be grateful to me for introducing him to you.

*Virago (with rising fury).* Don't you gammon *me!* Chancery! I'll put yer blessed 'ead there, if yer try any games on *me!*

*Mr. Larsny (aside).* Really, this interviewing of clients has its objectionable side. Wonder how Solicitors manage it. (*To her.*) I am very sorry I can't take up your case. It's against the rules of the Bar.

**THINGS ONE WOULD RATHER HAVE LEFT UNSAID.**

(A WINTER HEALTH RESORT.)

*Enthusiastic Lady Visitor.* "WHAT A DELIGHTFUL PLACE THIS IS, PROFESSOR. AND THE BATHS, HOW PERFECT! I COULD BATHE ALL DAY—COULDN'T YOU?"

*The Professor.* "WELL, YOU SEE, I'M A *RESIDENT*, AND THAT MAKES A DIFFERENCE!"

*Lady Visitor.* "AH! TO BE SURE. I SUPPOSE YOU NEVER EVEN *THINK* OF TAKING A BATH!"

*Virago (trying to get at* Mr. LARSNY, *who dodges behind various pieces of furniture, furiously).* Bar! You, &c., &c. What do *you* know of bars? Never a-bin inside one in yer life, or ye wouldn't 'ave a mug like a blank baker's ghost, yer wouldn't. Tell *me* to go to a S'l'otor! Go there yerself, yer——

[*Hurls a volume of abuse and the Law Reports at* Mr. LARSNY'S *head, takes up her money, and exit, violently knocking over the* Clerk *in her way out.* Mr. LARSNY *is left ruminating as to whether personal interviews with Clients are really consistent with the dignity of the Bar or not.*

AN EARLY RISER.—We have always held the talents of Sir HENRY LELAND HARRISON, I.C.S., the popular Commissioner of Police and Chairman of the Corporation of Calcutta, in respect, but we had no idea until we read the biography of the Hon. gentleman in DOD'S *Peerage, Baronetage, and Knightage of Great Britain and Ireland*, that his promotion had been quite so rapid as it seems to have been. According to DOD, Sir HENRY, who was born in 1857, entered in 1860, (after being educated at Westminster and Christ Church, Oxford) the Indian Civil Service when he was only three years old! At ten (1867) he was Junior (very junior!) Secretary to the Government of Bengal, a position he relinquished at the not very mature age of fourteen (in 1871) to become Magistrate and Collector of Midnapore. Seemingly he dispensed justice to the satisfaction of the Indian Government until he was promoted on coming of age (in 1878) to the post of Secretary to the Board of Revenue. A year later he was elected a Member of the Rent Commission, and at four-and-twenty (1881) appointed to the Commissionership of Police and Chairmanship of the Corporation of Calcutta, which he has "doubled" for the last seven years to the great benefit of that important city and its neighbourhood. If the rise of Sir HENRY in the future is as rapid as it has been in the past, there seems to be no reason why he should not appear in DOD as Governor-General of India long before he is forty. Finally, it is to be hoped that no mistake has been made in the date of Sir HENRY's birth (which DOD, it will be seen, declares to have occurred in 1857) as such an error may possibly cause disappointment in the breasts of those proud parents of precocious children who, encouraged by the brilliant career thus chronicled, may have already recognised in the Indian Civil Service the best and earliest possible opening for infants in arms.

A VERY-MUCH MARRIED MAN.—The "Hub" of the Universe.

## LONDON AS SHE IS.

(*An Intercepted Letter.*)

MY DEAR WIFE,—I am so glad I did not bring you up to Town to see the Cattle Show, as I feel sure (judging from my own experience) that you would not have enjoyed yourself. It has been *very* dull in London, and I am longing to return to you. You will remember that I proposed originally staying only three days in the great Metropolis, but I have been so terribly *triste* that I have lingered on and on for more than a week. As this is my first letter since I left Bumbleby-on-Brain, I fancy you will expect some account of what I have been doing during my absence from that much-loved spot, and consequently, to please you, I jot down a few particulars. Need I tell you that I visited the British Museum, the School of Mines in Jermyn Street, the Diploma Gallery at the Royal Academy, and Exeter Hall? No, I need not. I hope you believe that I paid at least one visit to each of these admirable institutions. I repeat, I hope that you do. However, all work and no play makes Jack a dull boy, so I determined to combine with information a little amusement. I rather fancy that that eminent divine, your uncle, the Rev. JEREMIAH CRABAPPLE, told me one day that he would like above all things to see a "boxing tournament." Finding that such a contest was indeed being held at Her Majesty's Theatre, I determined to be present, so that I might send him some report of the proceedings. Will you please tell him, with my affectionate but respectful regards, that the Indian club exercise and some wrestling were sadly, sadly frivolous, but that the fights in the ring were stunning. To wind up matters, JEM SMITH, the champion, was put on to box with his little brother. I pitied his little brother!

When your uncle comes to town to attend the May Meetings, he might really drop in to see "*Nadgy*."

*The Monk's Room*, which I visited out of compliment to the Reverend CRABAPPLE, is not half bad, and capitally played. HERBERT VEZIN and WILLARD are excellent, and so is ALMA MURRAY, who seems to have discovered the secret of perpetual youth. She is as comely as ever. I am afraid your revered relative will miss this piece, as it is already out of the bills. Perchance, as the author is a plucky gentleman who took a theatre himself in which to produce his own play, it may be revived. Any way Mr. CRABAPPLE cannot do wrong to reserve an evening from Exeter Hall for *The Monk's Room*. If it is not being played in May, we can go instead to the Empire, where we shall see a first-rate *ballet*.

On Tuesday I looked in at the Parnell Commission, where I found the same old game being played. Taking it all round, it was rather a better day than usual, for we were treated to the evidence of Captain BOYCOTT. The President made several amusing remarks, and Mr. Justice SMITH was also distinctly jocular, but the best things of the sitting were *thought* by Mr. Justice DAY who, however, kept them to himself. I was much pleased with the reticence of Mr. LOCKWOOD, who never speaks except when it is absolutely necessary, and evidently does his best to avoid being reported. Mr. SOAMES looked wonderfully well, in spite of his marvellous exertions, and seemed as fresh as ever. By universal consent it is admitted that the case of the *Times* has been admirably prepared. Mr. GRAHAME was not present during the whole of the sitting, but, in spite of his occasional absence, Sir HENRY JAMES and the ATTORNEY-GENERAL really seemed to get on very nicely without him.

And now, my dear Wife, I must bring this letter to a close, as I have important appointments to keep at Romano's (a meeting-house close to Exeter Hall) and the Pelican Club, a name which has been recently given to a well-known Sunday Society. Hoping to see you soon, I remain, Your ever affectionate husband,

*Grand Hotel, Trafalgar Square, W.C.* TOMMY SLYBOOTS.

## "ALL HAIL, MACBETH!"

THE revival of *Macbeth* at the Lyceum is postponed until after Christmas. It will be brought out Saturday, December 29. We are indebted to a private and thoroughly trustworthy source for the following particulars, exclusively communicated to our Representative:—

Sir ARTHUR SULLIVAN has composed charming and appropriate music for the revival. He breathes again, and says, with expansion of his chest-notes, "What a difference there is in writing for 'W. S.'—WILLIAM SHAKSPEARE—without the 'G.'!" As to whether any of the original music will be used, the answer is, that Sir ARTHUR's keys won't fit the old LOCKE.

For the finish of Scene 2, Act II., after the murder of *Duncan*, Sir ARTHUR has composed a characteristic Scotch melody, to which *Macbeth* and *Lady Macbeth*, with daggers in their hands, will reel off. This is one of the Realistic effects.

Real Whiskey will be served at the banquet. There is a great competition among advertisers to supply the article.

The combat between *Macduff* and *Macbeth* will be of so terrific a character that The Two MACS will probably give up their knock-about entertainment in despair. They won't be "in it" with The Two Macs at the Lyceum.

One line, originally written by W. S., has been restored to the text by Mr. FRANK MCMARSHALL, who will not, as previously arranged,

"THE TWO MACS."
Macbeth and Macduff at the Lyceum.

play *Banquo's* Ghost. *Macduff* retorts on *Macbeth*, who is shouting at him, and brandishing his sword of the period:—

"I will not be
Put down by claymore!"

It is finally settled that Mrs. LANGTRY, Miss VIOLET CAMERON, and Miss MAUD MILLET will *not* appear as the *Three Witches*.

The proposal made by Mr. CREMER, of Oxford Street, to practically illustrate the line, "all is but toys" (Act II., Scene 3), was, on consideration, declined with thanks.

There are two medical men in *Macbeth*, One an English Doctor, and the other a Scotch. Each will be "made-up" after well-known celebrities. The Scotch practitioner in attendance on *Lady Macbeth*, will be an easily recognisable portrait of another great "Mac,"—in fact "the very moral" of him. Miss ELLEN TERRY will not adopt the costume with which we are familiar in the picture of Mrs. SIDDONS as *Lady M.*, with a handkerchief round her face, suggestive of mumps, toothache, or of "holding her jaw."

A new reading has been introduced by the MACMARSHALL in Act IV., Scene 1., The Witches' Cave, when *Macbeth* on entering, will look at the cauldron, give a significant sniff, as if relishing the savour of national cookery, and exclaim—

"How now, you secret, black, and midnight Haggis!"

He will be then, in dumb show, invited to partake of the favourite dish.

## ANSWERS TO CORRESPONDENTS.

CHRISTMAS ENTERTAINMENT FOR SCHOOL CHILDREN.—The resolution of "VICAR" to attempt to produce, with the limited means at his disposal, the grand Opera of *Faust* as a Christmas treat for his youthful parishioners, does infinite credit to his energy and resource. The idea of substituting for the fiend *Mephistopheles* the genial figure of *Punchinello*, out of regard for the tender age and general theological scruples of his audience, is a happy one, but we doubt if he will find the fine musical effects of the Second and Fourth Acts satisfactorily rendered by a full chorus of three. His plan for representing the Apotheosis of *Marguerite* is a capital one, but we would warn him to be careful that the steps, clothes-horse, and arm-chair, which he is going to call into requisition for the purpose of producing the effect in question, do not give way.

BROKEN ENGAGEMENT.—You were certainly justified in resenting the remark of your future father-in-law in the little family *fracas* on the eve of your wedding, to which you refer; but it would, we think, have given your case a better look in the Police Court if you had not first torn his coat off his back, and then thrown him out of window. His offer to "square" the assault on your undertaking to pay for a portion of the wedding breakfast, though commercially mean, might, perhaps, under the peculiar circumstances, be entertained by you. With regard to the presents, you divide these, of course, with your *fiancée*, tossing for first choice. This is the etiquette invariably followed on such occasions in the best society. It is a pity that the three clergymen were kept waiting at the church two hours and a half before any one thought of informing them that the ceremony had been abandoned; but if they get troublesome about their fees, let them have a Solicitor's letter to tell them that if they want to recover them they must do it through the County Court.

## PLAY-TIME.

*Hands Across the Sea*, the Melodrama at the Princess's is capitally played. Young HENRY NEVILLE is first-rate as the hero, and more popular than ever. See him floor the Frenchmen. Song—

AIR—"*You should see me dance the Polka.*"

You should see him floor the Frenchmen,
You should see him cover the ground,
You should see his shirt-sleeves flying,
As he bangs the men all round;
You should see him in it revel,
You should see him full of "go,"
For our rollicking HENRY NEVILLE
Is a Melodrame's best hero.
*Chorus (all)*—You should see him, &c.

Then Miss MARY RORKE is charming, so is Miss WEBSTER, with double the life in her now she is away from the St. James's. Mr. PATEMAN's *Jean de Lussac* is repulsively clever, especially when he has on that tight fit which finishes him. As for GARDEN, it is quite a pleasure, GARDEN, to see you as *Tom Bassett*; and in fact, all are good, not forgetting such minor parts as Mr. H. H. MORELL's *Hiram Hickory*, a character sketch, adroitly worked into the plot by that sharp playwright, HENRY PETTITT, of whose work, however, this drama is not the best specimen. Less well acted, *Hands Across* might have resulted in Mr. PETTITT's determining not again to try a *pas seul*, but to make his bow and return to partner.

Mr. W. S. GILBERT seems to be considerably annoyed about the failure of his piece at the St. James's. He would like to sweep all the critics off the face of the newspapers, except one. Quite right; let us smash everyone whose opinion differs from our own. Noble

*Suggestion for making something of the St. James's Play at Christmas*:—

THE MAD MORTGAGE OF BAB-BALLAD HALL; OR, HARLEQUIN LONG-LOST LOVER, THE CONVICT'S COQUETTISH CHEYILD, AND THE CRITIC ON THE D.T.

| | | |
|---|---|---|
| *Harlequin* | .. .. | The Long-lost Lover. |
| *Columbine* | .. .. | Julia (Who's so "very peculiar"). |
| *Pantaloon* | .. .. | Broken-down Old Nobleman. |
| *Sprite* .. | .. .. | The Virtuous Villin. |
| *Clown* .. | by .. | The Great Pooh Bah-rington. |

sentiment! There was, at all events, one fond and faithful critic who liked it; namely, the critic of the *Standard*. So W. S. G. may henceforth reckon *Pooh-Bah-rington Hall* as specially a Standard Play. Approbation from Sir ALFRED STANDARD is praise indeed!

It is said that so disgusted was Mr. W. S. G. at his treatment by the critics generally, or by the conduct of one in particular, which nearly gave him a fit of *D. T.*, that he solemnly vowed "never again to write a serious play." I can't believe it. The threat is too awful. What! Boycott the public! This is intimidation indeed. But, if true, we must bear it as best we may. JACK IN THE BOX.

---

NO ATTRACTION FOR CHRISTMAS HOLIDAYS.—Why should Railway Companies advertise their "Late Trains"? Surely the public would much prefer "Punctual Trains."

---

PROBABLE.—Lord SALISBURY's Black Man is in a fair way to become his Lordship's "*bête noire*."

## OUR BOOKING-OFFICE.

MY faithful "Co." says he has been *very* hard at work reading a novel called *Mary Myles*. It is only in two volumes, but more than enough. "Co." does not like the heroine who gives her name to the book. He describes her as an artful minx, who, under pretence of being a governess from Girton, flirts with every boy, man, and grey-beard, she runs across. She has an unpleasant habit of walking about without her shoes and stockings, and after becoming an old maid, ultimately marries a man many years her junior. "Co." has also looked through a somewhat elaborate work upon *Kensington*, which he says contains several rather clever illustrations. The letterpress, he thinks, less satisfactory, as many interesting particulars about the Royal suburb are unrecorded. "Co." is surprised that there should be so many omissions, considering that the book is written by no less a person than that eminent *littérateur*, the compiler of the *Authorised Guide to the Tower*. He has also dipped into the *Aspern Papers* of Mr. HENRY JAMES, and read *The Modern Warning*, contained in the second volume. Written in excellent English, the characters are unpleasant, and he hopes unnatural. He says he can answer that there was never such a vulgar person as *Sir Rufus Chasemore, K.C.B.*, on this side of the Atlantic; and he hopes that the Yankee snob, *Macarthy Grice*, on the other side, is equally mythical. He fears that *Aspern Papers* will please neither Britishers nor their American cousins. Mr. JAMES should turn his attention to real foreigners, and then, perhaps, he would score a success. My faithful "Co." feels that Mr. JAMES is rather out of his element when he talks of Fifth Avenue and Piccadilly; and my faithful "Co." was out of *his* element when he called the clever *brochure* to which he referred the week before last the *Dawn of the Nineteenth Century*, instead of the *Dawn of the Twentieth*.

I don't go in for books much this week. Shall have to do so next week. Christmas Books and cheque-books. Hark! the merry Christmas Bills! They don't quite chime in with my idea of perfect happiness. "*Partons!*" Now, what says "Co."? Co. has gone in for crackers. That is "Co.'s" literature just now. He sings in praise of TOM SMITH's crackers, which, he says, reproduce the latest fashions. The costumes being twisted up inside the cracker, which may be known as "SMITH's Closure," and are most ingenious, quite "SMITH up to date." So much for the Smitheries.

At the Cremeries, the toy-purveyor should adopt as his motto the old French quotation, "*A Toy Toujours*." The great point here, says Co., is that there is such a variety to delight the genuine shilling customers. What boy or girl cares for a guinea toy, and other articles of rare price? No, give 'em a few good knock-about toys at a shilling a wooden head, and the quantity will please them as long as the quality is sufficiently enduring—say, for six weeks, when away back to lessons.

"Co." says I must mention GOODALL AND SON, for "Novelties in note paper," and a neat little box of cards with all appliances for whist, which is an education for a happy old age. GOODALL, all good. "My only books" are not "women's looks" this week, but children's books—charming little volumes, nursery rhymes and tales—old friends with new and attractive faces—by ERNEST NISTER. Bindings lovely; interior too good for little idle hands, accustomed to the use of scissors, and belonging to children possessed by scrap-mania. Scrap-maniacs are most destructive insects.

THE BARON DE B.-W. & CO.

---

## CONFOUND THEIR NAVY-ISH TRICKS!

OLIVER TWIST would not be "in it" with Lord CHARLES BERESFORD in "asking for more." The brave and breezy BERESFORD frankly avowed that he desired to add Twenty Millions to the Navy Estimates! What Lord GEORGE HAMILTON had to say in reply practically amounted to this; that the British Navy was better than it had been, but not so good as it ought to be. Between our salt water *Oliver Twist* and our naval *Micawber* there does not seem to be much comfort for JOHN BULL. The official *Micawber* said that the difference between himself and the tarry-breeked *Oliver Twist* was that in him (Lord GEORGE MICAWBER) "the sense of caution was more fully developed." He added that when the Government moved, he hoped their movement would be "genuine and prolonged." Well, if they don't do their duty by our naval defences, doubtless their movement, when it comes, *will* be "genuine and prolonged," and that its motor will be what Lord TENNYSON calls "the wild mob's million feet." But, meanwhile, events move; they move all the time, and do not wait for sessions, or for programmes, or even for Budgets. That is why Naval finance of the *Pip* and *Herbert Pocket* order affords *Mr. Punch* little satisfaction, and not very much hope.

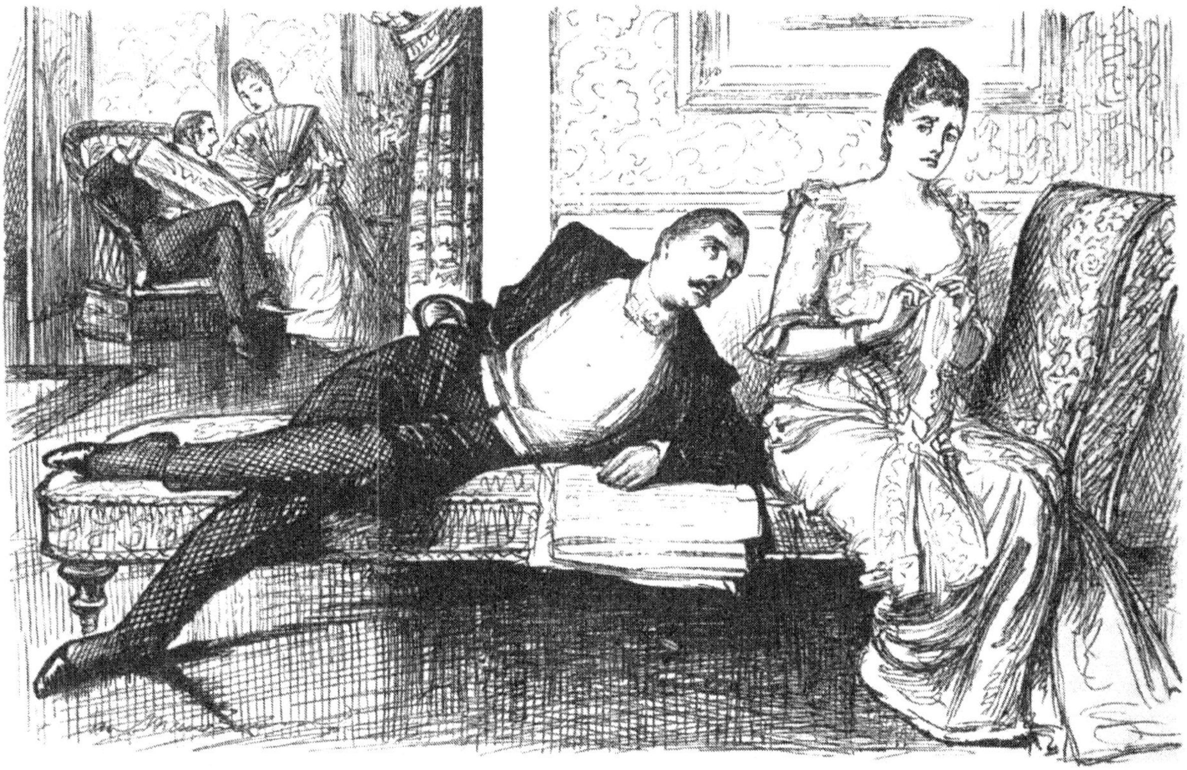

## FEMININE PERVERSITY.

*Aunt Betsy.* "I wonder, James, at your encouraging young Cadby to be so much with Madeline! He's a bad Match, and not a good fellow, I fear!"

*Papa.* "Confound him, no! I've given him *carte-blanche* to come when he likes, and she's getting rather tired of him at last, for I'm always cracking him up!"

*Aunt Betsy.* "And that nice fellow, Goodenough? He's never here now?"

*Papa.* "No; I've forbidden him the house, and won't even allow his Name to be mentioned. She's always thinking of him in consequence. I'm in hopes she'll marry him some day!"

## CHRISTMAS IN THE COMMONS.

### THE SPEAKER'S DREAM.

"Sleep, Mr. Speaker; it's surely fair,
If you don't in your bed, that you should in your chair."
So sang Praed, with much sympa*thee*,
In the year eighteen hundred and thirty-three.
What *would* he sing, did he live so late,
In the year eighteen hundred and eighty-eight?

"Christmas cometh but once a year, [here."
And when it comes—finds the Speaker still
That is the version to fit the Commons [mons
Of the old Yule tag. Shall the cheerful sum-
That gladly rings from the Christmas chimes
Find Parliament prating of Party crimes?

Sleep, Mr. Speaker; close an eye!
It is Christmas Eve, but they're still at
Tanner or Tim in a minute or two [Supply.
Some dreadful disorderly thing will do;
Or Labby will move to dock somebody's pay.
Sleep, Mr. Speaker—sleep, sleep while you may!

Sleep, Mr. Speaker; Conybeare soon
The power of the Chair will invoke—or im-
Hanbury soon will be raising a din [pugn.
On the subject of sixpence, or Suakin;
Grandolph will bother, or Jennings bray;
Sleep, Mr. Speaker; sleep, sleep, while you may!

Sleep, Mr. Speaker, dream of the time
When courtesy was not counted a crime;
When Gladstone was pupil in Peel's old school; [rule;
When Palmerston jested, but knew how to
How parties and principles pass away!
Sleep, Mr. Speaker, sleep, sleep, while you may!

And the Speaker slept; and what did he dream?
The House was filled with a fire-like gleam.
Something had clearly gone wrong with the place, [Mace?
The Table was altered, and where was the
And—really this was the rummiest rig!
A garland of holly encircled his wig.

He was wrapped in woollen from top to toes,
And that rubicund button was not *his* nose.
It was Father Christmas sat in his Chair;
And who—*who* was it advancing there,
With a dish borne high, and an apron? Look!
*Is* it Old Morality garbed as a Cook?

Cook? Faith, yes! And what does he sing?
And what is the dish that the Cook doth bring?
A Boar's Head? Ay! But 'tis plain to see
One must spell it here B O R E;
And, despite its tusks, what a likeness there
To the dreaded visage of C-nyb-re!

### The Bore's Head Carol.

Conybore's head in hand bear I,
Bedecked with bays and rosemary;
And I pray you, M.P.'s, be merry,
Ye must be glad to see it—very!

The Bore's head is a dainty dish;
That is, when dressed as all must wish,
With tongue that never more will wag,
Wide mouth—but with a lemon-gag!

Our steward hath provided this,
A seasonable boon and bliss.
To render all such Bore's heads dumb ones
Were worth a Christmas in the Commons!

The Speaker was roused by an Irish scream,
And he found it was but a Christmas dream.
But he said, as his robe round his form he drew,
And settled his wig, which had got askew;—
"A vision, bred of the Season, no more!
How I wish it were true—as regards the Bore!"

---

"Q. E. D."—which stands for "Quilter, Ed." of the *Universal Review*—deserves well of the public for the reproduction of poor Fred Walker's sketch for a Black-eyed Susan Envelope, and of "our Mr. Tenniel's" spirited likeness of the *Dame Hatley* of that period. No wonder the Burlesque had such a run, seeing the number of legs with which our Cartoonist has gifted the bounding old lady. Most interesting article about General Gordon too. Altogether a capital number. Lucky Quilter!

---

Surplice-age.—"I can't understand Canon Liddon's Sermons," observed one Chorister of St. Paul's to another. "No more can I," replied his friend, who had been reading a learned letter of Sir George Grove's in the *Musical World*. "I call him 'the enigmatic Canon.'"

# CHRISTMAS IN THE COMMONS.

*(A PROSPECT!)*

"CONYBORE'S HEAD IN HAND BEAR I,
BEDECKED WITH BAYS AND ROSEMARY;

"AND I PRAY YOU, M.P.'S, BE MERRY,
YE MUST BE GLAD TO SEE IT—VERY!"

## OUR NEW M.F.H.

*Mr. Topple.* "HI, BOY! PULL UP THAT HURDLE—SHARP!"
*Yokel.* "YES, SUR, I'LL *PULL IT UP!* HOW MUCH HIGHER DO EE WANT IT?"

## ROBERT ON TOASTS AT BANKWETS.

I DON'T quite kno what's a cumming to my good old friends the Members of the grand old Copperashun, but they seams to be gradooally a lessning of the number of their Toasteses when they nobly dines together.

Why, at wun of the werry nicest little dinners as I've waited at for a long time, the Cheerman, who was jest as fresh and as genial as I dessay he was sum fifty years ago, told his rayther estonished Gests, and us more estonished Waiters, that he shoodn't giv 'em more than too Toastes, and them wood in course be Her Most Grayshus Majesty the QUEEN, and the Rite Honrabel the LORD MARE, the too most principlest peeple in the country, and they coud talk, and they coud smoke, and they cood sing, without being bored—yes, bored was the word as he used—with a lot of tiresome toasts, and a lot of dreeary speeches! Yes, and, to our immense estonishment, the Gests all cried out, "Here! Here!" And I suttenly must confess that a merrier, or a larfinger, or a appyer party I hav seldom seen. They chatted away, and told most emusing storys, and wun rayther ancient Deputy acshally guv a commick ressetation, as made 'em all roar, Waiters and all; and one Gent, who was a wisiter, by the name of LANE, I rayther thinks—"most likely HUNNEY LANE," as BROWN rayther cleverly said—sang 'em three most luvly songs most sweetly, one on 'em being all about "holler arts wearing a mask"—more shame for 'em! Werry well—so far so good. But if wunse this sort of change is allowd, where's it a going for to stop?

Is it to be hexpected that Gents of great persitions in Sosiety, such as Dooks, and Markisses, and Haldermen, and Hadmirals, is to dress themselves in their werry best close, and put on all there horders and chanes and things, and not to be treeted to all the time-onered Toastes? No Royal Fammerly, and no Army and Nawy and Wolunteers, and no old Copperashun, and no Howses of Parlement! Why, the werry thort of it sends quite a shudder thro me as I writes.

Why, what did I hear a galliant Hadmiral say, ony larst week but wun, when returning thanks for the Nawy? Why, that whenewer he was a taking his Fleet into haction,—and he seemed to be doing it about wunce a week by the way he torked—the wun thort as filled his galliant sole was, that sum day, when the war was ower, he and his brave comrades wood all be drunk sumwheres in the City! and the nobel sentiment was cheered to the hecko. The same with the nobel Ouse of Lords. They has such preshus littel hoppertunities in their own gilded Chamber of making their woices herd, or their names nown, that if it wasn't for the thortful as well as geeniel orspitallerty of the Manshun Ouse and the great Livvery Cumpnys with their grand Toastes, nobody woodn't never hear on 'em, and they'd be like the flowers a wasting their sweetness on the dessert there.

I'm quite willing to allow that sumtimes, when the crittiele moment arrives, after the almost sacred Luvving Cup has gone quite round the table, that the warious Gests makes themselves as cumferal as they can, and assoomes a hair of demmy semmy resignashun, if not indeed of marterdom, that is sumwhat puzzling to us Waiters. BROWN, with his usual himperence, says as it's becoz they all thinks as they knows xactly wot's cumming, as they've herd it all so offen afore; but BROWN's rong, as ushal, for I wenturs to say, with dubble his xperience, that there's an amount of wariety interdooced in perposing the werry same Toastes as to me is puffekly surprizing.

It's sumtimes werry good fun to us when a werry stout Gineral, or a werry red Hadmiral, goes on a pounding away for sumthink like twenty minutes, and who takes the applause, that gits lowder and lowder every minnet, for encouragement, when it's really all hintended for chaff, and to drownd his poor woice. Sumtimes he finds it out, and then don't he jest set down quickly, pore feller!

No, Gennelmen Copporators, and Gennelmen Marsters, and Gennelmen Wardens, it won't do. Change in sum few things may posserbly mean himprovement, but any change in all the thortful derangements of a grand, scrumpshus, and almost hinterminabel Bankwet, wood be fatal to its sollem charackter, and lower it down to the levvel of a mere Dinner, at which all sorts of peeple are mingled together for mere eating, and drinking, and chat, and amoosement. Long be the day ere that sad change shall cum to pass in the grand old City of London, is the fervent prayer of one who is quite sattisfied with things as they is, and his name is ROBERT.

OLFACTORY.

*He* (*with a look of dissatisfaction at his dish—"He is so particular!"*). "My dear—I think——"
*She.* "Oh, I'm sure it's a very good Ham, George! A genuine Westphalia."
*He.* "Ah—well—yes, dear—I sм—certainly perceived it was a Failure o' some sort directly the Cover was taken off!!"

## KISSING GOES BY—PHONOGRAPH.

[Mr. Edison announces that he is able to transmit kisses by phonograph.]

Few, of true amorous orthodoxy,
Have ever cared to kiss by proxy,
But Cupid's realm looks clean awry
When Edison—beshrew the man!—
Produces this preposterous plan
For kissing by machinery!

"Make me immortal by a kiss!"
Cried Helen's lover. How would *this*
Strike learned *Dr. Faustus?*
Though Science dominates the earth,
One sometimes wonders is it worth
What it seems like to cost us?

Troy's paragon—pray do not laugh!—
Had she possessed a phonograph,
Might have bequeathed her kisses
To *Faustus*, or to you or me.
She *didn't*, and I don't quite see
That much a fellow misses.

Of course, to press one's lips to hers
Were rapture; but a man prefers
Direct and labial contact;
And, when one thinks of wax and wire
As media for love's "kiss of fire,"—
No, Edison, it *won't* act!

Closure v. Closure.—Mr. J. C. Stevenson—unmindful of the fate of Sir Andrew Agnew and Lord Robert Grosvenor,—favours a Bill for the total shutting up of public-houses on Sunday. The Public prefer the total shutting up of Mr. J. C. Stevenson. The Public is quite right.

## THE MOAN OF THE MOUNTED ONE.

(*By a London Rider.*)

Equestrians of London, who pace its miles of street, [the friction of our feet,
Whose "flags" have braved so many years

The glorious times of paving-stone and granite blocks fast flow,
Now Wood
Is thought good,
And Asphalte is all the go!
Now your horses slip on slimy blocks,
And Asphalte is all the go!

The gee-gees of your fathers the granite safely trod, [with iron shod;
For M'Adam was the faithful friend of steeds
Now brave Bucephalus must slip, and stagger, and lie low,
For Wood
Is deemed good,
And Asphalte is all the go;
The slithery wood-blocks funk our nags,
And Asphalte is all the go!

The Horseman finds no "halfpenny rolls," no "metal" firm and easy;
His ride is o'er the treacly wood, and o'er the asphalte greasy.
Damp blocks, *not* from our native oak, are spread his steed below:
What a bore,
To be sure!
Now Asphalte is all the go;
Malodorous timber paves our paths,
And Asphalte is all the go!

The Horsemen of Old England, they scarce know where to turn,
The danger of a fall to dodge. For the old days they yearn. [ye, fast or slow,
Then, then, ye park-pad amblers, safe went
Ere Wood
Was deemed good,
Or Asphalte was all the go;
Ere slippery wood-blocks lamed our steeds,
Or Asphalte was all the go!

The new Lyric Theatre, just opened, possesses a bath-room! Mr. Phipps, the architect, has thus afforded the Manager, Mr. Leslie, in the first place, and secondly any visitor, every facility for getting into hot water on the shortest possible notice. In Mr. Gilbert's new theatre of course there will be a dressing-room for critics. But which will provide the dressing?—the critics, for the author, as a rule.

*House of Commons, Monday, December* 10.—House full of fog to-night; obscures even Irish Question; Members flit ghostlike through the cloud; Irish Members suspect BALFOUR at bottom of it; CUNNINGHAME GRAHAM sure it was HOME SECRETARY. PLUNKET, questioned by Grand Young GARDNER, explains fog is entirely due to presence of Members. Air carefully introduced to Chamber through layers of cotton-wool; fog intercepted; only fresh air in House; all right up to Three o'Clock; then Members troop in, and everything in a fog.

House declines to accept this explanation, and Motion for Adjournment threatened. Things look bad for Ministry, when well-known figure looms through mist at table, and familiar voice is heard. It is OLD MORALITY, riding on the whirlwind and explaining the fog.

"Members brought fog in with them."

"Sir," he said, turning in direction where he thought he saw outline of Speaker's Chair, "the Hon. Member asks, What is the cause of the fog? Her Majesty's Government have nothing to hide in this matter. I will be quite frank with the House. These fogs, which occur generally in the winter time, are occasioned thus:—Some current of air being suddenly cooled, descends into the warm streets, forcing back the smoke in a mass towards the earth. Fogs would be more frequent but for the fact that the air will not always hold in solution a certain quantity of vapour, which varies according to its temperature, and when the air is not saturated it may be cooled without parting with its vapour. I have now given the House the fullest explanation in my power, concealing nothing, and extenuating nothing, it being my only wish to consult the convenience of Members on both sides, to do my duty to the country, and to perform the functions of the Government with the least friction possible."

That settled it. Fog denser than ever, but everyone satisfied. Irish Members with light hearts turned to boo for BALFOUR. Operation lasted till midnight, when Closure moved. Condition of affairs so exhilarating that COURTNEY dropped into a joke. Years ago now since JACOB BRIGHT made his reputation as humorist by alluding to GRANDOLPH as "the noble Lord, the Member for Woodcock." COURTNEY, cheered by the fog, and soothed by OLD MORALITY's oration, determined to outshine this flash. Struck a light on TAY PAY. TAY PAY from time to time emerged out of fog, yelled "Yah!" in somebody's ear, and disappeared. COURTNEY lay in wait for him; he swooped down, and caught him by left ear.

"This," he said, shaking him vigorously, "is the third time the Hon. Member for Scotland Yard has interrupted."

"'The Member for Scotland Yard,'" says FRASER, V.C., "lacks the brisk movement of 'TAY PAY'; but it will serve for Sundays and state occasions."

*Business done.*—Irish Votes in Supply.

Tay Pay, "Member for Scotland Yard" as seen in Mr. Courtney's mind's eye. Monday, Dec. 10.

*Wednesday*, 2 A.M.—Been here, or hereabouts, since three yesterday. Me and the SPEAKER took our chairs together. No present sign of getting home; daresay shall go on till Three o'Clock, which nicely divides the day.

And such a night too! Scotch Estimates on; Scotch Members don't often get a chance; when they do, don't easily let it go. ANDERSON, who led off at prodigious length, invented new process which extorted grunt of admiration from TIM HEALY. Moved to reduce salary of Secretary for Scotland by £1000; amid growing impatience from compatriots who had speeches ready, ANDERSON reached his seventhly and sat down; then came dreary procession of Scotch Members till ROBERTSON, vainly trying to catch the SPEAKER's eye, temporarily gave up pursuit and left House.

"It's amazing," he said glaring at ESSLEMONT, "how some people with nothing to say wag their tongues."

ROBERTSON back presently, and getting his innings, talked for half an hour. Meanwhile ANDERSON sprung his patent process on disheartened House; withdrew Amendment to reduce salary by £1000; moved another to reduce it by £200; this being new Amendment, he was in order in making new speech; which he did.

Thinking over these things sitting in limp condition on plank bench, startled by hearing curious whimpering, "Boo-ooh!" Turned round; found it was TANNER digging his knuckles into his eyes and whimpering like whipped schoolboy.

"What are you at now?" I asked. "Booing for BALFOUR?"

"Boo-ooh!" he said, with another outburst. "He's got my stick."

Tanner of the Broken Bâton.

"Who's got your stick?"

"Boo-ooh, FIELDEN, boo. I'll tell the SPEAKER."

So he did. Seems he'd brought in broken bâton; said to have been used by Irish Constable; left it on table whilst he went out to division; FIELDEN, coming in, put it in his pocket.

"Give me my stick!" screamed TANNER, when he came back, "or I'll tell my moth—I mean the SPEAKER."

FIELDEN playfully refused. TANNER stamped and screamed, tore his pinafore, whimpered, and finally peached. SPEAKER protested he was tired of these personal squabbles. Told FIELDEN to give the boy his stick. Nurse sent for, and TANNER carried off to bed, kicking and screaming. When we have come to this in House of Commons, it's time to wind up business.

*Business done.*—Scotch Votes in Supply.

*Thursday.*—Came down to-day in thoroughly depressed mood. Had a chat with BERESFORD yesterday: tells me it's all up with us: haven't got a ship in the Navy that could stand against a penny steamboat on the Seine; guns burst; engines won't work; ships run aground, and the Cavendish tobacco not at all what it should be. Worst of it is, the Government won't learn. CHARLIE wanted them to beach the *Agamemnon* or *Alexandra* opposite terrace of House of Commons, plant a few big guns on terrace and fire away at ship.

"Then you'd see," says CHARLES.

But HAMILTON won't see, and there we are. That is the truth about the Navy in a cockleshell. Cockleshell, however, couldn't hold all CHARLIE had to say. Prodigious effort; poured broadside after broadside into Admiralty; HAMILTON, with head hung down, tore up with busy fingers innumerable slips of paper in reply; a melancholy indictment, leaving us not a ship to sail in or a gun to fire. Curious part of it was that nobody seemed penny the worse. Carthage is as good as ruined—and Members went off to dinner just the same! So many went that at half-past eight House nearly Counted Out.

BROWN of Wenlock (ex-cornet in 50th Dragoon Guards), had come down determined to shed last drop of his blood for country.

"I'm a handy figure aboard a ship," he said, drawing himself out like a telescope, "and though not used to the sea, will enlist as a marine. In emergency, might serve as spare spar."

A Telescopic View.

But Cornet BROWN, finding how things were going, concluded he wasn't wanted; shut himself up a few feet, and went out. BERESFORD had several more speeches to make on other votes, but result of first oration not encouraging. In the end, votes ran through like greased lightning. England, dull-eared and blindfolded, went stumbling to her doom!

*Business done.*—Navy Votes agreed to.

*Friday.*—Army Estimates on to-day. Admirals retire, Colonels advance in fighting form. Navy bad; Army worse. An ancient nation tottering to its fall. Quite a cheerful Christmas Story, in two Parts. Part One: The Navy. Part Two: The Army. Conclusion: Both hopelessly bad.

Sir GEORGE ELLIOT sits out dreary debate, as last night he listened to lament over Navy. Wonder what *he* thinks of it all? Doesn't seem particularly depressed. Why don't they put him at head of War Office or Admiralty? Wouldn't matter which. Father wasn't a Duke, nor is his brother an Earl; but he's a man of great natural gifts, trained capacity, and infinite resources, a credit to Durham, an honour to Monmouth.

"That's the sort of man they ought to offer any inducement to leave his private affairs and look after the Nation's," said Serjeant SIMON, an Old Parliamentary Hand, looking in to see how the House is getting on without him.

Towards close of sitting, things took new turn; opposition melted away; money voted hand over hand; looks like adjournment before Christmas Day, after all.

*Business done.*—Army Votes.

Old Parliamentary Hand.

---

THE LAST OF A JOLLY OLD CHAP.—There was always something laughable in the absurd separation of Kensington Gardens from Hyde Park, and this ridiculous something was the old "Ha-ha wall" which has now disappeared for ever. It was removed bodily, both its sides shaking with laughter. Alas! never again will the glades of Kensington ring with the old Wall's merriment.

**A HINT FOR THE STICKY SEASON.**

FILL YOUR POCKETS WITH SAND, AND SCATTER AS YOU WALK. THEN, WHILE OTHER PEOPLE ARE PAINFULLY TOTTERING ALONG THE GLUEY PAVEMENT, *YOU* MAY MARCH WITH CONFIDENT STEP.

## CHOOSING A LADY GUIDE.

(AN ENTIRELY IMAGINARY FORECAST.)

SCENE—*The Offices of the New* "*Lady Guide Association.*" *Intelligent Gentlewomen,* "*Ladies by birth and education, of almost any age, and of different dispositions and capacities,*" *according to prospectus, discovered seated in background awaiting an engagement. In foreground, Clients are consulting Manageress.*

*Manageress* (*to Couple from the Country*). Exactly; this is your first visit to London, and you want to see everything during the week you are here. There is a lady there, the third from the end, with the short hair and the *pince-nez.* She is in charge of the Intellectual Sight-seeing Department, and you will find her a highly-intelligent companion, thoroughly acquainted with all the objects of interest in Sir Hans Soane's, the British, and the Geological Museums, Madame Tussaud's, and the Tower, where she will render a warder quite unnecessary. In the New Law Courts, for a small additional fee, she will explain the origin and growth of Common Law and Equity; she can translate the epitaphs in Westminster Abbey (if desired), and tell you the exact height of every public building in London.

*The Husband.* Hev she a eye for a beast? SUSY an' I be coom up fur Cattle Show maäinly.

*Manageress.* She has been through a course of lectures on Comparative Anatomy. Shall I call her?

*The Wife.* No offence to you, Ma'am, but I think I'd rather know what that young woman in the fur-trimmings can do, before I make up my mind, like.

*Manageress.* Ah, that lady? She is extremely well connected—a Baron's daughter—she undertakes the Social Sight-seeing, but she would be rather too expensive for you, perhaps?

*The Husband.* Oh, dang th' expense! let's hev' a good 'un while we're 'bout it. Kindly ask her to step out. (*The* Hon. Miss FREDERICA GEORGINA CHURCHMOUSE *steps forward.*) Now, Miss, me and my Missus here 'ud like to hear what you have to say for yourself.

*Miss Churchmouse* (*languidly*). I think I could show you something of Town while you are with us. Dear Lady PETTIFOORES kindly allows me to bring my friends in to tea on any of her afternoons, and I could get you cards for the Countess of HERRINGBARREL's crush, and Lady DARVISH's small dance, if you cared to go, that is. I would walk in the Row with you after Church on Sunday morning—(but that would be an extra)—and tell you who everybody was. If you thought of giving a little party while you are in Town, I could get some really smart people to come to you, and advise you how to do the thing, with or without supper and flowers—a brother of mine supplies a very fair champagne at a moderate price, and you would order the flowers from our hothouses at Brokeby, of course. I—ah—don't know if there's anything else you thought of doing?

*The Wife.* We did think of going to the Theayter.

*Miss Churchmouse.* Nothing worth seeing just now but the French plays—we have the back seats in an upper box for to-morrow, and I daresay I could get mother to take you in our party.

*The Husband.* And 'bout how much would it tot up to if we did the whole thing?

*Miss C.* Well, as nearly, as I can tell you, about—— (*Mentions a sum at which their eyes roll.*)

*The Husband* (*after whispered consultation*). Ah, thankee. I'll look in agëan when I'm this way maybe.

[*Country Couple retire. Enter an American party.*

*American Spokesman.* Good-day, Ma'm, we've looked in to ask if you've a smart high-toned Lady Guide to go around with us at a low figure. We're Amurrican citizens, and we mean having a real good time.

*Manageress.* Let me see—is there any lady on those seats there whose appearance takes your fancy?

*A Young American* (*insidiously*). That's a vurry attractive young lady with the blue eyes and a frizzy top-knot.

*His Wife.* HENRY CLAY BANGS, if you want to see me in a fit on the floor—go on!

*The Spokesman.* It's this way, Ma'm. We're a mixed party, and our ladies—well, they're not so darned partickler about having a *goodlooking* Guide. Birth and breeding we do take stock in. So, if you've got a female member of your pampered aristocracy, approaching middle-age, red-headed and squint-eyed, hitched up on these premises, I reckon we'll take her along.

*Manageress.* I'm afraid we have nothing but a Baronet's widow to-day, who, at all answers that description, and I'm sorry to say *she* doesn't squint.

*The Young American* (*in an undertone*). Say, couldn't we contrive to get along with one of the younger ones at a pinch? If they had a juvenile Duchess around now, it wouldn't signify much if she *did* happen to be personable, so far as *I'm* concerned.

*The Spokesman.* I believe you, BANGS—there's no prejudice about *you;* but if we're to preserve the harmony of this meeting—we've got to content ourselves with a plain patrician, or no one, that's so! And, as there's nothing of that kind in stock just now, I guess we'll hev to cavort around this effete old city without anyone to give us points. Come, Ladies! [*American party file out.*

*Enter* Provincial Lady, *much agitated.*

*Provincial Lady.* Oh, if you please, we've taken a house at Kilburn for the Winter Season, and the pipes have burst, and there's something wrong with the drains, and everything tastes of dry-rot, and the housemaids won't carry up the coals, and we're almost sure the cook sells our kitchen-stuff through the area railings, and we hear such very odd noises every night next door between eleven and twelve, and we have almost settled to give a quiet children's party, and I want someone to tell me the most fashionable shop in Kilburn to get a bonnet, and we fancy the baby has swallowed a button, and I don't know where to find a respectable sweep—*could* you recommend me a young person who would give me a little temporary household assistance, and *what* would be her charge for coming?

*The Manageress.* Certainly, Madam. You will find the charge stated in our Differential Tariff. Miss DE VERE, will you take this lady down-stairs to the Third Class Department, and show her the Confidential Companions?

[*Exit* Miss DE VERE *with Provincial Lady.*

*Enter a* Young Frenchman.

*The Y. F.* Pardon, Madame, I arrive at your Association, so desired, so distinguished, to select myself a leddi guide, *tout à fait comme il faut!*

*Manageress.* Certainly, Monsieur, I can give you a very superior Lady, whom you will find full of information and statistics of every kind, and who converses fluently in the Ollendorffian method. She possesses, too, a thorough knowledge of cab-fares, inside and outside the radius. May I ask how large your party is?

*The Y. F.* My party? But I am ze party—I am all alone!

*Manageress.* Ah, Indeed? Then I fear you must remain so, Monsieur. Our guides are not prepared to attend gentlemen travelling *en garçon.* I am very sorry, I can assure you.

*The Y. F. Ah, Madame, le plus désolé—c'est moi!*

[*Exit* Young Frenchman, *with a regretful glance at the bevy of* Lady Guides, *as Scene closes.*

---

### Mem. by One who Remembers.

"Suakin is the key to the Upper Nile."—*Pall Mall Gazette.*

DEAR me! The old, old talk! It mars my ease,
It comes upon me with a painful shock:
Whenever there is all this talk of "keys,"
Things seem so sure to come to a dead-lock.

---

MOTTO FOR THE PARNELL COMMISSION.—"*Sedet æternumque sedebit, Infelix Theseus.*" The unhappy Theseus is, of course, the President, "tied to the stake."

# ESSENCE OF PARLIAMENT.

## EXTRACTED FROM THE DIARY OF TOBY, M.P.

*House of Commons, Monday Night, December* 17.—Nice sort of preparation for Christmas. Thick fog outside; Benches crowded inside; debate on Suakin expected; GLADSTONE again in his place.

"You see I can't leave you, TOBY," he said, with sprightly air, but really apologetically. "Bade farewell to House three weeks ago. Then BALFOUR twitted me, so obliged to run up to Town and boo him. Really thought I was gone after that; but, having spare Saturday, spent it at Limehouse. Day after to-morrow set off for sunny South. No use going down to Hawarden for couple of days; so, being in Town, may as well come down to House; being in House, may as well deliver a speech. No trouble, I assure you."

GLADSTONE come, OLD MORALITY gone. In his place GOSCHEN sits nervously washing his hands with invisible soap in imperceptible water. Every prospect of a stiff debate. Holidays retire further into the dim and distant future. Things made worse by receipt of telegram from OLD MORALITY, dated Monte Carlo. Here it is:—"And how is TOBIAS, M.P.?" (TOBIAS!—that's his joke.) "Hope you are doing as well at Westminster as we are here. A bright sky overhead, peeps of blue Mediterranean between the palms in the garden, drives and walks through sunny atmosphere; delightful music, dinner *à la carte*, and the tables. I suppose you are beating this out and out? thoroughly enjoying yourself at Christmas time? Perhaps a little snow, but everything bright, crisp, sparkling, joyous and Christmas-like? No fog or slush or Suakin? I congratulate you. Kind regards to JOKEM. Dreamed last night that very first day he took my place in House GLADSTONE came back, and GRANDOLPH went on the rampage. But, of course, that only a dream. JOKEM quite happy. All the honours of leadership and none of the labours. Just going in to take walk round the tables and see that CHARLES RUSSELL isn't playing. By the way, you used to chaff me about pouncing. But what I've done in my little way, nothing to daily habit of the *croupiers* here. Pounce every six minutes; closure moved at every table; not, of course, in same words, since they speak French. '*Le jeu est fait. On ne va plus*,' which, being translated, means 'I move that the question be now put.' Here, as with you, no debate, not even division. Good bye and a Merry Christmas. *So* glad you're all enjoying yourselves at Westminster."

Something quite bloodthirsty about this pleasantry. Bad enough for Leader of House to run away to enjoy himself; too bad to jeer at us by telegraph from the sunny clime where he sojourns.

A regular tussle round Suakin. JOHN MORLEY led off attack from Front Bench; GLADSTONE brought up reserves; GRANDOLPH attacked Ministry in rear. Don't know what would have happened to Government if CHAPLIN hadn't thrown himself into breach and solemnly rebuked GRANDOLPH. GRANDOLPH laughed; but it was a hollow performance. *Business done.*—Suakin Vote agreed to.

*Tuesday.*—Met *Mr. Dick*—I mean Lord DENMAN, slowly making way down to House immersed in deep thought, with coronet under his arm. "How 's the Memorial getting on?" I asked.

"Pretty well," he said. "Head of CHARLES THE FIRST not been so troublesome lately. Have, however, laid manuscript aside for short time. Mind much occupied with Local Government Act; have my doubts about RITCHIE; Bill itself calculated to diminish the corn average and reduce the travelling weight of fat cattle. It must be seen to. So have brought in Bill for immediate repeal of Act. Down now to move Second Reading; sorry to embarrass the MARKISS; but public duty is a public trust. Expect the Government will resign if I carry my measure, and probably the Black Man would be sent for to Osborne. A nuisance at Christmas time; but there are higher considerations than plum-pudding. If you would like to see a bombshell drop in Ministerial Camp, better look in when I'm moving the Second Reading of my Bill."

An Anxious Moment.

Looked in accordingly. About a score of Peers present; *Mr. Dick*, seating himself close to woolsack so as to be ready when hour struck, looked round with triumphant glance. MARKISS not present; had probably received hint and stopped away. GRAND CROSS on Ministerial Bench, suffusing it with air of supreme respectability and profound sagacity. Public Health Acts Bill read Third Time; DUNRAVEN got Payment of Wages Bill read Second Time. A hushed moment of anxiety; then *Mr. Dick* discovered at table moving Second Reading of Local Government (England and Wales) Act, 1888, Repeal Bill. *Mr. Dick*, producing some pages of the Memorial, denounced Bill as "one of the most dangerous ever presented to their Lordships." GRAND CROSS nervously wiped his damp spectacles. No one had reckless audacity to deny *Mr. Dick's* statement. ABERDEEN sat bolt upright; clutched himself by the thighs; looked as if he was going to rise, but limbs refused to move.

"Great Heavens!" I murmured. "Is it possible the Act going to be sacrificed in this way? No one to say a word in favour of it. What Christmas Tidings for RITCHIE!"

LORD CHANCELLOR put the question. House stricken dumb. No one said either "Content" or "Not Content." Taking advantage of general condition of paralysis, LORD CHANCELLOR boldly declared "Not Contents" had it, and Bill thrown out.

"Au reservoir!"

"I shall draw up another Memorial," said *Mr. Dick*, sticking a pin in his cravat. "Shall be addressed to HER MAJESTY; briefly but firmly demand Head of HALSBURY. CHARLES THE FIRST never trifled with the Constitution in so reckless a manner. And where's *his* Head to-day?"

*Business done.*—In Peers, LORD CHANCELLOR saves Local Government Act; in Commons, Irish Votes in Supply.

*Wednesday.*—Booing all day for BALFOUR; last opportunity; must make the most of it; Windbag SEXTON does; House met at noon; Windbag started immediately after; went on for full hour without stopping; CLANCY took his place whilst he refreshed; came back again, continued his speech; end of second hour. TANNER volunteered to take a turn of duty; Windbag back again after brief interval puffing and blowing with welcome signs of growing feebleness. At last collapsed, and others got chance. BALFOUR all the while languidly prone on Treasury Bench thinking of pleasant days to come at the Chief Secretary's Lodge. Irish Members kept it going till Seven o'Clock, when last vote in Report of Supply agreed to. Appropriation Bill brought in and Session practically over.

"*Au reservoir*," said E. HARRINGTON, who hasn't sat near JOSEPH GILLIS for years without obtaining some smattering of the language spoken at Paris. "Some of us are going to spend the Recess in prison, but we 'll come back with the flowers in Spring and boo again for BALFOUR." *Business done.*—Practically, all.

## ROBERT BLAKE.

1598—1657.

"ADMIRAL BLAKE was the first man who made the name of England to be respected abroad, and also the first to see what the Supremacy of England on the Sea really meant."—LORD C. BERESFORD *at the unveiling of the* BLAKE *Memorial at St. Margaret's, Westminster.*

STOUT Sailor, pride of England's patriot sons,
  Who vanquished her most valiant foe, VAN TROMP,
  Cast forth from her great Abbey's glorious pomp,
Thy fame shines bright as when above the guns
At Santa Cruz thy keen eyes flamed and saw
  The path to England's Queenship of the Sea.
  What may not later patriots learn from thee,
In days of slackened will and shaken law?
Not swelling words but sturdy deeds were thine,
  Not conflicts voluble but valiant strokes.
  Thou, firm of fibre as our native oaks,
Didst bear our flag unchallenged o'er the brine;
Made England's name respected, and her power
  Acknowledged over all earth's watery ways.
  Englishmen, emulous of such splendid praise,
Sailors, who deem sea-sway our native dower,
Patriots who'd keep our greatness at full flower
  As in these strenuous days,
Scan that great record; as exemplar take
Our first of patriot Seamen, ROBERT BLAKE.

## IN THEIR CHRISTMAS HAMPERS.

*H.R.H. the Prince of Wales.*—Brand new Captain-General's and Colonel's Reversible Uniform of the Honourable Artillery Company, and £500 for military purposes sewn up in the tail coat pockets with the H.A. Co.'s compliments, thanks, and kind inquiries.

*Mr. Gladstone.*—The fancy dress costume of a Neapolitan Lazzarone, together with Mr. COOK's coupons for a circular three weeks' tour in Southern Italy.

*Lord Hartington.*—A bundle of "Grand Old Man" crackers, furnished with appropriate mottos.

*Lord Charles Beresford.*—A cheque on the Treasury for Twenty Millions, payable to "Naval Efficiency" or order.

*Lord Salisbury.*—A thoroughly New Egyptian Puzzle (Key wanting).

*Mr. Naoroji.*—Fancy portrait of Lord SALISBURY as the typical "White Man."

*Lord Grandolph.*—Gladstone bag containing Liberal-parti-coloured costume with false collars. Motto "*Suivez moi!*"

*Sir James Hannen.*—Diary showing Red Letter Day three years' hence as possible date for the termination of a certain protracted Commission.

*The Czar.*—*Bal Masqué* disguise of "Peace at any Price," with Handbook of Sentiments to match.

*M. de Lesseps.*—A draft at sight for £35,000,000, unlimited confidence of patriotic supporters, and no awkward questions asked about probable date of completion of the Canal.

*The Emperor of Germany.*—Shilling Handy Guide for the Conduct of Young Potentates, with special appended Essay on the use of the personal pronoun in public manifestos.

*Mr. Augustus Harris.*—Schedule from the Booking Office, showing the disposal, three months in advance, of all the Stalls and Dress Circle places at Drury Lane to witness his new Pantomime.

*Lord George Hamilton.*—A new pair of spectacles, not tinted *couleur de rose*, with which to survey the present condition of the British Navy.

*General Boulanger.*—A Dictator's trick hat, warranted to assume any new shape, according to circumstances.

*The Honourable Artillery Company.*—A Repaired Royal Charter with H.R.H. the Prince of WALES's best compliments and congratulations.

*Mr. Stanhope.*—Little volume, entitled, *Facts Controverted: or, a Hundred Ways of Shutting up the Parliamentary Awkward Questioners.*

*The Mahdi.*—Hymn of Jubilation over the general discomfiture of the British Cabinet.

AN ORIGINAL CORNER MAN.—*The Complete Angler.*

**LITTLE PUSS IN BOOTS; OR, THE CATS' MEET AND THE HUNTING KIT! (OUR PANTOMIME POEM.)**

THE Early Bird had done pecking the worm,
Who resented the act with a struggle and squirm;
The Bright Chanticleer had proclaimed the morn,
And the Huntsman already was sounding the Horn.

*Con spirito.*

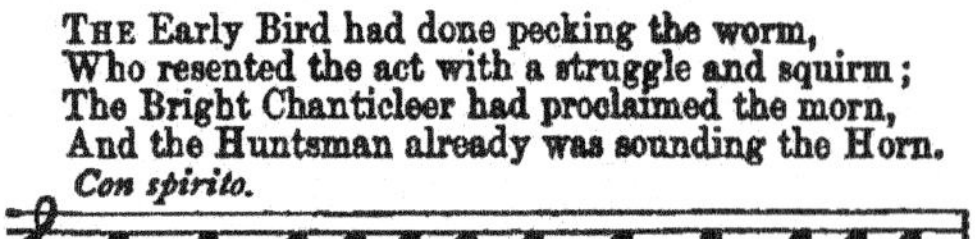

By way of parenthesis let us remark,
That the Bright Chanticleer was only a lark,
Who was kept in a very small cage on a shelf,
And who got up so early—he rose with himself.
The morning was bright, and the air was sweet.
Not a cloud in the sky—not a prospect of wet;
On the sward there assembled, a very smart set,
For there was to be—a special Cats' Meet.

Now Hunting Kit was the first to appear,
(The hounds were first—a detail mere);
Also to mention, I must not fail,
That the hounds were kittens (a mere detail),
And Hunting Kit had the pinkest of suits,
Including a marvellous pair of top boots.
Now People have often inquired how he kept in 'em—
We'll tell you, they fitted so tightly, he slept in 'em.
Now every huntsman with any *nous*
Was bent on hunting the wily mouse.
The Gay Lady Tabitha (rivals said "Tush!")
Was keen on securing the coveted brush.
A silly old Poodle turned up at the start,
Not mounted—oh no! never fear;
He came in a Lowther Arcade dog-cart,
To follow full well in the rear.

*Singing:—*

*With molto chic!!!*

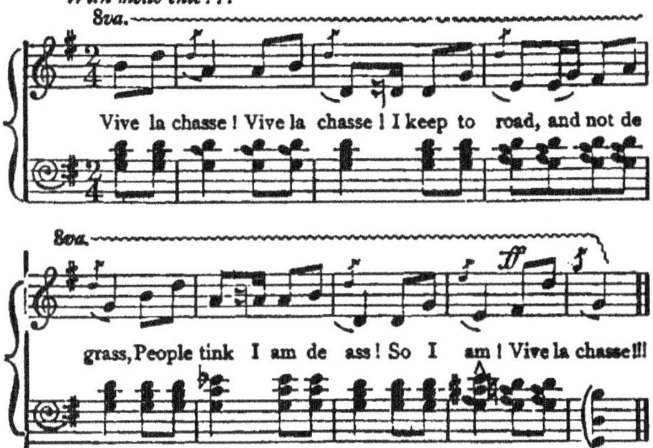


To every mouse-hunter the sweetest of sounds
Is the glorious purring and mewing of hounds.
Hurrah! We are off, and the air soon is ringing
With the sound of the unison song we are singing.

## OUR HUNTING SONG.

(*Cats' metre.*)

Hurrah, the View-halloa is heard—'tis a find,
"Hark forward!"—poor Poodle has "harked far behind."
Through everyone's property every one tears,
And (excepting the landlords) nobody cares.
We come to the farm of a grumpy old *owl*,
Who is armed with a pitchfork as well as a scowl.
He's very irate, as over his gate
Goes every hound, with leap and with bound,
There goes the mouse—right through his house,
And so do we—with heedless glee,
A truce to our mirth—we've run him to earth.
But tush!—never mind! Here's a much better find,
Superior to first;
A fine old mouse,
Who runs from the house—
A glorious burst!
What the Owl cried to Kit we never quite knew,
We heard what he said to a Groom,—
"To whip, To whip; To who, To who!"
(He ought to have said "*to whom.*")
And after a chase, though flooded field,
Poor mouse did yield;
And gay Lady Tabitha, short of breath,
Was in at the death.
Then came the best of the fun of the fair,
For Kit first was seen to stoop,
And, holding the mouse high up in the air,
He shouted "Who-hoop! Who-hoop!"
In spite of the rivals, who *would* say "Tush!"
Lady "Tab" was awarded the coveted brush.
Bemudded and splashed, we trudged along
Towards our home, with the usual song.

## THE HOMEWARD SONG.

(*To be Sung with the Huntsmen's remaining breath.*)

N.B.—"*God Save the Queen!*" may here be played if the Audience has not already departed, which is more than probable.

---

## THE HON'BLE ARTILLEREE.

(Air—"*The Ryal Artilleree.*")

Oh, have ye heard of what's occurred
In the Hon'ble Artilleree?
The town's alarmed for they were disarmed
Last Wednesday as it might be,
When they said: "we can't five hundred grant
For purposes militaree."
Then H.R.H. said, "I will tache
Them what 'tis to of-fend *me*.

So General, likewise Marshal
Of them I will not be;
An' if they don't mend, then there's an end
Of the Hon'ble Artilleree!"

*Refrain* (*sotto voce by Privates and Officers.*)

We don't intend this to be the end
Of the Hon'ble Artilleree!

---

Correct Cards.—Messrs. Birn Brothers—good fireside name for Christmas—have left their cards on us, and very pretty is the effect of the crystallised snow over roofs, trees, fields, and hedges. Picturesque, but, in reality, a nuisance, as it must end in a thaw, and then the slosh and slush—ugh! Still, so far, these are the Correct Cards for Christmas.

## THE FESTIVE SEASON.

*Policeman.* "Hullo, Sir! what are you doing here?"

*Enthusiastic Musician (who is mistaking a doorstep for the Key-board of an Organ).* "C-c-carntcher hear? I'm p-p-playin'—(*hic*)—Bach's Fugue in E Minor! Don'tcher know B-Bach's Fugue in E Minor?"

*Policeman.* "No, Sir; never heard of him. Come along, and let me see you Home, Sir."

*Enthusiastic Amateur.* "No; go away. I—(*hic*)—wouldn't be seen going Home with a Man that don't know B-Bach's Fugue in—(*hic*)—E Minor!"

## THE WASSAIL BOWL.

*Good gentles all, Christmas, like Love, is old, yet ever new:*
*Full eighteen hundred flying years have left that saying true.*
*The old Bodleian Wassail Song, a Carol in Black Letter,*
*Punch here adapts to instant needs. Can modern Muse do better?*

A jolly wassail bowl,
A wassail of good ale,
Will warm each drinker's soul.
Hail Christmas! and all hail
His jolly wassail!

Good gentles at our door,
Our wassail we begin.
Good health to rich and poor!
You all are welcome in
To our wassail!

Our wassail we do fill
With all that's sound and nice:
We ask you with good will
To taste; take good advice,
And our good wassail!

Without why should ye stand
All shivering in the cold?
It is our host's command
Ye enter and make bold
With his wassail!

Much joy to this our hall
With Christmas enters in,
*Punch*, just to start the ball,
Will first dip beaker in
To our wassail!

He drinks good health all round,
To little and to big,
Turn up all taps unsound,
And try a hearty swig,
Of our wassail!

Drop Party Spirit quite,
'Tis heavy, heady, stuff,
All men *Punch* doth invite
To tipple *quantum suff:*
Of his wassail!

Come, jovial Mr. Bull,
Our spicéd bowl you'll try,
Of stingo rare 'tis full;
No head-ache by-and-by
From *this* wassail!

Coy Miss Hibernia stands
Pouting red lips—in vain.
Come, Erin dear, join hands,
You can do nought but gain
From our wassail!

Come, Jonathan, old hoss,
And fur-clad Canada,
A right joint bumper toss!
You won't find "bitters" pay
Like our wassail!

Bismarck, my boy, no doubt
Our tipple is less "stiff"
Than your champagne and stout.
But let's drown every tiff
In our wassail!

No port South African,
Or Sherry of that ilk,
You'll find therein, old man;
'Tis strong, yet mild as milk
Is our wassail!

And William too, we hope,
Despite satiric shaft,
You'll join the genial Pope
In one deep generous draught
Of our wassail!

Boulanger—drop queer prank!—
De Lesseps—keep up heart!—
Whate'er his "flag," each Frank
Is welcome to a part
In our wassail!

Russia and Turkey, too,
And Italy, and Spain,
Dutchmen—you like stiff brew!—
Come *all*, and take a drain
Of our wassail!

It is a noble part
To bear a liberal mind,
And *Punch's* spacious heart
Holds room for all mankind—
So drink wassail!

Good luck betide you all!
One bumper more we'll fill;
*Punch* hopes, and ever shall,
For Peace and for Good-will.
That's his wassail!

Shakspeare for the Season (*by one surfeited with sensational shillingsworths*).—"I am ill at these (Christmas) numbers!"

# THE WASSAIL BOWL.

"DROP PARTY SPIRIT QUITE,
'TIS HEAVY, HEADY, STUFF,
ALL MEN *PUNCH* DOTH INVITE
TO TIPPLE *QUANTUM SUFF:*
OF HIS WASSAIL!

"GOOD LUCK BETIDE YOU ALL!
ONE BUMPER MORE WE'LL FILL;
*PUNCH* HOPES, AND EVER SHALL,
FOR PEACE AND FOR GOOD-WILL.
THAT'S HIS WASSAIL!"

## THE DIARY OF A NOBODY.

*November* 15.—Woke about twenty times during the night, with terrible thirst. Finished off all the water in the bottle, as well as half that in the jug. Kept dreaming, also, that last night's party was a failure, and that a lot of low people came, without invitation, and kept chaffing, and throwing things at Mr. PERKUPP, till at last I was obliged to hide him in the box-room (which we had just discovered), with a bath-towel over him. It seems absurd now, but it was painfully real in the dream. I had the same dream about a dozen times. CARRIE annoyed me by saying, "You know champagne never agrees with you." I told her I had only a couple of glasses of it, having kept myself entirely to port. I added that good champagne hurt nobody, and LUPIN told me he had only got it from a traveller as a favour, as that particular brand, "Jackson Frères," has been entirely bought up by a West-End Club. I think I eat too heartily of the "side dishes," as the waiter called them. I said to CARRIE, "I wish I had put those 'side dishes' *aside*." I repeated this, but CARRIE was busy, packing up the tea-spoons we had borrowed of Mrs. CUMMINGS for the party. It was just half-past eleven, and I was starting for the office, when LUPIN appeared, with a yellow complexion, and said, "Hulloh, Guv, what priced head have you this morning?" I told him he might just as well speak to me in Dutch. He added, "When I woke this morning, my head was as big as BALDWIN's Balloon." On the spur of the moment I said the cleverest thing I think I have ever said; viz., "Perhaps that accounts for the para*shooting* pains." We all three roared.

Nobody's Child.

*November* 16.—Still feel tired and headachy! In the evening GOWING called and was full of praise about our party last Wednesday. He said everything was done beautifully, and he enjoyed himself enormously. GOWING can be a very nice fellow when he likes, but you never know how long it will last. For instance, he stopped to supper, and seeing some *blanc-mange* on the table, shouted out while the servant was in the room, "Hulloh! The remains of Wednesday?"

*November* 17.—Woke up quite fresh after a good night's rest, and feel quite myself again. I am satisfied a life of going out and Society is not a life for me. I told SARAH not to bring up the *blanc-mange* again for breakfast. It seems to have been placed on our table at every meal since Wednesday. CUMMINGS came round in the evening and congratulated us on the success of our party. He said it was the best party he had been to for many a year, but he wished we had let him know it was full dress, as he would have turned up in his swallow-tails. We sat down to a quiet game of dominoes, and were interrupted by the noisy entrance of LUPIN and FRANK MUTLAR. CUMMINGS and I asked them to join us. LUPIN said he did not care for dominoes, and suggested a game of "Spoof." On my asking if it required counters, FRANK and LUPIN in measured time said, "One, two, three; Go! Have you an estate in Greenland?" It was simply Greek to me, but it appears it is one of the customs of the "Holloway Comedians" to do this when a member displays ignorance. In spite of my instructions that *blanc-mange* was brought up again for supper. To make matters worse, there had been an attempt to disguise it, by placing it in a glass dish with jam round it. CARRIE asked LUPIN if he would have some, and he replied, "No second-hand goods for me, thank you." I told CARRIE, when we were alone, if that *blanc-mange* were placed on the table again, I should walk out of the house.

*November* 18, *Sunday*.—A delightfully quiet day. In the afternoon LUPIN was off to spend the rest of the day with the MUTLARS. He departed in the best of spirits, and CARRIE said, "Well, one advantage of LUPIN's engagement with DAISY is that the boy seems happy all day long. That quite reconciles me to what I must confess seems an imprudent engagement." About nine o'clock to our surprise LUPIN entered, with a wild, reckless look, and in a hollow voice, which I must say seemed rather theatrical, said, "Have you any brandy?" I said "No, but here is some whiskey." LUPIN drank off nearly a wine-glassful without water, to my horror. We all three sat reading in silence till ten, when CARRIE and I rose to go to bed. CARRIE said to LUPIN, "I hope DAISY is well?" LUPIN, with a forced careless air that he must have picked up from the Holloway Comedians, replied: "Oh, DAISY? You mean Miss MUTLAR. I don't know whether she is well or not, but please *never to mention her name again in my presence*."

### Sympathy. (Finlay's Version.)

I SITS with a cynical look,
If the G. O. M. axes me why,
I (mentally) "cuts him a snook":
"Lack of Sympathy makes me," sez I.

## ROBERT ON THE EFFECTS OF BANKWETS.

MY rewelations on the subjek of Toastes has brort me lots of correspondents. Sum on 'em arsks me if I was serous in my statements. Why in coarse I was, tho' I'm not much surprized at the question. Why I remembers wun case as beat for downright imperance everythink as I hever herd on. The Chairman got up dreckly after dinner and acshally perposed all the reglar Toastes all at wunce! in wun full swoop, as BROWN said. It was at a Copperashun Dinner too. Sum of the yung fellers, of about 50 or 60, acshally larfed, but the old 'uns shook their heds gravely. By the by, no wun in the jolly Copperashun is considered as being old much hunder hayty.

Praps if I were arsked how it is as they lives so long and so jollily, I cood a tale unfoald, but as I sumtimes has the idear of retiring from my pressent perfeshun and starting as a consulting Feesishun for adwising all peeple as particklar wants to live well and to live long, how to do it, I wood rayther not unfoald that tale jest now.

I may praps add, that my xperience in that partickler line is probberbly almost quite uneek, and in werry speshal cases of rich and welthy and libberal old Gents as werry much wishes to live just a few years longer, both in good elth and good spirits, I may be priwetly hinsulted by letter addresst to the hoffiss. It may estonish sum peeple to hear that ony the summer before larst, when I was offishiating on bord the Grand City Barge, I was told, and I bleeves it, that in one squadreel as was being danced, the ages of the four gennelmen who was a dancing amounted to werry nearly three hundred years! and they all had werry yung and werry pretty partners.

One of the many results of my long xperience in the dining line is the conwicshun that the werry finest dygester of a reelly scrumshous Bankwet is Good Natur, or Good Temper, whichewer you likes to call it. I can always tell by the tone and manner in which a Gent addresses me at table, how he's a gitting on in that werry himportant respek. If he speeks sharply or surlyly to me, I knows at wunce wot's a goin on in his hunfortnite hinside, and I says to myself, ah! if you had the good temper of a hold Citty Deputy, that patty of *For Grar* wouldn't be a trubblin of you as it ewidently is, wile if he's a good-tempered feller, he smiles at me when we cums to the werry larst coarse, and says, "I'm not quite sure, ROBERT, as I wants any more, but it reelly looks so nice that I thinks I'll try jest a small peace." And so he does, and then tosses off another bumper of his speshal favrit drink, and then leens back in his chair smilin and appy and full.

And what grand fellers sum men are after a reel good dinner! Sum hignoramuses sumtimes wunders why, when sum of our werry grandest charitys wants jest a helpin and to help 'em to keep up their noble hinstitooshuns for all kinds of good and nobel hobjeks, they begins by arsking a lot of people to dinner, and says wot a waist! Bless their simple hignorance! Who nos, so well as we Waiters nos, wot the effeck of a good dinner is, how it hopens the art, and unloosens the tung, and unties the puss strings, and lets out the money. Why many and many an old cormudgeon who never praps gave away a suvverain to ewen a poor relashun when in his strickly sober and cawshus moments, after a reely grand dinner with plenty of fine old Clicko Shampain or the driest Pummery in his estonished hinside, will put down his name for five or ewen ten ginnys wen the fatal paper cums round, and wen he nos that whatever he gives will be enounced in a partickler lowd woice by the Lordly Tostmaster. The horful pangs of regret when, the next morning, he calls to his fatal remembrance the wild hact of ginerosity of which he has bin gilty owernite, is nuffin to me, and nuffin to the wise men who founded the feast. Having dewoted nearly fourty years of my waluable xistence to the study of mankind under these sumtimes rayther trying suckemstances, I arrives at this result,—that the one great hobjek to which all reelly sensibel peeple shood dewote themselves, supposing as they wishes to stand hi in the opinyuns of others as well as their own, is to dewote their cheef thorts, and their cheef study, to the eccomplishment of such a series of reelly nobel Bankwets, as, both by their present enjoyments and their subsekwent reflecksbun, will shed an halo ower their mortal xistence.

ROBERT.

### Suakin.

PLUCKILY done, and promptly! Here's a sample,
Even in Egypt, of the way to win.
Take, too long-halting Statesmen, an example
By that short, sharp half-hour at Suakin!

A VOCATION.

"AND WHAT ARE YOU GOING TO BE, TOMMY!"
"I'M GOIN' TO BE BIGGER DAN *YOU!*"

## A TENNYSONIAN INSPIRATION.

"We understand that Mr. W. S. GILBERT has expressed his determination—never again to write another SERIOUS PLAY."
*Evening Paper.*

WHEREUPON one of our Bards, inspired, sang:—

### ASK ME NO MORE!

Ask me no more—to write a Serious Play,
The crowd may stoop to "*Hands Across the Sea,*"
May troop to IRVING or to BEERBOHM TREE.
But from my loftiest Muse they turn away,
And do but smile, when they are bid to "*Pray.*"
Ask me no more!

Ask me no more—The Public's doom is sealed.
Never again, arrayed in sweetest "shapes"
(Of *my* design), shall BEAUTY stand revealed.
No more shall legal lore be turned to japes
And gibes, and "scriptural terms" provoke the gapes.
Ask me no more!

Ask me no more, I hate the empty jeer.
The critic's hollow "cheek"—his cruel eye.
Great Scott! Oh, *how* I loathe his damning leer.
And when he chaffs—I'd like his *Ruddigore,*
I'd love to see him weltering on the floor!
Ask me no more!

Ask me *no* more. Never again I vow
Shall the crass critic lift his empty roar
At *serious* work of MINE. And *now,*
I wish I'd vowed this vow BEFORE.
And kept to "*Pirates*"—(*Patience,* ruddy gore!)
Ask me no more!!

---

"THE OLD MASTERS' ALBUM."—(*Opinion of it by an Old Missis*).—Mrs. RAM was much struck by this handsomely got-up photographic album. "Indeed," said the good lady, "I do think it the finest book I've ever seen for keeping photographs. I suppose its publishers belong to some old City Guild; they generally do, my dear," she explained to her Niece, "and the Guild is named after some Saint." "Indeed, Aunt," returned LÆTITIA, "to what Saint's Guild would this firm belong?" "I don't absolutely know," replied Mrs. R. reflectively, "but, I suppose, to the Guild of St. Albums."

## THE WESTMINSTER PLAY.

SMITHICLES, a wealthy and prosperous Athenian, is ordered to go abroad by his medical adviser. Before doing so he entrusts the guardianship of his House at Westminster to his friend GOSCHENIDES, and at the same time requests him to look after the doings of a spendthrift nephew named CHURCHILLIO. He also bids GOSCHENIDES prosecute a law-suit, which he—SMITHICLES—and his friends have commenced against a foreigner called OSMANIKOS. All these commissions GOSCHENIDES readily undertakes. No sooner, however, is SMITHICLES safely abroad on his travels, than CHURCHILLIO breaks into the House at Westminster, snaps his fingers in the face of GOSCHENIDES and his friend STANHOPIS, and declares that the lawsuit against OSMANIKOS ought at once to be abandoned, or a heavier fee paid to the Counsel engaged. MORLÈS, a man who is not friendly to CHURCHILLIO, but is an enemy of GOSCHENIDES, joins in this demand; and in his confusion, GOSCHENIDES drops his purse containing a Bill on a Bank called "Employer's Liability"—which Bill is consequently lost. GOSCHENIDES and his friends are, of course, very angry with CHURCHILLIO, who, on this occasion is supported by a number of poor relations called PARNELLITI; when HARCOURTIAS, a comic slave, interferes, seeing that CHURCHILLIO and MORLÈS are going too far, and assures them that a buried treasure (called "Popular Favour") can only be obtained after a verdict against OSMANIKOS has been pronounced. At the same time a SYCOPHANTA (or Informer) appears on the scene pretending that he has brought a message from SMITHICLES ordering the suit against OSMANIKOS to be discontinued. It so happens, however, that SMITHICLES—who has been enjoying himself in Italy with an acquaintance named GLADSTONIDES—suddenly returns in person to his House at Westminster, sends the SYCOPHANTA about his business, and gets (by the help of an able advocate named GRENPHELLIOS) a verdict against OSMANIKOS. Thereupon MORLÈS and CHURCHILLIO apply to COOKION, an Athenian agent for personally conducting travellers to distant lands, and by his aid are enabled to absent themselves for a time from Athens; MORLÈS hastening to Naples to visit GLADSTONIDES, and CHURCHILLIO seeking rest and recreation amid the inhabitants of Chili and Peru. Thus all ends happily.

## BUMBLE ON BEER.

WE all know *Mr. Bumble's* opinion on the results of indulging paupers in meat. "Meat, Ma'am, meat," replied *Bumble,* with stern emphasis—"you've overfed him, Ma'am. You've raised a artificial soul and spirit in him, Ma'am, unbecoming a person of his condition; as the Board, *Mrs. Sowerberry,* who are practical philosophers, will tell you. What have paupers to do with soul or spirit? It's quite enough that we let 'em have live bodies."

It might be reasonably inferred from this passage how far this great and good man would have approved of Beer as a pauper beverage. *Punch* feels tolerably sure that, were *Mr. Bumble* alive to-day—as of course he is not—he would warmly commend the "practical philosophy" shown by the Dolgelly Board of Guardians, as lately recorded in a morning paper. A Guardian, we are told, "*offered to supply the paupers with a gratuitous cask of beer at Christmas. Several Guardians demurred. Poverty was, they said, created by drink, and it would be contrary to their duty to distribute liquors amongst the men and women, many of whom were paupers through drink. Ultimately the Board decided, by a majority, to refuse to accept the beer.*" What enlightened conscientiousness! What self-denial! What wise consideration for others! Think of the shocking and scandalous scenes that would certainly have been enacted on Christmas Day in Dolgelly workhouse, had "a artificial soul and spirit" been raised in those misguided, naturally high-spirited paupers by the unwise indulgence of a glass of beer a-piece! Thanks to the fostering care of their devoted Guardians, there is now every reason to hope that the festivities will be restrained within becoming limits. If one Guardian was weak enough to offer beer, the rest, it is pleasant at this season of universal charity and good-will to note, had the strength of mind to reply, "Skittles!"

---

SHAKSPEARE FOR THE SEASON. (PATERFAMILIAS'S VERSION.)
THERE'S a Yule-tide in the affairs of men
Which, taken at the flood, leads on to—indigestion!

---

"WHAT'S this I hear," said Mrs. RAM, "about H.R.H. and the Horrible Artillery Company?"

INDEX.

LARGE ENGRAVINGS.



SMALL ENGRAVINGS.



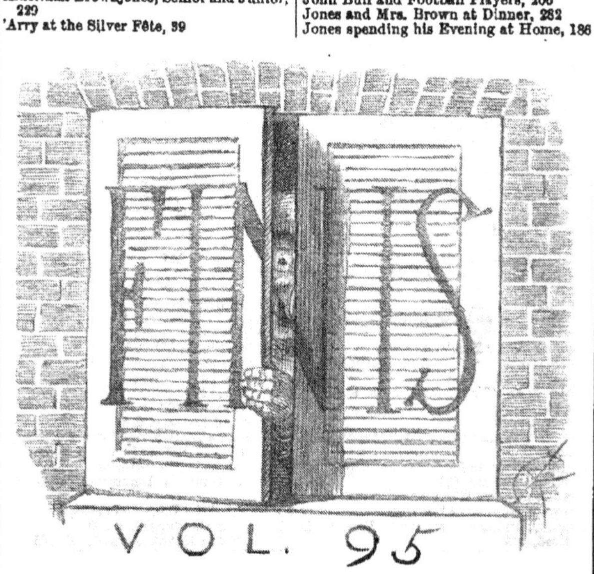


LONDON: BRADBURY, AGNEW, & CO., PRINTERS, WHITEFRIARS.

**JANUARY xxxi Days.**

| | | | | | |
|---|---|---|---|---|---|
| 1 | Tu | N. Year's D. | 17 | Th | Franklin b. |
| 2 | W | [illegible] | 18 | F | Prince. |
| 3 | Th | Hunt b. | 19 | S | Watt b. |
| 4 | F | Sambourne | 20 | S | 2 S. af. Epip. |
| 5 | S | Ed. Conf. d. | 21 | M | Agnes |
| 6 | S | Epiphany | 22 | Tu | Vincent |
| 7 | M | [illegible] | 23 | W | Pitt d. 1806 |
| 8 | Tu | P. A. Vict. b. | 24 | Th | Fox b. 1749 |
| 9 | W | [illegible] | 25 | F | Burns b. |
| 10 | Th | Ss. 4h. 10m. | 26 | S | Gordon kd. |
| 11 | F | Hil. Sit. b. | 27 | S | 3 S. af. Epip. |
| 12 | S | Lavater d. | 28 | M | Prescott d. |
| 13 | S | 1 S. af. Epip. | 29 | Tu | Capt. P. [illegible] |
| 14 | M | Oxf. L. T. b. | 30 | W | Chas. I bhd. |
| 15 | Tu | [illegible] plot | 31 | Th | B. Jonson b. |
| 16 | W | [illegible] | | | |

**FEBRUARY xxviii Days.**

| | | | | | |
|---|---|---|---|---|---|
| 1 | F | [illegible] | 16 | S | Buckstone. |
| 2 | S | Zulu War | 17 | S | Septuag. S. |
| 3 | S | 4 S. af. Epip. | 18 | M | Luther d. |
| 4 | M | Sr. 7h. 35m. | 19 | Tu | Copernic. b. |
| 5 | Tu | Galvani d. | 20 | W | J. Hume d. |
| 6 | W | Ss. 5h. 5m. | 21 | Th | Trinidad t. |
| 7 | Th | Dickens b. | 22 | F | Ferguson [illegible] |
| 8 | F | Hil. qr. Day | 23 | S | Sir J. Rey. d. |
| 9 | S | Darnley m. | 24 | S | Sexag. S. |
| 10 | S | 5 S. af. Epip. | 25 | M | Wren d. |
| 11 | M | D. [illegible] | 26 | Tu | T. Moore d. |
| 12 | Tu | Cellini d. | 27 | W | Benvenuto |
| 13 | W | Revol. 1688 | 28 | Th | J. Tenniel |
| 14 | Th | Valentine. | | | |
| 15 | F | [illegible] | | | |

**MARCH xxxi Days.**

| | | | | | |
|---|---|---|---|---|---|
| 1 | F | St. David | 17 | S | 2 S. in Lent |
| 2 | S | Wesley d. | 18 | M | [illegible] |
| 3 | S | Quinqu. S. | 19 | Tu | Lucknow t. |
| 4 | M | [illegible] | 20 | W | [illegible] |
| 5 | Tu | Sr. 6h. 40m. | 21 | Th | Benedict |
| 6 | W | Du Maurier | 22 | F | Goethe d. |
| 7 | Th | Ss. 5h. 50m. | 23 | S | Nat. Gal. f. |
| 8 | F | Will. III d. | 24 | S | 3 S. in Lent |
| 9 | S | Cobbett b. | 25 | M | Lady Day |
| 10 | S | 1 S. in Lent | 26 | Tu | [illegible] |
| 11 | M | In. T. [illegible] | 27 | W | Cam. L. T. e. |
| 12 | Tu | Gregory | 28 | Th | Hil. Sit. e. |
| 13 | W | Talfourd d. | 29 | F | B. Towton |
| 14 | Th | Byng shot | 30 | S | Sicil. Vesp. |
| 15 | F | Massinger d. | 31 | S | 4 S. in Lent |
| 16 | S | Dk. Kent d. | | | |

**APRIL xxx Days.**

| | | | | | |
|---|---|---|---|---|---|
| 1 | M | All Fool's | 16 | Tu | Thiers b. |
| 2 | Tu | Sr. 5h. 35m. | 17 | W | B. Culloden |
| 3 | W | Ss. 6h. 36m. | 18 | Th | Cam. E. T. b. |
| 4 | Th | Oxf. L. T. b. | 19 | F | Good Frid. |
| 5 | F | Nap. I. abd. | 20 | S | Nap. III. b. |
| 6 | S | O. Lady Day | 21 | S | Easter Sun. |
| 7 | S | 5 S. in Lent | 22 | M | Bk. Holiday |
| 8 | M | [illegible] | 23 | Tu | St. George |
| 9 | Tu | Fire Insur. | 24 | W | [illegible] |
| 10 | W | E. at Sit. b. | 25 | Th | Prs. Alice b. |
| 11 | Th | Canning d. | 26 | F | D. Hume b. |
| 12 | F | Young d. | 27 | S | Gibbon b. |
| 13 | S | Handel d. | 28 | S | Low Sun. |
| 14 | S | Palm Sun. | 29 | M | St. Cath. S. |
| 15 | M | [illegible] | 30 | Tu | Fitzroy d. |

**MAY xxxi Days.**

| | | | | | |
|---|---|---|---|---|---|
| 1 | W | May Day | 17 | F | Talleyrand d. |
| 2 | Th | Sr. 4h. 33m. | 18 | S | East. Sit. e. |
| 3 | F | Ss. 7h. 27m. | 19 | S | 4 S. af. Eas. |
| 4 | S | Sering. [illegible] | 20 | M | Columbus d. |
| 5 | S | 2 S. af. Eas. | 21 | Tu | [illegible] |
| 6 | M | [illegible] | 22 | W | [illegible] |
| 7 | Tu | [illegible] | 23 | Th | B. Ramillies |
| 8 | W | D. Jerrold d. | 24 | F | Q. Vict. b. |
| 9 | Th | Hl. qr. Day | 25 | S | Pr. Hel. b. |
| 10 | F | [illegible] | 26 | S | Rogation S. |
| 11 | S | Chatham d. | 27 | M | Ven. Bede |
| 12 | S | 3 S. af. Eas. | 28 | Tu | W. Pitt b. |
| 13 | M | O. May Day | 29 | W | Chas. II. res. |
| 14 | Tu | Grattan d. | 30 | Th | Ascen. Day |
| 15 | W | O'Connell d. | 31 | F | [illegible] |
| 16 | Th | B. Albuera | | | |

**JUNE xxx Days.**

| | | | | | |
|---|---|---|---|---|---|
| 1 | S | Nicomede | 16 | S | Trin. Sun. |
| 2 | S | S. af. Ascen. | 17 | M | St. Alban |
| 3 | M | Sr. 3h. 48m. | 18 | Tu | Waterloo |
| 4 | Tu | [illegible] | 19 | W | B. Worcest. |
| 5 | W | Weber d. | 20 | Th | Corp. Chris. |
| 6 | Th | [illegible] | 21 | F | Longest Dy |
| 7 | F | Reform Bill | 22 | S | [illegible] |
| 8 | S | [illegible] | 23 | S | 1 Su. af. Tr. |
| 9 | S | Whit Sun. | 24 | M | Midsum. D. |
| 10 | M | Bk. Holiday | 25 | Tu | Cam. E. T. e. |
| 11 | Tu | [illegible] | 26 | W | Geo. IV. d. |
| 12 | W | [illegible] | 27 | Th | [illegible] |
| 13 | Th | [illegible] | 28 | F | Q. Vic. Cr. |
| 14 | F | B. Naseby | 29 | S | St. Peter |
| 15 | S | Mag. Charta | 30 | S | 2 Su. af. Tr. |

**JULY xxxi Days.**

| | | | | | |
|---|---|---|---|---|---|
| 1 | M | B. Boyne | 17 | W | Punch b. '41 |
| 2 | Tu | Sr. 3h. 48m. | 18 | Th | Sherlock d. |
| 3 | W | B. Sadowa | 19 | F | Petrarch d. |
| 4 | Th | Ss. 8h. 17m. | 20 | S | Margaret |
| 5 | F | B. Wagram | 21 | S | 5 Su. af. Tr. |
| 6 | S | O. Mids. Da. | 22 | M | Salamanca |
| 7 | S | 3 Su. af. Tr. | 23 | Tu | [illegible] |
| 8 | M | A. Smith d. | 24 | W | Gibral. tkn. |
| 9 | Tu | Fire Insur. | 25 | Th | St. James |
| 10 | W | [illegible] | 26 | F | [illegible] |
| 11 | Th | [illegible] | 27 | S | Talavera |
| 12 | F | [illegible] | 28 | S | 6 Su. af. Tr. |
| 13 | S | [illegible] | 29 | M | [illegible] |
| 14 | S | 4 Su. af. Tr. | 30 | Tu | W. Penn d. |
| 15 | M | St. Swithin | 31 | W | [illegible] |
| 16 | Tu | [illegible] | | | |

**AUGUST xxxi Days.**

| | | | | | |
|---|---|---|---|---|---|
| 1 | Th | Lammas | 17 | S | Boulton d. |
| 2 | F | Blenheim | 18 | S | 9 Su. af. Tr. |
| 3 | S | Sr. 4h. 28m. | 19 | M | [illegible] |
| 4 | S | 7 Su. af. Tr. | 20 | Tu | [illegible] |
| 5 | M | Bk. Holiday | 21 | W | [illegible] |
| 6 | Tu | Dk. Edin. b. | 22 | Th | [illegible] |
| 7 | W | Ss. 7h. 33m. | 23 | F | Wallace ex. |
| 8 | Th | Otway b. | 24 | S | St. Bartholo. |
| 9 | F | Dryden b. | 25 | S | 10 Su. af. Tr. |
| 10 | S | C. Keene b. | 26 | M | P. Cons. b. |
| 11 | S | 8 Su. af. Tr. | 27 | Tu | Thomson d. |
| 12 | M | Grouse s. b. | 28 | W | B. Leipzig |
| 13 | Tu | Trin. Sit. e. | 29 | Th | Jno. Bap. bd. |
| 14 | W | Ld. Clyde d. | 30 | F | Paley b. |
| 15 | Th | W. Scott b. | 31 | S | Bunyan d. |
| 16 | F | [illegible] | | | |

**SEPTEMBER xxx Days.**

| | | | | | |
|---|---|---|---|---|---|
| 1 | S | 11 Su. af. Tr. | 16 | M | Jas. II. d. |
| 2 | M | Capt. Sedan | 17 | Tu | Lambert. |
| 3 | Tu | Sr. 5h. 18m. | 18 | W | [illegible] |
| 4 | W | Ss. 6h. 37m. | 19 | Th | B. Poitiers |
| 5 | Th | Comte d. | 20 | F | B. Alma |
| 6 | F | Colbert d. | 21 | S | St. Matth. |
| 7 | S | [illegible] | 22 | S | 14 S. af. Tr. |
| 8 | S | 12 S. af. Tr. | 23 | M | Autn. Q. b. |
| 9 | M | B. Flodden | 24 | Tu | S. Butler d. |
| 10 | Tu | [illegible] | 25 | W | Porson d. |
| 11 | W | S. of Delhi | 26 | Th | St. Cyprian |
| 12 | Th | O. P. Riots | 27 | F | [illegible] |
| 13 | F | C. J. Fox d. | 28 | S | Nicopolis |
| 14 | S | Holy Cross | 29 | S | 15 S. af. Tr. |
| 15 | S | 13 S. af. Tr. | 30 | M | Mich. Day |

**OCTOBER xxxi Days.**

| | | | | | |
|---|---|---|---|---|---|
| 1 | Tu | Cam. M. T. b. | 17 | Th | Etheldreda |
| 2 | W | Arago d. | 18 | F | St. Luke |
| 3 | Th | Sr. 6h. 7m. | 19 | S | Kneller d. |
| 4 | F | Ss. 5h. 25m. | 20 | S | 18 S. af. Tr. |
| 5 | S | [illegible] | 21 | M | Trafalgar |
| 6 | S | 16 S. af. Tr. | 22 | Tu | B. Edge Hill |
| 7 | M | Abp. Laud b. | 23 | W | Irish Reb. |
| 8 | Tu | [illegible] | 24 | Th | Mic. Sit. b. |
| 9 | W | St. Denys | 25 | F | St. Crispin |
| 10 | Th | Ox. M. T. b. | 26 | S | [illegible] |
| 11 | F | Old Mic. D. | 27 | S | 19 S. af. Tr. |
| 12 | S | Pekin tkn. | 28 | M | J. Locke d. |
| 13 | S | 17 S. af. Tr. | 29 | Tu | J. Leech d. |
| 14 | M | [illegible] | 30 | W | Tower burnt |
| 15 | Tu | Fire Insur. | 31 | Th | All Hallow |
| 16 | W | [illegible] | | | |

**NOVEMBER xxx Days.**

| | | | | | |
|---|---|---|---|---|---|
| 1 | F | All Saints | 16 | S | J. Bright b. |
| 2 | S | All Souls | 17 | S | 22 S. af. Tr. |
| 3 | S | 20 S. af. Tr. | 18 | M | Wilkie b. |
| 4 | M | P. Leigh [illegible] | 19 | Tu | [illegible] |
| 5 | Tu | Sr. 7h. 4m. | 20 | W | [illegible] |
| 6 | W | Ss. 4h. 21m. | 21 | Th | J. Hogg d. |
| 7 | Th | [illegible] | 22 | F | St. Cecilia |
| 8 | F | Milton d. | 23 | S | St. Clement |
| 9 | S | P. of Wales b. | 24 | S | 23 S. af. Tr. |
| 10 | S | 21 S. af. Tr. | 25 | M | Chantrey d. |
| 11 | M | St. Martin | 26 | Tu | [illegible] |
| 12 | Tu | Mi. qr. Day | 27 | W | Dk. Teck b. |
| 13 | W | Britius | 28 | Th | [illegible] |
| 14 | Th | Leibnitz d. | 29 | F | [illegible] |
| 15 | F | Machutus | 30 | S | St. Andrew |

**DECEMBER xxxi Days.**

| | | | | | |
|---|---|---|---|---|---|
| 1 | S | Adv. Sun. | 17 | Tu | Oxf. M. T. e. |
| 2 | M | B. Austerlitz | 18 | W | [illegible] |
| 3 | Tu | [illegible] | 19 | Th | Cam. M. T. e. |
| 4 | W | Richelieu d. | 20 | F | [illegible] |
| 5 | Th | [illegible] | 21 | S | Mich. Sit. e. |
| 6 | F | [illegible] | 22 | S | 4 S. in Adv. |
| 7 | S | [illegible] | 23 | M | Jas. II. abd. |
| 8 | S | 2 S. in Adv. | 24 | Tu | Christ. Eve |
| 9 | M | Vandyke d. | 25 | W | Christ. Day |
| 10 | Tu | Milton b. | 26 | Th | Bk. Holiday |
| 11 | W | [illegible] | 27 | F | St. John |
| 12 | Th | C. Cibber d. | 28 | S | Innocents |
| 13 | F | St. Lucy | 29 | S | Sun. af. Chr. |
| 14 | S | [illegible] | 30 | M | [illegible] |
| 15 | S | 3 S. in Adv. | 31 | Tu | Silvester |
| 16 | M | V. Weber b. | | | |

TIME AND TUNE.

*(By the Monster Zodiac Band.)*

*The Mayberds enjoyed their Trip on the Continent immensely this Summer, the only drawback being their ignorance of the Language.*

*Mrs. Mayberd (to her Sister).* "I WISH ALICE WOULD TRY AND PICK UP A LITTLE GERMAN. SHE 'S VERY CLEVER, AND IT WOULD BE SO PLEASANT TO——" *Aunt Jemima (single).* "GOOD GRACIOUS, JANE! WHAT ARE YOU THINKING OF!? I HOPE TO GOODNESS SHE WON'T. A NICE RESPECTABLE YOUNG ENGLISHMAN 'S WORTH A DOZEN OF 'EM!" [*Shows what she was thinking of.*

## MASTER TOMMY'S DOMESTIC ECONOMIES.

*How to Supply the House with a Cheap Hydraulic Lift.* — It being understood that the house is provided with a well staircase, fasten a pulley to the skylight, and over this pass a stout two-inch rope, to one end of which you have fastened a five-foot bath, and to the other the butler's tray, taking care that it is long enough to reach from the top to the bottom, Having landed your bath on the fifth story, proceed to fill it from the adjacent cistern. Now make the page-boy, who is about to take five o'clock tea to the drawing-room, take his place in the butler's tray in the hall, and your bath by this time being fully weighted with water, suddenly detach it from its position. It will rapidly descend, and, emptying itself with a crash on the pavement beneath, jerk the page-boy up to the fifth floor, where, letting go his tea-things, he will find himself clinging for safety to the outside of the balusters. Your Uncle, entering the house at this moment, and finding the water in his hall over his ancles, upon your briefly explaining the apparatus to him, will not fail to admit that, though it is not quite in satisfactory working order, you have at least supplied his premises with a cheap hydraulic lift.

DIES NON.—Night.

AT A SMOKING CONCERT.—*Basso.* "YES; I'VE JUST BOUGHT A CAPITAL ESTATE IN SURREY. JOIN OUR PARTY? SHOOTING OVER A THOUSAND ACRES!" *Flute (modestly).* "A THOUSAND ACRES? OH, I SHOULD NEVER BE ABLE TO HIT AT *THAT* DISTANCE!"

**LIKA JOKO'S PANTOMIME.**—The Haunt of the Demon Sweater.

A CLASSIC CALENDAR; OR, MYTHS FOR THE MONTHS.

A CLASSIC CALENDAR; OR, MYTHS FOR THE MONTHS.

### ANECDOTAGE FOR THE MONTHS.

JANUARY.—On the 27th, in 1859, the present German Emperor was born. Consequently he is thirty years old. So many anecdotes have been told of His Majesty, that it is difficult to find a new one. However, it may be interesting to note that the Emperor, about ten years ago, when he was staying in Sydney, New South Wales, during his honeymoon, was presented by the German residents of that place with a musical box, which played only one tune. On learning this, he turned round, and smilingly observed to a courtier, "This may be well called a musical box, as we can never visit it for *a change of air!*" The German residents of Sydney laughed at the witticism, but never forgave the sarcasm.

HOW TO TAKE AN EGG.—*Cum grano salis.*

### ODE BY AN ELDERLY GENTLEMAN.

*(An Apology to an Omnibus Conductor.)*

THE Omnibus is crammed,
We passengers are jammed
Extremely close together.
One more it can't contain.
'Tis coming on to rain;
Raw chill and cold the weather;
Or may be or may not,
The roof is broiling hot,
Whereas the interior's shady.
Room? None, Conductor; no.
"Will any Gentleman go
Outside to oblige a Lady?"
Oblige her? Wish I could,
How willingly I would
Accept your invitation;
Though I don't see the way
How she could e'er repay
That weighty obligation.
A Lady in the case,
Of course I should give place,
With pleasure, were I stronger.
Once I could scale a cliff,
But, now my limbs are stiff,
Can climb a 'bus no longer.
So, be the damsel fair,
Stout matron, old maid spare,
Or beauty past her heyday,
I must decline to ride
Your Omnibus outside,
Although "to oblige a Lady."

### ANECDOTAGE FOR THE MONTHS.

FEBRUARY.—On the 18th of the month, the late CHARLES LAMB was born as long ago as 1775. Had he lived until now, he would have reached the ripe old age of 114, which would have certainly been a prolonged life for a Lamb, or, if it comes to that (to quote Dr. JOHNSON), for a sheep either. On the 9th (in 1567) DARNLEY was murdered, and just twenty years afterwards (on the 8th, in 1587) poor MARY, Queen of Scots, was beheaded. It is only just to the memory of Queen ELIZABETH, to assert that the cruel jest ascribed to Her Majesty that "she had cut off her cousin's head to prove to the world that she had one," is supposed to have been invented some years before either Queen's birth, by WILL SOMERS, King HENRY VIII.'s reputed jester.

A VESTED INTEREST.

*Bystander (to excited Scot, whose Friend had been run over).* "NOT A NEAR RELATIVE, I HOPE, SIR."
*Scot.* "NA—BUT—HE HAS ON A PAIR O' MA BREEKS!"

### MASTER TOMMY'S DOMESTIC ECONOMIES.

*How to save your friends the expense of a visit to the Dentist's.*—Get your aunt to ask some young people to tea, and having looked out an old pair of pincers, a corkscrew, some hairpins, a pair of nutcrackers, some charcoal tongs, and other useful odds and ends of the same kind, place them on a little table in the back-study, facing the window of which you have arranged a roomy arm chair. Having everything prepared, get the young people into the room, and locking the door, make one of the ROBINSON girls sit down and open her mouth. As soon as she has done this, seize upon one of her teeth with the pincers. Now tug. You will probably be rewarded with an extraction. Having operated on all the company in turns, with more or less success, you can now let them out, to return to their respective Mammas, who, though you may have not taken out the right teeth, will be bound to admit that, as you have done it for nothing, you have certainly saved them the expense of a visit to the Dentist's.

Over the "Left."

### ANECDOTAGE FOR THE MONTHS.

MARCH.—On the 3rd of the month, in 1848, LOUIS PHILIPPE fled to England, where at first he was treated with some discourtesy. On learning that the name of his landing-place was Dover, he observed, "I am not surprised to find that this is Dover, as I do not admire its Folks' tone!" As LOUIS PHILIPPE did not speak a word of English, this ingenious and agreeable sally is worthy of recollection.

A CANVAS-BACKED DUCK.—The likeliest candidate to gain an election.

**LIKA JOKO'S PANTOMIME.**—**The Home of the Fairy Queen.**

## EXTRACTS FROM THE DIARY OF A DYSPEPTIC.

*January* 1.—Another dreary weary year to be lived through! Oh, to be done with it all! Got as far as Club in afternoon. Walked home despairing of Humanity. Considerable pain in epigastrium. *Query—internal!*

*February* 14.—Pairing time. No one pairs with Me! My doom to drag through the melancholy days unloved, uncared-for, alone! Remember passage in some poet—forget whom and exact lines—but to effect that the entire animal creation, down to the very rabbits, had a mate, with the single exception of the poet himself. Pathetic idea, and my own case exactly. Fortunately, I hold *all* women in secret contempt. Too depressed for regular luncheon, but snatched a Bath bun and some ginger ale at Confectioner's. Wished I was dead several times on way home.

28.—Dined with the GREENS. Took in SABINA. Was it fancy—or did she betray a passing emotion when I mentioned incidentally that I did not think I should live to see the Spring? SABINA distinctly a nice girl. Pretty, too—when she has that shy sympathetic look. But what is all that to *me?* Very fair dinner—oyster-patties especially good, but unwell all night.

*March.*—East winds. Blight in the air—and in my heart! What offensive worms are the majority of the people one meets—in the streets, nothing but hideous and malignant faces—nowhere a kindly look meets mine—how I hate the world! Call on the GREENS. Long talk with SABINA. Described my lonely lot, the singular fact that no woman's lips have ever yet murmured in my ears the confession that I was beloved. Had not intended to lead up to it—but somehow find myself engaged on coming away. She is a charming girl—but it *is* rather sudden. An engagement must make *some* difference in a man's life, and I hate changes. Melancholy presentiment, which I can't shake off, that Love will bring no happiness to Me. Possibly weather. Who can be blithe and hopeful without blue sky, and warmth, and the blessed sunshine?

*April.*—Still engaged to SABINA. The mockery of cloudless skies, and soft breezes, when there is no Spring in the heart. Cucumbers in season again. Uneasy about self. Pimple on left cheek—is it the precursor of some disfiguring eruption? Horrible to be unsightly to all the world, and to SABINA! Now I shall test her affection. Consult Doctor—prescribes "exercise and green food."

"IN TERROREM."

*Street Boy (to Old Lady).* "THE BOARD O' WORKS IS A COMIN' UP THE NEX' STREET, AN' IF THEY SEES YOUR DOOR AIN'T SWEP'—YOU 'LL KETCH IT!"

*May.*—Really affecting interview with SABINA. Begged her to visit my tomb at least once a day, suggested that she might stay in town for purpose, this year, at all events. Have an idea that she did not acquiesce with entire cheerfulness. Can she be selfish? New and curious symptoms after meals. Incipient—*what?*

*June.*—In better spirits all day. Composing my epitaph, and rather pleased with it. Took it to show SABINA, who wept. I quite composed and resigned. No regret (except for others) at the summons. Queer shooting-pangs about region of heart. Doctor's Prescription—"eat more slowly and less." And this is all that their boasted Science can do for me!

*July* 15.—I knew it! Always felt my happiness was not destined to endure. *Sabina is weary of me!* Would not see me in Row to-day—unmistakable cut. Met her at dance in evening, and would not see *her.* What Tragedies lie below the surface of Life! Sat at table in supper-room with my back to her, eating lobster-salad, while my heart was breaking.

16.—Letter from SABINA, imploring explanation, pretending ignorance of how she has offended me, &c., &c.; the unspeakable duplicity of Woman! Shall leave it unanswered,—the breach between us has gone too far to be mended *now.*

17.—Meet SABINA unexpectedly at picnic. All explained. She had no idea I was in the Row that day. How infinitely petty seem even the deepest injuries when Life is ebbing fast. Feel I can forgive and understand. We ate strawberries and cream together in silent harmony. Severe spasms in boat coming home.

*August* 8.—Down at the GREENS' Country house. Wish SABINA would be a little more *lively.* Hint to her that *I* do not break down—so why should *she?* Lawn-tennis. Prepare her, delicately, for my dropping a corpse on any violent exertion—won every sett easily.

26.—SABINA'S Cousin CHARLES staying here—a beast. I believe he would chaff me while I lay in my coffin!

*September.*—In town again. Had to make excuses before they would let me go. Left, ostensibly, to see my doctor; really, because I couldn't stand that confounded prig of a cousin. Wander disconsolate about empty squares, visit Her house, now all silent and shut up. She is enjoying her life away in the country, while *I*—oh, the heartlessness of healthy girlhood! No letter for last twenty-four hours, and I write regularly once a week.

*October.*—The fall of the leaf. Soon I too shall shed my leaves! (Mem. for letter to SABINA.) Find I have not lost my old relish for

# NEW

(*Mr. Punch's Design for a Grand H*

"THE OLD ORDER CHANGET

# NDON.

*legorical-Almaniacal Picture for 1889.)*

NG PLACE TO NEW."—TENNYSON.

"WHERE THERE'S A WILL," &c.

"HI! HI, SIR! WHERE ARE YOU COMING TO? THERE'S NO ROAD THROUGH HERE!"
"PRAY DON'T APOLOGISE, SIR. QUITE GOOD ENOUGH FOR ME, I ASSURE YOU!"

walnuts. Excruciating pain all day. Write to SABINA; tried to appear in my ordinary spirits. but could not refrain at end from warning her that if she wished to see me *alive*, she must lose no time.

*November*.—Life still flickering. Actually almost enjoyed stewed eels and venison last night at dinner. To day the inevitable reaction has overtaken me. The GREENS back in town. Explain to SABINA that I wish her to consider herself free to marry when I am no more. Make one exception—CHARLES.

*December*. — SABINA neither so pretty nor so sympathetic as she used to be. Less upset at any reference to mourning. Told her to-day *not* to send a wreath; she said (*dry-eyed*, too!) that she thought it "a senseless custom." How use habituates us to impending sorrow. I myself was almost gay last night, helping her to roast and eat chestnuts (ever a weakness of mine). Alas! since, impressive reminder that my state will *bear no trifling*.

25.—Dined with the GREENS. "*My last plum-pudding in THIS world*," as I said, in a solemn whisper, to SABINA. Think her laugh *may* have been only hysterical. If not—callous in extreme. She will think of my words *next* Christmas, perhaps!

31.—A Chapter closed in my life, not unwillingly. SABINA's shallow insensibility has revolted me at last! She actually told me to my face this morning that she "could not see there was so *very* much the matter with me!" If she could see *within!* But I have done with her. The shock almost seems to have revived in me the Will to Live. If I can only get rid of these swellings in the head, after eating, I may live yet to witness her remorse. Off to Monte Carlo to-morrow.

AN AWKWARD REPARTEE TO DEAL WITH.

*Head Master*. "IT'S DISGRACEFUL, SIR! WHY, YOUR BROTHER, WHO IS TWO YEARS YOUNGER THAN YOURSELF, KNOWS HIS GREEK GRAMMAR BETTER THAN YOU DO!"

*Dunce*. "AH, BUT MY BROTHER'S NOT BEEN HERE SO LONG AS I HAVE, SIR. IT'S ONLY HIS FIRST TERM!"

CALCULATION OF AGE.—If nonage is minority, how old is a Non-agenarian?

**LIKA JOKO'S PANTOMIME.**—The Grand Procession.

**AN OFFENSIVE WEAPON.**

*Careful Sportsman (whose gun has gone off, as he declares, "of its own accord").* "HULLO! BAILEY! YOU DON'T MEAN TO SAY THE CHARGE WENT THRO' YOUR HAT?" *Keeper.* "YES, SIR—NEARLY BLEW MY 'ED OFF!"
*Careful Sportsman.* "BY GEORGE!—*I'LL NEVER SHOOT WITH THIS GUN AGAIN!*"

MAXIM BY A MARTYR TO THE MULTITUDE OF (VOLUNTEER) COUNSELLORS.—Advice *gratis* is never worth what it costs.

CORRUPTIO OPTIMI PESSIMA.—Haunch of Venison too "high."

MOTTO OF THE FASHIONABLE FEMALE OF THE DAY (MORE SHAME FOR HER!).—A bird in the hat is worth two in the bush.

APOLOGY FOR SPIRITUALISM.—There 's a Medium in all things.

## MASTER TOMMY'S DOMESTIC ECONOMIES.

*How to Procure a Wild Turkey at a Moderate Outlay.*—Having purchased a tame turkey, bring it home, and shut it up in the coal-cellar. Now proceed to drive it wild. This you will do by bursting in upon it at odd times, now frightening it by beating a drum, and springing a large rattle, or by pelting it with squibs, crackers, and other detonating fireworks. Alternate this with waking it up suddenly at the dead of night, and jumping about it, enveloped in a sheet, with a dark lantern, and giving it an occasional chase round the back garden, pursuing it with a cab-whistle, and an open Japanese umbrella. After a fortnight of this, it will show signs of dementia; and when it has flown at the cook, and bitten the butler in the calf of the leg, may confidently be regarded as fit for table. Should it, however, not possess a distinctly gamey flavour, or eat "delicious," you may certainly point with triumph to the fact that the turkey with which, at a moderate outlay, you have provided the household, is, to all intents and purposes, undeniably quite "wild."

**EXPENDED!**

*Guest.* "WILL YOU GIVE ME A LITTLE CHAMPAGNE?"
*Hibernian Waiter.* "SHUMPANE, SOR! BEDAD, I'VE HAD NONE MESELF THIS TWO HOURS!"

THE LOGIC OF AGRICULTURE. — A Silogism.

**A CLASSIC CALENDAR; OR, MYTHS FOR THE MONTHS.**

**A CLASSIC CALENDAR; OR, MYTHS FOR THE MONTHS.**

**RESIGNATION.**

*Sympathetic Old Gentleman.* "I'M SORRY TO SEE YOUR HUSBAND SUFFER SO, MA'AM. HE SEEMS VERY——"
*Lady Passenger (faintly).* "OH DEAR! HE ISN'T MY HUSBAND. 'SURE I DON'T KNOW WHO THE GE'TLEMAN IS!"

**THE SWITCHBACK.**

HERE we go up, up, up!
And there we go down, down, down!
*I* feel as I do when on pork-chops I sup,
And I can't keep my hat on my crown.
My children have gammoned me in it;
I feel very frightened and hot.
Eh? Get in again, Pa! No, not for a minute!
Or may I be instantly shot.
Pheugh! *They* would be at it all day.
A wonderful thing is this youth!
For me, all my clothes seem to set the wrong way,
And I fear I have loosened a tooth.
There they go up, up, up!
And there they go down, down, down!
*I*'d almost as soon be shot out of a Krupp,
Or ride a wild horse. Not for BROWN!

**FROM THE "OTHER SIDE."**

"A—DO *YOU* PLAY, MISS VAN TROMP?"—"I GUESS NOT." "A—DO YOU SING?"—"WELL, NO, DUKE. I'VE BEEN TAUGHT NO *PARLOUR TRICKS!*"

**ANECDOTAGE FOR THE MONTHS.**

APRIL.—On the 10th the Battle of Toulouse was fought in 1814, when the Duke of WELLINGTON exclaimed, "Toulouse!—no, I mean *to win!*" On the 16th another memorable battle has its commemoration day — Culloden. It was here that the Butcher Duke of CUMBERLAND, in 1746, was informed by the then Duke of MARLBOROUGH of the death of his connection by marriage, Queen ANNE. Many aged females are wont to obtain their dividends on the 6th; it is consequently called "Old Lady Day."

**A QUESTION OF SOCIAL PRECEDENCE.**

*Scruby* (*the gifted but diminutive Author of "Lip to Lip under the Linden Trees," &c., &c.*). "FIRST LOW COMEDIAN AT THE PARTHENON, IS HE? I SEE! AN *ACTOR!!* *THAT* ACCOUNTS FOR THE SQUIRE'S GIVING *HIM* THE BIG BED AND THE BIG BED-ROOM, INSTEAD OF *ME!*"

**HAPPY THOUGHT.**—*Billy.* "OH!—*LOOK* AT GRANDMAMMA, DOTTIE! WHAT A CAPITAL SWITCHBACK SHE'D MAKE!"

*Rustic* (*to dismounted Horsey Equestrienne, who is on the Runaway's trail, in hope of his having been stopped*). "BE THIS YOURN, MEASTER!"

**A SOCIAL DIAGNOSIS.**

*Fair Visitor.* "THERE'S THAT LOVELY WOMAN AGAIN. I WONDER WHO SHE IS?"

*M. le Baron* (*an experienced observer*). "MADAM, I TINK SHE MUST BE A *ENGLISH DUCHESS*, BECAUSE SHE IS VER PRETTY, SHE DRESS VELL, SHE SPEAK SROO HER NOSE, SHE SAY, '*YOU BET*,' AND SHE TALK ABOUT *DOLLARS AND CARS!*"

**LIKA JOKO'S PANTOMIME.—Joko's Harlequinade. (Lika Joko Clown.)**

## ANECDOTAGE FOR THE MONTHS.

MAY.—On the 10th, in 1796, occurred the Battle of Lodi, memorable for the only recorded attempt of NAPOLEON BUONAPARTE at an English witticism. Referring to the use he made of his artillery, after the engagement, he said, "Good nameē for fighteē—fireē, fireē, after Lodi, Lodi!"

JUNE.—On the 4th, in 1859, the Battle of Magenta was fought, and appropriately gave its name to a popular *dye*. On the 15th, in 1215, Magna Charta was sealed, when, according to MACAULAY (in his unpublished MS.), King JOHN produced the wax. On the 18th the Battle of Waterloo was fought, in 1815, when WELLINGTON, meeting BLUCHER at the end of the engagement, is reported to have observed, "My Lord, this will be a great day for our boots!"—a prophecy verified by the subsequent popularity of Bluchers and Wellingtons.

## MASTER TOMMY'S DOMESTIC ECONOMIES.

*How to utilise the Family Portraits for the purpose of Christmas Amusement and Recreation.*—Get a ladder, and having taken a sharp pen-knife, cut out the eyes from all the family portraits in the dining room. Now fix behind the vacant spaces thus left a sliding slip of cardboard on which you have already made a large black spot as big as a threepenny piece to represent the pupil, and attaching a lever and string to this, bring it down at the back of the picture, so that when you pull it, the eyes will shift. The family being assembled on Christmas Day, work your string and call attention to the fact that *all their ancestors are winking at them.* Though he may deplore the cutting of the canvas, your Uncle, as head of the family, will be bound to admit that the effect is most grotesque, and has caused him no little Christmas amusement and recreation.

**"'APPY 'AMPSTEAD!"**

"IN THE SPRING"—(AND LIKEWISE IN THE SUMMER, AND IN THE AUTUMN ALSO; AND EVEN IN THE WINTER TOO)—"A YOUNG MAN'S FANCY LIGHTLY TURNS TO THOUGHTS OF LOVE!"

## ANECDOTAGE FOR THE MONTHS.

JULY.—On the 4th the Independence of the United States was declared, in 1776, since when the day has been observed by Americans in commemorating their escape from everything British save the Irish Vote. On the 30th, in 1689, Derry was relieved, to the great surprise of WILLIAM THE THIRD, who, in his quaint Anglo-Dutch, observed, with a smile, that "at dirst he was Derryfied!"

AUGUST.—On the 1st, in 1798, the Battle of the Nile was fought, when NELSON produced (after years of patient preparation) his celebrated classical witticism. "Can you tell me, my Lord," said Lady HAMILTON, "anything about your latest victory?" "Oh, Madam," returned the hero, "it was just nothing. *Nihil*—nothing—*Nile!*"

SEPTEMBER.—The 1st is usually known as the feast of St. Partridge, although it is really the *fête* day of St. Giles, and, equally popular, (as once sportively observed by WILBERFORCE, the philanthropist and jester) of St. James. This is a great month with accountants, who devote an entire day to the Leger with a running account. On the 20th the anniversary of the Battle of the Alma recalls the now half-forgotten *jeu d'esprit* of the present head of the British Army. Pointing to the officers of the Guards, Lord RAGLAN observed, "Our victory is attributable to their gallantry in a great degree," "A great degree?" repeated H.R.H. with emphasis, "certainly—this is neither Oxford nor Cambridge, and yet here is their *Alma mater!*"

OCTOBER.—On the 16th, in 1834, the Houses of Parliament were burnt, ending appropriately, however (as was observed by JOSEPH MILLER, wit and centenarian) in smoke. On the 20th, in 1875, the Deanery of Chichester went off the (P.) Hook. On the 25th, the Battle of Agincourt (or as it was anciently pronounced, A-gin-court) was fought, according to contemporary writers, most appropriately, with much spirit. On the same day, nearly four and a half centuries later, the Battle of Balaclava was contested, giving rise, as everyone knows, to a number of serious charges.

NOVEMBER.—The 5th and the 9th have for the last three hundred years been devoted, in London, to the processions of Guys. At the Mansion House the reign of Lord Mayor WHITEHEAD will expire on the latter date, if, like a torpedo, he does not go off sooner. On the 28th, in 1814, the *Times* was first printed by vapour-worked machinery. "How is it going?" hiccoughed Lord BYRON, who took an interest in all literary matters. "Like steam," replied the Archbishop of CANTERBURY, as he assisted the noble bard to rise from the gutter. The remainder of the anecdotage for November is lost in fog.

DECEMBER.—On the 10th, in 1768, the Royal Academy of Painting was instituted, a date which may be given for the commencement of the decay in the pavement pastel industry. Yule brings professional anecdotage to an end, as, at that joyous season of the year, everyone tells his own stories, the biggest of which is sometimes the wish that an objectionable acquaintance may enjoy "A Merry Christmas and a Happy New Year!"

---

CON FOR THE RACE-COURSE.—If a rascally "prophet" adapted a motto from the cricket-field what would it be?—"Tip and run!"

CPSIA information can be obtained at www.ICGtesting.com
Printed in the USA
BVOW09s0957130515

400213BV00016B/206/P

9 781148 739670